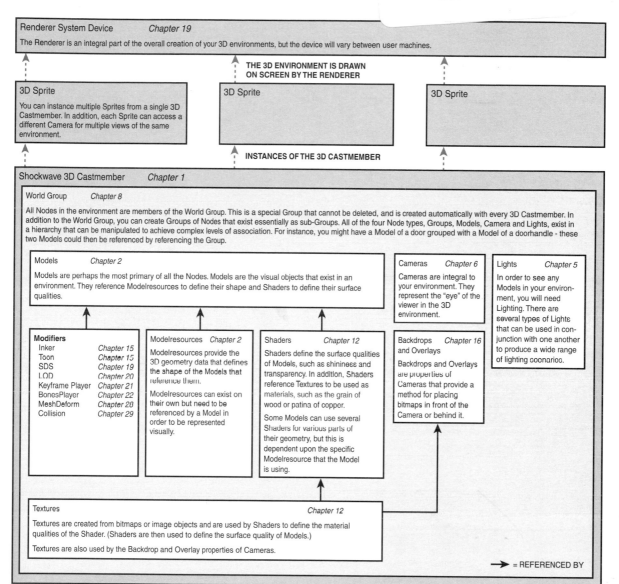

Renderer System Device   *Chapter 19*

The Renderer is an integral part of the overall creation of your 3D environments, but the device will vary between user machines.

THE 3D ENVIRONMENT IS DRAWN ON SCREEN BY THE RENDERER

3D Sprite

You can instance multiple Sprites from a single 3D Castmember. In addition, each Sprite can access a different Camera for multiple views of the same environment.

3D Sprite

3D Sprite

INSTANCES OF THE 3D CASTMEMBER

Shockwave 3D Castmember   *Chapter 1*

World Group   *Chapter 8*

All Nodes in the environment are members of the World Group. This is a special Group that cannot be deleted, and is created automatically with every 3D Castmember. In addition to the World Group, you can create Groups of Nodes that exist essentially as sub-Groups. All of the four Node types, Groups, Models, Camera and Lights, exist in a hierarchy that can be manipulated to achieve complex levels of association. For instance, you might have a Model of a door grouped with a Model of a doorhandle - these two Models could then be referenced by referencing the Group.

Models   *Chapter 2*

Models are perhaps the most primary of all the Nodes. Models are the visual objects that exist in an environment. They reference Modelresources to define their shape and Shaders to define their surface qualities.

Cameras   *Chapter 6*

Cameras are integral to your environment. They represent the "eye" of the viewer in the 3D environment.

Lights   *Chapter 5*

In order to see any Models in your environment, you will need Lighting. There are several types of Lights that can be used in conjunction with one another to produce a wide range of lighting scenarios.

Modifiers

Inker	*Chapter 15*
Toon	*Chapter 15*
SDS	*Chapter 19*
LOD	*Chapter 20*
Keyframe Player	*Chapter 21*
BonesPlayer	*Chapter 22*
MeshDeform	*Chapter 28*
Collision	*Chapter 29*

Modelresources   *Chapter 2*

Modelresources provide the 3D geometry data that defines the shape of the Models that reference them.

Modelresources can exist on their own but need to be referenced by a Model in order to be represented visually.

Shaders   *Chapter 12*

Shaders define the surface qualities of Models, such as shininess and transparency. In addition, Shaders reference Textures to be used as materials, such as the grain of wood or patina of copper.

Some Models can use several Shaders for various parts of their geometry, but this is dependent upon the specific Modelresource that the Model is using.

Backdrops   *Chapter 16*
and Overlays

Backdrops and Overlays are properties of Cameras that provide a method for placing bitmaps in front of the Camera or behind it.

Textures   *Chapter 12*

Textures are created from bitmaps or image objects and are used by Shaders to define the material qualities of the Shader. (Shaders are then used to define the surface quality of Models.)

Textures are also used by the Backdrop and Overlay properties of Cameras.

� → = REFERENCED BY

Paul Catanese

Director's Third Dimension

Fundamentals of 3D Programming in Director® 8.5

 A Division of Pearson Technology Group
201 West 103rd St. • Indianapolis, Indiana 46290 USA

Director's Third Dimension: Fundamentals of 3D Programming in Director

International Standard Book Number: 0672322285

Library of Congress Catalog Card Number: 2001089382

Printed in the United States of America

First Printing: October 2001

04   03   02   01   4   3   2   1

Trademarks

Warning and Disclaimer

Executive Editor
Jeff Schultz

Acquisitions Editor
Kate Small

Development Editor
Clint McCarty

Managing Editor
Charlotte Clapp

Project Editor
Heather McNeill

Copy Editor
Bart Reed

Indexer
Tom Dinse

Proofreader
Jessica McCarty

Technical Editor
Allen Partridge

Team Coordinator
Amy Patton

Media Developer
Dan Scherf

Interior Designer
Gary Adair

Cover Designer
Gary Adair

Contents at a Glance

Table of Contents

Part II   Data Visualization

10   Histograms   205

11   Pie Charts   237

About the Author

Paul Catanese is an experimental animator and interactive media artist residing in Chicago, Illinois. Paul has been working with interactive multimedia for over eight years. During that time he has used Director as well as many other interactive authoring solutions, including Hypercard, Oracle Media Objects, mTropolis, and Visual Basic. He has also worked with VRML, Java3D, and OpenGL. In addition, Paul has extensive experience with 3D modeling and animation, primarily with various versions of 3D Studio, AutoCAD, and LightScape.

Paul received his MFA in Art and Technology from the School of the Art Institute of Chicago (SAIC), where he now teaches digital animation and experimental imaging. Paul teaches methods that blend 3D, stop-motion, and traditional animation with experimental techniques that he uses in his own work. He also teaches how to create electronic input and output devices for building custom interfaces with computers. Paul is currently developing a class for SAIC to focus on the creation of physical objects that control or are controlled by virtual counterparts by combining the topics of 3D scanning, custom electronics, and Director 3D. In addition to his work at SAIC, Paul recently received a Technology Fellowship from Columbia College to develop a curriculum for a multipart class teaching 3D programming.

His animation has been screened internationally, notably at Animac99 in Barcelona, the Bangkok Experimental Film Festival, Enter Multimediale in Prague, and the Center on Contemporary Art in Seattle, Washington. Currently, his animations are distributed through Blackchair productions in Seattle as well as Offline Networks in Ithaca, New York. Other credits include consulting on various commercial projects, such as the Director 7 and 8 certification tests at Brainbench.com, onsite and offsite Director training for three years at Mac University, and the creation of the interactive multimedia consulting company skeletonmoon.com.

Dedication

To Mom and Dad for always believing in me.

Acknowledgments

I would first like to thank my companion and confidant, Lynn Baus, for her constant support, attention, and reassurance. Thank you for doing more dishes than you were supposed to, taking out the garbage when I let it pile up, and listening to me talk about 3D programming on a daily basis. This book could not have happened without you.

I would like to thank my Acquisitions Editor and book-writing spirit-guide Kate Small for her support and reassurance. Her dedication to this book was truly wonderful, and I appreciate her help in negotiating a process that was entirely foreign to me. In addition, I would like to thank my Executive Editor Jeff Schultz for his guidance on this project and for working with me to promote it even at the cost of turning me into a game show host for an afternoon at UCON.

I would like to personally thank my Technical Editor, Allen Partridge, for his advice and suggestions and for his diligence in checking several thousand lines of code. His suggestions and comments helped strengthen the book, and I appreciate his dedication and commitment to making this project as successful as possible. Also, I would like to thank Clint McCarty and the rest of the editorial team at Sams and Que for their hard work, feedback, and support during the months of development.

Special thanks go to Robert Wingate for allowing the use of his extremely helpful API for working with the MUI Xtra, which can be found posted on Director-Online.com. Additional thanks go to

Darrel Plant, Pat McClellan, and Zac Belado from Director-Online.com for making this material available as well. Also, I would like to thank Terry R. Schussler for including information about this book on his Web site, DirectorU.com.

I would like to thank Darrel Plant and James Khazar for reviewing the book proposal and for their feedback, which I found extremely helpful. In general, this book would not have been possible without the efforts of the Director development team from Macromedia and Intel, and I would like to thank those involved for doing a great job on their inclusion of 3D in Director. Specifically, I would like to thank Jeffrey R. Abouaf, Tom Higgins, Chris Nuuja, Christophe Leske, Gary C. Baldes, Adam Lake, and Carl Marshall for various conversations we have had clarifying specific details about the 3D environment that could only have been answered by those involved in creating it.

Finally, I would like to thank Chloe and Nico for overseeing the entire process with great interest. Although it meant suffering through a period of significantly fewer pets, both cats seem to have gained an appreciation for 3D programming that I had not anticipated.

Tell Us What You Think!

As the reader of this book, *you* are our most important critic and commentator. We value your opinion and want to know what we're doing right, what we could do better, what areas you'd like to see us publish in, and any other words of wisdom you're willing to pass our way.

As an Executive Editor for Que, I welcome your comments. You can email or write me directly to let me know what you did or didn't like about this book—as well as what we can do to make our books stronger.

Please note that I cannot help you with technical problems related to the topic of this book, and that due to the high volume of mail I receive, I might not be able to reply to every message.

When you write, please be sure to include this book's title and author as well as your name and phone or fax number. I will carefully review your comments and share them with the author and editors who worked on the book.

Email: ctfeedback@quepublishing.com

Mail: Jeff Schultz
           Executive Editor
           Que
           201 West 103rd Street
           Indianapolis, IN 46290 USA

Foreward

Outside of the game development community, interactive 3D is something that's been pretty much a pipe dream. Since the mid-1990s, several attempts have been made to get it off the ground, but barriers like low bandwidth and slow CPUs have always helped bring it to earth. The last element that was missing but wasn't really talked about was a tool that would let someone who wasn't a hard-core C++ programmer define the interactions between objects in a 3D scene. Plenty of applications existed to create 3D content. Not nearly as many tools let your average non-programmer develop interactive applications. And until recently, they two worlds didn't have any real overlap.

Even after just a few months it's already a cliché, but I'll say it anyway: Director 8.5 and Shockwave3D adds a whole new dimension to multimedia programming. It's the first tool that lets people combine 3D with the sort of real-time interactivity that's been available in Director for the past decade. A number of applications have been trotted out to fulfill the same goal, but with the exception of custom game development systems that cost tens or hundreds of thousands of dollars, nothing has come close to providing the type of control and complexity you find in Director 8.5.

With all of that control and complexity, though, comes a lot of learning. The Director 8.5 manual is just about the same size as the *Lingo Dictionary*, but it doesn't really tell you *how* to do anything; it's largely a reference for 3D Lingo. There's nary a word in there about making models, placing textures, how to light your scene, or what to avoid when you're creating a 3D world. Macromedia would have needed another book for that, but search as you may through your Director 8.5 box, you're not going to find it there.

This is that book.

Just about anyone interested in creating Shockwave3D should find plenty of interest in Paul Catanese's book.

Relatively few people have experience with interactive 3D programming and development. Long-time Director developers almost all have some experience with a 3D modeling application, but usually only for creation of bitmap or digital video assets. There are a lot of differences between preparing 3D for a static series of frames and a real-time interaction Shockwave3D model. You'll find a wealth of advice in this book on how to build scenes that will actually work on as many computers as possible.

3D content creators wanting to turn their models into something that can interact with the user will find in this book someone who understands their language and can communicate the concepts of Shockwave3D programming to them, as well as important information on how to prepare models and scenes. Whether you've been making intricate models for movies or low-resolution characters for games, you'll understand the path to Shockwave3D laid out here.

For people who are new to both 3D and Director, you've got a steep wall ahead of you. There's nothing easy about Director. There's nothing easy about 3D. But you should be able to take the first steps toward both after going through Paul's exercises.

Interactive 3D is an exciting and challenging world. Not as exciting and challenging as the real world — but it's getting there.

Darrel Plant

1 September 2001

Introduction

Many years of software and hardware evolution have raised the bar for interactive multimedia developers. It is extremely exciting to be talking to you about the recent developments that have changed the fundamental capabilities of Macromedia Director. This software product has matured from the Director of 5 and 10 years ago and now includes a robust 3D-programming environment. No small boast, Macromedia's vision has created a cross-platform 3D environment that is CD-ROM and Web deliverable and allows for deep control of geometry through Lingo. Partnering with Intel has provided support for extremely fast download times over even a 56K modem and runtime routines that scale the precision of geometry based on a given client machine's speed.

Director's Future

To only speak of the technical power of Director fails to address a key issue that Director developers think about quite often: Director's future. It is always a dangerous business making predictions about the future of a company or product. However, the tool that Macromedia has created with this iteration of Director is laden with possibilities for capital, artwork, learning, and perhaps even changes in the fundamental expectations for computer-based user experience.

Of course, desktop real-time 3D has existed for quite a while, and yet our interfaces are still primarily 2D. There have been other solutions in the past, such as VRML and 3D support in Java, but neither of these solutions is as well planned as the 3D support in Director. Macromedia's insight led to its partnership with the leaders in 3D animation software and hardware in order to create a product that is integrated into the professional development platforms that have been used for 3D animation and game development for years.

It is no small accident that you are able to create geometry in any of the leading 3D modeling and animation packages—3DS MAX, Maya, Softimage, Lightwave, Truespace, or Cinema 4D—and then import that information into Director. So, unlike VRML and 3D Java, authoring 3D in Director has been introduced at the right time, when 3D-accelerated hardware is standard on any new machine. Plus, the integration into existing 3D modeling and animation packages will ensure that you will be able to incorporate engaging professional assets created with tools that have had many years to be perfected themselves.

Learning 3D will be an effort for many current Director developers, many who may not have an immediate call for it. However, the new 3D capabilities of Director are going to draw many new developers specifically interested in this area. As well, the market for developers has changed over the past few years, especially in terms of individuals who are now graduating from four-year programs in interactive multimedia.

Although we may not be able to predict Director's future, it is certain that this product is poised and ready for developers to create truly interactive 3D environments. What will seal the success of this product will be the projects that you create with it. It is important to begin to think about the larger goals of an industry that is constantly changing by stepping up to the challenges and possibilities that this 3D programming environment affords by revolutionizing the meaning and scope of user experience.

Real-time 3D

You have probably heard the term *real-time 3D* (RT3D) at least once. If you have ever wondered what that means, I can tell you that there is a significant difference between RT3D and what game developers often call *2.5D*. 2.5D uses prerendered images to depict 3D, but there is no geometry to control because the environment is comprised of cleverly drawn bitmaps. Director's 3D environment is not made of prerendered images. Real-time 3D environments are rendered at runtime by the client machine.

This allows your users to change the environment—to change what they see and what is happening inside the worlds you create. Examples of this type of interaction that you may have encountered previously include the powerful game consoles such as the Sony Playstation and the Microsoft Xbox.

Director takes advantage of any 3D video hardware that your system might have. This means that if you have a 3D-accelerated video card, Director will use it to render the scene. If you don't have a 3D accelerator, Director will use a software renderer instead. This way, no one is excluded.

Hardware Considerations

The demos for this book are cross-platform; for your reference, I am using the following machines for development with Director 3D:

- Macintosh G4 400MHz

  MacOS 9.0.2, OpenGL 1.1.3

  Dual 10GB Fast ATA hard drives

  704MB RAM

  ATI Rage with 16MB VRAM

- Athlon 1GHz

  Windows 2000, DirectX7, DirectX5, OpenGL

  Dual 20GB Fast ATA hard drives

  768MB RAM

  ATI Radeon with 64MB VRAM

Although these machines represent some of the latest hardware, you can be assured that development is still possible with significantly slower machines, including those that do not have large amounts of RAM. Your first large investment should be a powerful video card with a 3D accelerator. This will allow you to develop on a machine where you can see the differences between hardware and software rendering, both in speed and quality. Luckily, the price point for many powerful 3D-accelerated video cards is aimed at game players, which tends to keep the price of this equipment quite reasonable.

How 3D Changes Your Production Schedule

Do not underestimate the amount of time it might take you to get up to speed with 3D in Director. It will involve a fairly steep learning curve, even if you have worked with 3D programming in the past. If you have not worked with 3D programming before, you'll have many terms, concepts, and issues to contend with that make learning 3D while working on a commercial project that needs it quite prohibitive. I suggest first working through the entire book. Then with what you will have learned, think of a project that is similar to the types of projects you want to do; once you complete that project, you should be ready.

There is much to be learned from working with a team, and I suggest this as you begin. The division of labor can be as simple as programmer and modeler/animator, but of course each shop and each project will have its own needs. I suggest that everyone working on the project at least understand Director and the scope of its 3D capabilities. In addition, you should have a variety of machines on which to check your project, because the differences from machine to machine can vary dramatically depending on the specific effects you are using. In the book, when you learn about items that tend to look very different depending on hardware, I will make a note of it.

To be direct, you can expect that the bottom line to producing a 3D project will be more demanding, time consuming, and resource intensive than a non-3D project. You can reduce these requirements through careful design of your projects, which can only be done with a thorough understanding of the media. In addition, if you are thinking about learning how to create 3D geometry concurrently, you should consider the costs involved in high-end 3D modeling software and whether you might only need an entry-level 3D modeling product instead.

When you're making a decision on which 3D modeling/animation software to invest in, here are some of the features that can save you time:

- Built-in scripting languages
- Control of function curves
- Bones animation
- The ability to import or create motion capture data

Learning how to work with each of these will have a learning curve of its own, but in the end these particular items can save you much time.

What Does this Book Cover?

Specifically, *Director's Third Dimension* starts by teaching you the basics of 3D in Director: the environment, primitives, transformations, Lights, Cameras, and so on. Then it presents two practical examples for data visualization and an approach for creating custom data types with object-oriented programming (OOP). Then the book takes a closer look at specific intermediate issues: surfacing (materials and textures), building mouse interaction, non-photo-realistic rendering, and special effects. This third section ends with several fully working interfaces for you to learn from. The fourth section centers on learning about download and performance optimization for your 3D projects. The fifth section examines keyframe animation, Bones animation, interpolation animation, and a custom scheduler for controlling each of these to build interactive 3D animation. The sixth section of the book teaches several advanced Camera control techniques, vector math, collision detection, Mesh deformation, and Mesh creation. Plus, there are several appendixes of support information about Imaging Lingo, trigonometry, 3D export from 3DS MAX, a custom color tool, the Havok physics engine, and resources.

I am very aware that most Director developers have not worked with 3D programming before and I am equally aware that you may want to learn how to create product demonstrations, data visualizations, 3D interfaces, or games. For that reason I will be showing as many examples as possible in the book that can be applied to each of these.

As you progress through the book, the topics will become increasingly more demanding, but the approach remains the same. At the end of every chapter, I have summarized what we have covered and answer frequently asked questions about the topic. Then, if there are other resources that I feel you should look at, such as books and Web sites, I direct you to them.

What You Should Know Before You Start

If you are trying to determine whether this book is correct for you, let me offer the following advice: I expect that you are well versed in the structure of Director, and beyond that have had experience with Lingo creating custom handlers, custom functions, and parent/child scripts. You will not need to be a master at parent/child scripting—you'll just need to understand its concepts.

Where you must understand Director and Lingo, it would be helpful if you understood OOP.

In terms of 3D, this book starts at the beginning and then steadily works its way up. Is there more to learn after the book? Yes, of course, but the topics that are beyond the scope of the book should be considered expert subjects, and they are not really subjects of 3D alone (topics such as building a cognitive AI model to control the actions of the 3D world and building multiuser 3D environments).

So, with that said, this book expects that you know Director but not 3D. If you do know 3D, this book can help you learn how the implementation of 3D in Director works. If you know 3D modeling/animation, this book shows that you can utilize and integrate what you already know. I hope this helps you in making your decision; I feel that the book is the most complete that you will find on this subject.

PART I

Hands-On Introduction to the 3D Environment

In this section, I will introduce you to the basic principles involved in working with the 3D environment in Director. You will also learn some basic ways to control the 3D environment that focus on the creation of your own control solutions rather than using the built-in 3D behaviors. Only after we have looked at the various concepts will I introduce you to some of the built-in behaviors that you may find useful. However, the point should be clear: You are going to be learning how to control the environment from scratch via Lingo. Even if you know that you are only going to use built-in behaviors, it is important that you understand the elements and concepts that make a 3D environment work.

CHAPTER 1

Shockwave 3D Castmember

The focus of this chapter is to introduce to you the Shockwave 3D Castmember. This newly introduced Castmember plays a central role in the development of any 3D environment in Director 8.5. Because understanding how to control the Shockwave 3D Castmember to create 3D environments is the central focus of this book, beginning with this Castmember is the most logical starting point.

However, this chapter is not just about the 3D Castmember—it is also an introduction to 3D environments and some of the specifics of the implementation of 3D in Director. You may find that working with 3D in Director is very different from how you might approach a non-3D project. Of course, there are similarities, too, but if you have avoided Lingo in the past, there is no way around it now.

Lingo provides you with an impressive level of control over the 3D environment in Director as well as methods for creating your 3D worlds. Learning to create and control your 3D worlds is dependent on the particular paradigm of 3D set forth by the 3D Castmember. Therefore, we will start by covering the basics of this Castmember and the vocabulary used when talking about 3D. You'll be provided with an orientation to this new feature so that you will be ready to begin 3D programming in Director.

What Is the 3D Castmember?

The 3D Castmember has similarities to the other Castmember types you have learned to work with in previous versions of Director. The 3D Castmember does not change what you already know about other Castmembers but rather builds on the relationships that have existed in

Director for quite some time. This is good news because it means the inclusion of the 3D Castmember does not change how you will work with other Castmember types. In addition, this means you should already understand some of the basic concepts that apply to the 3D Castmember and other Castmembers equally, including the following:

- The 3D Castmember can coexist with non–3D Castmembers.
- A movie can contain multiple 3D Castmembers.
- 3D Castmembers are placed on the Stage/Score.
- Instances of 3D Castmembers are called *Sprites*.
- Each 3D Castmember has its own Xtra, properties, and Lingo.

These are rather broad concepts you should have an understanding of from previous versions of Director. However, the 3D Castmember is not a simple asset such as a bitmap or sound. Unlike these basic Castmembers, the 3D Castmember contains many internal elements that form the basis of the 3D environments you will be building. These internal elements, which include Lights, Cameras, and Models, are not trivial; they are the essential elements of the 3D environment—the building blocks of your 3D worlds.

The first and most difficult conceptual hurdle that you must overcome when learning 3D programming in Director is understanding that the internal elements of 3D Castmembers are not visible on the Score. The internal elements cannot be manipulated via the mouse or keyboard as you would with Sprites—the internal elements are not Sprites. The 3D Castmember itself can have instances that exist on the Score but the internal elements of that 3D Castmember cannot be manipulated as you would a Sprite. In Director, one tool encompasses the range of creation and control of 3D worlds—and that tool is Lingo.

It is true that there are literally hundreds of new commands, functions, and properties that contribute to the creation of 3D environments, and that's part of the reason for the size of this book—there are many new things to learn. However, you'll need to learn more than syntax—you need to learn concepts and strategies as well. Understanding what the internal elements of the 3D Castmember are in addition to how to control them with Lingo is essential to learning how to work with 3D in order to create your own environments.

The 3D Environment

The 3D environment is not simply a picture or static image; it is a fully functioning dynamic environment that must be controlled with Lingo. Several behaviors are geared toward helping you eliminate the need for coding, but approaching 3D programming with behaviors is extremely limiting. The approach of this book is to show you how to work with 3D programming from the ground up.

Several basic elements comprise a 3D environment: Models, Cameras, and Lights. These elements, in addition to Groups of these elements, are properly referred to as *Nodes*. Nodes can be thought of as a type of code object that have their own properties and functions. In addition to the Nodes are secondary elements in the environment that are used in conjunction with the Nodes. You might think of these secondary elements as properties, but they are much more than that. The secondary elements each have unique relationships with the primary Nodes. Some of them are used to define the geometry of Models, and others are used to define surface properties or even control animation and collision detection. As you can see from these few examples, there is a wide range of secondary elements that cannot be properly defined as simple properties. It would be better if you thought about the secondary elements as code objects in their own right, each with their own properties and functions.

Nodes

The four primary elements in the 3D environment that are referred to as *Nodes* are Models, Lights, Cameras, and Groups. Each of the four Nodes has a location in the 3D environment. The methods for changing the locations of these four elements are identical, so the term *Node* is used to refer to all four of these elements at the same time. Table 1.1 lists the four Nodes, what they are, and where you will be learning about them specifically in this book.

Table 1.1   The Four Nodes

Node	Purpose	Introduced
Model	Building block of 3D environments. Used to represent all the solid objects in a scene.	Chapter 2: Creating Models from Scratch via Lingo

Table 1.1   Continued

Node	Purpose	Introduced
Light	Source of illumination that will influence how much of a Model you can see.	Chapter 5: Understanding Lighting
Camera	Your point of view in the 3D environment. Think of the Camera as your eye on the 3D world.	Chapter 6: Understanding Cameras
Group	Groups are special nodes that are used to control several Models, Lights, Cameras, and other Groups at the same time.	Chapter 8: Parents, Children, and Cloning

The secondary elements in the 3D environment have a wide range of purposes and methods of control. In general, they are used in conjunction with the four primary Nodes or with other secondary elements. Table 1.2 lists the secondary elements, their uses, and where you can expect them to be introduced.

Table 1.2   Secondary Elements

Element	Purpose	Introduced
Modelresource	Provides geometrical data that is used by Models to determine their form.	Chapter 2: Creating Models from Scratch via Lingo
Shader	Provides a method of control for surface qualities of Models.	Chapter 12: Basic Control of Surfaces
Texture	Controls the material qualities of Models.	Chapter 12: Basic Control of Surfaces
Modifier	Used to enhance many basic properties of Models, such as geometry, surface, and method of animation.	Chapter 15: Non-Photorealistic Rendering

Table 1.2   Continued

Element	Purpose	Introduced
Motion	Provides those Modifiers that control Model animation with data from external programs.	Chapter 21: Keyframe Animation

You will learn many concepts and strategies for control of the Nodes and secondary elements throughout the book. In fact, learning to control all these elements is the core of learning how to program in 3D in Director.

NOTE

Of the secondary elements, note that Modifier is a particularly broad category that includes optimization Modifiers for geometry, specialized 3D animation playback Modifiers, surface Modifiers, and a basic collision Modifier.

It is important to understand that each of the Nodes and secondary elements have complex interrelationships that comprise the environment in the 3D Castmember. As you know from other Castmember types, controlling the internal properties and code objects must be used in conjunction with your knowledge of non-3D Director development.

Controlling the Environment

The process of control for the 3D environment is executed on several levels. First, you will be controlling the 3D environment at the Castmember level. The creation, modification, and handling of Nodes are accomplished at this basic level. Note that changing properties of the 3D Castmember will change every instance of that Castmember on the Stage. However, unlike many of the assets you have worked with in the past, most of the work that you will be doing in 3D is at the Castmember level.

Second, you will control the 3D environment at the Sprite level. A *3D Sprite* is an instance of the 3D Castmember that offers you a particular view of a 3D environment. You can have several 3D Sprites of the same Castmember—and if you use different Cameras, each 3D Sprite can offer you a different view of the same environment at once. Sprites and Camera Nodes have a unique relationship because Cameras are used to build interaction between the mouse and Nodes inside the 3D environment at the 3D Sprite level. Chapter 13, "A 2D Mouse in a 3D World," explains the concepts involved with building interactivity into your environments and explains several strategies for direct visual control.

Third, there is the Renderer, which is a system-level device whose specific settings are provided by individual user hardware. The Renderer is the primary cause for 3D environments appearing differently among machines and platforms because it is dependent on the specific hardware of the user machine. The relationship between the Renderer and the environment is important to understand. The environment exists in RAM—it is a Castmember and a Sprite. The Renderer is used to draw the environment on the Stage.

The Renderer

The 3D Castmember/3D Sprite is drawn in real time on the Stage by the Renderer. The architecture, video hardware, and RAM that a computer has can change the final rendering of an environment. Many times, these differences are minimal; however, you must be aware that your 3D environments have the potential to look drastically different depending on the machines on which they are viewed. Of the three items that I have listed, the video hardware has the most immediate effect on the rendering of your environments.

NOTE

You will have to contend with many combinations of video hardware and platforms. Macromedia provides some information about which video hardware and platform architectures are problematic, and which are safe.

It is advisable to have several machines with less than optimal settings for testing in addition to your development machine.

I am going to divide video hardware into two rough categories. First, there are video cards with 3D accelerators. These accelerators allow Director to take advantage of the fast hardware rendering techniques that these cards are built for. There are several different methods of hardware rendering, and depending on the architecture of the machine, you may have access to several methods of hardware rendering.

The second category of video cards includes those that either do not have 3D accelerators or whose accelerators are not supported by Director. Most of the nonsupported cards are older, first-generation 3D accelerated cards made prior to 1998. If a system does not have an acceptable 3D accelerator, Director will use software rendering techniques rather than hardware. There is only one software Renderer provided with Director. Although it is not impossible that the software rendering could give you higher frame rates, this is not likely.

NOTE

When a user starts a project that uses the Shockwave 3D Castmember, by default the movie will determine what the best available Renderer on the system is. If there are no hardware Renderers, the movie will use the software Renderer. In addition, if the user has a 3D accelerator that is not supported or is known to cause problems, the movie will choose the software Renderer as well.

You do have the option as the author to try and force the user's system to use a particular Renderer, as well as options to merely suggest which Renderer would be best. However, realize that with Shockwave distributions, users are able to change the current Renderer by right-clicking (PC) or Option-clicking (Macintosh) on the movie.

Certain effects may not work or not work correctly in the software Renderer, but it will still allow your users to see your project.

To summarize, the Renderer and the Environment are two separate entities that work together to produce real-time 3D in Director. The Environment is comprised of at least one 3D Castmember and at least one instance of that Castmember on the Stage. The Renderer is then used to draw this Environment.

Rendering Pipeline

It is helpful to see the complex interrelationships among Nodes, secondary elements, Castmembers, Sprites, and the Renderer all at once. The tearcard, located at the front of the book, is intended to illustrate the connections between all these elements to show you what is often referred to as the *rendering pipeline*.

The rendering pipeline signifies the flow of information from the 3D Castmember and RAM-based code objects through an individual Sprite instance and then through the Renderer device. The next logical step in this conceptual pipeline would be the eyes of your user looking at the real-time rendering of the 3D environment. Also note that the tearcard references the chapters in which you will first encounter each of the discussed elements.

As you examine the tearcard, realize that many of the entities that I am describing exist purely as code objects in RAM—until they are drawn on the screen by the Renderer. The speed of this process of rendering the code objects that comprise the 3D environment is affected by several variables. Among the major speed factors are the number of Models and Lights, the amount of detail in the geometry, and the number and size of Textures that you are using.

Direct to Stage

If you have worked with digital video in Director in the past, you have probably encountered the DirecttoStage (DTS) property. 3D Castmembers have the option to be drawn "DTS" as well. However, differences in the implementation of DTS for 3D Castmembers make it important to read on even if you have worked with this property in the past for other Castmember types.

DTS is a method of drawing a Sprite that offers a significant performance benefit because it allows the system to draw Sprites directly to video memory without using Director's Stage video buffer. The main downside of DTS is that you cannot use any Sprite Inks other than the default Copy Ink. With 3D Castmembers, turning the DirecttoStage property off only allows you to use the Background Transparent Ink.

I strongly discourage you from using 3D Sprites with DTS turned off—the performance hit is difficult to deal with. Plus, it is possible to mimic the Sprite Inks to some degree with backdrops and overlays. These are two tools available to Camera Nodes that we will be discussing in Chapter 16, "Camera Tricks." They allow you to create custom borders, curtains, and backgrounds for your 3D environments.

Finally, if you have worked with DTS with video Castmembers in the past, the key benefit for DTS is that its Castmembers update regardless of the position of the playback head. However, even 3D Castmembers using DTS still rely on `exitframe` and `updatestage` events to update the visual information on the Stage.

So, should you use DTS? Yes, it gives you a performance increase. Is DTS on by default? Yes, if you do not want it on, you will need to turn it off yourself. Why would you consider not using DTS? Because you need to use the Background Transparent Ink or you need to composite conventional Sprites over the top of the 3D Scene. Is it possible to simulate background transparent as well as composite 2D images on top of the 3D Castmember in other ways that allow you to leave DTS on? Yes, with backdrops and overlays and Imaging Lingo you can re-create these effects. How much of a performance increase will you typically see? This is admittedly a debatable point. In some low-polygon count scenes, you may be able to get along without it. But the real problem is that your project may work fine on your development machine with DTS off, but on user machines it may grind to a halt. My advice is that if you have no reason to turn it off, leave it on.

Persistence of the Environment

You'll need to be aware of two methods for creating 3D Castmembers. First, there is the method of inserting a new, empty 3D Castmember. In this method, you will use Lingo to create your worlds from scratch. The Nodes that you create with Lingo cannot be saved with the movie. Therefore, environments created with Lingo need to be created and modified entirely in real time—generally at the beginning of a given movie. Purely Lingo-based environments are extremely lightweight in terms of file size and therefore download very quickly.

However, many times it will be difficult to create all the elements for your 3D environment through Lingo alone. The second method of creating a 3D Castmember involves creating Models and animation in external 3D programs and then exporting that information as a W3D file, which can then be imported into Director as a 3D Castmember. Any changes that you make with Lingo to the imported 3D Castmember will not be saved either.

NOTE

Files imported from 3D modeling programs tend to be small and quick to download because of the Intel optimization routines inherent when a W3D file is created. You can choose from many strategies for optimizing your projects and organizing the division of labor between external modeling programs and Director.

We will work with movies that create environments from scratch, movies that use imported W3D files, and movies that use combinations of both. You will not be learning how to model in external environments, but I will supply you with many Models and environments created externally. The goal of this book is to teach you how to control any 3D environment in Director as well as how to create them from scratch with code.

As a general strategy, it is possible to use a combination of imported 3D Castmembers and inserted 3D Castmembers to produce a final composite 3D Castmember that is used as the 3D Sprite to be presented to the user. No matter your approach, it is important to realize that the changes you make with Lingo to imported or inserted 3D Castmembers will not persist; they cannot be saved with the file. What you will save is the Lingo that creates or modifies the 3D Castmembers.

Summary

The Shockwave 3D Castmember is the basis for working with 3D programming in Director, which is the primary focus of this book. It is possible to have multiple instances of the 3D Castmember on the Stage at once, and it is possible to have multiple 3D Castmembers in a movie. In addition, you can combine Nodes and secondary elements from separate 3D Castmembers within a single environment.

The specific implementation of a 3D environment will vary from machine to machine; several areas have an impact on how the implementation will differ. Hardware architecture, platform, availability of 3D accelerators, and VRAM play the most significant roles in what the environment will look like. Processor speed and RAM always have an effect on the simulation of an environment; however, in software rendering mode, the processor speed and RAM will also affect what the environment will look like on a given user's machine.

The directtostage property is generally considered to provide a performance boost for your 3D projects, but the amount of boost will vary greatly from machine to machine. Although there are few reasons why you might want to turn this property off, it is better if you leave it on. Finally, it is important that you understand that it is not possible to save the environments that you create with Lingo. You can save the Lingo and then re-create the environments, but when the file is saved, the Nodes are not saved with it. This may seem like a drawback, but the fact that you will be generating environments on-the-fly means that your download times will be very small.

Overall, the Shockwave 3D Castmember is the framework for 3D in Director. Throughout the book we will be working with the 3D Castmember. You will learn how to manipulate it with Lingo, examine its properties and functions through a myriad of demonstrations, build custom tools to facilitate common tasks, and amass the skills and concepts to confidently and successfully design, develop, and program with 3D in Director.

FAQ

What kinds of projects is Director 8.5 prepared to handle?

Your first question about any new feature probably involves some amount of assessing what is actually possible versus what is promised. I will not promise that learning or implementing 3D is easy, fast, or without problems. However, Director 8.5 is the first attempt by any software manufacturer to build an authoring environment for 3D applications that is serious, feasible, and sober about itself. Among the possibilities for Director 8.5 that are easily recognized as viable sources of revenue are games, data visualization, product demonstration, 3D animations, 3D interfaces, and multiuser 3D environments.

Do I need any other software other than Director 8.5?

This is a difficult question because it has two answers. Do you need any other software? No. You can develop robust, powerful environments purely from scratch, purely from code. Might you need other software? Probably. If you need to develop complex Models or animation, you are going to need a 3D modeling and animation software package.

Are 3D modeling and animation software packages expensive?

They can be, but they do not have to be. I have provided a list of resources in Appendix H, "Online Resources," that includes the modeling and animation programs that currently support W3D export—and these range widely in price. However, this list is constantly growing, so you may want to check with Macromedia to see what programs are supported as well.

Which modeling/animation software is the best?

It depends. A wide range of products integrate well with Director, and there are as many opinions as there are people working with 3D. I am biased toward 3D Studio MAX because I have been working with it for many years. The thing you can learn from this is that the choice you make now may be one you stick with for a long time. No matter what, realize that each of the modeling/animation programs that are available to be integrated into Director 3D are stellar products.

The products range in price, user base, features, and many other factors that are difficult to quantify. For example, having a built-in scripting language in your 3D environment may not be important to you, whereas others will feel that it is an essential tool.

Aside from the specifics of the 3D tools, learning any one of them is a serious time commitment. 3D software tends to promote building your own unique methods of working so that you can develop a style that is dependent on the software. The methods you develop for one program may take years to master, and it may be difficult to shift your specific style from one 3D program to another.

How can I choose which modeling/animation software is right for me and my project?

If you have never worked with a 3D animation/modeling program, you need to find the one that fits your current budget and development requirements. Try to plan for your future needs, but realize that it is not impossible to learn more than one 3D package when your development needs to grow. It is always nice to be able to build on the method of 3D modeling/animation you are familiar with, but you do not always need the most expensive modeler to get access to the tools you'll most likely need for 3D development in Shockwave 3D.

I do not know how to create 3D models and animation. Should I learn this skill first?

Not at all—this book has been designed to teach both 3D novices and those who have worked with 3D modeling and animation in the past. The most important thing that you need to bring to this book is an understanding of Director, including the fundamentals of programming in Lingo.

Should I try to learn 3D programming and modeling/animation concurrently?

You could, but you should realize that each of these skills—modeling/ animation and programming—will require a very large time and monetary commitment. In addition, you will need to learn how to model before you learn how to animate. By learning how to program first, you can approach modeling and animation understanding the limitations that the programming end of development will have on your work. If you learn modeling and animation first, you will have a more visual understanding of the 3D environment and how to create assets, but there will still be a learning curve involved in 3D programming.

In general, once you have learned one of these skills, the concepts you have mastered can help you learn the other, but I would discourage you from trying to learn everything at once. Otherwise, you may become frustrated by no fault of your own. It is a lot to learn—take it slow, learn it right the first time, and it will work out.

However, realize that understanding how to create models and animate them in an external program is not the same as 3D programming. No matter where your assets are created, you will still need to learn how to control them through code.

In addition, if you are considering dividing the labor of 3D development between those who create assets and those who program, it is going to help the entire project if all involved have an understanding of the strengths and limitations of the 3D environment. As with any multimedia project, your development team should have an integrated understanding of its medium.

I already know 3D modeling/animation program X, but W3D export is not available. What should I do?

This depends. The OBJ importer, which is supplied with Director, is also available. In addition, there are many translator tools that can convert to OBJ. After this, the options are less enticing, such as changing your 3D modeling/animation software, writing Lingo-based code to convert from a proprietary format on-the-fly, and writing your own W3D exporter after licensing the W3D exporter SDK from Macromedia. Obviously, these options become increasingly difficult and may lead you back to an answer that you do not want to hear: You will probably need to change which software you are using for 3D modeling/animation.

Are Modifiers the only way to animate my Models?

Not at all. Modifiers allow you to use 3D animation data created in external modeling and animation programs within Director 8.5. You will still create much animation directly with Lingo. In addition, you will learn how to combine Lingo-based animation with Modifier-based animation for the maximum amount of control in Part V, "Animation and Interactive Control Structures."

What about traditional Score-based animation in Director? Is this supported for Nodes?

No. You have no visual representation of the Models on the Score. There is no way to select an individual Model and alter its properties visually. You will have to do this via code—at runtime. The smallest individual unit that you can control via the Score is the 3D Sprite.

CHAPTER 2

Creating Models from Scratch via Lingo

The creation of Models should be considered the first step toward learning how to control the 3D environment. Although it is possible to create all Models in programs other than Director, there are several reasons why we do not start there. First, the process of creating Models with Lingo provides a foundation for control of both Lingo-based Models and imported Models. Second, an efficient strategy for creating your worlds is to use Lingo-based Models with only a few key external Models to flesh out the environment. Third, even if you or a co-worker will eventually create an entire world in a 3D-modeling program, you cannot wait until the modeling is done to start programming. Creating Models with code allows you to create visual place-holders that will be replaced by the actual geometry when it is ready.

Inserting an Empty 3D World

Before we can create any Models, we need a world in which to create them. New, empty worlds are created by inserting a Shockwave 3D Castmember into the Cast, as demonstrated in Figure 2.1.

After you insert the Shockwave 3D Castmember, the Shockwave 3D window should immediately open with a black background. This is a view of the blank 3D world that you have just created. It is important that you name the 3D Castmember before you close the Shockwave 3D window. If you do not name the 3D Castmember and close the Shockwave 3D window, the Castmember will disappear. Figure 2.2 illustrates the section of the Shockwave 3D window where you should name your Castmember immediately after inserting it.

FIGURE 2.1

Inserting an empty Shockwave 3D Castmember.

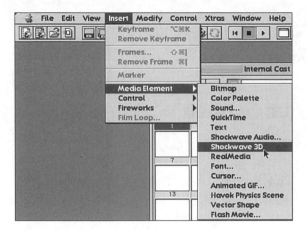

FIGURE 2.2

Don't forget to name your empty 3D world before closing the Shockwave 3D window.

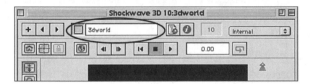

The name you choose for the 3D Castmember should be descriptive and easy to remember. Eventually, we will be working on Director movies that use several 3D Castmembers at once. I tend to create one 3D Castmember named "scene" and then name the other 3D Castmembers according to their functions (for example, dragonmodel, player_run, player_duck, and so on).

Consider adopting a naming convention for your 3D Castmembers that will aid you in debugging projects that you revisit. Elements in the 3D world are not referenced visually but rather by their name or number. Having a concise naming convention will aid you in controlling your environments more efficiently.

Persistence

Chapter 1 mentioned that changes made to your 3D world via Lingo do not persist. This means that you can change the 3D Castmember at runtime, but these changes will not be saved with the file. There is a slight addendum to this: If you are in Authoring mode, any changes made to the 3D environment persist between executions of a movie. Therefore, if you create a Model, stop the movie, and then run the movie again, you would end up with an error when the movie tries to create the object because it already exists. One way to solve this problem is to reset the world every time you start the movie. The resetworld() function will reset a 3D Castmember to its default settings. We will call the resetworld() function from the Startmovie handler, as follows:

```
On Startmovie
  Global scene
  Scene = member("3Dcastmembername")
  Scene.resetworld()
end
```

In Chapter 3, "Building a Simple API for Model Creation," we will examine the resetworld() function in depth. This example is good for Authoring mode, but I do not suggest using it for Projectors or Shockwave movies because the resetworld() function must not be called before the 3D Castmember is downloaded. Notice, in this example, that I created a global variable named scene. The value that I set for scene contains a reference to the 3D Castmember itself. The reason for this encapsulation is to save typing throughout all the scripts we will write pertaining to the 3D Castmember.

3D Castmember Defaults

The empty Shockwave 3D Castmembers that you insert into Director are not entirely empty. There are several elements that exist in the "blank" world by default. Your empty world contains one Camera, two Lights, one Shader, one Texture, and one Modelresource.

NOTE

Cameras are examined in Chapter 6, "Understanding Cameras," Lights are explained in Chapter 5, "Understanding Lighting," and Shaders and Textures are explored in depth in Chapter 12, "Basic Control of Surfaces."

After looking closely at this list, you may be curious—I say that you have one Modelresource but yet you do not see anything in the scene. This is because there is a difference between a Modelresource and a Model.

Modelresources and Models

The difference between a Modelresource and a Model is similar to the difference between a Castmember and a Sprite. Models are instances of a Modelresource that are visible on stage. Unlike Sprites, the score never contains any representation of Models in the 3D environment. All Nodes (Models, Modelresources, Shaders, Cameras, and so on) contained within the Castmember must be negotiated via code.

Models are code objects that visually express the properties of the Modelresource. If you were to change a Modelresource, every Model based on that Modelresource would change.

NOTE

It is possible to exploit this fact to create animations, similar to a flipbook for 3D models.

A Modelresource contains the geometric information that is used to create Models. This geometric information is referred to as a *Mesh*. A Mesh is comprised of Faces and Vertices. *Vertices* are points in a three-dimensional Cartesian coordinate system. Faces are triangular surfaces formed by connecting three Vertices. *Meshes* are objects or sections of objects defined by collections of Faces. Modelresources are comprised of one or more Meshes.

NOTE

By default, spheres only have one Mesh, whereas boxes have six—one for each side. The number of Meshes that a Modelresource has is determined by its type and how it was created.

The Modelresource is essential because it contains the geometric information used to create the Models that you will actually see. Therefore, before you can create any Models from scratch with Lingo, you have to create a Modelresource. The command to create a Modelresource is as follows:

```
Member("castmember").newmodelresource("name", #type, #facing)
```

The `newmodelresource()` command accepts several parameters. You must specify a name for the new Modelresource. You should specify a type, which is given as a symbol. Here are the five types of geometry that can be created with the `newmodelresource()` command:

- #plane
- #sphere
- #box
- #cylinder
- #particle (does not accept facing parameter)

These five Modelresource types are called *primitives*. Modelresources inherit properties based on their type. Some of the primitives, such as #plane and #sphere, have only a few properties, whereas #cylinder, #box, and #particle have many properties. Generally, a larger range of properties allows for greater variations of the basic shape of a primitive.

Table 2.1 lists the possible values for the optional #facing parameter. The #facing parameter influences how many Meshes will comprise a Modelresource and the orientation of those Meshes.

Table 2.1   Possible Values for the #facing Parameter

Value	Purpose
#front	Creates front-facing single-sided objects
#back	Creates back-facing single-sided objects
#both	Creates double-sided objects

There are two reasons why you might want to specify a #facing parameter during this process. The first reason is to create a double-sided object. The other reason is to create a single-sided plane. Table 2.2 compares the number of Meshes created by default and with the #both setting for each primitive.

Table 2.2   Number of Meshes for Primitive Model Types

Primitive	Default Facing	# of Meshes	Max # of Meshes
#plane	#both	2	2
#box	#front	6	12

Table 2.2   Continued

Primitive	Default Facing	# of Meshes	Max # of Meshes
#sphere	#front	1	2
#cylinder	#front	3	6
#particle	#front	1	1

The key difference is that with the #both value for the #facing parameter, double the number of Meshes are created. Creating double-sided objects should only be done if you absolutely need them. But what exactly is a double-sided object? Don't all objects have two sides? The answer to this is No. In order to optimize performance, the 3D engine only tries to draw the Faces of objects that are visible to the Camera. By default, Director does not create the geometry for the inside of Models. The #facing setting is one way to override this. Because the usage of double-sided objects is so closely related to the control of surfaces, I encourage you to read Chapter 12 for strategies for working with double-sided objects efficiently.

Primitives

The five primitive types are #plane, #sphere, #box, #cylinder, and #particle. These five types are known as primitives because they are considered the building blocks of 3D environments. With the exception of the particle system, they are simple shapes that can be created quickly by defining a small number of properties. However, although they are simple, they are not simplistic. Many of the projects that you work on will likely contain some primitives. The key advantage to creating worlds with primitives is that because they are created after the movie is downloaded, they require no download time.

One disadvantage of using primitives is that it is difficult at first to realize how powerful they can be. In addition to learning how to control primitives, overcoming the aesthetic challenges of using primitives requires some strategy. One strategy is to use primitives for broad, sweeping objects that satisfy large goals of an environment, such as the sky or the ground, as opposed to using primitives as focal points in your worlds. Another strategy is to combine primitives with advanced lighting (Chapter 5) and surface-control techniques (Chapters 12, 14, 15, and 17) to simulate complex geometry—without the performance costs. Yet another strategy is to mutate and complicate the geometry of primitives using the Meshdeform modifier (Chapter 28). These strategies can be used in conjunction with one another to achieve the most control.

#plane

The #plane primitive is one of the simplest types of geometry available in Director—arguably it is the simplest type, but simple does not mean simplistic or useless. In fact, planes are one of the most powerful tools in Director's 3D environment because they can be used for many purposes. Figure 2.3 illustrates several uses for the #plane primitive.

FIGURE 2.3

Sample uses of a plane, as a ground plane, a wall, and "billboard" trees.

Modelresources of the type #plane can be controlled via the properties in Table 2.3.

Table 2.3   Properties of the #plane Primitive

Property	Format	Default
Length	Float	1
Width	Float	1
Lengthvertices	Integer	2
Widthvertices	Integer	2

A plane is a simple geometry that requires a small amount of memory and is very efficient at certain tasks. One common use for a plane is for creating floors, ceilings, and walls. It is also often used to create "billboard" objects. A billboard can be described as a simple Model that has the image of a complex shape (such as a tree) pasted on it. Rather than needing all the memory to hold the complex geometry of the tree, one bitmap image can suffice. Billboard objects can be programmed to automatically face the viewer and update their images based on the angle at which they are viewed. This will require extra programming, but you begin to see the versatility of the plane. Figure 2.4 illustrates the difference between a plane with two Lengthvertices and a plane with eight Lengthvertices.

FIGURE 2.4

A #plane with two Lengthvertices and Widthvertices and a similar #plane with eight Lengthvertices and Widthvertices.

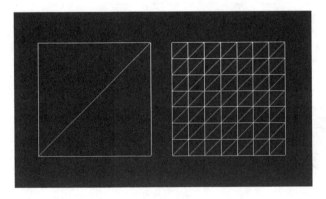

The Length and Width parameters control the size of the plane, but Lengthvertices and Widthvertices deserve some attention also. These two properties determine how detailed the geometry of the plane is. Figure 2.4 illustrates how the geometry of the plane is subdivided into smaller sections with higher values for these properties. At this point, you will not need to increase this value, but it is useful if you are going to create wire-frame grids or if you need to create terrain. See Chapter 12, "Basic Control of Surfaces," to learn about wire-frame surfaces and Chapter 28, "Mesh Deformation and Detailed Picking," to learn about Mesh deformation.

#box

The #box primitive type is a powerful tool that you will be utilizing throughout the book. Like the other primitive types, #box has several properties that can be used to create variations on its basic shape. Figure 2.5 illustrates several of the variations that are possible to achieve through manipulating the #box properties.

FIGURE 2.5

Views of a box, including a box with an open top and a box with open sides.

A box has three dimensions with which to express itself: height, width, and length. Table 2.4 lists these and the other Modelresource properties available to control the #box type.

Table 2.4   Properties of the #box Primitive

Property	Format	Default
Length	Float	50
Width	Float	50
Height	Float	50
Lengthvertices	Integer	2
Widthvertices	Integer	2
Heightvertices	Integer	2
Left	Boolean	true
Right	Boolean	true

Table 2.4   Continued

Property	Format	Default
Front	Boolean	true
Back	Boolean	true
Top	Boolean	true
Bottom	Boolean	true

From this list, you can see there is a wider range of controls for the #box primitive than the #plane. Length, Width, and Height are the most immediately accessible properties. In addition, we have talked about how Lengthvertices and similar properties affect a Model.

The Left, Right, Front, Back, Top, and Bottom parameters are used to remove sides of the #box. With these parameters, you can create a box with no top or missing a side. This is a Boolean value, and the default value is true. Therefore, boxes are normally created with all their sides intact. Setting any of these values to false will eliminate the appropriate side of the box. Keep in mind that these names (Top, Left, and so on) refer to the absolute sides of the box irrespective of their orientation on the Stage.

#sphere

The #sphere primitive is among the simplest and most basic of shapes. It has several properties that allow you to create interesting variations on the sphere, as illustrated in Figure 2.6.

FIGURE 2.6

Views of sphere, hemisphere, wedge, rough, and smooth.

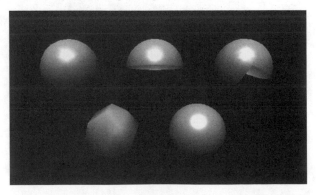

Spheres are widely used because, by default, they appear smooth and interact with light in interesting ways, as compared to flat surfaces. One word of caution: Spheres do require a bit more geometry than the other primitive types. Table 2.5 lists the properties of the sphere.

Table 2.5   Properties of the #sphere Primitive

Property	Format	Default
Radius	Float	25
Resolution	Integer	20
Startangle	Float	0
Endangle	Float	360

Note that among the properties listed in Table 2.5 is a property called Resolution. The Resolution property is similar to the Lengthvertices property for planes and boxes. Resolution limits the number of faces and vertices used to create the #sphere Mesh. Changing this property causes immediate visual and performance effects. The default setting of 20 produces a relatively smooth sphere. As you lower the Resolution setting, the sphere will become less and less rounded, until your reach a setting of 1, in which case you will have a tetrahedron. Although Resolution can be used to create tetrahedrons, dodecahedrons, and so on, it also has obvious optimization implications.

The Startangle and Endangle parameters allow you to create hemispheres and semispheres. Figure 2.7 illustrates the use of a hemisphere as a sky dome—it requires less geometry than a full sphere, yet it accomplishes the same goals.

FIGURE 2.7

Example of using a hemisphere for a sky dome with a plane for the ground. The Camera should then be located inside of the hemisphere, and the sky and ground should be properly textured.

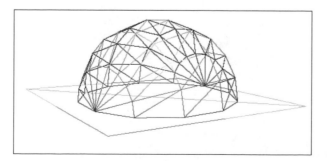

The Startangle property must not be larger than the Endangle property or less than 0. The Endangle property must be smaller than 360. If you set the Startangle or Endangle property outside of these ranges, it will cause a script error.

#cylinder

The #cylinder primitive is quite robust due to the number of variations that can be created via its properties. Figure 2.8 illustrates the possible variations on the geometry of the #cylinder primitive.

FIGURE 2.8

Examples of cylinder, cone, wedge, frustrum, tube, and hemicylinder.

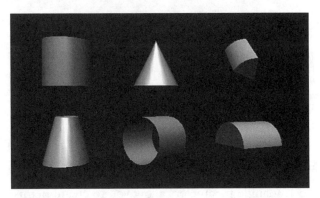

Table 2.6 lists the properties used to create these variations.

Table 2.6   Properties of the #cylinder Primitive

Property	Format	Default
Radius	Float	25
Topradius	Float	25
Bottomradius	Float	25
Height	Float	50
Resolution	Integer	20
Startangle	Float	0
Endangle	Float	360

Table 2.6   Continued

Property	Format	Default
Numsegments	Integer	2
Bottomcap	Boolean	true
Topcap	Boolean	true

We encountered several #cylinder properties, such as Radius, Resolution, and Startangle/Endangle, with the #sphere primitive. With the #cylinder, we have an optional degree of control over the radius with the Topradius and Bottomradius properties. When these values are not equal, the cylinder will begin to look like a cone. If you want the cone to converge to a sharp point, set Bottomradius or Topradius to 0.

The Bottomcap and Topcap properties are Boolean values that allow you to remove one or both ends of the cylinder. You can create the appearance of containers or cubes with these properties.

The Numsegments property determines how many horizontal segments define the cylinder. The default setting for this property is 2. Avoid increasing this value because it will affect the amount of geometry in the cylinder dramatically.

#particle

The #particle primitive is very different from the other primitive types. In most 3D environments, its peculiarities ensure that it is not a primitive. However, Director does define the #particle Modelresource type as a primitive, even though it is a rather advanced structure. Figure 2.9 illustrates one usage of the #particle primitive type to create an explosion.

In 3D programming, #particle primitives are referred to as *particle systems*. They are used to simulate many phenomena that would be difficult if not impossible to model. Particle systems can be used to create smoke, fire, star fields, and fireworks, for example. Notice how these examples are dynamic by their very nature. It would be incomprehensible to try and define one of these with a specific geometric model. A particle system defines how groups of very small "particles" will move. Using the many properties, you can define what these particles look like, alter how fast they move, and cause them to be influenced by physical properties such as gravity and wind. In essence, it is a primitive not of geometry but rather of motion. Particle systems deserve a good deal of attention, and for that reason, we will examine them in depth in Chapter 17, "Special Effects."

FIGURE 2.9

An example of an explosion created with the #particle primitive.

Non-Primitives

There are other ways of creating models with Director; therefore, there are other Modelresource types. The other three types that you will encounter are #extruder, #fromfile, and #mesh. None of these are created with the `newmodel-resource()` command; rather, they each have their own method of creation.

#extruder

When working with text, logos, or other simple shapes, you might consider using the #extruder Modelresource. Figure 2.10 illustrates several examples of Models created using this Modelresource type.

The #extruder Modelresource type is used when creating 3D Text or logos from a font file. Extruder Modelresources are created with the `extrude3d()` command. Chapter 7, "Text and Extrusion Capabilities," examines methods of working with 3D Text and logos.

FIGURE 2.10

Views of extruded text and logos.

#fromfile

Considering that the vast majority of 3D animation is not created with primitives, you might be concerned that your particular product or environment will not be able to be represented in Director's 3D environment. However, Director can import W3D files created externally, which is the case with the Models illustrated in Figure 2.11.

FIGURE 2.11

A star and wine glass from modeled software.

Models and geometry created in external 3D programs can be saved in W3D files and imported for use in Director. When a Modelresource is imported, it is given the #fromfile type, signifying that the geometric information was not created in Director. Chapter 9, "Working with Prebuilt Scenes and Behaviors," introduces the key concepts, limitations, and requirements for importing models created outside of Director.

#mesh

There are many situations in which primitive geometry will not suffice, and you may require complete control over the geometry of a Model. Rather than limiting you, Director includes functionality for a general, but robust, #mesh Modelresource type. Figure 2.12 shows an example of a terrain created from a #mesh Modelresource type.

FIGURE 2.12

View of terrain created from a #mesh Modelresource.

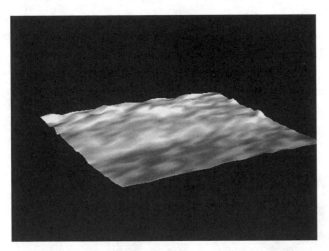

The #mesh Modelresource type is the most versatile type and also the most difficult to work with. Creating Meshes from scratch is a rather involved but rewarding process. Meshes can be used in a variety of situations. One common use for the #mesh Modelresource type is to create realistic terrain. However, to judge the purpose of the Mesh primitive by this example alone is limited in scope. Technically, the #Mesh primitive can be used to create a Model of any object. In a 3D-modeling program, you manipulate Vertices and Faces to create Models visually. Creating a Mesh is similar, but rather than a visual interface, you must manipulate the Vertices and Faces directly with math. Because of this, it is often considered very difficult to create Meshes. I think that the process is very rewarding, although it is involved. Chapter 27 is dedicated to the creation of Meshes, but if you are interested in this topic, you should read Chapter 26 and Chapter 28 as preliminary and supplemental information.

Generic Units

If you have not worked with 3D graphics before, you may be surprised to learn that the default unit that we work with is a generic unit. Normally, if I were to talk about the parameters of my favorite chair, I might tell you that it is 40 inches high by 22 inches wide and 30 inches deep—or I might describe it in feet or centimeters. It would be silly of me to describe it in microns or in miles because these units are relatively inappropriate to the relative size of my chair. This has always presented a problem for 3D graphics, because we can create a wide variety of realistic and nonrealistic environments. If we were to pick a unit type of inches as the default, a chemist making molecular models would share his woe with a cartographer making 3D maps of the ocean floor.

Inches is a terrible unit of measure for either of these individuals to use to describe the geometry of their 3D worlds. It is best not to limit the environment by requiring that a specific type of unit become the default; therefore, the generic unit is technically any unit you want it to be. When you work with generic units, it is more important that you make sure your measurements are correct in relation to one another. For example, if I were describing my chair as being 40 units high, 22 units wide, and 30 units deep, it would probably be a mistake to tell you that you were in the same room, standing 100,000 units away from it. You have to be aware of scale at all times when working with generic units.

When creating worlds from code, you can avoid problems relatively easily by keeping track of how large or small you create things. Most of the problems with generic units arise when transferring 3D data from one program to another, such as from a 3D-modeling program to Director—or worse, when trying to combine 3D data from more than one program.

Creating Models

We have examined the preliminary steps for the creation of a Model. Once you have created the Modelresource and assigned its properties, the next step is to create the Model. Models can be created with the following syntax:

```
Scene.newmodel("name", scene.modelresource("resourcename"))
```

This will create a new Model that we will be able to see. New Models are placed at the origin of the world, and the default Camera is pointed at the origin of the world. Chapter 4, "Transformations," examines how to move, rotate, and scale Cameras, Lights, and Models.

Like Modelresources, Models have many properties. Model-level properties allow you to control various aspects of the position of the Model and how it should be drawn. We will examine the range of Model properties throughout this book. At this point, we will concern ourselves only with the Shader property.

NOTE

Be aware that the term *Shader* is used to refer to a code object and a Model property. Also, be aware that this term has a different meaning outside of Director—particularly in 3D-modeling packages.

The Shader property allows us to control many aspects of a surface, but at this point, we will be using it to control the color of a Model.

Shader Basics

The subject of surfaces is much larger than what is explained in this section. Chapters 12, 14, 15, and 17 examine the details of creating many types of surfaces. In this chapter, however, we will consider a surface as merely the color of an object, and that color is defined via a code object called Shader. You may recall that I mentioned that an empty 3D world contains one Shader (and one Texture) in addition to the other default elements. Shaders are assigned to Models and determine how light will react with their surface. You create Shaders separately from your Models, and you can use a single Shader on multiple Models. Bear in mind that any change you make to a given Shader will affect every Model using that Shader. For this reason, it is often advantageous to create a Shader for each Model.

Here are the steps involved in the creation and application of a Shader:

1. Create a Shader. This sets up the Shader object.

2. Assign the Diffuse property. This assigns the color that the object will be.

3. Set the Texture property to void. This eliminates the default white and pink checkerboard Texture on all new Shaders.

4. Assign the Shader to a Model. This makes the Model use the color of the Shader.

Here is the syntax for this process:

```
Member("castmember").newshader("name", #standard)
Member("castmember").shader("name").diffuse = rgb(R,G,B)
Member("castmember").shader("name").texture = void
Member("castmember").model("modelname").shader =
\member("castmember").shader("name")
```

Notice that the format for the value that the Diffuse property expects is an rgb(R,G,B) color object. While using 3D in Director, you will assign colors using this system. The red, green, and blue parameters each accept an integer value between 0 and 255. These values are added together, and the resultant color is a mixture of some amount of red, green, and blue. If you are not familiar with the color object in Lingo, you should look at Appendix F, "Colorlut Custom Color Management System." It contains several useful examples for color conversions and goes into detail about how to work with the color object more effectively. Chapter 5 explains how light-based color is dramatically different from pigment-based color. Also, in Chapter 12, we examine how light-based color will react with pigment-based colors.

Model Creation Demo

Now that we have examined the parameters of creating a Model from scratch, it is time to examine a specific method of using code to accomplish this. The

CD-ROM contains a file called "model basics" that is used during this demo. The `Startmovie` event creates a Modelresource, Model, and Shader, as indicated in the following code:

```
1: On Startmovie
--declare scene variable as global
2:    Global scene
--create reference to sw3d Castmember object
3:    Scene = member("3dworld")
--reset sw3d castmember
4:    Scene.resetworld()
--create sphere modelresource
5:    Tempobjres = Scene.newmodelresource("sphereRES", #sphere)
--set sphere modelresrource radius to 40
6:    Tempobjres.radius = 40
--set the sphere modelresource resolution to 17
7:    Tempobjres.resolution = 17
--create a model from the sphere modelresource
8:    Tempobj = scene.newmodel("sphere01", tempobjres)
--create a new standard shader
9:    Tempshader = scene.newshader("sphereshd", #standard)
--set the diffuse color (in this case, a light green)
10:    Tempshader.diffuse = rgb(100,200,50)
--set the texture of the shader to void
11:    Tempshader.texture = void
-- assign the shader to the model
12:    Tempobj.shaderlist = tempshader
13: end
```

It is possible to alter this `Startmovie` event to create all the different primitives we have examined thus far. When the movie is running, you should see a sphere in the middle of the stage that is a bright green color. While the movie is running, it is possible to alter the properties of the sphere from the message window. For example, you can type the following in the message window and press Return:

```
Scene.modelresource("sphereRES").resolution = 3
```

This alters the shape of the sphere so that it appears faceted. Although this is a simple change, take note of how we can refer to the SW3D Castmember as "scene" because it is a global variable referencing the Castmember. Notice also that we can change Modelresource properties after a Model has been created, and those changes will be reflected in the Model without any extra effort.

NOTE

> Line 5 creates a local variable that temporarily retains the newly created Modelresource. This allows us to quickly refer to the Modelresource in line 6 and change its properties with a minimum of typing.

I encourage you to alter the Modelresource properties from the message window to become comfortable with the process. Also, stop the movie and play it again. If you have not altered the Startmovie event itself, notice how it creates the original sphere again, without any of the modifications applied to it in the message window. This is because you are creating the Model from scratch every time you run the movie. Even if you save the movie, changes you make to the SW3D will not persist.

I encourage you to alter lines 5–9 in the Startmovie event. Change those lines to the following:

```
--create cylinder instead
1:    Tempobjres = Scene.newmodelresource("cylRES", #cylinder)
--set radius at the top of the cylinder to 40
2:    Tempobjres.topradius = 40
-- set the radius at the bottom of the cylinder to 0
3:    Tempobjres.bottomradius = 0
--create a model from the cylinder modelresource
4:    Tempobj = scene.newmodel("cyl01", tempobjres)
--create a new standard shader
5:    Tempshader = scene.newshader("cylshd", #standard)
```

Now when you run the movie, the Startmovie event will create a cone. I have changed all references to the word *sphere* to *cyl*. Although this seems cosmetic, organizing the structure of your worlds through naming is crucial. Your workload will be eased if you refer to your models quickly and concisely. This is absolutely crucial if you are going to work in a team environment. Finally, note that you cannot create objects with duplicate names—if you do, it will cause a script error.

Although we could continue to alter this `Startmovie` event to create other primitives, we must remember that this event is fairly concise but not at all robust. There are several issues that arise from this strategy. The most serious of which is that this example does not deal with streaming. Because we are only running this movie in Authoring mode, we are not running into the problems that can occur due to the SW3D Castmember not being fully downloaded and ready at runtime.

Although I do not suggest this code for our applications, it is concise enough to serve as a learning tool to clarify the required steps for creating Models from scratch. Chapter 3 examines a strategy for working with streaming media and how to streamline custom handlers for the creation of primitives.

Summary

There is a difference between a Model and a Modelresource. Both these elements contribute to the creation of visual objects that we see onscreen, but they are two distinct code objects. They each have their own properties that are used to control various aspects of the visual objects. Because of this, it is important to distinguish between when we are controlling a Model property and when we are working with a Modelresource property.

The process of creating objects is broken into three crucial steps: creating a Modelresource, assigning Modelresource properties, and creating the Model. The structure of this process differs among primitive types, but overall it remains essentially the same. The creation of a Shader and the assignment of that Shader has been presented in a simplified form here. However, this process will suffice if the only changes you want to make to the surface of Models involve changing their color.

This process can become repetitive, and wasteful, in terms of typing code. At this point, we have utilized Lingo to create 3D objects, but we have not harnessed the power of Lingo (custom handlers and parent/child scripts) to streamline the process. The amount of control you have over your 3D world will depend on the degree of object orientation you bring to your code. The creation of objects with structured code is the first step toward understanding how to design, build, and control your 3D worlds.

FAQ

Primitives are so useless; how could I possibly utilize them?

I like to think of primitives as deceptively simple. Because they do not require a large amount of processor power and because they can be created quickly with Lingo, they do not have to be downloaded. This allows you to create relatively small documents (in terms of file size) that execute quickly and can contain complex scenes. If you can create a convincing world without using complex geometry, you will have a strong, light project. However, it is true that not everything can be done with primitives, but they should be part of your strategy if possible.

I would much rather just import the Models that I have been creating in my 3D software package. How can I do that?

This process is dealt with in Chapter 9. Also, Appendix A is dedicated to the issues surrounding the importation of Models, Animation, and so on, from 3D Studio MAX.

I don't understand—I can only control the color of objects?

You can control a very large amount of properties in terms of the surfaces of objects. This chapter only deals with one property: Diffuse. Refer to Chapters 12, 14, 15, and 17 to learn how to work with surfaces.

CHAPTER 3

Building a Simple API for Model Creation

Application Programming Interface (API) is the term used to refer to the commands of a programming language that allow you to control the inner workings of the operating system. This term is also used to refer to a group of commands built from a programming language that extend the capabilities of that language. Sometimes this is referred to as a *toolkit*, but I think the term *API* is more concise. I will use this term as we use Lingo to build a suite of custom handlers to deal with many common tasks. Among these tasks is the process of creating primitives, as discussed in Chapter 2, "Creating Models from Scratch via Lingo." We know that the creation of a primitive from scratch involves several steps that can become repetitive. Rather than bloating our code by typing these commands over and over, we will build custom handlers to deal with frequently repeated tasks. The elegance of building custom handlers to deal with these tasks is that you can make the handlers as specific as you need them to be.

The handlers that I present in this chapter create the basic primitives, such as boxes and spheres, and some variations on those primitives, such as cones and pyramids. The needs of your project will dictate which of these handlers you require and whether you need to customize them further.

World Cleanup Utilities

Attempting to perform operations on a 3D Castmember before it is fully downloaded will result in a script error. This does not mean that it is not possible to stream in 3D Data. The 3D Castmember contains 3D Data—and your movies may contain several 3D Castmembers. At this point, we are working with 3D Castmembers that are devoid of any Models and are therefore quite small (about 500 bytes). Our main concern is that the 3D

Castmembers are fully downloaded and ready for commands to be called on them. You can also work with 3D Castmembers from external casts, loading them as is required. This is a good method of approach for both online and offline work. We will explore streaming in Movies using 3D in Chapter 20, "Download Optimization."

When you're working with generated Models, there are two tasks you should handle at the beginning of any movie: making sure that the 3D Castmembers are fully loaded and resetting the 3D world. This is important in Authoring, Projectors, and Shockwave mode. Although this will become slightly modified when you learn to import Models, the overall schematic is the same.

To ensure that our 3D Castmember is fully downloaded, our efforts must be concentrated on this task from the very beginning of the movie. Recall that the order of events at the instantiation of a movie is as follows:

1. `PrepareMovie()` (sets up globals)

2. `BeginSprite()` (all Sprites in frame 1 initiate)

3. `PrepareFrame()` (occurs before anything is drawn on stage)

4. `StartMovie()` (suggest initializing non-3D elements here)

Figure 3.1 illustrates a sample score setup for a movie intended to run online or offline. The CD-ROM accompanying this book contains a file called "basic world setup." The illustration of the score in Figure 3.1 is derived from this file.

FIGURE 3.1

Example of a possible Score strategy for Movie download and initialization.

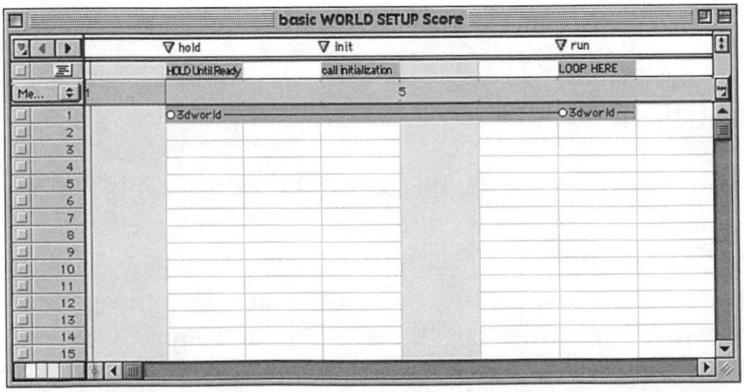

This movie contains two custom handlers designed to streamline the task of checking to ensure that the 3D Castmember is fully downloaded. One reason why I leave the first frame empty is because the 3D Castmember sometimes takes a moment to begin. If there is going to be a pause at the very beginning of the movie, you want to be able to control what the users see during that pause. They will see whatever was drawn on stage in the previous frame. If there is no previous frame, they will see the Macromedia load bar. Even if you are going to leave frame 1 empty, controlling the moment when the pause happens will allow you to make the process of beginning the movie more transparent to the user. The Behavior script attached to frame 2 contains an exitframe() handler. This handler calls upon a custom handler called check3Dready() that is used to determine whether the SW3D is ready. Here's the code:

```
1:on check3Dready(whichSW3D)
-- a state of 4 tells you the media is ready
2:if whichSW3D.state = 4 then
-- if it is ready, return true (for error checking & debugging)
3:return true
4:else
--if it isn't ready return false (for error checking & debugging)
5:return false
6:end if
7:end
```

This handler returns either true or false, depending on whether the 3D Castmember is ready. This information is used in the exitframe() handler attached to frame 2. The reason for this encapsulation is to create custom handlers that are robust enough to be used in several situations. In this case, check3Dready() is being used to determine whether we loop on a frame or jump to a new marker.

Line 2 of the check3Dready() handler refers to the State property of the 3D Castmember. The State property of a 3D Castmember contains information pertaining to the loading of that Castmember into RAM. Although we are primarily concerned with Castmembers fully downloading, the State property can be used to make sure that CD- or HD-based Director Movies are loaded correctly. The State property has six possible values that it can return, as indicated in Table 3.1.

Table 3.1   Values of 3D Castmember State Property

State Value	Meaning
-1	Error loading file
0	Not loaded
1	Loading has begun
2	High-priority Models downloading
3	Decompression
4	Media is ready for all 3D commands

When the State setting of a Castmember is 4, all 3D commands can be run on the Castmember without worry. It is possible to run some commands on 3D Castmembers with a State setting of 2 or 3. However, `resetworld()` should not be called unless the Castmember's State setting is 4.

NOTE

The priority of Model loading applies to Castmembers that contain Models created externally from Director. Check in Appendix A, "3D Studio MAX W3D Exporter," for information about changing the stream priority of Models.

The `check3Dready()` custom handler reports false when the 3D Castmember's State setting is not 4. The State property applies to other Castmember types as well as SW3D Castmembers. The State values for 3D Castmembers are unique to 3D Castmembers and do not reflect values for Shockwave Audio or Flash Castmembers.

When the 3D Castmember's State setting is 4, the `exitframe()` handler sends the Playback Head to the "init" marker. At init, the "call initialize" script contains an `enterframe()` handler. This handler calls a custom handler called `initialize()` and then sends the Playback Head to the "run" marker. The reason for all this jumping is to ensure that we have a specific moment that we can refer to when the `initialize()` handler will be called.

This strategy also allows us to separate the initialization of 3D and non-3D elements in our Movies. For example, although this demo does not contain a `Startmovie` event, it is a good location to initialize the non-3D portions of our Movie.

NOTE

This strategy can also be helpful if you want to "restart" a movie without stopping at some point by sending the Playback Head to the init marker.

Currently, the only operation of our initialize custom handler is to call yet another custom handler, shown here, called clearworld():

```
1: on clearworld(whichSW3D)
-- last minute double checking to make sure SW3D is ready
2:   if check3Dready(whichSW3D) then
-- if everything is ready, reset the world to default values
3:     whichSW3D.resetworld()
-- return true (for error checking & debugging)
4:     return true
5:   else
-- SW3D not ready, return false (for error checking)
6:     return false
7:   end if
8: end
```

The clearworld() custom handler is designed to make one final check to see whether the 3D Castmember's State property is ready, and then it calls the resetworld() function. Notice how in line 2 I call the check3Dready() custom handler to find out whether State is set to 4. This is a prime example of the reusability of the custom handlers we are building.

Most of the work of this handler occurs in line 3, where the resetworld() function is called. The resetworld() function is used to reinitialize a 3D Castmember to its default state. This means that after you call resetworld() on a 3D Castmember, it will only contain the defaults of one Camera, one Modelresource, one Shader, one Texture and two Lights.

If your 3D Castmember was created externally from Director, you should not use resetworld(). Rather, the reverttoworlddefaults() command reinitializes the 3D Castmember to its "saved" state. Chapter 9, "Working with Prebuilt Scenes and Behaviors," examines methods of working with 3D Castmembers created outside of Director.

One final precaution that we can take to avoid script errors is to actually turn off the streaming functionality for the Movie. You can accomplish this by editing your Movie Playback properties as noted in Figure 3.2.

FIGURE 3.2

Turning off the Play While Downloading Movie option from the Modify Movie menu.

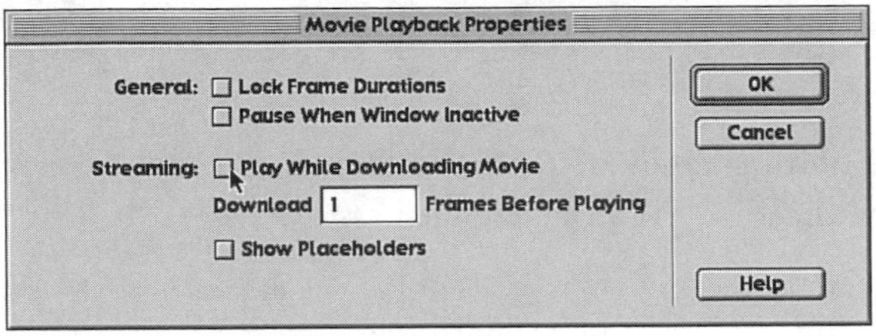

You can set the Movie Playback properties from the Modify, Movie menu to make sure that the movie fully downloads before playing. This is another method of ensuring that you or your users will not encounter script errors at the beginning of your movie due to bandwidth. However, this method does not take advantage of the ability to stream your data in dynamically.

Primitive Creation

We have now prepared the movie for the generation of 3D content on-the-fly. This section explains how to build an API of custom handlers for the creation of primitives. These custom handlers are designed to approach several of the primitive types discussed in Chapter 2: the plane, sphere, box, and cylinder. The particle primitive is explored in depth in Chapter 17, "Special Effects."

In general, the custom handlers for creating primitives utilize some of the properties of each Modelresource type. For instance, it is not useful to build an extremely specific API with features for every aspect of the cylinder unless you are going to need these features. We will revisit the box and cylinder primitive custom handlers in Chapter 10, "Histograms," and Chapter 11, "Pie Charts," respectively. The custom handlers that we are going to build in this section are quite general, allowing you to modify them as required for your individual projects.

Plane

The plane primitive is versatile, simple, and concise, and it can be used in a variety of situations. The plane primitive does not have an excessive amount of properties that define it. The two properties that are most critical are

Length and Width. For this reason, we will focus on the Length and Width properties as the controllable parameters for the `createplane()` custom handler, shown here:

```
 1: Global scene
 2: On createplane(planeName, L, W, planeColor)
 3:   If check3Dready(scene) then
 4:     Res = Scene.newmodelresource(planeName & "res", #plane)
 5:     Res.length = L
 6:     Res.width = W
 7:     Obj = scene.newmodel(planeName, res)
 8:     Shd = scene.newshader(planeName & "shd", #standard)
 9:     Shd.diffuse = planeColor
10:     Shd.texture = void
11:     Obj.shaderlist = shd
12:     Return scene.model(planename)
13:   Else
14:     Return false
15:   End if
16: End
```

The `createplane()` custom handler is called with the syntax `createplane("modelname", float, float, rgb(R,G,B))`. This custom handler is built to conserve your typing. Although calling it requires typing a long line of code, this is easier than typing the contents of the handler each time you want a plane. Also, you are probably aware that creating planes, boxes, and spheres is a good first step, but there are many other concerns to contend with. Because of this, it is best to simplify the parts of code that are crucial but not demanding. What's more, after you have established an API of custom handlers to deal with frequent tasks, it will become easier to perform these repetitive tasks with ease.

If we were creating an environment that called for two planes, it might be easier to create them in other ways. When you realize that you actually need an environment with 30 planes, this method may seem more approachable. This process is easily encapsulated inside of a repeat loop to accomplish the mass-creation of objects. Here's an example:

```
1: Repeat with x = 1 to 30
2:   Createplane("plane" & x, 10, 20, rgb(200,30,30))
3: End repeat
```

This example will quickly create 30 planes of a bright red color. If you decide later that you need another plane, you have a very concise way of changing the repeat loop to repeat until 31. Therefore, the time saved in typing accumulates as you develop a project.

NOTE

In this code example, you might expect that a wrong type error might occur, due to the fact that I am concatenating a string and an integer. Although you might disagree, Lingo is a very forgiving programming language when compared to others. Data types are not strongly enforced in Lingo, as they are in other languages. This logic is therefore a good programming trick for Lingo, but it's not a trick to take to other languages.

Finally, there are many occasions when you might be testing certain functions of the 3D environment on an isolated object. If you were to build a test Model to check one or two functions of a project, it would be tiring to have to type up all the commands to create a plane or a sphere. This method allows you to focus your attention on the needs of your project, rather than spending your energy reinventing the wheel (or in this case, the plane).

Sphere

The sphere is perhaps one of the more aesthetically pleasing types of primitives in the 3D environment because it exhibits visually interesting qualities. The smooth surface and the ability to simulate complex interactions with light make the sphere an attractive primitive. Even when you're working with primitives, it is obvious that some are more visually engaging.

One reason for this complexity is the curvature of the surface. When you are designing your 3D worlds and modeling many of the objects, you can use the visual interest that draws the eye to curved surfaces to create focal points in your worlds. Although you may not necessarily use a sphere to accomplish this, you might create complex objects with curved surfaces.

Curved surfaces tend to utilize more geometry and therefore more memory than flat-surfaced objects. For this reason, depending on your intended user, you will most likely need to limit the usage of highly descriptive geometry in your scenes. This can aid in emphasizing your choices for using curvilinear surfaces in areas of visual focus.

Finally, as a compositional element, spheres tend to have well-defined areas of highlight, midtone, and shadow. These three visual demarcations are used in a painting technique known as *chiaroscuro*. This technique is used to create the illusion of three-dimensional objects on a two-dimensional surface. By this description, the approach toward realistic painting techniques are similar to that of a 3D environment. For this reason, you may want to examine the vocabulary of formal composition as a method of learning how to control what you would like to see in your 3D world.

The custom handler for the creation of a sphere is similar to the `createplane()` handler. Note that the key difference is that the defining property of the sphere is truly its radius. For this reason, our handler will only deal with this one property. Here's the code:

```
1: Global scene
2: On createsphere(sphereName, R, sphereColor)
3:  If check3Dready(scene) then
4:    Res = Scene.newmodelresource(sphereName & "res", #sphere)
5:    Res.radius - R
6:    Obj = scene.newmodel(sphereName, res)
7:    Shd = scene.newshader(sphereName & "shd", #standard)
8:    Shd.diffuse = sphereColor
9:    Shd.texture = void
10:   Obj.shaderlist = shd
11:   Return scene.model(spherename)
12:  Else
13:    Return false
14:  End if
15: End
```

The critical lines of code that create Models in the `createplane()` and `createsphere()` custom handlers are encapsulated in an `if/then` statement. This `if/then` statement utilizes the `check3Dready()` custom handler we explored earlier. Note that after the successful creation of the Model, `createsphere()` returns a reference to the code object for the Model. This is true in `createplane()` as well. Also, upon failure, these custom functions will return false. The reason for this is twofold. Recall in prior examples, as well as in the `createsphere()` custom handler, that when we create code objects in the 3D world, we often save a reference to those objects in a variable to reduce our typing requirements. If we were to call the `createsphere()` function from the `initialize()` custom handler, the returning information allows us to create a reference to the new sphere's code object as follows:

```
Mynewsphere = createsphere("ball", 27, rgb(50,100,10))
```

This syntax allows us to refer to this sphere as `mynewsphere` throughout the `initialize()` handler. If we were to declare the `mynewsphere` variable as global prior to this line of code, we could easily reference the sphere throughout the rest of the Movie through this variable. Even as a local variable, this information affords us much latitude in our coding. One addition that we could make would be to encapsulate our creation of the sphere as follows:

```
-- create the sphere
1: Mynewsphere = createsphere("ball", 27, rgb(10,40,50))
then  --check to make sure that mynewsphere is not false
2: If not mynewsphere
-- take some action if mynewsphere is false
3:  Alert "problem!"
4: End if
```

Line 3 of this example is critical—we have decided to alert that there is a problem. We can do a few useful things here: We can either call an alert or halt the program, or we can redirect the Playback Head to a section of the movie where we can make the process of error handling more transparent to the end users. For example, you might send them back to the "hold" marker to make sure that the 3D Castmember is truly ready. Alternatively, you might have a marker called "error" where you could gracefully let the users know that something is wrong and give them a general idea of the problem. Error checking in this case is quite simple because the only error a user might encounter is that the Castmember somehow does not have a State setting of 4 when you are trying to create the sphere. The `createsphere()` custom handler could be expanded to include error checking to ensure that when the movie is loaded, the name you intend to use for the sphere is unique. Here's an example:

```
1: Global scene
2: On createsphere sphereName, R, sphereColor
3:  If check3Dready(scene) then
```

```
 4:    If scene.model(spherename) = void then
 5:    Res = Scene.newmodelresource(sphereName & "res", #sphere)
 6:    Res.radius = R
 7:    Obj = scene.newmodel(sphereName, res)
 8:    Shd = scene.newshader(sphereName & "shd", #standard)
 9:    Shd.diffuse = sphereColor
10:    Shd.texture = void
11:    Obj.shaderlist = shd
12:    Return scene.model(spherename)
13:    Else
14:    Return -2
15:    End if
16:  Else
17:    Return -1
18:  End if
19: End
```

Now this custom handler begins to develop some character, and more importantly a system for error checking. In this example, -1 informs us that the Castmember was not ready, and -2 tells us that we are using a duplicate name. It would not be difficult to modify these values to return -2001 and -2002. We could then easily say that error -2002 was generated when we tried to create a sphere, because we used a duplicate name. Perhaps −1002 could be reserved for when we try to create a plane with a duplicate name.

Box

Only the plane primitive rivals the versatility of the box primitive in the creation of basic architectural spaces. The box primitive will often be your first choice for walls, ceilings, and floors when describing interior spaces. Although a special case of the box primitive is the cube, rectangular boxes are viable building blocks. For this reason, our createbox() custom handler will be concerned with the Length, Width, and Height parameters of boxes. If we were more interested in only creating cubes, our custom handler would only need to accept one value for Length, Width, and Height. As it is, the createbox() custom handler is similar in form to createsphere() and createplane(), but it requires several arguments, as shown here:

```
1: Global scene
2: On createbox boxName, L,W,H, boxColor
3:   If check3Dready(scene) then
```

```
 4:     Res = Scene.newmodelresource(boxName & "res", #box)
 5:     Res.length = L
 6:     Res.width = W
 7:     Res.height = H
 8:     Obj = scene.newmodel(boxName, res)
 9:     Shd = scene.newshader(boxName & "shd", #standard)
10:     Shd.diffuse = boxColor
11:     Shd.texture = void
12:     Obj.shaderlist = shd
13:     Return scene.model(boxname)
14:    Else
15:     Return false
16:    End if
17: End
```

Lines 9 through 12 occupy themselves with the creation of a Shader dedicated to this Model. Note that the name of the Shader is the name of the box with the letters "shd" appended. Using a concise naming convention like this will aid you in controlling your worlds. Also, understand that the Shader object and Shader property are two separate entities.

This handler is quick and should suffice for the creation of basic box shapes. If we were interested in creating a maze-generation game, we might customize the box handler to build several boxes and position them correctly. We could then rename it the "createroom()" handler.

Cylinder

The cylinder primitive is intriguing because it can be reshaped into so many variations. Because of this, I have created two custom handlers: one to deal with common cylinder creation and another to deal with the creation of cones.

Basic Cylinder Handler

For a basic cylinder, the pertinent parameters we are interested in are its height and radius. Therefore, the custom handler looks like this:

```
1: Global scene
2: On createcylinder cylName, R,H, cylColor
3:  If check3Dready(scene) then
4:    Res = Scene.newmodelresource(cylName & "res", #cylinder)
```

```
 5:   Res.height = H

 6:   res.topradius = R
 7:    res.bottomradius = R
 8:   Obj = scene.newmodel(cylName, res)
 9:   Shd = scene.newshader(cylName & "shd", #standard)
10:   Shd.diffuse = cylColor
11:   Shd.texture = void
12:   Obj.shaderlist = shd
13:   Return scene.model(cylname)
14:  Else
15:   Return false
16:  End if
17: End
```

Notice in this example that in order to set the radius of the cylinder, I must set the Topradius and Bottomradius. Keep in mind that radius is not a property of the cylinder primitive. I will elaborate on the basic cylinder-creation handler in Chapter 11, where we will specialize this function to deal with the creation of pie charts.

Basic Cone Handler

You can also use the cylinder primitive to create cones by modifying the Topradius and Bottomradius properties. If our goal is to create a simple cone, we only need to modify one of these properties. In addition, we still need to modify the height. The revised cylinder handler becomes the simple cone handler and looks like this:

```
 1: Global scene
 2: On createcone coneName, R,H, coneColor
 3:  If check3Dready(scene) then
 4:   Res = Scene.newmodelresource(coneName & "res", #cylinder)
 5:   Res.height = H
 6:   Res.bottomradius = R
 7:   Res.topradius = 0
 8:   Obj = scene.newmodel(coneName, res)
 9:   Shd = scene.newshader(coneName & "shd", #standard)
10:   Shd.diffuse = coneColor
11:   Shd.texture = void
12:   Obj.shaderlist = shd
13:   Return scene.model(conename)
14:  Else
```

```
15:   Return false
16:  End if
17: End
```

Line 6 now sets Bottomradius as defined when you call the `createcone()` custom handler, and line 7 is "hard-wired" to set Topradius to 0. Although this will always create cones that point up, it is possible to rotate them into any position we want.

It would not be overly difficult to add a control for the resolution property to this handler in order to create a pyramid-creation custom handler. We could easily have a `createpyramid()` custom handler if we were to change all references of *cone* to *pyramid* and then insert the following line of code at line 7:

```
Res.resolution = 1
```

You can see that it is possible to develop an entire suite of frequently used primitive-creation handlers that are meant to ease your workload. Also, depending on the needs of your application, you may want to build error checking into your custom handlers. You will probably need more error checking if you are going to be building projects that generate Models on their own or via user manipulation. If all the Models you are going to create are known, you will most likely not need to have robust error checking for these operations. Aside from error checking, the strategy is clear: encapsulate and reuse. With this strategy, we can begin to focus our attention on how to work with the Models we have created.

Basic Shader Manipulation

The Models we have been creating allow us to specify an initial color, but beyond that we have very little control over the color of the objects. Because each of our Models has its own Shader, we can control the color of a Model with the following code:

```
Scene.model("whichmodel").shaderlist.diffuse = rgb(R,G,B)
```

Because this is only one line of code, I would probably not build a custom handler to control this one property. If you decide that you need more advanced surfacing for your Models, you may need to build a custom handler at that point. For now, this syntax will suffice for our demonstration.

Using Our API to Quickly Create Content

The CD-ROM accompanying this book contains a file called "basic primitives." This file contains all the custom handlers discussed in this chapter. If you play this movie, notice that nothing seems to happen. However, with the movie playing, type the following code into the message window and press Return:

```
Createsphere("firstsphere", 30, rgb(255,255,255))
```

You should see a white sphere directly in the middle of the Stage. If you stop the movie and start it again, the sphere should disappear. Take the line of code that you typed into the message window and insert it into the initialize() handler. Now when you restart the movie, the sphere is created automatically. While the movie is playing, type the following into the message window:

```
Scene.model("firstsphere").shaderlist.diffuse = rgb(255,0,0)
```

The sphere should turn a bright red color. If you restart the movie again, notice that the sphere is now white. This is because the sphere is created every single time you start the movie, no matter what its final state was. This leads to what can appear to be a difficulty: You cannot save changes made to the 3D Castmember. However, I believe that this difficulty is actually a positive benefit, because 3D Castmembers can be very lightweight. The code to generate Models is much smaller than the Models would be to download themselves.

One problem that you may encounter at this point occurs when you attempt to create multiple Models. Chapter 4, "Transformations," discusses the concepts and processes of moving, rotating, and scaling objects. By default, new Models are created at the "origin" of the world. Consider this the origin of our 3D Cartesian coordinate system. The default Camera of 3D Castmembers is pointed at the origin, which is the only reason why we can see newly created Models. Figure 3.3 illustrates what is happening when we create more than one Model.

FIGURE 3.3

Wire-frame view of primitives created on top of one another.

Notice that in wire-frame mode, it is apparent that the primitives are actually inside of one another. For now, we will work with one Model at a time.

To continue with our demonstration, open the file "sphere color cycle" on the CD-ROM. In this example, a slightly larger sphere is created, and the 3D Castmember takes up the entire stage. Also, the stage background is now black, so the transition from frame 1 to frame 2 is not obvious. The "loop here & color cycle" script provides the color changes:

```
--gain access to the scene global variable
 1: global scene
-- create a custom property which we will use to count up
 2: property pcount  4:
 3: on beginsprite
-- set the initial value of pcount to zero
 4:   pcount = 0
 5: end
 6: on exitFrame me
--stay on this frame
 7:   go "run"
--add one to the current value of pcount
 8:   pcount = pcount + 1
-- constrain the value of pcount to a number between 0 and 255
 9:   pcolor = pcount mod 255
-- find the rgb color located at the paletteindex of pclor*
10:   pcolor = paletteIndex(pcolor)
-- change the color of the sphere
11:   scene.model("firstsphere").shaderlist.diffuse = pcolor
12: end
```

Lines 12 and 13 deserve explanation. Remember that we are always adding 1 to the value of pcount; therefore, its value at any given time may well be very large (or more specifically, larger than 255). Because we are going to use the color palette to determine which colors we change the sphere to, we need to limit the value of pcount to within the range of 0 to 255. The mod (modulus) operator is a mathematical operator that has been in Lingo for quite some time, but it's often overlooked. It takes any numerical value and constrains it to a predetermined range. Appendix D, "2D Mathematics and Utilities," explains more about this useful operator. To continue, the current color palette of this movie is the "vivid" palette. Line 13 determines what the rgb(R,G,B) value of a given palette index number is. It is this RGB data that is then used to change the color. The reason for all of this is to make the color change very smooth. Try changing your color palette to the "grayscale" or "metallic" palette to see how this affects your color cycling.

Now open the "basic interaction" file on the CD-ROM. This example of basic interaction with the 3D Model we have created uses the following exit-frame() handler:

```
1: global scene
2:
3: on exitFrame me
--stay on this frame
4:   go "run"
5:
--offset the mouseloc by the center of the stage
6:   offsetML = the mouseloc - point(250,165)
--get absolute values of X & Y
7:   offsetML = point(abs(offsetML[1]), abs(offsetML[2]))
8:
--determine (roughly) how far from center of sphere we are
9:   if (offsetML[1] + offsetML[2])/2 < 255 then
10:    pcolor = (offsetML[1] + offsetML[2])
11:    pcolor = paletteIndex(pcolor)
12:  else
13:    pcolor = rgb(0,0,0)
14:  end if
15:
16:  scene.model("firstsphere").shaderlist.diffuse = pcolor
17:
18: end
```

This example determines a rough estimate of how far the mouse is from the center of the stage. If the mouse is roughly within 255 pixels, we change the color based on the palette index. If the mouse is outside that range, we automatically choose black as the new color of the sphere. The overall effect makes it appear as if the sphere is aware of the presence of the mouse. This method works well here, but with multiple Models, we will need a more concise way of determining mouse interaction. Chapter 13, "A 2D Mouse in a 3D World," explores methods of negotiating a two-dimensional mouse in a three-dimensional space.

Future Considerations

The custom handlers presented in this chapter can be expanded in several key directions. First, the error checking can be expanded depending on your needs. Error checking can become quite complex and can consist of both User mode error checking and Authoring mode error checking. Another consideration would be to develop a debugging mode used to turn on and off surfaces.

More importantly, though, perhaps the most robust change that we will explore is the move from simple custom handlers to dedicated parent/child scripts. This is explored in depth in Chapter 23, "Controling Time." Parent/child scripts are well suited to the objects we are creating in the 3D world. Remember, parent/child scripts are very similar to behaviors. The key difference is that parent/child scripts are not attached to the score in any way. Similarly, the Models, Shaders, Cameras, and other Nodes we are working with do not have a representation on the score.

Beyond this visual similarity, parent/child scripts allow us to connect our Models to robust systems of control. The systems that we will look at include creation and destruction methods, scheduling, and hooks for collision, physics, and basic AI. Because Nodes in the 3D world are not score based, advanced applications may avoid utilizing the score for most control issues. A dedicated scheduler can be used to take the place of most Playback Head functionality.

Summary

The creation of primitives is a simple but repetitive process that can be streamlined with custom handlers. The amount of complexity to build into your custom handlers can range from eliminating typing, to robust error checking and dedicated scheduling. However, the custom handlers presented are, in themselves, complete tools.

These tools allow us to quickly create a host of primitives. It is possible to quickly modify these handlers to create very specific variations of primitives, such as the pyramid handler derived from the cylinder primitive.

Perhaps the most important lesson of these examples is learning to decide what is necessary for your projects. The level of complexity that you employ should always be dictated by the needs of your project. In addition, the level of specificity of handlers should be dictated by these needs as well.

FAQ

Can I save my Models?

Unfortunately, no. Models created at runtime with Lingo cannot be saved inside your file. You must create them with code every time the movie runs. This actually saves download time in the long run.

Models exported from 3D-modeling software can be saved inside of a W3D file, and this file can be imported into a movie. But changes that you make to the Shockwave 3D Castmember with Lingo cannot be saved.

Can I move my Models?

Yes; Chapter 4 explores Model transformation—the process of moving, rotating, and scaling Models.

Am I going to have to build some extremely robust, non-Playback Head–based parent/child script system for my project?

It depends. Not knowing what your specific project is, I can say that from project to project, the answer to this question will vary. Games tend to need a larger degree of this type of functionality, whereas interfaces or charting applications can survive without it. However, these are hardly concrete guidelines. You could easily design an interface or data-visualization project that might require these. In general, more complex systems tend to be easier to implement with parent/child scripts. This does not mean that you must use parent/child scripts every time you want to create something in 3D.

Director comes with several custom behaviors in the behavior library that let me do the things that you have described. Why have you shown me these things if I can already do them with no work?

Good question. You are learning how to control your 3D world through Lingo. The custom behaviors will only get you so far—actually, they won't get you that far at all. But again, remember that you need to choose how complex your code is depending on your project. If you believe that you can control your 3D world within your needs using the behavior library, by all means use it. This book is intended to guide you from the limitations of "one size fits all" behaviors to being able to build your own.

CHAPTER 4

Transformations

A real-time 3D environment would not be interesting to look at or interact with unless we have a way of positioning, rotating, and scaling the Models, Lights, and Cameras in a scene. This chapter covers the basic principles of a rather large subject that performs these functions, commonly known as *transformations*. The concept of transformations is applicable to all Nodes; this chapter concentrates on transformations of Models.

We will be dealing with many terms and concepts that have similar names but whose meanings are different. I will give you extra warning when dealing with topics that are easily confused. In this chapter, I assume that you have had some experience with 2D geometry and perhaps trigonometry in the past.

This chapter is broken into several conceptual areas in order to work our way up to 3D transformations. We will first review some basic 2D concepts that will facilitate understanding their 3D equivalents. We will then look at `vector()` objects and `transform()` objects in order to understand the foundation of transformation. Next, we will apply what you have learned about `transform()` objects to Models. Finally, we will apply what you have learned in the chapter about transformations in several demos.

Before we begin, I must stress that this topic is classically difficult for first-time users. Keep in mind that 3D transformations can sometimes confuse even seasoned 3D coders because the result of transformations can often be difficult to "previsualize." If you find that any one section is not making sense, I encourage you to read through until the end of the chapter and then work your way back to the sections that did not make sense.

Two-dimensional Cartesian Coordinates

If you are going to position, rotate, or scale anything in the 3D environment, you need to have a firm understanding of the coordinate system that governs how geometry, algebra, and trigonometry correlate.

Cartesian coordinates are defined by some quantifying locations in number of dimensions. A good example of a one-dimensional Cartesian coordinate system would be a ruler or a line. The classic two-dimensional Cartesian coordinate system is illustrated in Figure 4.1.

FIGURE 4.1

A two-dimensional plane with X and Y axes and an origin point compared to the Director Stage origin and axis directions.

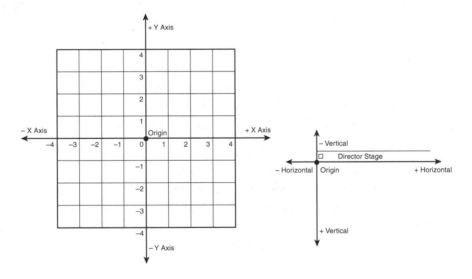

Figure 4.1 illustrates several of the key features of a two-dimensional Cartesian coordinate system: clearly defined axes representing each dimension, some form of measuring distances in each dimension, and an origin point where the axes converge. These key features are required for evaluating the coordinates of a specific location on the grid; specific locations on the grid are referred to as *points*. This information is compared with the Director Stage, whose origin is in the upper-left corner and whose vertical axis is measured in the positive direction as you move down.

Points and Vectors

Distinctions exist between points and vectors that make them unique. You should already be familiar with 2D points. Points consist of two components: the horizontal distance from the origin and the vertical distance from the origin that comprises a location in space. In Director, the Stage is a 2D coordinate system, and points() are the data type that are commonly used to describe locations in that space.

You may not be as familiar with the concept of vectors as you are with points(). Vectors represent dynamic information; an inclusive definition is that vectors describe a displacement in space. But what does that really mean? Vectors are comprised of two vital pieces of information: a direction and a magnitude. In short, vectors do not have a location in space—they represent a change from one place to another. For this reason, vectors have a very specific direction (which way they are pointing) and a magnitude (how far they displace in that direction). Figure 4.2 illustrates several points and several vectors in a 2D coordinate system.

FIGURE 4.2

2D points are represented as the measurement of two directions; 2D vectors are represented as a rotation and a magnitude.

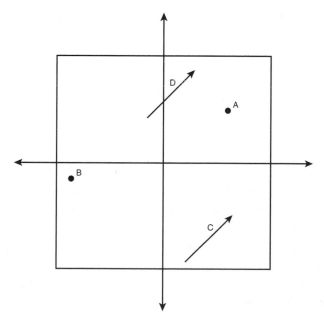

Figure 4.2 illustrates a distinction between points and vectors that can be difficult to understand. Would you say that point A and point B are the same? Probably not, because they are not in the same place. Would you say that vector C and vector D are the same? You should, because even though they are in different places, what makes these vectors the same is that they have the same displacement.

In order to be very clear about the distinction between points and vectors, I will clarify once more that points represent two pieces of information: a horizontal distance and a vertical distance from some origin point. The horizontal and vertical distances of a point can be referred to as its *location*. Vectors represent two pieces of information: a direction and a magnitude. The direction and magnitude of a vector can be referred to as its *displacement*.

Figure 4.3 illustrates a variety of vectors—I have drawn these without any indication of a coordinate system to stress that these vectors do not have a location.

FIGURE 4.3

Various vectors.

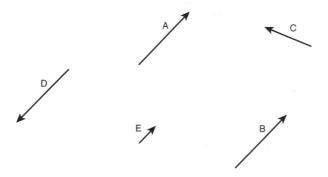

Let's closely examine some of the relationships between the vectors in Figure 4.3. Vectors A and B are the same because their directions and magnitudes are the same. Vectors A and C are clearly different because both their directions and magnitudes are different. Vectors A and D can be tricky: These are not the same. Even though their magnitudes are the same, their directions are not. The fact that both the direction and magnitude must be the same is easier to see in vectors A and E. Their directions are the same, but their magnitudes are different; clearly they are not the same vector.

Now, we know that vectors represent a direction and a magnitude, but often it is much easier to transcribe the values of a vector in terms of displacement on the X and Y axes. Figure 4.4 illustrates several vectors on a two-dimensional coordinate grid and a diagram of how to measure the displacement as components.

FIGURE 4.4

Various vectors on a coordinate grid and how to measure the displacement as components of displacement on the X and Y axes.

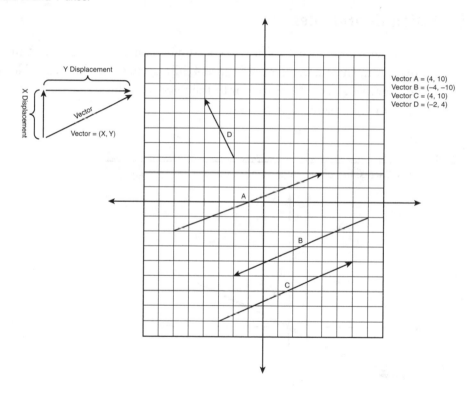

Looking at vectors A and B in this diagram, you can see that the values of displacement are different, thus making these two vectors different. Vectors A and C, although located in different quadrants, are the same because their displacements are the same. Finally, vectors A and D are obviously very different. I included vector D to show you that displacement can be either positive or negative.

If we were to quantify the net displacement (the length of vector A), that value would be referred to as the *magnitude*. If we were to measure the angle from 0 degrees (at 3:00) counterclockwise, this angle would be the direction. Making these measurements on graph paper is quite simple. But we do not have that luxury on the computer. It is easier to describe a vector in terms of components of displacement and utilize calculations to derive the magnitude and direction of the vector. This statement is even easier to defend, especially after the introduction of a third dimension.

3D Cartesian Coordinates

In a three-dimensional Cartesian coordinate system, a third axis of information is introduced: the Z axis. Figure 4.5 illustrates this third axis. Notice that the negative Z axis is pointing into the page, and the positive Z axis is pointing out of the page.

FIGURE 4.5

Three-dimensional Cartesian coordinate system.

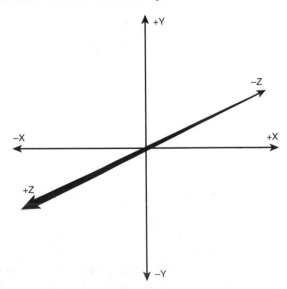

The introduction of the Z axis complicates our understanding of points and vectors. In terms of defining a point in three dimensions, there is little more to do than add a third point of data so that the three required components are *x,y,z*, where *x* equals the distance from the origin on the X axis, *y* equals the distance from the origin from the Y axis, and *z* equals the distance from the origin on the Z axis.

NOTE

> If you have worked in other 3D animation or programming systems before, make particular note of the positions of the axes in Figure 4.5. Because many 3D animation packages do not use the positive Y axis as up, you may want to make sure you have looked closely at this figure if you are having trouble getting your bearings in Director.

Defining vectors as three components of displacement is relatively easy as well. The calculations for determining the magnitude and direction of the vector become a bit more difficult—but those calculations have been built in to Director 8.5. It is important to remember that even in three dimensions, vectors still do not have a location in space—only a displacement.

The `Vector()` **Function and Vector Data Type**

In Lingo, you have probably encountered some of the more advanced data types that are both code objects and functions, such as the `time()` object and the `color()` object. Director 8.5 introduces a new data type known as `vector()`. The vector data type in Director is always a three-dimensional vector. The `vector()` function allows you to create new vectors and store them in a variable. Try the following code in the message window to create a vector:

```
myvector = vector(10,12,-3)
```

Now, the properties of the vector code object named "myvector" can then be accessed via dot syntax. Try the following lines of code in the message window:

```
Put myvector
Put myvector.x
Put myvector.y
Put myvector.z
Put myvector.magnitude
```

With these four examples, you can see that it is possible to access the `vector()` object and each of the components. You can even have Director evaluate the magnitude of the vector. Finding out the direction of the vector object is a little more involved. We will revisit this issue of direction in Chapter 26 "Advanced Transforms and Vector Math."

So far, we are still able to hold to our understanding about displacements. I will caution you that as we continue to examine the `vector()` data type in Lingo, you will learn that the vector information is used to position Models in the World. It may seem like vectors are used as locations, but they are not.

This can be more easily understood if you think about what I have said several times about vectors. If they are going to be used to position Models in the World, and the only thing that they can tell us is where to "move" a Model to, the all important question becomes, "Where are we moving models from?"

World Coordinates Versus Local Coordinates

If I asked you the fragmentary question "How far?", you would probably ask in response, "From where?" What if I ask you how far this book is from you? Before you answer, think about it—this question is still quite fragmentary. Am I asking you the distance from your eye to this page or am I asking you the distance from your toe to the upper-left corner of the book? I am going to guess that these two distances, whatever they might be, are different. So which one is the right answer? Technically, neither. The point to this is that if you ask Director incomplete questions about distances, you will most likely get the wrong answers—or you might be getting the right answers, but just not the answer to the question you felt that you asked.

In Director's 3D environment, it is important that you understand that all positions and rotations occur relative to some point. The origin point of the World is at 0,0,0. But not all positions and rotations occur relative to this point. Imagine if you had a square located 10 units on the positive X axis from the World origin. The World origin is still at 0,0,0, but the square is at 10,0,0. Figure 4.6 illustrates the issue of rotating around World coordinates versus local coordinates.

Just as measurements could be taken relative to yourself, the book, or even the center of the room in which you are reading, measurements in a 3D

Castmember may be specified relative to individual models or relative to the center of the 3D world. When working with a Model-relative coordinate system, we will refer to it as a *local coordinate system.*

FIGURE 4.6

Rotation around World coordinates versus local coordinates.

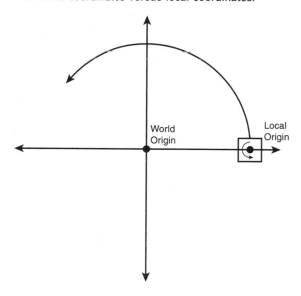

Notice how we could end up with highly different results if we rotate around the World origin or if we rotate around the origin of the Model (the local origin). This issue applies to rotation and positioning. You need to know what point you are positioning and rotating from; otherwise, Director may decide for you.

NOTE

This issue does not apply to scaling, although it does in other 3D programming environments. In Director, scaling always happens relative to a Model's local origin.

Transform() **and Transformations**

There is a difference between the nature and scope of the transform() object and the subject of transformation. The difference is that transform() is a data type and function in Director 8.5, whereas *transformation* is a process of changing the data contained by a `transform()` object. A `transform()` object can be used to position, orient, and scale Models, Lights, Cameras, and Groups.

A `transform()` object contains information about position, rotation, and scale. This information is quite complex, and it is easier to interface with `transform()` through its properties, which can be accessed with dot syntax. In particular, you will probably be interested in the `transform()` properties listed in Table 4.1.

TABLE 4.1   Transform Properties

Property	Default
position	vector(0,0,0)
rotation	vector(0,0,0)
scale	vector(1,1,1)

In terms of position, the `vector()` data that is contained by the `transform().position` property is as we would expect. Because `transform()` objects are always World relative, we can deduce that if the default position of the transform is explained as the displacement `vector(0,0,0)`, we know that the origin and the position are the same. The `position` property represents the amount of displacement on the World X, Y, and Z axes.

It is at this point that our understanding of vectors diverges from the `vector()` data type. If `vector()` describes a displacement, and we have been measuring displacements in terms of position, what if we described angles of displacement with `vector()`? In terms of rotation, the three components of the vector represent the rotation in degrees around the X, Y, and Z axes.

To further complicate the `vector()` data type, it is also used to represent scaling information. The `scale` property represents what is known as the *scalefactor*. There are components to the scalefactor for a given transform. Each of these components describes the amount of scaling in the X, Y, and Z directions.

A scalefactor component of 1 means that the scale of the transform in that direction is 100 percent to scale. At a scale factor of vector(.5,.5,.5), your transform() would be 50 percent, and so on. It is possible to have negative scalefactors, indicating that the transform is mirrored across the given axis. No scalefactor will ever be 0, nor should you try to set a scalefactor component to 0. It represents an impossible situation and will generate a script error.

You may still not be convinced about the transform() object and the properties that we have looked at so far—especially because of the way that it forces us to rethink our understanding of vectors. However, I think I can convince you with the following exercise. In the message window, create a new transform() object and save it in a variable with the following line of code:

```
Mytrans = transform()
```

Now, take a look at what you just created:

```
Put mytrans
-- transform(1.0000,0.0000,0.0000,0.0000, 0.0000,1.0000,0.0000,\
0.0000, 0.0000,0.0000,1.0000,0.00000.0000,0.0000,0.0000,1.0000)
```

This large 16-component list of information is revealed to us. However, it is much easier to ask for specific information from the transform() object with the following:

```
put mytrans.position
-- vector( 0.0000, 0.0000, 0.0000 )
put mytrans.rotation
-- vector( 0.0000, 0.0000, 0.0000 )
put mytrans.scale
-- vector( 1.0000, 1.0000, 1.0000 )
```

Notice that this information is easier to understand because it has been put into a format that we can comprehend with less work. When you are working with transforms, you are probably not interested in the whole entire transform() matrix.

NOTE

> It is recommended that you avoid accessing the `transform()` matrix directly because even if you do know what you are doing, you can create `transform()` matrices that have the wrong meaning or no meaning at all. Working with `transform()` matrices directly is well beyond the scope of this book. We will revisit `transform()` objects and vector math in greater detail in Chapter 26.

Although I encourage you to think of the properties of `transform()` objects as the public properties for accessing information about a `transform()`, I mention the matrix to show you that there are many levels of detail in Director's 3D environment.

Transforming the `Transform()` Object

Until now, we have only been examining the default `transform()` object that we created with the `transform()` function. The next challenge is to learn about the process known as *transformation* in order to actually change the data stored in the `transform()` object.

Although it is entirely possible to both get and set the `transform()` properties with Lingo, it is not recommended to set `transform()` properties in this way. Although not as consuming as setting the `transform()` matrix directly, setting the `transform()` properties does take some care and attention. In several examples in this book, we will set the `transform()` properties directly, notably in Chapter 13, "A 2D Mouse in a 3D World," where you learn to control a 2D mouse in a 3D environment.

The recommended way to perform transformations on a `transform()` object is via several dedicated commands, which are listed in Table 4.2.

TABLE 4.2   Transform Commands

Command	Expects
`Translate()`	`vector(Xdisplace, Ydisplace, Zdisplace)`
`Rotate()`	`vector(Xdegrees,Ydegrees,Zdegrees)`
`Scale()`	`vector(Xscalefactor,Yscalefactor,Zscalefactor)`

The difference in wording should provide some clues regarding the nature of these commands: notice that they are verbs—we are doing something with these commands. Translate() changes the position of a transform() object by displacing it with a vector representing three components of location change. Rotate() changes the rotation/orientation of a transform() object with a vector representing three angles of rotation in degrees around the three axes. Finally, Scale() changes the scale of a transform via a vector representing three components of scale factor.

The key is that each of these commands changes the transform() object. They are the public methods for changing the values of position, rotation, and scale. Also note that these commands are accumulative. In the message window, create a new transform() object called "t" and rotate it with the following code:

```
T = transform()
t.rotate(30,5,7)
put t.rotation
-- vector(30,5,7)
```

Now, rotate t again:

```
t.rotate(30.0000, 5.0000, 7.0000)
put t.rotation
-- vector( 60.5039, 5.7908, 15.5969 )
```

Did you expect that it would have returned vector(60,10,14)? Does it seem like these values are wrong? They aren't wrong—but they do offer a glimpse into the way that transformations take place. When you rotate a transform() object, Director first rotates the X component, then the Y component, and then the Z component. For this reason, the second time we rotate the transform() object, the final rotation is not quite what you may have expected. This is what makes it difficult to set the properties of the transform directly.

Another issue that you should be aware of is that the order of Rotate() transforms has to do with rotating Nodes back from where they came from. For example, let's create a transform() object called "a" and rotate it with the following code:

```
A = transform()
A.rotate(10,45,2)
Put a.rotation
-- vector(10.0000, 45.0000, 2.0000)
```

Now try to rotate the transform() object back with the following code:

```
a.rotate(-10,-45,-2)
put a.rotation
-- vector( 1.5242, -0.2442, -7.6520 )
```

The result of rotating and then rotating with negative values for each component is not what you might expect. Again, the reason for this is that rotations are performed in a specific order, and this can change the final transformation. If you do need to rotate a Node back from where it came, you can always use the following:

```
a = transform()
a.rotate(10,45,2)
put a.rotation
-- vector( 10.0000, 45.0000, 2.0000 )
b = a.inverse()
put b.rotation
-- vector( -12.0962, -44.5877, 7.1258 )
a.rotate(b.rotation)
put a.rotation
-- vector( 0.0000, 0.0000, 0.0000 )
```

In this case, we are using the transform().inverse() command, which returns a new transform that contains the inverted rotation and position information from the original transform. It is a helpful way to create a displacement for rotation or position that will return your Node to its previous position or orientation.

To learn more about vector math, transform() objects, trigonometry, and the 3D environment interact, look at Chapter 26, where we'll take what you have learned about vector() objects and transform() objects and apply this knowledge to Models.

Models, `Transform()`, and Transformations

Although a `transform()` object can exist as an independent object, every Model Node has a `transform()` "tied" to it. In short, every Model Node has a `transform` property that defines the location, rotation, and scale of a Model in coordinates relative to the Model's parent. This is a key difference between the transforms that are "tied" to Models and those that are independent `transform()` objects. Independent `transform()` objects have no parents—all coordinates are relative to themselves in their local space.

By default, a Model's parent is the World; this means that by default a Model's coordinates are reported as relative to the World origin. In Chapter 8, "Parents, Children, and Cloning," we will explore the subject of manipulating the Model and Scene hierarchy in terms of parents and children and how this affects transformations.

Although the `transform()` coordinates for a Model are parent-relative, it is possible to perform transformations on Models that are specifically World-relative, self relative, or relative to another Model or Node.

Transformation Demos

The CD contains several demos that we will examine in order to begin your understanding of the scope of transformations. In addition, we will look at several specific applications of transformation to accomplish common tasks.

Basic Model Transformation

If you open the "Basic Transforms" file on the CD and play the movie, you will be able to execute some transformations from the message window. When you play the movie, a box should appear in the center of the Stage. Type the following into the message window and then press Return:

```
scene.model[1].transform.rotate(20,10,10)
```

On the Stage, the box should rotate to a new position. Without stopping the movie, type the following into the message window and then press Return:

```
scene.model[1].transform.identity()
```

The Model should have returned to its original position. The `identity()` command sets the `transform()` object to its default values. It is a very easy method of resetting the Model to its default position. But what if in your movie the default `transform()` object that you would like for your Model is not the default `transform()` object that `identity()` sets it to? This is one reason why it is helpful to have independent transforms. Stop and restart the movie and let's try the following in the message window:

```
scene.model[1].transform.translate(0,-30,0)
```

The Model should have moved down vertically on the Stage. Now, rotate the Model with the following code:

```
scene.model[1].transform.rotate(0,45,0)
```

Save a new transform of the Model in World-relative coordinates in a `transform()` object that is independent from the Model:

```
homebase = scene.model[1].getworldtransform()
```

Now let's move the Model to a new location:

```
Scene.model[1].transform.translate(20,50,-150)
```

To set the Model back to its "home" position, we need only execute the following:

```
Scene.model[1].transform = homebase
```

In this example, you learned about the `identity()` and `getworldtransform()` functions. Both of these are useful utilities that will make many tasks much easier. However, the `getworldtransform()` function can only be run on Models. It cannot be run on independent `transform()` objects. The `identity()` function can be run on any `transform()` object. Stop and rewind the movie and we will continue with our demonstration.

Transforming Models: World-Relative and Model-Relative

In this section, I address how to work with World coordinates and local coordinates. Play the movie, type the following into the message window, and then press Return:

```
scene.model[1].translate(50,0,0)
```

Notice that I have removed the word "transform" from this code; you can use the typing shortcut for transforming Models. Now, rotate the Model with the following:

```
scene.model[1].rotate(0,10,0, #world)
```

Notice the fourth parameter that we have passed along with the `rotate` function: #world. This parameter forces the Model to rotate around the #world origin.

NOTE

By default, a Model transforms relative to its parent Node. Also by default, a Model's parent is the World. So, if you do not specify the "relative to" parameter when transforming a Model, and you have not changed the Model's parent, the Model will transform relative to the World. I think that it is better practice to be precise by including the "relative to" parameter.

Look at the Model; it just rotated around the World origin. You can find out information about its new position with the following:

```
put scene.model[1].getworldtransform().position
-- vector( 49.2404, 0.0000, -8.6824 )
```

Look at the values it returned; we translated the model by `vector(50,0,0)`, and after a rotation of 10 degrees around the World Y axis, the X and Z components of `position` have changed. What if you wanted to rotate the object in place? Stop and restart the movie and then move the Model again with the following code:

```
scene.model[1].translate(50,0,0)
```

Now, rotate the Model with the following:

```
scene.model[1].rotate(0,10,0, #self)
```

The Model should rotate 10 degrees around the local Y axis. Now, take a look at the position information with the following code:

```
put scene.model[1].getworldtransform().position
-- vector( 50.0000, 0.0000, 0.0000 )
```

The Model has not moved from the position that we moved it to, but it has changed its rotation. There are other options for the "relative to" parameter, such as #parent. In addition, there is also a way to use the "relative to" parameter to transform Models relative to another Model or Node.

Transforming Models Relative to Another Model or Node

Open the file "Relative Transform" and start the movie. A sphere and a box should appear on the Stage. We can rotate the box around the sphere with the following line of code:

```
Scene.model[1].rotate(0,0,30, scene.model[2])
```

By setting the "relative to" parameter to a Node, you can create objects that orbit other objects quite easily.

Orbits and Revolutions

Open the "Orbits" file on the CD and press Play. This effect is accomplished with the following exitframe handler:

```
global scene

on exitFrame me
  go "run"    --stay on this frame
```

```
 --rotate the box around the sphere
 scene.model[1].rotate(0,-3,0,scene.model[2])
 --rotate the box around itself
 scene.model[1].rotate(5,4,2,#self)
end
```

Because we are transforming the rotation of the Model the same amount on every frame, a smooth animation is produced. However, you should realize that this animation is being created with code in real time. While the movie is still running, type the following code into the message window and press Return:

```
scene.model[2].debug = true
```

If you are in software rendering mode, this will not have the correct effect. If you are in a rendering mode such as opengl or directX, you will see the sphere surrounded by a gray wire mesh. This is referred to as the *bounding sphere*. In addition, you should see a red and green line extending from the sphere, and a dark blue dot in the center of the sphere. The red line points in the direction of the local positive X axis, the green line points in the direction of the local positive Y axis, and the blue dot is actually the local positive Z axis (because it is pointing directly at us, it looks like a point). Type the following into the message window to turn on the local axes and bounding sphere for the box:

```
scene.model[1].debug = true
```

Now, the box has a bounding sphere, represented by the gray mesh sphere that surrounds the box. This sphere shows you the extents of the mesh of the Model. It is a helpful tool for visualizing how close objects are to each other. We will explore the bounding sphere again later when we deal with collision detection in Chapter 29. The local axes should be spinning all around as the object orbits the sphere and revolves around itself. This illustrates an important point: The local axes of the object are actually changing position.

Order of Transformations

The fact that the local axes are changing position is important because it can help you understand how the order of transformations affects your final transform. We have been focusing a lot of attention on rotation; in this demo, we will look at how rotation and translation can lead to unexpected problems. Open the file "Basic Transforms" again and play the movie.

In the message window, type the following line of code to rotate the object:

```
Scene.model[1].rotate(30,40,0,#self)
```

Now turn on the bounding box and local axis:

```
Scene.model[1].debug = true
```

Notice that the local positive Z axis for the Model is not pointing out of the screen toward us. When we translate the Model on the Z axis, notice what happens:

```
Scene.model[1].translate(0,0,30,#self)
```

Rather than moving toward us, the Model moves along the local Z axis. If you want the Model to move toward us, you can use #world as the "relative to" parameter. However, I am more interested in showing you what will happen if we try this example again in a different order. Without stopping the movie, type the following in the message window and press Return:

```
Scene.model[1].transform.identity()
```

Remember, the identity() function resets a transform() object to its default values. Now, rather than rotating and then translating the object, let's perform the transformations in the reverse order. Type the following into the message window and press Return after each line:

```
Scene.model[1].translate(0,0,30,#self)
Scene.model[1].rotate(30,40,0,#self)
```

The result of performing these transformations in reverse order has quite different consequences. You can see how this is important: It is possible to know what the correct transformations are, but this is not enough—you must know what order you need to perform them in.

Using Independent `Transform()` and `Vector()` Objects

I have mentioned that you can use the `transform()` function to create `transform()` Nodes that are independent of Models. We have also examined the `getworldtransform()` function as another method of creating a `transform()` Node.

In this example, you will need to open the "Independent Transform" file on the CD. While the movie is playing, create a `transform()` object in the message window with the following:

```
Mytrans = transform()
Mytrans.translate(10,2,0)
Mytrans.rotate(40,1,0)
```

Now set each of the Model's transformations equal to mytrans:

```
Scene.model[1].transform = mytrans
Scene.model[2].transform = mytrans
Scene.model[3].transform = mytrans
Scene.model[4].transform = mytrans
```

By the time you are done, it should look like all the Models have disappeared. They are all in the same exact place, because we positioned them according to the same `transform()` information. A `transform()` object contains information that is relative to itself, and for this reason you cannot use the "relative to" parameter when working with independent transforms.

Stop, rewind, and start the movie again. We will create a custom vector in the message window with the following code:

```
Myvect = vector(5,3,-30)
```

Now we will translate each model by this vector:

```
Scene.model[1].translate(myvect)
Scene.model[2].translate(myvect)
```

```
Scene.model[3].translate(myvect)
Scene.model[4].translate(myvect)
```

With this example, we were able to make a single independent vector and then displace several models in the same way based on that vector.

Scaling Demo

The scale() command always operates in Model-relative space, so you cannot use the "relative to" parameter. Although it may seem unimportant, in other 3D programming environments, this is not the case, which leads to many problems.

Open the "Scale Transforms" file on the CD and play the movie. A bright orange cone should appear in the center of the Stage. I have chosen the cone because it will make visualizing certain effects more apparent. If we scale the Model using the code

```
scene.model[1].scale(.5,1,1)
```

the Model should appear half as wide. Note that this function is not changing the Modelresource; instead, it is scaling the Model. Now scale the model again:

```
scene.model[1].scale(.5,1,1)
```

The Model is now a quarter as wide as the original. The effect of scaling accumulates the same way that rotation and translations accumulate. You can use the getworldtransform() function to learn information about the current scale of the Model:

```
put scene.model[1].getworldtransform().scale
-- vector (.2500, 1.0000, 1.0000)
```

On the CD, there is a file called "Scaling Demo." Open this movie and press Play. Here's the script that causes the pulsation effects:

```
1: property pScounter, spritenum, pfactor, pdir
2:
3: global scene
4:
5: on beginsprite me
6:   pScounter = 0 --counter used to determine period of throbbing
7:   pdir = .005  --used to scale in a positive or negative direction
8:   pfactor = 1  -- default scale factor used to scale object
9: end
10:
11: on exitframe
12:  -- increase counter by one
13:  pScounter = pScounter + 1
14:
15:  -- if the counter is a multiple of 5, flip the direction of scaling
16:  if (pScounter mod 5) = 1 then
17:   pdir = -pdir
18:  end if
19:
20:  -- add the value of pdir to the scale factor
21:  -- if the pdir is positive, pfactor will grow
22:  -- if pdir is negative, pfactor will shrink
23:  pfactor = pfactor + pdir
24:
25:  -- by using pfactor, we are able to scale
26:  -- in a linear manner, bypassing the
27:  -- accumulation of scaling via the
28:  -- scale command and performing the scale
29:  -- factor increase manually.
30:  scene.model[1].transform.scale = vector(pfactor,pfactor,pfactor)
31:
32:  -- rotate the model for demonstration purposes:
33:  -- to show that we can perform other
34:  -- transformations at the same time
35:  scene.model[1].rotate(.3,.4,.1)
36:
37: end
```

NOTE

There are two reasons why I have shown you this demo: First, to emphasize that, in Director, scale changes on an object do not interfere with rotation and position changes—this is classically not the case with other 3D environments. Second, creating objects that pulse slightly may seem like a minute task, but we will use this technique in Chapter 24 with Lingo-controlled Bones Animation to simulate breathing in our characters.

Controlling Objects with Keyboard Input

In the next several demos, we will use the keyboard as an input device for controlling Models in several different ways.

Keyboard Translation

Open the file named "Keyboard Translation" and press Play. Make sure that the Stage is the active window and use the arrow keys to control the position of the box. This demo uses the left and right arrows for X-axis translation and the up and down arrows for Z-axis translation. Here's the code:

```
 1: global scene
 2:
 3: on exitframe
 4:
 5:  --remember, chartonum() changes a character
 6:  --into its character map number equivalent
 7:  --30 = up arrow
 8:  --31 = down arrow
 9:  --28 = left arrow
10:  --29 = right arrow
11:
12:  case(chartonum(the keypressed)) of
13:   30: --up arrow
14:    scene.model[1].translate(0,0,-1)
15:   31:  --down arrow
16:    scene.model[1].translate(0,0,1)
17:   28: --left arrow
18:    scene.model[1].translate(-1,0,0)
19:   29:--right arrow
20:    scene.model[1].translate(1,0,0)
21:  end case
22: end
```

The approach of this demonstration utilizes the keypressed system property and an exitframe handler. You should avoid using repeat loops when you can, and this is certainly one of those cases. Notice how we are taking input from arrow keys and using their numeric keyboard mappings to decide what to do with the input in the case statement.

Notice in lines 14 and 16 that we are using the up and down arrows to move in the positive and negative Z directions. Before you look at the answer, think about how you might alter these two lines so that the box moves in the X/Y plane.

The answer is that you need to change the lines of code that deal with translation in the X/Z plane. In other words, change the lines

```
Line 14: Scene.model[1].translate(0,0,-1)
Line 16: Scene.model[1].translate(0,0,1)
```

to this:

```
Line 14: Scene.model[1].translate(0,1,0)
Line 16: Scene.model[1].translate(0,-1,0)
```

One last note about this demo: The frame rate has been set to 999 in order to try and move the box as fast as possible. You can alter the frame rate or the distance of translation to create some interesting effects. Also, note that you can rotate the box in addition to translating it.

Keyboard Harp

In this demo, we will utilize the number keys as input in order to create an instrument. Open the file named "Keyboard Harp" and press Play. Make sure that the Stage is the active window and use the number keys (1–8) to play with the keyboard harp.

The keyboard harp is slightly more involved than the previous demo. The initialization script is more advanced because the initial setup of the boxes in the environment is created on-the-fly. Notice how I have encapsulated the process of creating and positioning the boxes inside of a repeat loop to minimize the typing in the following code:

```
1: global scene
2:
3: on initialize
4:   clearworld(scene)
5:
6:   scene.light[1].color = rgb(20,20,20)
7:
8:   -- I am going to create 8 boxes, and then position them evenly across
```

```
 9:  -- the stage, and because no one likes to type, I am going to do this
10:  -- from within a repeat loop
11:
12:  repeat with x = 1 to 8
13:
14:    -- set a variable = to x * 25 this will generate
15:    -- a number from 25 to 200 depending on the value of x
16:    xcol = x * 25
17:
18:    -- when we create the box, append X on the name to make it unique
19:    obj = createbox("mybox" & x, 10,15,40, rgb(40,110,xcol))
20:    -- also, notice that I am using the variable xcol as the blue component
21:    -- for the diffuse property of the box - this is what generates
22:    -- the ramp of color from greenblue to bluegreen
23:
24:    -- move the object to this position initially
25:    obj.translate(-90,-30,0)
26:
27:    -- decide how far on the positive x axis you want to move
28:    -- the current model.
29:    xset = x * 20
30:
31:    -- move the object once again to its home position
32:    obj.translate(xset,0,0)
33:
34:  end repeat
35:
36: end
```

Now that the environment is set up, the keyboard input is handled through a custom script:

```
 1: property spritenum, homelist
 2:
 3: global scene
 4:
 5: on beginsprite me
 6:   -- create a blank list
 7:   homelist = []
 8:
 9:   -- store the default values for the Y displacement
10:   -- of each box in a linear list
11:   repeat with x = 1 to scene.model.count
12:     addat(homelist, scene.model[x].getworldtransform().position.y)
13:   end repeat
```

```
14: end
15:
16: on keydown
17:   -- if the user presses key 1 - 8 then
18:   if "12345678" contains the key then
19:     -- change the key from a character into a number
20:     -- and store this value in a variable
21:     wm = value(the key)
22:
23:     -- choose the model to translate
24:     -- based on what key was pressed
25:     scene.model[wm].translate(0,20,0)
26:
27:     -- if you haven't already, check out rateshift
28:     -- choose the sound channel to play in and the
29:     -- amount of rateshift to apply to the note
30:     sound(wm).play([#member: member("pluck"), #rateshift: wm])
31:     -- NOTE: shifting rates linearly does not
32:     -- produce an "in tune" scale, as you can hear.
33:   end if
34: end
35:
36: on exitframe
37:   --repeat this for each model
38:   repeat with x = 1 to 8
39:     -- find out the current y displacement of the model
40:     curpos = scene.model[x].getworldtransform().position.y
41:     -- if the model is not in its "home" y displacement then
42:     --move translate it "down" by one unit
43:     if curpos <> homelist[x] then
44:       scene.model[x].translate(0,-1,0)
45:     end if
46:   end repeat
47: end
```

In addition to applying what you have learned about translating to set up the 3D environment and then control it with the keyboard, this demo introduces a few concepts that we will revisit, such as the use of "homelist". Technically, I would call this list a look-up table. We will explore the possibilities of look-up tables in Chapter 18, "3D Interface Design." The last two demos have utilized the keyboard as an input device. The keyboard is very immediate, and you can see that it is not terribly difficult to use it to control the 3D environment. I encourage you to read Chapter 13, which explains how to utilize the mouse as an input device for the 3D world.

Summary

Transformation is a process that can be used to change the position, orientation, and scale of several Nodes. Among these Nodes are Models, Cameras, and Lights as well as transform() objects. Independent transform() objects do not have a visual representation onscreen, but the data they contain can be used to position Nodes.

Many factors affect the final outcome of transformations: the order of transformations, the World or local coordinate system used, and the accuracy of the vectors used to displace position, rotation, and scale. Several commands are used to affect the transformation of Nodes. These commands are easier to use than directly accessing transform matrices, although this advanced functionality does exist.

Finally, transformations can be approached on several levels of increasing complexity. However, at each level it is important to remember what you are trying to accomplish as well as how you are trying to accomplish it. Because transformations can be counterintuitive, your first tries may well be wrong. First, examine your requirements to see whether there is a built-in function, command, or behavior that performs that task you are looking for. Then create custom transforms, custom handlers, custom functions, and custom scripts, and then look into transformation matrices.

FAQ

This is my nth time through the chapter, and I still do not feel like I have a handle on this subject. What can I do?

First, don't panic. Transformations are classically difficult to master. I suggest first taking a good look at the demos in the chapter and then trying to re-create some of these demos. Start with the simpler tasks: Move a Model and then rotate a Model in place. Then move up to the more involved demos: Rotate a Model around a fixed point and see if you can cause it to revolve around itself at the same time. If you can get these to work, you are on the right track. If none of this math stuff is working for you, you might need a visual tool. Some transformation issues are easier to comprehend if you use a visual tool such as the 3D Property Inspector (3DPI). 3DPI runs as a tool Xtra and allows you to modify the properties of your environment visually, while the movie is playing. Although you cannot save your changes to the Shockwave 3D Castmember, you may be able to visualize where your logic has gone wrong in order to guide you through the math.

Do vector shapes and `vector()` *objects have anything to do with one another?*

No. Not at all.

I have a Model that I want to point at another Model. Is this possible?

There is a command that deals with pointing nodes called `pointat()`. We will first examine `pointat()` in Chapter 6, "Understanding Cameras," in terms of Cameras, but the lessons that I show there can be applied to Models and Lights as well.

I keep hearing about something called "gimbal lock," but I have no idea what people are talking about. Should I worry?

Yes and no. Gimbal lock is a side effect of rotating `transform()` objects with the `rotate()` command. When you are rotating your Models on more than one axis at a time, you may run into this problem. The problem is that your Model may rotate on the X and Y axes but not on the Z axis. The short answer is that this problem can be avoided with the `axisangle()` property, but it is more difficult to use. We will examine the problem of gimbal lock and its implications in Chapter 26. Until we deal with this problem, I would not worry about it.

CHAPTER 5

Understanding Lighting

In this chapter, we will be exploring the various types of Lights available to you when creating 3D worlds. In addition to an introduction to scene lighting theory, we will discuss the differences between physical lighting and the lighting tools available in Director. Performance issues limit the lighting capabilities of the computer in real time. These performance issues demand attention during the design stage of your projects. When lighting is incorporated into your design from the beginning, you can use it to limit the number of Models and illustrate areas of complex geometry.

The degree of impact that lighting has on your project will be determined by your understanding of the possibilities lighting provides. Without lighting in the 3D world, nothing is visible. Models that are not lit are not seen; Models that are improperly lit may look deceptively flat. Lighting should contribute toward the overall design solution of your project: from the basic goals of providing illumination and establishing mood, to the more understated possibilities of Lights playing an active role in performance optimization.

Developing an understanding of lighting will allow you to more accurately "previsualize" your projects and organize the parameters of your production. Director provides many tools for the creation of compelling compositions with lighting. This chapter focuses on providing a method for designing with lighting and a system for implementing those designs with Director.

NOTE

In this chapter, we are specifically discussing the way that Lights react with Models using the standard Shader. Non-photorealistic Shaders will react differently to the Lights in a scene, but the

Lights will be controlled with the same code as when the standard Shader is used. For more on non-photorealistic Shaders, see Chapter 15, "Non-Photorealistic Rendering."

Basic Scene Lighting

When designing your projects, it is helpful if you can describe the approach toward your overall lighting solution with words. Many times this will be similar to how you might describe the stylization of the Models or other elements of your project. The first step in lighting design is to define this solution as specifically as possible with words such as *cinematic*, *fantastic*, *realistic*, and so on. Each of these demands a slightly different approach that results in determining several key factors about the Lights in your design: How many Lights are required? What types of Lights are best suited? What colors should be used? What positions and angles work?

Design Priorities

Beyond defining stylization, you need to develop a method of prioritizing the needs of your lighting design. Each Light Node can be thought of as having a primary purpose—a specific goal that it must accomplish or a purpose that justifies its existence. Light Nodes that meet their primary goals and then fulfill secondary and tertiary goals have a higher priority. These are the types of Light Nodes you want to define. The purpose of each Light Node can be broken down into three categories: illumination, modeling, and focus.

Illumination is generally the first purpose of lighting, and most lighting scenarios require proper illumination in order to provide the information your users will need to understand your project. Without Lights in the 3D world, you will not see anything in your scenes. The goal of illumination is to allow users to see the environment, whereas the goals of modeling and focus are as much about revealing geometry as they are about concealing geometry. Because the sole purpose of illumination is to reveal the environment, the more Models that are affected, the better.

The second goal for lighting is to use Lights as modeling aids for describing the sculptural and dimensional qualities of Models and the spatial relationships within your scene. In addition, using Lights for modeling can also establish the time of day in your scene. The geometry of Models that are not modeled with Light will become very flat, even when that geometry is complex. The term *modeling* has two meanings in 3D development that must be clarified: In terms of geometry, we use the term *modeling* to describe the process of creating Models with 3D modeling software. In the sense of lighting design, *modeling* refers to how lighting can be used to reveal or conceal the sculptural form of Models.

The primary compositional element that fuels focus is *contrast*. By selectively lighting parts of a given Model or scene, you can direct the eye of the viewer to specific elements that you want him or her to look at. The eye tends to be drawn to areas of contrast, and this can be used to define areas of your composition with more importance.

These three purposes are not exclusive. Many times, you will use Lights to provide detail to a section of a Model, which also changes the contrast in that area of the scene. The primary purpose may be modeling, but when the Light Node begins to be used to describe parts of the Model and obscure others, its secondary purpose becomes focus.

NOTE

Because the 3D world is rendered in real time, certain performance issues must be noted. In particular, the more Lights your scene has, the more work the processor has to do and therefore the slower your runtime frame rate will be. Take a look at Chapter 19, "Performance Optimization," for lighting benchmarks and optimization tricks.

Types of Lights

There are several different types of Light Nodes available in Director—each with unique characteristics. Understanding how these Lights will react with Models on their own will aid you in learning how they work in conjunction with one another. With the three purposes of lighting in mind, it is time to introduce the four Light Node types: #ambient, #directional, #point, and #spot. The purpose of each of the Light Node types is detailed in Table 5.1.

TABLE 5.1   Light Node Types

Light Type	Primary Purpose
#ambient	Illumination
#directional	Illumination and modeling

TABLE 5.1   Continued

Light Type	Primary Purpose
#point	Illumination and modeling
#spot	Modeling and focusing

To successfully implement our lighting designs, it is necessary to utilize a combination of the Light Node types. Table 5.1 provides guidelines when deciding which Light Nodes are required for specific goals of the design.

NOTE

Although it is possible to use the #spot Light type for the primary purpose of illumination, proper modeling and focusing as the primary and secondary goals of a #spot Light will make illumination a tertiary goal.

#ambient Lights

Of the four types, #ambient Lights have the fewest parameters. Because of this, #ambient Lights tend to be overlooked or misunderstood as being simplistic. The #ambient Light Node type represents the reflected light within a scene. You experience the effects of #ambient Light constantly throughout the day. In the physical world, surfaces absorb and reflect the light that hits them. The light that is not absorbed is reflected and travels on to other surfaces to be absorbed or reflected until, ideally, there is no longer any light remaining.

In the computer, we are only simulating specific qualities of light. The calculation of numerous interreflections of light in a given environment is time consuming. Therefore, the reflected light that contributes to the illumination of Models in the real world is approximated with the #ambient Light type. Figure 5.1 illustrates the effect of lighting a scene with an #ambient Light only.

#ambient Light is omnipresent and permeates the scene affecting every Model. It does not have a position or orientation, and for this reason it is unique. It is a light level that is used to approximate the overall brightness and contrast of a scene. For this reason, #ambient Lights have one controllable property that affects how the scene is lit: Color.

FIGURE 5.1

This scene is lit with #ambient Light only. It looks flat because #ambient Light is good for general illumination, but not modeling.

#directional Lights

The #directional Light Node type is a versatile tool for lighting your 3D environments. It can accomplish the goals of illumination and modeling quite successfully. Figure 5.2 illustrates the manner in which Models are both illuminated and modeled by #directional Lights by defining three key areas on Models: highlight, midtone, and shaded regions.

FIGURE 5.2

A #directional Light emphasizes the geometric qualities of Models by defining them in terms of highlight, midtone, and shaded regions.

The #directional Light type is most often compared to sunlight. The reason for this comparison is the manner in which light from the sun reaches the earth. Because the sun is so massive and extremely far away, the rays of light from the sun that reach a given spot on the earth tend to be almost exactly parallel. The rays of a #directional Light are exactly parallel and affect the scene in a uniform manner.

Technically, a #directional Light reacts with any surfaces that are pointing in the direction of the light, irrespective of the position of those surfaces in the scene (see Figure 5.3). In short, every Model in your scene, no matter how distant, will be lit in the same manner by a given #directional Light.

FIGURE 5.3

The diagram illustrates how rays from the #directional Light Node affect only the surfaces pointing toward the Light. The image demonstrates how the rays in the diagram will resolve when the scene is rendered.

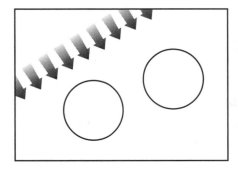 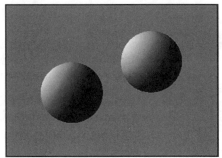

Because #directional Light does not have a position in space, there is no sense of Models being "closer to the light" or "farther away from the light." For this reason, #directional Lights can be used to create uniform illumination for all the Models in your scene.

A #directional Light has three defining properties: Color, Specular, and Rotation. Specular is a Boolean property (either true or false) that controls whether there is a highlight on the Models affected by the #directional Light.

The property that primarily defines how the Light will affect the scene is Rotation. Remember that the #directional Light does not have a location other than infinitely far away, but this cannot be altered. The Rotation property allows you to control whether the light is coming from above, below, behind, in front, and so on. Because of this, the #directional Light can be used for the purpose of modeling as well as illumination. The modeling that

#directional Lights provide is a uniform description of the Models in your scene—the highlights will be in the same place, and the shadow regions will be in the same place.

#point Lights

A #point Light Node can be compared with a bare light bulb—light rays emanate from the bulb in all directions. #point Lights have three defining properties: Color, Specular, and Position. Because light emanates in all directions from a #point Light, the primary defining property is its position. #point Lights will affect every surface in a scene that is facing the direction of the emitted light, so they are prime candidates for providing general illumination.

Because the rays of light emitted from a #point Light are not parallel, #point Lights can be used to represent local lighting sources—that is, light sources that have a perceived location in the scene, as illustrated in Figure 5.4.

FIGURE 5.4

The diagram illustrates how rays of light from the #point Light Node travel in an omni-directional manner. Notice how it is possible to localize the position of the #point Light in the rendered image.

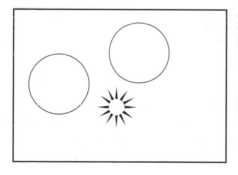 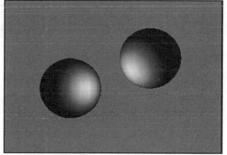

It is the capability of #point Lights to localize their position that allow them to serve as a modeling and illumination source. The modeling capabilities of the #point Light tend to be superior when you're creating interiors, especially when multiple #point Lights are used.

NOTE

It is also possible to alter the distance the light rays of a #point Light reach. See the section titled "Attenuation," later in this chapter, for a discussion of how to achieve this.

#spot Lights

#spot Lights have more properties than the other Light Nodes. For this reason, you have the most control over the use of #spot Lights. They are mainly used to draw focus to a specific area of a scene or for their power to accentuate the sculptural qualities of a surface. Used correctly, #spot Lights can add dynamism and dimensionality to a scene. Overused, they can cause the computer to grind to a halt. The properties that define the #spot Light are Color, Rotation, Position, Specular, Spotangle, and Spotdecay. Figure 5.5 illustrates how a #spot Light can be used to focus on particular areas of a Model.

FIGURE 5.5

The #spot Light can be used to pinpoint specific areas of your Models.

In the case of the #spot Light, both Position and Rotation play an extremely important role. Specifically, a #spot Light has a position in a scene, but it also must be rotated in order to point toward the Models you want to light. Whereas it is much easier to provide general illumination and modeling with the other Light types, the #spot Light is very specific and demands attention be paid to the geometry and spatial relationships within a scene. A metaphor that you can use for understanding this is a flashlight. You have to rotate the beam of light in order to point at Models you want to see.

Spotangle plays a crucial role in effectively utilizing #spot Lights. The #spot Light provides you with a beam of light that can be pointed at Models—Spotangle determines how wide that beam of light is. The rays of light emanate from the #spot Light's Position toward the angle of Rotation in a cone defined by Spotangle. The larger the Spotangle, the larger the cone, and the more Models affected by the #spot Light. This beam width can be described as an angle, as illustrated in Figure 5.6.

FIGURE 5.6

The beam angle of a #spot Light can be set between 0 to 180 degrees. This diagram demonstrates how the Spotangle property and the beam angle correspond.

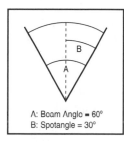 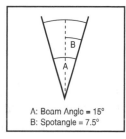 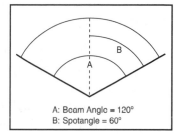

A: Beam Angle = 60°
B: Spotangle = 30°

A: Beam Angle = 15°
B: Spotangle = 7.5°

A: Beam Angle = 120°
B: Spotangle = 60°

Spotdecay is a very useful property whose value is a Boolean (either true or false). Using Spotdecay does affect performance, but the results are generally worth it. Note in Figure 5.7 the difference in the smoothness of the edge of the light on the sphere. The only property change between these two images is Spotdecay.

FIGURE 5.7

Notice how the edge of light in the right image is very coarse because the Spotdecay property has been set to false.

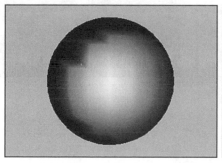 

A Method for Designing with Light

Key lighting diagrams are yet another design tool you can use to determine how many Lights you need and where they should be placed. The Light Node with the highest priority is said to be the "key" light. It is possible that you may have more than one key light if you have several lights with the same priority. The other lights in the scene take on the role of "fill" lights—that is, lights that supplement the illumination, modeling, and focus where the key light cannot.

Key Lights

The key light designs in Figure 5.8 have several features in common. Note that the diagram contains only the pertinent information necessary to assess how many lights are required for a scene, the colors that are needed, and the general positions and rotations that are going to be required. There's also a notation: high, mid, low, back, front, and so on. These words describe the relative position of the key light and the fill lights and what the shadows and highlights of those lights should look like.

FIGURE 5.8

This illustration of a key light diagram corresponds with the accompanying image. Key light diagrams are drawn as if viewing the environment from above. (A color version is included on the CD-ROM.)

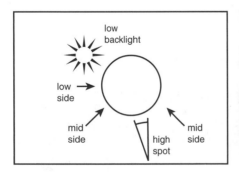

Fill Lights

Figure 5.9 demonstrates the relationship of highlights and shaded regions on Models with varying angles of incidence using only #directional Lights. Notice how the angles are described with terms such as *high side* and *low backlight*. The angle of incidence allows us to accentuate features of a Model and therefore can be thought of as an element that adds sculptural detail to a scene. It may be tempting to light a scene "dead on," similar to the way you might point a flashlight in the same direction you are looking.

FIGURE 5.9

This figure illustrates the effect of changing the rotation of a #directional Light on a Model. Notice how the top light and high-side lights are very dramatic, whereas the closer toward a direct front light the angle is, the flatter the geometry of the Model appears. Use this chart as a guide for learning to pre-visualize what you intend your lights to achieve.

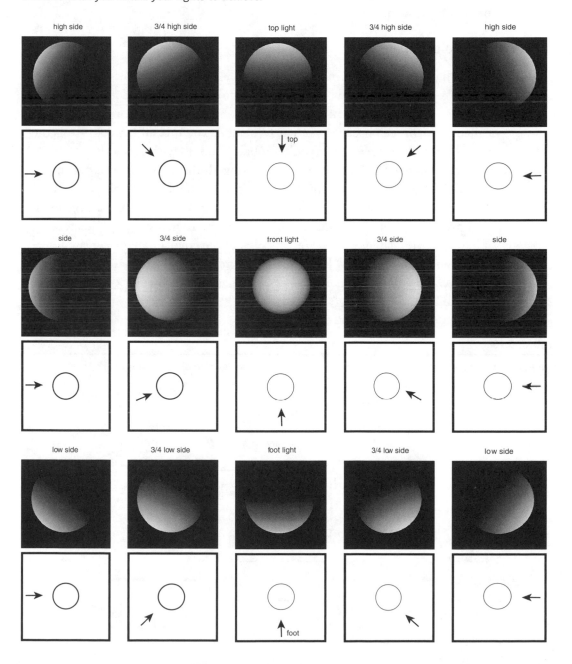

Note the dramatic differences in Figure 5.9 in the visual description of the geometry when using a front light versus a high-side light. Many times, the overuse of elaborate Model geometry can be avoided with lighting techniques by accentuating the detailed areas and obscuring the less detailed (or even nonexistent) areas.

Additive Color Mixing

If you have worked with mixing paint in the past, be aware that mixing light works very differently. Two physical color models define how colors will mix together: additive color and subtractive color. Subtractive color is sometimes called *pigment color* because, similar to paint, if you mix all the colors together, you should ideally get black (you'll probably end up with a muddy purple-brown, though). With additive color, mixing all the colors together ideally results in white. Have you ever seen a prism or a rainbow? White light is divided into its components, thus producing a spectrum of colors. This integral property of light is simulated by each of the Light types in Director. Therefore, you can utilize the effects of additive color mixing to create interesting and unique effects. Figure 5.10 illustrates the positions of color on the additive and subtractive color wheels, emphasizing how color combinations will mix.

FIGURE 5.10

The additive and subtractive color models. (A color version is included on the CD-ROM.)

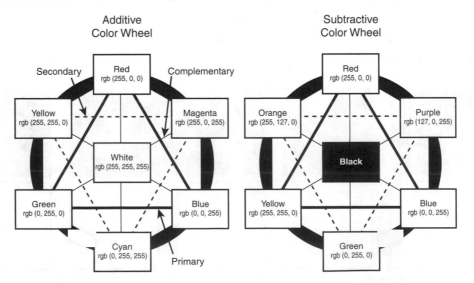

You may remember hearing that the primary colors are red, blue, and yellow. From these three colors, you can mix all the other colors. This statement is true—for pigments (subtractive color mixing). The primary colors of light are red, blue, and green (ever wonder why digital images are usually in RGB?). Notice in Figure 5.10 how yellow and blue will mix into green when the subtractive color model is used. Compare that to the additive color model, where yellow and blue will mix into white. In additive color, mixing complementary colors creates white (where mixing complementary colors in pigment will produce black). If you need help "pre-visualizing" the effects of additive color mixing, I suggest purchasing a gel-swatch book (a sample collection of translucent color filters) from a theatrical or photographic supply house. If you want a cheaper solution, you can buy various colors of cellophane. Observe how the colors mix and consult the color wheels in Figure 5.10 to test yourself.

This knowledge allows you to supplement what you have learned about key lighting. Using additive color mixing, it is possible to create varying shadow and highlight detail on a Model with both angle of incidence and color variation. Figure 5.11 illustrates a method of including information about color on your key light diagrams.

FIGURE 5.11

An additive color-mixing key diagram and rendered image. (A color version is included on the CD-ROM.)

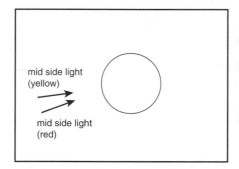

How to Choose #ambient Light Color

Because Color is the only parameter for #ambient Lights, it is important to understand what it represents. Technically, we know that it represents the reflected light in a scene. Visually, it can be understood as the color of the shadow regions on a Model. I am not speaking about the shadows that the Model casts—only the shadows on the Model itself. When used alone, #ambient Lights will affect each Model in the scene equally. Shader properties can be set to determine how individual Models react to the #ambient Light in a scene.

NOTE

> Models in a scene do not cast shadows. See the FAQ at the end of this chapter for more information.

The color you choose will depend on the goals of your lighting. When choosing a color for the #ambient Light, you should avoid absolute black or absolute white. I usually pick the color for the #ambient Light after determining the color of the background in a scene. Table 5.2 outlines a range of strategies for choosing the specific color.

TABLE 5.2   Ambient Color Strategies

Effect	Ambient	Background
High contrast	Dark color	Dark color
Low contrast	Light color	Light color
Model outlines	Dark color	Light color visible
Semitransparent	Same as background	Light color
Metallic	Same as background	Dark color

It is advisable that you set a specific #ambient Light in all situations. However, #ambient Light alone is just not enough; Models will have no definition, which is where the other Light types come in to action.

How to Determine the Direction and Color of #directional Lights

We have seen how the rotation angle of a #directional Light can affect a scene, but how does one decide which is best? This reverts back to the priority of the light and its specific purpose. The key decision is whether the scene is an interior or an exterior scene. Exteriors utilize #directional Lights as the key light; therefore, its color and highlight are dominant. Interiors usually have several areas of shadow and highlight, so you will usually need to have more than one dominant angle.

When the purpose of a #directional Light is for modeling, most likely you will turn the Specular highlight on. This will define Models in terms of a highlight, midtone, and shaded regions. The color for modeling lights is dependent on the stylization of the scene. For realistic lighting, it is often best to stay with colors that have bright luminosity but little saturation. Heavily saturated Lights tend to give a scene a theatrical or fantastical feel. But even when achieving a fantastical feel, it is easy to overdo the process. In most situations, you will want to stay away from absolute colors because they tend to do a poor job of modeling (which is the purpose of the Light in the first place).

A second reason to utilize the #directional Light is to give a scene a sense of time of day. See Table 5.3 for several methods of establishing the time of day with #directional Lights.

TABLE 5.3   Time of Day Settings

Time of Day	Rotation	Realistic	Fantastic
Morning	Low angle	Brown tint	Bright yellow
Noon	Overhead	Yellow tint	White
Afternoon	Mid angle	Pale orange	Orange
Dusk	Low angle	Orange-red tint	Deep orange-red
Night	Mid angle	Pale blue tint	Deep blue

Note that the rotation suggested for realistic and fantastic stylization for defining the time of day is the same—the difference is the saturation of the color.

In Figure 5.12, I have turned off the Specular highlight for establishing the time of day. The reason for this is that I am not interested in the modeling capabilities of the #directional Light, but rather I am more interested in the illumination capabilities.

FIGURE 5.12

These images of realistic and fantastic time of day are accompanied by a key lighting diagram that illustrates that the angles of the lights in each type of rendering do not change; rather, the difference between fantastic and realistic is expressed solely through color. (Color versions of these images are on the CD-ROM.)

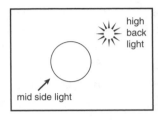 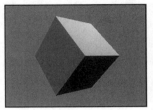 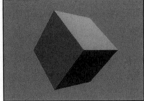

Where to Place #point Lights?

The main difference between using #point Lights for illumination or for modeling is that when illuminating, the #point Lights are far away from the scene, outside of the Camera view. When utilizing #point Lights for modeling, part of the objective is to create a sense of localized light—light that is emanating from one of the Models in your scene. Viewers will subconsciously determine the source of the #point Light, even though no physical representation is made. If you further accentuate this with a Model (for example, a lamp on a table), the connection will become solidified.

Specific Key Lighting Solutions

This section describes some design ideas for utilizing combinations of Light Nodes in order to achieve specific results. Pay close attention to the rendered images and the key light diagrams that correspond to them.

Two-Point Illumination

Two-point illumination can aid in the successful execution of exterior scenes, and it does not require a massive amount of processor overhead. The #point Lights are located off-camera, opposite one another. This allows the two #point Lights to illuminate most parts of the Models in a scene, while still leaving interesting shaded areas and moderate Model detail, as illustrated in Figure 5.13.

FIGURE 5.13

A key light diagram accompanied by a rendering of the two-point illumination technique. (A color version is included on the CD-ROM.)

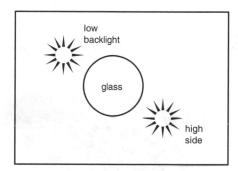

Overhead Illumination

Overhead illumination is a method of lighting interior scenes with a minimal amount of Light Nodes. The #point Lights are always located above the Models in the scene, putting the shadow regions on the lower halves of the Models. This tends to emphasize the gravity in a composition, leading the eye to believe that darker Models near the bottom of the composition are heavier. You can see this effect illustrated in Figure 5.14.

FIGURE 5.14

A key light diagram accompanied by a rendering of the overhead illumination technique. (A color version is included on the CD-ROM.)

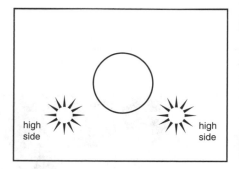

Backlight Modeling

Backlighting is a technique that is used to accentuate the outlines of Models with highlights, rather than allowing them to fade into the background, as illustrated in Figure 5.15. It is a very useful technique when lighting human figures or animals. If the Light source is very bright, the technique tends to become extremely theatrical and obviously stylized.

FIGURE 5.15

A key light diagram accompanied by a rendering of the backlight modeling technique. (A color version is included on the CD-ROM.)

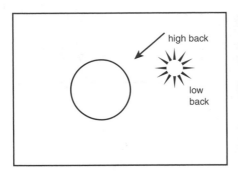 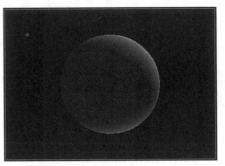

Footlight Modeling

Footlighting is a highly stylized form of lighting, as illustrated in Figure 5.16. The reason it is so dramatic (even when compared to a similar angle from above) is that we are not used to lighting situations that are lit from below. Therefore, the shaded regions on people's faces become distorted in ways we are not accustomed to seeing—this is disturbing and dramatic at the same time.

FIGURE 5.16

A key light diagram accompanied by a rendering of the footlight modeling technique. (A color version is included on the CD-ROM.)

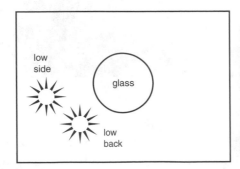 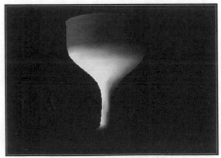

Practical Modeling

A *practical* describes a light source that is intended to seem to emanate from a local area of the scene or from a Model that is visible in the scene. Figure 5.17 illustrates how a #point Light can be placed in a central location in order to create the illusion of localization of a source of light from within a scene.

FIGURE 5.17

A key light diagram accompanied by a rendering of the practical modeling technique. (A color version is included on the CD-ROM.)

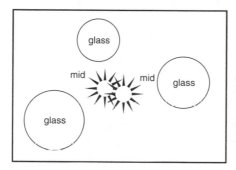 

This effect can be further enhanced by placing a Model that is intended to represent the physical source of light near the position of the Light Node. Because psychological associations between lighting and its source are so primary to human experience, understanding how to design lighting that has presence within your environments is an immediate method of developing your overall strategy of interaction.

Lighting Laboratory Demo

The Lighting Laboratory demo was developed as a controlled environment for you to learn about the various parameters of each Light Node type. You can create multiple Lights and control each parameter—as well as position and rotate the Lights. Included in the demo are four Models to choose from. The first two are basic primitive types: sphere and box. The others were modeled in 3D Studio MAX—one of which has a smooth surface (wineglass), and the other a faceted surface (star).

You are encouraged to use the Lighting Laboratory demo to observe the effects of single and multiple Light sources. Of particular note are the differences in the manner in which rectilinear and curvilinear surfaces will react with lighting. In addition, pay close attention to the subtle differences in speed and output when using different Renderers. The Lighting Laboratory demo can aid you in understanding how additive color mixing can be used to create interesting shadow and highlight regions on Models.

The Lighting Laboratory demo also provides you with a real-time key lighting diagram that updates as you work with the parameters of the Lights in the scene. With the Lighting Laboratory demo, you can generate a report about all the Lights in the scene as a general informational tool. Finally, the Lighting Laboratory demo can save and load your lighting scenarios so that you can compare several design methods rapidly. Figure 5.18 is a screenshot of the Lighting Laboratory demo that illustrates the purpose of each of the controls.

Try executing the key light diagrams within the Lighting Laboratory demo in Figure 5.19 to exercise your understanding of the Light types. Figure 5.19 illustrates key diagrams of several of the lighting techniques that have been discussed throughout the chapter. The purpose of this illustration is to function as an exercise for you; use the Lighting Laboratory to create working versions of these key diagrams.

Creating and Modifying Lights

We have looked at methods of organizing the lighting in your projects as well as a demonstration of those methods as a mode of design. In terms of code, Light Nodes can be created in Lingo with the following syntax:

```
member("castmember").newlight("name", #type)
```

Note that the Light type parameter is a symbol. All the Lights in the scene can be referenced by name or by number. The Lights are assigned numbers when they are created, so the first Light created will be 1, the second will be 2, and so on. When accessing a Light by number, you will use bracket access, as follows:

```
member("castmember").light[n]
```

FIGURE 5.18

Visual guide describing the controls of the Lighting Laboratory demo.

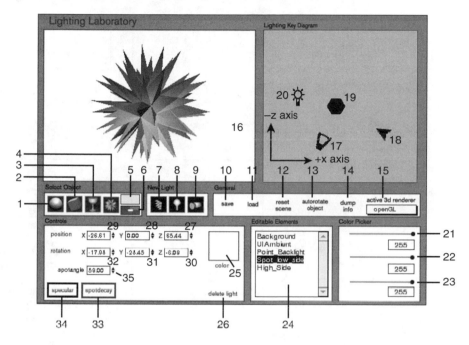

1 Use sphere model
2 Use cube model
3 Use wineglass model
4 Use star model
5 Use white texture
6 Use color texture
7 Create directional light
8 Create point light
9 Create spot light
10 Save lighting scenario
11 Load saved lighting scenario
12 Reset scene to defaults
13 Make model rotate
14 Dump lighting info to the message window
15 Active renderer drop down box
16 3D castmember (click to zoom in/out)
17 Spot light
18 Directional light

19 Model
20 Point light
21 Red slider
22 Green slider
23 Blue slider
24 Select current light mode
25 Current light color
26 Delete current light
27 Translate light on z axis
28 Translate light on y axis
29 Translate light on x axis
30 Rotate light around z axis
31 Rotate light around y axis
32 Rotate light around x axis
33 Use spot decay
34 Use specular highlight
35 Change spotlight beam angle

FIGURE 5.19

Additional key light diagrams.

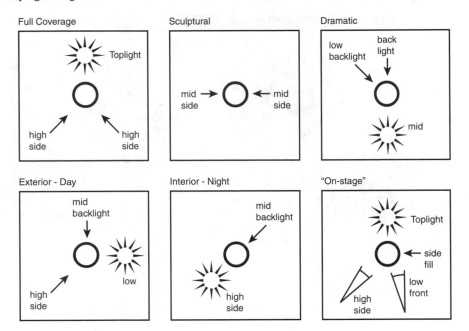

The only caution about using bracket access for Lights is to pay careful attention when you are deleting them. If you have five Lights in a scene and you delete light[3], light[5] will now become light[4]. However, the name will remain intact. Because Lights can be accessed via bracket access, the following is possible:

```
member("castmember").light.count
```

This will return an integer value of how many Lights are currently in the scene. This can be very useful when used with a repeat loop, like so:

```
repeat with x = 1 to member("castmember").light.count
    put "#" & x & ":" & member("castmember").light[x]
end repeat
```

This will put the number and corresponding name of every Light in the scene into the message window. The same code can be altered slightly to create a property list of Light names and numbers. The reason for this would be to sort the list. I find it helpful to create a sorted list of Light names so that I can easily modify groups of Lights at once. Clever naming conventions for your lights are certainly in order if you want to have absolute control over the environment. As a basic convention, you could use the first character of the Light type for the first character of the name. For more elaborate naming, you could include key information, priority, purpose, or color. It will entirely depend on how much real-time control you need over the Lights in your scene.

Light Node Properties

Control of the specific properties of Lights will be executed entirely via dot syntax. See Table 5.4 for a list of the properties, which Light types they apply to, and the expected formats.

TABLE 5.4 Light Node Properties

Property	Light Type	Value Format
Color	All	$rgb(R,G,B)$
Rotation	#Directional, #spot	$vector(x,y,z)$
Position	#Point, #spot	$vector(x,y,z)$
Specular	#Directional, #point, #spot	True or false
Spotangle	#Spot	0–90
Spotdecay	#Spot	True or false
Attenuation	#Point, #spot	$vector(C,L,Q)$

NOTE

Assigning properties to a Light Node type that is irrelevant (for example, assigning a #directional Light a position) will not generate an effect—or an error.

Light Node Color

The color value for Light Nodes is given as an `rgb(R,G,B)` data type. Refer to Appendix F, "Colorlut Custom Color Management System," for specific information and code for working with the RGB color object. There are examples of how to convert between color models via Lingo and strategies for creating lists of colors that can be referred to by name. Remember that Light colors will mix using the additive color wheel. More information on how the subtractive colors of Models will react with Lights can be found in Chapter 12, "Basic Control of Surfaces."

Light Node Transformation

The Light Node conforms to the standards for Node transformation. See the previous chapter for a discussion of Node transformation basics and Chapter 26, "Advanced Transforms and Vector Math," for more advanced techniques. I also suggest that you read the section titled "Camera Orientation Demo" in the next chapter. The information presented there about pointing Cameras directly applies to pointing #spot Lights at Models as well.

Spotangle

The Spotangle property expects a value from 0 to 90. However, this value can be deceptive. The value is a float value, meaning that it can have floating-point units, such as .5 or 12.234. The difficulty is that the number refers to half the actual beam angle. In order to create a #spot Light with a beam angle of 42 degrees, you must enter a Spotangle value of 21. Because the maximum Spotangle value is 90, the maximum beam angle for a #spot Light is 180 degrees. In general, #spot Lights with beam angles less than 15 degrees tend to become difficult to manage.

Attenuation

Attenuation is a property of #point Lights and #spot Lights that determines the calculations used to diminish the power of the light with distance. Attenuation accepts a vector value of `vector(constant, linear, quadratic)`, where `constant`, `linear`, and `quadratic` are float values. This means that unlike most all the vectors you will work with, this vector is not a position or a rotation. Rather, it is a vector comprised of three floating-point values that refer to three methods of calculating attenuation, each of which is slightly more precise than the preceding. The default Attenuation setting is `vector(1,0,0)`, which means that the light will attenuate at a constant rate of 1. The larger the value, the faster the light will diminish over distance. This default setting for Attenuation will likely be sufficient for your lighting solutions.

Summary

In order to design with Light, it is best if you can determine the stylization of lighting that you want to achieve before coding. In order to achieve the stylization your project requires, you must determine what the objectives of your lighting are. These objectives will aid you in determining what types of Lights you need and their multiple properties. The goal is to achieve your lighting objectives with the least amount of nodes necessary. There is always more than one way to achieve a lighting objective, so a solid understanding of how multiple Light Nodes will interact can guide you in choosing the best solution.

Even in the real world, lighting is a difficult medium to design with because it is intangible. Because of this, a standardized vocabulary and design shorthand is very important, especially when you're attempting to convey design ideas to others, without programming the lighting first. Key diagrams allow designers to experiment with the possibilities of a lighting scenario very quickly so that subjectivity is not lost.

It is important to control the lighting in the scene because the element of light can be used to reduce the amount of geometry the computer has to deal with. Also, light is a crucial and integral part of the 3D environment, allowing us to set the mood and tension of a scene. In addition, when light is considered part of the design of a project from the beginning, it can establish a stronger experience for the user, whether it is used to draw the eye to dynamic areas of contrast or to amplify the intensity of interactivity in a project.

Finally, Light Nodes do not have a very large amount of properties, but we know that we can achieve a very wide array of effects from these few properties. This suggests that the specific settings of the Light properties may not seem very different, but the effect is.

FAQ

Where are the shadows in my scene? I have a Model that should be casting a shadow on the ground, and nothing is showing up there.

The calculations for creating shadows are time consuming and prohibitive for use in real-time environments. Therefore, the lights in Director 3D do not cast shadows. If it is important that your users see shadows, it is possible to create a Model of the shadow—or to place a texture of the shadow on other Models.

I have worked with using lights as projectors before. Is this possible in Director?

In short, no. In high-end 3D-rendering programs, this is an option for projecting custom shadows, images (similar to a slide projector), or animations (similar to a movie projector). The images react with surfaces, conforming to the contours of the Model geometry. Although this feature is not provided, it is possible to utilize the texturing techniques discussed in Chapter 14, "Multitexturing," to produce effects similar to this.

What about raytracing and radiosity? Does Director do these?

Along the lines of the discussion about real-time shadows, raytracing and radiosity solutions are too time intensive to be viable. The hallmarks of raytracing—interreflections, refracted surfaces, and so on—are just not possible due to the processing load. Similarly, radiosity is a technique for accurately determining the bounced and inherited light in a scene, whose calculations are too intense for a real-time environment. It is possible to create prerendered textures to simulate raytracing and radiosity techniques.

I put a light in the middle of my scene. The objects seem to be lit correctly, but I don't see the light source anywhere. Where is it?

To be specific, the Lights that you are using have no physical representation. You are used to the term *light source* meaning that there is a physical object that emanates light waves when its atoms are excited by electricity or heat. Because your environment is just a simulation, it does not take several of the laws of physics into account. If you need to show a source for the lighting in your scene, you will need to create geometry to represent it. Chapter 12, "Basic Control of Surfaces," discusses methods of modifying the surface qualities of Models via Shaders so they appear to emit light.

I want to see atmospheric qualities, such as light beams in fog or dust. Is this possible?

Yes. You must create a cone slightly smaller than the beam angle of the Spotlight. Set the `shader.blend` property of the cone to less than or equal to 5. Also, if you can afford the performance hit, create an 8-bit mask in order to add a bit of gradient blending for the Model. Chapter 14 explains the details of working with Textures that have alpha channels.

I want to exclude several objects from the effect of one particular lighting node. How can I do this?

You cannot do this. All Models are "visible" to all Lights. Other than being outside of the rays of a #spot Light, do not expect any exclusionary methods for Lights. However, Cameras are a different story. See Chapter 25, "Advanced Camera Control," for an explanation of excluding Lights and Models from rendering with the Rootnode property.

I have an object that I do not want to be affected by any Lights. How can I do this?

Set the Ambient, Diffuse, and Specular properties of the Shader to `rgb(0,0,0)` and set the Emissive property of the Shader to a nonzero value. You'll find more information about this technique in Chapter 12.

I animated some Lights in 3DS Max, and when I export them, nothing happens. Why?

This is expected. If you are animating the colors of the Lights, it can be done through Lingo. If you are animating the positions of the Lights, you have several options, which will be discussed in Appendix A, "3D Studio MAX W3D Exporter."

In my 3D program, I can control Hotspot and Falloff for Spotlights. Does Director have this capability?

No. Consider the Spotdecay property the closest solution to this for now.

Can I create headlights or a flashlight?

Chapter 8, "Parents, Children, and Cloning," deals with learning about how Nodes can be linked together to create effects like this.

Supplemental Resources

- *A Method of Lighting the Stage*, by Stanley McCandless

  McCandless is the Father of Modern Lighting Design. His early work involved designing with lights and using instruments to design lights. His methods of lighting are still employed today.

- *Lighting Design Handbook*, by Lee Watson

  This is an excellent resource for theatrical and architectural lighting examples. Watson is extremely concise and thorough in his examination of the lighting profession.

- *Designing with Light*, by J. Michael Gillette

  This is a concise guide to the ideas of additive color mixing, key lighting, and lighting design for the theatre.

- *The Scenography of Josef Svoboda*, by Jarka, Burian

  Svoboda is a Czech scenographer whose work incorporates light, projections, and reflection, among other techniques. He is known for his creation of the "light curtain." His ability to utilize lighting in order to create utterly unique environments is highly inspirational.

- *3D Lighting: History, Concepts, and Techniques*, by Arnold Gallardo

  Gallardo's book on digital lighting is an extremely inclusive and thorough examination of the various elements that define physical lighting, from light waves to the human eye. He explains how these physical lighting principles are duplicated in the computer.

CHAPTER 6

Understanding Cameras

In this chapter, I will explain the basic principles of simulated Cameras in the 3D environment and how they differ from lens-based cameras. We will also explore how to create and control Cameras. In this chapter, you'll find several demonstrations explaining techniques that are important to master, such as moving Cameras and pointing Cameras.

This is one of three chapters dedicated to learning the various methods and techniques for 3D Camera usage—consider this chapter a primer to dispel what many first-time users consider inconsistencies for 3D Cameras. Because 3D Cameras are not lens-based cameras, many of the effects you expect from a "real-world" camera are not available natively in Director 3D.

Cameras are the eyes of a 3D environment; learning to control them will allow you to direct what people see, in addition to how they see and experience your environments.

How Are 3D Cameras Different from Lens-Based Cameras?

When speaking about a lens-based camera, I am referring to the cameras you know in the real world. A lens-based camera allows you to look through a lens at your subject, focus, and then take pictures. Lens-based cameras frequently have interchangeable lens systems, zoom lenses, and the ability to use specialty lenses, such as fisheye, wide-angle, and telephoto lenses. The detail that I am interested with lens-based cameras is that light passes through the lens system and is projected onto a flat piece of photosensitive film. In the case of the viewfinder, that visual information is passed on to your eye.

A common misconception about 3D Cameras is that they work on the same principle: that light is passing through a lens system. This is simply not true; everything about the 3D environment is about simulating what we expect to see. When you're working with "real" cameras, many desirable aberrations are caused by the lens system. For example, telephoto (zoom) lenses tend to foreshorten (flatten) the subject, whereas wide-angle and fisheye lenses have the effect of curving straight lines. Also, you can use focus for depth-of-field effects, where the subject is in focus, but the background is not.

These are all signifiers of the medium of photography, film, and video. Simulating these effects in real time is too intense for most user machines; therefore, native support is not included in Director. Because we are not simulating lenses, every Model in the scene is always drawn in focus. In addition, although perspective may be skewed, lines will not curve near the edges of your view of the 3D World. Because a 3D Camera does not use a lens system, the question becomes, How do 3D Cameras work? The answer is this: A 3D Camera is a "projection" of 3D geometry onto a 2D plane.

What Is a Projection?

A *projection* is a mathematical method of calculating how to draw three-dimensional geometry on a two-dimensional plane. This two-dimensional plane is referred to by several names in 3D programming, among them are *view plane* and *projection plane*. A more familiar name for the default view plane in Director's 3D environment is *3D Sprite*. Figure 6.1 illustrates the projection of a 3D vector onto a 2D plane.

From Figure 6.1, you can see that the process of drawing a 3D environment is quite intense. I have only drawn one vector—imagine the calculations needed to accurately draw whole Models.

It is important to realize that projections are a mathematical process; simulating a Camera in a 3D environment is one application of this process. To simulate a Camera in a 3D environment, several crucial elements are used to determine the 2D projection:

- The position of the Camera in the 3D environment
- The direction the Camera is pointed
- The Camera orientation

- The size of the Camera's view plane
- The type of projection

FIGURE 6.1

Projecting a 3D vector onto a 2D plane.

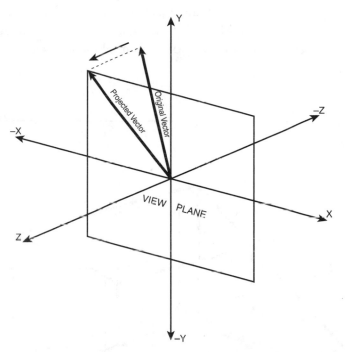

Many of these may seem obvious, such as where the camera is positioned and to what it is pointed. The Camera orientation is quite important and determines which way is "up." The size of the Camera view plane can be restated as the size of the Sprite, so this should be immediately understandable. Out of these, the last item is perhaps the most unfamiliar, especially because I have just introduced you to projections.

Several methods of calculating are used to determine how the three-dimensional geometry should be projected onto the view plane. These methods have an effect on the manner in which lines that are parallel in the 3D environment appear when projected. Director has an implementation of two types of projection: perspective and orthographic.

Perspective Projection

Perspective projection is the default type of Camera that is established for empty Shockwave 3D Castmembers. To better understand a perspective projection, try the following experiment: Close one eye and put your thumb close to your face. Now look at something far away that you know is much larger than your thumb. You know that your thumb is relatively small, but in *perspective* it seems as large as objects that are objectively larger. When perspective projection is used, the closer a Model is to the Camera, the larger it appears. Figure 6.2 illustrates how the view plane is produced for a perspective projection Camera.

FIGURE 6.2

Perspective view frustum.

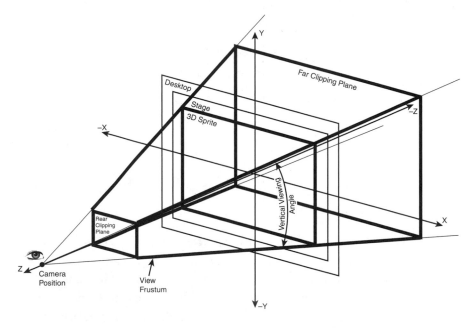

Figure 6.2 illustrates several important concepts. First, note the area designated as the "view frustum." A *frustum* is a cone or pyramid where the top has been cut off by a plane parallel to the base. Notice that the "bottom" of the frustum is labeled *far clipping plane* and the "top" is labeled *near clipping plane*. All Models closer than the near clipping plane or further than the far clipping

plane will not be projected onto the 3D Sprite (view plane). Every Model inside of the view frustum will be drawn.

Second, notice that there is an arc labeled *vertical viewing angle*. This angle is referred to as the "fieldofview" in Director. Many times, the term *fieldofview* is confused with the field of view for lens-based cameras. Do not be confused— our synthetic Camera has no lenses and no depth of field. Instead, it has a vertical height that is measured as an angle in degrees, and the arc labeled *vertical viewing angle* is that angle.

The horizontal viewing angle is determined by the width of the `Camera.rect` property. In Chapter 25, "Advanced Camera Control," I will explain how to utilize the `Camera.rect` property for advanced control of the aspect ratio and multiple Cameras.

Fieldofview

Because the fieldofview determines the vertical viewing angle, it is important to understand how this property will affect your Camera. Figure 6.3 illustrates three views of the same scene, taken from the same location, but with varying fieldofview settings.

FIGURE 6.3

Fieldofview diagrams: 120 degrees, 60 degrees, and 30 degrees, from left to right.

Notice the correlation between larger fieldofview settings and distortions of the geometry in the scene. Conversely, notice how with smaller fieldofview settings you cannot see much of the space in the 3D environment.

Hither and Yon

In Director, the near and far clipping planes are referred to as *hither* and *yon*, respectively. Geometry that is too close or too far from the Camera is excluded from being drawn. Setting the hither and yon is an effective way of increasing the performance of your movies dramatically. Figure 6.4 is a cross-section illustration of the view frustum, with emphasis placed on the hither and yon "clipping planes."

FIGURE 6.4

Hither and yon (clipping planes) diagram. Only Models and geometry within the view frustum (shaded area) will be drawn.

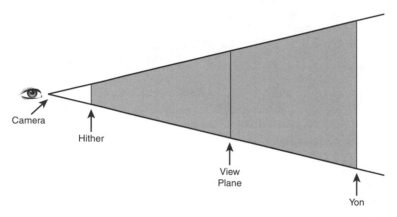

In general, it is best to limit the amount of geometry drawn onscreen by setting the yon to a lower value, thereby moving the far clipping plane closer to the Camera. What you may not realize is that even if you do not have a large number of Models and geometry or you do not have any Models that you want excluded, you should move the far clipping plane as close to your Models as possible. By following these directions, you should notice significant performance improvements in your overall frame rate.

The hither setting, used to control the near clipping plane, is not usually used for performance but rather as a visual tool. One common use for the near clipping plane is to "cut away" architecture so that you can see into buildings or structures. The most common use, which is accomplished with the default settings for hither, is to make sure your view is not completely obstructed if a Model comes too close to the Camera.

Uses for Perspective Cameras

Perspective Cameras are certainly more common than orthographic Cameras when working in real-time 3D. This is especially true if your subject matter is a game or is cinematic in nature. The perspective Camera excels at portraying two very distinctive styles of digital cinematography that have literary equivalents. In short, perspective projection is well suited for creating first-person and third-person Cameras. Figure 6.5 is a screenshot from a first-person point-of-view game, generally referred to as a *first-person shooter*.

FIGURE 6.5

A first-person Camera from the game Prism Boy. The mirror effect is faked through advanced texturing and Imaging Lingo.

A wide array of games utilize this style of camera work, among them Wolfenstein 3D and Doom. Of course, these are not the only reasons why you might need a first-person Camera—certainly architectural walkthroughs and exterior views lend themselves to this style of Camera.

The third-person Camera has a tendency to create a cinematic aesthetic that is useful for games as well as animation. Figure 6.6 is a screenshot of a third-person Camera utilizing a highly stylized camera angle, reminiscent of film noir.

In this example, the character is still controlled by the user, but the Camera is not assumed to be the eyes of the character. Rather, this has the effect of distancing the viewer visually while simultaneously enticing the user through input and interaction.

FIGURE 6.6

Third-person camera.

Orthographic Projection

The second type of Camera projection is called *orthographic*, and it is unlike perspective projection in several ways. The most noticeable difference is that the distance from the Camera does not modulate the apparent size of Models. The reason why this is true has to do with the view frustum of an orthographic Camera. The orthographic view frustum is quite technically known as a *parallelepiped*, which is a six-sided object whose sides are parallel parallelograms. Figure 6.7 illustrates the projection of an orthographic Camera.

In orthographic projection, parallel lines remain parallel no matter how far they are from the center of the view plane. In perspective projection, the farther an object is from the center of the view plane, the more skewed toward the edges of the view frustum it will appear. Because all sides of our "view volume" are parallel, the edges of objects cannot skew when projected onto a two-dimensional plane. Therefore, Model distance from the Camera does not affect Model size.

FIGURE 6.7

Orthographic projection.

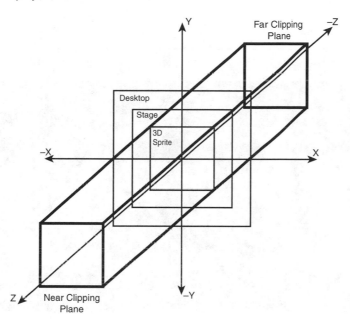

Because the sides of the "view volume" are parallel, the fieldofview property does not have any meaning. Rather, the orthoheight property is used to determine how many vertical units high the viewing plane is. Notice from Figure 6.7 that the near and far clipping planes apply to orthographic projections. These controls are still accessed via the hither and yon properties.

Uses for Orthographic Cameras

Orthographic Cameras are good at describing objects with architectural precision because they remove all issues surrounded by Models appearing relatively larger than Models that are actually smaller than them. They are useful in several situations, such as in charts and graphing applications, where you want the data to be observed objectively, rather than depending on where your viewpoint is. Also, they are strong candidates for technical drawing because they maintain a sterile, unbiased point of view. For the same reason, they are generally not used for cinematic or photorealistic simulations.

If you have worked in 3D modeling in the past, you have most likely worked with orthographic projection already. Figure 6.8 illustrates several orthographic views of a city block from the top and left sides.

FIGURE 6.8

Top and left orthographic views of a city block.

These types of descriptive Cameras are generally used in tandem to help visualize an object or Model from many views at once. This is helpful when you want to visualize the relationships of geometry in a precise manner.

In addition, orthographic Cameras can be used to create isometric and/or dimetric views of a scene or Model. An isometric view is a special type of orthogonal projection, where the Camera is situated at 45-degree angles from the subject. Figure 6.9 illustrates the city block from Figure 6.8 as an isometric view.

The strength of orthographic Cameras is revealed in this illustration. Notice how the spatial relationships between buildings are well represented. Isometric views lend themselves to cutaway maps, architecture, technical illustrations, and data-visualization applications. In addition, you may be familiar with a genre of computer games known as *iso-games* that include Zaxxon, The

Immortal, SimCity, and Ultima Online. Although this style of game is normally accomplished through tiling (2.5D) methods, it is possible to create a fully 3D environment and then present it in an isometric fashion. This affords you the added benefit of being able to control the point of view of the Camera with more options than you might have in 2.5D.

FIGURE 6.9

An isometric view of a city block.

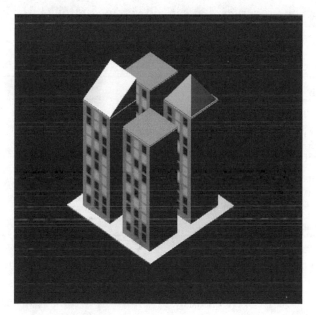

Modifying Cameras

The default Camera for Shockwave 3D Castmembers has the following defaults:

- Perspective projection
- 34.5160-degree field of view
- World position location at `vector(0,0,250)`
- Pointing at the World origin, no rotation
- Background color of black

Models that are created on-the-fly are automatically placed at the World origin, and the default Camera is pointing at the World origin. For this reason, when we have been creating Models on-the-fly, we have seen the Models appear in the World. Because the Camera is located at 0 units on the Y axis, and Models are located at 0 units on the Y axis, by default, we are looking directly (straight on) at new Models. For this reason, the composition of the default Camera is quite boring.

In order to gain control over our Camera, we need to pay special attention to several properties. The properties that can aid you in controlling the basic functionality of Cameras are listed in Table 6.1.

TABLE 6.1   Basic Camera Properties

Property	Usage
Transform	Uses transform commands (rotate and translate)
Projection	Is set to #orthographic or #perspective
Fieldofview	A float value greater than 0 and less than or equal to 180.
Orthoheight	The float value that's greater than 0
Hither	Near clipping plane; float value
Yon	Far clipping plane; float value

Here are a few points to note about these properties: First, Hither must not exceed Yon. Second, a fieldofview or orthoheight setting of 0 will result in no visual representation of the scene. Third, a fieldofview setting that's greater than 180 will produce an error.

Background Color

In addition to the other basic Camera properties, the background color of individual Cameras can be set via the Colorbuffer.clearvalue property. The syntax for changing the background color of a camera is as follows, where scene is a global variable containing a reference to the 3D Castmember:

```
scene.Camera("name").colorbuffer.clearvalue = rgb(R,G,B)
```

Keep in mind that when we begin to work with multiple Cameras, it will be necessary to reset the background color after changing active Cameras.

Camera Movement

Moving Cameras is quite easy once you have mastered transformations. The difficulty that you might experience with moving Cameras the first or second time has to do with knowing what will happen visually when you move them. When you move a Camera in one direction, the Models and geometry in the scene will appear to move in the opposite direction, as illustrated in Figure 6.10.

FIGURE 6.10

The visual effect of moving a Camera.

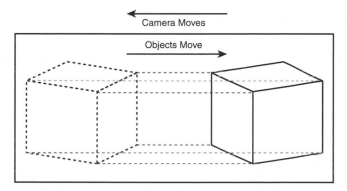

In short, if you move the Camera toward the Models on the negative Z axis, the Models will enlarge. If you move the Camera away from the Models on the positive Z axis, the Models will shrink—they are farther away. This can become difficult when you are moving both Models and Cameras at the same time.

Basic Movement and Modifications Demo

Open the file on the CD named "Camera Movement" and press Play. You should see a small red box in the center of the Stage. This box is located at the World origin, and the Camera is pointed at the World origin.

First, we should try to move the Camera vertically up a bit so that we are above the box. While the movie is still playing, type the following code into the message window and press Return:

```
scene.camera[1].translate(0,70,0)
```

The box should appear to move down on the screen because the camera is now higher than the box. Now, let's rotate the Camera slightly around the X axis with the following code:

```
Scene.camera[1].rotate(-15,0,0)
```

Now the box is oriented in the middle of the Stage, but because we are looking at the box from a higher viewpoint, the composition and geometry of the box is visually more interesting. Now, without stopping the movie, zoom in on the box by setting the fieldofview property with the following code:

```
Scene.camera[1].fieldofview = 22
```

Now that you have seen the box illustrated with a perspective projection, change the projection to orthographic with the following code:

```
scene.camera[1].projection = #orthographic
```

Notice how the box seems to be "farther away." This is because the orthographic Camera does not affect the size of a Model based on its size. To make the #orthographic projection of the box take up more room on the screen (that is, to zoom in), we need to use the orthoheight property while in #orthographic projection. While the movie is still running, type the following code into the message window and press Return:

```
scene.camera[1].orthoheight = 100
```

Now the box appears larger again. This is because we have set the view plane to only show 100 World units rather than the default 200. Because we are viewing less World units on the Sprite, the box appears larger.

Camera Orientation

So far, we have moved the Camera but we have not examined methods of pointing the Camera at specific locations. This process is simplified for us by the pointat() command.

NOTE

> The `pointat()` command applies to all Nodes: Cameras, Lights, and Models. It is easiest to learn how to use `pointat()` with a Camera and then begin to apply this knowledge to Lights and then Models.

The `pointat()` command relies on the pointatorientation property of a Node. To begin with, in order to point a Node in a particular direction, we must establish several parameters. First, we must know a vector describing which way the "front" of the Node is facing relative to the Node. Second, we must know a vector describing which way "up" is facing relative to the Node. Figure 6.11 illustrates a Camera frustum and a front vector pointing from the Camera location forward as well as an up vector pointing toward the up direction.

FIGURE 6.11

Camera orientation diagram: The front vector is `vector(0,0,-1)`, and the up vector is `vector(0,1,0)`.

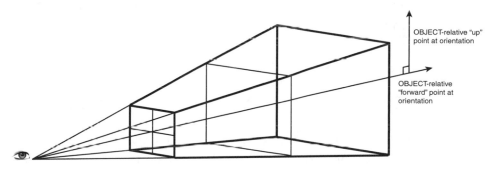

The vectors illustrated in Figure 6.11 comprise the default pointatorientation property of a Camera. Because the default front vector is `vector(0,0,-1)` relative to the Camera Node, the Camera is facing toward its relative negative Z axis. In addition, because the default up vector is `vector(0,1,0)` relative to the Camera Node, the Camera appears to be level. You will most likely not modify the front vector for a Camera, but you might modify it for some other Node, such as a Model of a cone. For a Camera, the up vector will determine whether the Camera rolls to the left or the right. For now, we will use the default pointatorientation setting:

```
Front = vector(0,0,-1)
Up = vector(0,1,0)
Scene.camera[1].pointatorientation = [Front, Up]
```

Because this is the default, we will not need to change the values. Notice, though, that the pointatorientation setting is a linear list comprised of the two vectors.

The method of pointing the Camera is achieved through the pointat() command. This command accepts two arguments that I will refer to as *direction* and *up*. If you do not want to roll the camera to the left or right, leave the "up" argument as vector(0,1,0). The direction vector should be the vector that displaces to the location to which you want to point the Camera. The syntax for this command is as follows:

```
Scene.camera[x].pointat(direction_vector, up_vector)
```

Stop, rewind, and play the "Camera Movement" file again. Type each of the following lines of code into the message window and press Return after each one:

```
scene.camera[1].translate(0,-30,0)
Scene.camera[1].fieldofview = 22
scene.camera[1].pointat(vector(0,20,0),vector(0,1,0))
```

In this example, we have moved the Camera vertically lower, reduced the fieldofview property, and then pointed the Camera. Because we are pointing the Camera at vector(0,20,0), the Camera tilts upward, and it appears as though the box is looming above us.

Camera Orientation Demo

Open the file on the CD named "Camera Pointing" and press Play. The three buttons below the 3D Sprite will automatically aim the camera at the three Models in the scene. This behavior is accomplished through the following custom script:

```
1: property pWM
2:
3: global scene
4:
5: on getpropertydescriptionlist me
6:   set plist = [:]
7:   setaprop(plist, #pWM, [#comment:"Which Model #", \
     #format:#integer, #default:0])
8:   return plist
9: end
10:
11: on mousedown
12:   obj = scene.model[pWM].getWorldTransform().position
13:   up = vector(0,1,0)
14:   scene.camera(1).pointAt(obj, up)
15: end
```

Notice that this script utilizes a getpropertydescriptionlist handler. This way, the same script can be used for each button. Of greatest importance is the mousedown handler. First, the position of the correct Model in World units is stored in a variable, obj. Then the "up" vector(0,1,0) is stored in a variable, up. Finally, the pointat() command is called using the information collected and stored in the obj and up variables. The result is quick and effective. It is possible to bypass the button Castmembers by utilizing Picking Lingo to determine which object the mouse is clicked on. Picking Lingo and mouse control is covered in Chapter 13, "A 2D Mouse in a 3D World." In addition, there are methods of smoothly animating the Camera from one position to the next, collectively known as *interpolation*. These techniques are discussed in Chapter 25.

Multiple Cameras Demo

There are several strategies for working with multiple view ports. In this demonstration, I will be showing you how to create multiple Cameras, set positions and orientation, and then use Lingo to change the "active" Camera. This process can be summarized as follows:

1. Create a new Camera.

2. Position, rotate, and point the Camera.

3. Repeat steps 1 and 2 for all required Cameras.

4. Set the Sprite's active Camera as required.

On the CD is a file named "Multiple Cameras." Open this file and Press play.
You'll notice three buttons near the bottom of the Stage. You can click these
to change the active Camera.

Two important scripts make this movie possible. First, the `initialize` handler
generates the Models and Cameras for the scene at the beginning of the
movie. Note that I have broken the following code down into several sections,
the last section of which is where I set up the Cameras:

```
1: global scene
2:
3: on initialize
4:   clearworld(scene)
5:
6:   --set up the scene
7:   obj = createpyramid("pyraA", 400,275, rgb(199,150,50))
8:   obj.rotate(0,112,0,#self)
9:   obj.translate(100,0,-500, #world)
10:
11:   obj = createpyramid("pyraB", 450,345, rgb(199,150,50))
12:   obj.rotate(0,122,0,#self)
13:   obj.translate(10,0,-900, #world)
14:
15:   obj = createpyramid("pyraC", 370,225, rgb(199,150,50))
16:   obj.rotate(0,12,0,#self)
17:   obj.translate(-300,0,-850, #world)
18:
19:   obj = createplane("sand", 2000,2000, rgb(121,90,30))
20:   obj.rotate(90,0,0)
21:   obj.translate(0,-100,0,#world)
22:
23:   --move the directional light
24:   scene.light[2].rotate(16,0,138)
25:
26:
27:   -- move the default camera into position
28:   scene.camera[1].translate(0,20,500)
29:   --rotate camera
30:   Scene.camera[1].rotate(-4,0,0)
31:   --set up initial background color
32:   scene.camera[1].colorbuffer.clearvalue = rgb(230,250,250)
33:
34:   --create second camera
35:   scene.newcamera("closeup")
36:   --position camera
```

```
37:    scene.camera("closeup").translate(100,200,75)
38:    --rotate camera
39:    scene.camera("closeup").rotate(-10,0,0)
40:    --set field of view
41:    scene.camera("closeup").fieldofview = 25
42:
43:    --create third camera
44:    scene.newcamera("vclose")
45:    --position camera
46:    scene.camera("vclose").translate(5,12,400, #world)
47:    --rotate camera
48:    scene.camera("vclose").rotate(1,0,0)
49:    --set field of view
50:    scene.camera("vclose").fieldofview = 11
51: end
```

Notice how new Cameras are created with the newCamera() command, and each Camera is uniquely named. When you need to reference Cameras, you will be able to access them by name or by number.

Once the Cameras and the scene is set up, we are presented with the three buttons that allow us to change between the available Camera views. The following code utilizes the getpropertydescriptionlist handler so that we can use one script for all three buttons:

```
 1: property pWM
 2:
 3: global scene
 4:
 5: on getpropertydescriptionlist me
 6:   set plist = [:]
 7:   setaprop(plist, #pWM, [#comment:"Which Camera #", \
      #format:#integer, #default:0])
 8:   return plist
 9: end
10:
11: on mousedown
12:    -- set active sprite camera to the camera saved from GPDL
13:    sprite(1).camera = scene.camera[pwm]
14:    -- re-init the background color
15:    scene.camera[pwm].colorbuffer.clearvalue = rgb(230,250,250)
16: end
```

The majority of work is done in the mousedown handler in this script. Notice that changing Cameras is relatively uncomplicated when compared to the initialization script. A large amount of Cameras really does not take up a large amount of RAM, so there shouldn't be many performance issues when you're using this technique.

Future Considerations

Several areas of consideration are left to explore in terms of Cameras. Among the topics that we have to deal with are special effects, trails, overlays, and backdrops in Chapter 16, "Camera Tricks," and Camera animation and navigation in Chapters 24 and 25, respectively. In addition, Chapter 26, "Advanced Transforms and Vector Math," covers details about vector math and transforms that are applicable to Cameras.

Summary

The Cameras used to view Director's 3D environment do not have lenses, nor do they simulate the effects of lenses. Because of this, all Models and geometry in the scene are always in focus. Any depth of field effects that you might need will have to be simulated via Lingo.

Two types of Camera projection styles are supported in Director 3D: perspective and orthographic. Perspective Cameras provide subjective viewpoints in the 3D environment that are good for cinematic and emotional stylization. Orthographic Cameras, on the other hand, provide objective viewpoints of the 3D environment that are good for data visualization and spatial relationship recognition.

The Camera is the most essential Node in a 3D environment. It doesn't define what you see but rather whether you see and how you see. Without the Camera, you do not have "eyes" in the 3D environment. Because the Camera contributes to the aesthetic and emotional stylization of your projects, you are justified to at least define what you want the Camera to accomplish when you're selecting a visual strategy for your project.

FAQ

I am having trouble with the pointatorientation property. It just does not make sense to me. Is there anything I can do to try and visualize it?

Have you ever taken a snapshot and then, after developing it, realized that the right side of the camera was higher than the left side? The image looks like it rolls slightly to the right. This is an example of changing the orientation of the Camera. Imagine the "pointat" vector that points straight out of the lens of the Camera. Now try to imagine the vector that begins on the "pointat" vector and points in the direction of the sky in your "rolled" snapshot. Okay, now imagine that you are watching someone take this crooked picture, and you are standing level. From your point of view, you can clearly see that the Camera is rolled slightly to the left. This angle is the important angle, because the pointatorientation property should be in World coordinates.

I thought isometric games were made with tiles and Imaging Lingo?

You are absolutely correct—there are many times when tile-based bitmap isometric games will be superior to fully 3D isometric games. The game logic and AI of each project are going to make demands of your ability to plan and accurately assess which method is correct for you.

How do I build a ray-casting Camera?

Actually, this has already been done for you. A ray-casting Camera shoots rays from the Camera into the 3D environment, looking for intersections with geometry. More importantly than having the ability to perform ray-casting is knowing what to do with the information it returns to you. Chapter 13 explains how to use a method of ray-casting to build mouse interaction. Chapter 25 details several methods of Camera navigation and Camera following that utilize ray-casting as well.

CHAPTER 7

Text and Extrusion Capabilities

In this chapter, we will examine several methods of creating and manipulating 3D Text with Director. Because there is more than one method of creation, we must establish the vocabulary of working with 3D Text.

The major difference between the two methods of 3D Text creation is the amount of control you have over the final product. The first method that we will examine is a very immediate method of working with 3D Text—it uses Text Castmembers rather than 3D Castmembers. This may seem unusual—and it is, because it is the only situation where we might create 3D content that is not inside of a 3D Castmember. In general, there are many disadvantages and limitations for controlling Text Castmembers in this way.

The second method focuses on creating 3D Text that conforms to the structure of the 3D Castmember/Modelresource/Model relationship. Creating "3D Text" in this way essentially is really just a new way of creating Models, and a different method of approaching how to construct Modelresources for those Models. The strength of working with 3D Text in this way is that you have full control over the Text as a Model in a 3D environment that can interact with your other Models and Nodes.

For the sake of clarity, we will use the term *3D Text* to refer to the first method—using Text Castmembers for Text that appears to be 3D. We will use the term *Extruder* to refer to Modelresources that we create from Text.

Creating 3D Text with Text Castmembers

The difference between normal Text Castmembers and 3D Text Castmembers is a property change. 3D Text is merely a mode of displaying a

Text Castmember. Essentially, the capabilities of the Text Castmember have been extended such that it can appear 3D as well as 2D. Figure 7.1 demonstrates the difference between a normal Text Castmember and a Text Castmember in 3D.

FIGURE 7.1

Two Text Castmembers, with the upper-left Text Castmember displayed in 3D.

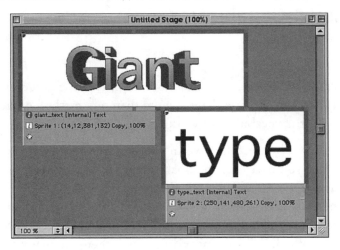

The first method of creating 3D Text is accomplished by changing the Displaymode property of a Text Castmember from #modenormal to #mode3D. You can do this from Lingo or from the Property Inspector. Be aware that the 3D properties of Text Castmembers are Castmember properties; therefore, every Sprite instance of a particular Text Castmember will have the same 3D properties. When you select #mode3D, a new panel on the Property Inspector will become available to you, as shown in Figure 7.2.

From the 3D Extruder tab on the Property Inspector, you are able to modify the 3D properties of Text Castmembers. Take a moment to examine the visual effect that these properties have on the 3D Text.

3D Text can be awkward to rotate and reposition with the Property Inspector. The reason for this is that you are actually rotating and repositioning the point of view rather than the Text. If you need to change the position or rotation of the 3D Text, I suggest that you modify your editor preferences under the File menu, where you will be given the choice to edit 3D Text with the

Text window or the Shockwave 3D window. If you choose the Shockwave 3D window as your editor for 3D Text, you will be able to control the rotation and position of your 3D Text with greater precision.

FIGURE 7.2

The 3D Text tab in the Property Inspector is only available when the Text Castmember is in #mode3D.

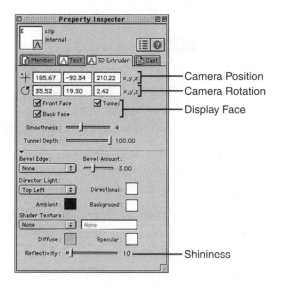

NOTE

Technically, you are still changing the position of the Camera when you edit Text in the Shockwave 3D window, but the controls are easier to manipulate. One reason you can tell that you are still moving the Camera is that the lighting on the 3D Text remains the same. We will discuss the Shockwave 3D window in depth in Chapter 9, "Working with Prebuilt Scenes and Behaviors," when we deal with imported objects.

The 3D properties you should be aware of are Tunneldepth, Smoothness, Beveltype, and Beveldepth. These four properties affect both the quality and the speed of your 3D Text dramatically. Along with the font that you choose and the number of characters in your text, the size of the font will affect the speed as well. Keep in mind that the upper limit is 65 characters for 3D Text in a given Text Sprite; any characters above that limit will be truncated.

The Tunneldepth property describes how "deep" the Text should be. With a low setting, the Text looks like it is carved out of thin paper; with a high setting, it looks like it is carved out of a mountain. Very deep text can be quite difficult to read especially if you are using a serif font.

The Smoothness property determines how accurately the vector-based font outline should be translated into the 3D environment. With a setting of 1 or 2, the font will look very coarse and may lose its definition altogether. Above 5, you will notice a speed decrease, but you may not see much better quality. Generally, serif fonts are going to require high Smoothness settings.

The Beveltype property allows you to decide whether the corners of the 3D Text are square, mitered at a 45-degree angle, or rounded. Normally, the edges of text are not beveled, making the edges look square. However, with most fonts, the 3D Text that this creates is very hard to read. By default, this property is set to #none. Setting this property to #miter or #rounded can greatly improve the legibility of 3D Text. When set to #miter or #rounded, the complexity of this property is dependent on the last property, Beveldepth.

The success of setting the Beveldepth property is dependent on the size of the font you are working with. You see, the beveling that takes place on the 3D Text does not cut *in* to the geometry of the text. Rather, the bevel cuts *out* into 3D space. This means that as you increase the Beveldepth, the geometry for the 3D Text will actually become larger. If your font is small and your Beveldepth is large, the bevels of individual letters will begin to cut into one another, to the point of cutting into the base letters themselves; however, if you use the same Beveldepth with a larger font size, you may not notice the problem. Figure 7.3 illustrates some of the variations you can achieve by altering these four properties.

Unfortunately, once in #mode3D, Text Castmembers lose much of their native functionality: Editable, Hyperlink Lingo, and Antialiasing are among the list of "exceptions." The full list can be found in the Director Help file under What's New, Using 3D Text, Exceptions. The full list includes 26 properties, commands, and functions that do not work with Text Castmembers in #mode3D.

FIGURE 7.3

Variations of 3D Text created by modifying the Tunneldepth, Smoothness, Beveltype, and Beveldepth settings.

Font Choices

If you are planning on utilizing 3D Text and your goal is to have that Text remain readable, you should choose your font carefully. Serif fonts tend to use more geometry, and they become more difficult to discern. This is especially true when the characters of the font have very tight ascenders and descenders, such as the Times New Roman and 540 Caslon Roman typefaces. Sans-serif and block fonts tend to work well for 3D Text and retain their readability. Script fonts can work, but I would suggest utilizing the #miter Beveltype to accentuate the edges of the characters. In general, if you are trying to use a font and find it hard to read, try altering the Beveltype and Beveldepth settings for the 3D Text. Many times, even a subtle change near the edges of the letters can help distinguish them enough so that they're useful.

Should I Use 3D Text Castmembers or Not?

So far we have examined the first method of creating 3D Text, which has several difficulties and limitations. You may still choose to utilize Text Castmembers for 3D Text—especially if your project does not have a 3D environment. However, because we are focusing our attention on the creation of 3D environments, we will concentrate on the second method of creating 3D Text.

Using `extrude3d()` for 3D Text and Beyond

A better way to work with 3D Text is to utilize the `extrude3d()` command. This command generates a Modelresource based on a Text Castmember and inserts that Modelresource into a Shockwave 3D Castmember. From that Modelresource, you can create Models that may be manipulated exactly how you control any other Model.

The only major change is that the Modelresource type will be noted as #extruder. You may recall that each Modelresource type defines what Modelresource properties are available. The Modelresource of the #extruder type are listed in Table 7.1.

TABLE 7.1   3D Properties for Text Castmembers

Property	Range
Displayface	Any combination of [#front, #back, #tunnel]
Beveltype	#none, #miter, or #round
Beveldepth	Float 1–10
Smoothness	Float 1–10
Tunneldepth	Float 1–100

The main purpose of the `extrude3d()` command is to allow you to avoid modeling your Text in an external 3D program. Creating 3D Text externally is actually discouraged because it will most likely be geometrically complex and will need to be downloaded rather than created at runtime. The `extrude3d()` command is powerful because it allows you to extrude the vector outlines of characters from a font file. The method of extruding is quite approachable, as demonstrated in the following code:

```
Member("textcastmember").extrude3d(member("3dCastmember"))
```

The most important observation about this code is that the `extrude3d()` command is executed on a Text Castmember object rather than on the 3D

Castmember. Also, this command creates a Modelresource, so you will still need to create a Model in order to see the Text.

Basic Extrusion Demo

This demo will use a file named Extrusion Basics on the CD-ROM that accompanies this book. Inside this file are several Castmembers, Sprites, and Scripts that initialize the 3D environment. Most importantly, there is a 3D Castmember named "3Dworld" and a Text Castmember named "basic." If you play the movie, a global variable named "scene," containing a reference to the 3D Castmember, will become available. We can walk through the steps of creating 3D Text in the message window while the movie is running. Type the following into the message window:

```
Res = member("basic").extrude3d(scene)
```

We have just created a new Modelresource in the 3D Castmember. Now let's create a Model from that Modelresource with the following code:

```
Obj = scene.newmodel("mytext", res)
```

The word "Hello!" should appear in the center of the 3D environment. Try using some of the rotation and translation methods that we examined in Chapter 4, "Transformations," on the new Model. Here's an example:

```
Obj.rotate(0,45,0)
```

Notice that when you rotate this Text around its local origin, it seems to rotate around a point that is located 5 or 10 units to the left. The reason for this is that the default local origin for the Text is the world origin. However, the origin for the 3D Text geometry is not in the same location. This is a difficulty that we cannot overcome until we examine Groups in Chapter 8, "Parents, Children, and Cloning."

Try removing the default texture of the Text (the pink and white checkerboard) with the following code:

```
Obj.shaderlist.texture = void
```

The method of controlling the Text Model is exactly similar to the methods used to control any other Model. However, because the Modelresource type is #extruder, the Modelresource properties are a bit different. Try changing the depth of the text with the following:

```
Res.tunneldepth = 20
```

Now try changing the Beveltype and Beveldepth properties:

```
Res.beveltype = #miter
Res.beveldepth = 7
```

These changes to the Modelresource are similar to the changes we made to Text Castmembers using the Property Inspector. Refer to Table 7.1 for the full list of #extruder Modelresource properties. As an exercise, try to modify these properties from the message window for varied effects. The process of creating 3D Text is immediate and rewarding.

Basic Extrusion API

Although the process of extruding 3D Text is quite simple, it can become repetitive, similar to how the creation of primitives can become repetitive. One of the benefits of creating 3D Text on-the-fly is to avoid downloading geometry. The problem is that we still need to download a Text Castmember to extrude Text from. The following custom handler is designed to streamline the process of extruding text as well as overcome the problem of downloading a Text Castmember:

```
1: global scene
2:
3: on create3Dtext modelname, whattext, whatfont, whatsize, \
howdeep, whatcolor
4:   if scene.model(modelname) = void then
-- create new text castmember
5:   newtext = new(#text)
-- set the font for the new text castmember
6:   newtext.font = whatfont
-- set the fontsize of the new text castmember
7:   newtext.fontsize = whatsize
```

```
-- assign text property of new text castmember
 8:   newtext.text = whattext
-- extrude a modelresource from the new text castmember
 9:   res = member(newtext).extrude3D(scene)
-- delete the new text castmember (we do not need it anymore)
10:   newtext.erase()
11:
--set the extruder modelresource tunneldepth property
12:   res.tunneldepth = howdeep
-- create a new model from the extruder modelresource
13:   obj = scene.newmodel(modelname, res)
-- create a new shader for the model
14:   shd = scene.newshader(modelname & "shd", #standard)
-- set the diffuse color for the new shader
15:   shd.diffuse = whatcolor
-- remove the default texture from the new shader
16:   shd.texture = void
17:
-- set the model's shader to the new shader
18:   obj.shaderlist = shd.
19:    return obj
20:   else
21:   return false
22:   end if
23:
24: end
```

The strength of this custom handler is that it creates a new Text Castmember on-the-fly, extrudes the Text from it, and then deletes the Text Castmember.

NOTE

The weakness of this custom handler is that it uses the `erase()` command to delete the Text Castmember. This can sometimes lead to memory leaks. If you are uncomfortable with this, a second handler `create3Dfromtext()` can be found on the CD-ROM that does not use the `erase()` command.

This custom handler is located in a file named Extrusion API on the CD-ROM. When we play the movie, nothing seems to happen unless we modify the `initialize()` handler with the following code:

```
Create3Dtext("mytext", "hi there", "geneva", 12, 10, rgb(255,100,50))
```

It is not very difficult to change "hi there" to anything you like. In addition, you can also embed fonts to extend the range of capabilities of the `extrude3D()` command.

Creating Custom Fonts for Director

Creating 3D Text is relatively simple, but many times you need to extrude a company logo or some other vector artwork into 3D. Rather than modeling this text in an external 3D program, you can use the `extrude3D()` command to generate a 3D logo from a font.

You may have encountered some fonts that Director will not recognize, even though you can use them in other programs. Among the fonts that are not recognized, you may find that some will not allow you to embed them. Now that you have been working with 3D Text, you may find that even fewer of your fonts are available for extrusion. The fonts that you cannot embed into Director are the same fonts you cannot extrude. Generally, I feel that it is good practice to embed fonts in Director before you use them for extrusions—this ensures that your users have the fonts they need to see your 3D Text. Also, if you try to extrude text from a font that is not supported, at best you will get a script error. Many times Director will crash if you try to extrude a character from a font with invalid information. On the other hand, with the font embedded into Director, you know that the font is ready to be extruded.

There are many reasons why your font's information may be invalid. One reason that Director does not allow a font to be embedded is that some fonts do not include outlines for all characters. One example of this would be a font with only uppercase letters and no numbers. Director only embeds fonts that have an outline for the lowercase, uppercase, and number characters. Even if you decide to only embed one or two of the letters, Director will not let you insert the font.

The workaround for this problem is to modify the font. A font-editing program such as Fontographer can make small changes to a font that allow it to be inserted into Director. Also, Fontographer enables you to create completely customized fonts. The CD-ROM contains a font file named "freefont" that you can use in your projects. Figure 7.4 illustrates the characters present in this file.

FIGURE 7.4

The main font window in Fontographer, displaying the glyphs for characters A–Z, a–z, and 0–9.

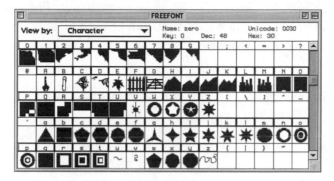

Notice in Figure 7.4 that the glyph for the characters Z and *l* are identical. This is meant to demonstrate that even though I did not have enough images for the 62 required characters, I was able to simply copy some letters in order to fill in the required blanks. If you have a font that will not embed, try opening the font in a font editor and make sure that there are characters for A–Z, a–z, and 0–9. If there are not, duplicate some of the letters to fill in where you need them. Also, try using TrueType fonts because the character information that is saved for each "letter" works best in Director.

The shapes in freefont were created in a variety of ways. Characters *A* and *B* were scanned into Photoshop, saved as bitmaps, and then traced with auto-trace in Freehand. Then, the outlines were imported directly into Fontographer. Many of the lowercase letters were drawn directly in Freehand and then imported. Several shapes, such as lowercase *z* and *y*, were drawn directly in Fontographer, which has many drawing and tracing tools of its own. Lowercase *z* was drawn with a pen tablet (Fontographer accepts pressure-sensitive information). This is a very immediate and gestural method of creating shapes that will later become 3D objects. The purpose of this is to emphasize that it is possible to create complex Models in Director without the use of high-end 3D modeling.

The Hidden Power of Extrusion

So far we have been looking at 3D Text for readable Text and company logos. However, the `extrude3d()` command is much more powerful than this if you utilize it with a broader scope than "3D Text." Notice that the custom font, freefont, falls into the category of a Wingdings style font. Essentially, it is a font created from small iconographic clip art–style drawings. These shapes will all extrude quite well as 3D Models and can be used in a variety of situations. The strengths of working with 3D extrusion are as follows:

- You don't need a 3D modeler to create complex 3D Models.
- Font files are relatively small (14–25KB) when embedded.
- Extrusions are created on-the-fly.
- No download time is required for Model geometry.

Paperclip Demo

The Paperclip demo only uses extrusion techniques for modeling. Open the file named Paperclip Demo, located on the CD-ROM. When you play this movie, the paperclip Model is created on-the-fly from the letter *B* in freefont. Figure 7.5 illustrates what this paperclip Model should look like after you start the movie.

FIGURE 7.5

A Model of a paperclip created from extruding a 2D character from a font. No 3D modeling was required to create this Model.

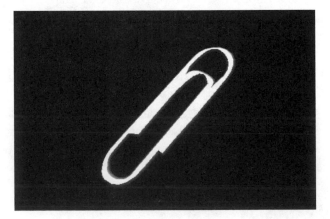

Although there is no real interaction in this movie, the goal of this demo is to show how powerful extrusion can be. The letter *B* was created by scanning a paperclip and then using this information to create vector outlines in Freehand. Several of the other objects in freefont were created this way, such as the letters *A* (a key) and *E* (a leaf). One reason why the Paperclip demo works so well is because of the #round beveling of the edges. This, in addition to the Beveldepth setting, creates the illusion of a believable paperclip.

State Quiz Demo

The characters 0–9 in freefont were used to generate the Models for the State Quiz file, located on the CD-ROM. Figure 7.6 is a screenshot from this small demonstration of how you might begin to think about using fonts to create custom geometry.

FIGURE 7.6

A practical use of Models created with the #extruder Modelresource type.

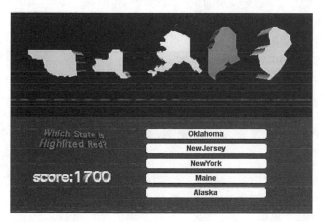

Note that the size of this demo file is small (148KB), and when it is compressed as a Shockwave file, it only occupies 24KB. It would not be very difficult to modify this game so that it uses all 50 states, or even all the countries of the world—the game size would remain essentially the same.

Further Notes on Extrusion

The freefont file includes many shapes that were designed to demonstrate the power of extrusion. I suggest extruding the sample characters to get a sense of what is possible. Among the glyphs that are included are those shown in Figure 7.7.

FIGURE 7.7

Several examples of characters in the freefont file.

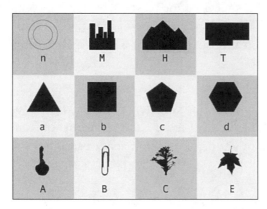

These examples from the freefont file can be used to derive a wide array of Models. The concentric circles can be used to create tubes that have an inside, outside, and some amount of wall thickness. The skyline characters can be used to generate distant mountains or cityscapes. The overhead plan views for buildings can be extruded to create a small housing development. Note that the shapes included range from geometric polygons for the creation of faceted tubes, to organic shapes such as the leaf and the whale skeleton. Observe the objects around you and try to imagine which ones could be expressed through extrusion.

One final bonus of using extrusion to generate Models is that your font resources are protected better than those imported in 3D Models. See Chapter 9 for a full discussion of the security problems related to importing 3D Models.

Summary

3D Text can be created by a simple property change for Text Castmembers or as a process that includes creating a Modelresource in your 3D environment. The first method is not very flexible, and the effects it can achieve could also be done with bitmaps. The second method is more robust because you are able to create Modelresources that can be used as geometry in your 3D environment.

Aside from the method you use to create 3D Text, there is the matter of how you conceptualize what 3D Text can accomplish. If you take a broad meaning to the term *3D Text* to include the ability to extrude 2D shapes into 3D Models, you can begin to see how extrude3d() is a powerful tool.

Creating custom fonts that are nontypographic is a skill that can be learned rather quickly. It provides you with a method for creating complex Models without 3D software. Considering that using 3D software may be a difficult option for some, extrusions allow for an immediate method of Model creation with little technical knowledge.

In conclusion, although there are two methods of creating 3D Text, the extrude3d() command is superior because of its ability to create Modelresources that can be used in your 3D environments. Also, extrude3d() reinforces the fact that you do not specifically need to create 3D Text when extruding any 2D shape into the 3D environment.

FAQ

What about modeling letters in my 3D software?

> You can do this, but it really is not worth it. The characters that you create in 3D software will have to be downloaded as geometry. In addition, the geometry that is created will most likely be more complex than you might need. One reason why you might do this is because the extrusions in Director are only along a straight-line path. If you need text that extrudes along a complex path, you will need to create that geometry externally.

I experience frequent crashes when embedding fonts. How can I stop this?

> Some fonts cause crashes when embedded. This is especially true of Windows 95 and 98. One possibility is to try to insert the font into castlib #1. Another is to make sure you are using TrueType fonts.

Supplemental Resources

Many resources for typography and fonts can be found in books and on the Web. However, many of the resources on the Web for fonts are less than desirable. The resources listed here are professional type foundries that have developed fonts for quite some time and are well respected.

Online Font Repositories

- T26 (www.t26.com). Carlos Segura's Digital Type Foundry offers a large range of professional quality typefaces, ranging from classical to contemporary and experimental.

- *Émigré* (www.emigre.com). *Émigré* is a design magazine that also produces custom typography. Many of the "body fonts" that *Émigré* licenses are designed to be quite modern and readable.

- Adobe (www.adobe.com). Adobe offers an extremely large range of professional-grade fonts. Also, Adobe produces the Adobe Type Manager—a professional font-organization tool.

Font-Creation Software

- Fontographer (www.macromedia.com). Macromedia distributes Fontographer, which is considered by some as the undisputed leader in font-creation software. It integrates well with Freehand and also with Fireworks, Photoshop, and Illustrator.

- Fontlab (www.fontlab.com). Fontlab is a highly respected tool for the creation of professional-quality fonts. It supports a wider number of font types and a more complete execution of TrueType hinting than its competitors.

CHAPTER 8

Parents, Children, and Cloning

This chapter deals with several topics that affect the scenegraph hierarchy of your 3D environments. Specifically, the topics of parents and children, cloning, and Groups will be covered. Note that the topic of parents and children is not the same topic as parent/child scripts in Director. A parent/child script is a type of code object that is related to programming Lingo. In terms of the 3D Castmember, the topic of parents and children refers to the hierarchy of Nodes in your 3D Castmembers.

Cloning is a process that provides a method of duplicating Nodes. Rather than creating multiple Nodes and then setting a myriad of properties for each, you can use cloning to quickly generate copies of a Node with its properties and hierarchy intact. I will show you several strategies for cloning and explain the advantages and disadvantages involved.

Finally, I will explain how Groups contribute to the overall hierarchy of Nodes. We will examine how you can apply Groups as a tool to simplify complex transformations. In addition, we will examine some of the subtleties of the basic hierarchy structure of all 3D Castmembers.

Scenegraph Hierarchy

The default hierarchy of the 3D environment is rather flat. Technically, each Node is dependent on the World origin and itself for position and rotation. Figure 8.1 illustrates a scenegraph hierarchy for a 3D Castmember that has had two Models created on-the-fly.

FIGURE 8.1

The scenegraph hierarchy for a 3D Castmember with two Models, and visual representations of how parenting, grouping, and cloning affect this hierarchy.

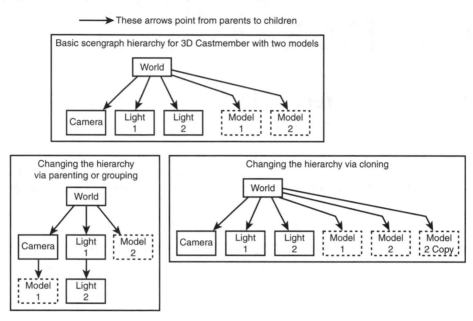

Figure 8.1 illustrates that there are two types of changes we can make to the scenegraph hierarchy. The first type of change creates links between Nodes through parenting or grouping. In this case, rather than depending on the World origin and itself for position and rotation, a Node will depend on another Node and itself for position and rotation.

The second change that we can make to the scenegraph hierarchy is to duplicate Nodes, thus expanding the scengraph hierarchy "laterally," as illustrated in Figure 8.1. Cloning can be thought of as simply copying Nodes, but that is not entirely true. When you clone a Node, you will clone that Node and every Node "linked" to it. Therefore, cloning can be used to copy one Node or whole branches of Nodes.

Parents and Children

You are probably familiar with the use of the terms *parent* and *child* in Director in reference to parent/child scripts. With the introduction of a 3D environment, these terms acquire additional meanings. *Parenting* is used to refer to a method of linking Nodes together in order to control the inheritance of position and rotation among Nodes.

The topic of parents and children applies to several Nodes, including Models, Lights, Cameras, and also Groups. Each of these Nodes has a parent property; the default value for the parent property of a Node is the World. In any 3D environment, the concept of "who" a Node's parent is can be changed at any given time. Changing the parent of a Node manifests itself through transformations.

In Chapter 4, "Transformations," you learned that a Model can be rotated and positioned relative to its parent or to itself. You also learned that, by default, a Model's parent is the World and that this means, by default, a Model's coordinates are reported as relative to the World origin. Through the parent property of Nodes, we have the ability to change this relationship, so rather than rotating or translating a Node relative to the World origin, we can make a Node transform relative to its parent's origin.

Basic Parenting

Open the file named "Parenting" from the CD and press Play. You should see two Models on the Stage: a cube and a cone. Below the 3D Sprite, you should see information concerning the current World position of each Model and its parent Node.

Changing the parent of a Node has several effects on that Node. First, the position of the Node will be translated into parent-relative space. This is most obvious if we change the cone Model parent Node from the World to the cube. While the movie is still running, type the following into the message window and press Return:

```
Scene.model[2].parent = scene.model[1]
```

As soon as you press Return, you should notice an immediate effect on the environment. The cone has moved relative to the cube rather than relative to the World origin. Note that the position of the cube is still being reported to us in World coordinates. To see immediate information about the cone position in World-relative space without stopping the movie, type the following into the message window and press Return:

```
Put scene.model[2].getworldtransform().position
-- vector( 0.0000, -15.0000, -60.0000 )
```

To see information about the cone position in parent-relative space, again without stopping the movie, try this:

```
Put scene.model[2].transform.position
-- vector( 50.0000, 0.0000, -60.0000 )
```

When you change the parent of the Model, that Model visually "jumps" to its new relative location. Because of this, I recommend that you avoid directly manipulating the parent property of Nodes. Rather, you should use the command addchild(), which offers more control over the process of linking Nodes together.

Stop, rewind, and play the movie again. In the message window, type the following line of code and press Return:

```
Scene.model[1].addchild(scene.model[2], #preserveworld)
```

The field box on the Stage reporting the value of model[2].parent informs you that the parent of model[2] is now model[1], but model[2] did not move. This is because the #preserveworld parameter will link Nodes together, but it won't move them. Rather, the position of the Node at the time the addchild() command is executed will be recalculated into parent-relative space. Then the child will be moved to that new location. The new location is the same location if we were to examine the coordinates in World-relative space; therefore, the change is visually imperceptible.

There are several things to note about the addchild() command. This command is run on the object that will become the parent rather than manipulating the child's parent property. The #preserveworld argument is the default method of linking Nodes with this command, so you can reduce typing by omitting this parameter when using addchild(). If you prefer that the child object reposition itself relative to the parent as a result of the addchild() command, use #preserveparent as the argument.

This approach to parenting is certainly the preferred method, because you will have more control over the position of the child at the moment of linking. This approach has other implications as well. While the movie is still running, type the following code into the message window and press Return:

```
Put Scene.model[1].child.count
--1
put scene.model[1].child[1]
--model("mycone")
```

You can see that it is possible to find out specific information about the child of a given Node; what may not be clear is that you can modify the child properties this way. For example, while the movie continues to play, try the following code:

```
Scene.model[1].child[1].translate(20,0,0)
```

Although this may not be the optimal choice for all situations, the preceding example demonstrates that it is entirely possible to modify a child Node directly through its parent. Finally, with the movie still playing, move the parent Node with the following:

```
Scene.model[1].translate(30,0,0)
```

Notice that both the parent and the child Node move—the child Node will maintain its relative position to the parent Node. This behavior is important because it provides a clear visual summation of the following:

- Translating a parent translates the parent and all children
- Translating a child translates the child (and its children)

The next demonstration that we will examine deals with how parent and child Node relationships affect rotation.

Chains of Parents and Children

It is possible to create detailed chains of parents and children in order to simulate complex relationships between objects. Think about your arms: Your torso is the parent object to your upper arm, your upper arm parent to your forearm, your forearm parent to your hand, and so on. Granted, your arms have certain limitations placed on rotation, but the hierarchy remains.

On the CD is a file named "Basic Chain" that demonstrates how parenting affects rotation. In this example are three Models: a yellow cube, a pink cube, and a blue cube. The blue cube's parent is the pink cube, and the pink cube's parent is the yellow cube.

When you toggle auto-rotation for the yellow cube, all its children (the pink and blue cubes) rotate along with it. This is similar to the behavior that you observed with translation and can be summarized as follows:

- Rotating a parent rotates the parent and all children
- Rotating a child rotates the child (and its children)

While the movie is playing, type the following code into the message window and press Return:

```
Scene.model[3].addchild(scene.model[1])
```

This code does not generate an error, but in this case, it is rather useless. Without stopping the movie, type the following into the message window:

```
put scene.model[1].parent
--group("world")
```

Notice that the parent of `model[1]` is still the `group("world")`. This is important because you tried to set the yellow cube to become a child of the blue cube. The blue cube is a "grandchild" of the yellow cube, and this type of chain is not supported. In this case, Director ignores the request.

NOTE

It is not possible to create circular chains in Director. That is, you cannot create a chain of parents and children, where a child is the parent of one of its "ancestors."

In summation, rotation and position are inherited by the children of a given Node. Scale is not inherited because scaling is always Node relative. Yet, with the capability for inherited rotation and position, there are quite a few possible strategies for utilizing parent/child chains.

Linear Chains

So far, the chains that we have looked at are rather small—they only involve three Models. Chains can contain many more Models, but to limit our discussion to Models is unfair. Lights, Cameras, and Groups can be members of a chain as well. You need not have a Model in the chain at all. For our examples, it will be easiest to observe these effects on Models, but do not forget that these rules apply to other Nodes as well.

I will use the term *linear chain* when referring to a chain that has several members and is a single, linear chain. To continue, a linear chain can be used to create fairly complex motions due to the inheritance of transformations of each child on the chain. I will also refer to the parents of parents of a child Node as its *ancestors*. This term is not meant to be confused with ancestors from parent/child scripting.

A good example of a linear chain might be a rope or a snake that has the ability to wriggle. Another example would be a stick or rod with the ability to bend. You can also use linear chains to create telescoping hierarchies and hierarchies with gear ratios.

On the CD is a file named "Linear Chain" that automatically creates several objects and manipulates their hierarchy such that they form a linear chain. Figure 8.2 is a screenshot of this scene with arrows illustrated to show the direction of the linkage of the chain.

The Models and the hierarchy of this chain are created during the initialization script of this movie. In the previous example, we created a chain with only three Models. Because there were so few Models to create and form the hierarchy, I coded the creation of each Model and each parent/child link. However, this approach is not feasible or advantageous for longer chains. The logical structure of a repeat loop is well suited to the creation of linear chains, although deciphering the overall logic of this code can be difficult. For that reason, first take a look at the repeat loop that we will use to create our linear chain in pseudocode:

```
Repeat some number of times
 Create New Model
 If this is not the first Model then
  Make New model the child of the previous model
 End if
Repeat again
```

FIGURE 8.2

The "Linear Chain" demonstration, with arrows to indicate the child Nodes.

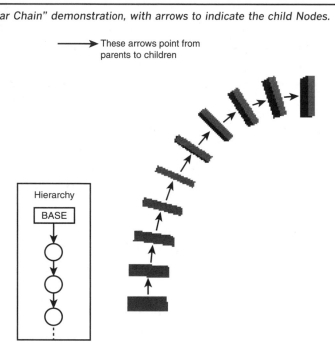

Of these steps, two logical elements are crucial. Because a chain must begin with some Node, it is important that we do not cause the first Node to become the child of some other Node (other than the World). This is why the if/then statement is encapsulated inside of the repeat loop. The second element is the logic to attach Nodes as children to the Model created previously. This actually forms the hierarchy of the chain.

This pseudocode has been implemented with slight additions for this specific demonstration; notably I have added code to move each child Node a set distance away from its parent. The following code is the initialization script for the "Linear Chain" movie:

```
 1: global scene
 2:
 3: on initialize
 4:   clearworld(scene)
 5:
 6:   --create a chain with ten Nodes
 7:   repeat with x = 1 to 10
 8:
 9:     --create a new model
10:     --this example utilizes the x variable to create
11:     --unique names, and also to vary the Model Color
12:     createbox("mybox" & x, 12,12,2,rgb(x * 20,100,0))
13:
14:     --if this is the first iteration of the repeat loop
15:     --skip this section, otherwise…
16:     if x <> 1 then
17:       --move the New model
18:       scene.model[x].translate(0,10,0)
19:       --Make the new Model become the child of the previous Model
20:       scene.model[x-1].addchild(scene.model[x], #preserveparent)
21:     end if
22:   end repeat
23:
24:   --non chain related
25:   --changes the color of the sprite background to white
26:   scene.camera[1].colorbuffer.clearvalue = rgb(255,255,255)
27: end
```

Notice that this script is quite concise because the linking is handled within the repeat loop. It would not be very difficult to change this repeat loop to create many more than 10 Nodes or to alter the distance between the Nodes.

After the hierarchy of Nodes has been established for this scene, it is possible to utilize the inheritance of Node position and rotation to create complex transformations. In this example, the linear chain repeatedly bends. Concurrently, the entire chain spins on the World's Y axis, which was done so that you can visualize the bending of the chain with greater perspective about the space that this bending occurs in.

The behavior of the chain can best be understood through a close examination of the following bending script:

```
1: Property pDirection
2:
3: global scene
```

```
 4:
 5: on beginsprite
 6:  pDirection = 1
 7: end
 8:
 9:
10: on exitframe me
11:
12:  --rotate the whole entire chain around the world y-Axis
13:  scene.model[1].rotate(0,.5,0, #world)
14:
15:  -- notice that we are repeating from 2 to 10
16:  -- this is because I do not want to "bend" the
17:  -- first Node in the chain in this example
18:  repeat with x = 2 to 10
19:
20:    --decide if the chain has bent "too far" in this
21:    --case if the current Node has rotated further than
22:    --45 or negative 45 degrees on the Z-axis. If we have
23:    --bent too far, then negate the direction of bending.
24:
25:    rlimit = scene.model[x].transform.rotation.z
26:
27:
28:    if rlimit > 45 or rlimit < -45 then
29:     pDirection = -pDirection
30:    end if
31:
32:    --determine how far to bend this particular Node
33:    --irrespective of the direction of bending
34:    bendAmount = float(x) / 25
35:
36:    -- if pDirection is positive, bendAmount will
37:    -- remain bending in the same direction. If
38:    -- pDirection is negative, the bendAmount will
39:    -- become negative
40:
41:    bendAmount = bendAmount * pDirection
42:
43:    --rotate the current Model along its parent's Z axis
44:    --an amount and Direction specified by bendAmount.
45:    --Remember, each child of the Current Node will bend
46:    --along with the current Node, thus creating the
47:    --cumulative effect of rotation.
48:
49:    scene.model[x].rotate(0,0,bendAmount,#parent)
50:  end repeat
51:
52: end
```

To reiterate, inherited rotations (and translations) can be used to create complex motions with a linear chain. Although the motion in this particular example is a bit mechanical, the basic principle of allowing changes to accumulate can be fine-tuned. It is important to realize that the creation of chains is not difficult, but the methods of control can be significantly more complex.

Forked Chains

In the previous example, our chain extended in one direction so that no one Node was the immediate parent to more than one other Node. When a single Node is parent to several other Nodes, chains are formed that fork and branch. On the CD is a file named "Forked Chain" that demonstrates how a forked chain is different from a single linear chain. Figure 8.3 illustrates the hierarchy created in this demonstration.

FIGURE 8.3

The "Forked Chain" demonstration, with arrows to indicate the child Nodes.

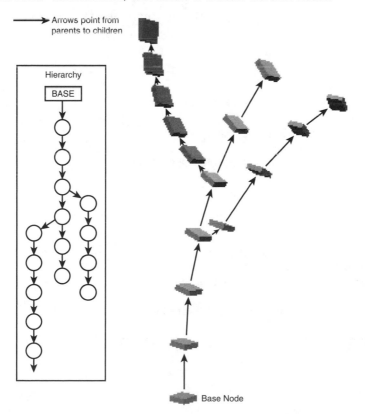

The code used to create a forked (or *branched*) chain is similar to the code used to create a linear chain. Here's the code that generates the Nodes and the forked hierarchy:

```
 1: global scene
 2:
 3: on initialize
 4:   clearworld(scene)
 5:
 6:   -- Create Main Chain (grey)
 7:   repeat with x = 1 to 7
 8:     --create New Model Node
 9:     obj = createbox("msCA" & x, 7,7,2,rgb(200,200,190))
10:
11:     -- if this is not the very first Model in the chain
12:     -- then set the initial position and rotation of the
13:     -- Model and then make it a child of the previous Model
14:     if x <> 1 then
15:       obj.rotate(0,0,5 + x,#self)
16:       obj.translate(x,20,0)
17:       scene.model[x-1].addchild(scene.model[x], #preserveparent)
18:     end if
19:   end repeat
20:
21:
22:   --Create Branch (light blue)
23:   -- notice that I am starting the repeat loop at 8
24:   repeat with x = 8 to 11
25:     --create a new Model. this will be the
26:     --first child in this branch.
27:     obj = createbox("msCB" & x, 7,7,2,rgb(100,200,190))
28:
29:     --set up the initial position
30:     obj.rotate(x,0,0)
31:     obj.translate(0,25,x)
32:
33:     -- if this is the first child in this branch, then
34:     -- attach the branch to model 3 (in this case)
35:     -- otherwise, attach the new model to the previous Model
36:     if x = 8 then
37:       scene.model[3].addchild(scene.model[x], #preserveparent)
38:     else
39:       scene.model[x-1].addchild(scene.model[x], #preserveparent)
40:     end if
41:   end repeat
```

```
42:
43:   --Create Branch (magenta)
44:   --this code is logically identical to creating the light blue
45:   --branch. Only note that we begin the repeat loop at 12
46:   repeat with x = 12 to 16
47:     obj = createbox("msCC" & x, 7,7,2,rgb(200,100,190))
48:     obj.rotate(0,0,12)
49:     obj.translate(10,2,-5)
50:
51:     if x = 12 then
52:       scene.model[5].addchild(scene.model[x], #preserveparent)
53:     else
54:       scene.model[x-1].addchild(scene.model[x], #preserveparent)
55:     end if
56:   end repeat
57:
58:   --non-chain related (set the sprite background color)
59:   scene.camera[1].colorbuffer.clearvalue = rgb(255,255,255)
60: end
```

A forked chain is essentially a chain with chains attached to it. Some examples of structures that possess a forked chain hierarchy are trees, insects, humans, and animals with appendages. From these examples, you can see that forked chains offer you development choices that mimic some physiological and biological hierarchies.

Bi-directional Chains

A bi-directional chain is a special variation of a forked chain that has unique properties. Technically, there are several variations of bi-directional chains, but not all these variations can be created in Director, although this is an issue in most 3D environments. The type of bi-directional chain that is possible has a base Node that is the originator of two chains. Figure 8.4 illustrates two variations on the bi-directional chain: the one that is possible and the one that is not.

I mention the chain that is not possible because this hierarchy is similar to a rope held from some point in the middle, with ends that are not tethered. This type of behavior can be simulated, but it cannot be accomplished with native parent/child hierarchical chains.

FIGURE 8.4

Two variations on the concept of a bi-directional chain. Note that only one of these is possible in Director.

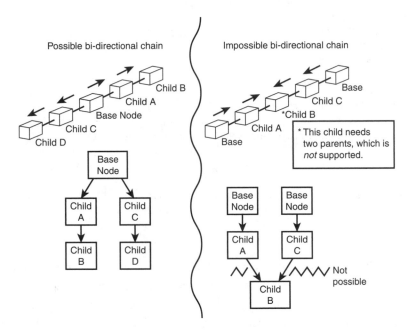

NOTE

Rope behavior is rather complex and can be simulated with varying degrees of "accuracy." If this type of interaction is required, I suggest using a parent/child script that defines a custom data type with handlers for grabbing, dragging, and releasing the rope. For a more realistic simulation of a rope, refer to Appendix G, "Havok Xtra," for information about the Havok Physics plug-in.

When I speak of a "bi-directional chain," I am speaking about the chain that we can create using the parent/child properties of Nodes. This hierarchy is similar to a rope tied semi-taught at both ends with a weight attached somewhere in the middle (for example, a swing). On the CD is a file named "Bi-directional Chain." Open that file and press Play. Note that Figure 8.5 is a screenshot from this demonstration of the bi-directional chain, with arrows indicating the scenegraph hierarchy.

FIGURE 8.5

The "Bi-directional Chain" demonstration, with arrows to indicate the child Nodes.

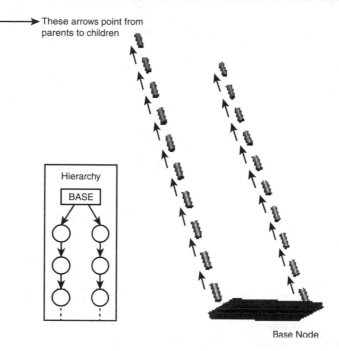

The creation of a bi-directional chain does not vary much from the creation of a forked chain. Remember, the bi-directional chain is just a special type of forked chain. This example is intended to demonstrate that the power of a bi-directional chain is in how you control it.

In this case, the seat of the swing is rotated around the X axis of its last child. Although the oscillation for the swing is simulated through Lingo, the values are not physically accurate (it's only a simulation). Here's the swinging script:

```
1: property pdirection --determines the direction of swinging
2: property swayLUT    --Look-Up Table of amount of "swing"
3: property pcounter   --enumerates the period of swinging
4:
5: global scene
6:
7: on beginsprite me
8:   paccumulate = false --by default do not rotate children
9:
```

```
10:  pdirection = 1
11:
12: --the swayLUT is a linear list that contains values
13: --that steadily increase and then steadily decrease
14: --these values are used to simulate the oscillation
15: --of the swing, without more complicated math.
16:  swayLUT = []
17:
18:  repeat with x = 1 to 50
19:    addat(swayLUT, (float(x) / 25))
20:  end repeat
21:
22:  repeat with x = 50 down to 1
23:    addat(swayLUT, (float(x) / 25))
24:  end repeat
25:
26:  pcounter = 1
27: end
28:
29:
30: on exitframe me
31:   --add one to the counter
32:   pcounter = pcounter + 1
33:
34: -- if the counter is larger than 101
35: --reset the counter and switch the direction of swing
36:   if pcounter = 101 then
37:     pcounter = 1
38:     pdirection = -pdirection
39:   end if
40:
41: --retrieve the "amount of swing" from the swayLUT
42: --based on the current value of pcounter
43:   bendangle = swayLUT[pcounter]
44:
45: --modulate the bendangle based on the direction
46: --of swing (positive or negative)
47:   bendangle = bendangle * pdirection
48:
49: --rotate the base node around the x-axis
50: --of its most distant child.
51:   scene.model[1].rotate(bendangle,0,0, scene.model[11])
52:
53: end
```

Other possibilities that you might consider would be to slightly bend each child of the chain in order to add a slight bend in the "ropes." Bi-directional chains can also be used for the control of physiological systems, such as bird or insect wings.

From these examples, you can see that the creation of chains and the method of approaching chains is one application of the parent/child hierarchy. The strength of chains is in your ability to control them. Learning how to control a chain is dependent on your understanding of how position and rotation is inherited down the chain. You can create controls that force the children to rigidly follow the base object, such as in the bi-directional chain demo, or you can create controls that utilize the inheritance of rotation and position to create more organic motions, such as in the linear chain demo.

Cloning

Cloning is a powerful tool that has several implications, advantages, and disadvantages. Cloning a Node in Director has the advantage of providing a method for you to download one complex Model and then create several instances of it, rather than needing to download multiple copies of the same geometry. In terms of disadvantages, cloning causes a performance hit that is affected by geometry complexity, machine speed, and the number of Nodes cloned at the same time, among other things. Cloning is not something that I recommend doing while your users are "in" your movie. Rather, it is the type of task you should handle during "loading" or similar sections near the beginning of a movie. Also, just because you clone something does not mean you need to show it to the user right away.

Cloning in Director implies more than simply copying a Node. There are two commands for cloning that affect Models, Cameras, Lights, and Groups. The first command, `clone()`, has the following qualities:

- It creates a new Node.
- The new Node has its own unique transform.
- The new Node has its own unique Modifiers.
- The children of the cloned Node are cloned.
- In the case of a Model, the new Model shares a Modelresource.
- In the case of a Model, the new Model shares Shaders.

In the case of the fourth item, be aware that when you clone a Node, you will clone all its children as well. This can cause major problems. Out of all these qualities, the fifth and sixth items have the most implications. Because the new Model shares a Modelresource with the cloned Model, any changes you make to the Modelresource of either will affect both Models. In addition, the Models share Shaders; it is more common that you would need to have unique Shaders when cloning.

The second command for cloning in Director is `clonedeep()`, which causes a larger performance hit regardless of the situation because, in addition to the first through fourth items, `clonedeep()` clones Modelresources and Shaders as well. `Clonedeep()` should not be used trivially—because you are actually loading more of the same geometry into RAM, you should only be doing so if you know that you are going to need to edit separate Modelresources. A good example of this would be if you cloned a box and you needed to remove the top from one but not from the other. One often overlooked implication of the fourth item in conjunction with `clonedeep()` is this: When you use `clonedeep()` on a non-Model Node, all its children are cloned. In addition, any children of the cloned Node that are Models will have their Modelresources cloned.

If you need to clone Nodes while the user is using your project, you should not to use the `clonedeep()` command. If you must create clones while the user is interacting with your movie, use `clone()`. The major drawback is that you won't have unique Shaders. One possible strategy that you might employ would be to create several identical Shaders near the beginning of the movie and then distribute them to the clones as required during the movie.

Basic Cloning

The file "Basic Cloning" on the CD contains the current demonstration. Open this file and play the movie. You should see a sphere slightly offset to the left side of the Stage. To clone this sphere, type the following code into the message window while the movie is playing and press Return:

```
scene.model[1].clone("sphereclone")
```

Although you have just created a clone, that clone is impossible to see because it is in exactly the same location as the original Model. While the movie continues to play, use the following code in the message window to move the clone:

```
scene.model[2].translate(60,0,0)
```

Now try changing the color of the original Model with the following:

```
Scene.model[1].shader.diffuse = rgb(0,200,100)
```

The color of both spheres should change, because when you use the `clone()` command, the spheres share a Shader. Rather than simply cloning again, this time we will use the `clonedeep()` command. Again, without stopping the movie, type the following code into the message window and press Return after each line:

```
Scene.model[1].clonedeep("spheredeep")
Scene.model[3].translate(0,60,0)
Scene.model[3].shader.diffuse = rgb(20,40,150)
```

Finally, with the movie still running, use the following commands in the message window to find out the names of the Shader objects used by the three Model Nodes:

```
Put scene.model[1].shader.name
-- shader("mysphereshd")
Put scene.model[2].shader.name
-- shader("mysphereshd")
Put scene.model[3].shader.name
-- shader("mysphereshd-copy1")
```

Note that the Model that was cloned with `clone()` shares a Shader with the original, whereas the Model that was cloned with `clonedeep()` has its own dedicated Shader object.

Duplicating Chains

This demo involves an important lesson about how you can use cloning to create variations of complex objects. Open the file named "Forked Chain" from the CD and start the movie.

While the movie is running, type the following command into the message window and press Return:

```
scene.model[1].clone("newchain")
```

By duplicating the first Model in the chain, we have effectively cloned every child attached to that parent. The second chain contains the same hierarchy as the first chain—the only similarities are the Shader and Modelresources shared between the clone and the original.

Stop the movie, rewind it, and play it again. This time we are going to clone a member of the chain that is not the first Model in the chain. Type the following code into the message window and press Return:

```
Scene.model[8].clone("newbranch")
```

When we clone a Node that is part of a chain, the clones will possess the same hierarchy as the original. This is important because while the movie is still playing it is visually impossible to determine that any Nodes have been cloned. Because we originally had 16 Nodes in our chain, the first new Model is Model 17. Use the following code to move Model 17:

```
Scene.model[17].translate(30,0,0)
```

Now it is possible to see the new branch that we created through cloning. Now we can use the following code to remove that new branch from the overall chain:

```
scene.group[1].addchild(scene.model[17], #preserveworld)
```

By using the `addchild()` command in this case, we are technically removing the child and all its children from the chain.

NOTE

> Although we have not yet discussed Groups, this command reveals an important detail that we will explore in the "Groups" section of this chapter. Specifically, this line of code assumes that you understand that `group[1]` is the World.

Because a Node can have only one parent, this command is powerful because we can use the #preserveworld argument to "leave" the branch in place.

Considerations for a Chain API

Working with chains can become quite complex. Also, you can see from the initialization scripts for the chain demos that creating chains is repetitive. If you know that you are going to be working on a project that will heavily involve chains, I suggest that you build a specific custom API to handle the functioning of those chains.

Many variations and levels of complexity for the application of the concept of chains can be implemented in Director. Because of the sheer number of options and the variations involved in each option, I have broken down the key tasks required for creating a chain API in order to help you plan your own:

- Creating linear chains on-the-fly
- Adding, removing, and duplicating branches
- Adding, removing, and duplicating children
- Unlinking all members of a chain
- Reconfiguring the base Node of a chain on-the-fly
- Removing the last child from a chain

Consider that several of these tasks—especially reconfiguring the base Node of a chain on-the-fly—are best implemented through parent/child *scripts*. An API of this complexity would likely use parent/child scripts to define a custom data type, where each of these tasks are methods of that data type.

You should also consider that cloning can be used not only for duplicating chains or children on chains but also as a method for creating the chains themselves. Rather than creating 30 Models and Modelresources to build a chain, you can create one Model, clone it 29 times, and link all the clones together.

Whichever route you decide to take, remember that chains can be approached with the basic logic that we have looked at in this chapter's demonstrations. The amount of streamlining that you contribute toward the control of chains is dependent on your specific project.

Groups

A *Group* is a special Node that can be used to associate several Nodes in order to refer to all members of the Group at once. Technically, a Group is similar in function to a parent. In fact, the members of a Group are children of that Group, and the Group is their parent. We will use the `addchild()` command to add Nodes to a Group (members of a Group are children of that Group).

The qualities that differentiate a Group from a simple parent are as follows: A Group is given a specific name that is used to refer to that Group as a single unit. The World space position of the Group is relative to the center of the Group bounding sphere, which is the smallest sphere that encapsulates all members of the Group.

You learned in Chapter 2, "Creating Models from Scratch via Lingo," about the creation of an empty 3D Castmember and how that Castmember is not entirely empty because it contains one Camera, two Lights, one Texture, one Shader, and one Modelresource. There is, however, one more Node whose inclusion both completes your knowledge of the default 3D Castmember and plays a primary role in your 3D environment. That Node is a Group whose name is *World*. In terms of the scenegraph hierarchy, this primary Node is often referred to as the *World origin*. However, the World origin itself is a special Group. Any Node that belongs to the World origin or whose parent belongs to the World origin is considered within the World. Only Nodes that are attached to the World origin are visible.

In the "Duplicating Chains" section of this chapter, we utilized the "World" Group to change the hierarchy of the new chain that we cloned from an existing chain. The command that we used to do this was the `addchild()` command, which is the standard method for adding Nodes to a Group. The World Group is a special exception to the fact that in order to add Nodes to a Group, you need to create the Group first. The World Group is a default element of every 3D Castmember, not to mention that you cannot delete it, even if you try (but you really wouldn't want to anyway).

The creation of Groups is handled by the dedicated command newgroup(). Open the file "Basic Group" on the CD and press Play. While the movie is playing, create a new Group with the following command in the message window:

```
grp = scene.newgroup("mygroup")
```

Now add each of the Model Nodes as children of the Group:

```
grp.addchild(scene.model[1])
grp.addchild(scene.model[2])
grp.addchild(scene.model[3])
```

Now, it is possible to manipulate the position of all members of the Group with the following command:

```
grp.translate(0,-10,0)
```

So far, this is very similar to how we would expect a chain to act, given that the chain needs to be moved by referencing the first member of the chain. The distinction between Groups and chains becomes punctuated as we begin to rotate the Group. While the movie continues to play, type the following code into the message window and press Return:

```
grp.rotate(0,5,5)
```

Observe that the members of the Group have rotated around the center of the Group. The center of the Group is a 3D point that exists in the center of the 3D space that all the members of the Group (and their children) occupy.

NOTE

Another special property of the World Group is that it cannot be rotated or translated. Any rotations or translations that you try to apply to it will be ignored.

Note that a Group can have children and that members of the Group can have children of their own. In addition, the Group can be the child of other Nodes. This is important because it will have an effect on the results of cloning. When you clone a Group or a chain that includes a Group, every Node that is either a child or grandchild of the Group will be cloned.

Rotating Text

In Chapter 7, "Text and Extrusion Capabilities," we discussed the creation of extruding text on-the-fly. While we were working with the Models created from extruded text, it was noted that the local origin of an extrusion Node is located to the lower left of the Node. This causes difficulty in rotating text around its center and positioning 3D text within the environment. Open the file "Grouping Text" on the CD and press Play. When this movie begins, a new Model will be created from a text Castmember. While the movie plays, type the following into the message window:

```
Scene.model[1].debug = true
```

Turning on the debug flag for the Model reveals that the local origin for the Model is located slightly to the left and lower than the center of the Node. Note that if you are in software rendering mode, setting debug to true does not show the axes for the Model and therefore you will not be able to see the local origin for the Model. If you were to rotate the Model with

```
Scene.model[1].rotate(0,0,45)
```

it would rotate around that local origin point. In addition, if you were to issue the command

```
Put scene.model[1].worldposition
--vector (0.0000, 0.0000, 0.0000)
Put scene.model[1].transform.position
--vector (0.0000, 0.0000, 0.0000)
```

in the message window, it is difficult to discern where in 3D space the center of the text actually is. However, there is still an option. In the message window, type the following while the movie is still running:

```
Put scene.model[1].boundingsphere
-- [vector( 72.5000, 34.5000, -25.0000 ), 68.9166]
```

The information that is returned to you is the location of the center of the bounding sphere of the Model and its radius. In this demonstration, we are not concerned about the radius, but the location of the center of the bounding sphere for this Model is also the location of the center of the Model. This is because the Model has no children.

From this information about the center of the Model, we can use a Group to simplify the task of rotating and translating the Model relative to its center. Here are the steps to take:

1. Create a Group.

2. Move the Group to the center of the Model.

3. Add the Model to the Group.

4. Rotate and translate the Model via the Group.

While the movie continues to play, type the following commands into the message window:

```
Obj = scene.model[1]
grp = scene.newgroup("mygroup")
grp.translate(obj.boundingsphere[1])
grp.addchild(scene.model[1])
grp.rotate(0,0,45)
```

The strength of this strategy for the hierarchy is that you can refer to the text directly through the Group for transformations. In addition, because Groups can become members of Groups, you could create chains of letters or groups of words that can be manipulated more easily than controlling them through their default local origins.

Other Possibilities for Groups

Groups are quite powerful and can contribute to your 3D worlds in many ways. You should consider that Groups offer you many possibilities. Remember that in this chapter we worked heavily with Models as Nodes within Groups, but other Nodes can be members of Groups as well. You can use a spotlight Node to create a flashlight or headlights for a car. Grouping a Model to a Camera can offer you a way to create a Model that is always in the Camera view at a specific location, such as a dashboard or a control panel.

When scenes are exported from external 3D modeling software into W3D format, their hierarchies are converted into Shockwave 3D hierarchies. You should read Appendix A, "3D Studio MAX W3D Exporter," for a discussion of exactly how the hierarchy will translate. The point is that you can access hierarchies created in external software as well as through Lingo.

Summary

Parents, children, cloning, and Groups are topics that affect the scenegraph hierarchy. The scenegraph is an integral part of every 3D Castmember that offers the developer unique possibilities capable of reducing the amount of effort required for complex transformations. In addition, the scenegraph for a 3D Castmember can be used to duplicate large numbers of Nodes.

The concept of *chains* is a method of approaching the scenegraph hierarchy whose functionality is implied with the inheritance of parent and child Nodes. Creating chains is no more difficult than parenting multiple Nodes—controlling chains is less trivial, but rewarding. Although chains can be expanded to fit your needs, they perform well in certain situations and less gracefully in others.

The concept of *grouping* is a method of approaching the scenegraph hierarchy whose functionality is included in Director. Grouping is much easier to apply than chains, even though they are similar. The strength of Director in this topic is in its ability to allow you to combine Groups and chains, control them with parents, and clone them with varying degrees of independence.

FAQ

I usually determine hierarchies when I work in my favorite 3D modeling program. Does Director support hierarchies from external modelers?

Good question. The answer, however, is a bit double edged. Yes, Director supports hierarchies from external modelers. At the time of this writing, there is only one exporter available, and that exporter does not support 100 percent of the hierarchy information. I can say that if you are working in 3DS MAX, it is best to look at the 3DS MAX exporter appendix for information about how hierarchies will export and what you can do to learn how to integrate external Models into a hierarchy.

When I try to clone a Model, I get script errors. What am I doing wrong?

It is possible that you are trying to clone a Node that does not exist. This issue becomes more prevalent when we begin to work with imported W3D files. For now, make sure you are referencing an existing Node that can be cloned. Another possibility is that you are trying to create a clone with a name that is already taken. If you are going to be creating clones dynamically during the runtime of the movie, make sure you have a system in place for naming the clones uniquely. One method I frequently use is to append the milliseconds onto the name of the clone so that I know that it is a unique name.

Is there a way to create self-referential parents?

No. A Node cannot be its own parent.

Is there a way to create circular linkage in a chain?

No. A child cannot be the parent of an ancestor.

Can a Model have more than one parent?

No. There is no built-in support for this type of chain.

How many children can a Node have?

There is no hard limit.

Is there a way to clone some of the members of a Group?

Yes, but this is not supported natively. You will have to ungroup, clone, and then regroup in order to achieve this type of function.

Is there a built-in constraints system for chains?

No. A constraint system for parent/child chains would be extremely helpful; however, constraints as well as inverse kinematics are not supported. Both of these could be implemented via Lingo, but it is doubtful that they would resolve in a timely manner.

CHAPTER 9

Working with Prebuilt Scenes and Behaviors

The focus of this chapter is to introduce you to the importation of W3D files created in external modeling programs. Keep in mind that we are not going to be dealing with how to create the W3D files themselves but rather how to import them after they have been created. This chapter introduces the topic of importation as well as a range of importation strategies, but several of these strategies are discussed later in the book because working with W3D files can range from the basic to the advanced.

In addition, we will examine how to work with the Shockwave 3D Viewer window to tweak Camera settings. The Shockwave 3D Viewer is a useful tool, whether you are working with imported scenes, scenes from scratch, or both. Finally, we will be looking at some of the prebuilt behaviors that ship with Director 8.5. I have mentioned that your primary focus is to learn how to build your own code, but several prebuilt behaviors are worth looking at as well.

Importing Objects from Modeling Software

The W3D format is a proprietary, binary file format that can contain both geometric and animation data. W3D files can be exported by a variety of professional 3D modeling and animation software packages that range dramatically in price. The CD that accompanies this book contains several sample W3D files you can work with if you do not currently have a method of creating W3D files.

Importing a W3D file is similar to importing any other asset into Director. You use the Import option from the File menu to create a Shockwave 3D Castmember from the W3D file. As with digital video, when you're working with imported W3D there are several different strategies you might use, depending on whether you are delivering over the Web or via CD.

We have been working with creating 3D from scratch, which we will continue to do. Part of the reason for this is to learn how to control every aspect of the 3D environment by learning how to create every part from code. Also, because we are eliminating the download of any Models, we are able to keep our file sizes extremely small. However, we will not always be able to create the Models that we want from code as efficiently as we could if we were to create those Models in an external 3D modeling/animation program.

The ability to use imported W3D Models expands the range of strategies you have when designing the internal structure of your projects. Specifically, you will be gaining the ability to incorporate complex Models and animations from external programs that would be difficult, if not impossible, to create with code alone. You should also consider that W3D files can change the way you manage your 3D Castmember assets; for example, consider the following four possible strategies:

- Create Models from scratch
- Import a single W3D file and use its Models/environment exclusively
- Create Models from scratch and combine them with Models and Nodes imported with a W3D file
- Merge the elements of external W3D files with internal 3D Castmembers

These strategies have been arranged from basic to complicated. We have been exclusively examining the creation of Models from scratch. In this chapter, we will continue by examining the second strategy—importing a single W3D file. The last two strategies are very powerful, and it is these strategies that we are moving toward. They are covered in Chapter 19, "Performance Optimization," and used heavily within Part V, "Animation and Interactive Control Structures."

Persistence

Once you have imported a W3D file, it is important to remember what you learned about persistence in the first chapter. Any changes you make to the imported W3D file will not be saved. This is actually a positive aspect of working with imported W3D files—you do not need to worry that changes you make to the Castmember will change the Castmember the next time you look at the project.

The downside is that if you need to make changes to the Castmember, you will need to make those changes every time the movie starts. If those changes involve the default Camera position and orientation, you should also read through the section on the Shockwave 3D Viewer, later in this chapter. The Shockwave 3D Viewer can make changes to the default Camera position and orientation of a Shockwave 3D Castmember, and these changes can be saved with the movie.

Resetworld() **versus** Reverttoworlddefaults()

The first time you begin working with imported files, you'll encounter two functions whose usage can be a bit difficult to understand: resetworld() and reverttoworlddefaults(). We have been using the resetworld() function in order to "clear" Shockwave 3D Castmembers to their "empty" default state, but we have only been working with Shockwave 3D Castmembers whose Nodes have been created from scratch.

You should not be concerned about the use of the resetworld() function on Shockwave 3D Castmembers created from imported W3D files—the Shockwave 3D Castmember will return to its default state. That is, any properties of Nodes in the 3D Castmember that you change will return to their defaults, any new Nodes you add to the Castmember will be deleted, and any Nodes in the file originally that you delete will be restored. The point is that there is no worry that resetworld() will destroy your scene—it will essentially return you to the original state of the Castmember when you imported it into your movie.

The other function, reverttoworlddefaults(), we have not examined yet. The definition of this function from the Lingo help file may be difficult to understand, but there is a clear difference between resetworld() and reverttoworlddefaults() that can be explained with an example.

Imagine that you have a Shockwave 3D Castmember created from an imported W3D file and that you have changed the contents of this Castmember by creating new Models, deleting some of the Lights that were in it, and moving the Camera around. When you run the reverttoworlddefaults() function on this Castmember, the Lights you deleted will be re-created and the Camera will return to its default location and orientation, but the Models you created will be left alone. The idea is that any properties of original Nodes in the W3D file that you change will be reset to their defaults. Any Nodes or secondary elements that you add to the World will be left alone.

The `reverttoworlddefaults()` command can be useful if you are going to be creating Nodes inside of a 3D Castmember based on a W3D file. For the most part, however, you will still be using the `resetworld()` command.

The difference between these commands is that `resetworld()` resets a Castmember to its state when loaded, whereas `reverttoworlddefaults()` restores a Castmember's Nodes to their state when created. Because you cannot save changes to a 3D Castmember, this may seem like a small point; however, as you are going to learn in the next section, it is possible to save changes to the position and location of the default Camera for a Shockwave 3D Castmember.

Shockwave 3D Viewer

The Shockwave 3D Viewer is a useful utility that allows you to inspect your 3D Castmembers and also make small changes to the Camera location and orientation that can be saved with the movie. The Shockwave 3D Viewer always shows you a view of the 3D environment with the default Camera for the 3D Castmember you are viewing. Until now, we have been creating Worlds from scratch, so using the Shockwave 3D Viewer to inspect our 3D environments has not had much use.

You can open the Shockwave 3D Viewer from the Window menu or by using Ctl+Shift+W on a PC or Command+Shift+W on a Mac. You will recognize this viewer as the window that opens when you insert a blank Shockwave 3D Castmember.

Inspecting Imported Models

One reason you will use the Shockwave 3D window is to inspect the W3D files that you import from external modeling programs. If you open the file named "Basic Import" on the CD, you will see that I have imported a single W3D file. Notice that I have set up the Score for this movie in much the same way I have set up the Score for a Shockwave 3D Castmember for which I would create Models from scratch.

Now, open the Cast window and double-click the Castmember named *3Dworld*. The Shockwave 3D Viewer should automatically open, as shown in Figure 9.1.

FIGURE 9.1

The Shockwave 3D Viewer window that opens when you double-click Shockwave 3D Castmembers is the same window that opens when you insert blank 3D Castmembers.

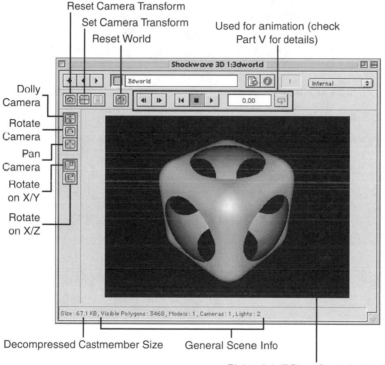

As you can see in Figure 9.1, this window contains several controls. In addition, at the bottom of the window is a list of information about the scene: the size of the decompressed 3D Castmember and the number of Models, Cameras, and Lights in the scene.

Along the left side of the window are a series of five buttons. If you click the preview window and drag your mouse, the Camera will move in different ways, depending on the first three buttons, which control dollying the Camera, rotating the Camera around the center of the scene, and panning the camera left, right, up, and down. In addition, the last two buttons affect the rotation control, allowing you to toggle between X/Y axis rotation and X/Z axis rotation.

NOTE

Note that when you rotate the Camera around the scene, the Lights are not moving with the Camera. Therefore, you may be able to rotate the Camera in such a way that the scene is not visible because you are changing your point of view—you are not moving the scene.

Setting Camera Defaults

Along the top of the window, but below the standard controls for all Castmember windows, is a row of several buttons. Several of the controls in this row are used with imported animation, which we will cover in Part V, "Animation and Interactive Control Structures." For now, we are interested in the Reset Camera Transform button and the Set Camera Transform button.

If you reposition and reorient the Camera and would like this new position to be the default Camera transform, click the Set Camera Transform button. Be aware that the Reset Camera Transform button cannot undo the setting of the Camera transform. If you close the Shockwave 3D Viewer after you have moved the Camera but before you set the Camera transform, your changes will be lost.

NOTE

If you are working with scenes and Models developed entirely in Lingo, you may find that it is often still difficult to accurately place the Camera position. Because you are still in the authoring environment, even though no changes in terms of your Models can be saved with the Shockwave 3D Castmember, any changes you make to the Camera position and orientation can be saved.

One trick that you might find useful is to create your 3D scene in Lingo and then stop the movie without calling the `resetworld()` function. After you have stopped the movie, but before you reset the World, open the Shockwave 3D Viewer. Then, position and orient the Camera as you would like and click the Set Camera Defaults button. Now when you save the movie, these default Camera settings will be saved along with the movie. This way, you don't need to code the initial Camera setup each time.

`Reverttoworlddefaults()` **Revisited**

Remember that the `reverttoworlddefaults()` function will restore a Shockwave 3D Castmember's Nodes to the state they were in when created. If you have set the Camera transform and later realize that you do not like the new default position of the Camera and would like to return to the original position and orientation of the Camera, you can run the `reverttoworlddefaults()` function on the Castmember. The changes you have made to the Camera position and orientation will be undone. Note that the `resetworld()` function will not destroy the modifications that you set with the Set Camera Transform button but rather will revert to the last "set" camera position.

3D Behavior Basics

The 3D behaviors in the library palette have been set up in an interesting way that needs some explanation. Note that the behaviors for 3D are divided into two groups: actions and triggers. The concept is that you can apply many actions to a given 3D environment and then apply triggers that are associated to those actions.

This relationship allows for complex associations between trigger and action to be developed by you, but they are still behaviors. Therefore, there are still going to be limitations for you as a designer or developer if you need to do anything that they cannot.

In addition to the action/trigger-based 3D behaviors are several automatic 3D behaviors that do not require a specific trigger. Therefore, they run automatically, without any user instigation.

NOTE

Note that some of the action behaviors are designed to act on a specific Model in the 3D Castmember. If you are planning on using these behaviors in conjunction with a 3D Castmember that has Models created from scratch rather than from import, the actions that are designed to act on a specific Model will not find any Models in your empty 3D Castmember.

There is a workaround to this limitation that you may encounter when assigning the Model-based action behaviors for 3D. If you stop your movie after the Models have been created but before `resetworld()` is called, the Models will still exist in the authoring environment. This is similar to the workaround described for setting the default Camera position for Castmembers that you are going to create the Models for from scratch.

Before you run the movie again, assign your behaviors to the Castmember, and the `getpropertydescriptionlist()` handler will be able to find the Models in the scene. Of course, you need to make sure you do not change the names of the Models that you are going to be creating after you do this.

Among the behaviors for 3D that ship with Director 8.5, I will highlight the following:

- Drag Model to Rotate
- Generic Do
- MouseLeft trigger

Before you can assign a trigger behavior, you must first assign at least one action behavior to a 3D Sprite. Although there are a variety of actions to choose from, we will work with only two. Make sure that you have the file named "Basic Import" from the CD opened before you proceed with the demonstration.

Drag Model to Rotate

First, open the Score window and look at how I have separated the Sprite timeline for the 3D Sprite into two sections. This is because in the first section, we are going to handle the loading of the 3D Castmember and any additional initialization, even though in this example there is no additional initialization. The 3D Sprite timeline that exists on the frame labeled "run" is the only section that we want to apply behaviors to.

We do not want users to be able to interact with the movie until it is on the "run" frame for two reasons. First, we want to make sure that the Castmember is fully loaded before any interaction takes place. Second, if we need to create any Models or perform any initialization, this should be separated from the interaction phase of the movie.

If you drop the Drag Model to Rotate behavior on the 3D Sprite at frame 7, a dialog box will pop up. Set the sensitivity slider to 1 and type **easy_rotate** into the field named What Group Does This Belong To?. We will be assigned several actions before we assign the triggers. Your task will be facilitated if you name each of the actions—later on, the triggers that we assign to control these actions will refer to the names we choose. For now, this is all we need to do with the Drag Model to Rotate action.

Generic Do

The Generic Do behavior is quite versatile because it allows you to specify Lingo that you would like to execute as the result of some trigger. In this case, we will use the Generic Do action to start and stop a sound while we drag and rotate the Model.

First, drop a single instance of the Generic Do behavior onto the 3D Sprite at frame 7. A dialog box will appear with two fields that need to be filled in. In the first field, you will type the exact Lingo command you want to execute; in this case, type in **puppetsound(1, member(12))**. Next, assign the name "easy_sound_on" to this action Group. Now, drop a second instance of the Generic Do action on the 3D Sprite at frame 7. This time, type in **puppetsound(1,0)** in the first field and name the action Group "easy_sound_off."

MouseLeft

At this point, we have assigned all the actions, but we still need to assign triggers for each action. This means that even though we are going to use only one trigger behavior, we will need to assign it once for each of the actions already attached to the 3D Sprite.

The MouseLeft trigger is a simple behavior that will map the user interaction via the left mouse button to various actions that have been assigned to the 3D Sprite. Drop an instance of the MouseLeft trigger onto the 3D Sprite at frame 7. In this case, you are presented with several drop-down choices. Set when this action occurs to Anytime the Left Mouse Is Down and set which action to perform to easy_rotate X-Y. Notice that in the drop-down list for actions, the easy_rotate Group has several options—this is because the Drag Model to Rotate behavior makes each of these choices available to you. Also, notice that the easy_sound_on and easy_sound_off Group actions are in this list as well.

Drop a second instance of the MouseLeft trigger onto the 3D Sprite at frame 7 and this time set when this action occurs to Once When the Mouse Is Pressed. Then set the Group for easy_sound_on. Finally, drop a third instance of the MouseLeft trigger and set when the action occurs to Once When the Mouse Is Released for the Group action easy_sound_off.

The only thing left is to test the movie to see whether you have it right. Rewind and play the movie; when you click the 3D Sprite and drag the mouse, the hollow box should rotate, and the sound should play. When you let go, the sound should stop. If you are having trouble, open the file named "Basic Import Completed" on the CD; this file contains the completed demonstration.

Final Words on 3D Behaviors

Because this is the last time we will be working with 3D behaviors in this book, I encourage you to look through the other behaviors in the library palette. If nothing else, these behaviors can help you set up some extremely basic interaction, which may be all you require. Beyond this chapter, you will be learning intermediate and advanced coding techniques for 3D that, among other techniques, will teach you how to create interaction that can duplicate and surpass the functionality of the 3D behaviors.

Summary

The importation of W3D files as Shockwave 3D Castmembers is one of the easier Castmember types to import because there are no options to contend with. If you have a W3D file, you are able to import it into Director. Any changes you make to Shockwave 3D Castmembers, whether they are inserted or imported from W3D files, cannot be saved with the movie. The only exception to this is that you can set the location and orientation of the default Camera with the Shockwave 3D Viewer. However, even after the movie has been saved, this can be undone with the `reverttoworlddefaults()` function.

Once imported, basic interactivity can be quickly added to a Shockwave 3D Castmember created from a W3D file with the 3D behaviors that ship standard with Director. It is important to remember that although these behaviors provide you with many basic types of interaction, if you need any control that they do not provide, you will need to code it yourself.

FAQ

Are there any resources for obtaining W3D files?

Yes. There are several W3D files on the Director 8.5 CD as well as the CD supplied with this book. In addition, several Model vendors are listed in Appendix H, "Online Resources," to help you get started.

Is there a list of 3D modeling/animation software that exports W3D files?

Yes. There is a list in Appendix H, but I also suggest checking the Macromedia Web site because the list of 3D software packages that support W3D continues to grow.

Is it better to code my own interactivity or use the behaviors? I feel like the behaviors save me time.

I agree. The behaviors do save you time, and if they meet your needs, then by all means use them. Just remember that they have limitations—especially in terms of building interactivity. That's why Part III, "Interface Applications of Shockwave 3D," is dedicated to examining how interaction can be approached from a more intermediate level. Part V, "Animation and Interactive Control Structures," centers on building advanced interaction code structures that involve the control of 3D animation. Finally, Part VI, "Advanced Techniques," examines a wide range of advanced techniques for building advanced Camera controls.

PART II

Section II: Data Visualization

One of the primary uses for Director's 3D environment is to provide a method of visualizing data. Far from being a small issue, data-visualization applications can range from monthly budgets to atomic models. In this section, we will be exploring the topic of data visualization. You will also see how to apply the tools you have learned so far to create two types of charts. The demonstrations in this section exemplify extensive integration of parent/child script control over the 3D environment. If you are not familiar with designing or working with object-oriented programming (OOP) scripts, do not be alarmed; Chapter 10, "Histograms," not only explains how to create histograms but also teaches how to approach creating an inclusive dedicated parent/child script to accomplish the task. The goal of this section is to show you two tools you can use for the most frequent types of data visualization you are likely to require. At the same time, it is organized to help you learn how to design your own customized systems for the visualization of data.

CHAPTER 10

Histograms

The methodology, structure, and purpose of this chapter and the following chapter are slightly different from many of the other chapters in this book. In this chapter, we will apply the knowledge from Chapters 1 through 9 and your prior Director expertise to synthesize a solution for the creation of histograms. A histogram is another term for a bar chart—a chart of rectangular bars that is used to represent numerical data. I will walk you through the process of how to make decisions about planning a custom data type for the creation of bar charts. Figure 10.1 is an example of the type of bar chart we are going to create with this custom data type.

FIGURE 10.1

A 3D bar chart created using the bar chart data type and custom functions discussed in this chapter.

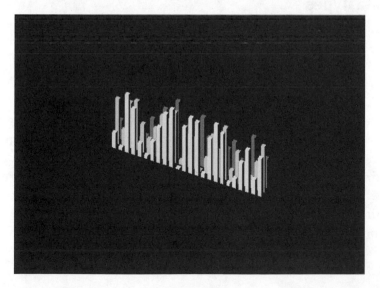

Note some of the capabilities of the bar chart as illustrated in Figure 10.1: Our 3D bar charts will be able to handle both rows and columns of data, and all data should be visible in the 3D Sprite.

This chapter expands on the notion of creating a custom API for tasks that are important to your projects. We have created several entries into our API that are intended to extend the basic capabilities of Director for reasons of reducing our typing load and simplifying the methods of working with the 3D environment without removing any of the functionality. Our API has centered on the creation of Models and World cleanup utilities. In this chapter, we will expand our API to include a custom data type for working with bar charts and a host of custom functions to manipulate that data.

In many ways, this chapter is as much about learning how to use object-oriented programming (OOP) as it is about how to create bar charts. The new 3D environment in Director can capitalize on the capabilities of parent/child scripting and custom functions that have existed in Director for several versions. If you are familiar with designing and implementing parent/child scripts, many of the discussions in this chapter will reinforce the lessons of OOP you already understand. If you are not familiar or comfortable with designing and implementing OOP, this chapter and the following chapter will help you harness a powerful tool that no serious Director developer can forego.

Custom Data Types

With all this talk about a custom data type, I want to be clear about what I mean by this. Director has several data types, many of which you work with on a daily basis, such as string data, integer data, and float data, and others that you might use less frequently, such as color data, time data, and so on.

With each of these types of data, you most likely will be storing results inside of variables. However, a variable is a container for many different types of data: It is up to you to choose the specific functions for accessing and manipulating that data. This is because each data type has a specific structure and specific methods of manipulation. Although some of the methods of manipulating data may overlap, generally each type of data has its own specific functions.

NOTE

For example, think about the multitude of functions that string data can be manipulated with in Director. There are functions for working with characters, regular expressions (chunks of characters), string conversions into other data types, operators, and so on.

Functions increase the versatility of a data type because they increase the number of ways you can manipulate data without having to program a custom function. However, it would be impossible for any programming language to predict every use of data that programmers will need. For this reason, the functions supplied with a programming language deal with the data in a general manner. The code you write deals with the data in a manner specific to your project.

When creating a custom data type, your job is to create code that does a little of both. Again, remember how we created a custom API for the creation of primitives and extruded text in previous chapters—in those examples, we tried to make the code as general as possible so that it would work in as many situations as possible. The same is true for a custom data type, except you will try to make the *handlers* as general as possible. Conceptually, you are attempting to encapsulate all the code required to perform a given task into a single handler.

NOTE

Programmers usually refer to this conceptual encapsulation as creating a *black box*—a piece of code to which you send arguments. The black box does work on the arguments you give it and then returns its "answer" to you.

The idea is that once the black box is set up, you only ask it questions, you believe its answers, and you do not "mess with" the internal workings of the black box. Another name for a black box that is related to Director is *custom handler*, or more specifically, *custom function*.

Many times the black boxes you create will need to perform certain tasks over and over, which you might encapsulate into even more custom functions. However, you are not expected to interface with these second, third, and beyond levels of custom functions—just the black boxes. The terminology commonly used to talk about these two types of custom functions is *public handlers* and *private handlers*, or even more generally, *public methods* and *private methods*.

A good example of the concept of a public handler versus a private handler is your kitchen sink. If you are thirsty and need water, would you go to the sink with a glass or the water main with a hacksaw? Hopefully, going to the sink sounds a bit cleaner, more sane, and legal.

Overall, one might say that when compared to chopping open the water main, getting a glass of water from the sink is a "graceful" if not "elegant" way to quench one's thirst. The sink is a public method of getting a glass of water. Still, the sink relies on the water main to complete its functionality, even though you do not interact with it directly; therefore, the water main represents a private method.

A custom data type can be as complex as the requirements of your project, but you will most likely need to have both private and public handlers to streamline the process of working with your data type. Overall, the goal is to create a tool that, once programmed, will function as a reusable tool rather than a piece of code that is only good in one situation.

However, if that were our definition of a custom data type, you might question how that is different from an API. For this reason, the creation of a custom data type takes the notion of creating a custom API one step further: You are creating functions that expect to work with a specific type of data that is defined by your code.

Brainstorming

It is important to write down all the elements you need to include, might include, and might never include into a single "brainstorming" document. However, to refer to such a document is ridiculous, because it usually exists on scraps of paper or napkins. Regardless of its form, it is important to have some type of document like this so that you can decide how best to implement a solution for your challenge.

In this case, we want to create a concise, easy, and quick way to create histograms. However, *histograms* is a rather broad term, referring to several types of charts; in order to make our work a bit more manageable, we will work to specifically create bar charts.

When you think about a bar chart, you need to break down the vital components and the purpose of the bar chart in order to decide which elements are essential. First, the data itself is essential. Second, the visual form that the data is represented by is essential. Because of this split between the actual data and the way it will be represented, it becomes clear that what is needed is a quick way to create bar charts as well as a robust method of handling a custom data type.

There are no tools in Director that rival parent/child scripts in their ability to create custom data types, replete with fully functional public and private handlers for the separation of code and data.

Designing the Data Type

With the key decision having been made to use parent/child scripts, the next stage is now important: We need to decide what the internal structure of the custom data type is. We know that we want to ultimately create bar charts with this data. We know that we want to create rows of bars as well as columns of bars. Finally, we know that the rows and bars are going to represent larger numbers as larger bars.

Because we are going to be working with both rows and columns, we need to create an array of data from lists. In this case, I want to store numeric data about each bar as well as some type of signifier as to what the bar data represents. For this reason, multiple property lists representing rows of data nested inside of a linear list is a strong candidate for the structure of the basic chart data. Here's an example of this structure:

```
[[#bar_1x1:value, #bar_1x2:value], [#bar_2x1:value, #bar_2x2:value]]
```

This leads to an important distinction in conceptualizing the outline for our code. If our custom data type is an array of data, that data exists separately from the Models we are going to create to express that data. Another way of saying this is that there is a distinction between the data and the visualization of that data.

NOTE

Depending on how complex your project and chart requirements are, you might decide to separate the parent/child script for your custom data type into two sections: one main parent/child
script for the visualization of the data and then *grandchild* objects that inherit properties of the
main parent/child script for manipulating the data in the array itself.

In this example, the parent/child script will contain the handlers required to
create and manipulate the data as an array as well as the functions required for
creating visualizations of that data as a bar chart.

Building the Handlers

After determining that we are going to use a custom data type with custom
functions to control both the data and the visualization of that data, we must
set up some parameters for our code. Specifically, we need to determine what
handlers we are going to need and what the purpose of each one will be. Table
10.1 lists the various custom functions we will create for the bar chart utility.

TABLE 10.1   Bar Chart Utility Handler Overview

Handler Name	Purpose
New()	Initializes the chart child object
BC_DataAdd()	Adds data to the list
BC_DataRemove()	Removes data from the list
BC_DataReport()	Accesses existing data for interaction
BC_ChartCreate()	Creates the chart from data
BC_ChartDestroy()	Destroys the chart
BC_ChartUpdate()	Quickly updates the chart
BC_ChartSpin()	Spins the chart on its Y axis
BC_ChartParams()	Sets the chart parameters
BC_ColorChange()	Changes the current colors for the chart
BC_ColorReport()	Finds out the current colors for the chart
BC_SetCamera()	Positions and orients the Camera toward the chart
BC_ColorAppend()	Appends colors to the color list (private)

Each of these handlers has a specific purpose that can be guessed from the name of the handler because all the names are descriptive. In addition, notice that some of the handlers deal with the data and others deal with the chart or colors. The point is that naming is important here as well as everywhere else in your code. Here's a good rule to follow: If you can't think of a concise name for your handler, think about what it is supposed to do. If you don't know what it is supposed to do, you have more of a problem than naming the handler, and you should reevaluate why you need the handler. In the following sections, we will examine each of these handlers so you can learn specifically how they work and how to control them.

Finally, in this section, we will look at the syntax for each handler. However, keep in mind that we will explore methods of using the Bar Chart Utility script later in this chapter, in the section "Creating Bar Charts."

New()

The new() handler of any parent/child script is an important place to start because you can learn a lot about the structure and the properties that are going to be used throughout the script. In this case, the new() handler requires one argument: the name of the chart you want to create. If you do not supply a name, the handler will return false. To create a new bar chart data type, use the following syntax:

```
ChildObjectRef = new(script "Bar Chart Utility", "name")
```

In this case, I am assuming that ChildObjectRef is a global variable. I am also assuming that you will give a name for the chart used in the naming of the Group that will contain all the Models in the bar chart. That name should be a string; if it is not, some type casting has been built in to the new() handler to ensure that the name is valid.

NOTE

Remember that when you're working with parent/child scripts, it is important that you store references to child objects in global variables or other persistent properties. If no references exist to a child object, the child object does not exist. In this demonstration, we will be utilizing global variables to store and reference the bar chart child objects we create.

Now that you know the syntax for creating a new bar chart, let's look at the code for the new() handler. In addition, note the basic properties that are set up for this custom data type, as shown in Listing 10.1.

Listing 10.1   The New() Handler for the Bar Chart Utility

```
 1: --PROPERTIES----------------------------------------------
 2: --property containing the chart data
 3: property pChartData
 4: --name of the chart
 5: property pChartName
 6: --how tall should the largest bar be in 3D units
 7: property pMaxSize
 8: -- how wide & deep should all bars be in 3D units
 9: property pBarWidth
10: -- how close should bars be (percentage of bar width)
11: property pBarCloseness
12: -- what colors will be used for each row of data
13: property pColors
14: -- what castmember will the chart be created in?
15: property pTargetCastmember
16: -- Integer: Camera Number
17: property pTargetCamera
18: -- used to hold on to a reference to a dummy model
19: -- that is used to rotate chart around the center
20: -- of the group
21: property pChartCenter
22: --boolean: is there a 3D manifestation of Chart?
23: property pChart
24: ----------------------------------------------------------
25:
26: on new(me, nameArg)
27:    -- you must supply a name for the chart
28:    -- if you don't supply a name,
29:    -- the script and returns false (zero)
30:    if nameArg = void then
31:      return false
32:    else
33:      -- if you do supply a name, this
34:      -- handler will set up the
35:      -- default values for various parameters
36:
37:      -- name of chart, this is the same as
38:      -- the name of the group that will be
39:      -- created in the 3D world
40:
41:      --but we must make sure that name is a string
```

Listing 10.1   Continued

```
42:      --(convert it to a string if it is not one)
43:      if nameArg.ilk <> #string then
44:        nameArg = string(nameArg)
45:      end if
46:
47:      --and that it contains no spaces,
48:      --(convert all spaces to underscores)
49:      tempName = ""
50:      repeat with x = 1 to nameArg.length
51:        if nameArg.Char[x] = " " then
52:          put "_" after tempName
53:        else
54:          put nameArg.Char[x] after tempname
55:        end if
56:      end repeat
57:      nameArg = tempname
58:
59:      --and that the first character is not a number.
60:      if "1234567890" contains nameArg.char[1] then
61:        nameArg = "a" & nameArg
62:      end if
63:
64:      --once all those changes are made to the name,
65:      --go ahead and set the property...
66:      pChartName = nameArg
67:
68:      -- pchartdata starts as an empty linear list
69:      -- each row will be a new property list nested
70:      -- inside of this linear list
71:      pChartData = []
72:
73:      -- by default, no visual representation of the
74:      -- chart exists as of yet
75:      pChart = false
76:
77:      -- set up the maximum bar height.  This number will
78:      -- also be used in determining the size of the
79:      -- camera's orthoheight parameter and helps to
80:      -- position the camera so that you can see the whole
81:      -- chart (when created)
82:      pMaxSize = 200
83:
84:      -- set up the default bar width & length, the bars in
85:      -- this demo are always "square tubes", feel free
86:      -- to expand this.
```

Listing 10.1   Continued

```
 87:       pBarWidth = 10
 88:
 89:       -- set up how close bars should be positioned near
 90:       -- each other.  notice that this value is given in
 91:       -- terms of a percentage.  If bar closeness is
 92:       -- 100, the bars will be flush against one another.
 93:       -- smaller than 100, the bars will be inside on another
 94:       -- so values greater than 100 will produce bars that are
 95:       -- set apart from one another.
 96:       pBarCloseness = 170 --(percent of bar width)
 97:
 98:       -- set up the default target castmember.  (the castmember
 99:       -- where the chart Models will be created)  this repeat
100:       -- loop searches through the first castlibrary, looking
101:       -- for the first 3D castmember it can find.  When it finds
102:       -- one, it uses that member.  You can change property with
103:       -- the BC_ChartParams() function
104:       repeat with x = 1 to the number of members in castlib 1
105:         if member(x).type = #shockwave3D then
106:           pTargetCastmember = member(x)
107:           exit repeat
108:         end if
109:       end repeat
110:
111:       --set up the value for the default camera
112:       --unless you have multiple cameras, 1 should be fine
113:       ptargetcamera = 1
114:
115:       --set up the linear list used to store the
116:       --colors used per-ro
117:       pcolors = []
118:     end if
119:
120:     -- return a reference to the child object
121:     return me
122: end
```

The new() handler is crucial; if you do not set up the child object, none of the other handlers will work because there will be nothing to work on. Also, remember that you must be careful to store the child object reference that is returned to you so that you can reference it later on. Finally, when you use this command, you might want to check to make sure a nonzero value was returned to you; if the value is zero (false), the child object does not exist for some reason. Most likely it is because you forgot to supply a name for the chart.

BC_DataAdd()

Instantiating the bar chart data type does not create a bar chart; rather, it creates a structure for you to load data into and then allows you to create 3D charts from that data. For this reason, the next logical handler to examine is the handler that allows you to add data to the data type.

One reason why you might choose to create a 3D bar chart is to compare rows and columns of data in a meaningful visual way. For this reason, the BC_DataAdd() function is divided into two sections: One section allows you to add rows of data, and the other section allows you to add columns of data.

Although the syntax for adding data to the data type will be very similar when we're adding either rows or columns, we will need some way of alerting the handler as to which type of data we are intending to add. For this reason, if you want to add a row of data, use the following code:

```
Childobjectref.BC_DataAdd(#row, propertylist, RGB_color)
```

Here, the propertylist argument represents a single property list that's the same number of items long as any rows that already exist—or if it is the first row, at least one item long. The RGB_color argument is optional and allows you to specify a color for the new row, or you can allow the handler to choose one randomly.

If you are going to add a column of data, the syntax is as follows:

```
Childobjectref.BC_DataAdd(#column, propertylist)
```

Notice that in this example I omitted the RGB_color argument. If you try to use this argument while adding columns of data, it will be ignored. In this case, the propertylist argument is still structured as a single property list, and the handler will reorganize the items and place them on the corresponding rows. It is important that this property list have as many items as there are rows of data; if this is the first column, you need at least one item. The specific code that comprises the BC_DataAdd() handler is shown in Listing 10.2.

Listing 10.2   The BC_DataAdd() Handler for the Bar Chart Utility

```
 1: on BC_DataAdd(me, addWhat, newData, rowColor)
 2:
 3:    --determine whether you are adding a row or a column
 4:    case(addwhat) of
 5:        --if you are adding a row...
 6:      #row:
 7:        --make sure that the newData is either the first row
 8:        --or if it is not the first row, that it has as many
 9:        --entries as the other rows
10:
11:        if pChartData = [] then
12:          nothing
13:        else if pChartData[1].count = newData.count then
14:          nothing
15:        else
16:          return false
17:        end if
18:
19:        --add unique identifiers to each property so that
20:        --(a) all entries have unique property names and
21:        --(b) you can refer to the chart entries by row and
22:        -- column position as well as by name
23:        rowNumber = pChartData.count() + 1
24:        fixedData = [:]
25:
26:        repeat with rowPosition = 1 to newdata.count()
27:          identifier = "_" & rowNumber & "x" & rowPosition
28:      ident = symbol(getpropat(newdata, rowposition) & identifier)
29:          setaprop(fixedData, ident, newdata[rowposition])
30:        end repeat
31:
32:        --add the "fixeddata" to the pChartData; the data with
33:        --row and column positions tacked onto end of each property
34:        append(pChartData, fixedData)
35:
36:        --IF you supplied a color for row with rowcolor argument
37:        --then add this to the list pColors so that the row will be
38:        --drawn in that color otherwise pick a random color.
39:        --change the colors using BC_ColorChange
40:        if rowColor <> void and rowColor.ilk = #color then
41:          BC_ColorAppend(me, #single, rowcolor)
42:        else
43:          randomcolor = rgb(random(255),random(255),random(255))
44:          BC_ColorAppend(me, #single, randomcolor)
45:        end if
46:
```

Listing 10.2   Continued

```
47:       --if we have made it this far, return true
48:       return true
49:
50:       --if you are adding a column...
51:    #column:
52:
53:       -- there must be as many column entries as rows in newdata
54:       --or that this is the first column you are adding.
55:       if pchartData = [] then
56:         nothing
57:       else if pChartData.count = newdata.count then
58:         nothing
59:       else
60:         return false
61:       end if
62:
63:       --determine the Column Number for this new data.
64:       -- if newdata is the first entry into the chart then...
65:       if pchartdata.count() = 0 then
66:         columnNumber = 1
67:         --figure out how many rows you intend to add data to
68:         iterations = newdata.count()
69:       else
70:         --if this is a newcolumn added to existing data then...
71:         --count how many bars are in row one
72:         --and then add one to that number
73:         columnNumber = pChartData[1].count() + 1
74:         --determine number of rows that you are adding data to
75:         iterations = pchartData.count()
76:       end if
77:
78:       --add unique identifiers to each property so that
79:       --(a) all entries have unique property names and
80:       --(b) you can refer to the chart entries by row and
81:       -- column position as well as by name
82:       fixedData = [:]
83:
84:       repeat with rowNumber = 1 to iterations
85:         identifier = "_" & rownumber & "x" & columnNumber
86:        ident = symbol(getpropat(newdata, rowNumber) & identifier)
87:         setaprop(fixedData, ident, newdata[rowNumber])
88:       end repeat
89:
90:
91:       --we need to take the list of data intended to be in
92:       -- columns, and reorganize that data into rows
```

Listing 10.2   Continued

```
 93:        if columnNumber = 1 then
 94:     --if this is the very first column of data being added to the
 95:     --list, then we need to add three property lists to the main
 96:        --pChartData so that each column has a new row to be in
 97:        repeat with x = 1 to fixedData.count()
 98:          columnData = [:]
 99:      setaprop(columnData, getpropat(fixedData, x), fixedData[x])
100:          addat(pChartData, columnData)
101:          columnData = void
102:        end repeat
103:
104:      else
105:        --if this is not the first row, then add this column data
106:        -- on to the end of the appropriate existing row
107:        repeat with x = 1 to fixedData.count()
108:      setaprop(pchartdata[x], getpropat(fixeddata, x), fixeddata[x])
109:        end repeat
110:      end if
111:
112:      --if we have made it this far, return true
113:      return true
114:
115:    otherwise:
116:      --if you did not specify #row or #column then return false
117:      return false
118:  end case
119: end
```

Notice in lines 41 and 44 I call the BC_ColorAppend() handler, which adds the given color to the end of the list pColors. This handler is a private handler; therefore, you should not use it directly. If you do, you will interfere with the type of data that is expected for the row coloring. For this reason, this handler is private and should not be called. The methods BC_ColorReport() and BC_ColorChange() are intended to be used in conjunction with one another to change and modify the colors of the rows.

Note that although the creation of data for the array is handled through a rather involved process, there is a custom handler to remove all data from the array that is much simpler to use and to understand. BC_DataRemove() will destroy all the data in the array, but it will not destroy the visualization of the data—that is handled separately.

The ability to add data to the array that will comprise our bar chart is a crucial step to creating our bar chart. Chronologically, the next step that you most likely would take after adding data to the array would be to actually create a chart.

BC_ChartCreate()

The BC_ChartCreate() function relies on the fact that there is data in the pChartData property. If there is no data, this command will return false. Otherwise, this command will perform the following tasks:

- Create a Group
- Create a Model for each bar of data
- Assign each Model as a child of the Group
- Position and orient the 3D Camera

The BC_ChartCreate() function does not accept any arguments and is called with the following syntax:

```
ChildObjectRef.BC_ChartCreate()
```

This code will call the BC_ChartCreate handler and execute the code shown in Listing 10.3.

Listing 10.3   The BC_ChartCreate() Handler for the Bar Chart Utility

```
 1: on BC_ChartCreate(me)
 2:    --determine whether there is chart data
 3:    --and that the chart data is a list
 4:    if pChartData <> [:] and pChartData.ilk = #list then
 5:
 6:       --create a group in the 3D world
 7:       --notice that I am using the pTargetCastmember
 8:       --property to determine which 3D world to create
 9:       --the bar chart group within.
10:       chartgroup = pTargetCastmember.newgroup(pChartName)
11:
12:       --figure out what the largest piece of data in the chart is
13:       --this repeat loop will create a temporary list
14:       --containing the max data value from each row
15:       tempmaxlist = []
```

Listing 10.3   Continued

```
16:     repeat with x = 1 to pChartData.count()
17:        addat(tempmaxlist, pChartData[x].max())
18:     end repeat
19:
20:     --then we can determine which of all of the data entries
21:     --has the largest value for the entire array
22:     maxData = tempmaxlist.max()
23:
24:     --this step is important.  we are going to figure out the
25:     --ratio between the maximum world-unit bar height that you
26:     --want to create, and the largest value in the array
27:     --this number will be used to scale up OR down all of the
28:     --heights of all of the bars in the chart, so that the entry
29:     --with the largest data value will have the largest bar
30:     --and that bar will be the size of the pmaxsize in world units
31:     --high.  The rest of the bars will reflect their values in
32:     --scale, so the relationships between data values is preserved
33:     dataToBarRatio = float(pMaxSize) / maxData
34:
35:     --use a nested repeat loop to create the bars
36:     --the first loop creates counter for the current row
37:     repeat with x = 1 to pchartdata.count
38:        --the second loop creates counter for data in current column
39:        repeat with y = 1 to pchartdata[x].count
40:           --determine the world unit height of the bar
41:           --from the current data value * the ratio...
42:           barHeight = pChartData[x][y] * dataToBarRatio
43:
44:          --get name of the property at the x,y position in the array
45:           barname = string(getpropat(pchartdata[x],y))
46:           --create box, give it the name from property list
47:           --set its width and length equal to the pBarwidth,
                -- set height based on the barheight we just computed
48:            -- and find the color from color list
49:           newbar = createbox(barname, pBarwidth,pBarwidth,\
barHeight, pColors[x])
50:
51:           --assign the bar as the child of the bar chart group
52:           chartgroup.addchild(newbar, #preserveparent)
53:           --calculate position of the bar based on the width of the
54:           --bar and how close it should be to other bars.
55:           baroffset = pbarwidth * (pbarcloseness / float(100))
56:           --this step is important.  Notice that we are moving the
57:           --bar based on the value of the counters from the loop
58:           --these help determine the position in the X/Z plane.
59:           --I am moving the bar in the y plane (barheight/float(2)).
```

Listing 10.3   Continued

```
60:          --the center of new models are positioned at the origin-
61:          --the bars in the chart are not flush with "zero". by
             -- figuring out how tall the current bar is
62:          -- and moving bar "up" vertically by half that distance,
63:          --all of the bars will appear to start at "zero".....
64:           newbar.translate(y*baroffset, \
(barHeight/float(2)),x*baroffset, #parent)
65:
66:       end repeat
67:     end repeat
68:
69:     --set up a dummy model and move it to the center of the chart
70:     --to ease the task of rotating the chart around its center
71:     pchartcenter = pTargetCastmember.newmodel("dummy")
72:     pchartcenter.translate\
(pTargetCastmember.group[2].boundingsphere[1])
73:
74:     --set the pChart variable to true, to ease checking
75:     --whether a visualization of the data currently exists
76:     pchart = true
77:
78:     --run the BC_ChartSetCamera handler.  This handler can
79:     --also be run as a public handler. Its purpose is to
80:     --orient the camera so that all of the bars will be visible
81:     --in the viewport.
82:     BC_ChartSetCamera(me)
83:   end if
84: end
```

First, line 33 is of particular interest and a quite important step in the process of creating a visualization of the data in the array. This line determines the ratio between the largest piece of data and the maximum World unit bar size. The reason for this is as follows: Imagine that you have an array with 10 entries, and each has a value well over 5,000 units. Rather than creating Models that are 5,000 units high, by figuring out the ratio between the largest data value and the largest bar unit, you can ensure that the largest bar will be as large as the largest size. In addition, the rest of the bars will use this ratio to scale their data respective to the size of the largest bar. Therefore, it becomes clear that the visualization of data does not necessarily need to be World unit accurate, but the relationship among the bars does need to be accurate. We are creating a visualization of data so that people can visualize the relationships between values in the data and also to spot trends in the data.

Finally, line 82 calls the `BC_ChartSetCamera()` handler, which is designed to automatically position and orient the Camera toward the bar chart. Listing 10.4 shows the specific code for this handler.

Listing 10.4   The `BC_ChartSetCamera()` Handler

```
 1: on BC_ChartSetCamera(me)
 2:   if pchart then
 3:     -- set a direct reference to the camera node
 4:     cam = pTargetCastmember.camera[pTargetCamera]
 5:     -- make sure that the camera is orthographic
 6:     cam.projection = #orthographic
 7:     -- reset the camera position
 8:     cam.transform.identity()
 9:
10:     -- find out the radius of the bounding sphere
11:     -- of the chart, this number will vary depending
12:     -- on the size of the data.  add that number to
13:     -- pmaxsize for the CF: chartfactor
14:     CF = ptargetcastmember.group(pchartname).boundingsphere[2]\
+ pmaxsize
15:
16:     --move the camera to the "upper corner" of the chart
17:     cam.translate(CF,CF, (CF * .6667),#world)
18:     --point at the center of the chart
19:     cam.pointat(pChartCenter)
20:     --make sure that the orthoheight of the camera is slightly
21:     --larger than the largest bar in the chart
22:     cam.orthoheight = pMaxsize * (CF / float(200))
23:     return true
24:   else
25:     return false
26:   end if
27: end
```

Even though this handler is being used privately, it can also be used publicly, and nothing about the bar chart or the data will break. In fact, it is a useful utility for positioning and orienting the Camera. Feel free to use this handler for that purpose. Beyond the handlers we have already looked at, there are several handlers that provide robust functionality for both the chart visualization and the array data.

BC_ChartParams()

Among the utilities for controlling chart visualization is the BC_ChartParams() handler. This is a general property setting handler—literally it is a single handler that is used to set the values of a variety of properties. This handler has a unique structure when compared to several of the other handlers we have looked at. Similar to creating public and private handlers, one secondary goal of a public handler is to have public methods of accessing private data. In a parent/child script, the properties are considered private data. This means that you should only access and change that private data via the public methods.

NOTE

> Previously I compared public and private methods to getting a glass of water from the kitchen sink versus the water main. If we were to continue with that analogy, the water represents private data.

We have many parameters to contend with in the bar chart utility, and to create a public method for each one might become rather tedious, and it might become difficult to remember all the given names of the handlers. The syntax for calling this handler is as follows:

```
ChildObjectRef.BC_ChartParams(#whatproperty, newval)
```

Notice how extremely general this syntax is, especially the newval parameter. Normally I might tell you that the newval parameter should be a string, an integer, or a list. In this case, the value of #whatproperty will determine what type of data the handler will be expecting.

Because there are many properties to access, I have created a structure for this handler to provide a public method for manipulating the values of several different properties, as outlined in Table 10.2.

TABLE 10.2   `BC_ChartParams()` Arguments

#whatproperty	Immediate Purpose	Purpose	newval
#barheight	Sets `pMaxSize`	Sets the maximum bar height	Float
#barsize	Sets `pBarWidth`	Sets the width and bar length	Integer
#spacing	Sets `pBarCloseness`	Sets the distance between bars	Float
#target	Sets `pTargetCastmember`	Sets the 3D member to create the bar chart Models in	Member
#camera	Sets `pTargetCamera`	Sets the camera to use for the chart	Integer

It is important when you're creating a handler that expects several different types of data to perform accurate type checking on the data you send via the newval argument. This is because it is likely that when working with this handler, you may confuse which type of data you are setting at a given time. The structure of this code is heavily dependent on the case statement, as show in Listing 10.5.

Listing 10.5   The `BC_ChartParams()` Handler

```
 1: on BC_ChartParams(me, aparam, newval)
 2:    --determine which property you intend to change
 3:    case(aparam) of
 4:      #barheight:
 5:        --make sure that the data is either an integer
 6:        --or a float and that number is larger than zero
 7:        if newval.ilk = #integer or newval.ilk = #float \
and newval > 0 then
 8:          pMaxsize = newVal
 9:        else
10:          return false
11:        end if
12:
13:      #barsize:
14:        --make sure that the value is an integer and
15:        --the value is greater than zero
```

Listing 10.5 Continued

```
16:        if newval.ilk = #integer and newval > 0 then
17:          pBarWidth = newval
18:        else
19:          return false
20:        end if
21:
22:    #spacing:
23:       --make sure that the value is an integer and
24:       --the value is greater than zero (you probably
25:       --also want to set this value greater than 100
26:       --otherwise bars will be placed inside of one
27:       --another...
28:       if newval.ilk = #integer and newval > 0 then
29:         pBarCloseness = newval
30:       else
31:         return false
32:       end if
33:
34:    #target:
35:       --make sure that the new value is a castmember
36:       if newval.ilk = #member then
37:         --make sure that castmember is a 3D castmember
38:         if newval.type = #shockwave3d then
39:           pTargetCastmember = newval
40:         else
41:           return false
42:         end if
43:       end if
44:
45:    #camera:
46:       --make sure that the value is an integer and
47:       --it is greater than or equal to 1
48:       if newval.ilk = #integer and newval >= 1 then
49:         --make sure that that number refers to a camera
50:         --that currently exists in the pTargetCastmember
51:         if newval <= pTargetCastmember.camera.count then
52:           pTargetCamera = newval
53:         else
54:           return false
55:         end if
56:       else
57:         return false
58:       end if
59:    otherwise:
60:       --if you did not specify or incorrectly specified a
```

Listing 10.5   Continued

```
61:        --parameter to alter, return false
62:        return false
63:    end case
64:    return true
65: end
```

Notice how the bulk of the BC_ChartParams() handler is spent ensuring that the data in the newval argument is in the correct format. Although I have created a public method for controlling a large number of the properties for the bar chart utility with this handler, other properties need to be controlled and other small tasks need to be performed in addition to setting these properties.

Color Handlers

Several properties are specific enough to warrant the creation of their own public handlers. Specifically, the handling of the color list is an important procedure that has two public methods. The first method, BC_ColorReport(), is extremely simple code. This method is used with the following syntax:

```
ChildObjectRef.BC_ColorReport()
```

As you can see, this handler accepts no arguments. It will simply return the contents of the property pColors, which is a list. Note that the structure of this handler is as follows:

```
on BC_ColorReport(me)
  return pColors
end
```

NOTE

BC_ColorReport() is a clear example of how you should go out of your way to create public methods, even for the reporting of the values of properties. This code embodies a timeless conceptual mantra of object-oriented programming that should constantly ring in your head as you design parent/child scripts: *Create public methods for private data.*

Whereas the BC_ColorReport() handler will only tell us the current colors, BC_ColorChange() allows us to change the colors used by the chart. The syntax for BC_ColorChange() is as follows:

```
ChildObjectRef.BC_ColorChange(newcolors)
```

Here, newcolors is a linear list of rgb(*R*,*G*,*B*) color values. There must be as many entries in this list as there are rows in the data array. This handler will overwrite the current values of the pColors list with the newcolors argument you supply.

Various Visualization Utilities

Three general utilities for working with the visualization of the bar chart are important to understand. The first of these utilities is the BC_ChartSpin() handler, which rotates the chart around the center of the Group. This is an important handler because it makes sure that the Group rotates around the center of the Group rather than the local Group Y axis, which is not in the same position as the center of the Group. This handler is called with ChildObjectRef.BC_ChartSpin(speed), where the speed parameter is the number of degrees to rotate the chart around its center.

The next two utilities are related. Both do not require arguments because they provide two very basic functions. BC_ChartDestroy() destroys the Group and the Models that comprise the visualization of the chart. However, it does not destroy the array of data. BC_ChartUpdate() destroys the chart visualization and then quickly re-creates it. If you change any of the chart parameters, such as the chart colors or the sizes of the Models, you will need to call BC_ChartUpdate() to see the changes.

The last handler we will look at before working directly with creating charts is the BC_DataReport() handler. This handler returns data from the array and can return either all the data or one specific piece of data. The syntax for returning all the data is quite simple:

```
ChildObjectRef.BC_DataReport(#full)
```

This essentially returns the current value of pChartData, but it gives you a public method for doing so. To access a specific piece of data, use the following syntax:

```
ChildObjectRef.BC_DataReport(#frommodelname, "modelname")
```

Notice that when you're looking for a specific value in the array, this handler expects two arguments: the #frommodelname symbol, to alert the script that you are looking for a single piece of data, and the "modelname" argument, which requires a string that is the name of the Model from the chart visualization of which you are interested in learning the specific value. The code for this script uses a case statement to determine what data to return, as shown in Listing 10.6.

Listing 10.6   The BC_ChartReport() Handler

```
 1: on BC_DataReport(me, detailLevel, aParam)
 2:
 3:    --determine what level of detail is required
 4:    case(detailLevel) of
 5:
 6:      #fromModelName:
 7:        --if you are looking for a specific value from
 8:        --the array based on the name of the model, we will
 9:        --convert the name of the model into a numerical
10:        --value for both the row and the column, and then
11:        --search the pChartData list via bracket access
12:
13:        --create three empty string placeholders
14:        row = ""
15:        col = ""
16:        temp = ""
17:
18:        --strip off all but the rowXcolumn data that was appended to
19:        --each model name when the data was added
20:        repeat with x = aparam.length down to 1
21:          if aparam.char[x] = "_" then
22:            temp = aparam.char[(x+1)..aparam.length]
23:            exit repeat
24:          end if
25:        end repeat
26:
27:        --separate the row and the column portions
28:        -- of the rowXcolumn data...
```

Listing 10.6   Continued

```
29:        repeat with x = 1 to temp.length
30:          if temp.char[x] = "x" then
31:            put temp.char[(x+1)..temp.length] after col
32:            exit repeat
33:          else
34:            put temp.char[x] after row
35:          end if
36:        end repeat
37:
38:        --convert the row and column string data to numbers
39:        row = value(row)
40:        col = value(col)
41:
42:        --look up that position in the array
43:        avalue = pChartData[row][col]
44:
45:        --return that value
46:        return avalue
47:
48:      #full:
49:        --if you are looking for the complete
50:        --array, just return it.
51:        return pchartdata
52:      otherwise:
53:        --if you did not specify what to report,
54:        --simply return false (zero)
55:        return false
56:    end case
57: end
```

In general, the BC_ChartReport() handler could be greatly expanded to report row and column data, or even to handle mild statistics. If the reporting were to be any more involved, to the point where other charts would be created from the report, I might suggest that you move toward the conceptual framework of totally separating your data type code from the visualization code. Many commercial databases are available that may already perform the advanced statistical analysis you require.

Creating Bar Charts

Now that we have looked at the various handlers and their syntax, we will work with two demonstrations so that you can see how to actually work with this custom data type and visualization tool.

Bar Chart Basics

First, we will examine how to create and modify bar charts on-the-fly from the message window. On the CD is a file named "Bar Chart Basics." Open this file and press Play. Do not stop the movie during this demonstration— both the parent/child script and the 3D environment require that you perform the following commands on a single contiguous execution of the movie.

First, create a new Bar Chart Utility child object and save a reference to that object in a variable by typing the following code into the message window and pressing Return:

```
Chartobj = new(script "Bar Chart Utility", "newchart")
```

NOTE

Remember that any variables created in the message window are automatically global. If we were going to create this child object from a script, we would need to declare the chartobj variable as a global variable prior to this line of code.

The next step is to add some data to the array. Add a row of data by typing the following code into the message window and pressing Return:

```
Chartobj.BC_DataAdd(#row, [#a:20,#b:45,#c:12,#d:7,#e:32], rgb( 120, 90, 100
➡))
```

This code also specifies that the color for the row should be light mauve. The next step we will take is to create a visual representation of the data with the following code in the message window:

```
Chartobj.BC_ChartCreate()
```

At this point, you should see the bar chart on the Stage. This bar chart can be worked with in many ways. You can rotate the chart with the BC_ChartSpin() function, or you can change the chart parameters. Let's change the size of the bars. To do so, type the following code into the message window and press Return:

```
Chartobj.BC_ChartParams(#barsize, 25)
```

In order to see the parameter change, you must update the chart with the following code:

```
Chartobj.BC_ChartUpdate()
```

Note that chartupdate() will automatically reset the rotation of the chart, because the chart is actually re-created. Now you should see the chart with different parameters for the size of the bars. Let's add another row of data onto the array with the following code (remember to update the visualization after changing the data):

```
Chartobj.BC_DataAdd(#row, [#a:50,#b:15,#c:1,#d:2,#e:5], rgb( 0, 0, 255 ))
Chartobj.BC_Chartupdate()
```

Now you should see two rows of data: one blue, the other mauve. Let's continue adding data. This time, add a new column of data with the following lines of code:

```
Chartobj.BC_DataAdd(#column, [#f:12,#f:35])
Chartobj.BC_ChartUpdate()
```

Now the charts have two rows, each with six columns of data. Just to make sure that you understand how the data in the array is currently organized, you can get a full report on the data with the following command:

```
Put Chartobj.BC_DataReport(#full)
-- [[#a_1x1: 20, #b_1x2: 45, #c_1x3: 12, #d_1x4: 7, #e_1x5: 32, #f_1x6: 12],
➥[#a_2x1: 50, #b_2x2: 15,
➥#c_2x3: 1, #d_2x4: 2, #e_2x5: 5, #f_2x6: 35]]
```

Notice how row and column positions have been appended to each of the properties in the list. These unique names were used for the Models that exist as the bars in the bar chart. This structure offers you a concise and powerful method of dealing with the data in your chart. I suggest that you continue experimenting with these various handlers for a few moments before continuing on to the next demonstration.

Basic Chart Interaction

Open the file "Basic Chart Interaction" from the CD and press Play. Note that this demo creates three rows of randomly generated data and allows the computer to pick the colors for the rows. If it is difficult to see any of the rows, simply rewind and restart the movie. In addition to three rows of data being created, the chart is constantly spinning around its center. This is accomplished via the BC_ChartSpin() handler called from within an exitframe handler.

Now, while the movie continues to play, click any of the bars. Notice how the bar you clicked lights up. In addition, the name and value of the bar are reported back to you in a small field Sprite near the lower-right corner of the Stage. Before we look at the script that creates this interaction in Listing 10.7, you need to know that two of the lines of code that make this script work are fully explained in other chapters.

Listing 10.7   Basic Bar Chart Interaction Script

```
 1: property pOffset, spritenum, plastclicked
 2: property pReturnWhere, pReturnMember
 3:
 4: global scene, chartobj
 5:
 6:
 7: on beginsprite
 8:   poffset = point(sprite(spritenum).left, sprite(spritenum).top)
 9: end
10:
11: on getpropertydescriptionlist
12:
13:   set templist = []
14:
15:   repeat with x = 1 to the number of members in castlib 1
16:     if member(x).type = #field then
17:       addat(templist, member(x))
18:     end if
19:   end repeat
20:
21:   plist = [:]
22:   setaprop(plist, #pReturnWhere, \
```

Listing 10.7   Continued

```
23:    [#comment:"Return to the Message window, or a Field?", \
24:    #format:#symbol, \
25:    #default:#field, \
26:    #range:[#field,#message]])
27:
28:    setaprop(plist, #pReturnMember, \
29:    [#comment:"If #field, which field?", \
30:    #format:#member, \
31:    #default:"Name of Field", \
32:    #range:templist])
33:
34:    return plist
35: end
36:
37: on mousedown
38:    curloc = the mouseloc
39:    cloc = curloc - poffset
40:
41:    --we learn "picking" in chapter 13...
42:    mdl = scene.camera[1].modelunderloc(cloc)
43:
44:    if mdl <> void then
45:      global ob
46:      answer = chartobj.bc_datareport(#frommodelname, mdl.name)
47:      case(preturnwhere) of
48:        #field:
49:          preturnmember.text = string(mdl) && "value:" && answer
50:        #message:
51:          put string(mdl) && "value:" && answer
52:      end case
53:
54:      --and we will examine the emissive property
55:      --in chapter 12
56:      scene.model(mdl.name).shader.emissive = rgb(150,150,150)
57:    else
58:      case(preturnwhere) of
59:        #field:
60:          preturnmember.text = "None Selected"
61:        #message:
62:          put "None Selected"
63:      end case
64:    end if
65:
66:    if plastclicked <> void then
67:      --again, emissive is explained in chapter 12
```

Listing 10.7   Continued

```
68:      scene.model(plastclicked.name).shader.emissive = rgb(0,0,0)
69:   end if
70:   plastclicked = mdl
71: end
```

This script expects that you have created a bar chart whose child object is stored in a global variable named chartobj. In addition, note that a major portion of this script is a getpropertydescriptionlist handler. The reason for this is so that you can utilize this behavior without needing to understand the functionality of several lines of code that are explained later in the book.

NOTE

Specifically, there are two lines that we have not yet worked with that are dealt with in separate chapters. This script utilizes a technique known as Picking Lingo, which is explained in detail in Chapter 13, "A 2D Mouse in a 3D World." Picking Lingo allows you to determine the names of Models that are underneath the current mouse position. Also, this script uses a specific Shader property known as the Emissive property. This property modifies the color of the Model in order to make it appear as though the surface of the Model is emitting light. The Emissive property of the standard Shader is explained in Chapter 12, "Basic Control of Surfaces."

I strongly encourage you to examine the respective chapters I have mentioned in order to learn how you can greatly expand the functionality of this script as well as the amount of possible interactions with the bar chart itself. In addition, you may be interested in several lessons in Chapter 25, "Advanced Camera Control," that examine methods of changing the viewpoint of the Camera via the mouse dynamically.

Future Considerations

Depending on the specific requirements of your project, you may need to expand this bar chart data type quite dramatically. In terms of the chart that is created, several items could be immediately considered for most charts, such as chart labels and a key.

In addition, there are several areas that we have not yet explored in the book, if you are reading chronologically, that you might want to consider. For example, you might expand the section of the bar chart script that deals with color to handle more advanced surfaces, which we will examine in Chapter 12, "Basic Control of Surfaces." You might also expand the color section to deal with Texture, as discussed in Chapter 12 as well as in Chapter 14, "Multitexturing."

Finally, you might also consider the possibility of expanding the methods in which users interact with the charts you create. Chapter 13, "A 2D Mouse in a 3D World," examines methods of building mouse interaction, and Chapter 25, "Advanced Camera Control," has several demonstrations of controlling the Camera with the mouse to allow users to dynamically change their viewpoint.

Summary

The creation of bar charts is a process that can be approached with varying levels of complexity. In this chapter, a decision was made to create a custom data type with custom functions to control the array of data as well as the visualization of that data.

The Bar Chart Utility parent/child script is quite robust and can satisfy most of your basic bar chart needs. If your project requires more statistical reporting or complex data visualization, you may want to consider expanding this parent/child script, or even building a new one to meet your needs.

The goal of this chapter was to show you how to create bar charts as well as how to integrate advanced object-oriented programming concepts of parent/child scripts with the 3D environment.

FAQ

Where can I find more examples of OOP and parent/child scripts?

Check the next chapter on pie charts, where we will create a custom pie chart data type. In addition, examine Appendix F, "Colorlut Custom Color Management System," for another example of parent/child scripting.

CHAPTER 11

Pie Charts

In the previous chapter, we examined a method for creating histograms through a custom data type and custom functions. In this chapter, we will apply similar methods of using parent/child scripts for creating a pie chart custom data type. Also, we will be creating the functions used to create visualizations of this custom data type. Figure 11.1 illustrates an example of a pie chart that we will be able to create with this utility.

FIGURE 11.1

Pie chart visualization created with the pie chart utility parent/child script.

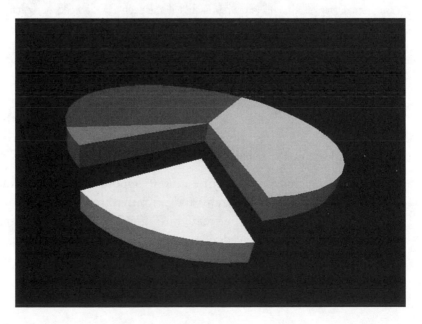

In Figure 11.1, you can see that one of the pie chart wedges is broken away from the main chart. The pie chart utility we will be examining creates charts where the wedges create a full circle by default. The hierarchy for the Models used for visualization is constructed so that the wedges can be easily manipulated individually as well as a whole group.

Brainstorming

In many ways, creating a utility for pie charts is easier than creating a utility for bar charts. The array of data required for a pie chart is much less involved than that for bar charts. Rather than the data requiring a wide array, it only really needs a single property list. This is because from a data management standpoint, a pie chart only represents a single *row* of data. Each of the wedges represents some percentage of the whole pie, which is derived from the raw value of the wedge. Therefore, the pie chart shows the relationship between data through the size of the wedges.

NOTE

Imagine a pie chart of the world's population with wedges to represent how many individuals inhabit each country. Some countries would have very large wedges, whereas others would have very small wedges. The whole pie represents all the people in the world, and each wedge represents some portion of that whole.

We will need to build several handlers that deal with the conversion of data from raw values into ratios that represent the size, in degrees, of each wedge. The important difference between pie charts and bar charts is that the data type itself is much less complex. Because the data is only a single property list, the handlers for the management of pie chart data are easier to develop.

However, pie charts do present a unique opportunity to test your understanding of the scenegraph hierarchy and primitive creation. The actual visualization of the pie chart will be created using cylinders. Cylinders are the obvious choice for the basic pie wedge shapes because of the Startangle and Endangle Modelresource properties that allow you to create wedge-shaped Modelresources.

The difficulty with creating wedges is that in Director the inside walls of the wedges are not capped off. In order to account for this, we will be creating caps for the inside walls of the cylinder. This is accomplished by creating two planes and rotating them into place where the inside walls of the cylinder should be. For this reason, we will need to build a specialized wedge-creation utility rather than using the primitive API we have been using for cylinders.

Building the Handlers

In this example, we will actually have several private handlers rather than just one private handler, as in the bar chart utility from the previous chapter. The reason for this is that the wedge-creation handler is going to be quite specific to this demonstration. It will be easier to eliminate type checking for this private handler by designing accurate type checking for the public handler that calls it. However, because type checking will be eliminated, it would not be wise to encourage others to use the handler publicly.

In addition to the specialized wedge-creation handler, we will be looking at another private handler that deals with the conversion of data from values into percentages and then into degrees. The reason for this is that when we enter data into our single-row array, we will be using the actual data values. Those values need to be converted into degrees so that we can create accurate pie wedges. In addition, we need to rotate each pie wedge so that all the wedges will line up correctly.

Several publicly accessible handlers have names that are similar to those in the bar chart utility but have slight differences in syntax, scope, or both. Table 11.1 lists the handlers we will be creating for the pie chart utility and their purposes.

TABLE 11.1   The Handlers of the Pie Chart Utility

Handler Name	Purpose
New()	Initializes the pie chart child object
PC_DataAdd()	Adds data to the list
PC_DataRemove()	Removes data from the list
PC_DataReport()	Accesses existing data for interaction
PC_ChartCreate()	Creates a chart from the data

TABLE 11.1   Continued

Handler Name	Purpose
PC_ChartDestroy()	Destroy the chart
PC_ChartUpdate()	Quickly updates the chart
PC_ChartParams()	Sets the chart parameters
PC_ColorChange()	Changes the current colors for the chart
PC_ColorReport()	Finds out the current colors for the chart
PC_SetCamera()	Positions and orients the Camera toward the chart
PC_ColorAppend()	Appends colors to the color list (private)
PC_CreateWedge()	Creates the pie wedge with inner caps (private)
PC_DataToDegrees()	Converts all data to degrees (private)

Again, although most of these handlers are similar in name, each has a slight key difference. We will examine all the handlers. However, I have eliminated comments in the code, where the code is identical to the bar chart utility, so that you can focus on those elements that are specific to the pie chart utility.

New()

We will begin with the new() handler for the pie chart utility. It initializes the various properties required to create pie charts. As you know, it is important to save a reference to the child object, which is returned from the new() handler. Here's the syntax for the new() handler:

```
ChildObjectRef = new(script "pie chart utility", "chartname")
```

In this script, if you do not supply a chartname argument, the script will abort. The new() handler is almost identical to the new() handler for the bar chart utility. The only differences can be seen in the following lines of code:

```
-- pchartdata starts as an empty linear list
-- each row will be a new property list nested
-- inside of this linear list
pChartData = [:]

-- Default Radius of the Pie Chart
pPieRadius = 100
-- Default Height of the Pie Chart
pPieHeight = 15
```

Because most of these lines are comments, you can see that the differences occur in three lines of code. Note that pChartData has a slightly different format—a single property list. Also note that because we are going to be dealing with cylinders, we need properties that accurately describe the radius and height of the cylinders we create.

PC_DataAdd()

The PC_DataAdd handler is quite easy to use because only one "row" of data is to be managed by the pie chart. For this reason, the structure of the data is a single property list. The property names will be used to generate the names of Models for the pie chart visualization. To append data onto the property list, use the following syntax:

```
ChildObjectRef.PC_DataAdd(#symbol, value, RGB_color)
```

Here, #symbol is the name of the property you will be adding to the list, and value is the value of the data that you would like associated with that property. The rgb_color argument is an optional argument that allows you to specify a color for the pie wedge. If you do not specify a color, one will be assigned randomly. You can examine the code that delivers this functionality in Listing 11.1.

LISTING 11.1   The PC_DataAdd() Handler for the Pie Chart Utility

```
 1: on PC_DataAdd(me, newprop, newdata, newcolor)
 2:
 3:    --determine that the newprop is a symbol and
 4:    --that newdata is some type of numeric data
 5:    if newprop.ilk = #symbol and (newdata.ilk = #integer or \
newdata.ilk = #float) then
 6:      --make sure that the data is positive
 7:      if newdata > 0 then
 8:        --go ahead and add the property and data
 9:        --to the pchartdata property list
10:        setaprop(pChartData, newprop, newdata)
11:
12:        --determine whether a color was specified
13:        --if so, add that color to the pcolors list
14:        if newcolor.ilk = #color then
15:          addat(pcolors, newcolor)
```

LISTING 11.1   Continued

```
16:        else
17:            --if not, choose a random color.
18:            rcolor = rgb(random(255), random(255), random(255))
19:            addat(pcolors, rcolor)
20:          end if
21:      else
22:          --if the data was not positive, return false
23:          return false
24:      end if
25:    else
26:      --if you did not specify a symbol for the property
27:      --or numeric data for the value, return false
28:      return false
29:    end if
30:
31:    --everything went ok, return true.
32:    return true
33: end
```

PC_ChartCreate()

This function of this handler is conceptually similar to its equivalent in the bar chart utility, in that this handler creates the visualization of the data. However, because we are creating a fundamentally different visualization, the code is quite different. The syntax for calling this handler remains similar:

```
ChildObjectRef.PC_ChartCreate()
```

Several tasks need to be accomplished when we're creating the pie chart. Conceptually, the tasks are as follows:

- Create the pie chart Group.
- Convert the raw data values into number of degrees for wedges.
- Create the wedges.
- Set up the Group center.
- Set up the Camera.

Of these five tasks, I have singled out the second and third tasks and created custom private handlers that are called from the PC_ChartCreate() handler. First, let's look at the structure of the PC_ChartCreate() handler, as shown in Listing 11.2.

LISTING 11.2   The PC_ChartCreate() Handler for the Pie Chart Utility

```
 1: on PC_ChartCreate(me)
 2:
 3:    --create pie chart group
 4:    grp = ptargetcastmember.newgroup(pChartName)
 5:
 6:    --convert each of the values into a number
 7:    --of degrees representing some percentage
 8:    --of the 360 degrees in the whole pie.
 9:    --store that information in a separate list
10:    --from the original pChartData
11:    ChartDataDegrees = PC_ConvertToDegrees(me)
12:
13:    --determine that the pie wedges are going to
14:    --begin at 0 degrees on the total pie
15:    startpoint = 0
16:
17:    --cycle through every member of the "fixed" list
18:    repeat with x = 1 to ChartDataDegrees.count()
19:       --determine the ending angle of the current
20:       --wedge based on the number of degrees in
21:       --the current wedge plus the current startpoint
22:       endpoint = chartDatadegrees[x] + startpoint
23:
24:       --determine the name of the Model from the
25:       --name of the current property in the property list
26:       wedgeName = string(getpropat(chartdatadegrees, x))
27:
28:       --create the wedge
29:       obj = PC_createwedge(me, wedgename, \
startpoint, endpoint, pcolors[x])
30:
31:       --add the pie wedge to the group
32:       grp.addchild(obj, #preserveworld)
33:
34:       --increase the value of the startpoint so that
35:       --it is equal to this wedge's endpoint.  That way
36:       -- the next wedge will begin where this one ends
37:       startpoint = startpoint + chartDatadegrees[x]
```

LISTING 11.2   Continued

```
38:    end repeat
39:
40:    --create a dummy model at the center of the group
41:    pchartcenter = pTargetCastmember.newmodel("dummy")
42:
43:    --set the pchart flag true so that it will be easy to determine
44:    --whether a visualization of the data currently exists
45:    pchart = true
46:    --set up the default camera position
47:    PC_ChartSetCamera(me)
48: end
```

PC_ConvertToDegrees() is the first private handler that this script calls. This private handler performs the task of converting the raw data values from the property list into degrees. Note in Listing 11.3 how the structure of this private handler does not include error checking because this handler is not intended to be called publicly.

LISTING 11.3   The PC_ConvertToDegrees() Private Handler

```
 1: on PC_ConvertToDegrees(me)
 2:    --create a blank property list
 3:    output = [:]
 4:
 5:    --we need to find out what the sum of
 6:    --all pieces of data in the property
 7:    --list is, this way we can figure out
 8:    --how each individual piece of data
 9:    --relates to the whole.  first we will
10:    --set a new variable named total = 0
11:    total = 0
12:    --then we will cycle through each value in
13:    --the list and add its value to the total
14:    repeat with x = 1 to pchartdata.count()
15:      total = total + pchartdata[x]
16:    end repeat
17:
18:    --next we will need to cycle through each
19:    --value in the list again.  This time our
20:    --goal is to actually perform the conversion
21:    --now that we have all the required information.
22:    repeat with x = 1 to pChartData.count()
```

LISTING 11.3   Continued

```
23:     --this next line is important.  we multiply the
24:     --current raw value by 360, and then divide by
25:     --the total value of the chart.  this will reveal
26:     --the degrees in that particular wedge.
27:     wedgeDegrees = pChartData[x]  * 360.0 / float(total)
28:     --find out the name of the property for this wedge
29:     --from the raw property list
30:     pname = getpropat(pchartdata, x)
31:     --set a new property with the same name as the property
32:     --from the raw property list, but with the degrees as the value
33:     setaprop(output, pname, wedgeDegrees)
34:   end repeat
35:
36:   --when you are done, return the list with property
37:   --names correlated to the number of degrees in each wedge
38:   return output
39: end
```

As you can see, the result of this handler (the list stored in output) is returned to the PC_CreateChart() handler at line 11 in Listing 11.2. Note that this list of converted values is kept separate from the original data so that the original data is preserved.

The next private handler called by PC_CreateChart() is perhaps the most complex handler in the pie chart utility. As mentioned earlier, when you create cylinder primitives that are less that 360 degrees, you will create a wedge. However, the inside walls of the wedge are not created, and because of that you can see inside of the wedge. If our pie charts were simply going to be static, this might not be a problem, but because we are working with a dynamic 3D environment, it is best to plan for a situation where these inside walls are capped up.

The process of capping the wedges is a bit more involved than just simply creating a cylinder, as you can see from the code in Listing 11.4.

LISTING 11.4   The PC_CreateWedge() Private Handler

```
1: On PC_CreateWedge(me, wedgename, startang, endang, cylColor)
2:
3:   Res = ptargetcastmember.newmodelresource(wedgename & "res", #cylinder)
4:   --set the height of the cylinder (soon to be wedge)
5:   Res.height = pPieHeight
```

LISTING 11.4   Continued

```
 6:   --set the radius of the cylinder (soon to be wedge)
 7:   Res.topradius = pPieRadius
 8:   Res.bottomradius = pPieRadius
 9:   --set the start and end angle properties
10:   --for the modelresource, thereby actually
11:   --changing the geometry into a wedge
12:   res.startangle = startang
13:   res.endangle = endang
14:   --reduce the number of height segments to one.
15:   res.numsegments = 1
16:   --dynamically increase or reduce the resolution
17:   --of the wedge based on the number of degrees that
18:   --the wedge spans making sure that it is at least 1
19:   detail = (endang - startang) / 12 + 1
20:   res.resolution = detail
21:   --create the wedge Model
22:   Obj = ptargetcastmember.newmodel(wedgename, res)
23:   --create a new shader
24:   Shd = ptargetcastmember.newshader(wedgename & "shd", #standard)
25:   --assign the diffuse color of the shader
26:   Shd.diffuse = cylColor
27:   --make sure to eliminate the default texture from the shader
28:   Shd.texture = void
29:   --assign the shader to all sides of the wedge
30:   Obj.shaderlist = shd
31:
32:   --create a plane Modelresource
33:   Res = ptargetcastmember.newmodelresource\
(wedgename & "capres", #plane)
34:   --set up length and width properties of plane Modelresource
35:   --based on the height and radius of the pie chart...
36:   Res.length = pPieHeight
37:   Res.width = pPieRadius
38:   --create the plane Model
39:   capa = ptargetcastmember.newmodel(wedgename & "capa", res)
40:   --set the shaders of capa to the same shader
41:   --that the wedge uses.  No sense in creating a ton
42:   --of shaders and setting them all the same, this way
43:   --if you want to change what the wedge looks like, you
44:   --just change the properties of one shader.
45:   capa.shaderlist = shd
46:   --capa was created at the center of the world.
47:   --we need to move it half of its length to the
48:   --right so that it is pointing toward 3:00 on
49:   --the pie chart.  the left edge of the cap will be
50:   --at the center of the pie chart by doing this
51:   --and will make rotating the wedge into position
```

LISTING 11.4 Continued

```
52:    --rather easy.
53:    capa.translate((pPieRadius * .5),0,0,#world)
54:    --make a copy of capa
55:    capb = capa.clone(wedgename & "capb")
56:    --rotate cap a and cap b into position
57:    capa.rotate(0,270-startang, 0, #world)
58:    capb.rotate(0,270-endang, 0,#world)
59:    --assign the caps as children of the wedge
60:    obj.addchild(capa, #preserveworld)
61:    obj.addchild(capb, #preserveworld)
62:    --return a reference to the wedge Model
63:    Return obj
64: End
```

Notice that this private handler creates the wedge, caps the wedge, assigns the caps as children of the wedge, and then returns a reference to the wedge Model. In Listing 11.2, this information is returned to line 29. That reference is then used to add the wedge (and its children, the caps) to the pie chart group.

Various Utilities

The PC_ChartDestroy(), PC_ChartUpdate(), PC_ColorReport(), and PC_ColorChange() handlers still have the same functionality as their bar chart utility counterparts, as well as the same syntax and usage. Of the utilities, PC_ChartParams() has not changed in syntax, but some of the switches have changed. Recall that the syntax for the handler is this:

```
ChildObjectRef.BC_ChartParams(#whatproperty, newval)
```

Several properties can be accessed and controlled via this handler, so I have created a structure for this handler to provide a public method for manipulating the values of several different properties, as outlined in Table 11.2.

TABLE 11.2 The PC_ChartParams() Arguments

#whatproperty	Immediate Purpose	Purpose	newval
#pieradius	Sets pPieRadius	Sets the radius of the pie chart	float

TABLE 11.2 Continued

#whatproperty	Immediate Purpose	Purpose	newval
#pieheight	Sets pPieHeight	Sets the height of the pie chart	integer
#target	Sets pTargetCastmember	Sets the 3D member in which to create the pie chart Models	member
#camera	Sets pTargetCamera	Sets the camera to use for the chart	integer

The data visualization of the pie chart is fairly straightforward. Most likely, you will not need to alter these parameters, although if you are planning on creating multiple pie charts, it makes sense to have control over these parameters.

PC_DataReport()

The final handler that we will examine is the PC_DataReport() handler. Again, because of the relative simplicity of the data structure in this script, the code required for the PC_DataReport() handler is fairly straightforward. There are two ways to find out information about the data. First, you can always use

```
ChildObjectRef.PC_DataReport(#full)
```

This will return a full listing of the pChartData property list. Of course, you will need to do something with the data that it returns. The other possibility is to return a single piece of information on the list from a Model name using the following syntax:

```
ChildObjectRef.PC_DataReport(#frommodelname, "modelname")
```

Here, the modelname parameter is the name of the Model that you want to know the specific value for from the pChartData property list. You can see how the PC_DataReport() custom handler functions in Listing 11.5.

LISTING 11.5   The `PC_DataReport()` Handler for the Pie Chart Utility

```
 1: on PC_DataReport(me, detailLevel, aParam)
 2:
 3:    --determine what level of detail is required
 4:    case(detailLevel) of
 5:
 6:      #fromModelName:
 7:        --convert the model name to a symbol name
 8:        --which will correspond to a property
 9:        --in the pchartdata property list
10:        namesymbol = symbol(aparam)
11:
12:        --look up that position in the list
13:        avalue = getaprop(pChartData, namesymbol)
14:
15:        --return that value
16:        return avalue
17:
18:      #full:
19:        --if you are looking for the complete
20:        --array, just return it.
21:        pChartData.sort()
22:
23:        return pchartdata
24:      otherwise:
25:        --if you did not specify what to report,
26:        --simply return false (zero)
27:        return false
28:    end case
29: end
```

Now that we have looked at the syntax and the specific code that performs that pie chart script functionality, we will examine several methods of implementing this code.

Creating Pie Charts

In this section, we will be examining how to use the handlers to create and manipulate a basic pie chart. Then we will examine a small demonstration of how to use the pie chart utility with a prebuilt behavior to create some simple but useful interaction.

Pie Chart Basics Demo

On the CD is a file named "Pie Chart Basics" that contains the pie chart utility script. Open this file and press Play; keep in mind that in this demo we are going to walk through the steps of creating a pie chart from the message window. It is important that you execute all commands in the demo in a single, contiguous execution of the movie. If you run into an error, stop and rewind the movie and then press Play. You can then start entering the commands again from the beginning.

The first step that we need to take is to create a new child object from the script and store the reference in a variable. Type the following code in the message window and press Return:

```
Chartobj = new(script "pie chart utility", "mychart")
```

This will initialize the child object, and we are now ready to add data. To do this, use each of the following lines of code:

```
Chartobj.PC_DataAdd(#food, 250, rgb(0,200,100))
Chartobj.PC_DataAdd(#rent, 700, rgb(200,100,0))
Chartobj.PC_DataAdd(#fun, 110, rgb(10,100,200))
Chartobj.PC_DataAdd(#savings, 400, rgb(0,0,190))
```

Now that we have entered the data for a simulated monthly budget, let's visualize the data with the following line of code:

```
Chartobj.PC_ChartCreate()
```

At this point, you should see a chart in the center of your Stage. Because the Camera has been automatically positioned for you, you will have a good view of the chart. Let's add another element of data to the chart and then update the chart with the following lines of code:

```
Chartobj.PC_DataAdd(#bills, 230, rgb(200,0,0))
Chartobj.PC_ChartUpdate()
```

Finally, let's move the pie wedge that indicates bills up on its local Y axis with the following code:

```
Scene.model("rent").translate(0,10,0,#parent)
```

If you were to move the Group named mychart at this point, all the wedges would move and retain their relationships with each other. This way, you can position wedges and then control all of them via the Group.

Pie Chart Interaction Demo

In this next example, we are going to take a look at an interesting method for interaction with the pie chart that combines picking techniques, data reporting, and code to lift the chart wedges into a controlled experience for the user to learn about the data in the visualization. Open the file named "Pie Chart Interaction" on the CD and press Play. You will be presented with a pie chart; use your mouse to click the various wedges in the pie chart. This will allow you to glimpse some of the possibilities for controlling the pie chart that we will be covering throughout the next section of the book. Specifically, we will be examining an expanded version of this demonstration in Chapter 18, "3D Interface Design." The functionality for interaction in this demonstration is provided through a specialized behavior script that is similar to the one used in the previous chapter for bar chart interaction.

Future Considerations

You might want to consider how we are approaching both histograms and pie charts, especially if you are going to be dealing charting as a primary application. Because these two data types treat their data exclusively, we have been able to simplify some of the functions and build a somewhat-robust structure.

However, if you need one set of data to be viewed as bar charts, pie charts, stem/leaf plots, surface plots, and so on, you should really consider expanding the structure we have started. I suggest that you consider separating the data and the 3D models created from that data much more than we have done.

In fact, I would suggest that your solution be flexible enough to support not only 3D visualizations of data, but 2D visualizations as well. You might approach the 2D visualizations via Imaging Lingo. In Chapter 17, "Special Effects," we will examine a method of using Imaging Lingo to create dynamic textures for the 3D environment. You might consider combining 2D visualizations into the 3D environment.

You could utilize Director's capabilities to create inheritance for properties of your code, using ancestors in your parent/child scripts. The overall goal would be to create one database data type that fits your needs; then you could create parent/child scripts that use your database data type to create visualizations of specific parts of the database.

Another reason why I might suggest going in this direction is if you need robust statistical functionality built in to your project. Consider that statistics are performed on the database, not on the charts. This separation of data and visualization is crucial.

You should think about the data itself as well as where it is coming from. It is possible to build functionality that allows users to enter data either through a Shockwave front end or via scripting languages. You could create a Shockwave movie that loads data via JavaScript or VBScript from a Web page with values stored in it—and that Web page could be created on-the-fly so that the data can have been pulled from a remote server.

Finally, you might consider that several databases and database engines already exist that can be used to handle the data part of your visualization. You may still need to create specific statistical analysis on your data, but the structure of the database would already exist. I suggest several database possibilities for use in Director in the "Supplemental Resources" section near the end of this chapter.

Summary

The pie chart is a powerful tool that can be used to visualize a wide variety of data. In this chapter, you have seen that a robust method of handling the creation and maintenance of pie charts in Director can be accomplished through parent/child scripts. In addition, parent/child scripts can be used to develop a larger system of data visualization based on a separation of data management and data visualization.

The method you choose to implement for data visualization should be thought out carefully. A data visualization system integrated into a professional back-end Web-driven database could save you enormous amounts of time if you require that kind of power. However, if you just need a few charts, it doesn't really make sense to create such an involved solution. The most difficult decisions can arise when you are making a visualization system that may need to expand and grow with your project. This is why you should learn to separate data management and data visualization, even on this small scale. If you ever need to expand your system of visualization, it will be easier to expand into a full-fledged system if you have been thinking about expansion from the beginning.

Finally, the notion of expansion doesn't need to mean "visualizing more data." It could simply mean visualizing the same data in many different ways. However, that might not be simple if your system of data management is too tightly intertwined with your system of data visualization.

FAQ

Is there a similar method of creating the inner walls of cylinders when I am trying to create a cone or a sphere wedge?

For the cone, you might consider examining the Meshdeform Modifier, which is explained in Chapter 28, "Mesh Deformation and Detailed Picking." This Modifier could be used to modify the geometry of planes to create caps for a pie wedge created from a cone.

For a sphere wedge, the process is a bit different—you might use the top cap of a cylinder to create a circular cap for the inside walls of the sphere.

Is there a way to create a surface plot for my data?

Yes. It is possible to do this by creating a custom Mesh using the Mesh Modelresource. We will examine how to use this Modelresource in Chapter 27, "Creating Meshes from Code." In that chapter, we will examine a technique to create terrain, which is essentially a surface plot.

Supplemental Resources

- V12: `http://www.integration.qc.ca/products/v12director/`

  V12 is a cross-platform database engine that supports the V12 database but can import data from Access, FoxPro, Excel, and Microsoft SQL

Server. Some encryption routines are built in to the engine, and overall it is a solid reliable system.

- Valentina: `http://www.paradigmasoft.com/product/v4md.html`

  Valentina is another cross-platform database engine that also has ports to several other development platforms, such as RealBasic, C++, and Director. It is a powerful solution that is worth exploring.

- SMUS and Multiuser Xtra: `http://www.macromedia.com`

  It is possible to use the Shockwave Multiuser server in conjunction with the Multiuser Xtra to build custom databases and a database management system of your own. The Shockwave Multiuser server currently runs on Macintosh and Windows machines.

- ColdFusion: `http://www.macromedia.com`

  ColdFusion was recently added to the Macromedia product line through a merger with Allaire. ColdFusion is a powerful database server that can run on a variety of platforms, including Linux, and can be integrated into your Director projects either through the Multiuser Xtra or through netLingo calls.

PART III

Interface Applications of Shockwave 3D

Perhaps one of the most challenging design problems of working with real-time 3D graphics is learning how to create effective interfaces that communicate their intent and method of use. Part III expands your understanding of the 3D environment by introducing several new design elements. In addition, we will examine practical solutions for common interface issues. Among these issues are methods of negotiating a two-dimensional mouse in a three-dimensional environment, advanced techniques for animating textures, and effective usage of the Camera as a dynamic component.

CHAPTER 12

Basic Control of Surfaces

Before I can accurately describe how to work with a surface, it is probably best to answer this question: What is a surface? The 3D environment we are working with utilizes Mesh-based surfaces. This means that the surfaces of Models are infinitely thin. Models in our environment are not solid geometry—nor are they simulated solid geometry. If you were to cut a sphere primitive in half, you would see that the inside is hollow. We are not used to this in the real world. If I hand you a wooden sphere with weight appropriate to its size, you would most likely expect that the sphere is solid wood. This is not the case in Director's 3D environment.

A good way to understand a Model is to imagine a box made of squares of paper, glued together at the corners. If you cut the paper box in half, it is hollow inside, and it is revealed that the surface of the box is actually "infinitely" thin.

The Models that we create are illusory; surfaces are simulated through the usage of Shaders and Textures. Shaders define the simulated effects of reflected light: For example, metal is shiny and glass is semi-transparent. Examples of Textures are the grain of wood and the patina of oxidized copper. For clarity, I use the term *surface* to refer to the net result of the Shaders and Textures that define how a Model reacts to light, and what physical material it appears to be constructed of.

Models, Shaders, and Textures

It is important to clearly understand that Models, Shaders, and Textures are created as separate Nodes. Each of these Nodes exist as separate code objects with properties of their own. Shader objects are assigned to the Shader property of a Model or Models; Texture objects are assigned to the Texture property of one or many Shader objects. This means that changes that you make to Shader and Texture objects will affect every Model that references those Shader and Texture objects. Figure 12.1 illustrates the relationship between Models, Shader objects, and Texture objects.

FIGURE 12.1

Shader objects are assigned to the Shader properties of Models; Texture objects are assigned to the Texture properties of Shader objects.

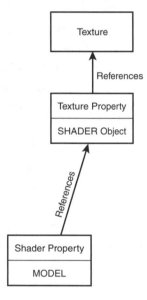

Because of the intricate relationship between these three Nodes, it is crucial that you do not confuse Model object properties with Shader object and Texture object properties. This can be especially difficult because the vocabulary that is used to refer to properties is similar to the names of the Nodes themselves. For example, the Model Node has a Shader property, to which Shader objects are assigned as the value of that property.

Model Properties

Control of the overall look of a surface begins with several Model properties. Table 12.1 lists the Model properties that are pertinent to the control of surfaces. These properties are used in conjunction with Shader and Texture object properties to define the final surface.

Table 12.1 Model Properties Pertaining to Surfaces

Model Property	Purpose
.Shaderlist	Linear list of Shaders attached to Model
.Shader	Shortcut to Shaderlist[1]
.visibility	Method of drawing the object

Shaderlist **and** Shader

The number of Shaders available to a Model is exactly equal to the number of Meshes that the Model has. When speaking of a Mesh or Meshes, I am referring to the Vertices (3D points) and Faces (plane segments) that comprise the geometry of a Model.

NOTE

When creating Modelresources with the newModelresource() function, you can specify the optional #facing parameter to control the number of Meshes created. This number cannot be changed once the Modelresource has been created.

The number of default Meshes that are created for primitive Modelresource types and the maximum number of Meshes that can be created for each of these types is compared in Table 12.2.

Table 12.2 Number of Meshes for Primitive Model Types

Primitive	Default Meshes	Maximum Meshes	Represents
#plane	2	2	Two sides
#box	6	12	Six sides in and out
#sphere	1	2	One side in and out
#cylinder	3	6	Three sides in and out
#particle	1	1	Only one-sided
#extruder	Varies—one Mesh for each letter extruded		

Each Mesh supports only one Shader at a time. To access which Shaders are applied to each Mesh of a Model, you can utilize the `Shaderlist` property. The `Shaderlist` property supports bracket access so that `Shaderlist[1]` gives access to the first Shader, `Shaderlist[2]` gives access to the second Shader, and so on.

NOTE

> Chapter 28, "Mesh Deformation and Detailed Picking," deals with the creation of custom Models. Custom Models are non-primitives created from code, with varying numbers of Meshes. In addition, any Models imported from 3D Modeling software may have any number of Meshes, and therefore any number of Shaders available.

The most concise example of a Model that has more than one Mesh is the #box primitive. By default, a #box has six Meshes—one for each side. Each Mesh has its own Shader, which means that each side of the #box can be treated as though it were created from a different material (one side made of metal, another side made of wood, and so on). A helpful function to find out how many Shaders are available to a given Model is

```
member("Castmember").Model("Modelname").Shaderlist.count()
```

The `Shaderlist.count()` function returns the number of Shaders available to a given Model. This information is vital because the `Shaderlist` is manipulated via bracket access as follows:

```
member("Castmember").Model("Modelname").Shaderlist[1]
```

Often, even though you have a Model with multiple Shaders, you might want each Shader assigned the same. Rather than accessing each Shader one at a time via bracket access, it is possible to reference all of a Model's Shaders at once by omitting the brackets as follows:

```
Member("Castmember").Model("Modelname").Shaderlist
```

Finally, because some Models have only one Shader available to them, it is often helpful to save a bit of typing with the following shortcut:

```
member("Castmember").Model("Modelname").Shader
```

This syntax is exactly equivalent to bracket access of item 1 on the `Shaderlist`.

Visibility

Model visibility is a unique property that deserves some attention. There are generally three situations in which it is used: semi-transparent objects, wire-frame objects, and with Models whose geometry has become corrupted. This chapter deals with the first two situations; Chapter 27 deals with geometry corruption.

Real-time 3D environments require a large amount of processor power to render with useful frame rates. The more efficiently a real-time engine can deal with the constant tasks of drawing objects on the screen, the more time there is for other code such as AI, game logic, keeping score, streaming media, playing audio, and so on. To free up more processor time, corners are cut as often as possible. One of the ways that a large amount of processor time can be recovered is by drawing only those faces of objects that are facing the camera. Imagine you have a sphere with 100 faces. If you have to draw only the 50 that are visible to the camera at once, you have split your processor load in half.

The visibility setting is related to performance optimization as well as surface control. It allows you to decide which Model faces will be drawn: those facing the camera (#front), those facing away from the camera (#back), all the faces (#both), or none of the faces (#none). There will be times when you want to draw #both faces, such as when creating semi-transparent objects. #back can be difficult to understand because it creates the optical illusion shown in Figure 12.2—it looks like the box is upside down, but really it is inside out.

FIGURE 12.2

Examples of a sphere and cube rendered with visibility set to #front, #back, #none, and #both, respectively. Note that #none is not visible, and that at this point, because #both enables visibility on the front and back of the 3D Model it is impossible to see this effect in the 2D illustration without using this setting in conjunction with others, such as Model.Shader.blend.

Shaders

You have worked with Shaders and Textures before, but you have not examined them in depth. Understanding the relationship between a Shader and a Texture is critical to creating surfaces for your objects. As with Models and Modelresources, Shaders are code-based objects. The purpose of a Shader is to provide a method of drawing the surfaces of a Model. The purpose of a Texture is to provide a method of applying a bitmap to the surface of a Model.

Several types of Shaders are built in to Director, but the most common is the #standard Shader. This Shader is designed for the creation and implementation of photorealistic surfaces. Of the built-in Shader types, the #standard Shader is the only one that utilizes Textures. Throughout this chapter, you are dealing with the properties of the #standard Shader. Chapter 15 deals entirely with non-photorealistic rendering methods.

To create convincing surfaces, it is necessary to examine several Shader properties that are often overlooked. These Shader properties pertain to how an object absorbs and reflects light.

Standard Shader Properties

Table 12.3 details the basic #standard Shader properties. In general, these properties provide a wide range of control over the surfaces that you create. Chapter 14, "Multitexturing," examines the advanced #standard Shader properties, which are used for multitexturing techniques.

Table 12.3 Standard Shader Properties

Property	Format	Default
Ambient	rgb(R,G,B)	rgb(63,63,63)
Diffuse	rgb(R,G,B)	rgb(255,255,255)
Specular	rgb(R,G,B)	rgb(255,255,255)
Shininess	0–100	30
Emissive	rgb(R,G,B)	rgb(0,0,0)
Blend	0–100	100
Transparent	Boolean	True
Renderstyle	#fill, #wire, or #point	#fill
Flat	Boolean	False
Texture	Texture code object	"defaultTexture"
UsediffusewithTexture	Boolean	False

Ambient, Diffuse, and Specular

The Ambient, Diffuse, and Specular properties of the #standard Shader are responsible for producing realistic highlights, mid-tones, and shadow areas on an object. These three parameters define what colors of light will be reflected from an object. Remember that you encountered these terms when dealing with lighting—it is no accident that these properties are controlled at the Shader level. The Ambient, Diffuse, and Specular properties essentially define how the surface of a Model reacts to the light that hits the Model's surface. Figure 12.3 illustrates how and where the effects of the Ambient, Diffuse, and Specular properties are expressed on a Model.

FIGURE 12.3

The effects of Ambient, Diffuse, and Specular properties are expressed on a Model.

Highlight (specular)

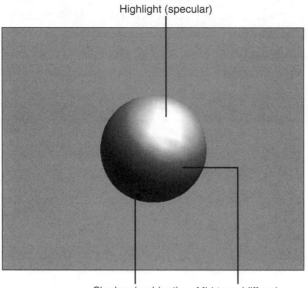

Shadow (ambient)   Mid-tone (diffuse)

Of the three properties, Diffuse is the easiest to understand. In essence, the Diffuse property defines the color of the object. However, this is not enough information to understand how to control a surface. To accurately understand how to control a surface, you need to know how the lights in your scene are going to react with the Diffuse property. This is because surfaces are not created through one Shader property; they are created through a conjunction of several Shader properties and the lights in the scene.

Figure 12.4 illustrates a scene in which a Model's Shader property has a Diffuse setting of green, and is being struck by white light. In this example, all the light that is not green is absorbed by the surface, and all the available light that is green is reflected by the surface. The end result is that the Model appears green.

Figure 12.5 illustrates a similar scene; however, the key difference is that the light color is now blue-green. The Model absorbs all the available non-green light. Because the light color does not contain enough green light to reflect the true color of the object, the color of the object appears dull.

FIGURE 12.4

White light hitting a green object.

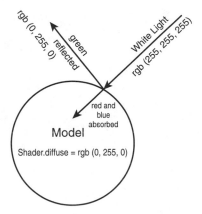

FIGURE 12.5

Blue-green light hitting a green object.

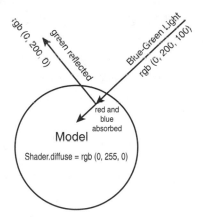

Figure 12.6 illustrates the same scene, this time with the green object struck by magenta light. In this situation, remember that pure magenta light contains no green. Because the object can reflect only green light, the object appears black. This is why it is important to understand that although the Diffuse property contributes to the final color of a surface, it does not determine it.

FIGURE 12.6

Magenta light hitting a green object.

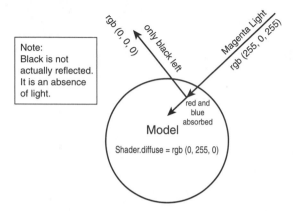

From your observations of the Diffuse property, your understanding of the Ambient and Specular properties should be much clearer. Remember that a general ambient light node color level was set, and it was suggested that this color not be absolute black or absolute white. The reason for this is that the color of the ambient light node in a scene contributes to an often-overlooked area of a Model: the shaded area of Models. The Ambient property of the #standard Shader can reflect light only if ambient light is hitting the Model. If you choose an ambient light color of black, no matter what you do to the Ambient Shader property, you will not see a reaction.

In the real world, the shaded areas on an object are defined by the color of the object, and the light that hits the object contributes to the color of the shaded areas as well. However, because the ambient light level affects all Models in the scene evenly, it is often difficult to choose a good color for the ambient light. One strategy is to choose a very dark, non-black color such as rgb(50,50,50). Then you set the Ambient Shader property to a darker shade of the Model's color. This will at least create shaded areas on the Model that are similar to the mid-tone areas of the Model.

Finally, the Specular setting provides a method of controlling the color of the specular highlight on a Model. Changing this setting will have no effect if there are no light nodes in the scene with their Specular property set to true. A general guide to setting the Shader Specular color is that nonmetallic shiny surfaces should have a white Specular color. Metallic shiny surfaces should have a Specular color that is similar to the Diffuse setting, but much brighter.

Several strategies of determining settings for the Ambient, Diffuse, and Specular properties are discussed near the end of this chapter in the "Surface Techniques" section.

Shininess

The Specular property for Shaders allows you to set the color of the specular highlight; the Shininess property allows you to set its size. The concept that underlies how the Specular property works can be explained with the following example. Imagine that you have a Model with a Diffuse value of rgb(0,255,0) green. Let us also say that this Model has a Specular value of rgb(255,255,255) white. This Model is struck by a directional light colored rgb(255,255,255), as illustrated in Figure 12.7.

FIGURE 12.7

A green object with a white highlight struck by white light.

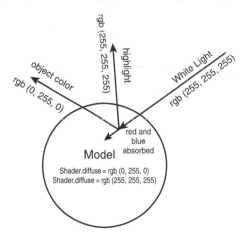

Figure 12.7 illustrates that some of the white light that strikes the Model will be immediately reflected and some white light will be absorbed. The areas of the Model that immediately reflect the white light will create areas of highlight. The areas that absorb some of the light absorb all but the green value of the light; therefore, you see a green-colored object with a white highlight. The key to the size of the highlight is controlling what percentage of the light

striking the Model is immediately reflected as a highlight, and what percentage is absorbed.

The acceptable values for the Shininess property are between 0–100, but in light of the concept outlined earlier, the effect that these values produce can be deceptive. The higher the Shininess value, the smaller the specular highlight will be. With a Shininess value of 100, a Model will have a tiny, moderately crisp highlight. This might seem like an inconsistency, but it is not.

The shinier an object is, the smaller its specular highlight should be. Metallic objects are characterized by a tiny, crisp highlight. They also are characterized by reflections of the environment contained in the mid-tone areas of their surface—but Shininess does not deal with these reflections. They must be handled differently, and are discussed in Chapter 14. Models with a low Shininess property setting have very large highlights; values of 1–10 produce extreme results. Be aware of this if you set values for Shininess in this range.

Setting the Shininess to a value of 0 is a special case. It produces a surface with no specular highlight at all. Figure 12.8 illustrates the relationship between the value of the Shininess property and the size of the specular highlight.

FIGURE 12.8

Note how a value of 0 produces no highlight, whereas a value of 1 produces a very large highlight.

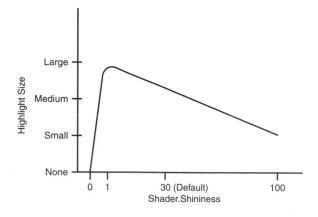

A surface without a specular highlight is often referred to as a *matte surface*. Creating believable matte surfaces through a combination of Shader properties is discussed near the end of this chapter in the "Surface Techniques" section.

Emissive

The Emissive property is used to simulate the effect of a glowing surface. This does not cause the surface to actually emit light, but it causes the surface to become dramatically brighter. It also has the effect of eliminating shaded areas on the Model and, eventually, all mid-tone regions of an Model. At the highest settings, Emissive visually flattens the geometry of a Model.

The Emissive property is by default set to rgb(0,0,0) black. With this setting, the surface does not appear to emit any light. With a setting of rgb(255,255,255) white, the Model appears to have no geometry. The Emissive property is useful when expressing a localized light source in a scene, such as a lamp. It also can be carefully used in conjunction with the creation of matte surfaces. Both of these are discussed in the "Surface Techniques" section at the end of this chapter.

Blend and Transparent

The Transparent Shader property is a Boolean value that determines whether the Blend setting for the Model is ignored. When Transparent is set to true, the Model has the capability of becoming semi-transparent. The Blend property is similar to the blend property for Sprites. It accepts a value between 0–100, where 0 is entirely transparent and 100 is entirely opaque. Creating believable semi-transparent objects takes some tweaking, and certainly calls for the use of several properties in conjunction with one another. I try to plan situations in which the areas of semi-transparency will "look through" to generally dark areas or relatively neutral areas. The strongest way to create the look of semi-transparency is to utilize diffused colors for the object that are identical to the background color.

In addition, I recommend experimenting with various levels of blend in conjunction with altering the settings of `Model.visibility`. Figure 12.9 illuminates the difference between a semi-transparent object whose `Model.visibility` is set to #front, and one that has been set to #both.

FIGURE 12.9

Transparent objects with Model.visibility *set to #front, and with* Model.visibility *set to #both.*

Notice how with Model.visibility set to #both and a Shader.blend less than 100, you can see through the object—but you can also see the opposite side of the object. This helps to visually distinguish the boundaries of the object, while still allowing you to see through it.

Renderstyle

Shader.renderstyle is a helpful property that allows you to switch between three modes of drawing your Model: #fill, #wire, and #point. The #fill setting is the default, and by now you are accustomed to its result: The Model's Mesh is filled in and shaded, such that the Model appears to be a solid object. The #wire setting is used when you want to draw the object in wireframe mode so that you can see the geometry of the Model. The last mode, ##point, takes this one step further so that the only geometric elements drawn are the vertices of a Model's Mesh. Figure 12.10 illustrates all three modes.

Shader.renderstyle and Model.visibility can produce useful effects when used in conjunction with one another. Figure 12.11 compares two Models, both using wireframe Renderstyle, but the left Model has a setting of Model.visibility = #both. Figure 12.11 illustrates that it is possible to see through the wireframe to the backside of the object.

FIGURE 12.10

#fill, #wire, and #point.

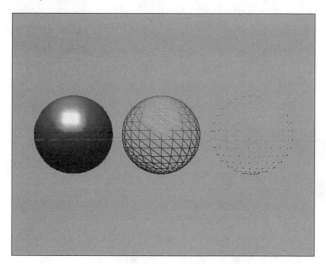

FIGURE 12.11

#wire mode Renderstyle comparison between `Model.visibility` *= #both and* `Model.visibility` *= #front.*

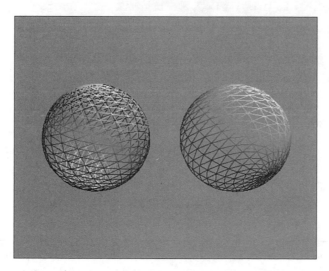

Flat

Flat is a Boolean property that determines whether the individual Faces of a Mesh will be shaded smoothly (with Gouraud shading) or with flat shading.

The default for Shader.flat is false. When set to true, objects that were previously smooth, such as spheres, will appear faceted. In terms of performance, there is a minor boost when using flat shading—but I do not recommend the sacrifice in visual quality for performance reasons. Flat shading is helpful when attempting to Model faceted objects or objects whose surface is not smooth. Figure 12.12 illustrates the visual difference between smooth and flat shading.

FIGURE 12.12

Gouraud shading versus flat shading.

Texture Object Versus Texture Property

Texture is both a property of the #standard Shader, and a code object created from a bitmap Castmember via Lingo (or imported with a .w3d Castmember).

NOTE

The creation of Textures is one of the largest areas for performance and download optimization. Please see Chapters 19, "Performance Optimization," and 20, "Download Optimization," to learn about effective techniques for Texture optimization.

To create a Texture object from a bitmap Castmember so that it can be assigned to a surface, use the following code:

```
member("Castmember").newTexture("name", #fromCastmember, member("Castmem
➥ber"))
```

This allows you to assign the Texture object as the value of a Shader's Texture property. The assignment process can be accomplished as follows:

```
Member("Castmember").Shader[x].Texture =
member("Castmember").Texture("name")
```

The Texture property of the #standard Shader is a shortcut for referencing the first Texture of a Shader. Chapter 14 examines how to utilize multiple Textures.

NOTE

When a Texture is created from a bitmap Castmember, that Texture is an image of how the bitmap currently looks. If the bitmap that a Texture is based on is updated later in the course of a movie, the Texture does not change.

Because the Texture object and the Texture property are two separate items, you must first learn about them separately.

Texture Object

There are three methods of bringing image data into the 3D environment of Director for use as Textures:

- Creating Textures from Castmembers with `newTexture()`
- Creating Textures from Lingo image objects with `newTexture()`
- Importing Textures exported as .w3d files from 3D software

This chapter is primarily concerned with the creation of Textures from bitmap Castmembers. Chapter 17, "Special Effects," discusses the creation of Textures from image objects, and Chapter 9, "Working with Prebuilt Scenes and Behaviors," explains the concepts surrounding the importation of .w3d scenes.

Figure 12.13 compares the original bitmap Castmember that was used to create a Texture object, and what that Texture object looks like when applied to a Model in the 3D environment.

FIGURE 12.13

A bitmap Castmember compared with the Texture created from that Castmember applied to a Model.

By default, a Texture stretches to the size of the Model. There are several recommendations when making Texture maps. First, try to keep the aspect ratio of the Texture map similar to the final usage. For example, if you are going to place the Texture on a rectangular object, make sure that the Texture is rectangular. Second, the size of the Texture (in pixels) will be determined by two factors: speed and download versus quality. Large Textures adversely affect performance, but they look very good. It is your job to find out how small you can get a Texture while still getting the correct amount of detail out of the bitmap.

NOTE

See Chapter 19 for performance issues dealing with Textures, such as a discussion of the `scaledown()` function, "powers of 2," Mip-mapping, and Nearfiltering.

Texture Property of the #standard Shader

The Texture property accepts a Texture object as its value. If you try to assign a Texture that does not exist, you will get an error. At its most basic, Texture mapping allows you to place images on the surface of your objects.

The Shader properties that we have looked at have all contributed directly to the simulation of the absorptive and reflective qualities of light. By default, the Texture property overrides the surface color set with `Shader.Diffuse`. When using Textures to develop realistic surfaces, I recommend that you examine the Shader property UsediffusewithTexture. This property is a Boolean that determines whether the current Texture should be influenced by the `Shader.Diffuse` color. White and neutral areas of the Texture will fade toward the Diffuse color when this property is set to true. It allows you to avoid areas of pure white in your Textures, but leaves a bit of the overall surface color as if that color were bounced off the white.

Finally, Textures that contain alpha-channel information will create surfaces that are transparent. The `Shader.transparent` property controls whether the Texture object is rendered with transparency. You can utilize alpha-channel information to modify the look of geometry. See Chapter 14 for information on opacity mapping techniques.

Seven Steps for Creating a Basic Surface (Demo)

We have examined the properties of Models, Shaders, and Textures that are pertinent to the creation of basic realistic surfaces. This demonstration is intended to give a hands-on explanation of how to create a surface. Refer to the Basic Shader Demo on the CD to see the code in action. There are several steps involved in this process, which are as follows:

1. Create new Shader object of the appropriate type
2. Assign ambient color property for the Shader object
3. Assign diffuse color property for the Shader object
4. Assign specular color property for the Shader object
5. Create new Texture object referencing a Castmember

6. Assign Texture object to Texture property of the Shader object

7. Assign Shader object to Shader property of the Model

Listing 12.1 is set up as a custom handler that can be called from any script, as well as from the message window.

LISTING 12.1   Texturize Custom Handler

```
1:on texturize scene, obj, ntext, nshade, sAmb, sDiff, sSpec
2:  -- type casting, making sure that the arguments passed are valid
3:
4:  --check scene argument -- name of shockwave 3d Castmember to work on
5:  -- exit script if the argument scene does not refer to a sw3d Castmember
6:  if member(scene).type <> #shockwave3d then return false
7:  -- if scene argument is indeed a valid sw3d
8:  -- then modify the variable so that it will reduce typing later
9:  scene = member(scene)
10:
11: --check obj argument -- name of Model to texturize
12: -- this line checks to see if there is indeed a Model
13: -- named obj in the scene, if not it jumps out of the handler
14: if ilk(scene.Model(obj), #Model) <> true then return false
15:
16: --check ntext argument -- name of bitmap Castmember to turn into Texture
17: -- this line checks to make sure that ntext refers to
18: -- a bitmap cast member, if not it jumps out of the handler
19: temptype = member(ntext).type
20: if temptype <> #bitmap then return false
21:
22: -- check nshade argument
23: -- if a Shader named nshade exists jump out of the handler
24: if ilk(scene.Shader(nshade), #Shader) then return false
25:
26: -- check sAmb, sDiff & sSpec
27: -- if any one of these is not a color, then jump out of the handler.
28: if ilk(sAmb, #color) <> true then return false
29: if ilk(sDiff, #color) <> true then return false
30: if ilk(sSpec, #color) <> true then return false
31:
32: --if we have made it this far in the handler we are ready
33: --to create the Shader, set up its default values
34: --to create the Texture, apply it to the Shader
35: --to apply the Shader to the object
36:
37: --create a Shader named nshade in Castmember scene
```

LISTING 12.1   Continued

```
38:  theNewShader = scene.newShader(nshade, #standard)
39:  --set the ambient, diffuse, and specular colors
40:  theNewShader.ambient = sAmb
41:  theNewShader.diffuse = sDiff
42:  theNewShader.specular = sSpec
43:
44:  -- one last check to see if ntext is already a Texture in the world
45:  -- if it already exists as a Texture, just keep going,
46:  -- if it does not exist as a Texture, create it as a Texture.
47:  if ilk(scene.Texture(ntext), #Texture)  = false then
48:    theNewTexture = scene.newTexture(ntext, #fromCastmember, member(ntext))
49:  end if
50:
51:  -- apply the new Texture to the new Shader's first Texture layer
52:  theNewShader.Texture = theNewTexture
53:
54:  -- apply the new Shader to all of the available Shaders of the Model obj
55:  scene.Model(obj).Shaderlist = thenewShader
56:end
```

The method for calling this handler is described in the file on the CD, and I will also describe it here. The custom handler texturize() requires six arguments. It is called with the syntax:

```
texturize(scene, obj, ntext, nshade, sAmb, sDiff, sSpec)
```

Table 12.4 lists the arguments of the Texturize Custom Handler and explains what values are expected for each argument.

Table 12.4   Arguments of the texturize() Custom Handler

Argument	Expected Value
scene	The name of the Shockwave 3D Castmember
obj	The name of the Model to "Texturize"
ntext	The name of the bitmap to turn into a Texture
nshade	The name of the Shader to create
sAmb	The rgb color value for Shader.ambient
sDiff	The rgb color value for Shader.diffuse
sSpec	The rgb color value for Shader.specular

The demo file includes several bitmaps that can be turned into Textures and applied to the sphere very quickly. Make sure that you play the movie, and while the movie is running, type the following into the message window and press Return:

```
texturize("test", "sphere", "water", "wShader", rgb(10,30,100), /
rgb(10,50,100), rgb(200,200,250))
```

This line creates a Texture object called "water" and a Shader object named "wShader." It assigns the Texture object ("water") as the value for the Texture property of the Shader object ("wShader") and then applies the Shader object ("wShader") to the Shader property of the Model named "sphere."

NOTE

Stopping the playback of the movie will destroy the Shader ("wShader") and will prevent code from functioning as expected. While working through the examples in this section, make sure that you are entering code in the message window during a single contiguous session of movie playback.

Try changing some of the other Shader properties from the message window:

```
Scene.Shader("wShader").emissive = rgb(150,150,150)
Scene.Shader("wShader").blend = 50
```

Or try changing some of the Model properties:

```
Scene.Model[1].visibility = #both
```

The `texturize()` custom handler can be expanded or simplified as you need. One particular note that you should be aware of is that new #standard Shaders have a default Texture applied. This default Texture looks like a white-and-pink checkerboard. If you want to create a new Shader that does not use a Texture, you must remember to set `Shader.Texture = void`. By doing this, you will remove any Texture object that was applied to the Texture property of a given Shader object. In the case of a new Shader, this will remove the default Texture object that looks like a white-and-pink checkerboard.

Surface Techniques

In this section, I want to address strategies for developing specific surface types. The values that I suggest are a starting point and you will need to tweak the values depending on your specific situation. These examples assume that you have an ambient light color of rgb(80,80,80) as well as other lighting sources, at least one of which with its Specular property set to true.

Matte Surfaces

FIGURE 12.14

An example of a matte surface; refer to CD for a color version of this image.

Matte surfaces are those that do not have a specular highlight (see Figure 12.14). Although you might refer to them as dull as opposed to shiny, it is often difficult to create matte surfaces that are realistic rather than very flat. Here are some suggestions for creating a gray matte surface. Of particular importance is that you set the shininess to 0, but also notice the Emissive setting. Even though they are not shiny, matte surfaces tend to have an extremely faint glow to them.

- `Shader.ambient` = rgb(160,160,160)
- `Shader.diffuse` = rgb(128,128,128)

- Shader.emissive = rgb(15,15,15)
- Shader.Shininess = 0
- Shader.Texture = void

Shiny Non-Metals

FIGURE 12.15

An example of a shiny non-metal surface; refer to the CD for a color version of this image.

Shiny non-metal materials tend to have a large specular highlight (see Figure 12.15). Try to set your Shininess property below 40 and above 5 to keep the highlight size believable. Also note that the Specular property is set to absolute white. I recommend not changing this; one characteristic of non-metallic surfaces is that their specular highlight is white. Finally, note how dark the ambient color is in respect to the diffuse color.

- Shader.ambient = rgb(60, 60, 60)
- Shader.diffuse = rgb(128,128,128)
- Shader.Specular = rgb(255,255,255)
- Shader.Shininess = 20
- Shader.Texture = void

Shiny Metals

FIGURE 12.16

Example of a shiny metal surface; refer to the CD for a color version of this image.

Metals are characteristically very shiny, and therefore have a small specular highlight (see Figure 12.16). Also, the specular highlight of a metal tends to be a lighter shade of the diffuse color. Chapter 14 discusses how to create reflections as well, which will aid in creating believable metal surfaces.

- `Shader.ambient` = rgb(10,10,10)
- `Shader.diffuse` = rgb(75,10,10)
- `Shader.specular` = rgb(150,20,20)
- `Shader.Shininess` = 60
- `Shader.Texture` = void

Semi-Transparent Objects

Transparency works very well in Director (see Figure 12.17). However, keep in mind that there is no built-in way to easily simulate the refraction of light through materials. The success of a semi-transparent object is dependent on the background color of the camera. I feel that the best results are achieved when the background color is the same as the diffuse color of the Shader. Unfortunately, this is not always possible because you might not be able to see the background at all if you have built an inclusive environment.

- `Model.visibility` = #both
- `Shader.ambient` = rgb(100,100,100)
- `Shader.diffuse` = rgb(80,80,80)
- `Shader.blend` = 50
- `Shader.Shininess` = 100
- `Shader.Texture` = void

FIGURE 12.17

Example of a semi-transparent surface; refer to the CD for a color version of this image.

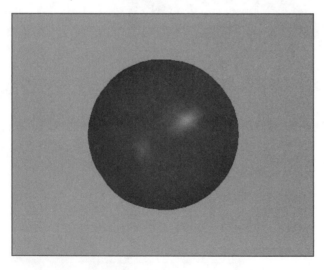

Glowing Light Sources

The Emissive property of Shaders can be used to create surfaces that appear to emit light. When used in conjunction with a light source, the effect can be quite convincing (see Figure 12.18). In terms of the surface for the light, try to choose an emissive color that is similar to the light color. The following example works for an amber light.

- Shader.ambient = rgb(100,100,100)
- Shader.diffuse = rgb(255,255,255)
- Shader.emissive = rgb(250,180,50)
- Shader.Shininess = 0
- Shader.Texture = void

FIGURE 12.18

An example of a glowing light source surface; refer to the CD for a color version of this image.

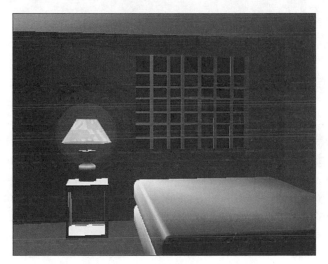

Figure 12.19 demonstrates another technique for creating glowing objects. Create several clones of the glowing Model and scale them successively larger. By setting each these copies very transparent, you can simulate the effect of atmosphere. Try setting the background color to a color similar to the glow color to make it look like the object is luminous.

FIGURE 12.19

An example of a glowing Model with atmospheric effect; refer to the CD for a color version of this image.

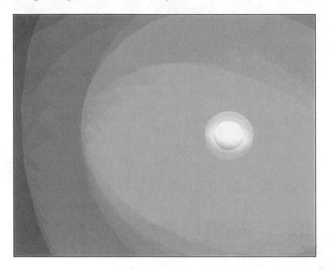

Summary

The surface of an object is the result of a combination of three elements: Models, Shaders, and Textures. Each of these elements contains properties that affect the final outcome of the surface of a given object. Realistic surfaces begin at the Model level, but are most heavily influenced at the Shader level. Many times Textures are overused because they can cover up a misunderstanding of what the Shader properties are meant to do. Do not overlook the Shader properties, especially if photorealism is your goal. Textures do not have many properties, and the ones that they do have deal mostly with performance optimization.

FAQ

I want to make animated Textures. Is this possible?

Yes. Chapter 17 explains animated Textures. There are several procedures for this technique.

Can I create tiling Textures or decal Textures?

Yes. Chapter 14 explains how to create Textures that tile over the surface of an object, as well as how to create decals (Textures that appear once on an object).

You mentioned that I could use Lingo image objects as Textures?

Yes, this is explained in Chapter 17.

What is (and can I use) opacity mapping?

Opacity mapping is the ability to create Textures that modulate the opacity of a 3D object. It is possible to create opacity maps, and this is discussed in Chapter 14.

What is (and can I use) bump mapping and displacement mapping?

Bump mapping utilizes the luminosity information in an image to distort the surface of an object so that the geometry looks as though it has bumps or ridges on it. *Displacement mapping* is very similar, except that it does actually change the geometry. Unfortunately, neither of these is currently supported in Director.

What are (and can I use) reflection maps?

Reflection maps are a visual trick that simulates the reflection of an environment on a surface Texture; they are very helpful when creating metals. Yes, Director supports reflection maps, and this is examined in Chapter 14.

Does Director support multiple Textures?

Yes, the Texture layers are discussed in Chapter 14.

Supplemental Resources

The following is a list of online, book, and software resources that can help with the creation of Textures.

Online Texture Resources

```
http://www.3dcafe.com/asp/textures.asp
```

3d Café has many free Textures, as well as resources for purchasing CDs of Textures.

```
http://www.turbosquid.com/
```

Turbosquid is a very good commercial resource for both Textures and Models.

Technique Books

Jeremy Birn: *Digital Lighting & Rendering*, New Riders ISBN 1-56205-954-8

Birn's book contains information about creating Textures and examines how they interact with lighting. It does not center on any one package, so the techniques he mentions are applicable to many situations.

3D Texture Software

Deep Paint

Deep Paint is a powerful painting tool that many 3D artists use to develop Textures. It is particularly good at painting with Textures. In addition, it is capable of importing Models from 3D software and allows you to paint Textures directly onto the surface of your Models.

MeshPaint

MeshPaint is another 3D painting tool that allows you to paint directly onto objects imported from 3D Modeling software.

Painter and Painter 3D

Painter is a powerful natural-media paint tool that takes full advantage of pressure-sensitive tablets. The brushes are realistic and convincing and customizable. In addition, there is a similar version of Painter (Painter 3D) that allows you to import 3D Models and paint directly on them.

Lightscape

Unlike the other tools listed here, Lightscape is not a paint tool, nor is it used only for creating Textures. Lightscape creates both photorealistic and photo-accurate data. It utilizes actual physical information about the objects in your scene to create a real-time rendering of the lighting in your scene. Lightscape contains a tool called Mesh-to-Texture, which allows you to take the high-quality real-time rendering from Lightscape, and create Texture maps for your environments from it.

CHAPTER 13

A 2D Mouse in a 3D World

This chapter explores a subset of 3D Lingo known as *Picking Lingo*—Lingo that can be used to develop how the mouse interacts with Models and to determine the location of the mouse in the 3D environment. This chapter also covers several issues that affect the development of 3D environments; specifically, learning how to design the method of user interaction with your interfaces.

3D Interface Design Challenges

The most common input device you will be designing your environments for is the mouse. The mouse provides two coordinates of information to the computer and translates those coordinates onto the screen. When personal computers became available in the late 70s and early 80s, emphasis was focused on familiarizing users with the relationship between the 2D mouse and the 2D screen.

Since then, we have come to hold basic assumptions about what users will know about how to interact with our interfaces. This has made the task of designing a 2D interface seem fairly straightforward. Over the past 30 years, a complex vocabulary of visual signifiers has developed. Once learned, these signifiers guide users toward accomplishing tasks with software by manipulating the software interface.

Among the visual vocabulary, you will recognize the terms that refer to these signifiers: rollovers, buttons, sliders, check boxes, radio buttons, and even windows and menus. Coders usually refer to these as *widgets*. These 2D widget types have had decades of development and refinement. I cannot imagine a

GUI-based operating system without at least some variation on all these items. Although these widgets can be translated into the 3D environment, much of their familiarity is lost; therefore, the expectations for these translations tend to outweigh the reality.

A majority of users have not interfaced with a real-time 3D application via a mouse. Rather, the average user has probably interfaced with real-time 3D environments either through games played on the personal computer or on standalone entertainment systems. With an entertainment system, the interface is manipulated through dedicated and specialized devices such as joysticks and game pads. These devices and interfaces have their own vocabulary.

In terms of games played on personal computers, players have a wide variety of input choices, including joysticks, game pads, steering wheels, pedals, and thrusters, in addition to the mouse and keyboard. Although this does include a very large number of individuals, there is no standard language of design for interaction with 3D environments. In this case, we lack the 30-year history of experiments, failures, and successes associated with commercial interface design for 2D software.

What we do not lack is a broader, much older history of working with reality; we understand 3D space because we live in it. Therefore, we should take inspiration for the design of interaction from the world around us. At some point, you learned how to use a fork, cup, pencil, book, and so on. You do not need to relearn these things—the same way that you do not need to relearn how to use a scroll bar. In short, the difficulty of interface design for 3D environments is that your users will need to learn the signifiers of interaction as well as the visual language.

Although this may seem like a small issue, the overall success of 3D on the Web or anywhere else will rely on the user's ability to learn how to interact. If it is perceived that it is difficult to interact with a 3D environment, it will become impossible to convince average users to look at real-time 3D projects. For this reason alone, this issue should be considered critical.

3D Interface Design Solutions

The key difficulty of designing a 3D interface is that we need an input device that can negotiate three dimensions—the mouse can only negotiate two.

Normally, your mouse moves in two dimensions, which are translated on to the screen as horizontal and vertical coordinates. Working with three dimensions demands as many as six unique types of control: x/y coordinates, y/z coordinates, z/x coordinates, and control of rotation around the X, Y, and Z axes. This type of control is often referred to as having "six degrees of freedom."

Meta Keys

One design solution to this problem has been to implement the use of meta keys and meta-key combinations. You are probably most familiar with the names of meta-keys, such as Shift, Ctrl, Command, Alt, and so on. Meta-keys change the significance of the other input—whether that means keyboard keys, mouse buttons, or mouse coordinates.

In practice, it is possible to use any key or key combination on the computer as a meta-key, but the choices that Lingo allows us to use are Shift, Ctrl or Command, and Option or Alt. You can also combine meta-keys to generate a wider range of combinations. The meta-key combinations modify the method of translating coordinate information from the mouse.

NOTE

When the keyboard interface was first introduced, some systems had very large numbers of meta-keys; those systems were difficult to learn and use because the keyboard interface had too many complexities, too many combinations.

Although keyboard/mouse combinations can be cumbersome, with time they can be learned. Unfortunately, there are no standards; therefore, users need to learn and adapt to keyboard/mouse combinations for each project they look at.

A variation on meta-keys that is used to increase the number of unique controls relies on the use of a two-button mouse. In this approach, the meta-keys are present on one input device, allowing for single-handed control of the environment. Although this is a step in the right direction, for cross-platform delivery, this type of strategy is not an option.

Total Keyboard Control

Another possibility is to control the environment entirely from the keyboard. This has many advantages because the large number of input keys can represent all of the six unique controls we would like from our input device. The problem with this solution is that the keyboard was made for typing, and it's optimized as such. The rows of keys are staggered, and you cannot rely on your users always having a number pad.

The keyboard is a binary input device; conceptually, each key can only speak the words "on" and "off." Gradients of input are required for controlling aspects of interaction, such as velocity, acceleration, and gesture. This solution requires that the user learn how to remap his understanding of keys on the keyboard so that gradations of input are equated with duration or rhythm.

Many times when using a solution like this, you might want one key to represent a gas pedal (the longer you hold it, the faster you go). You might then need another two keys to represent turning left and turning right (the longer you hold the key, the more toward left or right you go). Depending on your key choices, this may be difficult for Director because it can sometimes become confused when dealing with multiple, persistent keyboard inputs. Even if you can overcome these obstacles, you are still limited by the trappings of a tool optimized for typing. The mouse excels as an input device because it visually expresses gestures and verbs.

3D Widgets

One method of approaching the 3D interface is to design universal 3D widgets in the style of classical 2D widgets. Essentially, *widgets* are the visual elements that we manipulate with the mouse. We grab, drag, drop, click, double-click, slide, and otherwise "fiddle" with widgets in order to elicit some response from the computer.

Translating successful 2D tools into the 3D environment does not always work. Some of the more traditional types of widgets, such as scrollbars, make for difficult translations. Others, such as buttons, have more immediate and successful translations but lack a sense of conceptual depth, considering that buttons are a 3D concept that was translated to make 2D interfaces easier to understand. Still, many designs seem drawn to the success of 2D widgets, and perhaps there is some lesson that can be learned from them.

The most important lesson that we can glean from widgets is the way that the user learns to expect how the system will react. Essentially, within an operating system or an application, the widgets used are very similar if not exactly similar. When the user learns how to use a scrollbar or a button, he has learned how to use all scrollbars or all buttons. Rather than forcing users to learn overtly complex patterns of manipulation, widgets allow the user to manipulate different ranges of data by manipulating concise visual elements. Each element relates to a different range of data: scrollbars deal with a linear range of data, buttons deal with Boolean data, and so on. Elements should be able to react to each other, and in this way a complex language of interaction can be built.

2D Dashboard

A common method of designing a 3D interface essentially avoids having a 3D interface. Rather, with the 2D dashboard, traditional 2D controls such as sliders and buttons are used to manipulate the 3D environment. This approach is quite successful because users do not need to learn how to interact with the 3D interface. It is a good solution because users can immediately control your 3D environment through recognizable tools; it is good for projects where you want the user to have precise control over the environment or to feel conceptually removed from the environment. This particular approach is used in several of the demos throughout this book—particularly any of the demos of the "laboratory" variety. Still, what this solution lacks is the immersive qualities of interaction with a 3D environment that create captivating experiences for the user.

Intuitive Solutions

The classic solutions for transforming 2D mouse input for the 3D world create as many problems as they solve. It may seem that the only viable solution for intuitive input that remains is to utilize custom devices. Although this is an interesting possibility, it is beyond the scope of this book. Also, a dedicated nonstandard device will not be available to a vast majority of computer users by definition. If you can control the immediate environment of your project, such as a kiosk or an installation, you should consider this as a possible solution. At the end of this chapter is a list of resources for uncommon input devices.

At minimum, your users will have a mouse that can move in two directions, with one button. If we limit our solution to a single-handed input device with one-button manipulation, our strategy will be extremely inclusive. In order to derive a range of control, we must closely examine the three values of input from the mouse: horizontal motion, vertical motion, and the mouse click.

What Does Horizontal and Vertical Motion Signify?

Generally when moving the physical mouse horizontally and vertically with our hands, we expect that the graphic representation of the mouse will move horizontally and vertically as well. When we begin working with 3D, because there is a third dimension, often moving the mouse vertically is used to signify "in and out" of the screen. In addition, generally the movements of the physical mouse and the graphic mouse are thought of as existing on a rectilinear Cartesian grid. Later in this chapter is a section where we will also be dealing with how to convert mouse movements into polar coordinates.

What Does Clicking Signify?

Traditionally, clicking the mouse has several different meanings, the most common of which is an affirmative gesture. The double-click has an associated meaning of the double affirmation. Coupled with moving the mouse, clicking can signify grabbing, dragging, and rotating, among other expressions. The critical issue here is that the mouse is a visual tool that allows us to manipulate items on the screen. For this reason, the mouse and the click have come to signify an extension of the hand placed onto the desktop. Rather than manipulating through words, the action is more immediate—you point, you click.

Because so much in the 3D world is about the recognition of spatial relationships, what if proximity was equated with an affirmative action? Or rather, what if proximity led to gradations of affirmation?

Other possibilities include taking advantage of the click velocity. Double-clicking versus single-clicking is a perfect example of utilizing the rhythm and velocity of the click to signify multiple levels of input through a single button. What if the first click signifies an affirmation and the second click modulates the method of how that affirmation is enacted?

Introduction to Picking Lingo

The mouse button confers a Boolean state: on or off. The position of the mouse can be quantified as the resultant of two directions: X/Y. Because we will be dealing with describing locations in the 3D environment using `vector(x,y,z)` coordinates, I will refer to the horizontal and vertical space that the mouse moves in as the H/V plane for clarity. This basic principle is illustrated in Figure 13.1.

FIGURE 13.1

Relationship between the mouse's H/V plane and the coordinates of the Director Stage.

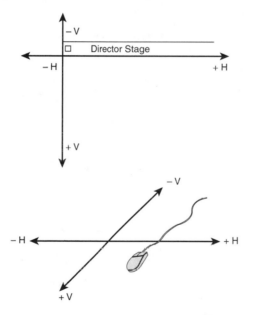

Methods of working with the 2D mouse in the 2D environment of Director usually concentrate on `mouseup/mousedown` handlers and `mouseloc` coordinates. Many Lingo elements deal with the mouse that have existed long before 3D in Director. Also, several new Lingo functions deal with relating the 2D coordinate system to the 3D coordinate system, and vice versa. Table 13.1 lists some of the Lingo elements that we will be utilizing in our examination of various techniques for developing interface strategies.

TABLE 13.1   Properties and Functions for Mouse and Picking Lingo

Element	Type	Purpose/Usage
On Mousedown	Handler	Intercepts a mouse button press.
on mouseUp	Handler	Intercepts a mouse button release.
Cursor	Command	Changes the mouse cursor.
the mousedown	Property	Boolean. If the mouse is currently being pressed, this value will be true; otherwise, it will be false.
MouseH	Property	Number of pixels (H) from stage left.
MouseV	Property	Number of pixels (V) from stage top.
Mouseloc	Property	point(mouseH, mouseV).
the lastroll	Property	Returns ticks since the last move.
the lastClick	Property	Returns ticks since the last click.
the Clickloc	Property	Returns point(h,v) of the last click.
flushInputEvents()	Function	Empties the input event queue.
New 3D Functions		
modelUnderLoc()	Function	Returns the Model closest in -Z.
spriteSpaceToWorldSpace()	Function	Converts from the H/V plane to the vector(x,y,z) space.
worldSpaceToSpriteSpace()	Function	Converts from the vector(x,y,z) space to the H/V plane.

You most likely recognize many of the elements among the entries in Table 13.1 (although some items, such as lastroll and lastclick, are not used as often as some of the others). Among these familiar items are several 3D functions that establish the core of Picking Lingo. There are also two additional Picking Lingo functions, modelsunderloc() and modelsunderray(), which we examine in Chapters 25, "Advanced Camera Control," and 27, "Creating Meshes from Code."

Picking Demonstrations

The subject of Picking Lingo is demonstrated with a small amount of code and a slightly larger amount of planning. Technically, we are examining Basic

Picking Lingo—in Chapter 28, we will examine some advanced variations on these functions, known as Detailed Picking.

I will define Basic Picking to mean "to click on Models in the 3D environment with the 2D mouse." In this case, the purpose of Mousedown changes—it will be used to determine whether a Model has been picked. Then it will trigger custom handlers that perform the reactions of the environment to the mouse. Because Models are not represented by individual Sprites, mouseenter and mouseleave handlers have little practical usage when working with Models. We will examine the simulation of these handlers through custom code.

The Basic Pick

You know that the H/V mouse coordinates relate to the Stage, as illustrated in Figure 13.2. In addition, the vector(x,y,z) coordinates of the 3D environment are illustrated in this example.

FIGURE 13.2

Correlation of the 2D mouse, 2D screen, and 3D environment coordinates.

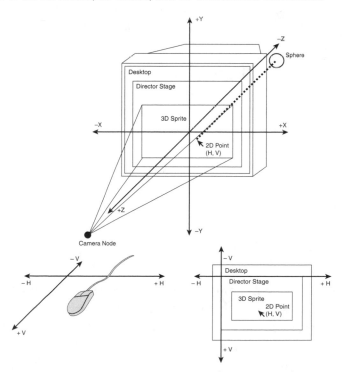

Note the dotted line that extends from the 2D point on the surface of the screen, orthogonal to the screen and infinitely in the positive Z direction. The information for the first Model that this "ray" encounters will be returned by the `modelunderloc()` function. Here's the syntax we will use:

```
scene.camera("whichCamera").modelUnderLoc(whichpoint)
```

The key to working with `modelunderloc()` is maintaining the value of `which-point` as coordinates relative to the Sprite's upper-left corner. Note that `which-point` is a `point(x,y)` data type. The following behavior script is designed to account for this. Also, in this script, `on mousedown` is treated as a logical trigger that exists separately from the actions taken by the `on hit` handler.

```
 1: Property spritenum, porigin
 2:
 3: On beginsprite me
 4:   porigin = point(sprite(spritenum).left,sprite(spritenum).top)
 5: end
 6:
 7: On mousedown me
 8:   finpoint = the clickloc - porigin
 9:   modelhit = sprite(spritenum).camera.modelunderloc(finpoint)
10:
11:   if modelhit <> void then
12:    hit(modelhit)
13:   else
14:    hit(false)
15:   end if
16: end
17:
18: on hit whichmodel
19:   if not whichmodel then
20:    put "No Hit"
21:   else
22:    put whichmodel
23:   end if
24: end
```

At line 4, we set the custom property `porigin` equal to the upper-left H/V coordinate of the 3D sprite so that we can refer to it quickly later in the script. At line 8, we calculate `finpoint` by subtracting the value of `porigin` from the clickloc. This will convert Stage-relative coordinates into Sprite-relative coordinates. Notice that I am using the clickloc property rather than mouseloc. If the user is moving the mouse very quickly, the value of mouseloc will be changing. The value of clickloc will remain constant until the user clicks again. In this situation, where we are interested in Models under the location of the click, we need this constancy to maintain some degree of accuracy with the modelunderloc() function.

At line 10, we begin an if/then statement designed to determine whether any Models were hit. If so, the statement passes the name of the Model to the on hit custom handler. If no Model was hit, on mousedown passes false to on hit. That way, the hit handler will manage all mouse action and inaction. For this reason, the on hit handler is where we will concentrate most of our customizations. In the previous example, on hit reports to the message window. In the "Basic Picking A" file on the CD, the on hit handler reacts to messages as follows:

```
1: On hit whichmodel
2: if not whichmodel then
3:   member("outbox").text = "No Hit"
4:   else
5:   member("outbox").text = whichmodel.name && "Hit"
6:   end if
7: end
```

In this example, "outbox" is a field on the Stage through which the name of the last model clicked will be reported to the user. If the user does not hit any models, this is reported as well.

In "Basic Picking B," the on hit handler is further expanded to demonstrate the use of a case statement to control the range of possible actions. Rather than report the names of the models, the environment generates audible and visual responses to user actions:

```
1: on hit whichmodel
2:  global scene
3:  scene.shader("redboxshd").blend = 30
4:  scene.shader("blueboxshd").blend = 30
5:  scene.shader("greenboxshd").blend = 30
6:
```

```
 7:  if not whichmodel then
 8:    puppetsound 1, "miss"
 9:  else
10:    puppetsound 1, "hit"
11:    case(whichmodel.name) of
12:      "redbox":
13:        scene.shader("redboxshd").blend = 100
14:      "greenbox":
15:        scene.shader("greenboxshd").blend = 100
16:      "bluebox":
17:        scene.shader("blueboxshd").blend = 100
18:    end case
19:  end if
20: end
```

This demonstration utilizes the `blend` property to alter the opacity of the current last object selected. If no Models are selected, they all remain semitransparent. Another variation on this example would be to continually fade the blend of all Models at a constant rate down to a minimum of 30 or so. This way, clicking the boxes will generate an environment that appears to react fluidly rather than in a binary manner.

Translation of 2D Design Elements

In the previous examples, we examined a method of "Picking" an object, and several methods of interpreting the information from the "Pick." In this section, we will be examining the success of translating 2D design elements—specifically rollovers—into the 3D environment.

Because individual Models are not represented on the score, we must simulate the functionality of the `mouseenter` and `mouseleave` handlers. The difficulty with simulating these two handlers is that we need to perform a process known as *polling*; we need to continually ask Director what Model, if any, we are on top of. The difficulty in this process involves the `modelunderloc()` function, because it is relatively slow. If you are not clever about calling this function over and over, you can slow down even the fastest machines.

Some other events that might seem viable candidates to poll from are on `prepareframe`, on `enterframe`, and on `idle`. `Prepareframe` and `enterframe` are going to perform about as well as `exitframe`. However, on `idle` is a poor choice because `modelunderloc()` takes a relatively long time to execute. The on

idle handler is a classically terrible event for handling slow code because it
will maximize on slowing down the machine.

In short, there are two choices: Either enhance the exitframe handler by
polling after checking the milliseconds or use a persistent timeout object with
the on timeout handler. In this chapter, I am going to demonstrate the exitframe handler technique rather than the timeout handler for two reasons.
First, on timeout uses ticks, and I would prefer to use the slightly more accurate milliseconds. Second, Chapter 23, "Controlling Time," examines detailed
methods of working with timeout objects that allow for a larger discussion of
the issues of polling for multiple conditions.

The direct approach of putting the modelunderloc() function in an exitframe
handler relies on several nested if/then statements. In order to clarify the
logic of polling for simulated "mouseenter" and "mouseleave" handlers, I have
demonstrated the process in pseudocode:

```
Exitframe
(1) Has enough time passed to check for "mouseenter"?
 (1) Yes:
   check to see what model we hit?
   (2) Did we hit a model?
     (2) Yes:
       (3) Is it the same model we hit the time before?
         (3) Yes:
           Do Nothing
         (3) No:
           Send the old model a "mouseleave"
           Send the new model a "mouseenter"
     (2) No:
       Send the old model a "mouseleave"
       Update how long to wait until next poll
 (1) No:
   Do Nothing
END
```

The realization of this pseudocode as a script is as follows:

```
1: Property porigin, spritenum, pskip, pTime, pfrequency
2:
3: Global scene
4:
```

```
 5: On beginsprite me
 6:   --set up the sprite origin
 7:   Porigin = point(sprite(spritenum).left, sprite(spritenum).top)
 8:   -- pskip holds on to the name of the last model hit
 9:   -- the -1 is used to signify that there was no "last model"
10:   Pskip = -1
11:   -- hold on to the time in milliseconds right now
12:   Ptime = the milliseconds
13:   -- a setting of 100 refers to 100 milliseconds,
14:   -- or 1/10 of a second
15:   Pfrequency = 100
16: End
17:
18: On exitframe me
19:   -- find out the current time in milliseconds
20:   Curtime = the milliseconds
21:   -- find out the change in time since the last time we checked
22:   Deltatime = curtime - pTime
23:    -- is the change in time is greater than 100 milliseconds?
24:   If deltatime >= pfrequency then
25:    -- notice we are using the mouseloc, rather than clickloc
26:   Finpoint = the mouseloc - porigin
27:    -- find out what model we hit
28:   Test = sprite(spritenum).camera.Modelunderloc(finpoint)
29:
30:    -- did we indeed hit a model?
31:   If test <> void then
32:   -- is the model we hit different than the model we hit last?
33:    If pskip <> test then
34:   -- did we hit a model last time?
35:     If pskip <> -1 then
36:   -- yes, we did, send that model an exitaction
37:       Exitaction(me,pskip)
38:      End if
39:   --send the model we just hit an enteraction
40:       EnterAction(me,test)
41:    -- set the name of the model last hit to the model we just hit
42:      Pskip = test
43:    End if
44:   Else  -- we didn't hit a model
45:   -- did we hit a model the last time we checked?
46:    if pskip <> -1 then
47:   -- yes, therefore, send an exitaction to that model
48:   exitaction(me, pskip)
49:     pskip = -1
50:    end if
51:   End if
```

```
52:    -- since we just checked for hits, update the time
53:    PTime = the milliseconds
54:  End if
55: End
```

Notice the pskip property is used to generate the simulated "mouseleave" handler and to make sure that this code acts more like mouseleave and mouseenter rather than mousewithin. Rather than sending events every time a Model is hit, it sends events only when there has been a change in the Model hit.

In this example, pFrequency determines how often we should poll the environment. At a setting of 100 milliseconds, we will poll the environment every tenth of a second. By creating a property called pFrequency, we've made this code ready for performance optimization. Specifically, we could create a custom handler to change the frequency of polling depending on the current speed of the machine.

The Basic Rollover

On the CD is a file named "Surface Rollover" that uses the simulated "mouseenter" and "mouseleave" handlers we created with an exitframe handler. In addition, it utilizes the following custom handlers to control what action to take at the precise moment for simulated "mouseenter" and "mouseleave" events:

```
 1: On exitaction me, whichmodel
 2:  Case(whichmodel.name) of
 3:  "redbox":
 4:    scene.shader("redboxshd").emissive = rgb(127,127,127)
 5:  "bluebox":
 6:    scene.shader("blueboxshd").emissive = rgb(127,127,127)
 7:   end case
 8: End
 9:
10: On enteraction me, whichmodel
11:  Case(whichmodel.name) of
12:  "redbox":
13:    scene.shader("redboxshd").emissive = rgb(0,0,0)
14:  "bluebox":
15:    scene.shader("blueboxshd").emissive = rgb(0,0,0)
16:   end case
17: End
```

Variation on the Basic Rollover

This example shows how to generate a very basic rollover that changes the surface quality of the model "rolled" onto. There is another file on the CD, called "Geometry Rollover," that I would like to look at next. This demonstration is made possible by switching the Modelresource of a Model, similar to how you might switch the member of a Sprite to create a rollover. The process is initiated in the `initialize` custom handler.

```
1: on initialize
2:   clearworld(scene)
3:   scene.camera[1].colorbuffer.clearvalue = rgb(230,230,230)
4:
5:   rbox = createbox("RedBox", 60,60,60, rgb(200,20,10))
6:   bbox = createbox("BlueBox", 60,60,60, rgb(10,20,200))
7:
8:   temp = scene.newmodelresource("redsphere", #sphere)
9:   temp.radius = 30
10:
11:   temp = scene.newmodelresource("bluesphere", #sphere)
12:   temp.radius = 30
13:
14:   rbox.translate(45,0,0)
15:   bbox.translate(-45,0,0)
16: end
```

In this example, we are mainly concerned with lines 8–12. In these lines, we create geometry for the "roll-on" state. Notice that we are only creating the Modelresource. Because we are not creating a Model, there is no visual representation of that Model in the 3D World. Next, the `exitaction` and `enteraction` custom handlers are modified, as follows:

```
1: On exitaction me, whichmodel
2:   Case(whichmodel.name) of
3:     "redbox":
4:       scene.model("redbox").resource = scene.modelresource("redboxres")
5:     "bluebox":
6:       scene.model("bluebox").resource = scene.modelresource("blueboxres")
7:   end case
8: End
9:
10: On enteraction me, whichmodel
```

```
11:  Case(whichmodel.name) of
12:   "redbox":
13:    scene.model("redbox").resource = scene.modelresource("redsphere")
14:   "bluebox":
15:    scene.model("bluebox").resource = scene.modelresource("bluesphere")
16:   end case
17: End
```

Notice in lines 4, 6, 13, and 15 that I am referring to the Resource property of the Model. By changing the value of this property to the sphere Modelresources we created earlier, the result is a change from a box to a sphere upon rollover.

Game Board Demo

In the "Basic Game Board" example, the mouse coordinates are related to the 3D environment by changing the surface quality of Models. The position of the game board Models can be changed by clicking and dragging. In addition, the mouse cursor is invisible only when the user is on top of the game board squares. This variation on the simulated "mouseenter" and "mouseleave" strategy is achieved through the following code:

```
1: On exitaction me, whichmodel
2:  if (whichmodel.name) <> "cone01" then
3:   scene.model(whichmodel.name).shader.emissive = rgb(0,0,0)
4:   cursor -1
5:  end if
6: End
7:
8: On enteraction me, whichmodel
9:  if (whichmodel.name) <> "cone01" then
10:   scene.model(whichmodel.name).shader.emissive = rgb(127,127,127)
11:   member("outbox").text = "Position:" && string(whichmodel.name)
12:   cursor 200
13:  end if
14: End
```

This code is not dramatically different from some of our previous examples. The functionality of the individual handlers are encapsulated in if/then statements to ensure that users only interact with the squares of the game board, rather than the edges of the board. In addition, a small amount of reporting information is given to let the users know what game square they are on.

The structure of the Models is a large part of the demo. The game board W3D file was created in 3D Studio MAX from 64 planes and one cone. Although the Director file is currently 112KB, we could achieve a very small file size (20–30KB) if we were to create the board from scratch via Lingo from primitives. In terms of this demo, all the Models are grouped at the beginning of the Movie. This way, the Models can be referred to individually and also as one unit. In addition, the `initialize` custom handler creates a unique Shader for each Model so that we can refer to the surface qualities of each Model individually. The fusion of imported Models and Lingo can be quite rewarding.

In terms of performance optimization, the frame rate of this demo would not gain much from creating the board through Lingo primitives. The reason for this is that every single Model has to be drawn by the Renderer one at a time. The more Models, the longer it takes to draw each frame. The most powerful, but equally difficult solution for the creation of the game board is to create a custom mesh—we will work with this topic in Chapter 27, "Creating Meshes from Code."

The 3D Mouse Demo

In order to develop a language of interaction, we need to signify the presence of our hand in the 3D environment in a more robust manner than in the previous example, where the mouse pointer is still obviously a 2D pointer. It is similar to looking out a window and placing your finger on the glass, believing that you are touching the tree across the street. In short, the degree of interaction possible for the user is very removed from the real-time environment we are creating. However, this may well be exactly the type of interaction you are looking for. A removed viewer has certain advantages over a user who is immersed in a given system.

The first alternative that we will look at is the "3D Mouse Cursor" file on the CD. This demonstration is based heavily on coordinate transformation; Figure 13.3 illustrates the logic behind this demo.

This method utilizes the rectilinear mouse coordinates that occur in the H/V plane as the basis for setting the position of a Model in the X/Z plane. Notice that in this example I have turned the mouse cursor off to heighten the implication that the Model is the cursor. Moving the mouse "up" on the screen moves the object farther into the screen; moving the mouse "down" on the screen moves the object toward the viewer.

FIGURE 13.3

Mapping the H/V motions of the mouse onto the X/Z plane.

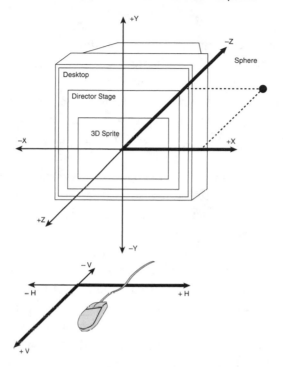

This technique is achieved with the spritespacetoworldspace() function. This function accepts a two-dimensional point as its input and returns a 3D vector. Here's the script that is used in this demo:

```
 1: Property spritenum, porigin
 2:
 3: global scene
 4:
 5: On beginsprite me
 6:   porigin = point(sprite(spritenum).left,sprite(spritenum).top)
 7: end
 8:
 9: on exitframe
10:   cursor 200
11:   finpoint = the mouseloc - porigin
12:
13:   newloc = scene.camera[1].spriteSpaceToWorldSpace(finpoint)
```

```
14:  newlocb = vector(newloc.x,-50,-newloc.y)
15:  scene.model[2].transform.position = newlocb
16: end
```

There are several items of note about this code. First, the `spritespacetoworld-space()` function requires point data in Sprite-relative space. Second, the `cursor 200` command sets the mouse cursor to a blank cursor. Most importantly, notice line 14; in this line, we are creating a new vector from the vector information returned from the `spritespacetoworldspace()` function. The `vector(x,y,z)` coordinates returned to from this function are remapped as `vector(x,-50,-y)` into the `newlocb` vector. This accomplishes several goals. The x coordinates remain constant, so this is understandable. A constant setting of -50 for the y coordinate constrains the sphere to a plane -50 units below the World origin. Perhaps the most difficult setting to understand is using the -y coordinate from the original vector as the z coordinate. The reason for this is that the original y coordinates are relative to the vertical space of the Stage, but we are interested in moving the mouse "into" the space of the stage, into the Z direction. Literally, we are taking the vertical motion of the mouse and "remapping" it into the Z direction. The reason for the negation is to achieve the "up on the Stage equals farther away from the viewer" relationship. Finally, note that in line 15 we are setting the `transform.position` property directly, rather than using the `translate()` function. The reason for this is that rather than needing an accumulative movement, we need to move the Model to a very specific location in World space, depending on the location of the mouse.

Polar Mouse Coordinates

In the previous examples, we transformed the rectilinear H/V coordinates into rectilinear `vector(x,y,z)` coordinates. The mouse coordinates can also be transformed into polar coordinates. Figure 13.4 illustrates how the mouse position can be considered a single vector with rotation and magnitude.

Because we know the Cartesian coordinates of the mouse, we can convert these into polar coordinates quite easily with the following formulas:

- `PolarMagnitude = sqrt(power(x,2) + power(y,2))`

- `PolarAngle = atan(x/y)` * 57.29577951

FIGURE 13.4

Polar mouse coordinates are measured in angle and magnitude.

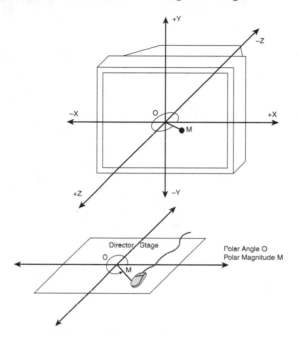

We will need to clean the values that this code produces, depending on where we want 0 degrees to point. Normally, you will want 0 degrees to point toward three o'clock and the angles to run counterclockwise. Keep in mind that the following demos generate angles that conform to this range. The magnitude is less trouble, because its value needs no cleaning.

Polar Mouse Demo

The file "Polar Mouse Cursor" demonstrates the usage and implementation of interpreting the mouse location in polar coordinates, as opposed to rectilinear Cartesian coordinates. That information is used to rotate and translate a Model that functions as the cursor in 3D space. Try moving the mouse in a circle and watch the corresponding movement of the box. I have color-coded the sides of the box using the `shaderlist[]` property so that you can visualize how the box is actually rotating in space.

NOTE

You can find a full discussion of the `Shaderlist[]` property in Chapter 14, "Multitexturing."

Now try moving the mouse vertically and horizontally. Notice how when moving the mouse vertically, you pass a point about halfway through the Sprite where the box flips 180 degrees. This is essentially the point you are rotating around. The code for this technique is as follows:

```
1: property spritenum, centerofsprite
2:
3: global scene
4:
5: on beginsprite me
6:  centerofsprite = point((sprite(spritenum).width / 2), \
     (sprite(spritenum).height / 2))
7: end
8:
9: on exitframe me
10:  curloc = the mouseloc
11:
12: -- offset the mouseloc to make the values sprite-relative
13:  sideA = curloc[1] - centerofsprite[1]
14:  sideB = (curloc[2] - centerofsprite[2]) + .1
15:
16: -- generate the angle, and convert from radians to degrees
17:  myangle = atan(sidea/sideb) * 57.29577951
18:
19: -- orient the results such that zero points toward 3:00
20: -- and also so that the angles run counterclockwise
21:  if sideb < 0 then
22:    myangle = myangle + 90
23:  else
24:    myangle = myangle + 270
25:  end if
26:
27: --generate the magnitude
28:  mymagnitude = sqrt(power(sidea,2) + power(sideb,2))
29:
30: --(optional) report the results back to a field on stage, so you \
     can watch the numbers
31:  member("outbox").text = "Angle:" && string(myangle) && "-" && \
     "Magnitude:" && string(mymagnitude)
32:
```

```
33: -- transform.identity() will reset position of box to world origin
34:  scene.model[1].transform.identity()
35: --next we will move box on the x axis distance of the magnitude
36:  scene.model[1].translate(mymagnitude,0,0,#world)
37: --finally, we will rotate around the y axis the correct angle
38:  scene.model[1].rotate(0,myangle,0,#world)
39: end
```

Polar Game Board Rotation

In the file "Game Board Polar Rotate," you will see this technique applied to the Game Board demo we were working with previously. There are some slight changes to the script. Notably, the script has been encapsulated in a toggle switch. Also, because of the way that the geometry was created for the board, it is necessary to rotate around a different axis. Finally, we do not need (or want) to reposition the game board on each frame; rather, we only want to rotate it. The modified script looks like this:

```
 1: property spritenum, centerofsprite, ptoggle
 2:
 3: global scene
 4:
 5: on beginsprite me
 6:  centerofsprite = point((sprite(spritenum).width / 2), \
    (sprite(spritenum).height / 2))
 7:  ptoggle = false
 8: end
 9:
10: on exitframe me
11:  if ptoggle then
12:   curloc = the mouseloc
13:
14:    sideA = curloc[1] - centerofsprite[1]
15:    sideB = (curloc[2] - centerofsprite[2]) + .1
16:
17: -- figure out the angle
18:    myangle = atan(sidea/sideb) * 57.29577951
19:    if sideb < 0 then
20:     myangle = myangle + 90
21:    else
22:     myangle = myangle + 270
23:    end if
24:
25: --since we do not need the magnitude, we are not generating it
```

```
26:
27: --transform.identity()resets transform of all models in the group
28:   scene.group("board").transform.identity()
29: -- rotate group around a model hidden in the center of the group
30:   scene.group("board").rotate(0,0,myangle, scene.model("center"))
31:   end if
32:
33: end
34:
35: --controls for the "toggle switch"
36: on mousedown me
37:   ptoggle = true
38: end
39:
40: on mouseup me
41:   ptoggle = false
42: end
43:
44: on mouseupoutside me
45:   ptoggle = false
46: end
```

In this example, we are using rectilinear mouse coordinates for determining our rollovers and polar coordinates to determine the rotation of the board. This is precisely the type of modulation of the mouse click I have been speaking about: mousedown changes the character of the coordinates of the mouse and how they are used. You can see that there are many variations on how you can decide to utilize two "simple" coordinates.

Learning to master the control of the environment through mouse input is a crucial skill. If you are having difficulty with the transforms, I strongly suggest rereading Chapter 4 on basic transformations. Keep in mind that transformations can confuse even the most hardened of 3D programmers from time to time—it is pretty much expected that you are going to make some mistakes with them in the beginning, and you will get better with practice.

Summary

Creating intuitive interfaces is a challenging design problem that has not been fully solved for 3D environments. Classically, there has been a range of solutions, but none is recognized as the standard. Because there is no standard, users need to learn how to interact with each interface they encounter.

Designing your solutions based on the mouse is a strong choice—it can allow the user to express gestures, emotions, and commands, and the mouse can be used with a single hand. What's more, the mouse is ubiquitous.

We have examined Picking Lingo, the branch of Lingo programming that concerns itself with correlating 2D locations with 3D Models as the basis for developing interaction with an interface. Because Picking Lingo is robust, we can develop 3D interfaces based on classic solutions or experiment with alternative designs for interaction.

FAQ

When I "pick" a Model, can I only find out more information about the Model that I hit?

Yes. We have been exploring basic picking. In Chapter 28, we will examine the subject of detailed picking, which returns information about the Mesh, Vertices, and Faces as well as other in-depth information.

I need to control the camera with the mouse and/or keyboard rather than (or in addition to) the objects in the scene. Is that possible?

Yes, absolutely. Chapter 25 is dedicated to advanced camera control.

Supplemental Resources

The following resources are divided into three sections: "Hardware," "Bibliography," and "Artists." This section is intended to inform you about several nontraditional input devices, provide bibliographic information on experimental 3D interface design, and highlight several artists who have created successful and innovative nontraditional input devices for 3D environments.

Hardware

The following list of hardware includes 3D mice, specialized monitors, custom I/O boards, and even MIDI solutions. It is not intended as an inclusive list but rather as a list of solutions that offer interesting possibilities that I have worked with and that are approachable. However, many of these solutions do require the use of Xtras, and some require a basic knowledge of electronics.

- Flock of Birds

  This is a "six degrees of freedom" motion-tracking device that can function as a three-dimensional mouse. The device can be configured to work within a 16-foot sphere range. Multiple "birds" can be used to input several locations at the same time. The Flock of Birds is a serial input device, so it requires the use of Xtras to communicate with Director.

  www.ascension-tech.com/products/flockofbirds/

- Spaceball

  The Spaceball is a desktop device that provides information on six degrees of freedom. The controller is a ball mounted to a pedestal that you grasp. The ball can be twisted and manipulated to send input in a very fluid fashion.

  www.labtec.com/spaceball3003.cfm

- Touchscreens

  A *touchscreen* is a monitor that users can directly touch to manipulate the environment with their fingers. Traditionally, touchscreens are not pressure sensitive. There are several types of technologies that are used to achieve a touchscreen, some of which require detailed calibration, some of which are fragile, and some of which are not very accurate. Because there are many manufacturers and many different options for the specific technology used to create touchscreens, there is an extensive list of manufacturers. I have not included links for these because the list is simply too long, and there are too many parameters. However, if you are interested in this type of manipulation, you should investigate touchscreens.

- LCD tablet screens

  One intriguing input device is the LCD tablet screen, which is a pressure-sensitive screen whose interface is a wireless pen. This enables the user to draw directly on the screen with a familiar device (a pen), to control the environment of the computer. Two manufacturers for this type of product are Sony and Wacom.

  www.wacom.com/lcdtablets/index.cfm

  www.sonystyle.com/vaio/pentablet/index.html

- EZIO

  The EZIO is an interface board that allows you to perform "easy" serial input and output communications. This controller can be used to build input devices from electronic components. The EZIO offers support for binary digital input/output, analog-to-digital conversion, and pulse-width management. The EZIO is extremely extensible because it is a device you can use for both input and output. It does require a knowledge of basic electronics, but it can be very rewarding to develop with because many electronic components are fairly inexpensive: pressure sensors, photocells, ultrasonic proximity sensors, passive infrared motion detectors, and so on. These can all be used to control your Director environments. Because the EZIO is a serial communication device, you will need to utilize Xtras to communicate with Director.

  www.ezio.com

- I-CubeX

  The I-CubeX system is a robust suite of modular MIDI-based controllers. Essentially, there is a base unit that you then can use for MIDI-based input and output devices. Many devices are available that are prebuilt and ready to be integrated into your system, including tap controllers, heat sensors, acceleration/deceleration sensors, ultrasonic proximity sensors, bend sensors (for fingers), and light sensors. Because these are MIDI-based devices, you will need to utilize Xtras to communicate with Director.

  www.infusionsystems.com

Bibliography

The *3D User Interface Bibliography* compiled by Ivan Poupyrev and Ernst Kruijff is one of the most extensive documents on the subject, with over 170 entries. The papers and research that are listed are quite advanced, but it is worth a look if you are interested in alternative interfaces.

www.mic.atr.co.jp/~poup/3dui/3duibib.htm

Artists

I have chosen to mention two installation artists whose work with real-time 3D and experimental interfaces are innovative, unique, and inspiring.

- Char Davies

  Char Davies is well known for her immersive installations. In particular, "Osmose" is a powerful example of alternative input. The input device is a vest that the user wears that measures the amount of air in his lungs. Its design was inspired by methods of locomotion when scuba diving, where breath control and buoyancy are interrelated.

- Maurice Benayoun

  Maurice Benayoun has done extensive work in interactive installation and has won numerous awards for his work. I would like to highlight his installation "World Skin." In this installation, users interact with the environment through what appear to be 35mm cameras, taking snapshots of the 3D environment. The 3D environment itself is a highly stylized simulation of a war shown through historical photographs that have been extruded in the 3D environment. When users take "photos," they erase the scenes of war that they are surrounded by, but the objects appear quicker than users can click, and the sounds of war become increasingly loud. The environment is designed such that the more you interact with it, the more violent it becomes.

CHAPTER 14

Multitexturing

In this chapter, we will cover several concepts and techniques dealing with Textures. Because of the relationship between Textures and the standard Shader, we will be looking at specific advanced properties of both so you can learn how they can be used together.

The techniques in this chapter range from creating reflective surfaces, using opacity maps to vary Model transparency, creating decal Textures, and using hand-tuned multitexturing. Texturing is an extremely important aspect of building your 3D environments; a poorly textured environment can often stem from a misunderstanding of the advanced concepts and techniques that we will be exploring in this chapter.

Finally, although this chapter is named "Multitexturing," you might consider the subject matter "intermediate and advanced standard Shader and Texture techniques." The technique of multitexturing is a very large portion of this and encompasses many intermediate and advanced concepts. In short, to understand the topic of multitexturing, you must first examine many preliminary concepts. The organization of this chapter is broken into several laboratory-style demonstrations to isolate the individual concepts of advanced texturing. Then you can slowly apply these concepts together toward multitexturing.

Advanced Texture Properties

All Textures, regardless of their method of creation—imported from Castmembers or from image objects—have several advanced properties. These advanced properties are used to control several aspects of individual Textures from the Texture object level, such as the quality of Textures when they scale and how to handle alpha channel information. These changes affect every instance of the Texture object in question. Therefore, the choices you make are important for individual Textures, but these choices can be made independently of other Texture objects.

Texture.Quality

When you create a Texture, it has a specific width and height; therefore, it has a specific number of pixels and contains a specific amount of information. When you apply a Texture to the Shader of a Model, the Texture will automatically stretch to fill the Model. Models can change location in 3D space, and when they do, they get bigger or smaller, depending on their distance to the Camera (if you are using perspective projection).

If Models increase or decrease in size, the Textures applied to them scale along with the Models. Sometimes, when Models are very far away, you will not be able to see much detail, if any, of the Texture on the Model. This is where the Texture.Quality property comes into play.

The Quality property allows you to improve the appearance of Textures through a process called *mip-mapping*, which creates three consecutively smaller versions of a Texture, called *mip-maps*, and loads them into memory in addition to the base Texture. If a Texture on a Model is far enough away from the Camera, the display of the Texture will be much smaller than the actual Texture. In such cases, the mip-map whose size best corresponds to the size of the Texture onscreen is used rather than the full-size Texture.

You will need to understand three possible values for the Quality property: #low, #medium, and #high. With a setting of #low, mip-mapping is disabled. This means that when a Model using a Texture moves far from the Camera, all the Texture information will be scaled down on-the-fly. The visual quality of this setting tends to look quite poor.

The default setting is #medium; this setting uses a particular mathematical method of scaling the Texture down to create the mip-maps. This method is known as *bilinear scaling* and is a relatively fast way of creating the three mip-maps. However, as the name implies, #medium-quality Textures may not seem as smooth as they could be.

With a setting of #high, a mathematical method of scaling the Texture known as *trilinear scaling* is used. This method is superior, but it is computationally much slower than the #medium setting. The mip-maps created through this process will look very good, but they may take a moment or so longer to create when the Texture object is first created, or if you change the Texture.Quality property. Figure 14.1 shows a Texture used to create a tiling effect with its Texture.Quality property set to #low, #medium, and #high.

FIGURE 14.1

Comparison of no mip-mapping, bilinear mip-mapping, and trilinear mip-mapping, respectively.

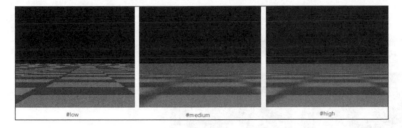

I suggest turning mip-mapping on if you are concerned about the visual appearance of your projects—it is an important process that can add to the overall quality of your work. However, you should be aware that when you're working in software rendering mode, mip-mapping is not supported; therefore, anyone viewing your projects using the software rendering mode will not gain the benefit of mip-mapped Textures.

Keep in mind that mip-mapping helps the visual quality of Textures as they recede from the Camera; if you are working with scenes that are going to be very deep, you may want to use the #high setting. Note that the difference in computation time between #medium and #high is not double but rather more akin to four times as long. How long it actually takes to perform the mip-mapping depends on the size of the Texture itself as well as processor speed.

NOTE

Note that mip-mapping only needs to be calculated once, unless you change the Texture.Quality property, in which case the mip-maps will be calculated again. Therefore, you should not change the value of the Texture.Quality property over and over again.

Texture.Nearfiltering

The Texture.Nearfiltering property is similar in spirit to Texture.Quality; its purpose is for improving the visual quality of your Textures in real time. When Models approach the Camera and their Textures stretch to sizes that are larger than the source for the Textures, you will begin to see pixelization. The Texture.Nearfiltering property is a Boolean that determines whether Textures close to the Camera should be slightly blurred to try and eliminate some of this pixelization. Figure 14.2 compares the difference between a Model whose Shader uses a Texture with Nearfiltering set to True and the same Texture with Nearfiltering set to False.

FIGURE 14.2

A nearfiltered Texture (left) compared to the same Texture not nearfiltered (right).

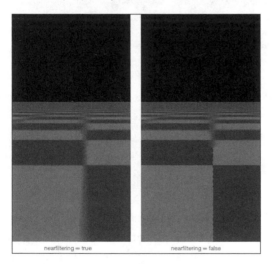

You may encounter problems with Nearfiltering if you have not set your Camera.Yon value. By default, Camera.Yon (far-clipping plane) is extremely far away. The process of Nearfiltering uses the distance between the clipping planes to determine which Models are "near" the Camera. Those Models that are determined to be "near" the Camera will be blurred. If your far-clipping plane is inordinately far away, the area defined as "near" can become quite large. If this happens, you may have Models that are *not* relatively near the Camera whose Textures are blurred.

NOTE

Many times you may want to turn Nearfiltering off, especially if you are working with text that you would like to remain crisp. Another reason to turn Nearfiltering off is if you are working with alpha channels that you would like to remain crisp.

Texture.Renderformat

The Texture.Renderformat property can have a great impact on performance and visual quality. The range of possible values for the Texture.Renderformat property will vary from machine to machine, depending on the specific Renderer, system architecture, and video card the machine uses.

NOTE

Chapter 19, "Performance Optimization," explains the specifics of why the possible values for this property vary from machine to machine.

Texture.Renderformat controls the bit-depth of the individual pixels in a Texture. This value includes information about whether the Texture should include alpha channel information and how detailed that information should be. Table 14.1 lists the possible values for this property.

TABLE 14.1   Possible Values for Texture.Renderformat

Value	Purpose
#default	Instructs the Texture to use the Renderformat setting for the movie specified by the `getrendererservices().texturerenderformat` property
#rgba4444	12 bits of color, 4 bits of alpha
#rgba5550	15 bits of color, 0 bits of alpha
#rgba5650	16 bits of color, 0 bits of alpha
#rgba5551	15 bits of color, 1 bit of alpha
#rgba8880	24 bits of color, 0 bits of alpha
#rgba8888	24 bits of color, 8 bits of alpha

The first thing to note concerning the possible values for the Texture.Renderformat property is that the #default setting will force a Texture object to use the Renderformat specified for the movie. The Renderformat specified for the movie is stored in the `getrendererservices().texturerenderformat` system property.

NOTE

Controlling the `getrendererservices()` function is explained in Chapter 19. In this chapter, we will focus on how to work with the Renderformat at the individual Texture level.

Notice that other than #default, the range of values begin with the letters *rgba*, which refers to the fact that these values determine the bit-depth for the red, green, blue, and alpha channel information of a Texture object. For example, a Texture.Renderformat setting of #rgba4444 has 4 bits of red, 4 bits of blue, 4 bits of green, and 4 bits of alpha information, for a total of 16 bits.

The possible values for Texture.Renderformat add up to 15, 16, 24, and 32 bits, although #rgba5550 is actually considered a 16-bit Texture as well because the extra bit is not used, but the space is still required in memory. Of the six possible values, four of them are 16-bit Textures. Three of the Texture.Renderformat values allow alpha channel support, and three do not. Of the three values for alpha channel support, you are able to use 1-bit, 4-bit, and 8-bit alpha channels.

This range of possibilities is quite good because you are able to create simple 1-bit masks as well as more-complex 8-bit masks with 256 possible levels of transparency. In addition, you have the flexibility of a 4-bit alpha channel, which allows you some graduation within your alpha channel but does not require as much memory as a full 32-bit Texture. Table 14.2 lists the Texture.Renderformat values and explains these formats in terms of the number of possible colors and levels of transparency as well as the total required bit-depth for each setting.

TABLE 14.2   Ranges Represented by the Renderformat Values

Value	Number of Colors	Number of Alpha Levels	Total Bit-Depth
#rgba4444	4,096	16	16
#rgba5550	32,768	0	16

TABLE 14.2   Continued

Value	Number of Colors	Number of Alpha Levels	Total Bit-Depth
#rgba5650	65,536	0	16
#rgba5551	32,768	1	16
#rgba8880	16,777,216	0	24
#rgba8888	16,777,216	256	32

If you are working with a Texture and do not need the alpha channel information, you should set Texture.Renderformat to a value that does not store the alpha information, because even if you do not have alpha information, the Texture object will store the memory for the information anyway. This is a waste, so setting Texture.Renderformat to a value that does not store alpha information is an easy way to reduce memory requirements.

The Renderformat you choose should be dictated by the needs of your project. In addition, you should be aware that some Renderers do not deal with alpha channel information as well as others. For example, DirectX 5.2 tends to have difficulties working with alpha channel information, although the software Renderer tends to do a rather good job of working with alpha channels.

The system architecture and video card of the user machine dictate alpha channel performance. Unfortunately, too many hardware configurations exist to come up with a general rule, but you should keep one point in mind: If you are working with alpha channels in your Textures, you are most likely excluding someone from viewing those parts of your project that rely on alpha channels.

NOTE

When you are working with Textures, make sure their widths and heights are powers of 2 (that is, 2, 4, 8, 16, 32, 64, 128, 256, 512, 1024, and so on). Note that the width and height do not need to be the same value—they just need to be some power of 2. Refer to Chapter 19 for a more detailed discussion of powers of 2 and how the Texture.Quality, Texture.Nearfiltering, and Texture.Renderformat properties affect movie performance.

Opacity Mapping Demo

Alpha channels should be considered an important and useful tool for achieving a variety of effects. One reason for this is that you will use alpha channels to create Textures that express themselves by making parts of Models transparent. When alpha channels are used in this way, they are often referred to as *opacity maps*. An opacity map is a Texture with an alpha channel, but the alpha channel expresses itself by making portions of the Model it is applied to opaque, transparent, or semitransparent, depending on the black, grayscale, and white pixel information saved in the alpha channel.

This is an important tool because you can use opacity maps to make simple geometry look much more complex as well as create interesting atmospheric lighting, to name a few examples. Note that Figure 14.3 compares the alpha channel information saved in a Texture object with a Model in the 3D environment using a Shader with this Texture.

FIGURE 14.3

Alpha channel information compared to a Model using the Texture with alpha channel information.

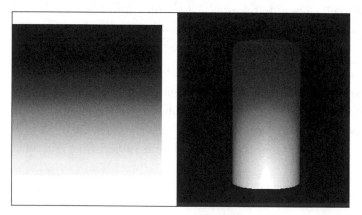

You can see in Figure 14.3 that the Model is completely transparent near the top, semitransparent in the middle, and completely opaque near the bottom. In order for this to work, the Texture.Renderformat property for the Texture object must be set to one of the Renderformats that allows the Texture to use alpha channel information. In addition, you need to make sure that the Shader.Transparent property is set to True. Note that it is possible to change the Shader.Blend property in addition to using opacity maps to further apply a constant level of transparency to a Model. Also, keep in mind that because the Model is transparent, you may want to work with the Model.Visibility property so that the internal Faces of the Model are visible as well. You can see in Figure 14.4 the difference in quality between 4-bit and 8-bit alpha channels.

FIGURE 14.4

The differences in gradation between 4-bit and 8-bit alpha channels.

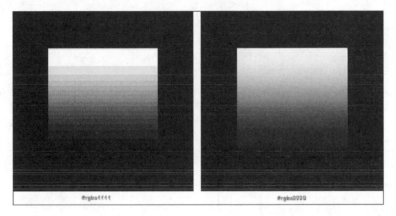

Keep in mind that you may not always need an 8-bit alpha channel to achieve your goals. Reducing your Textures from 32 bit to 16 bit is a wise move, considering that you most likely want your projects to run on as many machines as possible.

Often, I will use a 1-bit alpha channel if I am trying to create the look of complex geometry with alpha channel information. In Figure 14.5, you can see how I have applied a Texture of a grid to a box Model to create the look of a cage.

In Figure 14.5, I set Texture.Quality to #low to avoid mip-mapping, and I set Texture.Renderformat to #rgba5551 to use 1-bit of alpha channel information. To complete the cage effect, I set the Model.Visibility property to #both. This way, you can actually see through the Model and see the grid on the opposite interior wall of the box. Again, note that this cage is being created with Textures, not with wire-frame rendering.

FIGURE 14.5

A 1-bit alpha channel used to create the illusion of complex geometry.

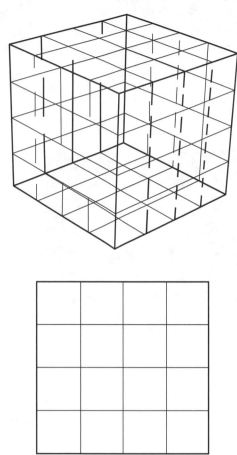

Another example of opacity mapping that you should be aware of is the use of 8-bit alpha channels to create atmospheric lighting effects. Remember that Lights do not cast shadows, nor do they have any atmosphere. In order to simulate atmosphere, you can create a Texture with alpha channel information. This Texture can be applied to a simple Model, such as a plane, to simulate atmospheric effects. Figure 14.6 illustrates the usage of an 8-bit alpha channel to create the atmospheric effect surrounding a Model representing a light bulb.

FIGURE 14.6

Using an 8-bit alpha channel to create atmospheric lighting effects. A color version of this figure appears on the CD.

Note that in this example, the Texture.Renderformat property of the atmosphere Texture is set to #rgba8888. This use of alpha channels can help evoke moody, dark scenes in a way that emphasizes the location of light. It also gives the light a sense of placement in the scene.

Texture Layers of the Standard Shader

When working with the standard Shader, we have been assigning Texture objects to the Shader.Texture property. However, the Shader.Texture property is only a shortcut that is used to reduce typing. Every standard Shader actually has eight Texture layers available to it. These eight Texture layers are accessed through the Shader.Texturelist[*x*] property, where *x* is a number between 1 and 8. If you were to reference Shader.Texturelist[1], this is exactly equivalent to the Shader.Texture property we have been using until now.

You can decide to work with the available Texture layers in two ways: First, you can use predefined layer "modes" that allow you to easily assign multiple Texture objects to a Shader for specific effects that are quite common uses of multitexturing. Second, you can decide to control every aspect of every layer to create your own unique effects. In this section, we will be looking at how to work with both predefined layer modes and advanced layer control.

NOTE

Note that this section might be difficult because of the way the standard Shader is set up. You see, you are going to learn shortcuts to advanced properties as well as how to control the advanced standard Shader properties directly. What you need to remember is that often there will be more than one way to accomplish your goals in this section. As we begin to work with the advanced properties, you may begin to see some overlap between properties that you learned as shortcuts. What you might want to consider is learning the shortcuts first and then, when you need more control, look into the advanced standard Shader properties.

Predefined Layer Modes

We will be working with four types of predefined layer modes through special shortcut properties defined for the standard Shader. These shortcut properties define automatically many of the advanced layer controls you will learn in the next section. Four shortcuts for predefined layer modes extend the capabilities of the standard Shader: Shader.Reflectionmap, Shader.Glossmap, Shader.Diffuselightmap, and Shader.Specularlightmap.

NOTE

When you work with any of these Shader properties, you will likely control the main Texture for the Shader through the Shader.Texture property. Only until you need advanced control will you begin to use the Shader.Texturelist [x] property.

Reflection Map Laboratory

You need to understand the scope of what is meant by a *reflection map*. Many often misinterpret the capability of the Shader.Reflectionmap property to mean that the standard Shader can be used for real-time reflections of the environment. This is simply not true. A reflection map uses a Texture to make it look as though the surface is reflecting the Texture, rather than the Texture being applied directly to the surface. This means that it is possible to create the look of chrome or metal; however, it does not mean that you can use reflection maps to create mirrors. You are not reflecting the environment, but rather, you are using a map to simulate what would be reflected if the environment happened to look like the given map.

To understand what a reflection map is, you need to remember that everything in the 3D environment is simulated to look as if it is real. As with many other aspects of Texturing, it is very important that you understand the impact of the choices you make in code as well as how these choices are impacted by the assets you choose to work with.

It is possible to use reflection maps to create some rather convincing demonstrations of reflective surfaces. However, the overall effect of reflection maps will not reproduce well on paper because part of their appeal is the way they change, depending on the orientation of the Model. If you open the file named "Reflection Map Laboratory" on the CD and press Play, you will be presented with several choices. Figure 14.7 is a screenshot from the Reflection Map Laboratory that explains the function of the various controls for the laboratory.

FIGURE 14.7

Screenshot from the Reflection Map Laboratory.

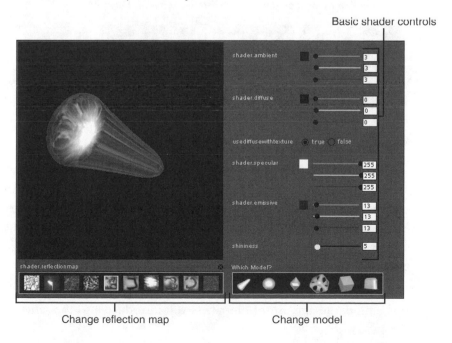

In the Reflection Map Laboratory, you have access to a wide number of bitmaps to use as reflection maps. In addition, I have provided several different types of Models—curved, flat, and Models with combinations of both. Note that some of the reflection maps that work well on curved Models do not work as well on flat ones. In addition, pay attention to the fact that I have given you control over many of the standard Shader parameters in this demo. This is because you must understand that setting the reflection map property does not mean you can ignore all the basic surface properties. Pay close attention to your Ambient, Diffuse, Specular, Emissive, and Shininess settings when trying to build a spectacular reflective material.

I realize that this can be difficult, so here are a few pointers: Take close note of the reflection maps I have provided. There is an art to creating really good reflection maps, of which there are a few general tips that can help you as you begin to create your own. Remember that the reflections are simulated; you will not be able to actually reflect other Models in the environment or have interreflections (reflections of reflections). Figure 14.8 illustrates all the images provided for reflection maps in this demonstration.

FIGURE 14.8

Examples of all the reflection maps included with the Reflection Map Laboratory.

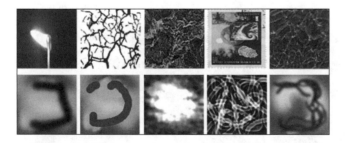

From these choices, you can see that the reflection maps can be divided into roughly two groups: photographic images and drawings. If you are trying to create a reflection that *looks* like it is reflecting the environment, you should consider using a more photographic reflection map. If you are trying to create a generally reflective material, you might use a drawn reflection map.

When drawing a reflection map, you should keep in mind a few general rules. For example, the amount of blurriness you introduce into the reflection map will translate into the *finish* of the final material. Blurry maps will produce dull metals, whereas sharp maps will produce highly polished metals. When drawing a reflection map, you generally want some amount of blur rather than a map dominated by sharp lines. Try to create large swaths of dark and light areas rather than small noisy maps. Finally, if there are specific colors in your scene, try to use these in the reflection map; otherwise, leave the reflection map only levels of gray.

In addition to the reflection map you choose, you need to work with the basic Shader settings in order to build convincing materials. Often, you will want to have a dark, ambient, diffuse color and a bright, specular color. I often add some amount of Emissive into my metals to give them a bit of warmth as well.

Try some of the following settings for the standard Shader properties to achieve various types of metals. By altering the reflection map you use for each, you can adjust the "finish" of the given metal. Exploring these examples will help you gain a better understanding of how these standard properties work in conjunction with reflection maps to create dramatic materials.

Bright, hot gold:

- Shader.Ambient—rgb(217,97,3)
- Shader.Diffuse—rgb(178,20,0)
- Shader.Specular—rgb(255,255,145)
- Shader.Emissive—rgb(116,62,13)
- Shader.Shininess—2

Icy, cold platinum:

- Shader.Ambient—rgb(5,5,5)
- Shader.Diffuse—rgb(0,0,5)
- Shader.Specular—rgb(250,250,255)
- Shader.Emissive—rgb(0,0,4)
- Shader.Shininess—3

Electric chrome:

- Shader.Ambient—rgb(255,255,255)
- Shader.Diffuse—rgb(0,0,0)
- Shader.Specular—rgb(190,220,255)
- Shader.Emissive—rgb(0,0,255)
- Shader.Shininess—2

Also, be sure to change Models often while you are testing—some Models will create reflections better than others, depending on the reflection map you use. If you observe what is successful and what is not in this closed environment, it will be easier for you to create your own reflective materials later.

Additional Mapping Shortcuts

In addition to the Shader.Reflectionmap property are the Shader.Glossmap, Shader.Diffuselightmap, and Shader.Specularlightmap properties. I will explain each of these separately, but we will look at a demonstration that combines all four of these shortcuts on the Shader.Texture property at the end of this subsection. In addition, remember that these properties are only shortcuts to Shader properties that you will learn about later in this chapter in the section "Advanced Standard Shader Controls."

The Shader.Glossmap property allows you to define a Texture as a *gloss map*, which is a type of Texture used to determine which areas on a given Model are bright and which are dark. It is often difficult to create scenes in which your Models appear affected by the lighting in the scene. Areas of a gloss map that are bright will be affected by lighting, whereas other sections will trail off into darkness. Gloss maps work well when combined with the Shader.Texture property—or when used alone. Using gloss maps is a great way to introduce subtleties and small glowing areas into your Models without requiring a lighting Node.

The next standard Shader property shortcut we will be looking at is the Shader.Diffuselightmap property. A diffuse light map will be affected by the direction or position of the first nonambient Light Node in a scene but not by the color of lights. You can use a diffuse light map to create the appearance of many lighting Nodes in a scene without needing the actual Nodes. In addition, the last of the standard Shader property shortcuts is the Shader.Specularlightmap property. Whereas a specular light map will change its orientation based on the lights in a scene, you can use the Shader.Shininess property to affect the size of the specular light map, as expressed on a given Model. A specular light map will be much brighter than the diffuse light map. You should consider combining these with other map types to gain a very wide variety of effects.

Predefined Layer-Mode Laboratory

On the CD is a file named "Layer-Mode Laboratory" that gives you access to all the standard Shader properties you have learned so far, in addition to the ability to set the Texture, Reflectionmap, Glossmap, Diffuselightmap, and Specularlightmap properties. Figure 14.9 illustrates the various controls you will find in this laboratory for learning about these properties visually.

FIGURE 14.9

A screenshot from the Layer-Mode Laboratory.

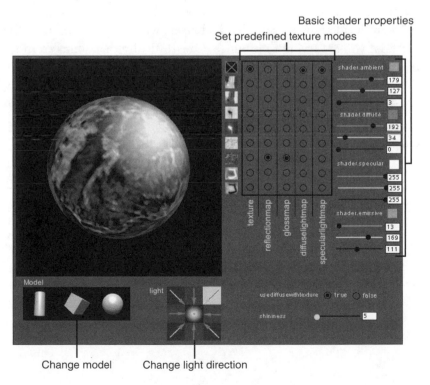

In the Layer-Mode Laboratory, I suggest that you first focus on the individual layer modes and then examine combinations of layer modes. Many combinations of layer modes are available in this demonstration. I suggest testing the success of layer mode combinations when applied to different Models. Many times, choices you make for the box Model will not work at all for the sphere Model, and vice versa.

Advanced Standard Shader Controls

In this section, we will be working with the advanced controls over the individual Texture layers of the standard Shader. Remember that the predefined layer modes from the previous section are merely shortcuts to the properties we will be examining in this section. Also, keep in mind that because of the nature of this advanced topic, the results of working with advanced Shader.Texture layer controls can vary from machine to machine more so than in other areas.

Texturelist

The Shader.Texturelist property is a linear list that contains eight available Texture layers. You are able to assign several Textures to a single Shader, and you can decide how these individual layers will blend together for the final material you are trying to produce. One difficulty that stems from the fact that there is a Shader.Texture property and a Shader.Texturelist property is that there are also many other properties of the standard Shader that have shortcut and "list" versions. Table 14.3 lists the advanced standard Shader properties we will be working with in this section and the next section in this chapter.

TABLE 14.3   Advanced Standard Shader Properties

Property	Purpose
Texture/Texturelist	Assigns Texture objects to the eight texture layers.
Texturemode/Texturemodelist	Determines the method of applying textures to Models and Meshes.
Blendfunction/Blendfunctionlist	Determines how the Texture layers will blend together.
Blendsource/Blendsourcelist	Determines whether the alpha information in a Texture is also used to control layer blending.

TABLE 14.3   Continued

Property	Purpose
Blendconstant/Blendconstantlist	Used to control layer blending that does not use alpha information.
Texturetransform/Texturetransformlist	This property is a transform that allows you to scale, rotate, and position Textures.
Wraptransform/Wraptransformlist	This property allows you to control some of the methods of applying Textures to Models with greater detail.
Texturerepeat/Texturerepeatlist	This property controls whether a Texture will tile or only be drawn once.

Note that the list is separated into those properties that you will be learning in this section and those you will be learning in the next section. The ultimate goal is to learn how to use all these properties together. As you look at the sheer number of properties and settings represented by this list, remember that you are not going to be using every one of them for each material you build. Many times, you will only use one or two of them. However, while you are learning the scope of the advanced standard Shader properties, this still might feel intimidating. That is why I have broken these properties into two sections. Also, they address two slightly different aspects of the concepts behind multitexturing.

Texturemodelist

The Shader.Texturemodelist property is used to determine how a Texture layer is applied to a Model's geometry. When you create a Modelresource with Lingo, not only does Director create coordinates for Model geometry but also coordinates that describe how to apply Textures to that geometry. Geometry coordinates are referred to as *XYZ coordinates*, and Texture coordinates are referred to as *UVW coordinates*. The letters *U*, *V*, and *W* are used to differentiate the fact that these coordinates are used for Textures, but the locations that are referred to with these coordinates are coordinates in XYZ space.

Normally, when you apply a Texture object to one of the Texture layers, the Texturemode property for that layer will tell the Texture to use the UVW coordinates stored with the Modelresource for the Model. However, you can decide to ignore the UVW coordinate information that was saved with the geometry and use several other methods of applying the Texture to the geometry. The possible choices for the Shader.Texturemode property are listed in Table 14.4.

TABLE 14.4 List of Possible Texturemode Settings

Value	Purpose
#none	Uses the UV mapping coordinates that have been supplied with the geometry. When you're creating Modelresources via Lingo, this UV information is created for you. In external Modeling programs, you would need to make sure you specifically create this mapping information for Director.
#wrapplanar	Projects the Texture onto the Model as if it were shined on the Model from an overhead projector. Pixels at the edge of the Texture will repeat.
#wrapspherical	Wraps the Texture onto the Model as if the Model were placed in the center of the Texture like a blanket, and then you pick up the blanket from the corners of the Texture. With this Texture mode, the seams can be very obvious, unless you are working with a sphere.
#wrapcylindrical	In this Texture mode, imagine that you place the Model at the edge of a blanket that is the Texture and then roll the Model up with the Texture. The top and bottom seams tend to be noticeable, but this mode is very useful.
#diffuselight	This Texture mode will apply the Texture in the direction of the first non-ambient Light in the scene.
#specularlight	This Texture mode will apply the Texture in the direction of the first non-ambient Light in the scene. In addition, you can control the size of the mapping with the Shader.Shininess property.
#reflection	The Texture is applied to the Model, similar to #wrapspherical, but when the Model rotates, the Texture does not rotate with it. Rather, the Texture rotates "through" the Model, creating the appearance of reflection. (This is also the reason why spherical objects do not do as well as semicurved objects when you create reflective materials.)

The settings for the Shader.Texturemode property are among the most difficult to grasp the first time you work with them. We will be looking at several more properties, but before you try to absorb any more properties, open the file named "Texture-Layer Laboratory" on the CD and press Play. This laboratory is quite complex due to the sheer number of properties you are able to control as well as the fact that there are eight layers of these properties—one for each Texture layer. Figure 14.10 illustrates the controls for this laboratory we will be working with in this section.

FIGURE 14.10

A screenshot from the Texture-Layer Laboratory on the CD.

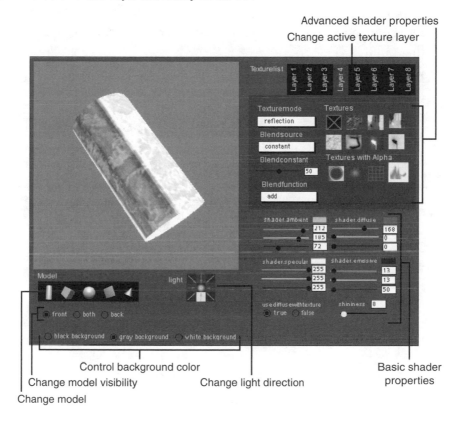

Select the box Model and apply the Texture of the match to the first Texture layer. The match Texture stretches to fill the sides of the box Model. Note that the Shader.Texturemode property is set to #none in this case. However, this does *not* mean the Texture is not being mapped to the Model. Look at the Model—it has the Texture of the match mapped to it. The #none setting forces the standard Shader to use the UV coordinates saved along with the Modelresource when it was first created. The default UVW coordinates are plotted in the same locations as the outermost edge Vertices in a Model. In

Chapter 28, "Mesh Deformation and Detailed Picking," we will look at how to control these UVW texture coordinates as well as the geometry.

Note that with an external 3D modeling program, you will have control over the UV coordinates. You can actually move them around and create extremely complex texture mapping. But as you know, we are focusing on the creation of 3D worlds from within Director. This is important because even if you are working with 3D programs, at some point the Models will be coming into Director, and you will need to understand what controls are available to you at that point.

If you change the Shader.Texturemode property to #wrapplanar, the Texture wraps around the Model much differently. Note that the UV coordinates supplied with the Modelresource are now ignored and instead the Texture is applied to the Model, as illustrated in Figure 14.11.

FIGURE 14.11

Example of how a Texture will wrap around a Model when the #wrapplanar Texture mode is used.

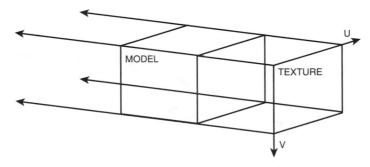

Note that the edges of the Texture will repeat along the sides of the box, creating a streaking effect. Creating an alpha channel that renders the edge pixels transparent can eliminate this streaking effect. However, this effect will not be as noticeable on some of the other Model types; try changing your current Model to see what I mean.

Now, change the Shader.Texturemode property to #wrapspherical. It may be very difficult to see what is actually happening with this texture mapping. Try also changing your Model to a sphere; change your Texture to the green grid and set the Model.Visibility to both. This will allow you to see through the Model to the other side. Often, this can help you at least visualize how the

Texture is applied in this mode. In addition, refer to the illustration in Figure 14.12, which shows how the Texture is wrapped onto a sphere and then applied to the Model.

FIGURE 14.12

An example of how a Texture will wrap around a Model when the #wrapspherical Texture mode is used.

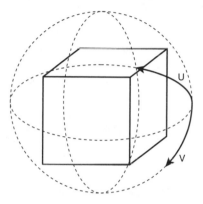

The #wrapspherical Texture mode is an important one to understand because it is also used for the #reflection Texture mode. The only difference is that for #wrapspherical, the Texture coordinates move with the Model. When Texturemode is set to #reflection, the Texture coordinates do not move at all.

If you now change Texturemode to #wrapcylindrical, you can see that there is yet another way to map your Textures on to Models. Figure 14.13 illustrates the method that is used to apply the Texture to the Model for #wrapcylindrical mapping.

Again, you may want to change between different types of Models to observe how this type of mapping will change depending on the type of Model you are mapping onto. It is important to remember that the Texturemode property only refers to the first layer of Texture information. You are able to set the Texturemode property of each layer independently of one another to create a wide variety of effects. However, in order for you to understand how multiple Textures interact with one another, we will need to look at how the blending of Texture layers can be controlled.

FIGURE 14.13

An example of how a Texture will wrap around a Model when the #wrapcylindrical Texture mode is used.

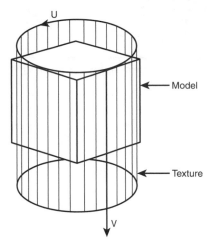

The #specularlight and #diffuselight settings generate mapping coordinates differently from the previous Texturemode settings. They generate one Texture coordinate per Vertex of the Model. If there are more Vertices, there will be more texture coordinates. However, the final result of these two Texturemode settings is affected by the position or rotation of the first non-ambient Light Node in the scene, but it is *not* affected by the Light color.

This is important because these two settings are difficult to learn how to control at first. You see, these settings tend to be easier to learn if the Models they are applied to are not moving through the scene. In general, you can use both these settings to create materials that appear to be interacting with lighting in the scene, without requiring additional lighting Nodes.

NOTE

Note that several of the Texturemode choices—#reflection, #specularlight, and #diffuselight—may remind you of some of the choices you learned about for the standard Shader shortcut properties for creating reflection maps, diffuse light maps, and specular light maps. This is no accident—for example, when you assign a reflection map through the shortcut Shader property, the Texturemode property as well as several other advanced properties are set for you. Controlling Texturemode directly allows you a greater degree of control over the overall texture itself.

Also, if you are experiencing problems with the Texture modes, keep in mind that it is recommended that you do not skip any layers in the Texture list. This means that you should assign Textures to contiguous Texture layers, starting with the first layer. Although this problem will not affect every video card, because you cannot predict what video cards your user will have, it is best to plan your multitexturing solutions with this issue in mind.

Blendfunctionlist

As you begin to apply multiple Textures to a single Shader, it becomes necessary to control the method by which the layers of Textures blend together. Four methods of blending Textures are supplied with the standard Shader that will have a great effect on the overall visual quality of the final composite material. Table 14.5 lists the four possible values for the Shader.Blendfunction and the Shader.Blendfunctionlist properties.

TABLE 14.5 Values for the Shader.Blendfunction Property

Value	Purpose
#multiply	This is the default Blendfunction setting. Colors from the current Texture layer will be multiplied with the colors from the layers beneath. This has the effect of revealing Texture layers in the sections of the Texture that are light and concealing areas that are dark.
#add	This Blendfunction setting adds colors together and clamps the colors at white. This means that as you add the rgb() values for each pixel, if a pixel adds up to white, it will remain white (and not circle back around to black again). This Blendfunction setting creates very bright, dynamic materials.
#replace	This Blendfunction setting acts similar to the "normal" blending mode in Adobe Photoshop. That is, all Textures below this level will be replaced by the current Texture. This mode can be helpful if you want to hide the layers beneath this one. If you are working with a Texture with an alpha channel, you can use #replace so that the areas of opaque Texture will replace everything below, and transparent areas will blend, depending on how semitransparent they are.
#blend	This Blendfunction setting works in conjunction with two more Shader properties to blend the Texture with the layer below. In addition, the #blend Blendfunction setting can be used to control the amount of blending between the first Texture layer and the Shader.Diffuse color.

Blendsourcelist and Blendconstantlist

When the Shader.Blendfunction property is set to #blend, the Shader will depend on the Shader.Blendsource and Shader.Blendconstant properties to determine exactly how to blend with the other layers. When Shader.Blendsource is set to #constant, the Shader will use Shader.Blendconstant to determine what percentage of the composite material should be from the current Texture layer and what percentage from the previous Texture layers. If you set Shader.Blendsource to #alpha, Blendconstant will be ignored and any alpha information that the current Texture layer contains will be used to blend the Texture with the previous Textures. In this way, the Blendsource/Blendconstant properties allow you to decide whether you want to control the opacity of the Texture layer in a linear way or with predefined alpha channel information.

Shader.Texture Transformations

In this section, we will be working with the advanced topic of Texture transformations. When applying a Texture to a Shader, we have been using several of the tools available for making sure that the Texture stretches correctly onto the Model. We know that for Lingo-generated Models, UV coordinates are generated that can provide hints for the Texture to wrap around the Model. In addition, we know that we can override these settings with the Texturemode and Texturemodelist properties. Rather than using the UV coordinates supplied with the geometry of a Model, we can try to wrap the Texture around the Model using built-in methods—or we can even use reflection-style mapping. No matter the choice of mapping, we still have more options.

In this section, we will be looking at the Shader.Texturetransform property and the Shader.Wraptransform property. These two properties are mildly similar, but there are differences that make them exclusive to one another.

When you apply a Texture to a Shader, you are able to apply transformations to that Texture in UV space. Essentially, you are able to scale, rotate, and reposition where the Texture lies in UV coordinates. Controlling the UV coordinates through Texture transformations allows you to perform two specific tasks: control the tiling of Textures and build decal Textures.

Tiling Textures

By default, the Shader.Texturerepeat property is set to True when you apply a Texture object to the Texturelist of a Shader. If you do not change this setting, Textures will tile infinitely in both the U and V directions. However, you also know that when you apply a Texture to a Shader, it automatically stretches to fill the current Model geometry. You are able to alter how the Texture stretches by changing the relative scale of the Texture after it has been applied to a Model. Scaling the Shader.Texturetransform property can be approached with the following syntax:

```
Scene.shader[x].texturetransform.scale(U,V,1)
```

Look closely at the values I have suggested as the arguments for this function: U, V, and 1. Note that the 1 will never change—and there is a very specific reason for this. You see, when you scale a Texture layer via its Texturetransform, you are only scaling it on the U/V axis—you do not have any control over the W axis, but at the same time, it would not make sense for you to have control over this because the scaling of the Texture layer happens in the space of the Texture, which only exists in two dimensions.

If you scale Texturetransform between 0 and 1, the tiling of the Texture layer will become much more obvious. As the scaling decreases, you will be able to see more tiles of the individual Texture fill the Model. It is also possible to scale the Texture beyond 1, but in this case you will not see any tiling—in fact, the Texture layer will scale such that you will not be able to see the whole Texture object itself. Note that as with regular Node transformation, you must not set the scale to 0; otherwise, you will get a script error.

Decal Textures

Remember that the Shader.Texturerepeat property is set to True by default; if you set this to False, you can create what are generally known as *decal Textures*. A *decal* is a Texture that is applied once to a Mesh. Because of this, it is often very important to be able to rotate, scale, and reposition that decal exactly where you want it on the Mesh. What better time than now to introduce the rotation and translation of the Texturetransform property?

In addition to controlling the scale, you are also able to rotate and change the position of the Texture layer—but again, be aware that this will take place in U/V space. If you try to reposition the Texture layer, you will need to use the following syntax:

```
Scene.shader[x].texturetransform.translate(U,V,0)
```

Note that, in this case, the U and V coordinates are not scalar but rather are used to reposition the Texture itself. Texture coordinates exist in Texture layer space—this is important to understand. You see, positional Texture coordinates are going to range from 0 to 1. You can give coordinates larger than this, but the Texture will be applied to the Mesh beyond the scope of the Mesh so that it will be impossible to see. If you stay within the 0–1 range, the decal will remain within the boundaries of the Mesh.

Finally, you are also able to control the rotation of the Texturetransform property. In this case, you will only control one parameter with the following syntax:

```
Scene.shader[x].texturetransform.rotate(0,0,angle)
```

In this case, `0,0` refers to the upper-left corner of the Texture in U/V space, and `angle` is the angle around that point where you intend to spin the Texture. As with Node transformation, you should use the `rotate()`, `scale()`, and `translate()` functions to change the Texturetransform property. In addition, realize that it is equally possible to call `texturetransform.identity()` to reset Texturetransform to its initial state.

Texture Transformation Laboratory

Texture transformations are among the most difficult transformations to learn and understand the very first time you begin to work with 3D environments. I strongly encourage you to work with the Texture Transformation Laboratory that I have put together until you can predict what will happen when you make changes to the Texture transform. This laboratory gives you access to many of the standard Shader properties as well as control over the transformations you can apply to Textures. Figure 14.14 is a screenshot from the "Texture Transformation Laboratory" file included on the CD; open this file and press Play.

To begin working with Texture transformations, stop the rotation of the Model first and choose the box Model when you begin. Apply one of the tiling Textures, such as the match. Then, work with the scaling—watch how the Texture scales. Now try rotating the Texture; then try repositioning it.

FIGURE 14.14

A screenshot from the Texture Transformation Laboratory.

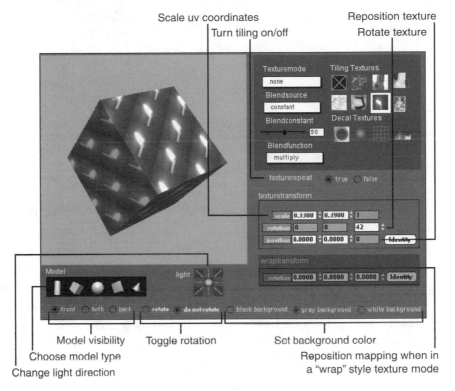

Next, use the green grid Texture that has an alpha channel. If you set your Model to be double sided, you will be able to see the mapping on both sides of the Model at once. Because you should have an intrinsic sense of the grid, it is often easier to visualize what is happening to the grid as it is applied to the Model. Continue to scale, rotate, and reposition the grid so that you can begin to predict how the grid will Move. In addition, try changing Models to see how the grid is applied to different Models with the same Texture transformation.

Finally, choose one of the Textures and set the Texturerepeat property to False. This will allow you to control the Textures as decals. Try using some decals with alpha channels, and others without. Note that if you are using software rendering, changing this setting will have no effect on the Texture. In short, Textures will always tile if you are working in software rendering mode.

NOTE

> On those decals without alpha channels, and even on some of the Textures with alpha channels, you will probably notice that the edge pixels of the Textures repeat across the Model. This is a known problem, but one with a workaround. When creating a Texture that is to be used as a decal, you need to create an alpha channel that surrounds the entire Texture. This way, when the edge pixels repeat, those pixels will be transparent.

Texturetransform Versus Wraptransform

Notice near the bottom-right side of the Texture Transform Laboratory is a section named *Wraptransform* that should be grayed out (so that you do not have access to the control panel). This is because the Wraptransform property is a special portion of Texture transformations that has a subtle difference from the transformations you have been learning. Unlike Texturetransform, Wraptransform does not apply to a Texture but rather to the coordinates it uses to wrap around the Model. However, the Wraptransform property only applies if you are working with a Texture mode that uses a "wrap" mapping style, such as #wrapplanar, #wrapcylindrical, or #wrapspherical. Note that in the Texture Transform Laboratory, you are able to change the Texturemode property—and if you change it to any of these three mapping styles, the Wraptransform panel will become available to you.

The Shader.Wraptransform property can be rotated so that the Texture layer to be wrapped around the Model can be changed in terms of its orientation. The one important note you must understand is that `Shader.wraptransform.rotate(U,V,W)` is rotated in three-dimensional space— literally, you are rotating the mapping coordinates used to apply the Texture layer, not the Texture layer itself.

This means you can actually use Texturetransform and Wraptransform together. Often, you will only need to rotate Wraptransform 180, 90, or 45 degrees in order to apply Textures correctly to a Model. Of all the transformations, Wraptransform can be one of the most difficult to learn how to control.

Animated Texture Transforms

In addition to the two examples we have looked at—tiling and decals—you may also want to look at the file named "Animated Texturetransforms" on the

CD. This file is a very small example of how you might continuously translate the Texturetransform property to easily create a type of animated texture. Figure 14.15 is a screenshot from this example that shows a semitransparent Texture applied to a box.

A screenshot from the "Animated Texturetransforms" file.

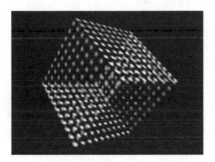

Notice in this figure that you are able to see both the inside and outside of the box, and when you play the example, these dots will endlessly slide across the surface of the box. Using this method, you could create sliding, rotating, or scaling Textures, which is often just enough for certain projects. If not, continue on to Chapter 17, "Special Effects," where we will examine many ways to create animated Textures for your Models. Detailed comments in this file explain how this effect was achieved. Although the initial setup of the scene contributes much in this example, the animation effect only requires one line of code.

Texturetransforms and Texture Layers

In case there weren't enough options for you as a developer in terms of Textures, I need to tell you that in addition to the fact that there is a Shader.Texturetransform property, there is also a Shader.Texturetransformlist property. Remember that with many of the other Shader properties, the "base" property is merely a shortcut to the first Texture layer. This is also the case with the Texturetransform property as well as the Wraptransform property.

I have created a small example for you to look at that combines control of individual Texture layers and Texture transformations for layers. Figure 14.16 is a screenshot from the "Layered Texturetransforms" file on the CD.

FIGURE 14.16

A screenshot from the "Layered Texturetransforms" file.

Note that this example has two Texture layers—the background image of a building and a Texture layer containing a stamp. The stamp has been designed as a decal Texture so that it does not tile. In addition, it has alpha channel information that allows it to still have a complex edge—although this may be difficult to see unless you open the file. Detailed comments in this file explain how this effect was achieved. One final note on this demonstration: If you are using software rendering mode, the texture will always repeat no matter the setting of Texturerepeat. Unfortunately, this means that on some machines, users will not see the second Texture as a decal but rather as a tiled Texture.

Summary

Textures are easily one of the largest areas of confusion in any 3D environment. If you are reading this chapter for the first time, you may feel overwhelmed by the number of properties and the depth of those properties while trying to learn how to apply the concepts.

As with every other chapter in this book, I offer you the following advice: Go slowly at first, master the sections you need to, and continue adding individual skills as you go. The standard Shader is perhaps the most complex element in Director's 3D environment, just based on the sheer number of properties— and the fact that these properties multiply due to the number of layers of Textures available.

We have looked at methods of controlling Texture/Model opacity and Texture scaling quality as well as creating reflective materials, Texture transformations, and decal/tile Textures, in addition to Texture layers. All these loosely fall under the blanket of "multitexturing" because they are used in conjunction with one another to achieve many multitextured effects.

Shaders and Textures are used to create surfaces and materials. Multitexturing is an important part of controlling the material aspects of a surface, but as you have seen, you cannot overlook the basic surface qualities of a Shader when designing a multitexture. Often, you will only need a handful of the advanced properties coupled with a strong background in the basic properties.

FAQ

Does Director support bump maps?

> *Bump maps* are a type of map commonly used in 3D animation programs, and sometimes in real-time 3D environments, to modulate the surface of a Model so that it appears to have dents, embossments, or raised areas. Bump maps are powerful because they provide another method of simulating the effects of complex geometry without the detail and overhead of complex geometry. However, bump maps are not currently supported in Director. It is possible that you could create your own bump map solution with the Meshdeform Modifier. The Meshdeform Modifier is explained in Chapter 28. However, realize that simulating bump maps with the Meshdeform Modifier is a nontrivial application of the Meshdeform Modifier that is beyond the scope of this book.

I need to control UV coordinates much more precisely than anything I have seen inside Director. What are my options outside of Director?

> This is an important question. Many times, it is just not possible to create believable Textures without using advanced UV coordinate mapping. You will want to look at the specific features, but every advanced 3D modeling solution I know of offers some method of visually controlling the UV coordinates through a visual 3D tool. That is, most 3D modelers have some method of allowing you to "grab" Texture coordinates and reposition them. This type of control is essential when you're learning how to create low-poly-count Models and also when you're learning how to combine many materials into a single Texture object. You should consider what your needs are and look at the tools available for working with Texture coordinates. Of course, even if

you learn to create Texture coordinates outside of Director, it is still important to learn how to control Texture mapping and coordinates inside of Director with the standard Shader properties. This is especially true if you are going to be creating the majority of your environments via Lingo, because when applying Textures to those Models, you must use the standard Shader mappings.

CHAPTER 15

Non-Photorealistic Rendering

This chapter explores techniques of non-photorealistic (NPR) rendering with built-in nonstandard Shaders in Director. In addition, we will examine several NPR techniques involving Modifiers. The methods examined in this chapter are offered as an alternative to photorealism.

NPR rendering has several advantages over photorealistic rendering. First, nonstandard Shaders and Modifiers have a relatively small number of properties; therefore, the effects we'll create will be achieved without an excess of code. Second, NPR rendering does not utilize textures, so you can use these methods to reduce the download requirements for a project.

The beauty of working with NPR rendering is that it offers you unconventional stylistic options capable of both abstract and descriptive visuals. Learning to control these uncommon tools provides you with a way to set your projects apart from others. However, making the choice to use NPR is not as simple as flipping a switch; I will explain the techniques and strategies to applying NPR rendering in this chapter.

In this chapter are a variety of demonstrations, many of which are of the laboratory style. I encourage you to look closely at the figures in this chapter and try to re-create the effects illustrated with the laboratories. The NPR Shaders tend to be overlooked because the settings that you must make to produce interesting results are generally within a very small range. For that reason, experimenting with the laboratories in this chapter should be given a lengthy session so that you can grasp the substantial range of these powerful tools.

What Is NPR Rendering?

NPR rendering differs from standard rendering techniques in several ways. Visually, the final product does not attempt to achieve verisimilitude. Rather, NPR rendering simulates traditional cartooning and drawing techniques with some degree of success.

NPR rendering can be achieved in several ways in Director. The first way is through using one of the built-in nonstandard Shaders: Newsprint, Engraver, or Painter. The second way to achieve NPR rendering is through the use of the Toon or Inker Modifiers. The third approach combines Modifiers with both photo-realistic and NPR Shaders for a variety of effects.

Nonstandard Shaders have access to all the properties of the standard Shader. However, they will ignore the vast majority of these properties because they do not apply. Second, the properties of the standard Shader that they do use—Diffuse, Ambient, and Renderstyle—do not always control the surface quality of Models in the same way you have learned in the past. They utilize the same names, but they have different meanings.

NPR with Nonstandard Shaders

You will find that the implementation of nonstandard Shaders varies with the renderer and video card. These variations sometimes change the final rendering enough to warrant this caution. I have designed the demos in this chapter primarily using OpenGL acceleration. If you are using DirectX or software rendering, some of the effects may not be as dramatic.

This presents a difficulty for both the designer and developer. If you are going to deliver your projects via Shockwave, you may want to create a set of property values for each renderer and then detect which renderer is being used by the system and use the property values that you predefined for that renderer. It is more work, but if your project demands precision, you may need to take this extra step.

Newsprint Shader

The Newsprint Shader is intended to look like the stippled ink of newspaper photography. Objects are rendered in a monochromatic spectrum that defaults to white and black. Although the black must remain, you can change the color used for highlights to any color you wish. Figure 15.1 illustrates several Models rendered with the Newsprint Shader.

FIGURE 15.1

Several examples of the Newsprint Shader.

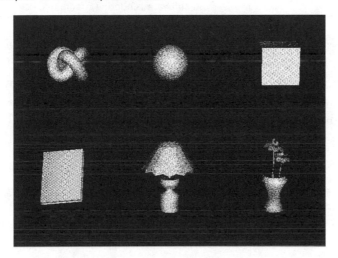

Figure 15.1 shows several types of Models. In the bottom row you see several Models of real-world objects: a book, a lamp, and a vase with flowers. Each of these has been stylized through the use of the Newsprint Shader. In the top row you see several "ideal" objects: a torus knot, a sphere, and a cube. These are represented to show how abstract or ideal objects become less characteristic, less predictable.

Newsprint Properties

Although the Newsprint Shader has a surprisingly small number of properties, you have several possible ways to utilize this Shader to achieve different results. Table 15.1 lists the properties that are available to this Shader.

Table 15.1   Newsprint Shader Properties

Property	Range	Purpose
Brightness	0–100	Controls the size of the highlight area.
Density	0–100	Controls amount of "stippling" used to define the Model.

Table 15.1   Continued

Property	Range	Purpose
Diffuse	rgb(r,g,b)	Controls the highlight color.
Renderstyle	#fill #wire #point	Controls the method of displaying the faces of the Model. Does not work in software-rendering mode.

The Diffuse property of the Newsprint Shader is not well documented. The purpose of the Diffuse property in this case is to provide the highlight color of the Model. The shaded areas used to describe the geometry are always black, and the amount of shading is defined by the Density property. However, the density of shading can be undermined by the Brightness property. With the highest settings of brightness, the Model will appear to have no detail.

NOTE

For each of the nonstandard Shaders, the Renderstyle property still works; if you are using OpenGL or DirectX hardware rendering, you can still use the #fill, #wire, and #point modes of rendering in conjunction with these Shaders.

One interesting quirk that you should keep in mind while you utilize the Newsprint and Engraver Shaders is that the highlighted and shaded areas of the Model will only be determined by the first directional or first point Light Node in a scene. The directional or point Light Node with the lowest index will be the only Light considered when the direction of the highlight is determined.

In addition, the color of the Light Node does not affect the final rendering, including luminance. Therefore, even if the first directional or point Light Node color is black, you will still be able to see your Models. It is possible to exploit this fact if you are going to create a scene that utilizes both nonstandard and standard Shaders in order to create a Light Node that affects certain Models and not others.

Newsprint Laboratory

On the CD you'll find a file named "Newsprint Laboratory." Open this file and press Play. On the Stage are two Models—one rectilinear and the other curvilinear. Adjust the sliders to create a range of effects and note the way that each of these Models reacts to the various settings. Figure 15.2 illustrates several examples from "Newsprint Laboratory" you can try to emulate.

FIGURE 15.2

Several examples from the Newsprint Laboratory file.

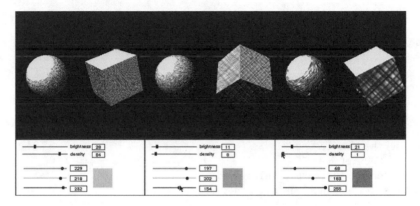

In this laboratory, the Models rotate to demonstrate the effect of the Newsprint Shader on a Model that is moving. Notice how the surface quality of the box seems to "pass through" the Texture. This can produce interesting visual effects when combined with Bones-based animation, which is covered in Chapter 22, "Bonesplayer Modifier."

The Jitter Technique

In this section, we will examine a technique for utilizing the Newsprint Shader. The purpose of this technique is to attempt to "jitter" the grain of the newsprint. The technique is applicable to other situations as well. There is a file on the CD named newsprint jitter that contains the code for this technique. Press Play and observe the visual effect of the jitter technique.

Several steps are required to set up the scene. The syntax used to create a Newsprint Shader utilizes the `newshader()` command, as follows:

```
Scene.newshader("shadername", #newsprint)
```

In the "Newsprint Jitter" file, several Newsprint Shaders are created on initialization of the movie. These Shaders are strategically assigned to Models in the environment so that the surface quality of several Models can be controlled via a single Shader. In total, three Newsprint Shaders are used in this example.

After the initialization and assignment of Shaders to the Models in the environment, the jittering of the Density property is accomplished through the following script:

```
1: property pCounter
2:
3: global scene
4:
5: on beginsprite
6:  pCounter = 0
7: end
8:
9: on exitframe
10:  -- increase the counter
11:  pCounter = pCounter + 1
12:  -- as the counter increases, selectively
13:  -- determine which shader.density to change
14:  if pCounter > 3 then
15:    scene.shader("walls").density = random(90,100)
16:    pCounter = 0
17:  else if pcounter > 2 then
18:    scene.shader("table").density = random(40,90)
19:  else if pcounter > 1 then
20:    scene.shader("lampbase").density = random(30,70)
21:  else if pcounter > 0 then
22:    scene.shader("lampshade").density = random(3,20)
23:  end if
24: end
```

The strength of this script is its ability to create surfaces in the room that are animated, even though we are technically looking at a static scene. By adding this layer of visual depth to the scene, we can draw focus by varying the amount of "jitter" in different areas. The eye will be drawn to areas of excitement rather than areas of rest. Therefore, with this strategy, you might make the areas you want users to look at jitter more.

Note that this technique is not only achieved through "jittering" the Density property but also through accurate choices for the diffuse color. The choice for three Shaders was determined due to the number of levels of luminosity required for the scene; only three levels of luminosity were required to distinguish the walls, lamp, and table.

Engraver Shader

The Engraver Shader is intended to simulate the aesthetic of engraved metal; it is successful at creating what appears to be more of a screen-printed graphic. Figure 15.3 illustrates several examples of geometry rendered with the Engraver Shader.

FIGURE 15.3

Examples of the Engraver Shader.

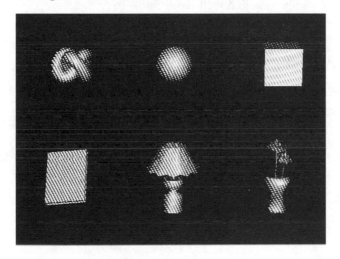

Notice how in each of these Models, the size of the white space varies in between the intersection of lines. It is through the size of these spaces that the geometry of the Model is conveyed. Because of this, the Engraver Shader tends to work well on most rectilinear Models and does not require much detail for curvilinear Models. The key is making sure that the boundaries of the Model are well defined.

Engraver Properties

The Engraver Shader is similar to Newsprint in terms of its low number of properties. Table 15.2 lists the properties used to control the Engraver Shader.

Table 15.2   Engraver Shader Properties

Property	Range	Purpose
Brightness	0–100	Controls the size of the highlight.
Density	0–100	Controls the size of lines.
Rotation	0–360	Controls the angle of lines.
Diffuse	rgb(r,g,b)	Controls the color of the highlight.
Renderstyle	#fill #wire #point	Controls the method of displaying the faces of the Model. Does not work in software-rendering mode.

Simulating lithography requires that you have control over more than the density of the lines and the brightness of the highlight. You also have control over the angle of rotation of the engraved lines. Control over the angle of the lines provides you with more variation than you might expect. Try experimenting with this property at specific angle degrees, such as 0, 30, 45, 60, 90, 120, and so on.

Engraver Laboratory

The Engraver Laboratory was designed to give you visual control over the properties of the Engraver Shader. On the CD you'll find a file named "Engraver Laboratory" that you should open and play. This laboratory provides you with a visual interface for controlling the properties of the Engraver Shader. Figure 15.4 illustrates several examples of NPR rendering created with the Engraver Shader.

FIGURE 15.4

Examples from the Engraver Laboratory.

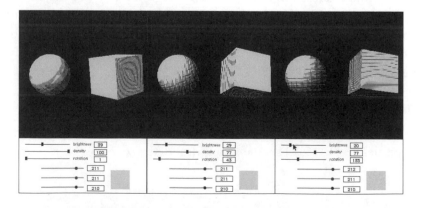

Notice how subtle changes in the properties of the Engraver Shader result in different visual styles. As you tweak the values for the properties, make sure you observe the quality of the Models in relation to the combination of properties. Setting a medium brightness and a low density will create visuals that may not seem engraved at all.

Multi-Shader Technique

If you were to draw an object on paper, you would need to utilize different types of shading, crosshatching, and angles to describe various sections of that object. Most likely you would need to describe various sections of the object in different ways. In the following technique, we will examine how to create multiple Shaders for greater control over the visual style of a Model.

Open the file named "Multi Shaders" on the CD and press Play. In the middle of the Stage you should see a book. This book was created in 3D Studio MAX and was comprised of two models: one for the pages and the other for the cover and binding. Before being exported from MAX, the binding and the pages were linked together. When MAX exports models that are linked, the hierarchy collapses into a single Director 3D Model. However, this single Model contains two Meshes and therefore has the ability to have two separate Shaders—one for each Mesh (the pages and the binding).

Notice the button named "switch model." If you click this button, you will be presented with flowers in a vase. Each flower and the vase belong to one Model. The "switch model" button will toggle between the book and the flowers. Figure 15.5 illustrates what each of these Models should look like.

I have created two custom handlers, named `initbook` and `initvase`, that contain the code used to create, assign, and modify the Shaders for the book and the vase, respectively. In general, these handlers reset the scene, set up new Shaders, clone the correct Model from another Castmember, and then assign the Shaders. Here's the specific script used to accomplish these tasks for the book:

```
1: on initbook
2:   --reset the world
3:   clearworld(scene)
4:
5:   --set up shader for the outside of the book
6:   shdA = scene.newshader("binding", #engraver)
7:   -- choose a dark brown color for the diffuse
```

```
 8:  shdA.diffuse = rgb(70,30,6)
 9:  -- set up the density, brightness and rotation
10:  shdA.density = 60
11:  shdA.brightness = 0
12:  shdA.rotation = 80
13:
14:  --set up shader for the pages of the book
15:  shdB = scene.newshader("pages", #engraver)
16:  --choose a cream color for the diffuse
17:  shdB.diffuse = rgb(230,230,199)
18:  -- set up density, brightness and rotation
19:  shdB.density = 99
20:  shdB.brightness = 2
21:  shdB.rotation = 14
22:
23:  -- clone the book from its castmember into the 3dworld
24:  obj = scene.cloneModelFromCastmember("book", "book", \
     member("book"))
25:
26:  -- assign "binding" shader to outside of book
27:  obj.shaderlist[1] = shdA
28:  -- assign "pages" shader to inside of book
29:  obj.shaderlist[2] = shdB
30:
31:  -- adjust camera
32:  scene.camera[1].fieldofview = 50
33: end
```

FIGURE 15.5

Book and flower vase Models utilizing multiple Shaders.

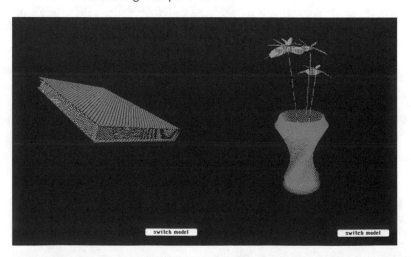

Note that in lines 27 and 29, I am assigning the new Shaders by index number. These Shader properties are in the first and second position because they were created this way in 3D Studio MAX. Near the end of the `initbook` handler is a small modification to the Camera that makes sure you can see the entire book as it rotates around. A similar section near the end of the `initvase` handler is dedicated to positioning the Model and the Camera. Here's the custom handler used to create, assign, and modify the Shaders for the flowers and vase:

```
1: on initvase
2:  --reset the world
3:  clearworld(scene)
4:
5:  --set up shader for the vase
6:  shdA = scene.newshader("vase", #engraver)
7:  --choose a muted green color for the diffuse
8:  shdA.diffuse = rgb(45,75,10)
9:  --set up density, brightness and rotation
10: shdA.density = 90
11: shdA.brightness = 60
12: shdA.rotation = 80
13:
14: --set up shader for the flowers
15: shdB = scene.newshader("flowers", #engraver)
16: --choose a medium green color for the diffuse
17: shdB.diffuse = rgb(50,130,10)
18: --set up density, brightness and rotation
19: shdB.density = 99
20: shdB.brightness = 0
21: shdB.rotation = 45
22:
23: --clone the vase from its castmember into the 3Dworld
24: obj = scene.cloneModelFromCastmember("vase", "vase", \
    member("vase"))
25:
26: --assign vase shader to the vase mesh
27: obj.shaderlist[1] = shdA
28: --assign the flower shader to each
29: --of the flower meshes
30: obj.shaderlist[2] = shdB
31: obj.shaderlist[3] = shdB
32: obj.shaderlist[4] = shdB
33:
34: --adjust the model
35: obj.rotate(-90,0,0)
36: obj.translate(0,680,-330)
```

```
37:
38:  --adjust the camera
39:  scene.camera[1].fieldofview = 50
40:  scene.camera[1].translate(0,250,0)
41:  scene.camera[1].rotate(-16,0,0)
42: end
```

Note that the initvase handler is similar to the initbook handler. The only large changes are the specifics of the Shader. If you were to plan a project that would use this type of Shader strategy, I would suggest converting these scripts into more general custom functions that accept arguments and are capable of reassigning multiple Shaders to many different Models with varying numbers of Meshes.

Painter Shader

The Painter Shader is unlike the previous Shaders we have looked at in several ways. The Painter Shader has a larger number of properties that are used to control the visual style. Because of this, it is important to understand that the Painter Shader is capable of a wider variety of stylizations. Figure 15.6 illustrates the usage of the Painter Shader in its most basic form, reducing objects to regions of black and white.

FIGURE 15.6

Examples of the Painter Shader.

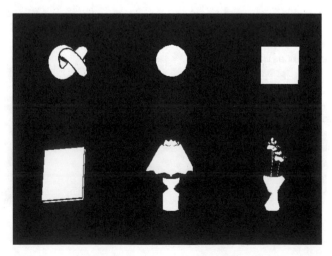

Figure 15.6 is intended to illustrate how the Painter Shader affects many different types of Models while using the same settings. Notice how extreme the reduction in internal geometrical detail is in this example. Although this example demonstrates how extreme the effects of the Painter Shader can be, it is possible to achieve many variations of these effects.

Painter Properties

The properties of the Painter Shader are among the most difficult to decipher from the available documentation. Table 15.3 provides a complete list of the properties of the Painter Shader that have an effect on the final rendering of a Model.

Table 15.3   Painter Shader Properties

Property	Range	Purpose
Style	#toon #gradient #blackandwhite	Determines how to use the other Shader properties when rendering the Model.
Colorsteps	2,4,8,16	Determines the number of gradations to use when the style is set to #gradient.
Shadowpercentage	0–100	Depends on shader style.
Highlightpercentage	0–100	Depends on shader style.
Shadowstrength	float	Depends on shader style.
Highlightstrength	float	Depends on shader style.
Diffuse	rgb(r,g,b)	Depends on shader style.
Ambient	rgb(r,g,b)	Depends on shader style.
Renderstyle	#fill #wire #point	Controls the display of the Models' faces. Does not work in software-rendering mode.

Notice that we are able to set both the Diffuse and Ambient properties for the Painter Shader. These properties have a great effect on the colors used in the final rendering. One difficulty with understanding how these properties will affect the final rendering stems from the fact that you have learned these properties in the context of the standard Shader. In the Painter Shader, they have a slightly different functionality, which I will explain as we continue. Also, note that most of the purposes for these properties depend on the specific style you are using for the Painter Shader. As we continue through this section, I will explain how these values are used in relation with each style.

NOTE

In addition to these properties, the first directional or first point Light and any ambient Light Nodes in the scene will affect the final rendering of this Shader. The rotation or position of this Light Node will be considered, and unlike the Newsprint and Engraver Shaders, the Light Node color will affect the final rendering as well.

Of all the properties of the Painter Shader, Style deserves primary attention because it affects both the final rendering and how you will utilize the other properties. The three possible choices—#toon, #gradient, and #blackandwhite—affect the number of colors and how they are applied to the Model. Figure 15.7 illustrates the Model of a torus knot with identical settings, except for the Style property.

FIGURE 15.7

The Painter Shader with its Style property set to #toon, #gradient, and #blackandwhite, respectively, from left to right.

Notice the marked difference between the #toon style and the #gradient style. Whereas #toon has reduced down the number of colors and created crisp divisions between highlight, midtone, and shaded regions, #gradient has created several divisions of color with soft changes from highlighted to shaded regions. Using #blackandwhite reduces the number of colors to only black and white and creates crisp divisions between the highlighted and shaded sections of the Model. To understand how to use each of these styles, it is important to realize that each style will depend on the other painter Shader properties differently.

#Toon Style

When you're working with the #toon style, the properties that will affect the final rendering are Shadowpercentage, Highlightpercentage, Shadowstrength, Highlightstrength, Diffuse, and Ambient.

Although I have not listed it, Colorsteps does have a visual effect on the #toon style. If you are using OpenGL acceleration, you can use Colorsteps in conjunction with the #toon style to achieve a specific effect, as discussed in the "Posterization Technique" section later in this chapter. For now, leave this property at a setting of 2.

To better understand the relationship between the properties, consider that the Shadowpercentage, Shadowstrength, and Ambient properties control the shaded areas of the Model, whereas the Highlightpercentage, Highlightstrength, and Diffuse properties control the highlight areas of the Model.

The Diffuse property will determine the base color for the highlight areas; the Ambient property will determine the base color for the shaded areas. Remember that both of these areas will be affected by the Light Nodes in your scene. Many times the Painter Shader is underutilized because users forget to set a non-black value for the ambient Light Node.

The Shadowstrength and Highlightstrength properties determine how bright or dark the color used to fill in the shaded and highlighted areas of the Model are. Keep in mind that even if we are speaking about the "shaded" area, that does not necessarily mean that the color used to fill this area is dark. Essentially, the luminosity of colors defined by the Diffuse and Ambient settings are fine-tuned with these properties. A setting of 1 corresponds to no change.

You should consider values in the range of 0.0 to 5.0 for the Shadowstrength and Highlightstrength properties. Although these properties will accept any floating-point value, values outside of this range have little effect. In most cases, you will not see any difference after a value of 2. For this reason, realize that the difference between a setting of .89 and .88 can be quite dramatic.

Finally, the Shadowpercentage and Highlightpercentage properties are used to determine the size of highlighted and shaded areas of the Model. Because of the way that these two properties interact, their sum cannot exceed 100. If you set one of these properties such that the sum does exceed 100, the value of the other property will recede such that its sum equals 100.

#Gradient Style

If you are using #gradient style, the properties that will affect the final rendering are Colorsteps, Shadowstrength, Highlightstrength, Diffuse, and Ambient.

The Colorsteps property has a strong effect on the way that the #gradient style will render. The number of "color steps" will determine how many divisions of color should be created to define the Model. A setting of 8 or 16 tends to create rather soft edges, whereas a setting of 2 or 4 provides you with crisper definition.

The Diffuse and Ambient properties still determine the base color for highlighted and shaded areas, but Colorsteps determines the ramp of colors between these two that comprise the midtone values of the Model. The #gradient style is more consistent across OpenGL and DirectX acceleration than the #toon style.

#Blackandwhite Style

The #blackandwhite style is the easiest to understand. The properties that will affect the final rendering when this style is used are Shadowpercentage and Highlightpercentage.

Unlike the other styles, #blackandwhite will only render the Model in two colors: black and white. The highlighted and shaded areas will be divided by a crisp boundary with no midtone area. The Shadowpercentage and Highlightpercentage properties determine how large the shaded and highlighted areas are, respectively.

Of the three styles, #blackandwhite is the most consistent across OpenGL, DirectX, and software-rendering modes.

Painter Laboratory

On the CD is a file named "Painter Laboratory" that has been designed in the same fashion as the other laboratories—to provide you with visual control over the properties of the Shader. Because the Painter Shader has several properties that are interdependent, I suggest you experiment with this laboratory for some time if these relationships are unclear to you. Figure 15.8 illustrates several examples of Models rendered with the Painter Shader.

FIGURE 15.8

Various examples of Models rendered with the Painter Shader.

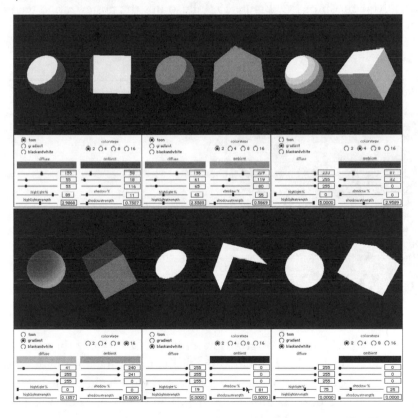

Note that these examples are intended to provide you with a starting point for understanding the scope of the Painter Shader. In the "NPR with Modifiers" section later in this chapter, we will examine an element called the *Toon Modifier*, which uses the Painter Shader to achieve its varied effects. If you can learn how to manipulate the Painter Shader here, your understanding of the Toon Modifier will be facilitated.

The Posterization Technique

Posterization is the name of a technique from photography that utilizes chemistry to reduce the number of colors in an image. You may be more familiar with the term from Adobe Photoshop or similar image-editing software tools. In this technique, I will explain how to set your properties to create an effect similar to posterization in the 3D environment utilizing the Painter Shader.

The final rendering of this technique will vary depending on whether you are on a Macintosh or PC. Figure 15.9 illustrates the posterization technique rendered with a Macintosh using OpenGL hardware acceleration.

FIGURE 15.9

The posterization technique on a Macintosh with OpenGL hardware acceleration rendering.

Open the file named "Posterization" on the CD and play the movie. Notice how the Model is described by three distinct color regions: highlight, midtone, and shade. Each of these areas is filled with highly stylized colors that underscore the posterization technique. The following code was used to set the properties of the Model:

```
1: global scene
2:
3: on initialize
4:  clearworld(scene)
```

```
 5:
 6:  --set up the background color for the camera
 7:  scene.camera[1].colorbuffer.clearvalue = rgb(45,75,10)
 8:
 9:  --set up the ambient light color
10:  scene.light[1].color = rgb(255,255,255)
11:
12:  --adjust the rotation of the directional light
13:  scene.light[2].transform.identity()
14:  scene.light[2].rotate(48,0,124)
15:
16:  --set up shader for the vase
17:  shdA = scene.newshader("vase", #painter)
18:  --choose a medium green color for the diffuse (highlight)
19:  shdA.diffuse = rgb(90,100,40)
20:  --choose a dark green color for the ambient (shaded area)
21:  shdA.ambient = rgb(5,30,2)
22:  --set up properties
23:  shdA.style = #toon
24:  shdA.colorsteps = 4
25:  shdA.shadowpercentage = 52
26:  shdA.highlightpercentage = 48
27:  shdA.shadowstrength = .4
28:  shdA.highlightstrength = 1
29:
30:  --set up shader for the flowers
31:  shdB = scene.newshader("flowers", #painter)
32:  --choose a medium green color for the diffuse (highlight)
33:  shdB.diffuse = rgb(90,100,40)
34:  --choose a dark green color for the ambient (shaded area)
35:  shdB.ambient = rgb(5,30,2)
36:  -- set up properties
37:  shdB.style = #toon
38:  shdB.colorsteps = 4
39:  shdB.shadowpercentage = 35
40:  shdB.highlightpercentage = 65
41:  shdB.shadowstrength = 1
42:  shdB.highlightstrength = 1.4
43:
44:  --clone the vase from its castmember into the 3Dworld
45:  obj = scene.cloneModelFromCastmember("vase", "vase", member("vase"))
46:
47:  --assign vase shader to the vase mesh
48:  obj.shaderlist[1] = shdA
49:  --assign the flower shader to each
50:  --of the flower meshes
51:  obj.shaderlist[2] = shdB
```

```
52:  obj.shaderlist[3] = shdB
53:  obj.shaderlist[4] = shdB
54:
55:  -- the following is not specific to
56:  -- the posterization technique
57:
58:  --adjust the model
59:  obj.rotate(-90,0,0)
60:  obj.translate(0,680,-330)
61:
62:  --adjust the camera
63:  scene.camera[1].fieldofview = 50
64:  scene.camera[1].translate(0,250,0)
65:  scene.camera[1].rotate(-16,0,0)
66:  end
```

I will highlight several key lines in this code. In line 7, notice how I have set the background color of the Camera to a green value that is in the family of colors used by the Shaders. This establishes the background as an element in your color scheme. If you choose a neutral color, you might not be as convinced by the results unless your Shader will be using neutrals.

Compare lines 19 and 21 with lines 33 and 35. In the first pair, I am setting the properties for the highlight and background of the "vase" Shader; in the second pair, I am doing the same for the "flowers" Shader. Notice that I have chosen the exact same colors. When you look at the final rendering though, it is obvious that the flowers and the vase are using slightly different shades of green. This is because I have used the Shadowstrength and Highlightstrength properties to keep the colors in the same family but to vary their luminosity.

Notice that at line 10 I have made certain that the ambient Light Node color is white. In this case, it is easiest to use white in order to ensure that the shaded areas of the Model will be seen. Although I could have used a non-white value, be aware that this can cause counterproductive results in your final rendering. In short, if you use non-white values, you will be altering the hues of the colors you choose for the shader.ambient property.

Finally, if you are working on a PC, even if you use OpenGL acceleration, you may not see this effect. If this is so, change the style of the "vase" and "flower" Shaders to #gradient. This will result in several zones of midtone, but it is better than the alternative.

NPR with Modifiers

In addition to the NPR rendering techniques we have looked at using non-standard Shaders, several Modifiers are available that can alter the method of rendering your 3D environment.

What Is a Modifier?

A *Modifier* is a rather broad type of Node that adds extra capabilities to a Model. These capabilities range from Subdivision Surfaces (SDS) and Level of Detail (LOD), which modify the geometry of Models, to Bonesplayer and Keyframeplayer, which add animation functionality. In addition to these Modifiers and several others, the Inker and Toon Modifiers change the way that a Model is drawn.

The Inker and Toon Modifiers have their own specific strengths. Inker is powerful because you can use it in addition to any of the other Shaders we have looked at. The capabilities it gives you strengthen the effects of both standard and nonstandard Shaders. The Toon Modifier is helpful because it combines the power of the Painter Shader and the Inker Modifier into one element. Rather than tweaking the properties of several different elements, you can use the Toon Modifier as a shortcut.

There are drawbacks to using the Inker and Toon Modifiers. Because they both essentially involve using Inker properties, it is important to understand that Inker relies heavily on the geometry of the Model. In short, the primary drawback is that you cannot use the SDS modifier in conjunction with the Inker Modifier. SDS is a powerful performance-optimization tool that enhances the detail of geometry, depending on the speed of the user machine. Chapter 19 explains how to utilize the SDS modifier, but you must realize that the choice to use Inker or Toon eliminates the possibility of using SDS.

Inker Modifier

The strength of the Inker Modifier lies in the fact that you can use it with any of the Shaders—standard or nonstandard. Figure 15.10 illustrates several Models using the Inker Modifier in conjunction with various Shaders.

FIGURE 15.10

Examples of Models utilizing the Inker Modifier.

Modifiers are applied to Models a bit differently from Shaders. You add a Modifier to a given model with the following syntax:

```
Scene.model[x].addmodifier(#modifiername)
```

In the case of the Inker Modifier, the #modifiername argument will be #inker. In addition, once you have added the Inker Modifier to a given Model, that Model will now have an Inker Modifier attached, through which you will assign the properties of the Inker. This relationship is easier to understand through the following syntax:

```
Scene.model[x].inker.inkerproperty
```

Notice that the Inker is now a property of the Model, and the Inker's properties are accessed via the Model.

Inker Modifier Properties

The Inker Modifier has several properties that control the style of drawing. In general, you can use Inker to draw the boundaries, silhouette, and internal geometry of a Model. You can alter the color of the line, and you can modulate the line so that it is solid or broken. The properties of the Inker Modifier are listed in Table 15.4.

Table 15.4   Inker Modifier Properties

Property	Range	Purpose
Linecolor	rgb(r,g,b)	Determines the color of the Inker line
Silhouettes	Boolean	Draws around the outside of the Model
Creases	Boolean	Draws the internal geometry
Creaseangle	-1 to 1	The maximum or minimum threshold angle between Mesh faces that determines how much of the internal geometry to draw
Boundary	Boolean	Draws a boundary of Meshes
Lineoffset	-100 to 100	Determines how close to the surface of the Model the line will be drawn in 3D space
Uselineoffset	Boolean	Determines whether or not the Lineoffset property is used

Here are a couple notes concerning the properties in Table 15.4: First, the Lineoffset property determines how close to the surface of the Model the line is drawn—positive values will draw the line slightly inside the Model, and negative values will draw the line slightly outside the Model. This allows you to decide whether the line will be clean (negative values) or variegated and rough (positive values).

Second, the Creaseangle property accepts floating-point values. If you want to create highly descriptive renderings of your geometry, use a setting of 1 or −1. I do not recommend this though, because it is not visually interesting and is little better than wire-frame mode rendering. Rather, try setting the value close to 1, such as .97 or .98, and see how this changes the quality of the description of the geometry.

Inker Laboratory

The "Inker Laboratory" file on your CD provides you with a concise method of learning about the various Inker properties visually. Figure 15.11 illustrates various examples utilizing different settings for the properties of the Inker Modifier.

FIGURE 15.11

Various examples of the Inker Modifier.

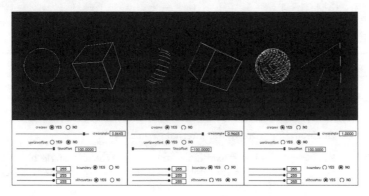

Note that although the strength of the Inker Modifier is in its ability to utilize different Shaders, this laboratory demonstrates the Inker's capabilities outside of being used in combination with Shader techniques. This enables you to acquire an understanding of the Inker properties on their own.

Engraver Embellishment Techniques

The Inker Modifier provides strong accompaniment to the Engraver Shader. Utilizing these two elements in conjunction can solidify the visual weight of geometry while providing a highly stylized method of rendering. On the CD is a file named "Engraver Embellishment." Open this file and press Play. You should see a Model of a torus knot in the center of the Stage, as illustrated in Figure 15.12.

FIGURE 15.12

A torus knot Model using the Engraver Shader and Inker Modifier.

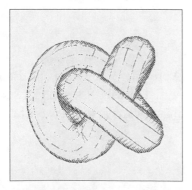

Notice how the Engraver Shader provides gradation information, and the Inker Modifier adds a desirable broken line that emphasizes the geometry of the Model. In this example, the Brightness property of the Engraver Shader is set quite high (60). If I were to use a setting of 60 for the Brightness property and did not use the Inker Modifier, it would be difficult to distinguish what the geometry of the Model is. The following initialization script is used to create this effect:

```
1: global scene
2:
3: on initialize
4:  clearworld(scene)
5:
6:  --set up the background color for the camera
7:  scene.camera[1].colorbuffer.clearvalue = rgb(255,255,170)
8:
9:  --set up the ambient light color
10: scene.light[1].color = rgb(255,255,255)
11:
12: --adjust the rotation of the directional light
13: scene.light[2].transform.identity()
14: scene.light[2].rotate(48,0,124)
15:
16: --set up shader for the torus knot
17: shdA = scene.newshader("vase", #engraver)
18: --choose a bright color for the diffuse (highlight)
19: shdA.diffuse = rgb(250,250,190)
20:
21: --set up Shader properties
22: shdA.rotation = 5
23: -- set to quite bright
24: shdA.brightness = 60
25: -- make sure the dots are small
26: shdA.density = 80
27:
28: --assign vase shader to the vase mesh
29: scene.model[1].shaderlist[1] = shdA
30:
31:
32: --add the inker modifier to the model
33: scene.model[1].addmodifier(#inker)
34:
35: -- use the lineoffset property, so that the
36: -- inker lines drawn can be drawn slightly
37: -- below the surface of the Model, creating
38: -- a desirable broken line.
```

```
39:  scene.model[1].inker.uselineoffset = true
40:  scene.model[1].inker.lineoffset = 53
41:
42:  --make sure that we are using creases
43:  --and set the creaseangle very close to 1
44:  scene.model[1].inker.creases = true
45:  scene.model[1].inker.creaseangle = .97
46:
47: --set the linecolor of the inker to a dark brown/yellow
48:  scene.model[1].inker.linecolor = rgb(70,70,10)
49:
50: end
```

Notice how I have correlated the background color of the Camera with the diffuse color of the Shader so that they aid each other in the overall aesthetic of this scene. Also, notice that I have chosen a line color of dark brown/yellow to emphasize the correlation between colors further. If you are having trouble choosing colors that work well, I suggest reading Appendix F, "Colorlut Custom Management System," which explains RGB color picking and provides methods of choosing colors via HSV as well as by user-defined names.

Toon Modifier

The Toon Modifier is both useful and unusual. It is a bit of a conceptual anomaly in Director because it creates a shortcut to the Inker Modifier and a Painter Shader. To clarify, when you add the Toon Modifier to a Model, you are technically changing the Model's Shader into a Painter Shader and adding the Inker Modifier. The properties for both of these elements will then be accessed via the Toon Modifier with the following syntax:

```
Scene.model[x].toon.toonproperty
```

Remember that *toonproperty* will specifically be controlling the Painter Shader now attached to the Model as well as the Inker Modifier attached to the Model. Because the Toon Modifier is using the Inker Modifier, you cannot use the SDS Modifier in conjunction with Toon.

Realize that the Toon Modifier does not really add functionality to the environment; rather, it provides a shortcut for you to access properties. That being said, the combination of the Painter Shader and the Inker Modifier is important enough to warrant the implementation of this shortcut. Consider that the Toon Modifier emphasizes the importance of using these two elements in conjunction with one another. Figure 15.13 illustrates examples of several Models utilizing the Toon Modifier.

FIGURE 15.13

Various examples of the Toon Modifier.

Rather than list the properties of the Painter Shader and Inker Modifier again, I will direct you to Table 15.3, which lists the Painter properties, and Table 15.4, which lists the Inker properties. The Toon Modifier allows you to access all these properties through one shortcut.

Cartooning Techniques

The power of combining the Painter Shader with the Inker Modifier can be seen in the "Cartooning" file on the CD. Several combinations of property settings can be used to provide interesting NPR rendering aesthetics. I will demonstrate how to utilize the Toon Modifier to create a highly cartooned style of rendering.

Cartoon drawing is typically separated into two critical areas: the line and the ink. The borders of objects are traced in heavy colors, whereas the interiors of objects are filled with solid, flat colors. Figure 15.14 illustrates a cartoon character head drawn using the Toon Modifier.

FIGURE 15.14

A cartoon head rendered with the Toon Modifier.

This technique is accomplished by emphasizing the boundaries and silhouettes of the Model and using the #gradient style. The properties for Lights, Camera, and Toon Modifier are set in the following initialization script:

```
 1: global scene
 2:
 3: on initialize
 4:   clearworld(scene)
 5:
 6:   --set up the background color for the camera
 7:   scene.camera[1].colorbuffer.clearvalue = rgb(160,160,160)
 8:
 9:   -- set up the ambient light
10:   scene.light[1].color = rgb(255,255,255)
11:
12:   --reposition the directional light
13:   scene.light[2].transform.identity()
14:   scene.light[2].rotate(77,80,4)
15:
16:   --add toon modifier
17:   scene.model[1].addmodifier(#toon)
18:
19:   --create reference to model[1]
20:   --to reduce typing load
21:   obj = scene.model[1]
22:
23:   -- use gradient style for several internal colors
```

```
24:  obj.toon.style = #gradient
25:  obj.toon.colorsteps = 4
26:  obj.toon.shadowpercentage = 39
27:  obj.toon.highlightpercentage = 61
28:  obj.toon.shadowstrength = .5
29:  obj.toon.highlightstrength = 1
30:
31:  -- since we do not want to see
32:  -- the geometry of the head,
33:  -- I will turn off creases
34:  obj.toon.creases = false
35:
36:  --creaseangle has a slight affect
37:  --on the boundary and silhouettes settings
38:  obj.toon.creaseangle = -1
39:  obj.toon.boundary = true
40:  obj.toon.silhouettes = true
41:
42:  --make sure that we are using the
43:  --lineoffset property, and draw
44:  --the lines in front of the
45:  --Model so that the lines are clean
46:  obj.toon.lineoffset = -100
47:  obj.toon.uselineoffset = true
48: end
```

Notice that in this example I have not set the diffuse or ambient colors for the Model. This is because the Model was created in 3DS MAX. At modeling time, you can assign specific colors to the MAX Models that will be inherited by their W3D versions. However, it is still important to set the ambient Light Node color and reposition the directional Light in order to get the correct highlight and shadow regions on the Model.

Abstract Techniques

Throughout this chapter are demonstrations involving specific applications of Shaders and Modifiers. The applications of those techniques are general enough to apply to a wide variety of situations. In this demonstration, I want to emphasize some of the possibilities of combining many techniques to create an abstract, atmospheric visual environment. Figure 15.15 is a screenshot from this demonstration.

FIGURE 15.15

An abstract environment created through multiple Models, Shaders, and Modifiers.

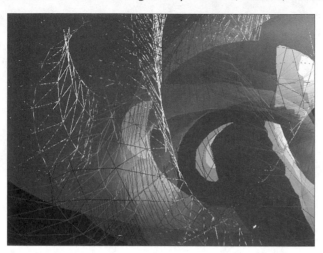

Essentially, this demonstration is more conceptual in nature, emphasizing the power of diverse combinations of techniques. On the CD is a file named "Abstract Environment." This particular example combines several of the techniques from earlier chapters. Specifically, this environment utilizes the Polar Mouse Coordinates demo in conjunction with a directional Light that has been parented to a group.

That group is comprised of several concentric spheres from the Glow demo in Chapter 12, "Basic Control of Surfaces." In addition, the environment was modeled in 3DS MAX and consists of "concentric" torus knots. These torus knots utilize several of the NPR rendering effects. If you play the movie and move your mouse, you should see how it is possible to control a visually complex environment with only the tools we have examined thus far.

One of the reasons why I mention this is that Chapter 16, "Camera Tricks," and Chapter 17, "Special Effects," deal with the Camera and general special effects. This demonstration shows that it is possible to create a complex environment even before broaching the typical methods of adding special effects. Finally, look at the size of the Shockwave version of this file; at 38.7KB, this demonstration proves that NPR rendering can be used without Textures to great effect.

Summary

Non-photorealistic rendering is a powerful but often-overlooked tool. The possibilities for this technique range from simple stylization to more complex treatment of the environment. The strength of NPR rendering is its ability to provide complex renditions of geometry without the need for Textures, thereby reducing the size of projects dramatically.

One of the key conceptual shortcomings that many designers and developers are faced with is an unswerving desire to create verisimilitude. The impact of this is that some of the key strengths of the 3D environment are overlooked, such as NPR rendering. Although it may not be right for all projects, NPR rendering offers possibilities for your 3D environments that challenge many of the overplayed signifiers typical of real-time "3D."

FAQ

In the Director 8.5 help system are references to the nonstandard Shaders in entries on properties that you have not mentioned in this chapter. Am I missing something?

There are many references to nonstandard Shaders, true. Certainly you can set the Reflectionmap and Texture properties of the Engraver Shader—you just won't see any visual effect. In fact, for the vast majority of standard Shader properties (33), only three have a visual effect on nonstandard Shaders: Ambient, Diffuse, and Renderstyle.

NPR rendering just does not look good. Why should I use it?

Although it is rather easy to create bad-looking rendering with NPR methods, this is equally true for the standard Shader. The reasons you should consider using NPR rendering are as follows: First, because there is no need for Textures, you can achieve quick download times. Second, NPR rendering provides visual stimulation for projects that might otherwise become stale using realism. Finally, some of the shortcomings of lighting in Director (no cast shadows) can be balanced by using NPR Shaders. Because NPR Shaders are so stylized, the fact that Models do not cast shadows is not brought to the attention of the viewer.

Supplemental Resources

The following nonstandard rendering resources are provided to help you gain a better understanding of the possibilities of NPR rendering beyond the scope of Director 8.5.

Bibliography of Siggraph Papers on NPR Rendering

```
http://www.cs.utah.edu/npr/papers.html
```

This link contains links to papers from Siggraph on NPR rendering. You can see how over the past five years this topic has been gaining popularity. This is good because the more time high-end developers and researchers devote to this area, the more implementation we can expect to see.

Information on NPR Rendering from Intel

```
http://developer.intel.com/ial/3dsoftware/doc.htm
```

The Intel Web site contains several PDF documents about NPR rendering that are informative and reveal some of the methodologies that contributed to the implementation of NPR rendering in Director.

CHAPTER 16

Camera Tricks

In this chapter, I will expand on the capabilities of the Camera in terms of several "tricks" that can add depth, realism, and interest to a 3D environment. Specifically in this chapter, we will be covering the topics of Backdrops and Overlays, fog, and trails. These topics can be used to incorporate 3D environments into your media-rich projects in a fluid and organic manner.

The Camera plays a primary role not only in what your users see but also how they see it. Because of this, many times it is not enough to simply point the Camera at your scene. The techniques in this chapter will give you more options when designing your 3D environments. In addition, these techniques are designed to help you think about how "tricks" can be used for spectacle and efficiency.

Each of these topics has the capability to change the way you approach your projects and therefore your production schedule. Techniques involving Fog can especially be used to reduce the amount of 3D modeling you might do on a project, whereas techniques involving Overlays can be used to change the overall structure of your design narrative. As with any "trick," the dangers for the design of your projects are general overuse and misuse. You can avoid both of these by incorporating "tricks" into your design rather than simply using them because they are available.

Backdrops and Overlays

Backdrops and Overlays are similar in nature as well as in the way they are manipulated. Both Backdrops and Overlays are properties of a Camera—each of these properties has properties of its own. Technically, a Backdrop allows you to place a Texture object behind all Nodes drawn in the scene. An Overlay allows you to place a Texture object in front of all Nodes drawn in the scene. It is possible to have several Backdrops and Overlays on a Camera at once. You can control their opacity as well as utilize Textures with alpha channel transparency.

Because they are similar, Backdrops and Overlays share the same common properties; if you learn how to control a Backdrop, you will essentially have learned how to control an Overlay as well. You can see that Backdrops and Overlays are controlled via a relatively small number of properties, which are listed in Table 16.1.

TABLE 16.1   Backdrop and Overlay Properties

Property	Data Type	Purpose
Loc	`point()`	Backdrop/Overlay position relative to 3D Sprite Loc.
Regpoint	`point()`	2D registration point for a Backdrop/Overlay.
Source	`texture()`	Texture object image used for a Backdrop/Overlay.
Scale	Float	Scale of the Backdrop/Overlay. Note that this property scales the entire Backdrop/Overlay constrained to its aspect ratio.
Rotation	Float	Rotation of a Backdrop/Overlay around the Regpoint in degrees.
Blend	Integer	Opacity of the Backdrop/Overlay.

Backdrops and Overlays use an existing Texture object for their source material. Many times you will be creating Textures from bitmap Castmembers, but there are other ways of creating Textures, which we will address in Chapter 17, "Special Effects," that utilize Imaging Lingo. Remember that a Texture object can contain alpha channel information to create areas of transparency in addition to the general changes in opacity through the Blend property.

NOTE

Note that the Regpoint property for Backdrops and Overlays exists separately from the Regpoint of bitmap Castmembers. When you create a Texture object from a Castmember, the Castmember Regpoint information is not used. When you create a Backdrop or Overlay from a Texture, a Regpoint is created. Realize this: When you create a Backdrop/Overlay, you are creating it from the Texture object.

Because Backdrops and Overlays utilize Texture objects, you may need to optimize the properties of the Texture in order to get the right effect. This can be especially important in the case of utilizing alpha-transparency, which we will discuss in the "Fancy Borders" demo. The processes for creating Backdrops and Overlays are also similar, as you can see by the commands to add, insert, and remove them in Table 16.2.

TABLE 16.2   Backdrop and Overlay Commands

Command	Purpose
Addbackdrop	Adds a Backdrop to the Camera
Removebackdrop	Removes a Backdrop from the Camera
Insertbackdrop	Inserts a Backdrop between, behind, or in front of other Backdrops
Addoverlay	Adds an Overlay to a Camera
Removeoverlay	Removes an Overlay from a Camera
Insertoverlay	Inserts an Overlay between, behind, or in front of other Overlays

From this list of commands, it is again reinforced that the methods you will use to control Backdrops are extremely similar to those you will use to control and create Overlays. Also, you may notice that in addition to adding and removing Backdrops and Overlays, you have the ability to insert Backdrops and Overlays. This is because you can have multiple Backdrops and Overlays—multiple Backdrops and Overlays are useful if you are modifying their opacity or using alpha-transparent Textures.

Backdrop Basics

In this demonstration, we will be taking our first look at understanding how to create and manipulate Backdrops. Overall, you should consider that the methods used to create and modify Backdrops are extremely similar to those used to create and modify Overlays. Therefore, as you work through this demonstration, which presents a concise method for creating Backdrops, remember that we will shortly be applying these rules to Overlays as well.

At least two steps are required for creating a backdrop: creating a Texture object and then adding the Backdrop to the Camera Node. On the CD is file named "Backdrop Basics." Open that file and press Play. You should see a red cube spinning in the center of the 3D Sprite with an orange background.

In order to create a Backdrop, you need a Texture object in memory. While the movie is playing, we can load a Texture with the following command from the message window:

```
bg = scene.newtexture("bgimg", #fromcastmember, member("grid"))
```

Now that we have the Texture object in memory, we will utilize the addback-drop() command; the syntax for this command is as follows:

```
Scene.camera[x].addbackdrop(textureobject, location, rotation)
```

Here, location is a point() data type and rotation is a floating-point number relating the degrees of rotation around the Backdrop/Overlay registration point. By default, the registration point for a Backdrop/Overlay is at point(0,0). The location that we specify for the Backdrop/Overlay is the displacement from the upper-left corner of the 3D Sprite to the Regpoint of the Backdrop/Overlay. You can use the following code to add a Backdrop with no rotation, flush to the top and left sides of the 3D Sprite:

```
scene.camera[1].addbackdrop(bg, point(0,0), 0)
```

The background of the Camera should now have the image of the "grid" placed behind the Model. Although the process of adding a Backdrop is not difficult, several "behind-the-scenes" events take place that you need to understand.

While the movie is still running, check how many Models are in the scene with the following code in the message window:

```
put scene.model.count
-- 2
```

Now you know that there is only the cube Model in the scene, so what is the second Model?

```
put scene.model[2]
-- model("Backdrop-copy1")
```

This is a clue to the nature of implementation of Backdrops and Overlays. Unfortunately, it might give you the wrong idea about how you can manipulate them. It is important that you do not alter the backdrop Model—if you translate it or try to work with it directly the way you would any other Model, the Backdrop will disappear, and you will not be able to get it back.

This inconsistency is perhaps one of the largest, immediately noticeable drawbacks to using Backdrops/Overlays. The fact that a Model that exists in the Model index is created that should not be translated can cause problems with your existing code. The danger is that when you insert a Backdrop, it is going to get a Model index number—the next available Model index number. Therefore, if your code blindly translates Models based on their indexes, you are going to need to be careful about not "touching" Models that are actually Backdrops/Overlays.

If you are using `repeat` loops to cycle through scores of Models in order to translate them and you are also using Backdrops/Overlays, I suggest working the following logic into your `repeat` loop:

```
Repeat with x = 1 to scene.model.count
  Modelname = scene.model[x].name
  If modelname contains "backdrop" or modelname contains "overlay" then
    Do nothing
  Else
    -- make your translation here…
  end if
end repeat
```

The idea is that you are going to encapsulate commands such as these to ensure that you do not touch a Model that is really a Backdrop/Overlay. The other way to deal with this situation is to refer to Models by name. Unfortunately, the problem with this method is that too many times you will need to cycle through via number.

Another way that you might consider is to encapsulate all the Models you use inside of a Group, in addition to the World Group. Then, you can cycle through the members of this Group using the Child property. For example, imagine that we have a Group named "modelsonly" that has every Model in the scene as a child. Every time we create a new Model, we add it to this Group. Then we can cycle through every child in that Group using the following code:

```
Repeat with x = 1 to scene.group("modelsonly").child.count
  --Make your translation here
End
```

Keep the movie playing as you continue with this demonstration. Now let's alter the Blend property of the Backdrop. This can be accomplished with the following code:

```
Scene.camera[1].backdrop[1].blend = 50
```

Notice that the Backdrop properties are accessed via the Camera. Also notice that we are accessing the Backdrop via bracket access. This is because we can add several Backdrops/Overlays—in fact, you can add as many Backdrops/Overlays as your RAM will allow, but you really should not need more than two or three of each to achieve even the most complex effects. Also notice that because the Backdrop is now semitransparent, we can see the background color of the Camera through the Backdrop. If there were multiple Backdrops, we would be able to see through to them.

More importantly, this shows you that you can use a grayscale texture to create a duo-tone-like effect for the backgrounds of your environments. The grid image works well because it has obvious changes in luminosity. While the movie continues to play, insert a Backdrop behind this one with the following commands:

```
bg = scene.newtexture("bgimgB", #fromcastmember, member("water"))

scene.camera[1].insertbackdrop(1, bg, point(0,0), 0)
```

Notice that `insertbackdrop()` requires four arguments, the first of which is an index number. Because there is only one Backdrop, and that backdrop is index 1, inserting a new backdrop at index 1 will cause what was `backdrop[1]` to become `backdrop[2]`. In short, we have inserted a new Backdrop behind the semitransparent one. To continue, let's remove the semitransparent backdrop, as follows:

```
Scene.camera[1].removebackdrop(2)
```

The image of water that is currently the Backdrop for the scene has a very different use of luminosity. Try setting this Backdrop so that it is semitransparent:

```
Scene.camera[1].backdrop[1].blend = 40
```

Again, we are able to see through to the background of the Camera. However, there is an additional way we might work with this luminosity (although it is unsupported). First, reset the Backdrop opacity to 100%:

```
Scene.camera[1].backdrop[1].blend = 100
```

Now, take a look at the number of Shaders in the scene:

```
put scene.shader.count

-- 3
put scene.shader[3]
-- shader("BackdropShader-copy2")
```

Notice that the third Shader in this scene is the Shader for the Backdrop. Although I do not recommend altering any properties of the Backdrop Shader, one trick that you might consider is the following:

```
Scene.shader[3].texturemode = #wrapplanar
```

Changing the `texturemode` setting of the Texture used by the Backdrop Shader has the effect of mirroring the Texture over its vertical axis. Remember that this trick is not supported, so you should test it thoroughly in any project you use it in.

To summarize, the supported method of working with Backdrops is via the `camera.backdrop` property. The second level of tweaking Backdrops should be executed on the Texture object level. Keep in mind that you should not alter any properties of the plane Models created by the `addbackdrop`/`insertbackdrop` type commands.

NOTE

> When working with Backdrops and Overlays, you should keep in mind several things that will aid the overall process. First, try to make sure that the Textures you are using follow the "Powers of 2" rule. That is, the width and height in pixels of the bitmaps used to create the Texture should conform to a power of 2 (that is, 2, 4, 8, 16, 32, 64, 128, 256, and so on).
>
> The width and height do not necessarily need to be the same—they just need to be powers of 2. This is especially true if your Backdrops or Overlays contain text that you intend users to read. See Chapter 19, "Performance Optimization," for optimization issues dealing with Textures, such as a full discussion of "Powers of 2", the `scaledown()` function, mip-mapping, and nearfiltering.

Conceptually, it may be difficult to understand "where" the Backdrop is. No matter how far on the World negative Z axis you translate the Model, it will not be able to go behind the Backdrop. What you can do is configure the `camera.yon` property in such a way that the Model will disappear behind the clipping plane at a certain point. Backdrops are not affected by the Yon property; consider that a Backdrop is basically at the Yon position but is not affected by it. In short, when you use Backdrops, they are always pasted behind every Model in your scenes.

Fading Curtain

In the previous example, we examined how to create and modify a Backdrop and the various implications that this has on the environment. In this demonstration, we will examine a method of using Overlays as a curtain that can reveal a 3D World. You may have noticed that many times when you initialize your 3D Worlds, it may take a moment for all your Models and Textures to load up. This is often not desirable, and you may wish to hide this from the user. For that reason, this demonstration will show how you can hide the initialization process from the user. However, keep in mind that curtains can be used not only to hide but also to relate information. For example, you might utilize the first curtain to show your company logo or the name of your project.

On the CD is a file named "Curtain." Open this file and press Play. This demo utilizes the Overlay of the Camera and its Blend property. In addition, the structure of the score in this demo is slightly enhanced to create the fade-in effect. Figure 16.1 illustrates how the score has been enhanced for this movie.

FIGURE 16.1

The score for the "Fading Curtain" movie.

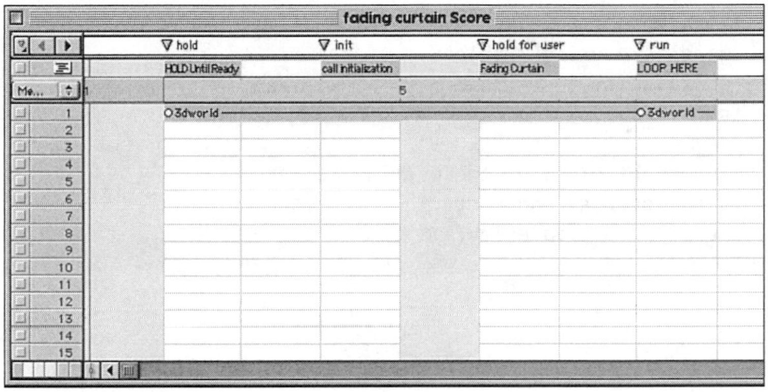

In this movie, rather than sending the playback head to the "run" marker directly after initialization, the playback head is sent to the "wait for user" marker. On that frame is a script that handles both the fading and the waiting, as follows:

```
1: property pfade -- used to toggle fading
2:
3: global scene
4:
5: on beginsprite me
6:   pfade = false -- initially curtain does not fade
7: end
8:
9: -- if the user clicks, set pfade to true
10: on mousedown
11:   pfade = true
12: end
13:
14:
15: on exitframe
16:   -- if the user has not clicked stay on the frame
17:   if pfade = false then
```

```
18:    go the frame
19:   else
20:     -- if the user has clicked…
21:     -- find out what the current overlay blend is
22:     cfade = scene.camera[1].overlay[1].blend
23:     -- if the current blend is not zero
24:     if cfade <> 0 then
25:       -- subtract 5 from the current blend
26:       cfade = cfade - 5
27:       -- set the blend of the overlay to the modified blend
28:       scene.camera[1].overlay[1].blend = cfade
29:       -- stay on this frame
30:       go the frame
31:     else
32:       -- if the current blend of the overlay is zero
33:       -- remove the overlay and go to the "run marker"
34:       scene.camera[1].removeoverlay(1)
35:       go "run"
36:     end if
37:   end if
38: end
```

This example makes use of a simple one-way toggle switch. Once the user clicks the mouse, he does not have a way of stopping the fading of the Overlay. All the fading happens on this frame. Because the cube is not animated until the "run" frame, the cube is static until the Overlay is removed. It would not be difficult to incorporate the fading in a manner that appears as though we are fading in on a scene that is "running"—this example is very dramatic in that the environment looks frozen until the curtain is entirely lifted.

NOTE

Note that while you are in authoring mode, the second time you play this movie during the same Director session before saving the file, you may notice an undesirable artifact. That is, you may notice the cube is visible before the "curtain" hides it the second time you play the movie.

This is because of the way information about the 3D environment remains in RAM between sessions of playing a movie. Try saving the movie, even if you have not made a change, and play it again. You should not notice the flashing this time through. This is not a problem that you need to worry about for your users because this only occurs in authoring mode.

In addition to using Overlays at the beginning of a movie as a curtain, consider the possibility of using Overlays as an inter-title between sections of a movie. You might use curtains as a method of hiding the scene from the user momentarily for blackouts or to convey information. Fading the scene out is as easy as fading the scene in. You might use this technique to transition between 3D content and 2D content in order to orchestrate a seamless experience for the user.

Irregular and Nonrectilinear Borders

Because Textures can contain alpha-channel transparency and because Backdrops and Overlays support this transparency as well, you can use an Overlay to create a nonrectilinear or irregular border for your 3D Sprite. In this section, we will examine this technique first utilizing a Texture with a 1-bit alpha channel and then a Texture with an 8-bit alpha channel.

NOTE

Use Textures with alpha channels with caution because differences in Renderer or video card capabilities can affect the final effect dramatically. In general, Textures with alpha channels are essentially unusable with DirectX 5, and OpenGL on the PC platform may cause undesirable "flashing." Chapter 14 examines the problems associated with alpha channels in textures.

When you intend to use a Texture with alpha-channel information, that Texture information can utilize much of a system's available VRAM. For this reason, I encourage you to make sure your project absolutely requires a nonrectilinear border. If you can use a 1-bit alpha channel, this will reduce the amount of VRAM required tremendously.

There is a file named "Irregular Border" on the CD. Open this file and start the movie. In this example, I have utilized an Overlay that has a 1-bit alpha channel that causes most of the Overlay to be transparent. Figure 16.2 is a screenshot from the "Irregular Border" demo—note that because this demo uses Textures with alpha channels, some hardware Renderers will have difficulty with this demo. If this project does not look like Figure 16.2 on your machine, switch to software rendering.

FIGURE 16.2

Screenshot from the "Irregular Border" demo.

Notice that the border of the 3D Sprite is nonregular. As the Models pass from right to left, the border clips them off. This technique can be used to create a wide variety of effects. You might consider using Overlays to create the illusion of using binoculars or a periscope.

NOTE

You should be cautious when using Backdrops and Overlays in Shockwave movies that you intend to "scale up" to the size of the browser window. Scaling a Shockwave outside of its aspect ratio can ruin the effect of a good Backdrop or Overlay. If you must scale the movie, I suggest setting it to scale maintaining aspect ratio rather than stretching the Shockwave to fill the browser window.

There is also a file named "Non-Rectilinear Border" on the CD. Open this file and press Play. This movie uses several effects that we will be learning about. Figure 16.3 shows what this demo should look like; if you are having trouble, switch to software rendering.

First, and most importantly, I am using an Overlay whose Texture has an 8-bit alpha channel. This means I can create 256 levels of transparency throughout the Overlay. This is why Models seem to fade out as they approach the borders of the Stage.

Not to miss an opportunity to be rather gratuitous, this demo also matches the Overlay with a swirling Backdrop, which is slowly rotated with the following code:

```
1: property bgRotate
2:
3: global scene
4:
5: on beginsprite
6:   bgrotate = 0
7: end
8:
9: on exitframe
10:    --subtract 9 from the current value
11:    --backdrop rotation
12:    bgrotate = bgrotate - 9
13:    --take that value and constrain it
14:    --between 0 to -360
15:    cbgrot = bgrotate mod 360
16:
17:    --rotate the backdrop to its new position
18:    scene.camera[1].backdrop[1].rotation = cbgrot
19: end
```

FIGURE 16.3

A screenshot from the "Non-Rectilinear Border" demo.

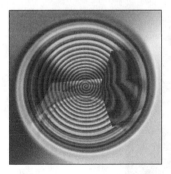

Here are the other three elements that contribute to this effect-laden demo:

- The Camera Fieldofview property is set to 110.
- Two models use the Backdrop Texture as a reflection map.
- Two Models use the foreground Texture with an alpha channel.

If you are in a hardware rendering mode, I suggest forcing your system into software mode via the Property Inspector to get a sense of how much of a drain an 8-bit alpha channel can have on your system. Depending on your specific hardware settings, it is not impossible that this demo might look horrid; if this is the case, you should change to software rendering mode to get a look.

Multipane Effect

Multipane animation is a term taken from traditional cel animation. Multipane animation refers to shots in which the different elements of the background need to move at different speeds. For example, if you look out a car window as you are driving on the highway, objects close to the car speed by while objects far away hardly move at all. Although that specific effect is best accomplished via Imaging Lingo, which we will address in Chapter 17, the concept of moving multiple panes of information can be used to great effect with Backdrops and Overlays. Figure 16.4 is a screenshot from the "Multi-Pane" demo—keep in mind that this demo utilizes 1-bit alpha channel–based Textures in case you have any display problems.

FIGURE 16.4

Using multiple Backdrops to create Multi-Pane animation.

On the CD is a file named "Multi-Pane" that the figure was taken from. Open this file and press Play. In this example, I am using both an Overlay and a Backdrop of 2D "waves" that shift back and forth for a simple effect. The textures used for this effect have a 1-bit alpha channel, and they are both 512 pixels wide by 64 pixels high. The Stage is only 482 pixels wide. Among other items handled by the initialization script are these two lines:

```
scene.camera[1].addbackdrop(bg, point(0,187), 0)
scene.camera[1].addoverlay(fg, point(-20,192), 0)
```

These lines from the initialization script for this movie add the Backdrop and Overlay. In addition, notice that we're setting the initial position of the Backdrop and Overlay at point(0,187) and point(-20,192). Essentially, this code places the waves at the bottom of the 3D Sprite and moves the Overlay slightly to the left.

Once the movie is at the "run" marker, a behavior script handles the motion of the waves moving back and forth:

```
 1: property pdirection, pcounter
 2:
 3: global scene
 4:
 5: on beginsprite
 6:    pcounter = 0
 7:    pdirection = 1
 8: end
 9:
10: on exitframe
11:    pcounter = pcounter + 1
12:
13:    if pcounter = 21 then
14:       pcounter = 1
15:       pdirection = -pdirection
16:    end if
17:
18:    fgposition = scene.camera[1].overlay[1].loc
19:    bgposition = scene.camera[1].backdrop[1].loc
20:
21:
22:    newFGpos = fgposition + point(pdirection,0)
23:    newBGpos = bgposition - point(pdirection,0)
24:
25:    scene.camera[1].overlay[1].loc = newFGpos
26:    scene.camera[1].backdrop[1].loc = newBGpos
27: end
```

This script is similar to several examples that we have looked at in the past. The logic is similar to the "Swing" demo from Chapter 8, "Parents, Children, and Cloning," and it is also similar to the logic that causes the boat to rock back and forth. In this example, we are moving the waves over a range of 20 pixels, back and forth in a linear manner. Although this is a rather simplified use of multipane animation, the concept should be clear: Multiple animated 2D images can be used to augment the sense of depth and motion within a scene. If you are extremely interested in multipane animation, examine the techniques of Imaging Lingo explained in Appendix C, "Imaging Lingo." Although Imaging Lingo is not specific to multipane animation, it certainly offers you a wider range of choices for compositing very wide bitmaps over time.

Depth of Field

When lens-based Cameras are used in the real world, one desirable effect that is caused by the nature of lenses is known as *depth of field*. This effect can be summarized as being able to selectively focus on objects in the foreground, midground, or background, while leaving objects in the other areas slightly or completely out of focus. You know that Director's Camera cannot simulate this effect on its own, but we can use Backdrops to create a believable version of depth of field.

Open the file named "Depth of Field" on the CD and press Play. This demonstration combines the techniques for remapping the mouse coordinates onto the X/Z plane with a change of source for the Backdrop. Figure 16.5 illustrates the two images used for the Backdrop in this demo.

FIGURE 16.5

Using Backdrops to simulate depth of field.

In Figure 16.5, I have emphasized the blurred areas by lightening them significantly. Notice how the whole image is divided into two halves: foreground and background. The idea is that only one half of the Backdrop will ever be in focus at a time. The movie will determine which image to use for the Backdrop based on the position of the Model, which is based on the position of the mouse. I have chosen to structure the demo such that the Backdrop changes based on the Model position because you might want to apply this effect to Models that are not controlled by the mouse.

There are several crucial elements that make this demonstration work that may not be clear. The photograph that I chose for this demonstration is hardly accidental. In fact, I had to take the photo just for this demo. That is the first lesson: You will most likely need to create the image. If you can do it with photography, fine. If you can render the image from 3D modeling software, it will make this job much easier, if not invisible. I am showing this demo with a photograph because it is harder to get it to "work right," and you might want to work from actual photos (or even video).

In order to get this effect to work, I had to decide where to "draw the line" between foreground and background. You can decide where this line is based on the horizon and the vanishing point for perspective. Specifically, this is the reason why I have chosen this photograph—it has an extremely well-defined vanishing point, as illustrated in Figure 16.6.

FIGURE 16.6

Determining World space coordinates from "photograph" coordinates.

The goal of this exercise of drawing the lines of perspective to find the vanishing point also helps us determine where the horizon is in this image. As you can see from Figure 16.6, the horizon is about halfway—again, this photograph was planned.

So many of my decisions are based on the vanishing point. Only the area below the vanishing point is important to me, because above the vanishing point, the Model will have vanished. Therefore, I took half the distance between the vanishing point and the bottom of the image to determine where to cut the image. In addition, I decided to follow the vertical line of the shadow on the building on the right side of the image. On the left side, I followed the areas of shadow that were clearly defined. Notice how the three-story tenement and the tower in the background are brightly lit? The fact that the foreground is much more brightly lit draws our eyes to it. Separating the image along those lines is almost natural.

After determining where to split the image, I made two copies of it. In one I selected the foreground and blurred it; in the other, I selected the background and blurred it. The blurring was very slight—a Gaussian blur with a radius of 1.2 pixels. In this example, I intentionally left the border between the foreground and background "hard." Once you have mastered this technique, I suggest that you feather the edge of blurring. Not so much on the walls but on the roadway.

Once I had determined where the key lines of perspective were, and therefore the vanishing point, the next step was to figure out where the vanishing point is in 3D World space. Accomplishing this requires a bit of trial and error, informed by an educated guess. In general, the first item to determine is the fieldofview property for your 3D camera. The approach that I take on this is to make a cube and also a backdrop from one of the images. Then, I try to move the cube to see whether I can make the corners of the cube match the corners of the alleyway.

Because the perspective in this photo is fairly straightforward, the corners align quite well at a point that's -105 units on the Y axis. Now I must try to move the cube along the wall in the photo until I reach a real-world object—the garbage can. If I adjust the fieldofview property until the garbage can and the cube are roughly the same depth, I've got it. It just so happens that this point is at about 35 degrees. The default fieldofview setting for the 3D Camera is 34.516, which will do just fine in this case.

Once the fieldofview property is set and the groundplane has been determined (-105), the next step is to determine the yon distance for the camera. In the photo, the yon is the distance to the vanishing point. We know where the vanishing point is on the photo. We know that the garbage can is 50 World units deep, and we know that the garbage can is about 50 percent of the vertical distance to the vanishing point. So, 50 times 50 is 2,500, which is the value I use for yon.

NOTE

3D Studio MAX has a tool for Camera matching. It can make the process of matching a 3D Camera to a real-world photograph much more accurate. I will *not* say that it makes your overall workload any easier, because it demands extremely accurate measurements and it still assumes that you were taking good photographs. When used correctly, though, the results that it produces are of superior quality.

By this point, only a few steps are left. I move the cube "into" the photo on the negative Z axis until it reaches the point where I want the Backdrop to switch from foreground to background. After I learn that number, −520, I know that when the Model is farther than −520 units from the Camera, I should use the background; otherwise, I use the foreground. The following script handles the motion of the cube in the space and is also used to determine the last element—the correlation between Sprite space, World space, and the space of the photo:

```
1: global scene
2:
3: on exitframe
4:    -- force the cursor to be invisible
5:    cursor 200
6:    -- correlate the mouseloc into worldspace coordinates
7:    newloc = scene.camera[1].spritespacetoworldspace(the mouseloc)
8:
9:    -- transpose the X/Y vector into X/Z data.
10:   nnloc = vector(newloc.x, -105, -newloc.y * 21)
11:   -- notice that the X vector remains the same
12:   --      - the Y vector is the same as the groundplane (constant)
13:   --      - the Z vector is derived from the old Y vector.
14:   --   notice how I multiply the Y information by 21
```

```
15:    --  this is because if I use unmoderated Y data, the
16:    -- mouse does not correspond well to the Z placement
17:    -- of the cube.  Through trial and error, I try to find
18:    -- the number to multiply Y by so that when the mouse
19:    -- cursor is at the top of the sprite, the cube has just
20:    -- gone through the vanishing point, and at the bottom
21:    -- of the sprite, the cube should disappear into the foreground
22:
23:    --move the cube to its new position
24:    scene.model[1].transform.position = nnloc
25:
26:
27:    -- if the cube is further than -520 units, use the background
28:    -- image as the source for the backdrop, otherwise use the
29:    -- foreground image.
30:    if nnloc.z < -520 then
31:      scene.camera[1].backdrop[1].source = scene.texture("bg")
32:    else
33:      scene.camera[1].backdrop[1].source = scene.texture("fg")
34:    end if
35: end
```

Notice that I change the Backdrop through the Source property. By changing the source of an existing Backdrop to a different existing Texture, you can quickly change the image of the Backdrop.

Remember that the photograph from this demo was chosen because it has several elements that make it easier to use—well-defined lines of perspective, a well-defined vanishing point, areas of light and shadow in both the foreground and background, and several real-world objects that can be used for comparing the space of the real world with the 3D world.

You should consider other possibilities for expanding this demo by dividing the vertical space into several areas of focus. Another possible enhancement would be to limit horizontal movement of the cube so that it cannot move into the walls of the buildings.

Fog

Most 3D environments contain support for a type of effect known as *fog*; Director supports fog as well. The problem that many first-time 3D developers have is that they confuse 3D fog with aspects of fog that they expect from the real world.

In general, it might help if I told you that the fog in a 3D environment works more like mist or haze. I make this distinction because it is easy to believe that fog in the 3D world can be used to create fog that lies near the ground. This is not the case in Director—although there are 3D environments that support this type of fog. Another common misconception is that the fog can roll or creep—although you may find methods to accomplish effects like this, the Fog property is not the way to implement it.

Therefore, rather than define what fog is not, I will say that fog is a method of creating a gradient from transparent to some opaque color of your choosing. Unlike gradients that you might apply in Photoshop or Fireworks on a 2D image from left to right, this gradient exists in 3D space. That is, the "fog gradient" extends along the Camera's negative Z axis—the farther from the camera, the more opaque the fog is. Fog is a property of Cameras that has several properties of its own. The properties that you can use to control the fog are indicated in Table 16.3.

Table 16.3   Fog Properties

Property	Value	Purpose
Enabled	Boolean	Determines whether fog is used on a given Camera
Near	Float	The distance from the Camera where the fog begins
Far	Float	The distance from the Camera where the fog becomes 100-percent opaque
Decaymode	#linear #exponential #exponential2	Determines the "weight" of the fog gradient
Color	rgb(R,G,B)	Determines the color of the fog

Fog is a wonderful tool, but it does take some skill to get it to work well. There are several guidelines that you can follow to get the best (foggiest) results. First, I would suggest starting with the #linear decaymode setting: *linear decay* means that the fog will become more opaque at a constant rate. Second, choose a background color for the Camera that is the same as the fog color—avoid using a backdrop and opt for a flat color, preferably neutral, between 50-percent gray and white. Third, choose the fog.far distance, which is the distance at which the fog becomes 100-percent opaque. Beyond that point, you will not see your Models.

NOTE

> Just because your Models are lost in fog does not mean that they are excluded from rendering. A good practice is to set `camera.yon` just slightly beyond the `fog.far` value. This way, anything beyond the fog will clip out and will not be considered for rendering.

The last step you should take is to alter the `fog.near` value, but this is usually not required. Generally, once you have set good values for the other properties, you can try testing the other decaymodes to see whether any are better for your current situation. If not, stay with #linear—it tends to work the best in the most situations.

Fog Laboratory

The file "Fog Laboratory" on the CD contains a useful tool for learning about fog visually. Open this file and press Play. Notice that the Fog Lab is designed so that you can control the pertinent properties that affect the quality of the fog. Figure 16.7 contains several screenshots from this laboratory, illustrating several different possibilities for the Fog settings.

FIGURE 16.7

Various examples from the Fog Laboratory.

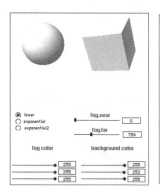
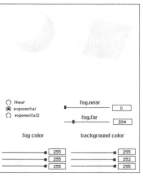
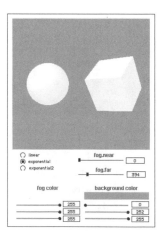

Try configuring the values of the properties for Fog in several different ways to see how the fog reacts. Especially test what happens when you set the fog color and the background color differently. In addition, once you have found settings that you like, try the other decaymodes.

Fog Demo

In this example, I have created a 3D environment that utilizes fog to create a heightened sense of depth. The "Fog" demo on the CD is taken from the "Swing" demo in Chapter 8, only this time fog has been added to heighten both the depth and the drama of the scene. Figure 16.8 is a screenshot from the "Fog" demo.

FIGURE 16.8

Utilizing fog in a 3D environment can emphasize depth in the scene.

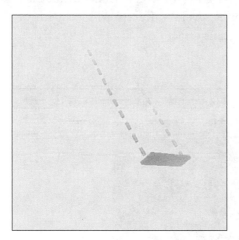

The fog in this demonstration was created with the following settings, configured during the initialization handler at the beginning of the movie:

```
-- FOG SETTINGS

scene.camera[1].fog.enabled = true
scene.camera[1].fog.color = rgb(240,240,240)
scene.camera[1].colorbuffer.clearvalue = rgb(240,240,240)
scene.camera[1].fog.far = 275
scene.camera[1].fog.decaymode = #linear
```

In general, fog is a solid component of the 3D environment. It is very good at providing mood, depth, and drama for scenes, but it should not be used with Backdrops. If you feel you want a Backdrop, make sure that it is very "foggy" itself—or at least mostly a neutral color. It is difficult to match the fog color and backdrop colors, so keep in mind that if you are in 100-percent fog, you really shouldn't be able to see any "backdrop" at all.

Trails

One effect that is extremely easy to use is the "trails" effect. You are probably familiar with the Trails option for Sprites. With this effect, you have the option to turn trails on for all the Models in your scene. Unfortunately, this implementation can only turn on trails for every Model. Still, the effect is quite good. Figure 16.9 illustrates several different Models with varying opacities rotating and utilizing the trails effect.

FIGURE 16.9

Comparison of an opaque object with trails and a semitransparent object with trails.

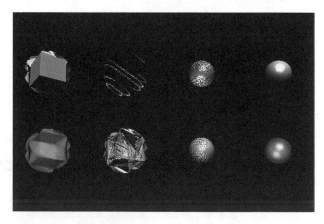

Trails are created with the following code:

```
Scene.camera[x].colorbuffer.clearatrender = false
```

This tells the 3D Sprite that it only needs to redraw pixels that are changing. Remember that trails are either on or off. If you turn them on and then off, your trails will disappear. Also notice in Figure 16.9 the effect that opacity has on trails. It is easier to see this effect in the "Trails" file on the CD. Keep in mind that trails do not work in software rendering mode.

Summary

Cameras are complex Nodes with many options and tricks available to them through their properties. Other than simply positioning, rotating, and pointing your Cameras, you can use properties for adding Overlays, Backdrops, fog, and trails. Each of these properties offers you, as the designer, many avenues of effects to choose from.

Many of these tricks are exclusive: Most do not work well in conjunction with one another. However, with the exception of trails, all require careful planning and correlation with the basic Camera properties. In addition, each of these properties has certain drawbacks—the majority of which center on the Renderer used to draw the scene. This makes sense because the Camera is the viewpoint from which the scene will be drawn. It has to be the most basic and critical effect on the final rendering, so it goes without saying that effects applied to the Camera have the most dramatic effect on the Renderer.

Finally, tricks should be used to further the goals of your project. If the only goal of your project is to show a trick, it will get very stale, very quickly. How long did you need to watch the "Non-Rectilinear Border" demo before you became bored with it? How many more projects of its ilk would you be satisfied with seeing? As far as eye candy goes, the demo is great, but beyond that, the content is nil. The best projects are those that marry their special effects to motivations, the same way you would expect characters in a novel to react to situations because of the way they are, not the way that they could be.

FAQ

How many Backdrops and Overlays can I have?

As many as your RAM will allow.

Is there any way to put Models between Backdrops or between Overlays?

No. Backdrops are behind everything in the scene; Overlays are in front of everything in the scene.

Fog never seems to work right. What am I doing wrong?

Fog is tricky. First, try changing the decaymode setting. I find that #linear is most agreeable to my sensibilities about how I want fog to act. You should really set the background color of the environment to be similar to the fog color. I would also discourage you from using a Backdrop with fog, unless you are going to blend the Backdrop to be almost totally transparent. Finally, keep in mind that the distance of your models from the Camera affect how fog will work, because `fog.near` and `fog.far` are relative to the Camera's World position.

I want to create fog that creeps along the ground. Are there any ways to do this?

It would be difficult, at best, to accomplish this with an animated Texture or particle system. What is certain is that you cannot do this with the Fog property—remember, the fog is more like mist or haze.

I have 10 Models in my scene. Is there any way to apply trails to just one of the Models?

Sort of. See the next question.

Can I create trails of a set length?

Rather than using the `camera.colorbuffer.clearatrender` property, applying trails with a set length to a Model can be achieved with clones. You could create several clones of the Model in question, each blended to be slightly more transparent than the one before. Then, each of these clones would constantly reposition itself based on the position of the previous clone, until the very last clone moves to the position of the "original" Model, which then translates itself normally, and the "trails" will follow.

CHAPTER 17

Special Effects

In this chapter, we will be examining two topics that can best be described as *special effects*. First, you will be learning about how to create animated Textures for your 3D Models. We will look at several approaches—one with bitmap Textures and the other with Imaging Lingo. Animated Textures are very approachable and can add a great deal to your scenes, although performance and download optimization issues are involved with both techniques.

Second, we will be working with particle systems; more specifically, you will be learning how to create and control the #particle primitive. This primitive type is an unusual but powerful tool. Creating fire, exhaust, explosions, water, and fog are common uses for particle systems. We will be examining these and other possibilities for this often misunderstood tool.

Animated Textures

Several functional and efficient methods are available for creating animated Textures in your 3D environments. We are going to examine some of these methods. Then you'll learn about how to build a custom script to handle the animation of Textures.

Simple Animated Textures

The first method of animating Textures that we will look at involves creating a flipbook-style animation. This technique works well, but you should be concerned with the number of frames in your animation, especially if you are creating a Web-based project. That said, you might think that it is necessary to create several Textures and then "flip" between them. Rather, Textures created from bitmap Castmembers have a Member property, and this property tells the Texture which bitmap to use as its source. Fortunately, you can "get" or "set" that property, meaning you can change the source of a Texture on-the-fly. Unlike the creation of the Texture itself, this operation is quite fast. Therefore, it is possible to use the Texture object as a container for images while quickly cycling through the frames of bitmap animation.

To look at a simple example of this, open the file named "Simple Animated Texture" on the CD and press Play. In the center of the stage is a rotating box with an animated Texture on each side. This rather basic cycling is created with the code in Listing 17.1.

Listing 17.1   Basic Animated Texture Script

```
 1: property pcount
 2:
 3: global scene
 4:
 5: on beginsprite
 6:   --initialize the counter
 7:   pcount = 0
 8: end
 9:
10: on exitFrame me
11:   --add one to the counter
12:   pcount = pcount + 1
13:
14:   --constrain pcount to the range 1 - 8
15:   txtnum = (pcount mod 8) + 1
16:
17:   --use txtnum to look up a reference to
18:   --a castmember from the "anim" cast
19:   newframe = member txtnum of castlib "anim"
20:
21:   --use this new cast member as the source
22:   --for the texture on the box
23:   scene.texture("myanim").member = newframe
24: end
```

This script is rather simple; you should get the impression that there are many ways to achieve this cycling. With a little effort, we can craft this concept into a more useful utility for animating Textures. The issues are not merely a lack of code elegance but also include timing issues that can affect the coherence of your visual aesthetic. In short, my reason for complicating this code is not arbitrary but rather based on the level of control you will most likely want from your animated Textures.

Advanced Animated Textures

The primary problem with using the `exitframe()` handler to cycle through the Textures is that, depending on the actual frame rate of the user's machine, your Textures will animate at different speeds. In addition, you have no way to control the playback when using the basic animated Texture approach.

Because cycling is a rather simple task, you should consider thinking about using a parent/child script to create a much more robust animated Texture. Rather than simply cycling through animation frames, we should be able to build a structure to alter at least a few items, such as the following:

- How fast the animation is playing
- Whether the animation is playing or paused
- The ability to "rewind" the animation
- The ability to play the animation in forward or reverse

I have chosen the parent/child structure rather than a behavior because if we create a parent/child script, we will be able to instantiate new animated Textures from code. I prefer a method that does not need to be attached to the 3D Sprite itself, but rather one that lives as a code object. Because we will be working with a parent/child script that needs the functionality of the `exitframe` handler, we will need to use the `stepframe` handler instead.

NOTE

Because parent/child scripts are strictly code-based objects, they are not attached to any frame event, per se, and therefore do not receive `exitframe` events. If you have an `exitframe` handler attached to a parent/child script, that handler will not receive messages.

The special event and handler known as `stepframe`, on the other hand, occurs directly after the `exitframe` event and before the `prepareframe` event. However, not all parent/child scripts receive the `stepframe` event. Rather, parent/child scripts need to be added to a special list known as the *actorlist*. All parent/child scripts registered with the actorlist will receive `stepframe` events.

Finally, if you are going to be working with the actorlist, it is recommended that you clear it on `stopmovie` in order to ensure that all references to the child object are destroyed.

To begin, open the file named "Advanced Animated Texture" on the CD and press Play. Note that at the bottom of the screen you have an array of controls that you can use to start, stop, and rewind the animation, as well as change its speed and order of playback.

In this example, I have taken advantage of the fact that we can create behaviors to interact with and control the properties of a parent/child script. That parent/child script performs the majority of the animating. Essentially, this script performs the function of switching the Member property of a Texture, but with more control than we have previously had.

First, I'll explain the syntax we will use to create and control the animated Texture parent/child script. In the code I have provided, before we create a new instance of the parent/child script, it is important that we have already created a target Texture in the 3D environment. It is also important that we set up all the frames we want to use for the animated Texture as consecutive Castmembers, beginning at member(1), in their own Cast, with unique names for each Castmember.

Once we have these initial steps taken care of, we can create a new instance of the animated Texture parent/child script with the following syntax:

```
ChildRef = new(script "Animated Texture", 3Dcastmember, Texture, Castlib)
```

Here, 3Dcastmember is a reference to the 3D Castmember that we want to use in the format member("3Dcastmembername"). Texture is the name of a Texture object that currently exists in the 3D world, and Castlib is the name of that Cast we want to use as the source for the animation. By default, the parent/child script will set the animation playing at the fastest possible speed.

Many of the controls for the animation have been consolidated into a single handler that accepts symbols for changing properties about the currently playing animation. We can use the transport() handler with the following syntax to control various properties of the animation:

```
Childref.transport(#action)
```

Here, #action is the name of the command we would like to perform. If we do not specify an #action or use an invalid #action, the handler will return False.

The `transport()` handler can accept the symbols in Table 17.1 as `#action` arguments.

TABLE 17.1   Acceptable Arguments for the `Transport()` Handler

Argument	Purpose
#play	Plays the animation
#pause	Pauses the animation
#rewind	Rewinds the animation to frame 1 (does not stop the animation)
#forward	Specifies that the animation should be played in forward order
#reverse	Specifies that the animation should be played in reverse order

In order to control the speed of playback, we will use the `playspeed()` handler with the following syntax:

```
Childref.playspeed(milliseconds)
```

Here, `milliseconds` is the number of milliseconds we want to have elapse between updates. This effectively separates the speed of the animation from the speed of the frame rate. However, bear in mind that we cannot play the animation any faster than the current frame rate. For this reason, it is advisable that you set a fairly high frame rate for your movies. Also, realize that because we are giving values in milliseconds, 1000 milliseconds means an update speed of 1 frame per second.

Other than these two handlers, the majority of the work done by this script is accomplished during the `stepframe()` handler and the `changeframe()` private handler. You can see how these handlers interact to produce the animated Texture in Listing 17.2.

Listing 17.2   Animated Texture Parent/Child Script

```
1: -- counter used to determine which frame we are on
2: property pcount
3: -- list of frames used by the animated texture
4: property pframes
5: -- castlib used for the frames
6: property pCast
7: -- name of the Texture in the 3D environment
8: property pTexture
```

Listing 17.2   Continued

```
 9: -- last update time
10: property pOldTime
11: -- number of milliseconds between updates
12: property pSpeed
13: -- play animation forward or reverse
14: -- 1 = forward, -1 = reverse
15: property pDirection
16: -- Boolean, true = play animation false = pause
17: property pPlaying
18: -- which 3D Castmember to use
19: property ptargetcastmember
20:
21: on new(me, whichcastmember, whichTexture, whichCast)
22:     --ensure that you have specified a 3d castmember
23:     if whichcastmember.type = #shockwave3d then
24:       ptargetcastmember = whichcastmember
25:     else
26:       return false
27:     end if
28:
29:     --ensure that you have specified a texture
30:     if ptargetcastmember.texture(whichtexture) <> void then
31:       pTexture = whichtexture
32:     else
33:       return false
34:     end if
35:
36:     --make sure that you have specified an existing cast
37:     jumpout = true
38:     repeat with x = 1 to the number of castlibs
39:       if whichcast = castlib(x).name then
40:         jumpout = false
41:         pcast = whichcast
42:       end if
43:     end repeat
44:     if jumpout then
45:       return false
46:     end if
47:
48:     --initialize the counter
49:     pcount = 0
50:
51:     --create a list that contains all of the names of the castmembers
52:     --from the cast that you want to use for your animation
53:     pframes = []
54:     repeat with x = 1 to the number of members of castlib pcast
```

Listing 17.2   Continued

```
55:     addat(pframes, the name of member x of castlib pcast)
56:   end repeat
57:   put pframes.count
58:
59:   --hold on to the current time, which is used
60:   --to determine when to update the texture
61:   pOldTime = the milliseconds
62:
63:   --the number of milliseconds to allow to pass
64:   --before updating the texture
65:   pspeed = 1
66:
67:   --the direction to play the animation in
68:   -- 1 means forward,  -1 means reverse
69:   pdirection = 1
70:
71:   -- set the animated texture to play by default
72:   pPlaying = true
73:
74:   --add child object reference to the actorlist
75:   --so that it receives stepframe events
76:   add the actorlist, me
77:
78:   --return a reference to the child object
79:   return me
80: end
81:
82: on transport(me, dowhat)
83:   -- many controls for the animation have been
84:   --consolidated into the transport handler.
85:   --note the range of actions that this handler performs.
86:   -- playing, pausing, rewinding, forward and reverse play
87:   case(dowhat) of
88:     #play:
89:       pPlaying = true
90:       return true
91:     #pause:
92:       pPlaying = false
93:       return true
94:     #rewind:
95:       pcount = 1
96:       changeframe(me, pframes[1])
97:       return true
98:     #forward:
99:       pDirection = 1
```

Listing 17.2   Continued

```
100:        return true
101:      #reverse:
102:        pDirection = -1
103:        return true
104:      otherwise:
105:        return false
106:    end case
107: end
108:
109: on playspeed(me, newspeed)
110:   -- this will change the speed of animation.
111:   --higher values will mean slower playback,.
112:   --values should be integers, and in milliseconds
113:   if newspeed <> void and newspeed.ilk = #integer then
114:     pspeed = newspeed
115:   else
116:     return false
117:   end if
118: end
119:
120: on stepframe(me)
121:   if pplaying then
122:     if the milliseconds - pOldTime > pSpeed then
123:        --add one to the counter
124:        pcount = pcount + pDirection
125:
126:        --make sure that we are still in "range"
127:        --meaning: if you have counted up to a number
128:        --that is too high, set pcount back to 1
129:        --or if you are counting down, and pcount = 0
130:        --set pcount = to the highest frame
131:        if pdirection = 1 then
132:          if pcount > pframes.count then
133:            pcount = 1
134:          end if
135:        else if pdirection = -1 then
136:          if pcount = 0 then
137:            pcount = pframes.count
138:          end if
139:        end if
140:
141:        --find the name of the frame that
142:        --corresponds with the value of pcount
143:        currentframe = pframes[pcount]
144:
```

Listing 17.2   Continued

```
145:        --call the changeframe handler to
146:        --actually handle changing the frame
147:        changeframe(me, currentframe)
148:        --reset the pOldTime
149:        pOldTime = the milliseconds
150:      end if
151:    end if
152: end
153:
154: on changeframe(me, whichframe)
155:    --set a reference to the castmember
156:    newframe = member whichframe of castlib pcast
157:    --change the member property of the texture
158:    --to the new reference...
159:    ptargetcastmember.texture(pTexture).member = newframe
160: end
```

This demonstration provides two sets of animated Textures. The first is a set of bitmaps with numbers on the front. You can use a set of bitmaps like this to easily test the functions of your handler—to make sure that #reverse truly plays in reverse, and so on. Also, I have taken the frames of animated fire from the previous example and created versions of those frames with an alpha channel in order to reinforce the fact that animated Textures do not need to be simple—nor do they need to be opaque.

Future Considerations for Animated Textures

Many future considerations exist that you may want to think about when working with this script. Among some of the enhancements you might add to the script are the following:

- Playing frames in ping-pong order (back and forth)
- Changing the list of Castmembers on-the-fly
- Interpolating multiple lists of Castmembers
- Changing the period of animation
- Animating other Shader properties as well (for example, Blend)

I strongly caution against using a behavior rather than a parent/child script for this functionality because the Nodes in the 3D environment do not exist on the Score. Because this includes Textures, I feel that it is best to achieve these effects with code that does not technically exist on the Score.

Imaging-Based Texture

In this example, you will be learning about a slightly different approach than those used for the previous animated Textures. When new Textures are created in Director, you can create them from bitmap Castmembers or from Lingo-based image objects. If you are not familiar with Imaging Lingo, this may present a bit of a challenge. In this example, I expect that you understand the basics of Imaging Lingo; if you do not, Appendix C, "Imaging Lingo," will help you learn the basics.

The beauty of using Imaging Lingo is that you can create images from code, thereby reducing the number of Textures users need to download. The list of possibilities that Imaging Lingo provides is quite impressive, but we hardly need to become imaging gurus in order to take advantage of this wonderful tool.

In this demonstration, I am going to keep the imaging quite simple because it is secondary to how we will use the Lingo image object and update that information in a useful way in the 3D environment.

Thus far, when we have created Textures for the 3D environment, we have been using the #fromcastmember flag and then specifying a source bitmap Castmember to use for the Texture. Then, when we animate, we have been changing the `texture.member` property. In this demonstration, we will be creating Textures for the 3D environment with the #fromimageobject flag, specifying a Lingo image object. But rather than modifying the `texture.member` property, we will need to modify the undocumented `texture.image` property that's available only when you create Textures with the #fromimageobject flag.

Basic Imaging Animation

In this first example of using Imaging Lingo to create animated Textures, I have kept the imaging quite simple. First, open the file named "Simple Imaging Texture" on the CD and press Play. You should see a cube spinning in the center of the Stage with a colorful, randomly generated animation creating rather garish red, green, and blue circles all over the cube.

Two locations in the code for this movie are used to create this effect. First, the Texture and Model are set up in the initialize() handler; then a specific exitframe() handler manages the generation of the random images. So, first we will look at how to create a new image object, create a Texture based on that object, and then apply the Texture to a Model (see Listing 17.3).

Listing 17.3   Initialization of a Simple Imaging-Based Texture

```
 1: on initialize
 2:   clearworld(scene)
 3:   --create a box
 4:   obj = createbox("fred", 64,64,64,rgb(30,120,40))
 5:
 6:   --create a new global variable, img
 7:   -- which will store an image object
 8:   global img
 9:
10:   --create the image object, a 128x128
11:   --8-bit image object...
12:   img = image(128,128,8)
13:   --fill the image object with yellow
14:   img.fill(0,0,128,128, rgb(255,255,0))
15:
16:   --create a new texture from that image object
17:   txt = scene.newtexture("f", #fromimageobject, img)
18:
19:   --set the texture of the object to the new texture
20:   obj.shaderlist.texture = txt
21: end
```

As you can see from Listing 17.3, the initial Texture is a yellow square entirely created on-the-fly. Creating the Texture this way can save you download time, because the image itself was created in code. The next step is to draw random circles on the image object and then update the image of the Texture based on the new image object. This can be seen in Listing 17.4.

Listing 17.4   Simple Imaging Lingo–Based Animation

```
 1: on exitframe
 2:   global img, scene
 3:
 4:   --choose a random point within the image map boundaries
```

Listing 17.4   Continued

```
 5:    randompoint = point(random(128), random(128))
 6:    --choose a radius for the random circle
 7:    randomradius = random(10,30)
 8:    --use the radius value to create a point
 9:    --that will then be use to figure out the
10:    --uppercorner and lower corner of the random circle
11:    radiusoffset = point(randomradius, randomradius)
12:    uppercorner = randompoint - radiusoffset
13:    lowercorner = randompoint + radiusoffset
14:
15:    --choose a random color: red, green or blue
16:    whichcolor = random(3)
17:    case(whichcolor) of
18:      1:
19:         rcolor = rgb(255,0,0)
20:      2:
21:         rcolor = rgb(0,255,0)
22:      3:
23:         rcolor = rgb(0,0,255)
24:    end case
25:
26:    --fill the circle in on img, the image object
27:    --that we will be using as the texture
28:    (img).fill(uppercorner,lowercorner, rcolor, [#shapetype:#oval])
29:
30:    --set the image of the texture to img
31:    scene.texture("f").image = img
32: end
```

For this example, you need to understand line 31. Essentially, we have updated the image that the Texture object uses—remember, the Image property of Texture objects is undocumented, but you need to update the Image property rather than the Member property if your Texture was created from an image object initially.

Mouse Image Mapping

Now that you have seen a rather simplified usage of Imaging Lingo to create an animated Texture, we can approach this more practical demonstration. I have mentioned that one of the strong points for Imaging Lingo is that it can create images on-the-fly, thus saving download time. Although you might use Imaging Lingo to create a wide variety of animated Textures, Imaging Lingo excels at creating images based on the 3D environment in real time. In addition, do not forget that Imaging Lingo allows you to draw RGB as well as alpha channel information.

Recall the "3D Mouse Cursor" demonstration from Chapter 13, "A 2D Mouse in a 3D World." In that demonstration, the mouse coordinates were used to move a sphere on the X/Z plane. In this demonstration, we are going to use the power of Imaging Lingo to draw RGB and alpha information with the power of an Overlay in the 3D environment to create a real-time map of the position of the sphere. Open the file named "3D Mouse with Map" on the CD and press Play. Note the map in the upper-right corner of the 3D Sprite and the real-time dot that moves in accordance with the mouse.

In this example are several items you should understand before we look at the code for this demonstration. First, look at the Cast for this movie. Notice that there are two bitmap images—one named *grid* and another named *gridmask*. Grid is a 32-bit image of a green grid with alpha channel information knocking out the white background of the grid, whereas *gridmask* is an 8-bit image of the same grid, but the grid is black.

The initial setup for this demonstration is quite easy. We create a Texture based on the 32-bit grid and then use that Texture to create an Overlay. This process is completed in the excerpt from the `Initialize()` handler shown in Listing 17.5.

Listing 17.5   An Excerpt from the `Initialize()` Handler

```
 1: --create image object based on 32-bit grid
 2:   imgmap = member("grid").image.duplicate()
 3:
 4:   --create texture based on image object
 5:   map = scene.newtexture("map", #fromimageobject, imgmap)
 6:
 7:   --set various parameters for the texture
 8:   --low quality will eliminate blur
 9:   map.quality = #low
10:   -- renderformat  rgba5551 will only use
11:   -- one bit of alpha information for the mask
12:   --(this way the mask will be very crisp)
13:   map.renderformat = #rgba5551
14:
15:   --create an overlay from the texture
16:   scene.camera[1].addoverlay(map, point(465,7), 0)
17: end
```

Once the Overlay has been initialized, a dedicated `exitframe()` handler creates the real-time animation. Before we look at the code, let's examine the reasons for the existence of the 8-bit mask and the general order of events in the pseudocode:

- Finding out where the sphere is in World coordinates
- Using the X/Z coordinate information to create X/Y coordinates
- Creating a new version of the image object based on the grid
- Creating an image object based on the gridmask
- Drawing a red circle on the 32-bit grid (correctly placed)
- Drawing a black circle on the 8-bit gridmask (placed the same)
- Using the gridmask as the alpha channel for the 32-bit grid
- Setting the 32-bit grid image object as the new value for `texture.image`

Notice that in this demonstration, we are actually drawing the position of the mouse twice—once on the grid in red, and once on the gridmask in black. However, realize that we are only drawing on image objects created from the bitmaps, so the original bitmaps are not changed. This is why the dot does not leave trails, but the map is redrawn at every frame, depending on where the mouse is. Now that you have looked at the pseudocode, take a look at the actual code used in this demonstration (see Listing 17.6).

Listing 17.6   The Mousemap Script

```
 1: global scene
 2:
 3: on exitframe
 4:    --find out the location of the sphere
 5:    --in world coordinates
 6:    sphereloc = scene.model[2].getworldtransform().position
 7:
 8:    --turn the X/Z world coordinates into X/Y point
 9:    -- that will be used to draw the dot on the grid.
10:    --note that I am adding and subtracting 64 from the
11:    --coordinates so that point(0,0) is at the middle
12:    --of the grid...
13:    spherepos = point(sphereloc.x + 64, sphereloc.z-64)
14:
15:    --figure out the upper and lower corners
```

Listing 17.6   Continued

```
16:    --of a rect based on the X/Y position of the sphere
17:    uppercorner = spherepos - point(4,4)
18:    lowercorner = spherepos + point(4,4)
19:
20:    --create an image object from the 32-bit grid
21:    imgmap = member("grid").image.duplicate()
22:
23:    --create an image object from the 8-bit grid
24:    mymask = member("gridmask").image.duplicate()
25:
26:    --draw a red dot on the 32-bit grid in the correct location
27:    imgmap.fill(uppercorner, lowercorner,\
       rgb(255,0,0), [#shapetype:#oval])
28:    --draw a black dot on the 8-bit grid in the same location
29:    mymask.fill(uppercorner, lowercorner,\
       rgb(0,0,0), [#shapetype:#oval])
30:
31:    --use the 8-bit grid as the mask for the 32-bit grid
32:    imgmap.setalpha(mymask)
33:
34:    --update the Texture.image property
35:    scene.texture("map").image - imgmap
36: end
```

Although this example uses a bit of swapping, the overall technique should be rather approachable. It is possible to create the grids on-the-fly as well, but for this example, the bitmaps do a good job for our purposes. In addition, they are not very large—and most likely if you were creating a grid, you would want to use a bitmap that was more complex than what you might create with Imaging Lingo on-the-fly. In addition, you might consider looking into the copypixel() command as a way to create a more interesting "red dot." Rather than simply drawing a dot, you can use this command to composite a small but interesting bitmap with the grid to show the location on the map.

Future Considerations

Imaging Lingo is an extremely powerful tool that should not be overlooked—especially now that Director developers also have a 3D environment. These two tools work quite well together. Realize that highly skilled developers used Imaging Lingo by itself to create robust 3D environments in Director before Director 8.5 introduced the 3D environment. To continue, Imaging Lingo offers several dramatic possibilities that should not be overlooked. Other than animated Textures, here are some of the uses you might consider for Imaging Lingo:

- A Texture-based menu system
- A 3D compass or radar animation
- A heads-up display or targeting display
- A multipane background animation
- Lens flares, glows, trails, and flat mirrors

If you are not familiar with Imaging Lingo, be sure to read through Appendix C as well as look through the links provided in the "Supplemental Resources" section at the end of this chapter.

Streaming Video Grabber Texture

Another possibility for animated Textures that is worth examining is using the RealMedia Xtra that's supplied standard with Director 8.5 for streaming video as the source for a Texture. Using a Real Video stream is similar to using a QuickTime video sprite, but because you have the ability to use Imaging Lingo to grab frames from the Real Video stream, it is a bit more versatile for creating animated Textures.

What this means is that while the video is playing, we are able to use Imaging Lingo to access the image information of the current frame of the Real Video stream. By updating the source of the Texture using this image data, we are able to effectively create video-based Textures.

Unless you have access to a Real streaming server, you might think your options are extremely limited. However, a little-known fact that you may be interested in learning is that Real Networks freely distributes a basic version of its encoding product, RealProducer. With RealProducer, you can encode any existing digital video file you might have into the Real format.

This file can then be used inside of Director. You will still need to use a dsw-media folder, because this streaming video will be loaded externally, but there is a clear advantage: The example we will be looking at is a 28KB file that uses a 15-second video clip. It only takes a moment for the movie to download, and then the remainder of the video Texture streams in. Open the file named "Real Video Texture" on the CD and press play.

NOTE

Be certain that if you copy this file to your hard drive, you also copy the dswmedia folder that accompanies the file. You should keep the dswmedia folder in the same directory as the Director movie—don't put the Director movie inside the dswmedia folder.

You should be presented with a television that has a small video clip playing on the screen. The television oscillates back and forth so that you can see the screen from a variety of directions. In this particular demonstration, I have made several modifications to the Shader the screen uses in order to try and capture the essence of the screen. Note how the screen itself is semitransparent, yet this can only be observed when the television is viewed from an oblique angle. Also, I have set the Texturemode property of the Texture to #reflection, but these Shader-level modifications are, of course, minute compared to the goal we are trying to achieve: animated Textures based on a RealMedia Castmember.

You may find it helpful to open the RealMedia viewer while the Director movie is playing. Director simultaneously updates the RealMedia viewer as well as the video stream we will be using for the animated Texture. This allows you to gain a better sense of where the frames for the animated Texture are coming from and what changes will occur for these frames when they're used as Textures.

In this example, I have decided to once again use a dedicated parent/child script in order to gain the animated Texture functionality. In order to use the parent/child script, some light preliminary setup must be performed at the initialization. Note the excerpt from the Initialize() custom handler in Listing 17.7.

Listing 17.7   An Excerpt from the Initialize() Handler

```
1:   -- start the realmedia clip playing
2:   member("smbouy").play()
3:   -- grab the image of the realmedia clip
4:   -- holding on to it in a variable
5:   imgobj = member("smbouy").image
```

Listing 17.7   Continued

```
6:
7:    --create a new texture from that image object
8:    txt = scene.newtexture("video", #fromimageobject, imgobj)
9:    --set some basic variables to avoid
10:   --high quality and nearfiltering since the texture
11:   --is animated, it will be difficult to focus on anyway.
12:   txt.quality = #low
13:   txt.nearfiltering = false
14:   txt.renderformat = #rgba5550
15:
16:   -- create a global to hold on to the child object that
17:   -- will "drive" the animated texture
18:   global animtxt
19:   -- initialize the animation of the texture
20:   animtxt = new(script "RealMedia Texture",\
 scene, "video", member("smbouy"))
21:
22:   -- set the texture of the screen Shader to the new texture
23:   scene.shader[9].texture = txt
24:
25: end
```

Note that there is a large difference between the reference to the Texture represented by txt and the child object represented by animtxt. The reference to the Texture, txt, must be used to set the Texture property of the Shader. The animtxt variable merely holds onto the child object reference that actually handles switching out the image objects so that the txt Texture appears animated.

Also, note the syntax in line 20; this line of code invokes the new() handler of the RealMedia Texture parent script. Note that this line must be called after you have created a Texture object that you want to animate. The syntax for initializing this parent script is as follows:

```
Ref = new(script "realmedia texture",\
 3Dcastmember, Texture, RealmediaCastmember)
```

Here, 3Dcastmember and RealmediaCastmember are references in form member("castmembername"), and Texture is the name of the Texture we want to animate. The parent script that this invokes is shown in Listing 17.8.

Listing 17.8   RealMedia Texture Parent Script

```
 1: property ptargetcastmember
 2: property ptargettexture
 3: property ptargetRM
 4:
 5: property pOldTime
 6:
 7: on new(me, which3Dcastmember, whichtexture, whichRM)
 8:    --make sure that you have specified a 3D castmember
 9:    if which3Dcastmember.type = #shockwave3D then
10:      ptargetcastmember = which3Dcastmember
11:    else
12:      return false
13:    end if
14:
15:    --make sure that you have specified a texture Node
16:    if which3Dcastmember.texture(whichtexture) <> void then
17:      ptargettexture = whichtexture
18:    else
19:      return false
20:    end if
21:
22:    --make sure that you have specified a realmedia castmember
23:    if whichRM.type = #realmedia then
24:      ptargetRM = whichRM
25:    else
26:      return false
27:    end if
28:
29:    --set up the initial poldtime
30:    --which is used to determine when to update the texture
31:    pOldTime = the milliseconds
32:    --add the child object reference to the actorlist
33:    --so that it receives stepframe events
34:    add the actorlist, me
35:    --return a reference to the child object
36:    return me
37: end
38:
39: on stepframe(me)
40:    -- since there is no built in looping
41:    -- for realmedia members, check to see
42:    -- the current time of the stream,
43:    -- if it is at 0, restart the playback
44:    if ptargetRM.currenttime = 0 then
45:      ptargetRM.play()
46:    end if
```

Listing 17.8   Continued

```
47:
48:    --check to see that at least a few milliseconds have elapsed
49:    if pOldtime - the milliseconds < 10 then
50:       -- grab the current image from the realmedia stream
51:       currentimage = ptargetRM.image
52:
53:       -- update the image of the texture property
54:       ptargetcastmember.texture(ptargettexture).image = currentimage
55:
56:       -- set the old time to the current time
57:       pOldTime = the milliseconds
58:    end if
59: end
```

Notice how there are two distinct handlers in this script: the new() handler, which is used to initialize the animated Texture, and the stepframe() handler, which is used to handle the image object swapping. In many ways, the functionality of this code is very similar to the others we have looked at for animated Textures. The prime difference lies in where we are getting the source image object material from.

RealMedia Issues

Unfortunately, working with RealMedia has several issues you should be aware of before you decide on using this method. First, realize that there is no built-in method for rewinding and restarting the video stream gracefully. When you play the RealMedia Castmember, there may be a small pause that affects the environment.

Second, you can only play one RealMedia stream at a time. Therefore, it is not possible to have more than one long animated Texture running at the same time. You can use several Textures in one movie, but they cannot play at the same time.

Finally, although Director 8.5 ships with the RealMedia Xtra installed standard, you or your users will need to have the RealMedia player installed as well. If your users do not, it will be installed automatically the first time they try to play a Shockwave movie that needs it. If it is any consolation, the RealMedia player is installed on a staggering number of machines, both PCs and Macintoshes.

Although these three issues are daunting, it is still obvious that RealMedia can be used to create Textures that are either live streams or extremely long, where it would be prohibitive to download all the frames. Also, keep in mind that this RealMedia clip could have included a soundtrack.

NOTE

Several resources can be found near the end of this chapter in the "Supplemental Resources" section, including links to RealMedia and a document on the Macromedia site you should look at before you begin to work with the RealMedia Xtra.

Particle Systems

Although Director 8.5 defines #particle as a primitive type, particle systems are generally not thought of as primitives. This is because they are radically different from the other primitives that #particle has been grouped with. A particle system is not defined by geometry but rather by motion. Particle systems are comprised of tiny "particles." In some 3D animation packages, you can define geometry as the particles, but this is not the case in Director. With Director, the particles are by default small, flat "planes." You can use Textures to modify the look of these planes, as you will in several of the demonstrations in this section. However, the basic principle still applies: A particle system is comprised of particles.

Because particle systems are a primitive of motion, time and physics figure heavily into the properties that define them. Other characteristics of the particle system include the following:

- How many particles there are
- How long they live
- How fast they are moving
- In which direction they are moving

The uses for this type of primitive can vary greatly—from explosions to fog to flames. Before we begin, you should note that particle systems have several "quirks" that place them outside of many of the rules that you have learned. Also, they have many properties. Setting any one of these properties "incorrectly" may ruin the effect you are trying to achieve.

With that said, you should also note that particles, although not impossible to use, can be difficult to learn how to control. For that reason, we will look at several examples in order to help you understand how you can gain control over the basic and advanced features available with this useful tool.

Particle Properties

To understand what a particle system is, you need to understand what a particle is. For now, think of a particle as a small square of paper. A particle system defines how many of these squares will exist at any given time, what direction they might be moving in, how large they are, and how long they will exist before they disappear. It is possible to change the color, size, and opacity of the particles and have these properties "tween" over time between values. It is also possible to define particles as continually emitting, like a stream of water, or bursting at a particular interval, like fireworks. In addition, we can set several properties to approximate the effects of wind and gravity on the particles.

When you create a particle system, these are some of the types of properties you will need to set. In addition, you need to understand that you cannot control individual particles in a particle system; rather, you set general parameters for the system, and the particles in the system follow those properties as rules. Some properties will be followed more strictly than others, creating various effects (such as some particles moving slower than others).

The best way to learn about particle systems is to see several examples of what they can do while noting some of the various basic properties they use. Table 17.2 is a rather large list of basic particle system properties.

TABLE 17.2   Particle System Modelresource Properties

Property	Value	Purpose
Lifetime	Milliseconds	Determines how long each particle will last.
Emitter.mode	#stream #burst	#stream creates aflowing effect, whereas #burst creates explosions.
Emitter.loop	Boolean	Continually emits particles or emits them just once.
Emitter.numparticles	Integer	Number of particles.

TABLE 17.2   Continued

Property	Value	Purpose
Emitter.direction	Vector	Direction that particles flow toward.
Emitter.angle	0–180	Determines whether particles flow more like a line or a sphere.
Emitter.distribution	#linear #gaussian	Determines where particles are placed when emitted.
Emitter.minspeed	#float	Slowest particle speed.
Emitter.maxspeed	#float	Fastest particle speed.
Sizerange.start	#float	Initial particle size.
Sizerange.end	#float	Final particle size.
Blendrange.start	0–100	Initial particle blend.
Blendrange.end	0–100	Final particle blend.
Colorrange.start	rgb(R,G,B)	Initial particle color.
Colorrange.end	rgb(R,G,B)	Final particle color.
Tweenmode	#velocity #age	Determines current blend and size based on particle age or speed.
Drag	0–100	Percentage to which the wind affects the particle.
Wind	Vector	Direction and strength of the wind.
Gravity	Vector	Direction and strength of gravity.

The most important thing you must understand is that all these properties are Modelresource properties. The majority of control over the look of the particle system will be done at the Modelresource level, more so than for any other Modelresource type. For this reason, it is very difficult to create an API for this Modelresource that would be easier to deal with than simply setting the properties.

Finally, before we look at the first demonstration, understand that particle systems are based on motion, not on geometry. No geometry is involved in a particle system. There's no Mesh—only squares of color that float about in 3D space. If it helps to think of these squares of color as flat planes, do so, but realize that no geometry is involved.

Particle Laboratory

Several times now I have mentioned that particle systems are systems of motion. They are defined by motion, time, and change—all these things make particle systems essentially impossible to visualize in a book. The best we can do is look at a snapshot of a particle system at a given point in time, but like a speeding car, it does not do the particle system justice.

Because there are so many properties to deal with just to begin learning what a particle system looks like, let alone what you might be able to accomplish with it, I have created a laboratory-style demonstration for you to learn about particle systems visually. Even if you have worked with particle systems in the past, I suggest you work with the "Particle Laboratory" file on the CD. This demonstration provides you with a visual interface for controlling all the basic properties of the particle system in real time.

This first demonstration is intended to give you a sense of how you can use the basic parameters to shape the particle system into a variety of different effects. We are going to look at several different parameters that I want to draw your attention to. During this demonstration, I expect that you have the "Particle Laboratory" file open and playing.

Emitter

The emitter is one of the basic properties of the particle system Modelresource. It is quite important, but you must understand that the emitter itself is not as important as the properties of the emitter. Look again at Table 17.2 and notice how many of the properties begin with the word *Emitter*. Each of the subproperties of the emitter controls some of the basic functions of the particle system.

While the particle laboratory is playing, try changing the mode from stream to burst. Changing this subproperty to burst has the rather dramatic effect of creating more of an explosion with the particle system. Now try changing the emitter.maxspeed property to a value of 200. Notice how when the particle system explodes, it does so much less violently. Continue this demonstration by changing the emitter.angle property to a value of 50. Notice that now the particles seem to explode toward the right side of the screen in a conical pattern rather than a sphere. You may also note from Table 17.2 that several of the particle system properties are not subproperties of the emitter. These other primary properties—Lifetime, Gravity, Wind, and Drag—control aspects of a particle system that are related to physics: time, force, and friction.

Lifetime

While the movie continues to play, we are going to alter the Lifetime property. This property determines how many milliseconds will elapse in the life of a particle. If you set this value quite low, notice how quickly the system bursts over and over. Now, set a rather high value, such as 5000, for Lifetime. Notice how the particles explode and then slowly continue to drift away from the origin.

The Lifetime property controls how long each particle in the particle system will "live." The particles in a particle system are generated according to the properties you set in the particle system Modelresource. Whereas the emitter settings control properties such as what direction particles are moving in or how many particles there are in a system at a given time, the Lifetime property controls how long the individual particles will exist to follow these rules. Once the lifetime of a given particle has elapsed, the particle is destroyed. However, the particle system itself lives on with new particles being created to follow the rules set up by the emitter.

Gravity, Wind, and Drag

The last few properties I want to examine during this demonstration are the Gravity, Wind, and Drag properties. The Gravity property is quite simple. You set a vector for the direction and strength that gravity will pull on each particle. While the movie is still playing, set Gravity to vector(0,-2,0). The particles should explode but slowly be pulled toward the bottom of the screen. Gravity affects all particles equally. Set Gravity back to vector(0,0,0) and then set the Wind property to vector(5,0,0). It might not seem like the Wind property has done much until you set the Drag property to 5. Now the particle system explodes and then slows down. Notice that while the particle system slows down, it is still drifting toward the right, because the wind is pushing the particles whose initial burst velocity has been dragged down to zero.

The particle laboratory is a large demo and a powerful tool. Before you continue, work with it for a while. Other than the properties I have singled out, try working with the color, size, and blend ranges and see how altering these affects the particle system as well.

Particle Mouse Demo

This next demonstration is rather short and straightforward. I have created a basic particle system, and I'm using the code from the "3D Mouse Cursor" demonstration in Chapter 13 to move the particle system in real time with the mouse. Open the file named "3D Particle Mouse" on the CD and press Play.

As you move the mouse, the particle system will move in 3D space. Notice how all the particles retain their relationship to each other. This is important. Realize that the particles are part of a system that has a single location in space—you cannot control the location of individual particles. You can only control the location of all the particles in a system at once.

Intermediate Particle: Texture

In this demonstration, we will be examining one method of altering the basic particle used for a particle system. Essentially, we are able to specify a Texture object as the particle to be used by the system. However, this is an intermediate exercise because you must understand how its implementation is quite odd when compared to similar operations in Director 8.5.

You already know that the #particle Modelresource type is strange as compared to the other types. In addition to the fact that this primitive is not really created of geometry, Models created from this primitive do not utilize their Shader property. The #particle Modelresource type contains a Texture property that you assign Texture objects to. This is unlike any of the other Models or Modelresources that we will be working with, so it should stand out in your mind as an irregularity.

The Texture object that you assign to the Texture property of #particle Modelresources can be any Texture object you can create in the 3D environment. So, you can use Texture objects with or without alpha channels, although using alpha channel–based Textures tends to look much better.

Open the file named "Particle Texture" on the CD and press Play. Note that the particles in this basic particle system are created from a small red circle with alpha transparency. These particles are created from a 32-bit Texture that looks like a fuzzy red ball. Remember, any image you can turn into a Texture can be used as the basic particle. However, any given particle system can only have one Texture at a time.

Using basic Textures in combination with particle systems can generate a wide variety of effects. Here's a short list of possibilities you might consider:

- Snowflakes or rain

- Dust or dirt

- Underwater air bubbles or plankton

Adding plankton and air bubbles to an underwater environment can dramatically increase the sense of realism—or at least help to signify underwater much better than without them. The point is, you do not necessarily need to use this technique in an obtrusive way to use it effectively.

Intermediate Particle: Animated Texture

Because it is possible to use Texture objects to change the overall look of the particle system, it is equally possible to combine the animated Texture techniques we examined previously in this chapter with particle systems to great effect.

First, open the file named "Advanced Particle Texture" on the CD and press Play. Wait a few moments for the slow-moving particle system to begin to populate. Small butterflies should flitter across the stage after a few moments. Although it is not possible to assign geometry to particles, nothing can stop you from creating a well-designed animation with alpha transparency that can look like geometry in a 3D environment. In fact, this animation was quickly generated in 3D Studio MAX.

Take a look at the butterfly cast that is included in this file and you will be able to see the individual frames that comprise the butterfly animation. Note that the butterfly essentially flaps its wings but does not change its registration point in this animation. Essentially, the butterfly is flapping in place. The beauty of the particle system is that we can allow the particles (the butterflies in this example) to slowly get smaller and smaller.

The use of animated Textures in combination with particle systems can be used to generate a slightly different set of techniques than the previous list we looked at for static Textures and particle systems. Here are some of the possibilities you might want to consider:

- Bugs, bees, or birds
- Schools of fish
- Herds of animals

Although this list highlights the animation of groups of organisms, animated Textures with particle systems can certainly be used for inorganic clusters of asteroids, glass shards, and so on.

Advanced Particle: Regions

Several properties of particle systems are used to create advanced effects that are not included in the Particle Laboratory demonstration. This is because each of these advanced properties will take a little longer to understand on their own.

The first of the advanced particle system properties we'll look at is the emitter.region property. Normally, you are accustomed to particles emanating from a single point in space. However, with the Region property, we are able to essentially create areas from which particles emanate.

We will examine two methods of creating regions in this demonstration. First, open the file named "Particle Regions" on the CD and press Play. At the bottom of the Stage are four buttons labeled Line, Rectangle, Line as Waterfall, and Rectangle as Fog, respectively. Test each of these to get a sense of what I mean by an "emitter region" and also to see two possibilities for its use.

The emitter.region property accepts a list of either two or four vectors. These vectors should be considered locations in 3D space relative to the particle system local coordinates. If you specify a list of two vectors, you will specify a region that is a line from which particles will emanate. If you specify a list of four vectors, you will be specifying a region that could look like a rectangle or square. However, be aware that the order of the vectors and specific values you choose can create unexpected results when you're attempting to create rectilinear regions.

Advanced Particle: Paths

The next advanced particle system property we will be examining is the emitter.path property. This is perhaps one of the most difficult properties to learn how to work with because it requires tweaking several of the other particle system properties in order to elicit the desired effect. In addition, creating the emitter path itself is a daunting task that can be difficult without a visual modeling tool such as 3D Studio MAX.

The emitter.path property accepts a list of vectors that describe the points on a three-dimensional curve. The difficulty with describing such a curve from scratch is obvious. To make curves that exist on a single plane can be approached with graph paper and diligence. Anything more than this would prove fairly difficult. In this demonstration are several paths I have created with the help of 3D Studio MAX.

Luckily, that program has the capability to export a list of vertex values for any three-dimensional curve I might happen to draw. This list can then be painstakingly converted into vectors and delimited with commas rather than colons to convert the list from a 3D Studio MAX ASCII file into a linear list of Director vectors.

The curves I have created range from a simple arc, a square, a complex arc, and finally an inward and upward spiraling helix. First open the file named "Particle Path" on the CD and press Play. You'll notice four buttons with the picture of a different path on each. Try clicking the buttons to see the different paths in action.

Aside from the difficulty of creating the path itself are the difficulties of how to implement the path. Realize that all the basic properties of the particle system are still working. Changes that you make to the speed, size, and so on will have a definite effect on the particles following the path. However, two properties in particular have a most dramatic effect on the path.

The first property is one that you have not yet learned: emitter.pathstrength. The emitter.pathstrength property determines how closely to the path particles attempt to follow. Be warned that setting this property incorrectly can ruin a perfectly good path. A setting of 0 means that the particles should not follow the path at all. The default value is 0.1. Strangely enough, more often than not, you will set too a high value for Pathstrength.

A good rule to figuring out what Pathstrength value to use is to start with the default setting of .1. If you cannot see any particles, try .01, then .001, and so on until you reach .00001. If you still cannot see any particles, reset

Pathstrength to 0.1. Then try setting the second property that affects the path dramatically: the Drag property. We have worked with Drag before. Previously, I defined Drag as the amount of effect the wind vector will have on your particle system. In terms of the path, the Drag property will cause particles that stray from the path to slow down. Generally, when you're trying to control the particles on a path, a relatively low Drag value should help (a value in the range of 1 to 20 usually will help keep enough particles on the path so that you can see them).

You may be wondering why anyone would want to use a particle path if it is so difficult. The overriding reason is that using the path property gives you the most control over the placement of particles over time. In addition, you can change the path over time. Imagine defining several paths that describe the path for letters of the alphabet or a company logo.

Summary

In this chapter, we have explored two areas of special effects that can be used in a rather large number of techniques. Animated Textures and particle systems both have the property of motion and time in common. The level of dynamism that these effects offer to you as a designer and developer for your 3D environment is quite exciting. As with any other element you plan on using in a given project, special effects should be planned for inclusion from the beginning.

We began by looking at both animated Textures and particle systems simply as effects. By the end of each section, however, you should have begun to realize how these elements remain effects on their own—but when coupled with each other (or other tools such as Imaging Lingo), they can become much more for your projects.

FAQ

Is there a way to create animated Textures without code?

No. There are no built-in mechanisms in the 3D environment to accomplish animated Textures without the help of code.

Do I have to use parent/child scripts to create animated Textures?

No, remember that the first demonstration in this chapter for the simple animated Texture used an `exitframe()` handler to accomplish the cycling of the

Texture. In addition, the animated particle Texture demonstration used simple `exitframe()` handler–based Texture cycling as well. Do not feel that you must use parent/child scripts for animated Textures, but I do recommend them if you need advanced control of the animation for interactivity, timing, or simply to have the extra level of control.

Do animated Textures cause a performance drain on systems?

Generally, no. However, this is going to be dependent on the size of the Texture you are attempting to animate. I recommend that you look at Chapter 19, "Performance Optimization," and Chapter 20, "Download Optimization," to gain a clear understanding of the developmental concerns you should have surrounding the use of animated Textures.

Are particle systems affected by Light Nodes?

Unfortunately, no. For the simplest method of approximating light, you can modify the Colorrange and Blendrange properties to simulate the cast of light on a particle system. A slightly more elegant approach would be to use a Texture for the particle system that appears to be affected by light. Using Textures that have the effects of lighting already applied to them are said to have the lighting "baked" onto them.

I don't understand the basics of Imaging Lingo. What can I do to learn more about it?

First, refer to Appendix C at the end of this book. Then, take a look at the links provided in the "Supplemental Resources" section of this chapter for more demonstrations of Imaging Lingo on the Web.

Supplemental Resources

- Director Online

    `www.director-online.com/quickLink.cfm?id=392`

    Director Online has created a quick directory link to all its articles dealing with Imaging Lingo.

- Setpixel

    `www.setpixel.com`

    Charles Forman has created several impressive demonstrations explaining Imaging Lingo, in addition to using Imaging Lingo in several projects that you can see at his Web site.

- Imaging help

  The dirGames-L listserv has quite a few members who use Imaging Lingo on a daily basis. If you are interested in learning more about Imaging Lingo, you should consider the members of this list highly skilled with this branch of Lingo. Remember that the focus of this listserv is game development, and they are quite strict about "on topic" questions. Even if you are not interested in game development, though, many Imaging Lingo tricks can be learned here.

- Animated textures

  You might consider many methods for the creation of animated Textures. Other than using digital video equipment or various hand-drawn animation techniques, consider that 3D Café (www.3dcafe.com) has animated Texture CDs for sale.

- Real Networks RealProducer

  If you are interested in working with RealProducer, you will need to go to www.realnetworks.com. There are two versions of RealProducer: Basic and Plus. The basic version is free, but it has limited capabilities as compared to the relatively inexpensive Plus version. Also, make sure you look at the Developer section to read about your server and legal requirements when using RealMedia.

- Macromedia PDF about RealMedia

  www.macromedia.com/support/director/soundvideo/realmedia_xtra

  Macromedia has produced a downloadable PDF that explains the commands and functions for RealMedia Castmembers. In addition, several links and resources in this document deal with basic RealMedia creation and distribution.

CHAPTER 18

3D Interface Design

We have been examining many aspects of the 3D environment in Director in terms of creation and control. In this chapter, we will be looking at combining the concepts that you have learned in previous chapters to develop three interfaces that utilize 3D as a main component. Although we will be combining many concepts from previous chapters, several concepts will be introduced in this chapter that have not been addressed yet.

The new concepts we will be discussing are look-up tables and sound localization. In addition, we will be discussing how interaction design and interface design are two different but interrelated aspects of your project that need to be addressed. These skills are important because in addition to learning how to create and control 3D, you must also learn how to integrate it with other non-3D assets. This is true whether you are creating immersive 3D environments or a hybrid application that combines 2D and 3D elements on the same Stage.

Charting an Application Interface

The first interface we will be looking at is a charting application. Recall from Part II, "Data Visualization," that we worked with a parent script to help us visualize 3D charts from data we supplied. In this interface, we will be combining the lessons from Section II along with Picking Lingo, Imaging Lingo, Backdrops, Overlays, and basic surfacing techniques. In addition, we will be incorporating the interactive 3D data visualization with 2D interface elements. Figure 18.1 is a screenshot from the file named "Visualization Interface," which can be found on the CD accompanying this book.

FIGURE 18.1

A screenshot from the charting application interface.

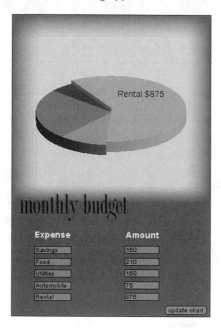

In this interface, the 3D elements and the 2D elements on the Stage need to able to occupy the same Stage but visually exist in the same "place." In this example, the pie chart appears to exist on a background that is integrated into the background of the movie.

Normally when achieving this effect, you might be tempted to set the Directtostage property to False and then use a Sprite Ink to achieve a transparent background for the 3D Sprite. However, I strongly discourage you from doing this because the performance hit is downright terrible. Instead, in this example, I have created a Backdrop for the 3D Castmember that integrates with the 2D Sprites on the Stage to create the look of the Stage background.

Because the 3D Sprite will be drawn "Directtostage," it is important that you avoid overlapping any other sprites with the 3D Sprite. Because of this, the other Sprites used to create the skin of the background for the Stage are created in sections that surround the 3D Sprite. Figure 18.2 illustrates the boundaries for the 2D Castmembers that comprise the background skin for the Stage.

FIGURE 18.2

In this figure, the boundaries of the 2D Sprites used to create the background for the Stage are indicated.

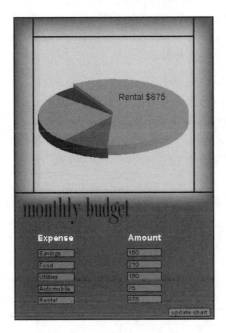

Note that all these 2D Sprites have been combined into a single film loop to conserve as many Sprite channels as possible. I prefer this multiple-Sprite method because I am able to create 16-bit Castmembers for the background images rather than wasting space on one gigantic 32-bit Castmember with an alpha channel "hole" for the 3D Castmember. Also, even with an alpha channel "hole," the 2D Sprite will need to occupy the same space as the 3D Sprite, which is something we want to avoid for performance reasons related to the fact that the 3D sprite should remain "Directtostage."

The second issue about this interface is related to the method of interaction that is built in to the 3D Sprite. We worked with code that creates pie charts in Chapter 11. In that chapter, there was even a rudimentary version of the interaction that has been created for the pie chart in this example. However, this example is enhanced by the fact that users can change the values and labels for the pie wedges, and they can also receive feedback about the individual wedges if they click them.

In this particular demonstration, it is possible for users to enter their own information and labels for the chart through the editable text fields present on the Stage. Then they can force the chart to update with their new data via a button within the interface. The point here is that this demonstration moves beyond explaining the usage of the pie chart API and now incorporates this code into an interface that is ready for users.

In this example, when you click an individual wedge of the pie chart, it reacts in several ways to indicate that it is the selected wedge. The wedge will raise up and use the Emissive property to look lighter in color. Also a label appears at the location of the mouse click. This label informs the user of the name of the wedge as well as the amount associated with that wedge.

Changing the Location and Emissive properties of the individual wedge is easy enough, but adding the label is a bit more complicated. This is because we are not able to use another Sprite to perform the labeling process. Rather, in this example, we are using an Overlay. You already know that an Overlay is created from a Texture object. In this case, the source for the Texture object will be generated from a Text Castmember via Imaging Lingo in real-time, based on the choices the user makes. Listing 18.1 shows the code for the wedge click behavior, with comments about the function of each line.

LISTING 18.1   Wedge Click Behavior

```
 1: Property spritenum
 2: -- pOffset is used with modelunderloc
 3: property pOffset
 4: -- plastclicked saves the name of the wedge that was clicked last
 5: -- this information is used to "un-select" wedges.
 6: property plastclicked
 7:
 8: global scene
 9: -- a reference to the pie chart child object
10: global chartobj
11: -- a reference to the Texture Object used for the Overlay
12: global labelimage
13:
14: on beginsprite
15:   poffset = point(sprite(spritenum).left, sprite(spritenum).top)
16: end
17:
18: on mousedown
19:   -- determine the location of the click
```

LISTING 18.1   Continued

```
20:   curloc = the clickloc
21:   -- offset the location of the click so that
22:   -- it is in sprite relative coordinates
23:   cloc = curloc - poffset
24:
25:   -- determine if the user has clicked on a Model
26:   mdl = scene.camera[1].modelunderloc(cloc)
27:
28:   -- determine if there is an Overlay
29:   -- and if there is, remove it
30:   isoverlay = scene.camera[1].overlay.count
31:   if isoverlay >=1 then
32:     scene.camera[1].removeoverlay(1)
33:   end if
34:
35:   -- If the user has clicked on a model then
36:   -- mdl will not be void
37:   if mdl <> void then
38:     -- make sure that the user did not click on the two
39:     -- planes that are used to cap off the ends of the
40:     -- wedge.  If they did, change the name of the Model
41:     -- to the parent Model of the cap - which will be the wedge
42:     if mdl.name contains "capb" or mdl.name contains "capa" then
43:       mdl = mdl.parent
44:     end if
45:
46:     -- determine if the last model that was clicked is the
47:     -- same as the model that was currently clicked.
48:     if plastclicked <> mdl then
49:       -- if the last model clicked and the current model
50:       -- are different then …
51:
52:       -- find out the value of the data
53:       -- associated with that wedge
54:       answer = chartobj.pc_datareport(#frommodelname, mdl.name)
55:       -- put the name of the wedge and
56:       -- its data into the text castmember named "outbox"
57:       -- this castmember is not on the score or stage.
58:       member("outbox").text = mdl.name  && "$" & answer
59:
60:       -- use the emissive property of the wedge to
61:       -- hilite the Model
62:       scene.model(mdl.name).shader.emissive = rgb(70,70,70)
63:       -- Also translate the wedge 5 units in the positive
64:       -- Y direction, thereby "lifting" the wedge
```

LISTING 18.1   Continued

```
65:        scene.model(mdl.name).translate(0,5,0,#parent)
66:     end if
67:
68:     -- duplicate the image source of the "outbox"
69:     -- text castmember.  Remember that this has
70:     -- stored the name and data associated with
71:     -- the wedge that has just been clicked.
72:     tempimage = member("outbox").image.duplicate()
73:     -- set the source of the Texture to the source
74:     -- that we just created from the "outbox" castmember
75:     labelimage.image = tempimage
76:
77:     -- offset the current location a bit for better
78:     -- placement of the Overlay
79:     cloc = cloc - point(10,0)
80:     -- add an overlay to the camera based on the
81:     -- labelimage Texture object and place it
82:     -- at cloc: the location of the mouse in sprite
83:     -- relative coordinates…
84:     scene.camera[1].addoverlay(labelimage,cloc, 0)
85:  end if
86:
87:  -- determine whether the plastclicked property
88:  -- is different than the name of the current model
89:  -- and that it is not void.  (we are trying to determine
90:  -- if the user clicked on the background or a different
91:  --  wedge in the 3D environment)
92:  if plastclicked <> void and plastclicked <> mdl then
93:     -- "un-select" the previous model clicked
94:     scene.model(plastclicked.name).shader.emissive = rgb(0,0,0)
95:     scene.model(plastclicked.name).translate(0,-5,0,#parent)
96:  end if
97:
98:  --record the name of the current Wedge as
99:  -- the name of the last Wedge that was clicked.
100:  plastclicked = mdl
101: end
```

This method of labeling has implications that go beyond pie charts—of course this includes other types of charts, but in reality it includes possibilities for all 3D interfaces. You can use this method to provide functionality, ranging from a type of tooltip to an Overlay-based 2D menu system.

NOTE

> You want to be careful, because this method requires the use of alpha channel–based Textures. Remember that some video cards do not support alpha channel–based Textures, and you may end up limiting the number of users who can see your labels. Also, remember that your Textures should be powers of 2. In this example, the Text Castmember named "outbox" is a fixed size that will always produce a 128×16 pixel image. This ensures that the Texture object will not be stretched, making it difficult to read. In addition, Texture.Nearfiltering and Texture.Quality have been turned off in order to avoid any blurring of the Overlay text.

3D Menu System Interface

In this demonstration, rather than incorporating 2D and 3D elements, we will build a menu system completely from 3D Models. In this approach, the idea is to create an interface that allows the user to interact with elements in the 3D Sprite in a uniform manner. In addition, the Models in this interface were created in an external 3D modeling package and then imported into Director. Figure 18.3 is a screenshot from the file named "3D Menu System" on the CD. Open this file and click the Models of teapots.

FIGURE 18.3

A screenshot from the "3D Menu System" demonstration.

The strength of this interface is its ability to create a seamless experience for the user in terms of interaction with the 3D environment. The user is able to click the Models in this example, and they will automatically float to a predetermined location in 3D space that allows the user to see the Models much closer. In addition, when a Model is in this "selected" position, it will spin, thus allowing the user to view the Model from all sides.

The idea with a menu system like this is to allow the user to always see the range of choices available. We can use the 3D space to foreground those details that are important and hide those details that are not. This particular example is a good method of displaying multiple products to a user so that he can get a sense of the scope of a product line. The motion of the Models is one of the most elegant and captivating parts of this interface, but as of yet we have not covered the function that makes this possible.

This Motion is made possible with interpolation; we will be working with interpolation not only in this chapter, but in many of the demonstrations in the chapters following this one. Because interpolation is an important concept, I suggest that you take your time reading through the explanation in this chapter so you are ready to apply it many more times in the future.

Interpolation

The concept of *interpolation* is one you have most likely worked with before in Director. Sprite-based keyframe animation is a form of interpolation. Essentially, you have two endpoints, and Director figures out where a Sprite should be in 2D space, depending on the difference in time between the two endpoints.

In the 3D environment, the function `interpolateto()` accepts two Transform objects and a percentage. This function then changes the value of the first Transform object to that of the location and orientation some distance between the two provided Transforms, depending on the percentage supplied with the function. The syntax for this function is as follows:

```
TransformA.interpolateto(TransformB, Percentage)
```

Note that the `interpolateto()` function is a destructive process that will immediately change the value of `transformA` in this example. If you would rather store this new position and orientation in a third Transform object, use the interpolate() function, as follows:

```
TransformC = TransformA.interpolate(TransformB, Percentage)
```

Whether you use interpolate() or interpolateto() really depends on the particular situation. In this demonstration, we will be using interpolateto(). Both the interpolation functions can provide a method of animation for your Nodes that is quite helpful. Remember that because these functions interpolate Transform objects, they are capable of interpolating between both orientation and position.

In general, the interpolation commands tend to provide the most dramatic results when used in conjunction with an exitframe()-based loop. The reason for this is that you are able to create the effect of a simple keyframe-based animation. In addition, the percentage you choose can influence the path of the animation, so you can allow the path to ease in, ease out, or remain constant. Figure 18.4 illustrates how the interpolation function can be used to generate a set of points between two points that slowly eases toward the second point.

FIGURE 18.4

An illustration of the set of points created by determining a third point between two source points.

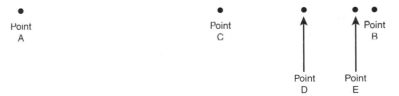

Note that in this figure, point A and B are the original endpoints. Point C is the point 75 percent between them, biased toward point B. Point D is the point 75 percent between points C and B. Point E is the point 75 percent between points D and B, and so on. Using this method with interpolation in the 3D environment allows us to create relatively smooth motion.

Calculating Distances

I will address the problems associated with interpolation after we look at the menu script. At this point, it is important to understand that these problems will be resolved by using another function we have not yet looked at: `distanceto()`. This function accepts two Vectors and calculates the distance in World units between those two Vectors and returns a floating-point value. The syntax for this function is as follows:

```
Distancebetween = vectorA.distanceto(vectorB)
```

Remember that this function accepts two Vectors and returns a floating-point value, rather than a third Vector. This is because the value that's returned is the shortest distance between the two supplied vectors.

Look-up Tables

The next item you need to know about before we start to look at code is a concept known as a *look-up table* (LUT). A LUT can be thought of as a list of values that have been precalculated or are calculated when the movie is initialized. This list is then referred to during the execution of the movie rather than those values being calculated in real time to optimize performance. Many times using a LUT is a better solution than creating an elaborate formula that is time consuming and generally too precise for the needs of multimedia.

This interface uses a LUT to reduce processor time as well as to generally store a range of values. Because list access in Lingo is quite fast, it is often easier to create a table of precalculated values in order to save time as well as for optimization. A LUT can be used to store a wide range of values, and the format of the list is entirely up to you. More importantly, a LUT is not just a list; rather, it is a way of using a list.

NOTE

Many examples of LUTs in action appear throughout the book. Specifically, Appendix D, "2D Mathematics and Utilities," shows ways for creating cosine and sine LUTs to save processor time, and Appendix F, "Colorlut Custom Color Management System," is entirely devoted to a particular LUT created to manage colors that actually takes the form of an API parent/child script.

3D Menu Behavior

Now that you have a basic understanding of interpolation, `distanceto()`, and LUTs, you are ready to take a closer look at the 3D menu interface. In this subsection, we will be looking at the code used to create the interaction with the 3D menu interface. Note that within the first few lines of the `begin-sprite()` handler in Listing 18.2, we are creating a list named *homelist*—this is our LUT, which contains the names of the teapot Models and their original `transform()` objects in World coordinates.

In general, the 3D menu behavior uses an `exitframe()` event in conjunction with a `mousedown()` handler. The `mousedown()` handler is used to determine whether the user has clicked a Model. If she has, the `exitframe()` event is used as a loop to move the Model to a predetermined location. If the user chooses a subsequent Model, the first Model is returned to its original position. In addition, if the user clicks empty space, the Model will return to its original position. Take a look at Listing 18.2 and read through the comments that accompany the code to learn how this behavior works.

LISTING 18.2 Code for the 3D Menu Behavior

```
 1: property spritenum
 2: -- homelist is used to store the values of the original
 3:    transforms for each Model in world relative coordinates
 4: property homelist
 5: -- used with modelunderloc
 6: property poffset
 7: -- phittransform stores the transform object that marks the
 8: -- position and orientation of a Model when selected.
 9: property phittransform
10: -- pmoving is used to store the name of the Model that
11: -- is currently moving between two points
12: property pmoving
13: -- plast is used to store the name of the last Model that
14: -- was clicked
15: property plast
16: -- phold is used to determine whether a model has reached its
17: -- destination and if so, causes the model to rotate at the
18: -- "selected" location noted in phittransform
19: property phold
20:
21: global scene
22:
23: on beginsprite
```

LISTING 18.2   Continued

```
24:   -- record the name of each Model and
25:   -- store this in a property list along with
26:   -- the original transformation for each
27:   homelist = [:]
28:   repeat with x = 1 to scene.model.count
29:     mdlname = scene.model[x].name
30:     setaprop(homelist, symbol(mdlname),\
31:     scene.model[x].getworldtransform())
32:   end repeat
33:
34:   -- determine the poffset
35:   poffset = point(sprite(spritenum).left, sprite(spritenum).top)
36:
37:   --create a new transform object
38:   phittransform = transform()
39:   -- hit is a vector that describes the location
40:   -- that I would like to use for the "selected"
41:   -- Model
42:   hit = vector(-15,-430,-15)
43:   -- displace the phittransform object
44:   -- based on the hit vector
45:   phittransform.translate(hit)
46:
47:   -- no model is moving by default
48:   pmoving = 0
49:   -- there is no previously hit model
50:   plast = 0
51: end
52:
53: on mousedown
54:   -- determine whether any Models are moving
55:   -- or not (you can only select a new Model
56:   -- if none are currently moving)
57:   if pmoving = 0 then
58:     -- determine location of the click
59:     curloc = the clickloc
60:     -- offset that amount for sprite relative coords.
61:     cloc = curloc - poffset
62:     -- determine if you clicked on a Model
63:     mm = scene.camera[1].modelunderloc(cloc)
64:
65:     -- if you did click on a model, then…
66:     if mm <> void then
67:       -- make sure that plast and phold are the same
68:       -- this is used to make sure that only one model
69:       -- can be selected at a time…
```

LISTING 18.2   Continued

```
70:        plast = phold
71:        --make sure that pmoving is a reference
72:        --to the model you want to move
73:        pmoving = mm
74:     else
75:        -- if you did not click on a model, then
76:        -- also "move" the value of phold to plast
77:        plast = phold
78:        -- and then set phold to 0 (nothing is held)
79:        phold = 0
80:     end if
81:   end if
82: end
83:
84: on exitframe me
85:   --determine if any models have been selected
86:   --and if they are currently Moving
87:   if pmoving <> 0 then
88:     --if there is a model moving, then find out
89:     -- its current position
90:     currentposition = pmoving.transform.position
91:     --and figure out how close it is to its destination
92:     dist = currentposition.distanceto(phittransform.position)
93:
94:     -- if it is within 5 units, stop the motion
95:     if dist < 5 then
96:        -- pass the value of pmoving on to phold
97:        -- so that the system will know which model
98:        -- is selected…
99:        phold = pmoving
100:       -- but then set pmoving to 0 so that no
101:       -- model will move until another selection is made
102:       pmoving = 0
103:    else
104:       -- if the distance is not within 5 units,
105:       -- move the model 70% closer to the destination
106:       pmoving.transform.interpolateto(phittransform, 70)
107:    end if
108:  end if
109:
110:  -- next, we must take care of any models that are
111:  -- moving back to their original position
112:  -- if the last model clicked is not empty and the
113:  -- last model and the current model clicked are not
114:  -- the same, then this means that you clicked on a
115:  -- new model or the background while some third model
```

LISTING 18.2   Continued

```
116:    -- was selected... we need to move that model back "home"
117:    if plast <> 0 and plast <> pmoving then
118:        -- use the LUT homelist to determine where the
119:        -- original position of the Model is
120:        mdlname = plast.name
121:        homepos = getaprop(homelist, mdlname)
122:        -- Move the model 90% of the way there.
123:        plast.transform.interpolateto(homepos, 90)
124:
125:        --determine if we are within 5 units of the destination
126:        currentposition = plast.getworldtransform().position
127:        dist = homepos.position.distanceto(currentposition)
128:        if dist < 5 then
129:          --if we are within 5 units of the destination,
130:          -- then stop the Model from moving
131:            plast = 0
132:          phold = 0
133:        end if
134:    end if
135:
136:    --in case some Model is currently selected, but not moving
137:    -- and therefore in the "hold" position - rotate it.
138:    if phold <> 0 then
139:      scene.model(phold.name).rotate(0,0,2)
140:    end if
141: end
```

A slight problem exists that you should be aware of when working with repeated interpolations. If you continually move an object half the distance between two points, eventually the distances you are moving are extremely small—but you are still moving nonetheless. This is a waste of processor power, and the Model will never really arrive at its destination (but it will get really close). In order to remedy this situation, note that there are two places in this script at lines 90-95 and 126-128 where we use the distanceto() function to determine whether the Model has moved close enough to its target destination. If it has, we stop the Model from interpolating.

This is the reason for the plast and phold properties. The plast property is used to determine which Model was the last one clicked, whereas phold is used to determine whether the selected Model has moved into its "selected" position. If the Model is in the "selected" position, lines 138–140 cause the Model to spin.

An added bonus of interpolation is that it not only affects position but also orientation. So, when the user clicks a different Model or the background and the selected Model returns to its original position, it also returns to its original orientation.

Also note the use of `transform()` objects in general in this example. Note that `phittransform` stores a location and orientation, and this is used in the interpolation of the selected Models. However, that `transform()` is not attached to any Model—it exists like any other variable, but it is special because it is a Transform object. Therefore, many functions are available to this object that can be used for a variety of reasons. If you would like to learn more about Transform objects, be sure you understand transformations from Chapter 4. Also, look at Chapter 26, which deals with vector math and advanced transformations.

NOTE

Another consideration for this example that you might want to consider would be creating secondary and tertiary levels for the menu system. Also, although I have only chosen to show different colored teapots in this example, the individual Models need not be the same. In addition, you might consider combining this menu system with the Modelresource rollover techniques covered in Chapter 13.

Incorporating a Sound Interface

In this demonstration, we will be examining an interface that is a bit more abstract in nature. This interface uses the spatial relationship between Models and the Camera to change the qualities of the sounds playing to make them seem as though they are related to the positions of the Models.

With this interface, you can move the Models in 3D space, and the apparent location of the sound will change. Figure 18.5 shows a screenshot from this interface, which shows three spheres that can be moved within the 3D environment by dragging them. Each of these spheres has a sound associated with it, but because sound is one of the key elements of this interface, it will be difficult if not impossible to understand a more specific explanation without first looking at the file "Sound Localization" on the CD.

FIGURE 18.5

A screenshot from the Sound Localization application interface.

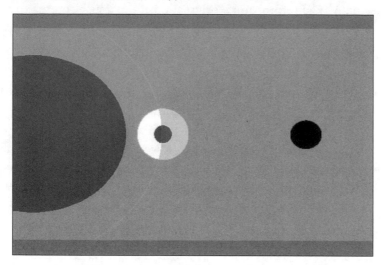

To control the sounds in this demonstration, click and drag the spheres to new locations in the 3D space. As you move the spheres farther away, the sound diminishes; as you move them closer, the sound becomes louder. In this simple way, we can at least determine "closer" and "farther away." In addition, you may notice that the sounds will pan left or right, depending on the location of the spheres.

NOTE

In this particular demonstration, the effect of localized sound works much better if you can listen to the demonstration on a pair of stereo headphones.

In this demonstration, we are using three clues to help the user understand where the sound is coming from: volume, pan, and visual clues. Note that the spheres play a crucial role in helping the user determine the location of a sound. In addition, the volume is used to determine proximity to the sound, whereas panning is used to determine the direction of the sound.

In this particular method, you must understand that certain limitations exist. It is very difficult to determine whether a sound is coming from "behind" using this method. In addition, none of the changes to a sound (high-pass filtering) that take place, depending on changes in the vertical direction, are possible. Therefore, in this example, all the sounds are spatialized on a flat plane. However, this method still has certain advantages that are worth looking at because the method itself is rather simple.

Some of the most complicated pieces of the code are based on the visual clues of the "expanding" spheres used to signify the waves of sound in a stylized fashion.

The initialization of this demonstration creates three groups of two spheres, for a total of six. The second sphere in a group is the child of the first sphere. The first sphere is opaque, and the second sphere uses the #add blendfunction and a very small red Texture. The parent spheres are named base1, base2, and base3. The child spheres are named effect1, effect2, and effect3. Once the environment has been initialized, two separate behaviors are used to create the overall interface.

The first behavior controls the method of interaction with the spheres, and the second behavior handles the localization of the sound. The 3D Mouse Cursor script in this demonstration is similar to the one discussed in Chapter 13, but this one also utilizes a flag variable in order to limit the effect of moving the spheres, unless the user has clicked a Model.

In addition, this script uses the `modelsunderloc()` command rather than the `modelunderloc()` command. `Modelsunderloc()` is a bit more robust, because rather than returning just the first Model hit, it returns a list of Models hit. In addition, you can limit the number of Models included in the list that this returns. This is necessary because the "effect" spheres could interfere with the ability to interact with the "base" spheres, which are the only spheres we want users to be able to interact with. With these requirements in mind, take a look at Listing 18.3, which explains the code used for the 3D Mouse Cursor demo.

LISTING 18.3   3D Mouse Cursor

```
1: Property spritenum
2: -- used with modelsunderloc()
3: Property poffset
4: --holds on to the name of the model that is currently
5: --selected, or zero if none are selected
6: Property whichmodel
7:
```

LISTING 18.3 Continued

```
 8: global scene
 9:
10: On beginsprite(me)
11:   poffset = point(sprite(spritenum).left,sprite(spritenum).top)
12:   whichmodel = 0
13: end
14:
15: on mousedown(me)
16:   -- determine the location of the click in
17:   -- sprite relative coordinates
18:   curloc = the clickloc - porigin
19:
20:   --use modelsunderloc to determine the first
21:   --four models that are hit at that location
22:   mdl = scene.camera[1].modelsunderloc(curloc, 4)
23:
24:   --if this is an empty list, do not do anything
25:   if mdl = [] then
26:     nothing
27:   else
28:     --otherwise, search through the list
29:     -- for the name of the first model whose
30:     -- name contains "base"  -- if there is one
31:     -- set whichmodel = the name of that model…
32:     repeat with x = 1 to mdl.count
33:       if mdl[x].name contains "base" then
34:         whichmodel = mdl[x].name
35:         exit repeat
36:       end if
37:     end repeat
38:   end if
39: end
40:
41: on mouseup(me)
42:   -- if the mouse goes up
43:   -- release any model that was
44:   -- being dragged
45:   whichmodel = 0
46:   cursor -1
47: end
48:
49: on mouseupoutside(me)
50:   --make sure that you do the same
51:   -- in case the mouse goes up
52:   -- outside the 3D sprite…
53:   whichmodel = 0
```

LISTING 18.3   Continued

```
54:    cursor -1
55: end
56:
57: on exitframe(me)
58: --if whichmodel is not 0, then
59: if whichmodel <> 0 then
60:      -- make the cursor invisible
61:      cursor 200
62:
63:      --determine the location of the mouse in
64:      --sprite coordinates (note that I am using
65:      -- the mouseloc this time rather than the clickloc)
66:      finpoint = the mouseloc - poffset
67:
68:      --figure out the location of the mouse in 3d space
69:      newloc = scene.camera[1].spriteSpaceToWorldSpace(finpoint)
70:      --translate the XY plane into XZ plane
71:      newlocb = vector(newloc.x,0,-newloc.y)
72:      --move the selected model to the new position
73:      scene.model(whichmodel).transform.position = newlocb
74:    end if
75: end
```

You can see from this script that we have essentially created a hybrid behavior for dragging Models that uses parts of the code for the 3D Mouse Cursor script from Chapter 13. In general, this part of the interface is highly reusable, even in situations that are not working with sound, because nothing in this script is dependent on sound.

The next behavior we will look at uses the locations of the base spheres to change properties about the sounds playing. This script is rather simple in nature, but in the interest of compartmentalizing, I have created several custom handlers that take care of a majority of the work in this script (see Listing 18.4).

LISTING 18.4   Sound Control Script

```
1: -- the effectlist is a structured list that contains
2: -- several values used in this demonstration.
3: -- note that the format for this list is defined
4: -- in the beginsprite handler
5: property effectlist
6:
```

LISTING 18.4   Continued

```
 7: global scene
 8:
 9: on beginsprite(me)
10:    --effectlist is a nested linear list
11:    --each of the lists nested inside the large list
12:    -- contain three values
13:    --effectlist[1][1] is a boolean that
14:    --stores whether the sound is playing
15:    --effectlist[1][2] stores the scale factor
16:    --for the effect sphere
17:    --effectlist[1][3] stores the blend for the sphere
18:    effectlist = [[0,1,30],[0,1,30],[0,1,30]]
19: end
20:
21: on exitframe(me)
22:
23:    -- on each exitframe determine if the sound has
24:    -- stopped playing in each channel.  If it has,
25:    -- restart the given sound, and set the corresponding
26:    -- value on the effectlist to true
27:    if soundbusy(1) = false then
28:      puppetsound(1, "soundA")
29:      effectlist[1][1] = true
30:    end if
31:
32:    if soundbusy(2) = false then
33:      puppetsound(2, "soundB")
34:      effectlist[2][1] = true
35:    end if
36:
37:    if soundbusy(3) = false then
38:      puppetsound(3, "soundC")
39:      effectlist[3][1] = true
40:    end if
41:
42:    -- if any of the sounds are playing, then call the
43:    --expand custom handler that causes the effect sphere
44:    -- to expand over time, and localizes the sound as well.
45:    if effectlist[1][1] then
46:      expand(me,1)
47:    end if
48:
49:    if effectlist[2][1] then
50:      expand(me,2)
51:    end if
52:
```

LISTING 18.4   Continued

```
53:   if effectlist[3][1] then
54:     expand(me,3)
55:   end if
56:
57: end
58:
59: on expand(me, whichmodel)
60:   --determine if the scale factor has grown too big,
61:   -- if so, reset the sphere
62:   if effectlist[whichmodel][2] >=1.1 then
63:     effectlist[whichmodel] = [0,1,30]
64:     scene.model("effect" & whichmodel).shader.blend = 30
65:     scene.model("effect" & whichmodel).transform.scale = \
        vector(1,1,1)
66:   else
67:   --if not, expand the scale of the effect sphere
68:   -- and lower the blend
69:     effectlist[whichmodel][2] = effectlist[whichmodel][2] + .002
70:     effectlist[whichmodel][3] = effectlist[whichmodel][3] - .5
71:
72:     newscale =  effectlist[whichmodel][2]
73:
74:     scene.model("effect" & \
        whichmodel).scale(newscale,newscale,newscale)
75:     scene.model("effect" & whichmodel).shader.blend =\
        effectlist[whichmodel][3]
76:   end if
77:
78:   --call the modelvolume() custom handler to determine
79:   --the new volume of the sound
80:   sound(whichmodel).volume = modelvolume(me, "base" & whichmodel)
81:   --call the modelpan() custom handler to determine
82:   -- the new pan of the sound.
83:   sound(whichmodel).pan = modelpan(me, "base" & whichmodel)
84: end
85:
86:
87: -- so far, most of this code has been very related to this
88: -- particular demo, but the modelvolume and modelpan
89: -- handlers are used to actually change the sound properties
90: -- based on the locations of the base models
91:
92: on modelvolume(me, whichone)
93:   --determine the distance between the camera and
94:   -- the Model in question
95:   modelposition = scene.model(whichone).transform.position
```

LISTING 18.4   Continued

```
 96:    dist = modelposition.distanceto(scene.camera[1].transform.position)
 97:
 98:    -- divide that number by three (dependent on this demo)
 99:    dist = dist / 3
100:
101:    -- reverse the sequence of numbers, so that when the Model is
102:    -- close to the camera, large values are returned
103:    newvolume = 255 - dist
104:
105:    --limit the range of numbers between 0 - 255
106:    if newvolume < 0 then newvolume = 0
107:    if newvolume > 255 then newvolume = 255
108:
109:    --return the newvolume
110:    return newvolume
111: end
112:
113: on modelpan(me, whichone)
114:    -- use the horizontal distance of the model
115:    -- to determine the pan of the sound.
116:    mypan = scene.model(whichone).transform.position.x
117:    if mypan > 100 then mypan = 100
118:    if mypan < -100 then mypan = -100
119:    return mypan
120: end
```

Note that the methods we are using to change the volume and the pan of a sound have room for expansion. In general, if you look at the modelvolume() custom handler, you'll see that this function modulates the volume of the sound in a linear way. That is, the farther away a sound is, the lower it is. However, sounds do not attenuate like this at all. I have used this method to avoid a square root function because sounds attenuate closer to an inverse square relationship, depending on the specifics of the environment. If you wanted to, you might create a LUT of volumes to use, depending on the distance of the "sound" from the Camera.

Additional Enhancements for Localizing Sound

Sound localization is a difficult area because Director does not take advantage of any 3D sound acceleration you might have on your machine. If you are interested in this capability, you have several options to consider. First, carefully consider the assets you are working with in relation to the environment you are trying to create.

The method of localizing sound we have just examined has many drawbacks that you should understand. The ability to control the pan and volume of a sound allows you to successfully localize sounds on a single plane. However, when trying to localize sounds above or below your point of view, you may have some trouble.

In the following subsections, I will address several additional elements that affect the overall use of sound in your projects, such as silence, reverberation, convolution, delay, multiple sounds, and pitch shift. Some of these elements can be created and manipulated with Director, whereas others will need to be created externally. In addition to explaining what these elements are, I will be explaining where you will be working with them.

Silence

When designing your overall sound design for a project, you need to think seriously about *silence*. If you are trying to generate a sense of space, you should consider avoiding silence altogether. This does not mean that your work should be loud. By "avoiding silence," I mean avoiding a *lack* of sound. Have you ever closed your eyes in a room where everything was silent? Soon you begin to hear small ambient noises—noises that are always present that contribute to the sonic makeup of the environment.

If you are trying to create space, creating this ambient noise is very important, especially if you have chosen to avoid background music.

Reverberation

When localizing sounds in the real world, we use many clues about the sound that are often difficult to reproduce in real time on the computer. *Reverberation* is the effect that occurs when sounds strike objects and bounce around a room many times. This can be extremely pronounced, such as in a cathedral, or flat, such as in a small room. The key to understanding reverberation is the physics of a space and how the materials in that space will affect the way a sound reverberates.

The physics of the space is important. Large spaces will allow sounds to travel longer and bounce around longer; therefore, you will hear sounds for a longer period of time. Small spaces have the opposite effect on sounds. In addition, the shape of the interior is important—think of the sound of the inside of a tunnel, where the walls are curved. Curved versus sharp corners can heavily affect sound. Sharp corners can filter sounds, whereas curves will allow for repeated reflections. In addition, in a space with hard, flat surfaces, you will have more sound reflections than in a space with carpets and drapes. Certain objects will absorb sound rather than reflect it, and this will tend to dampen sound.

Although real-time reverberation is not a tool built in to Director, nothing can stop you from carefully creating your assets with reverberation to help describe the space you are trying to create.

Convolution Filters

Getting a bit fancier about your reverberations, you might think about using a convolution filter. In a given space, different sounds will create relatively similar reverberations. Factors such as frequency, volume, and location can change this, but the reverberation of a room can be thought of as a type of signature for the space. A convolution filter will take a sound without any reverberation and mathematically apply the "reverberation signature" of a given room to the sound. Many different sound software packages provide this functionality, but all rely on the same basic principle. You will provide the software with two sound files: one that does not contain any reverberation, and one that contains a classic signature of a room. This "classic signature" is often created by recording the sound of a balloon popping in a room whose reverberation you are trying to capture. These two sound files are then convolved, and a third sound is produced.

Delay

One of the more difficult signifiers of a sound's location to achieve with Director is the delay between the time you hear a sound in your left ear and right ear due to the space that your head occupies. Sounds coming from the extreme left or right often have an exceptionally slight delay between the two ears—in the range of 0.5 milliseconds.

Multiple Sounds

One possibility that requires a very different approach to your sound design is to work with multiple sound Castmembers to create a single *localized sound*. I stress the difference between the sound Castmembers and the sound itself because this is the key toward understanding this approach. Rather than use Lingo to change the sound, you can decide to work with multiple sounds, where the localization has been "baked" into the given sound. In this sense, you will have multiple copies of the same sound recorded as if it were coming from different locations. Then you can play the correct sound, depending on where you would like the sound to be coming from. This technique can be difficult, not in the programming, but in the acquisition of the sounds. For this particular technique, you may want to consider reading more about the Beatnik Xtra in the "Supplemental Resources" section at the end of this chapter.

Pitch Shifting

Director 8 introduced the Rateshift property for sounds, and in Director 8.5, this property has been documented. Pitch shifting is very useful when you're reproducing the Doppler effect. You are most likely familiar with this effect if you have ever seen a car race. As a car speeds toward you, the frequency of the sound of the engine increases. After the car passes you, the frequency immediately decreases. The speed and the direction of the sound source affect the apparent frequency of the sound. With the Rateshift property for sounds, you are able to shift a sound to a higher or lower frequency. Therefore, you could use Rateshift to create a relatively believable approximation of the Doppler effect.

Interface, Interaction, and Information

As you begin to design your first 3D project, you're probably not asking yourself "How do I do this?" but rather "What do I do?" The 3D environment in Director has a lot of potential because you have many options and a deep level of control, much of which we have not yet even covered. But, even with the depth of control we have covered so far, the 3D environment offers many possibilities.

The amount of planning required to design a 3D interface is a bit different from that needed for designing a 2D interface. This is not to say that 2D interfaces cannot be extremely complex and time consuming. Instead, successful 3D interfaces tend to be more difficult to design. One of the first things you will need to determine in any project is what the role of the 3D Castmember will be.

In terms of 3D programming, the majority of 3D interfaces you are likely to have encountered in the past are games. This is most likely going to continue to be true. But if you are not a game developer and are still interested in working with 3D, where does this leave you? Perhaps you are creating a navigation system, a visualization system, or something entirely different altogether.

Regardless, there are few, if any, standards for (non-game) 3D interface design that rival the standards firmly in place for 2D interface design. After years of working with 2D interfaces, computer users have learned the signifiers of the 2D interface. Users understand buttons, sliders, and so on. It is generally considered poor form for a 2D interface to include directions such as "click here." When this happens, the user is forced to disengage from interaction with the interface and begin to interpret and translate the instructions from the interface.

Solid 2D interface designs are not only praised for their aesthetic and production value but also for how intuitive they are. Part of user intuition has grown from the short history of computer-based 2D interface design—users are going to expect buttons to act in a certain manner, the same way they expect a doorknob to work in a certain manner. If it doesn't, to the user the button may appear broken rather than unique.

This same level of standards with 3D interfaces has not yet been achieved for the general user. I realize that you might disagree, but remember, in a majority of cases, we are not designing 3D interfaces for users who will have interacted with them before. It may be very difficult for them to learn the signifiers of control because there are few standards.

I would define a similar weakness for 3D interfaces that need to include directions for users to interact with them. If you are designing games, this is hardly a rule, but again, I am not speaking about game interfaces with 3D. Interaction and interface combine to create the experience for your users. In this way, it is much like theatre. The bond between your users and the interface is much like the relationship between actors and the audience; those willing to participate will "suspend their disbelief"—the obvious understanding that what we are looking at is mediated. However, if the mediated experience is broken, so is the suspension of disbelief.

At the moment the user is rudely transported from the space of the media to the place of his own seat, he may lose interest in interacting with the project. It is our job as developers and designers to ensure that the experience will be a wholly positive one. If it is perceived that Director 3D is difficult to use, it will be difficult to convince clients to use it.

This is why the issue is larger than you might think. This is really the first time the Web has had the capability to deliver 3D content from a serious application. VRML, Java3D, and other solutions have not proved themselves in the long run for various reasons. However, Director has a serious chance for playing a crucial role in developing a new style of Web-based interaction— and that chance will depend on the interfaces you build. Think about it.

Summary

Interface is not merely a word that indicates the skin of a project; it includes the methods users will learn in order to interact with the project. In addition, the notion of *interface* includes the possibilities for the exchange of information through the interface as a protocol. It is more than a visual look, and it's deeper than what is often called a "feel." An interface is as much about *using* as it is about *learning to use* through observation and the study of reactions.

This learning process is not a long one—or at least it should not be. There are many ways we can aid users as developers to ensure that our projects are as clean as possible. However, as you may have realized by now, this chapter is not specifically about development but rather about the times when design and development need to learn about each other without taking away from a project.

In this chapter, we have looked at several ideas: an interface for data visualization, a 3D menu system, and a method for working with localized sound. Each of these interfaces requires that the users learn quickly about how to use the interface without forcing them to *read* about how to use this interface. It is much like the learning process for a physical interface such as a doorknob. Even if you do not immediately understand how to use a doorknob, after a few attempts, you should be able to get it working without reading instructions.

FAQ

Is there a "sound" Node in the 3D environment?

> No. In this case, I highly suggest that you send this suggestion to the Director wish list (e-mail `wish-director@macromedia.com`) if you are interested in the inclusion of a real-time 3D sound handled by Director's 3D environment.

Supplemental Resources

This section includes several links to technical articles and a bibliography about 3D sound. There are also several links to Xtras that deal with sound in Director on a variety of levels. Finally, I have included a list of digital sound software packages that span the gamut in terms of price, learning curve, and power.

Links

- *3D Sound Synthesis*, by Cindy Tonnesen and Joe Steinmetz

  `www.hitl.washington.edu/scivw/EVE/I.B.1.3DSoundSynthesis.html`

  This is a great article on the subject of 3D sound. It introduces you to some of the more scientific aspects of 3D sound synthesis, written for the point of view of a virtual reality developer.

- *Subject-Oriented Audio Bibliography*, by Geoffrey Glen Martin

  `pages.globetrotter.net/heisen/geoff/audio/bibliography/`

  An outstanding resource on all aspects of sound, including Internet links, books, and much more. This is an extremely inclusive source that you may find very helpful when beginning to look for articles on particular subjects. However, be aware that the resources in this bibliography are excellent from a scientific viewpoint.

Books

- *3-D Sound for Virtual Reality and Multimedia*, by Durand R. Begault (Academic Press, ISBN 0-12-084735-3)

  A wonderful but advanced book about learning the technical aspects of working with 3D sound. This title is geared toward those interested in building sound tools with low-level programming languages. It can be extremely technical at times. However, you can consider this an expert technical book on the subject of 3D sound that truly has no parallel.

Xtras

- DirectSound Xtra

  www.tactilepix.com/dsx5ref.html

  The DirectSound Xtra has recently become available as an Open Source utility. Among other great tools for controlling sound, this Xtra gives you the capability to use the 3D spatializing routines for sound that are built in to DirectX 5 and greater. Therefore, this Xtra is an outstanding method for working with high-quality 3D sound, with the only downside being that its 3D sound capabilities only work on the PC platform.

- Beatnik Xtra

  www.beatnik.com/software/xtra_director.html

  The Beatnik Xtra is widely respected for its ability to allow Director developers to provide high-quality sounds very quickly over the Net. Another reason to consider the Beatnik Xtra is the number of sound channels it makes available to Director: 64. This means you can build much more robust sonic environments because of the number of channels you have access to. In addition, the Beatnik Xtra can help you change your method of approaching 3D sound localization in general because you can be much more liberal with your use of sound channels.

- Amplitude Xtra

  www.marmalademedia.com.au/amplitude.htm

  The Amplitude Xtra is a great tool that provides a method for finding out the amplitude of a sound that is currently playing on the system. This is an outstanding Xtra that is worth looking into because it provides a basic function that can be used in a variety of ways.

Sound Software

- Soundhack

  www.soundhack.com

  Soundhack is a powerful freeware tool for the Mac that provides a wide array of filters and sound tools, including convolution and binaural filtering. In addition, the Web site is an extremely good resource for how to use the filters and tools included with Soundhack.

- Metasynth

  www.uisoftware.com/PAGES/soft.html

  This Mac-only product is an interesting package that offers a wide array of effects. In addition, it offers a unique method of "sound image synthesis" for creating sounds from digital images.

- Sound Forge

  www.sonicfoundry.com

- Peak VST

  www.bias-inc.com

  This professional-level package includes a powerful convolution filter as well as many other effects that are not available in the base package. In addition, because VST is enabled for this version of Peak, you will be able to use any plug-ins that are VST compatible with it.

- SoundEdit 16

  www.macromedia.com/software/sound

  This Mac-based sound-editing solution from Macromedia is a powerful tool, but it has had limited support within the past several years. The effects are quite good, but the level of control you have over each tends to be limited.

- Native Power Pack

  www.waves.com

  The Native Power Pack is a suite of audio plug-ins available for either the Macintosh or PC and will work with a variety of sound programs. This suite of audio filters is quite impressive—especially trueverb, a powerful reverberation utility. Also there is a great visual parametric equalizer, among the other tools.

- Deck

  www.bias-inc.com

  Deck is a powerful, Macintosh-based, multitrack recording and editing package. This tool is mainly used as a mixing device, although it has a number of effects and features. It is a worthwhile tool to look into if you are creating soundtracks or working with high-end audio capture.

- Cool Edit Pro

  www.syntrillium.com

  Cool Edit Pro is a powerful PC-based sound-editing solution that offers a wide variety of filters, including convolution, and several methods for adding delays and reverberations. In addition, Cool Edit Pro has the capability for working with multitrack recording and mixing.

PART IV

Project Optimization

When designing, executing, and testing your projects, you will begin to develop techniques that may or may not work well on the machines of your users. This section is organized into two chapters: one to deal with performance optimization and another to teach about download optimization. I have split the topic of project optimization into these two areas because you may be developing offline projects in addition to online ones. With online work, you will need to have a firm understanding of both areas of optimization. Keep in mind that one of the reasons why the 3D environment in Director is so enticing is due to the optimizations provided by Intel that allow for extremely fast download times and scalable geometry resolutions. Finally, optimization is not an afterthought or an element that you work into your project the last week of development. It is an important element that you must incorporate from the design stages and may help determine the aesthetic choices that you make. Consider that the reason to optimize projects is so that they will run faster, download faster, and work on more than your development machine.

CHAPTER 19

Performance Optimization

In this chapter, we will focus on performance optimization for your movies. In addition to examining techniques for using some of the properties you already know about from previous chapters, you will be learning how to control the Renderer. Because so much about the visual performance of your movies is tied up with the specifics of the Renderer used to draw your environments on a given machine, we will take a close look at the options available to you at the Renderer level.

In addition to the Renderer, we will look at methods of optimizing Textures, geometry, and Lighting. Keep in mind that some of these methods will have a bit of crossover with the next chapter on download optimization.

Renderer Optimization

In terms of performance optimization, it is important to understand the relationship between performance and client hardware. The Renderer is a system-level device that is dependent on the specifics of client hardware. Director is able to utilize many accelerated 3D video cards; when a compatible accelerator is found on a system, Director will opt in favor of hardware rendering. If compatible accelerated 3D hardware is not found, Director will instead use built-in software rendering.

If the client machine is using software rendering, the execution of the movie and the display of the movie will be handled by the system processor. It is not impossible that the system processor could actually be faster than hardware rendering in certain situations, but software rendering is considered inferior to hardware rendering because the quality of the playback will generally be inferior to hardware rendering.

Software rendering does not support some of the features of the environment, such as wire-frame and point rendering, nor does it support the Model.Debug property used to see the axis and bounding sphere of a Model. In general, the visual appearance will be inferior and most likely slower.

Other than having an unsupported 3D accelerated video card, or no 3D accelerator, users can be dropped into software rendering mode through a variety of ways. The first reason has to do with running out of video RAM (VRAM) on the video card (see the subsection on VRAM within the "Texture Optimization" section, later in this chapter). The second reason is that if the user is in 8-bit color mode, hardware rendering can only be used if the display is currently 16 bit or higher. If a user changes the display bit depth while the movie is running, this can sometimes cause the movie to drop into software rendering, even if the user changes between two supported bit-depth modes.

It is less common, but if the Shockwave movie is set to scale with the browser and the user changes the browser size, sometimes this can cause a drop into software rendering. Another reason that can cause users to switch to software rendering is the users themselves; Shockwave movies display a contextual menu to users who right-click (Windows) or Command-click (Macintosh) a Shockwave movie playing in a browser. From this menu, users are able to change the Renderer they are currently using—and you cannot override settings they make this way.

If you like, you can disable the contextual menu from the Shockwave Safe tab in the Publish Settings dialog box in Director before you publish the movie. However, I do not recommend you do this because users may experience trouble with the preferred Renderer you assign for their system. Because there are so many combinations of video cards, system architectures, and other devices that can affect Renderer performance, I suggest allowing the users to make the final decision on the best Renderer for themselves.

Getrendererservices()

The getrendererservices() function is a system-level function that allows you to determine several pieces of information about a client machine. You interface with the `getrendererservices()` function through its various properties, which are listed in Table 19.1.

TABLE 19.1   The `Getrendererservices()` Properties

Property	Purpose
Renderer	Gets or sets the Renderer to be used
Rendererdevicelist	A list of available Renderers
Currentrenderer	The Renderer that is used or will be used
Modifiers	Modifiers available to the system
Primitives	Primitives available to the system
Texturerenderformat	The default Render format for color depth that new Textures will use
Depthbufferdepth	The size of the depth buffer
Colorbufferdepth	The size of the color buffer

To gain access to these properties, use the following syntax:

```
Getrendererservices().propertyname
```

There are several points to note concerning this list of properties for the `getrendererservices()` function. Of these properties, modifiers and primitives do not really change. Until Xtras are available that can add to the modifiers and primitives a system can use, these properties will always return the same thing on every system.

Although you can get the value of the Renderer property at any time you can only set the Renderer while there are no 3D Sprites on the Stage. In Shockwave, users can override the settings you set for this value, which can be difficult to deal with.

If you need to set the Renderer, make sure you first read through the section "Active3Drenderer and Preferred3Drenderer," later in this chapter. Finally, if you are going to set the value of the Renderer, that value must be present in the Rendererdevicelist, which only shows those Renderers available on a particular system.

Another name for the depth buffer is the *Z-buffer*. The value of the Depthbufferdepth property will be either 16 or 24, depending on the hardware of the system. You cannot change these values, but this does bring up an interesting piece of information: Each pixel is given a Z value so that when the Renderer actually draws the scene, it knows which pixels to draw first. A larger Depthbufferdepth value allows you to create scenes where the distance between Models is greater.

Also, you must understand that as the distance between the two farthest Models increases, the Depthbufferdepth remains the same, so the precision of depth Rendering is spread out over a larger area. Therefore, when working with 3D scenes, you should be careful to limit the amount of area in units your scenes take up. Limiting the distance between Models is one way; another way is to make sure you set values for the clipping planes. Setting values for the clipping planes is described further in the section "Performance Optimizations for Cameras," later in this chapter.

NOTE

The Depthbufferdepth is not linear; rather it is biased toward the Camera. Models in the foreground will need more depth buffer information, because it is easier to see the difference in depth between Models that are closer to the Camera than with Models that are far away.

This may be easier to understand with an example. Imagine that you are walking down a city block and someone passes you. As that person passes, he gets smaller and smaller quite rapidly because he is relatively close to you. Now imagine that you can see a building that you are walking toward that you know to be far away. The building hardly changes in size as you approach it until, all of a sudden, it looks huge.

Here's a hint: Remember that Backdrops are rendered just behind the far-clipping plane. Use Backdrops to show objects that are far away in order to increase the apparent depth of the scene. The Backdrop can depict a background that is supposedly very far away from the Camera, but you can limit the view volume of your scene by setting the distance from the Camera to the far-clipping plane to a small value. This will ensure that the gradation of Z (depth) values remains smooth across the depth of the view volume.

The Colorbufferdepth property is much easier to understand—this is the color depth of Renderer, which is the color depth of the 3D Sprite. Generally, this number will be the same as the color depth of the screen. Both the Depthbufferdepth and the Colorbufferdepth are important numbers when we begin to talk about how to calculate the amount of VRAM required by a given movie later in this chapter.

Finally, the last property I'll comment on is Texturerenderformat. Recall that you learned about the Renderformat property of Textures in Chapter 14, "Multitexturing." The Texturerenderformat property defines the default Render format for Textures for a movie if you do not specify a Render format for a Texture. How to utilize this property in conjunction with Textures is fully explored in the subsection "Bit Depth" in the "Texture Optimization" section, later in this chapter.

In addition to the properties we have looked at so far for getrendererservices(), you need to know the gethardwareinfo() function, which you access through the getrendererservices() function. The syntax for the gethardwareinfo() function is as follows:

```
Getrendererservices().gethardwareinfo()
```

This function returns a property list containing information about the specific video card used by the system. Whereas getrendererservices() gives you general information about the Renderer device, gethardwareinfo() gives you specific information about the hardware that determines the choices for the Renderer device.

The property list the gethardwareinfo() function returns contains a lot of information, and it is often easier to access the specific properties with the following syntax:

```
Getrendererservices().gethardwareinfo().propertyname
```

The property names you can access and their purposes are detailed in Table 19.2.

TABLE 19.2   The Getrendererservices().Gethardwareinfo() Properties

Property	Purpose
Present	A Boolean that returns True if 3D acceleration is present
Vendor	A string value representing the name of the manufacturer of the video card

TABLE 19.2   Continued

Property	Purpose
Model	A string value representing the name of the model of the video card
Maxtexturesize	A list containing the maximum width and height of Textures the video card can accept
Supportedtexturepixelformat	A list of the formats that can be used by the Renderformat and Texturerenderformat properties
Textureunits	The number of Texture units present on the video card
Depthbufferrange	A list of possible values for the Depthbufferdepth
Colorbufferrange	A list of possible values for the Colorbufferdepth

You cannot change any of these values because they represent information about system hardware. Keep in mind that the vendor and model information will not be standardized among manufacturers. It would be very helpful if all manufacturers included the amount of VRAM for the card in the model name, but many do not.

We will examine what to do with the values from the Maxtexturesize property in the section "Texture Optimization," later in this chapter (specifically in the subsection "Scaledown()"). The Depthbufferrange and Colorbufferrange properties tell you the possible values for the Depthbufferdepth and Colorbufferdepth, respectively, but you cannot set these properties.

NOTE

The number of Texture units a video card has is an interesting bit of information. If you are really interested in this level of information, you need to know some other hardware properties to make useful decisions. Of course, you would also need much more low-level control to utilize these properties. The short explanation is that the more Texture units you have, the faster the video card will be to render multiple composite Textures.

Active3Drenderer and Preferred3Drenderer

The Active3Drenderer and Preferred3Drenderer are system-level properties you can use to control the current Renderer for the system. Note the language used to describe these properties: *active* and *preferred*. You can get information about the active 3D Renderer, but you cannot set it. Instead, you can influence the Renderer that is used through the Preferred3Drenderer property.

By default, the Preferred3Drenderer property is set to #auto, which allows the client machine to decide which Renderer is best. Generally, this will do a good job of picking the best Renderer. However, if you are working on a movie that has specific requirements for the specific Renderer that should be used, you can change this setting. Table 19.3 lists the possible values you can set for the Preferred3Drenderer.

TABLE 19.3   Preferred3Drenderer Values

Value	Purpose
#auto	Allows the client machine to choose the best Renderer based on the available choices
#openGL	Uses OpenGL rendering
#directX7_0	Uses DirectX 7.0 rendering
#directX5_2	Uses DirectX 5.2 rendering
#software	Uses software rendering

The valid choices for the Preferred3Drenderer property other than #auto must be present on the list of Renderer types returned via `getrendererservices().rendererdevicelist` in order for the movie to switch to your preferred Renderer. If you specify a preferred 3D Renderer that is not present, the computer will choose the best Renderer, as if you had specified #auto.

Working Cross-Platform

If you are working on 3D projects with Director, you most likely intend for them to be delivered "cross-platform," considering that this is one of the key reasons to use Director. Macromedia worked hard to ensure that the new 3D functions would be equally viable on both the Macintosh and Windows platforms, and for the most part, this was a successful endeavor.

As you begin to plan cross-platform projects with 3D in Director, one of the issues you will need to contend with is choosing a preferred 3D Renderer with the understanding that not all the Renderer types are available across both the Macintosh and Windows platforms. Of the Renderer types, both software and OpenGL rendering are supported on all platforms.

I encourage you to avoid choosing the software Renderer, only because it should be thought of as a "last resort." It's the workhorse Renderer that you know will definitely work if all else fails—but at the cost of visual quality. However, note that the quality of the software Renderer is not specifically *bad*; it simply has a hard time competing with the performance and quality of the hardware Renderers—that is, when they are available and working correctly.

In terms of hardware Rendering, OpenGL performs quite well, with the possible exception that you may need to adjust your surface and lighting settings because OpenGL is a bit darker than other Renderer types. In addition, you should check your colors across platforms because you may notice some luminosity differences between Macintosh- and Windows-based implementations of the OpenGL Renderer. One thing's for certain: OpenGL is the only hardware Renderer that is available for all platforms, and for all versions of the PC platform.

If you are working on a PC and either of the DirectX Renderer types are available, you may find that they perform extremely well. So what strategy should you take? The auto setting for Preferrerd3Drenderer will look for DirectX 7.0, DirectX 5.2, OpenGL, and then software rendering, in that order. Note that this order is generally accurate, but you still have to contend with the fact that you may not have tweaked your color settings for OpenGL.

So, what should you do? One solution is to choose #auto as the Preferred3Drenderer setting and give users access to the contextual menu in Shockwave. As you develop your project, test it with all Renderers, on all platforms, and try to choose settings that are good for all of them. If this is not good enough, you might specify settings based on the active 3D Renderer and the current platform, which could be determined at the beginning of a movie. In this case, you might consider taking away the contextual Shockwave menu.

The last strategy is a bit more severe, and it has limitations. You might decide that your project must use one of the particular Renderers, perhaps because you are using a specific effect that must be present or you just want to limit the use so that you are certain of what users will see. In this case, you should warn users that they do not have the Renderer you intend for them to use, and then put them into software rendering mode.

Texture Optimization

In general, Textures are the one area of performance and download optimization that you should be constantly thinking about as you build your projects. In this chapter, we will center on the rules that you should use working with Textures in terms of performance, but realize that many of these lessons apply to downloading as well.

Size of Textures, VRAM, and the Software Renderer

It goes without saying that you should keep your Textures small, but how small? You know that you can access getrendererservices().maxtexturesize to get a list of the widest and tallest sizes that a given Renderer will support, but that really does not help you much if you have already designed your projects with gigantic textures in mind. Some cards are going to support sizes of 1024×1024 and beyond! However, I do not recommend using Textures that large.

Textures in the 3D environment must be loaded into the VRAM of the video card when performing hardware rendering. If you use more VRAM than is available on the card, Director will switch to software rendering. Therefore, in general, you should design Textures no larger than 256×256 (preferably even smaller, if possible).

Bit Depth

You can dramatically reduce the amount of VRAM required for a Texture by using smaller bit depths. If you do not need an alpha channel, design for 16 bit—those 32-bit Textures can eat up VRAM very quickly.

However, you should take note of this small but important addendum: Remember that you can check the Texturerenderformat of individual textures as well as the global value used for Textures when they are first created. Note that all the Texturerenderformats add up to between 16 bits or 32 bits.

You see, when you create a new Texture, the amount of VRAM allocated in terms of bit depth is based on the default Texturerenderformat. You can change the Renderformat of an individual Texture, but you should try to do this during moments in the movie while the user is not expected to be interacting with the movie, because this can cause a pause. I would suggest using the default Texturerenderformat of #rgba5550 for your Textures. If your Texture has an alpha channel, you will need to change to an appropriate format; otherwise, leave it alone.

Even textures with 1-bit alpha channels can consume a great deal of performance resources. In addition, not all users will be able to see alpha channels, depending on their specific hardware setup. Of course, so many stunning effects can be achieved with alpha channels that you certainly wouldn't want to totally eliminate their use. Instead, just limit their use, and have solid reasons for when you use them.

Size of Textures and the Powers of 2

The one rule you should absolutely never break when working with Textures is the "powers of 2" rule. This rule refers to the sizes that you should choose as the width and height of the Textures in your projects.

The width and height of your textures should each be some power of 2 (that is, 2, 4, 8, 16, 32, 64, 128, 256, 512, 1024, and so on), keeping in mind that you should avoid exceeding 256. Note that the width and height can be different—for example, 16×32, 256×2, and 128×64 are some examples of Textures whose sides are not equal but are powers of 2.

The powers of 2 rule stems from the fact that the Renderer requires Textures to have dimensions of the powers of 2. In fact, they will be automatically scaled to a power of 2 if they are not already, and this can cause Textures to look terrible because the scaling can be nonuniform. In addition, Textures are normally scaled at some point when they are used in your 3D environment and displayed onscreen, causing a second generation of scaling artifacts.

Although the quality of scaling can be an immediate reason to avoid this, the initial scaling itself causes a performance hit that can be easily avoided. Therefore, make sure you design the width and height of your Textures as powers of 2.

Scaledown()

The `scaledown()` function can help you with Textures, scaling, and the powers of 2. It's a powerful function, but it can easily be misused. The function of `scaledown()` is to literally scale the size of Textures down to the next smallest available power of 2.

You should use this function on Textures that are powers of 2, not as a solution to scale Textures that are not powers of 2. You would use this command when a client machine does not support the size of Textures you are using. You can avoid this situation by designing your Textures to be smaller than 256×256. However, designing a Texture to be within that range is not always possible.

Remember that `getrendererservices().maxtexturesize` reports the maximum width and height for Textures. If you create a Texture on a user's machine that cannot be supported, the Texture will be scaled automatically to the largest available size. As a general rule, most 3D-accelerated cards will accept at least 256×256 Textures. After 512×512, however, it becomes questionable whether the sizes will be available (although I have seen advanced cards that support 2048×2048).

If a video card cannot accept a Texture that is smaller than 512×512, the chances of that video card having very much VRAM are slim. At that point, you can use `scaledown()` on numerous Textures to reduce the overall VRAM footprint required for the Textures in your project.

NOTE

Do not use the `scaledown()` function on Textures that are 2 pixels in any dimension. You will experience unexpected results that vary from machine to machine—none of which are desirable.

Instantiating and Removing Textures

Once you have designed your Textures to be powers of 2 and you are ready to begin instantiating Textures, the question of when to instantiate becomes highly relevant. You see, calling the `newTexture()` command causes a slight performance hit during the moments that the VRAM is being allocated for the Texture. In fact, even Textures that are generated from within W3D files take a moment to instantiate—they have to allocate VRAM for themselves as well.

Therefore, you need a strategy when working with Textures. My first suggestion is that you always create Textures at the beginning of a movie—before users are interacting with the 3D environment. If you create a new Texture while users are interacting with the movie, there may be a pause during playback, which is something you should always strive to avoid.

Even if you are not going to use a Texture right away, you can create it at the beginning of a movie. This way, when you need to use it, it is ready. Textures that already exist do not take long to be assigned—or even changed. Recall in Chapter 17, "Special Effects," that we worked with changing the .image and the .member properties of Textures to create animations. When you create Textures, the performance hit is due to the allocation of the VRAM. Once VRAM has been allocated for a Texture, there are no further performance hits when you assign that Texture to a Shader.

The one difficulty in this strategy is that you will need to have all the Textures loaded into VRAM at the same time. A variation on this strategy is to compartmentalize the sections of your movie. If you are designing a game with levels, for example, users are less likely to notice a slight pause if you load the Textures for the next level during a statistics screen. You can also use some aesthetic device that informs the user that he may take a break from the 3D world for just a moment before you immerse him in the 3D world again.

Finally, another item you should remember when working with Textures is to remove any Textures that you know you will not be using. If you are done with a Texture and will not need it again, use the deleteTexture() function to remove it. This function takes no time at all, so feel free to use it while users are interacting with your project.

Texture.Quality and Mip-Mapping

The size of the Texture onscreen does not always match the size of the Texture. As Models recede from Cameras using perspective projection, they will get smaller and the Textures on them will scale. The Texture.Quality property uses a process known as *mip-mapping* to create three successively smaller versions of each Texture so that lower-resolution Textures can be used when it's not possible to see the detail in them due to their distance from the Camera.

Three settings are available with the Texture.Quality property: #low, #medium, and #high. The #low setting will not use mip-mapping; therefore, no copies of the Texture will be made.

The difference between the #medium and #high values for quality is that they are computationally different. That is, both methods create three copies of the Texture, but they use different algorithms to determine what these copies look like. As you might expect, the #high setting looks much better, but it costs more computationally. However, once the mip-maps have been created, they do not have to be re-created unless you reset the value for quality.

So, mip-mapping really has two issues: the immediate performance costs required to create the maps and the VRAM costs to store the maps. Because three copies of the maps are created with #medium and #high mip-mapping, the VRAM cost for mip-maps is 33-percent greater than the same Texture without mip-maps.

NOTE

Software rendering does not support mip-mapping, and this is one of the larger reasons why the visual quality of software rendering is considered inferior when dealing with Textures.

Texture.Nearfiltering

As Models approach Cameras using perspective projection, they will get larger, and the Textures on them will scale along with the Models. It is entirely possible that the Textures will scale to a size onscreen that is much larger than the actual resolution of the Texture. Nearfiltering is a process that attempts to blur Textures as they grow larger onscreen than their actual size to reduce the effect of pixelation. The performance boost of turning Nearfiltering off is minimal, however. It's more of a decision of visual aesthetics.

3D Sprite and Desktop Size

Two major areas for performance optimization are the height/width of the 3D Sprite and the size of the user's desktop. This is because VRAM is allocated for both the desktop and the 3D Sprite. The amount of VRAM that is required by the desktop is dependent on both the size of the desktop as well as the color depth. Very large desktop sizes require a considerable amount of available VRAM. In general, this is one of the reasons why some 3D games created outside of Director will force systems into a lower screen size before they start.

The 3D Sprite itself will need to allocate an amount of VRAM that is dependent on the size of the Sprite, the color depth of the screen, and the Z-buffer for the active 3D Renderer. Due to the fact that so many items influence the amount of VRAM required for a 3D Sprite, the amount of VRAM for the 3D Sprite can often exceed the amount required for the desktop. Because one of the key areas of performance optimization is preserving VRAM, we need to look at the options you have available for controlling the 3D Sprite and the desktop.

If you are delivering your project via Shockwave, you have no options in terms of the user's screen size and color depth. At that point, the size and depth your users choose is beyond the reach of Lingo, but you can always try making strong suggestions about the size of the desktop and its color depth. If you are delivering a projector, you have more options in terms of switching color depth or using Xtras to switch monitor resolution.

In terms of the 3D Sprite, your option is clear: Try to reduce the size of the 3D Sprite if you can. In addition, if you are going to be working with Backdrops and Overlays that need to fill the entire Sprite, consider making the size of the Sprite a power of 2. This will make it easier to create Textures that can fill the Backdrop or Overlay without wasting any VRAM.

Determining the Amount of VRAM on the Video Card

With all this talk about VRAM, you might be curious how to find out how much VRAM is available on a given system. Unfortunately, there is no built-in method for determining the amount of VRAM on a system in Director. In addition, there are no built-in utilities for determining the amount of VRAM a project will require. However, there are strategies for working with both of these important tasks.

In terms of estimating how much VRAM exists on a client machine, you have to make an educated guess. You have two ways of informing this guess. First, consider that most current consumer 3D cards are going to have somewhere in the range of 4 to 64MB of VRAM. With this in mind, you can make a general assumption about what the median amount of VRAM your users will have. I suggest planning that your users will have between 16 and 32MB of VRAM available. Of course, you can always choose a more aggressive range of values, such as between 4 and 16MB of VRAM, in order to deliver your projects to a wider audience.

Another method you can use is to figure out how much VRAM is required by the current user's screen (this process is described later in this section) and then multiply this number by some value, depending on the level of user you are shooting for. For a low-end user, you might multiply by 4. For a median user, you might multiply by 8 to 12, and for a high-end user, from 20 to 32. If nothing else, this second method does not suffer from a lack of vagueness.

The third method takes a different approach. Unfortunately, VRAM information is not accessible via the `getrendererservices().gethardwareinfo()` function, but we can use this function to find out the model name of the video card. I have compiled a list of model names cross-referenced with the amount of VRAM for each card from manufacturer data as well as from the contributions of many helpful individual Director users who filled out an online survey. It was important to conduct the survey because the actual name of the video card one buys and the model "string" information that is returned via the `getrendererservives().gethardwareinfo()` function are usually very different.

Bear in mind that this list of video cards is not exhaustive, and you may need to add to it. However, the functionality to search the list is in place, and if you add entries to the list in the same format, you will have little trouble determining the VRAM for new cards.

If you open the file named "Performance Utilities" on the CD, you will find a movie script named "VRAM LUT." The VRAM LUT script is essentially a look-up table utility that contains one function: `videoCardVramLUT()`. This utility determines whether the model name of your current card is on the list and then returns the known value of VRAM for this card. If the card is not on the list, the `videoCardVramLUT()` function returns `false`.

The only question is, once you have determined how much VRAM there is, what can you do with it? You have many strategies to choose from; I will list these choices in order from moderately passive to increasingly aggressive strategies:

- Warn users who have too little VRAM for your project.
- Do not allow the movie to play for those who have too little VRAM for your project.

- Scale down Textures (using scaledown()) as they are loaded based on the ratio between the amount of VRAM required and the amount present.

- Have multiple external cast libraries ready with premade Textures for various VRAM configurations.

- Create a stub-style movie that determines the amount of VRAM and then auto-navigates the user to the correct version of the movie to choose an appropriate 3D Sprite size.

- On the Web, auto-navigate between movies that have the ability to scale and those that lack this ability based on the VRAM.

- Optimize a version of your project for software rendering mode that is scaled back on Textures, Lighting, geometry, and so on. If users are below a certain amount of VRAM, force them into software rendering mode and use this version of the movie.

Of course, all these choices are dependent on your knowledge of the second critical piece of information: How much VRAM your project requires.

Estimating the Amount of VRAM a Project Requires

Based on information that Director has access to, it is possible to estimate the VRAM size requirements of a project. Many different factors come into play. Here are three key areas that use VRAM:

- The screen
- 3D Sprites
- Textures

Of these three items, the screen is the most difficult for you to control but the easiest to calculate VRAM requirements for. The VRAM footprint for the screen is based on the desktop width, height, and color depth. Here's the general formula that returns the number of bits of VRAM required:

(ScreenWidth * ScreenHeight * ColorDepth)

NOTE

You can transform from values in bits to other more useful units quite easily. There are 8 bits in a byte, so if you divide the bits by 8, you will know the bytes required. Also, there are 8,192 bits in a kilobyte, and 8,192,000 bits in a megabyte.

Calculating an estimate for 3D Sprite VRAM requires one additional piece of information. We will need to know the 3D Sprite width and height, the Colorbufferdepth for the Renderer, and also the Depthbufferdepth. Remember that the Depthbufferdepth refers to the Z-buffer (memory used to determine the depth of pixels). The formula for determining the VRAM cost looks like this:

Spritecolor = (SpriteWidth * SpriteHeight * Colordepth)

Spritedepth = (SpriteWidth * SpriteHeight * Z-Buffer)

TotalSpriteVRAM = spritecolor + spritedepth

You are using the width and height of the screen to calculate the requirements for the array of X and Y bits. The Colorbufferdepth takes care of how many colors you can describe with each X/Y pixel, and the Depthbufferdepth describes the memory required to store the value of the Z-axis for each pixel in the scene.

Take a look at Table 19.4, which lists the amount of VRAM a project needs based on screen size, color depth, and 3D Sprite size—before any requirements for Textures. (This table assumes a 32-bit depth buffer for the Sprites and a color buffer for the Sprites equal to the color depth for the screen.)

TABLE 19.4   VRAM Estimation Table

Screen Size	Color Depth	Sprite Size	Screen VRAM	Sprite VRAM	Pre-Texture Total VRAM
640×480	16 bit	320×240	600KB	450KB	1.5MB
640×480	24 bit	320×240	900KB	525KB	1.4MB
640×480	32 bit	320×240	1.2MB	600KB	1.8MB
640×480	16 bit	640×480	600KB	1.8MB	2.4MB
640×480	24 bit	640×480	900KB	2.1MB	3.0MB
640×480	32 bit	640×480	1.2MB	2.4MB	3.6MB

TABLE 19.4   Continued

Screen Size	Color Depth	Sprite Size	Screen VRAM	Sprite VRAM	Pre-Texture Total VRAM
800×600	16 bit	800×600	930KB	2.8MB	3.7MB
800×600	24 bit	800×600	1.4MB	3.3MB	4.7MB
800×600	32 bit	800×600	1.9MB	3.8MB	5.8MB
1024×768	16 bit	1024×768	1.5MB	4.6MB	6.1MB
1024×768	24 bit	1024×768	2.3MB	5.4MB	7.7MB
1024×768	32 bit	1024×768	3.1MB	6.1MB	9.2MB
1280×1024	16 bit	1280×1024	2.6MB	7.7MB	10.3MB
1280×1024	24 bit	1280×1024	3.9MB	9.0MB	12.9MB
1280×1024	32 bit	1280×1024	5.1MB	10.0MB	15.1MB

From this list, you can see that the size of the screen alone can use a serious amount of VRAM. However, the real culprit, before Textures, is the 3D Sprite itself. Notice how dramatically the required VRAM changes based on the size of the Sprite. In addition, the 3D Sprite estimations are per 3D Sprite; if you have two or more 3D Sprites, you need to calculate for each of them.

In terms of Textures, the formula is a bit different again. For Textures, we are interested in the width, height, and color depth. In addition, we will need to find out whether the Textures have been mip-mapped, because this increases the overall VRAM footprint as well. Remember that the Texture.Quality property determines whether Textures are mip-mapped; all settings other than #low are mip-mapped. Mip-mapping will cause a 33-percent increase in size, due to the fact that three successively smaller copies of the Texture are created.

Here's the formula when you are not mip-mapping the Texture:

(Width * Height * ColorDepth)

If you are mip-mapping, you need to use the following:

(Width * Height * Colordepth) * 133 / 100

For a general idea about the various sizes of Textures and their performance costs, refer to Table 19.5.

TABLE 19.5   Estimated VRAM Costs for Textures

Dimensions	Color Depth	Mip-mapped	VRAM Cost
64×64	16	No	8KB
64×64	16	Yes	11KB
64×64	32	No	16KB
64×64	32	Yes	21KB
128×128	16	No	32KB
128×128	16	Yes	43KB
128×128	32	No	64KB
128×128	32	Yes	85KB
256×256	16	No	128KB
256×256	16	Yes	170KB
256×256	32	No	256KB
256×256	32	Yes	341KB
512×512	16	No	512KB
512×512	16	Yes	681KB
512×512	32	No	1.0MB
512×512	32	Yes	1.4MB

You can see from Table 19.5 how quickly the memory requirements for Textures can become quite large. Note the differences between mip-mapped and non-mip-mapped versions of the Textures. In addition, keep in mind that these costs are per Texture. Several medium-sized Textures can wreak havoc on a low-end system. Texture optimization is a combination of reducing the size of Textures as well as the number of Textures—in addition to issues such as reducing the color depth and mip-mapping, if possible.

I took these basic algorithms and built a suite of custom functions that you can use in your projects; open the file named "Performance Utilities" on the CD. In this file is a movie script named "Basic VRAM Utility." This script contains comments throughout that explain, line by line, how the functions work.

Now, let's examine how to use the functions. There are six public custom functions that you can use to calculate the values of VRAM. These functions are listed in Table 19.6.

TABLE 19.6   Basic VRAM Utilities Custom Functions

Custom Function	Arguments
CheckSpriteVram	(spritenumber, outputstyle)
CheckScreenVram	(outputstyle)
CheckTextureVram	(3DCastmember, Texturename, outputstyle)
CheckAllSprites	(outputstyle)
CheckAllTextures	(3DCastmember, outputstyle)
CheckProjectVram	(outputstyle)

Note that the outputstyle argument for all the custom functions in this set will accept the symbols #megabytes, #kilobytes, #bytes, and #bits. In addition, if you are checking the required VRAM for a Sprite, you will need to be on the frame that contains it. The CheckprojectVram() function checks all the VRAM required for the current frame, including all the Sprites, the screen, and all Textures in use by all the 3D Sprites.

Geometry Optimization

Another area for performance optimization is geometry—regardless of whether that geometry was created inside of Director via Lingo or imported via a W3D file. 3D artists and programmers typically speak about the number of polygons in a scene, an environment, a model, and onscreen to define boundaries for their projects.

If the geometry for a Model was created inside of Director via Lingo, the only option you have for optimizing that Model for performance is through the Resolution property of the Modelresource. One strategy is to lower the resolution of Modelresources that are farther away from the Camera.

However, if the geometry for a Model was imported from an external modeling program, your options are much more impressive. You see, when Models are exported, information is saved along with the geometry about which details of the geometry are most important and which are peripheral. Director normally ignores this extra information unless you use the Level of Detail (LOD) Modifier.

The Level of Detail Modifier

The Level of Detail (LOD) Modifier available to you in Director provides one method of greatly increasing performance—you should certainly consider using it in all your projects that utilize imported Models. LOD can dynamically reduce the amount of geometric Model information in real time, thus reducing the polygon count and speeding up performance.

LOD can be used in three basic ways: First, you can decide that you would like LOD to work automatically, using the distance from the Camera to each Model as the basis for geometric reduction. Second, you can use a property called Targetframerate that allows the computer to decide whether it is running too slow and needs to reduce geometry. Third, you can build manual control through your own custom Lingo to control the amount of geometry reduction based on your own needs. We will be looking at an example of all three of these techniques later in this section.

NOTE

Deciding to use LOD on a Model is a choice you cannot accurately make until you learn about the SDS (Subdivision Surfaces) Modifier in the next chapter. I do not recommend using both the LOD and SDS Modifiers in conjunction because they each have opposite purposes. The LOD Modifier is used to reduce detail and thereby increase performance. The SDS Modifier is used to increase detail and thereby reduce the amount of geometry a user needs to load. Using both of these Modifiers at the same time is akin to burning a candle at both ends.

To enable LOD, you will need to add the Modifier to the Model that you want to use it on via the `addmodifier` command. Adding LOD can be accomplished via the following syntax:

```
Scene.model("modelname").addmodifier(#lod)
```

It is possible to turn LOD and SDS on concurrently, but this is not a very good idea. Although it is possible, realize that LOD removes detail, and SDS adds detail. Therefore, if you use both of these concurrently, you will be wasting your time.

LOD Properties

Once you have enabled the LOD Modifier, three LOD properties are available to you. The settings for these three properties are interesting because they work together in several ways, depending on how you are using the LOD Modifier. In other words, there are several strategies for using the LOD Modifier that change the meaning of the three properties listed in Table 19.7.

TABLE 19.7   LOD Properties

Property	Purpose
Auto	A Boolean used to decide whether the computer should automatically control the reduction of geometry.
Bias	If Auto is set to True, Bias is used to determine how quickly the Model is 100-percent reduced.
Level	If Auto is set to False, you are able to set the level of reduction directly through this value.

Because these three properties have such a complex relationship, I will explain their usage with the three following strategies.

Automatic LOD

The easiest way to use LOD is to allow the Modifier to automatically decide how much to reduce geometry. Using automatic LOD will determine the amount of reduction based on two items. First, you will need to set the Lod.Bias property to decide how quickly the Model will reduce by 100 percent. At 100-percent reduced, the Model will have no geometry. The second item that will be used is the distance from the Camera to the Model, so that the farther from the Camera the Model is, the faster it will reduce.

In this first strategy, the Model distance from the Camera and the bias work in conjunction to decide how quickly to reduce the geometry of the Model. It is a quick and easy solution, and if you are considering using LOD, it is the most approachable method. The reason for this is that you only have to worry about setting the Bias value. Because you set the bias on a Model by Model basis, you might set the bias of an important model relatively high, whereas less important Models can lose their detail much more quickly.

Targetframerate LOD

The second strategy for using LOD is also an automatic method, but this method requires that you also understand two properties for 3D Sprites that we have not yet examined. These two properties are Targetframerate and Usetargetframerate.

Targetframerate is an integer that you will set to tell the computer what real-time frame rate you would like to achieve with the movie. Typical values are between 15 and 60, although you can set this value higher or lower.

Usetargetframerate is a Boolean, and if it is True, and LOD is set to Auto—the LOD Modifier will not use the Bias value in the same way it did in the previous example. Instead, the computer will determine whether it is meeting its target frame rate. If it is, the computer will ignore the LOD Modifier. If the computer is not meeting its target frame rate, it will automatically lower the level of detail on its own, lowering it until the Models in the scene reduce their geometry enough so the target frame rate is met. You can further influence this with Lod.Bias settings to control the level of detail based on distance as well.

NOTE

Realize that if you set an unrealistically high Targetframerate value, the LOD Modifier will simply reduce all Models to 0-percent geometry. If you set an underwhelmingly low Targetframerate value, the geometry will always remain at 100 percent. I would suggest using Targetframerate-based LOD if you feel comfortable with the fact that LOD can turn on and off. I prefer this method because, this way, if a client machine is fast enough to view my project, there will be no reduction in geometric detail.

Manual LOD

The third method for controlling the LOD is to set the Lod.Auto property to False. In this case, the Lod.Bias property will be ignored. You will be able to directly control the LOD of each Model via the Lod.Level property. A value of 0 will reduce the geometry to 0 percent, and a value of 100 will not reduce the geometry at all.

The only reason why you might decide to control the LOD in this way is if you are working with a project in which you want to reduce the geometry of Models in a nonlinear or nonregular way. For example, you might want to reduce the geometry of Models very slowly, or not at all, while they are within a certain number of units from the Camera and then reduce the level of detail dramatically. Another possibility would be to not reduce detail for a certain distance, and then reduce it slowly, and then reduce it all at once.

You might even decide that you want to reduce geometry based on reasons other than the distance to the Camera. For instance, if you are trying to draw the user's eye toward a certain area of the screen, you might reduce detail for Models in parts of the scene that you do not want the user to focus on.

LOD Laboratory

On the CD is a file named "LOD Laboratory." Open this file and press Play. You'll find a variety of visual controls to use in order to examine the various strategies for working with LOD. Figure 19.1 illustrates the various controls for this laboratory.

FIGURE 19.1

The LOD Laboratory is designed to give you visual controls over the various properties of the LOD Modifier.

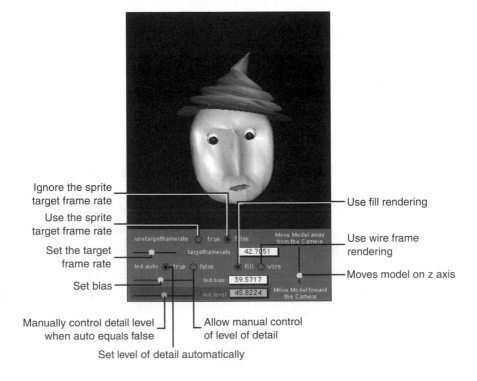

Note that the Model in the demonstration can be moved farther away from the Camera so that you can see the effect of automatic geometry reduction based on Camera distance. Also, try changing between wire-frame and fill rendering to get a better sense of how dramatic the geometry changes actually are.

Lighting Optimization

Lighting is another important area of performance optimization. There are two basic areas of lighting that affect the speed of the scene. First, and most important, is the number of Lights you use in a scene. I suggest as a general rule that you avoid using more than five Light Nodes, and you should absolutely stop adding Lights if you get to 10. These numbers may seem low, but if you recall the section on key lighting diagrams from Chapter 5, "Understanding Lighting," we were always using only a handful of Lights.

Of the Light types, Ambient Lights are the least computationally intensive, then Directional, then the Point Light, and finally the Spot Light type. Understanding the impact of the Light types can help you decide on a more value-based system for lighting rather than the aforementioned general strategy. Think about each Light as having a "lighting cost." Because you should always have an Ambient Light, do not even consider it in evaluating your lighting cost. Directional Lights might cost 1, Point Lights 2, and Spot Lights 4. Every time you want to use a Light, add its cost to your overall scene lighting cost. If the cost exceeds a certain number, you should stop. But what certain number? With the values I have suggested for the individual Light costs, I would suggest a low-end total project cost of 6, a medium total project cost of 12, and a high-end total project cost of 16 or 20.

Performance Optimizations for Cameras

As you know, Cameras are integral components of the 3D environment that determine what we will see in our worlds. One way you can gain a bit of performance is to monitor your usage of the Hither and Yon properties. Most likely, you will not be changing the Hither property, but it is likely (and suggested) that you always set the Yon property.

Remember that Yon defines the far-clipping plane. To the Renderer, anything beyond the far-clipping plane does not exist to be drawn. In addition, anything closer than the near-clipping plane, defined by the Hither property, will not be drawn either. The Hither property is set extremely close to the position of the Camera, and for most purposes, this is fine.

NOTE

You might change the near-clipping plane if you want to use the Camera to "cut away" from a scene in order to achieve techniques similar to cross-section views in architectural rendering.

In terms of the Yon property, the simplest performance strategy is to set this property as close to the Camera as you can, while still being able to see everything in your scene. This will reduce the view volume. Recall from Chapter 6, "Understanding Cameras," that the view volume can be a parallelepiped or a frustum, depending on the projection type. The view volume (literally the volume of this frustum or parallelepiped) affects performance simply because the larger the volume is, the more the Renderer has to think about—even if there are no Models in sections of the view volume. Therefore, you can essentially limit the boundaries of what the Renderer needs to think about for an easy performance gain.

NOTE

In addition to setting the Yon property as purely a performance gain, realize that mip-mapping and near-filtering also utilize the distance from the near-clipping plane to the far-clipping plane. They take this distance and divide it into areas based on percentages—if your far-clipping plane is extremely far away, the "near" zone for near-filtering may extend too far to be useful.

Another strategy involves the use of Fog. Remember that you learned how fog can be used to help the sense of depth in a scene in Chapter 16, "Camera Tricks." We even looked at ways to use particle systems to create our own type of foggy conditions in Chapter 17. Just because a Model has been enveloped by fog does not mean that the Renderer will ignore it. Therefore, if you are working with Fog, try to place the Yon value just a drop beyond the

Fog.Far value. This allows you to gain the aesthetic of fog, and it works as a performance gain as well.

Frames Per Second Utility

When you are doing performance benchmarks for your projects, nothing is more important than having some way of determining the actual frames per second of the project. You know that you can see an approximation of the actual frames per second (FPS) on the Control Panel window, but this only exists in the authoring environment—and you cannot get access to that value via Lingo.

Really, you are not interested in the speed that the project will run at inside of the authoring environment—you are more interested in how fast it will run on your client machines. Therefore, what is needed is some method of determining the FPS outside of the authoring environment. This means that we will have to perform these tests from Lingo itself.

We must contend with certain issues when trying to determine the actual FPS   the most important one is to make sure the FPS checker itself does not slow the project down. There are two key areas in which the FPS checker can cause trouble. First, the math required to calculate the actual FPS can cause a slight bit of performance trouble, but not too much. To deal with this, we will only check the FPS at a set interval. More important is how you decide to display the FPS that you have calculated.

If you choose to dump the FPS into a text Castmember or a field Castmember, you can expect a significant slowdown. One choice is to not display the FPS, but this hardly seems productive. If nothing else, you should be able to turn on and off the display of the FPS to the user.

In the behavior I have designed to check the actual FPS of the scene, the code relies on Imaging Lingo; specifically, we will be using the copypixels() function (because it is extremely fast) to create a composite bitmap version of the FPS to be drawn into a bitmap Castmember that lives on the Stage. For this to work, I had to draw a custom graphic font of the numbers 0–9 and the decimal point. These numbers were then compiled into a single bitmap Castmember, as illustrated in Figure 19.2. Note that this figure has been enhanced with grid marks to show you the uniform size of the number Modules.

FIGURE 19.2

The custom graphic font of numbers used by the FPS Counter script in the Performance Utilities demonstration.

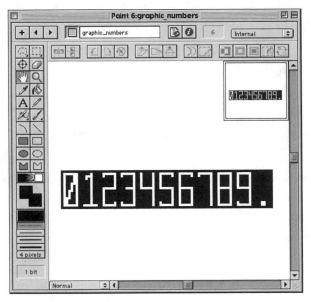

Each graphic number in Figure 19.2 is the same width and height, including the area that surrounds each number. Note that even the decimal point is given the same amount of room. The size of the rectangle that encloses each number can be described with rect(0,0,8,16); that is, each number fits into an 8×16 square. However, this bitmap is a composite of all the numbers into an 88×16 bitmap.

If you open the file named "Performance Utilities" on the CD and press Play, you can see the FPS Counter behavior in action. Granted, this movie does not have any 3D elements in it, but the point is that you can use this FPS Counter in any movie.

The FPS Counter script has been set up as a true behavior—you can only place it on Sprites created from bitmap Castmembers because it utilizes the isoktoattach() handler. In addition, it uses the getpropertydescriptionlist() handler, which will prompt you for the update speed in milliseconds. This is the speed at which the FPS will be calculated and displayed onscreen. Table 19.8 lists the custom handlers of the FPS counter behavior and their purposes.

TABLE 19.8   FPS Counter Behavior Handlers

Handler Name	Purpose
FPSupdate(float)	Takes any number, floating point or integer, and converts it into a bitmap version without using any text Castmembers.
FPSreport()	Reports the current FPS.
FPStoggle()	Toggles the FPS Counter on/off.
FPSinterval(milliseconds)	Changes the interval of FPS updating.
exitframe()	Checks to see whether enough time has elapsed to calculate the update and whether it should perform the update. If so, it calculates the FPS and then sends that data to FPSupdate().
Beginsprite()	Initializes the handler.
Endsprite()	Sends the last known FPS to the message window.
Getpropertydescriptionlist()	Sets the initial update interval.
Isoktoattach()	Ensures that you may only attach a behavior to bitmap-based Sprites.

Because of the way this behavior has been set up (using Imaging Lingo to display the FPS), it is a good model to use in case you would rather display the FPS as an Overlay in your 3D world. Listing 19.1 shows the FPSupdate() handler, the handler used to create a bitmap-based version of any floating-point number.

LISTING 19.1   The FPSupdate() Handler from the FPS Counter Behavior

```
 1: on FPSupdate(me, int)
 2:    --create an empty image object 32X16 at 1-bit
 3:    outputBuffer = image(32,16,1)
 4:    --create an arbitrary rectangle that is the size
 5:    --of a single digit from the display font
 6:    croppingRect = rect(0,0,8,16)
 7:    --create an arbitrary rectangle that will be used
 8:    --to determine where in the outputbuffer to draw
 9:    --each of the digits, starting at point(0,0)
10:    destinationrect = rect(0,0,8,16)
11:
12:    --create a list of the offset values which will
13:    --be used to move the cropping rect into
14:    --the correct position when copying digits from the
```

LISTING 19.1   Continued

```
15:    --display font image
16:    theoffset = [8,16,24,32,40,48,56,64,72,80]
17:
18:    -- turn the number passed to this handler into
19:    -- a string, so that each character can be evaluated
20:    int = string(int)
21:
22:    --this repeat loop cycles through the first four
23:    --characters of the int variable, and composites
24:    --the correct number from the display bitmap font
25:    repeat with i = 1 to 4
26:      --first, determine if this is the decimal point.
27:      if (int.char[i]) = "." then
28:        -- if this is the decimal point, choose the last
29:        -- position from the offset list
30:        cOffset = theoffset[10]
31:        -- if this is a zero, the offet is 0 as well
32:      else if (int.char[i]) = "0" then
33:        cOffset = 0
34:      else
35:        -- if this is any other digit, than choose the
36:        --corresponding offset from the list.
37:        cOffsetIndex = value(int.char[i])
38:        cOffset = theoffset[cOffsetIndex]
39:      end if
40:
41:
42:      --once you have chosen the correct offset amount,
43:      --move the croppingrect arbitrary rectangle by that
44:      --offset amount, using the offset command
45:      croppingrect = croppingrect.offset(cOffset, 0)
46:
47:      --copy pixels from the image object of the display font
48:      --(created in the beginsprite handler) and paste the results
49:      -- at the current position of the destination rect
50:      outputBuffer.copyPixels(pNums, destinationRect, croppingRect)
51:
52:      -- move the destinationrect 8 pixels to the right
53:      destinationrect = destinationRect.offset(8,0)
54:      -- reset the croppingrect
55:      croppingRect = rect(0,0,8,16)
56:    end repeat
57:
58:    --paste the output buffer into the image of the
59:    --bitmap that you are using for display on screen
60:    sprite(spritenum).member.image = outputBuffer
61: end
```

Note that this script has been set up to only display four digits. This is because the digits in the display font are 8 pixels wide; therefore, the final output bitmap is 32 pixels wide (and 16 pixels high). Because these dimensions are powers of 2, the final output bitmap could easily be used as the source for a Texture.Image property. Note that this would only require changing line 60 in Listing 19.1 to something like this:

```
Scene.texture[x].image = outputbuffer
```

If you would like more digits of output, you can increase the size of the output to eight digits by changing line 3 so that it creates an output buffer that is 64 pixels wide and by changing line 25 so that it repeats eight times rather than four. Of course, another option would be to create your own display font that's not as wide as the one I have created for you.

Additional Performance Tips Quick List

The following list includes several items that are not specifically 3D based, although some are. Each of these items is short enough to be mentioned in this fashion. Where more information is required, I will note it.

- Avoid using the sqrt function if you can. The square root function is classically slow. Consider using look-up tables if you can sacrifice precision. Appendix D, "2D Mathematics and Utilities," has some examples of look-up tables that you might be interested in.

- Avoid slow functions/commands in Repeat loops, such as updatestage. Instead use exitframe() events to perform slow tasks that need to be executed in a loop—this will allow Director to perform other tasks, such as rendering the environment, moving the playback head, and so on.

- Avoid the getpixel() and setpixel() Imaging Lingo functions—they are quite slow. Although it's a little more difficult to implement, you can use copypixels() to duplicate the functionality of setpixel() by creating a destination rect() that is one pixel in size and then offsetting it to the pixel location you need to change. You should especially avoid using getpixel() or setpixel() within a repeat loop.

- Try to avoid cloning Nodes during periods of user interaction. Clones can be created prior to user interaction and then referred to as needed.

- When you're using cull-backfaces, avoid using the #both setting for Model.Visibility. #Both essentially increases the number of Faces that need to be drawn, and they will be drawn, even if you do not see them, when #both is used. This is why is it useful with transparency, but transparency itself can cause a performance hit. Backface culling is the process of ignoring those Faces that are not facing the Camera, thus greatly reducing the load on the Renderer.

- In Director, the number of Model Nodes has a severe impact on the rendering process. If you can create W3D files that collapse all the static Models in your scene into a single Model, this will greatly increase the speed of rendering and, in turn, your frame rate. Keep in mind that this issue affects you even if the Models are not complex. It is a performance problem based on the number of Models irrespective of their complexity. LOD is one method of working with geometry complexity; SDS is another method that we will discuss in the next chapter.

- If you need to move the playback head to a frame where the 3D Castmember is not on the Stage, and then is on the Stage again, I suggest keeping an instance of the 3D Castmember somewhere off the Stage, rather than off the score. The beginsprite event for 3D Castmembers takes a moment to run and could momentarily pause your movie.

- Chapter 25, "Advanced Camera Control," describes two processes for creating multiple Camera viewports. One of these methods uses multiple 3D Sprites; the other does not. Remember when calculating the VRAM estimates for your movie, you must include all the 3D Sprites that are on the Stage at the same time.

- Generally, non-photorealistic (NPR) rendering works very well, but it can cause a performance hit on some systems; there is little you can do for those systems that are hardest hit. Understand that when you decide to use NPR rendering, there will be those users who may not be able to see your work, but that number is not large enough to avoid using NPR.

- Everything is a performance hit. Essentially, this is important to remember, too. Everything you do is going to use some amount of processor time. You should not cut out every interesting effect in a project just because someone, somewhere might not be able to see it. There are those without computers who won't be able to see your work at all. My point is, at some point you do need to draw the line with performance optimization. I am not against using esoteric means to increase performance, but when the performance gained outweighs the effort put in, you should consider whether it's really worth it.

Summary

Performance optimization is an extremely important facet of development that you should be thinking about from the very beginning stages of any project. It will work best if you are thinking about performance optimization during the design phase; allow yourself to incorporate performance optimizations into the aesthetics of the project.

Much of performance optimization has to do with Texture optimization. Texture optimization is time consuming and makes the creation of assets much more difficult. However, it is a rewarding process that can greatly increase the speed of your projects. If you overlook every other area of performance optimization, do not overlook Texture optimization.

The Renderer, VRAM, client system, desktop settings, Sprite size, geometry, number of Models, and lighting are all among the many areas that have a large effect on performance optimization. These areas should not be overlooked in any professional project.

Finally, as much as performance optimization is important, it is also important to remember that sometimes you are going to need to use effects, functions, and algorithms that are processor intensive. Performance optimization is a plan. It is part of your design; it is something that you incorporate into your work. When done well, you will make decisions on both sides of the issue—sometimes opting in favor of building a roundabout method of avoiding some function, and other times deciding that a 32-bit Texture is just worth it.

Performance optimization is a battle that you will wage with every variable and every function you use. Your coding skills are therefore very important, but they are not the only factors. Understanding how the structure as well as the design of your projects affect performance is critical. Although every effort should be made to win the battle of performance optimization, there are limits to what can be feasibly achieved in a given amount of time. A lack of planning is no excuse for poor performance, whereas a Pyrrhic victory is no more enticing for your clients. Therefore, setting realistic goals on the minimum requirements for your users and being able to explain these goals are part of your responsibility as a developer.

FAQ

Director does not do real-time cast shadows, motion blur, volumetric lighting, mirrors, real-time reflections and refractions, and many other things that work in game X on my machine just fine. Why is feature Y not in Director?

Real-time 3D means maintaining a real-time frame rate. Persistence of vision occurs around 8 frames per second—film is shown at 24 fps, video at 29.97 fps, IMAX movies at 72 fps. 3D games usually strive for 30 fps or 60 fps—achieving these speeds would not be possible with these effects without eliminating much of the user base.

Is there an order of importance to the performance and download optimizations?

You need to look at the "Optimization Cheat Sheet" in Appendix D. I have created a "Top 10" list of performance/download optimization concerns.

I have two video cards on my system, and two monitors. Is there a way to do 3D on both monitors?

This is not supported. Only the first monitor on the system will be able to use 3D acceleration, even if the second card/monitor is better.

Are there hooks into the Renderer for me to use my shutter glasses for stereoscopic 3D rendering?

Unfortunately, no. Shutter glasses, such as CrystalEyes, require that you control the refresh rate of the monitor. This is simply not possible with Lingo. You could simulate red/blue stereoscopic 3D, but this method is not as efficient as the shutter glasses approach.

Supplemental Resources

- *Tech Note 15428: Macromedia Shockwave Player 3D Readme*

  This tech note has specific information about the differences between hardware and software rendering. In addition, there are several links to video card manufacturers in order for you to obtain the most current drivers for your card.

- www.macromedia.com/support/director/ts/documents/
  3d_rendering/udl.htm

This link contains the official "unsupported drivers list" for Shockwave 3D and explains why each driver was excluded. You can use this list if you are having problems with rendering or to find out whether your card/driver is unsupported.

- `www.macromedia.com/support/director/ts/`
  `3d_rendering/video_card_tested.htm`

This link contains a list of all the graphics cards and drivers that have been tested by Macromedia with Shockwave 3D. This is another useful link for information about cards and drivers that you may want to look at if you are having trouble with real-time rendering.

CHAPTER 20

Download Optimization

This chapter examines the second major area for optimization: download time. Often, download optimization works in conjunction with performance optimization, but there are also instances when choices that you make to create a better downloading project will result in poorer performance. Yet, even in these situations where performance is affected, the results are not too terrible or unexpected.

Similar to performance optimization, Textures and geometry figure heavily into those areas that need to be streamlined for the fastest download speeds. However, the areas of download optimization are not as difficult to master as performance optimization. You should, of course, consider the techniques in this chapter as important issues that must be incorporated into your projects from the very beginning—geometry optimization especially, because this area will surely affect your scope of work outside of Director when modeling with external programs. Primarily we will be examining the usage of the Subdivision Modifier, the `clonemodelfromcastmember()` command, and the `loadfile()` command. In addition, we will look at strategies for setting up your Score for streaming when working with very large amounts of data. Overall, the techniques in this chapter are presented to help you understand the major issues involved with download optimization and how to plan to avoid them or deflect their negative effects as best as possible.

Textures

If you were to examine a breakdown of the memory storage requirements of assets used for a 3D project, you might be surprised to find out that the largest amount of space generally is used by Textures. Although geometry may be large, Textures truly take up the majority of space in most projects.

Because Textures are the largest area for download optimization, we will begin by examining several guidelines for Texture optimization. Although you may not be able to apply each guideline to a given project, I suggest that you strongly consider each before deciding against its use. The guidelines for Texture optimization that I suggest are as follows:

- If you can do without a Texture, remove it. If the Texture is a flat color or if you can get the same visual result with lighting, remove the Texture.

- If you can create a Texture on-the-fly with imaging, remove the Texture and generate the Texture on-the fly with code. Flat colors, grids, ramps of color—all of these are quite easy to generate with imaging.

- If you include a Texture to be downloaded, try to make the use of every bit. If you can reuse the Texture, do so—do not ever include multiples of the same Texture.

- Reduce the bit-depth. If you are not working with an alpha channel, reduce the bit-depth to 16. The Texture will take up half as much space.

- If you're working with animated Textures, be careful. Flipbook-style animated Textures can take up a large amount of space. If you can avoid them, do so; if you cannot, reduce the number of frames in them. Persistence of vision occurs at 8 frames per second. If you can limit your flipbook animation frame rates to between 6 and 8 frames per second, you will save much room. Also, look into the RealMedia-based Texture options that are outlined in Chapter 17, "Special Effects."

- Take a good look at the size of your Textures. Can you produce the same effect in half the size? A quarter of the size? Try it out. Evaluate the difference in quality before you make a judgment on what is too small. Remember that the actual size of Textures and the size in which they are shown onscreen usually will differ. If the objects using the Texture will be far from the Camera, you should absolutely reduce the detail.

- If possible, try to generate the alpha channel information on-the-fly with Imaging Lingo. This may not always be possible if the alpha information is complex.

Realize that although this section of the chapter is short, the greatest reduction in download time is going to lie in your Textures. Sounds will often play a substantial role as well, but in terms of the 3D environment, Textures will take up a bulk of your file size.

Geometry

If you are working with geometry created on-the-fly, this is good, because you will not have to download that geometry at all. A project created entirely from scratch with Lingo can be extremely small, but it is possible that the startup time for the environment could be large. It's a tradeoff, and you will have to decide which way to go.

If you are working with W3D files or a combination of W3D files and Models from scratch, the geometric information that is contained by a W3D file will contribute to the overall size of the download. There are aggressive modeling techniques, often referred to as *low-poly-count modeling*, that can help both performance and download speed. Keeping your Models at lower resolutions is certainly one of the traditional goals of 3D asset development.

You may hear many numbers when dealing with geometry; the key that you should remember is that Vertices and Faces may be small, but they add up. In general, you can use the geometry-compression options to reduce geometry size.

Creating low-poly-count Models is a skill that is unfortunately beyond the scope of this book. I do encourage you to learn techniques of low-poly-count Modeling for your intended modeling program. One of the strengths of Shockwave 3D is its capability to work with low-poly-count data to create higher-resolution data on-the-fly, after the download. Scaling up the resolution of a non-primitive Mesh is a nontrivial task—if we were to approach it mathematically. Luckily, the Subdivision Modifier adds this capability to Director, with a minimal amount of effort.

Subdivision Surfaces

The Subdivision Surfaces (SDS) Modifier is one of the most intriguing and powerful aspects of Director's 3D capabilities. In addition, it is not very difficult to use or understand. The SDS Modifier uses the speed of the client machine to increase the number of polygons in a Model.

NOTE

> The SDS Modifier cannot be attached to Models using the Inker or Toon Modifiers; if either of these Modifiers is attached, adding the SDS Modifier will have no effect. If the SDS Modifier is already attached to a Model, you will not be able to attach Inker or Toon. However, the beauty of the Toon modifier is that it does an excellent job with Models that have low or high geometry resolutions—keep this in mind as you make your decisions.

The SDS Modifier can be thought of as both a performance and a download optimization, because it adjusts the number of polygons based on the speed of the machine. However, the SDS Modifier should not be used in conjunction with the Level of Detail (LOD) Modifier. With the LOD Modifier, you are going to create relatively high-resolution Models and then reduce this amount based on processor speed or other factors. With SDS, you are going to create low-resolution Models and then increase this amount based on processor speed or other factors.

You might be curious where this detail will be coming from. There are two methods of adding detail to Models with SDS—the first method adds geometry to the entire Model by subdividing sections of the Model evenly and adding more geometry. The second method only adds geometry to those parts of the Model that are visible to the Camera.

Finally, you should be aware that the SDS Modifier can be applied to any Model, whether it was created externally or via Lingo, because the SDS Modifier actually performs calculations to add geometry dynamically without any hinting. Because of the real-time calculations involved, you should be concerned about the SDS Modifier's effect on overall movie performance.

SDS Properties

The SDS Modifier is added to a Model much like the other Modifiers, and its properties are accessed similarly as well. In order to add the SDS Modifier to a Model, use the following syntax:

```
Scene.model[x].addmodifier(#sds)
```

Note that adding the SDS Modifier to a Model will make several new properties available for the Model that are used to control the SDS Modifier itself. These properties and their purposes are listed in Table 20.1.

TABLE 20.1   SDS Modifier Properties

Property	Purpose
Enabled	Boolean. Determines whether the SDS Modifier has any effect on the Model.
Subdivision	Possible values are #adaptive and #uniform. Determines the method of adding geometry to the target Model.
Depth	Determines the number of recursions—that is, the number of times the Model is subdivided.
Tension	Determines how closely to the original surface the new subdivided geometry will be created. Lower values produce bumps in the surfaces of Models.
Error	Only used when Subdivision is set to #adaptive. Reduces the number of errant Faces created with a low Tension value.

Note that the Enabled property is True, by default, if you turn on the SDS Modifier. In addition, note that the Error property does not take effect unless the Subdivision property is set to #adaptive.

SDS Strategies

You need to be aware of the two basic strategies for using the SDS Modifier: uniform and adaptive subdivision. Each of these strategies will have a slightly different effect on performance. It is often quite necessary to test each of these strategies on a given Model in order to decide which is best, because the SDS Modifier works directly on the geometry of the Model—literally on the Modelresource. Differences in the Modelresource, how it is constructed, and how dense its geometry currently is will have a profound impact on your Models.

Uniform Adjustment

Setting the `sds.subdivision` property to #uniform will cause the Model to subdivide all its surfaces evenly, depending on the depth of recursion. This strategy is extremely easy to implement because few factors affect the adjustment.

You will need to set the `sds.depth` property. I suggest that you try a setting of 2 or 3, but avoid a setting of 4. A uniform change to the Modelresource will affect every Face, regardless of the position or distance to the Camera. You will need to pay attention to the `sds.tension` property as well. Remember that Tension will determine how closely to the original Model geometry you intend to create the new geometry. Most often, you will leave this setting at 100, because all other values can introduce unwanted artifacts into your Models.

Finally, uniform adjustment tends to be less of a performance hit on the processor than the adaptive adjustment, because the calculations for uniform adjustment are made once and then the Modelresource is left alone—unless you change the Tension or Depth property.

Adaptive Adjustment

If you set the `sds.subdivision` property to #adaptive, the Model will subdivide a bit differently than in the prior example. Rather than simply subdivide all the Faces of the Model, adaptive subdivision determines whether the position or orientation of the Model has changed. If it has, the subdivision for the Model is recalculated.

In addition, only those Faces that are facing the Camera are subdivided—this is meant to serve as a method of limiting the number of polygons created. However, because the subdivision calculations occur constantly with a moving Model, this is a prime cause for performance degradation.

Note that adaptive subdivision also uses a third property: `sds.error`. The Error property will try to limit the number of errant Faces created by low `sds.tension` values. A high Error value will eliminate most every change to the geometry, and a low Error value will allow every change. It is better to set Error to a median value—this way, some of the anomalies will be allowed to get through, and others will be ignored.

Finally, realize that adaptive subdivision depends heavily on the Camera. If the Camera is not pointed at the Model, it will not subdivide. If the Camera is moving and the Model is visible, the amount of subdivision may change as well.

SDS Laboratory

In order to help you best understand the settings for the SDS Modifier, I have constructed a laboratory-style demonstration so that you can examine the various properties of the SDS Modifier and observe the changes that take place on the Model. Open the file named "SDS Laboratory," which you can find on the CD, and press Play. Note that the laboratory has several controls, as shown in Figure 20.1.

FIGURE 20.1

A screenshot from the SDS Laboratory.

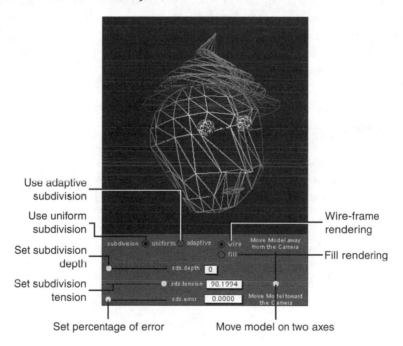

In this case, I am using a low-resolution version of the "head" Model that we saw in the LOD Laboratory in the previous chapter. In this demonstration, the head will automatically rotate so that you can see the effect of changing the geometry. In addition, you can move the Model closer and farther from the Camera to observe the effects of Camera relationship and SDS.

NOTE

> Although I have made a strong warning against it and I continue not to recommend it, you can use LOD and SDS at the same time. The reason and strategy for doing this is to attempt to elicit some amount of performance optimization as well as download optimization.
>
> The method you would employ is to create a Model of a medium resolution that would be able to download quickly. Then, you would set `lod.auto` to False and then set the base value for `lod.level`. Next, you would turn on the SDS Modifier and enable it—try using uniform subdivisions and a low depth.
>
> Finally, you'll need to determine some distance when you will decide to control SDS or LOD. Let's suppose you choose 300 units from the Camera as being the threshold. You will need to check the distance between the Camera and the Model; if you are closer than 300 units, enable SDS and set `lod.level` to its base value. You might even increase `sds.depth` as the Model continues to get closer to the Camera. If the Model moves beyond 300 units, set `sds.enabled = false` and manually control `lod.level` to reduce the geometry detail as the Model continues to move away from the Camera.

Streaming Options

In this section, we will be examining alternative methods of setting up your movies in order to optimize download speed based on your method of streaming data. Here are the three methods we will be examining:

- Cloning Models from internal Castmembers
- Loading Models from external Castmembers
- Using low-resolution proxy Models

Clonemodelfromcastmember() Demonstration

In the first method of optimizing for download speed, the goal is to try to compartmentalize as many of the 3D elements in the scene and then reassemble them into a single 3D Sprite for the viewer. `Clonemodelfromcastmember()` is similar in speed to `clonedeep()`, but it can be used to copy a Model between 3D Castmembers. In addition to copying the Model, it will copy all its children and all the family resources, including Textures and geometry.

In general, this command is not so much a download optimization, but it leads to a method for using cloning for download optimization. Because you can quickly create clones of clones, this method is very good if you are planning on working with multiple copies of the same Model. Rather than creating a single W3D that contains all the Models, you can save room by cloning this Model at initialization.

The `clonemodelfromcastmember()` function has the following syntax:

```
Scene.clonemodelfromcastmember(newmodelname, modelname, sourceMember)
```

Because you are copying from another 3D Castmember, make sure the state of both Castmembers is 4 before you execute this command. There are two ways of making sure the state of the Castmember is 4. First, you could put the Castmember on the off-Stage, but on the Score you can try to force it to load.

The proper way, though, would be to link the Castmember you are going to clone from as external media. Then, you set the `member.preload` property to True and run the `member.preload()` function. This will force the Castmember to load without requiring it to be on the Stage. You will still need to check to make sure the Castmember state is 4 before cloning from it. The benefit of this setup is that the externally linked Castmember will not need to download before the main movie can start playing.

For this type of strategy, we will need to modify the basic setup of the Score we have been working with. Rather than simply wait for the scene to be ready, we have two periods of waiting and two initializations. Figure 20.2 illustrates this change to the structure of the Score.

Here's an explanation of the function of each script based on the names of the frame markers:

- *Preload marker.* Tells the linked W3D file to preload.

- *Hold marker.* Waits until the 3Dscene, internal SW3D file is loaded. When it is ready, it sends the playback head to the init marker.

- *Init marker.* Initializes the movie (in this case, a cube with the word *loading* written all over it). When it is done, it sends the playback head to the loading marker.

- *Loading marker.* Waits on this frame until the linked W3D file that was set to preload has a state of 4. In addition, this script checks the Streamsize and Bytesstreamed properties of the loading W3D file and displays the percentage currently streamed to the user. When it is ready, it sends the playback head to the clone marker.

- *Clone marker*. Destroys the rotating box and clones a Model from the W3D file that was just loaded. When done, the playback head is sent to the run marker.

- *Run marker*. Stays on this frame.

FIGURE 20.2

Detail from the Score for the clonefromcastmember movie.

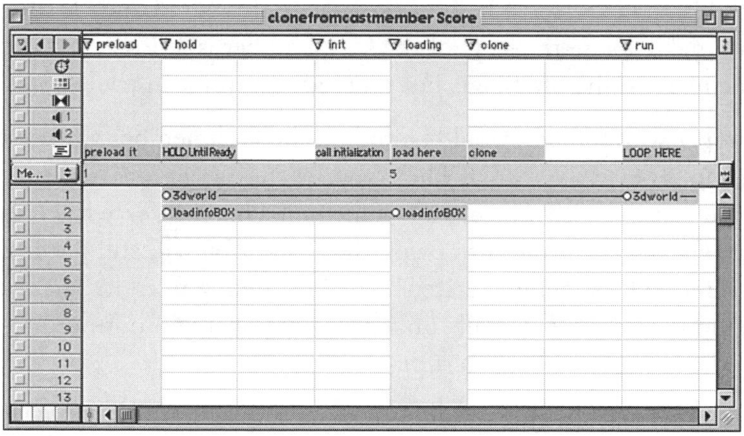

Notice that I have chosen a purposefully large W3D Model of a tree. This Model has quite a lot of detail, which is why the W3D file size is so high. Also, note that the linked Castmember "treemodel.w3d" exists in the dswmedia folder; because the file is external media, make sure you place it in the dswmedia folder for ease of download.

If you open the file named "clonefromcastmember," you can press Play to see this movie in action. There is still a slight pause at the clone frame, because the clone command takes a moment to run and also because the Model it is cloning is gigantic. Finally, this movie will load rather quickly if you open it locally, so I suggest uploading it to a Web server to test it over the Net as well.

Although this movie downloads one very large tree Model, we could have downloaded dozens of small items and then cloned them as they became ready. Essentially, we could end up letting our users watch the screen being built. Of course, this may not be preferable, especially if you are building a game. In such cases, you may want to recall the example of using Overlays as curtains from Chapter 16, "Camera Tricks." The cloning of Models can occur behind the screen, and then the World can be displayed when it is ready.

Loadfile()

A more aggressive form of download optimization is to download sections of the 3D World after the user has begun looking at your project. You can add these elements to the current World or hold onto them so that they are ready when the user moves to a different section of the World, or if there are multiple levels, such as in a dungeon-based game. In addition, you can use this method to build proxy Models—low-resolution Models that download extremely quickly that will be replaced by high-resolution Models as they stream in.

Both these strategies are possible with the powerful `loadfile()` command. This command will load a W3D file that is external to the movie itself. You can give the `loadfile()` command the name of a local file or a URL. The syntax for this command is as follows:

```
Scene.loadfile(filename, overwrite, generateNames)
```

The `overwrite` and `generatenames` properties are both optional, and they're also both Booleans. One way you can think of the `loadfile()` command is essentially as a scene merge. It will take all elements from an external W3D file and import them into the scene you specify. If you set `overwrite` to `true`, any Models and resources that share names will be overwritten by the merged Models and resources. If you set `overwrite` to `false`, you have the option of allowing Director to generate new names for any Models that may have duplicate names.

Basic `Loadfile()` Demonstration

In this example of the basic usage of the `loadfile()` function, we will be appending scene data via the syntax

```
Scene.loadfile(filename, False, True)
```

This will load Models but not overwrite any—and when duplicate names exist, it will generate new ones. Essentially, this is a classic merge that can be called multiple times. This method may seem very similar to the `preload()` function we used in the clonefromcastmember demonstration—and in theory, it is similar. But in practice, `loadfile()` is a more elegant solution because the Models are streamed directly into the Castmember that needs them, thus eliminating the need to clone and, therefore, the slight system pause for cloning.

As elegant as the theory of `loadfile()` may seem, learning how to control it in practice can be a trying exercise. I strongly encourage you to do many tests with `loadfile()` before incorporating it into a professional project because you will encounter quirks when using this command. Realize that you can use `loadfile()` for CD projects if you need, but in this case, I am going to present a method of `loadfile()` for streaming online files.

Because we will be loading files from the Internet, we will need to use the dswmedia folder, in which we will place all the files streamed off of the network. However, unlike most uses of the dswmedia folder, you will also need to put your movie into that folder in order for the `loadfile()` function to work properly.

In addition, realize that directly after you call `loadfile()`, the State property of the 3D Castmember you are loading files into will change. During the time you are actually loading files, the state will not be 4; therefore, you must check the state again before making any changes to the 3D Castmember.

Open the file named "Basic Loadfile" on the CD and press Play. This movie will quickly load six external W3D files that comprise a bathroom scene. Listing 20.1 is the `exitframe()`-based looping behavior that has been designed to load multiple external W3D files into the current scene.

LISTING 20.1 Multiple `loadfile()` Loop

```
1: property loadcount, loadlist
2:
3: global scene
4:
5: on beginsprite
6:   --set an initial value for a counter
7:   --used to cycle through the files to load
8:   loadcount = 1
```

LISTING 20.1   Continued

```
 9:  --create a list of file names that you want to
10:  --load in --NOTE in this case, capitalization counts
11:  loadlist = [ "room.W3D","tub.W3D", "sink.W3D", \
12:  "door.W3D", "misc.W3D", "showercurtain.W3D"]
13: end
14:
15: on exitFrame me
16:   --this exitframe loop checks the current value of loadcount
17:   -- if the value of loadcount is from 1 - 6 ...
18:   if loadcount >= 1 and loadcount < 7 then
19:
20:     --check to see if the scene is in state 4
21:     if scene.state = 4 then
22:
23:       --if it is, load the next file in, merging any elements
24:        --that have differing names
25:     scene.loadfile(the pathname & loadlist[loadcount], false, false)
26:       --add one to loadcount
27:       loadcount = loadcount + 1
28:     end if
29:
30:   else if loadcount = 7 then
31:     -- if loadcount is 7, again check the state
32:     -- of the 3D Castmember
33:     if scene.state - 4 then
34:       -- if it is ready, make the showercurtain
35:       -- semitransparent, and then go to the rest of the movie
36:       scene.model("showercurtain").shader.blend = 60
37:       go to "run"
38:     else
39:       go the frame
40:     end if
41:   end if
42:   go the frame
43: end
```

Listing 20.1 contains several items of importance you should be aware of. Note that in lines 11 and 12, the filenames contain capitalized letters. This is important because the actual files will be accessed via the Internet and most likely on a Unix-based server. Therefore, when you refer to external files from within Lingo, you need to understand that these file names are case sensitive. This can cause much distress when you are testing remotely for the first time. You see, on a local file system, the case-sensitivity issue is lax, and Director will be able to find the files, but it will not be able to find these same files on the Internet. This is one of the major causes of stress when working with external files delivered via a network.

Next, notice in line 21 that we are checking the state of the 3D Castmember before running `loadfile()` to add more elements to it. This is important because you can only call the `loadfile()` command on a 3D Castmember whose state is 4. Once you have called the `loadfile()` command, the state of a 3D Castmember will change from 4 to a lower value, until the external file has been fully loaded. This is how the `exitframe()` loop determines how to only download one file at a time into the 3D Castmember.

Also, notice in line 33 that prior to changing the transparency of the shower-curtain Model, we are making sure the state of the 3D Castmember is 4. It is important that you do not execute any commands on a 3D Castmember whose state is not 4; if you do, you will get a script error.

Finally, make note of line 25, where we are executing the actual `loadfile()` function. This is an important line because we are concatenating the path-name with the name of the file when downloading it. This ensures that the file will work locally and on the Internet, as well as across platforms, because the path delimiters as well as the actual path will be contained by the pathname variable.

NOTE

> Another strategy for using `loadfile()` is to stream in Models from external W3D files into 3D Castmembers that are off the Stage while the user is working with 3D Castmembers that are on the Stage. Once the external W3D files have been loaded, you can clone them into the current 3D Castmember. Most likely, you will do this cloning at a moment when the user is not expected to be interacting with the movie to avoid the pause that takes place during cloning.

Proxy Model Strategy

Another strategy that you should consider is to use the `loadfile()` function for proxy Models. Basically, you create a base 3D Castmember that contains very low-resolution proxy Models of a scene that can download very quickly. Once these files have downloaded, you issue the `loadfile()` function with the following syntax:

```
Scene.loadfile(filename, true)
```

Because overwrite is set to true (and the names of the loading Models are the same as the low-resolution Models), the Models will be overwritten as the high-resolution versions stream in and take their places.

NOTE

One possibility for proxy Models that you might consider is to download very low-resolution Models that use the SDS Modifier to dynamically increase the Model detail. At the same time, download a high-resolution Model that will replace the low-resolution one. Then, when you have made the switch, use the LOD Modifier to ensure that the Model geometry is not too large for the client machine.

Another possibility is to check the performance of the client machine after the user has downloaded the low-resolution Models. If the machine is able to maintain some minimum frame rate, the high-resolution versions can be downloaded. Otherwise, you simply leave the user with the low-resolution versions.

General Download Tips

Don't forget about optimizing the non-3D elements in your projects. Sound can eat up extreme amounts of file space—consider Shockwave audio, RealMedia, or QuickTime audio for streaming sound.

Some projects are going to be big—custom load bars are a great way to keep people interested while they are watching your movies download. Essentially, if people are going to sit and wait, you need to give them something to look at—something to read, something that changes.

A method of working with Director that involves Linked Director Movies (LDM) is also available. However, this method of building projects is beyond the scope of this book. An excellent article that deals with this subject can be found on Director-Online. The "Supplemental Resources" section has more information about this article.

Summary

Download optimization can be achieved in a variety of ways, but certainly Texture optimization is the most immediate form of optimization, and you must be diligent about it. Because Texture optimization also is the largest part of performance optimization for 3D Worlds, it's a good idea that you make sure you understand your options concerning this vital component.

In addition to Textures, Model geometry plays an important role in your 3D Worlds. The easiest way to reduce geometry is to create geometry on-the-fly using Lingo. However, many Models are too complex to create with Lingo or are not worth the effort. In such cases, you will need to create Models in an external modeling program, and these Models will need to be downloaded.

Remember that download optimization is a process that democratizes the Web—not everyone has high-bandwidth connections. If you want to reach the maximum number of people, you will need to ensure that your projects load quickly and easily. It is entirely possible to have miniscule download times—even for large projects. Download optimization occurs at a level that is removed from code as well. For example, think about structure—compartmentalize your 3D assets, stream these assets while a movie playback is in progress, and overall reduce the amount of geometry and Textures you use.

FAQ

Is there any way to change the streaming priority of Models?

Yes. However, this must be done from within a 3D modeling program before export to W3D. Check your exporter documentation to see the specific methods for your particular 3D program. In general, the process will involve assigning parameters to the Models in the 3D environment prior to export. The method with which you assign those parameters is different for every 3D modeler, which is why you should check your exporter documentation.

Is there a standard for Shockwave file sizes—industry standards that can be used to determine how big is "too big" for a project?

No. Everyone has an opinion on this, but there is no industry standard. There are "shop" standards, but no agreed-on file size that has been deemed "too large." However, here are a few things to realize: Just because we are working with 3D does not mean that file sizes need to be large— many projects will be able to fit under 100KB. Also, although these are not industry standards, I would suggest the following: Keep an ideal target size in mind for all projects—as you continue to develop, write down actual sizes to learn how close your expectations and reality meet. Always push for smaller sizes. If the file size is larger than 100KB, provide a simple custom load bar. If it is above 500KB, send the user to a load bar that has a little more to it—something that follows the mouse, for instance. If it is larger than 1MB, you have a problem, and you need to chop the file up into sections.

Why would I use uniform or adaptive subdivision?

This is a very good question. Uniform subdivision affects the whole Model and can create a very large number of polygons, but in practice, it tends to work faster than adaptive subdivision, which performs its calculations constantly on any moving Models. You should choose uniform subdivision if you want to avoid the performance drain or if your Models will be moving a lot. You should choose adaptive subdivision if your Models will not be moving much but your Camera might be.

Supplemental Resources

Linked Director Movies, by Rob Romanek, can be found at `http://www.director-online.com/accessArticle.cfm?id=439`.

This article is an excellent introduction to a little-known aspect of Director development that can be used to dramatically compartmentalize your projects into smaller components. LDMs excel in their ability to allow you to download a base movie and then download additional components of the movie as you need them. Even if you do not use it for your 3D projects, this technique is a worthy addition to your Director toolbox.

PART V

Animation and Interactive Control Structures

The subject of 3D animation is intriguing and powerful. In this section, you will learn about the tools that Director has for incorporating real-time 3D animation into your environments. In addition, we will examine several concepts and techniques that you will need to understand when working with interactive animation. In this section, you will specifically learn about controlling keyframe- and Bones-based animation. Then you will learn about how to control these types of animation in even your entire environment with a dedicated scheduler and parent/child scripts. Finally, we will examine several specific implementations of interactive animation that utilize combinations of the techniques learned in the three previous chapters.

CHAPTER 21

Keyframe Animation

This chapter introduces the Keyframeplayer Modifier. This is the first of two Modifiers used to control the playback of animation. The Keyframeplayer and the Bonesplayer (discussed in the next chapter) can control Motions—that is, animations embedded within W3D files that have been exported from external modeling programs. In this chapter, we will be examining the basics of the Keyframeplayer Modifier to control animation as well as several intermediate strategies for managing multiple Motions. In addition, I will explain several strategies for exporting Motions for use with the Keyframeplayer from 3D Studio MAX.

Motions and the Keyframeplayer Modifier

A *Motion* is a special type of resource that can exist in a 3D Castmember that has been imported from a W3D file. The purpose of a Motion is to store animation data that is used to control Models in the 3D environment. Two types of Motion resources can be stored within the 3D Castmember: keyframe animations, which control position, rotation, and the scaling of Models, and bones animations, which you will be learning about in the next chapter.

Motions are used to control Models, but they need to do so with the help of the Keyframeplayer. The Keyframeplayer Modifier will be added to the Modifier list of an individual Model. This way, you will be able to play keyframe Motions with that particular Model. For this reason, Motions are interesting because although they are saved within a W3D file, they are not hardwired to a single Model in that environment. Therefore, it is possible to use a single Motion to affect many different Models.

NOTE

Keyframe Motions cannot be created with code. They must be imported into a 3D Castmember from a W3D file. Several 3D animation packages support exportation of W3D files. These packages each have specific methods and procedures for exporting Motions. In this chapter, we will be working with Motions that were created in 3D Studio MAX version 3.1. However, the basics of the Keyframeplayer Modifier are going to remain the same no matter where your Motions were created.

Exporting Motions from 3D Studio MAX

Because keyframe Motions cannot be created within Director, you need to understand how they can be created outside of Director. 3D Studio MAX is one tool that allows you to export Motions of both the keyframe and bones varieties. In terms of keyframe Motion export, several issues arise during export that can affect the final W3D file.

Position, rotation, and scaling animation that is attached to meshes in 3D Studio MAX will export correctly—all other animation will be discarded. In addition, there are several guidelines you should understand when working with hierarchies in MAX. The type of hierarchy (linked or grouped) and whether that hierarchy contains meshes, non-meshes (lights and cameras), or both will determine exactly what will export and what will not. For this reason, I have categorized what you can expect to happen in terms of Motion export in the following four situations:

- A 3D Studio group that contains only meshes will collapse into a single Model in W3D. The name of the group in 3D Studio will be used for the Model name in W3D. That W3D Modelresource will contain each of the meshes from 3D Studio, and you will be able to access a separate Shader for each. In terms of animation, all animations on individual meshes in the group will be ignored. All animations on the group as a whole will be exported to Motions.

- A 3D Studio linked hierarchy of meshes will collapse into a single W3D Model. The name of the parent of the hierarchy will be used for the Model name. All animations on the children in the hierarchy will be lost. All animations on the parent will be retained.

- A 3D Studio group that contains meshes and non-meshes will do the following: The meshes will collapse into a single Model. The lights/cameras will become the children of that Model. Animations on the lights/cameras are always discarded. Animations on the child meshes will be discarded. Only animations applied to the group as a whole will be converted into a Motion.

- The last case that you might work with is a 3D Studio linked hierarchy of non-meshes and meshes. In a linear linked hierarchy, meshes that retain immediate parent/child relationships will collapse into a single Model. If a non-mesh Node is encountered, it will halt the process of collapsing the chain at that point. However, further parent/child relationships between meshes in the hierarchy will collapse into a single Model. Animations on the parent meshes will be retained and exported as Motions. Animations on child meshes or non-meshes will be discarded.

The discarding of non-mesh animation and the collapse of hierarchies may seem like limitations. However, there are two workarounds to these limitations that you might want to consider.

First, only animations attached to Meshes will be exported into Motions. This means that animation on Cameras and Lights will not export. However, there is a way to work around this problem. While you are in 3D Studio, create a Model and make it the parent of the Camera or Light. Then animate the Model. When you export the scene, the Motion will be converted, and so will the hierarchy. This is a great way to create flythrough style animations for 3D. Note that you should use free Cameras rather than target Cameras. Also, I tend to put the dummy Model used to control the Camera behind the Camera. This way, I won't need to see it in the scene.

Second, many times you may want to create a hierarchy and then animate each child in the hierarchy so that it rotates and moves relative to its parents. Because linked or grouped meshes will totally collapse into a single Model upon export, this may seem impossible. However, there is a workaround—but this workaround should be used with caution because it is not a very elegant solution (although it does work). In addition, you should first consider using nondeformable bones for this (explained in the next chapter). This method has the advantages that each mesh will become its own Model, each Model will preserve its place in the hierarchy, and each Model will retain its Motion.

If you create a linked hierarchy in 3D Studio MAX and alternate between meshes and non-meshes, the non-meshes will stop the meshes from collapsing into one another. I will caution you once again: This is an extremely ugly way to work because you will be creating many seemingly superfluous Nodes. In addition, these Nodes will become part of the hierarchy in Director (if they change position or orientation, so will their children). Also, if you choose to use Lights for this technique, I suggest setting the color of the Lights to black and placing them inside of the Models they are parents to.

Once you have exported a W3D file with Motions and then imported it into Director, those Motions will be available for use. You can test the number of Motions that have been imported into a 3D Castmember by using the `count` function with the following syntax:

```
Scene.motion.count
```

This will return the number of Motions currently within a given 3D Castmember. In addition, each Motion has properties that can be tested: `name`, `duration`, and `type`. The name of a Motion is dependent on the 3D animation software you used to create it. You can access this property with the following syntax:

```
Scene.motion[x].name
```

The `duration` property of a Motion refers to the number of milliseconds that the Motion will play at normal speed. This property can be accessed with the following syntax:

```
Scene.motion[x].duration
```

Finally, the `type` property is important because it returns the type of Motion stored within the Motion file: #keyframe, #bones or #none. Here's the syntax used to access this information:

```
Scene.motion[x].type
```

Here, #keyframe and #bones refer to keyframe and bones animation, respectively. A `motion.type` setting of #none will be designated for `scene.motion[1]`. This Motion is a default Motion that is attached to every 3D Castmember, but it does not actually contain Motion data. There are other situations when you may encounter Motions with a type of #none, but we will be examining these situations in the next chapter when we discuss Motion mapping.

Basic Keyframeplayer Control

The Keyframeplayer Modifier will need to be attached to any Model you want to animate with Motions—even the Model that was originally animated. The current version of the 3D Studio Exporter for version 3.1 should automatically attach the Keyframeplayer Modifier to the original Model. If it does not (or if you are using a different exporter that does not), make sure you add the Keyframeplayer Modifier to the Model that you want to animate with Motions with the following syntax:

```
Scene.model[x].addmodifier(#keyframeplayer)
```

Once the Keyframeplayer is attached to a Model, you will have access to several commands and properties that allow you to play Motions with that Model. A range of commands and properties allow for various levels of control of the Keyframeplayer Modifier. In this first demonstration, we will be using the Keyframeplayer Modifier to play back a single Motion on a single Model. Open the file named "Basic Keyframeplayer" on the CD and press Play. Figure 21.1 is a screenshot from this demonstration. You can see that there is a 3D Castmember and several buttons along the right side of the Stage.

While the movie is playing, test the function of each button to see the effect it has on the Motion of the car. The two commands we will discuss for controlling the playback of Motions are `play` and `pause`. In its simplest form, the `play` command can be used to start the current Motion on a Model with the following syntax:

```
Scene.model[x].keyframeplayer.play()
```

FIGURE 21.1

In the Basic Keyframeplayer demonstration, the car Model is controlled via simple behaviors attached to buttons on the Stage.

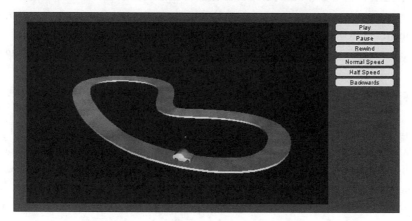

The `play()` command has a slightly more sophisticated syntax that will be used when we're working with multiple Motions. This technique is discussed in the next section. In terms of pausing a currently playing Motion on a Model, you will need to use the following syntax:

```
Scene.model[x].keyframeplayer.pause()
```

In addition to playing and pausing, several basic properties can be used to control the playback of Motions. The `playrate` property is both testable and settable and controls the speed of the playback of Motions. With a `playrate` value of 1, the Motion will play back at its normal speed. With a `playrate` value above 1, playback will be at a speed faster than normal. With a floating-point `playrate` between 0 and 1, playback will be slower than normal. Finally, with negative `playrate` values, the Motion will play backward (where -1 is backward at normal speed). Here's a breakdown of the possible uses of the `playrate` property:

- Forward, normal speed:
  ```
  Scene.model[x].keyframeplayer.playrate = 1
  ```
- Forward, faster-than-normal speed (where y > 1):
  ```
  Scene.model[x].keyframeplayer.playrate = y
  ```

- Forward, slower-than-normal speed (where y > 0 and y < 1):

```
Scene.model[x].keyframeplayer.playrate = y
```

- Backward, normal speed:

```
Scene.model[x].keyframeplayer.playrate = -1
```

In addition to the `playrate` property, we have the `currenttime` property. The `currenttime` property is testable and settable and refers to the current playback time of the Motion in milliseconds. Because you can set the playback time of a Motion, you can easily create a "rewind" button by issuing the following command:

```
Scene.model[x].keyframeplayer.currenttime = 0
```

The last of the basic Keyframeplayer properties is the `playing` property. This property is a Boolean that returns True if the Keyframeplayer is currently playing a Motion and False if it is not. This property is testable only—you must use the `keyframeplayer.play()` command to start a Motion.

These basic commands and properties of the Keyframeplayer Modifier can be used to create basic but useful controls for your 3D animation, as you can see from the Basic Keyframeplayer demonstration. If you examine the behavior scripts attached to the buttons, you will see that they are no more complex than the examples of code demonstrated in this section.

NOTE

Motions will play back at the speed at which they were recorded when exported from your 3D animation software. However, the Stage will only update when there has been an `exitframe` or `updatestage` event. Therefore, the apparent speed of the animation should be the same as when recorded, but how smooth the animation looks depends on Director's real-time frame rate.

In addition to building simple controls such as these, you may want to build more of a "slider" user interface for Motions. By a slider interface, I am referring to the style of interface you might expect to see with a QuickTime movie, where you are able to scrub through the video using a slider near the bottom of the video Sprite. You have access to the duration of the Motion and the `currenttime` of playback from the Keyframeplayer (in addition to the ability to reset that time). Therefore, creating a slider is perfectly possible.

Open the file named "Keyframeplayer Slider Controller" on the CD and press Play. Figure 21.2 is a screenshot from this demonstration that shows how I have built a custom slider located at the bottom of the 3D Sprite that will be used to control the current time of the playback of the Motion.

FIGURE 21.2

Screenshot from the Keyframe Slider Controller demonstration.

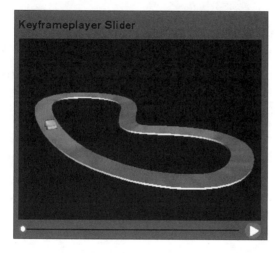

Note that the slider will move as long as the Motion is playing and will return to its starting position when the Motion loops back to its beginning. Try dragging the slider back and forth to scrub through the animation. This style of interface is extremely accessible for users because they are certain to be familiar with it. However, you should understand how we are creating this style of interface.

The functionality for this demonstration exists in several behaviors. The first of which is the toggle switch that allows you to start and stop the Motion, as shown in Listing 21.1.

LISTING 21.1   Motion Start/Stop Toggle Switch

```
1: property spritenum
2: property ptoggle
```

LISTING 21.1 Continued

```
 3: property whichmodel
 4:
 5: global scene
 6:
 7: on getpropertydescriptionlist(me)
 8:   plist = [:]
 9:   setaprop(plist, #whichmodel, \
10:   [#comment:"Which Model to control", \
11:   #format:#integer, \
12:   #default:1, \
13:   #range:[min:1, max:scene.model.count]])
14:   return plist
15: end
16:
17:
18: on beginsprite(me)
19:   ptoggle = false
20: end
21:
22: on mousedown(me)
23:   if ptoggle then
24:     pauseanim(me)
25:   else
26:     playanim(me)
27:   end if
28: end
29:
30: on playanim(me)
31:   scene.model[whichmodel].keyframeplayer.play()
32:   sprite(spritenum).member = member("pausebutton")
33:   ptoggle = true
34: end
35:
36: on pauseanim(me)
37:   scene.model[whichmodel].keyframeplayer.pause()
38:   sprite(spritenum).member = member("playbutton")
39:   ptoggle = false
40: end
```

Note that in this example I have encapsulated the code for starting and pausing the animation within the custom handlers playanim() and pauseanim(), respectively. This is because I will need to be able to call these functions from another Sprite—namely, the Sprite that is used as the slider. The slider Sprite has the "constrain to line" behavior attached to it. This behavior comes with all copies of Director. This is an extremely useful behavior that allows you to build a variety of sliders, among other tools. However, in order to create the slider for controlling Motions, it is necessary to also use yet another custom handler in conjunction with the "constrain to line" behavior to complete the effect. The slider behavior script is shown in Listing 21.2.

LISTING 21.2   Motion Slider Behavior Script

```
1: property spritenum
2: property pDuration
3: property ptoggle
4: property pwasplaying
5: property whichmodel
6: property whichmotion
7:
8: global scene
9:
10: on getpropertydescriptionlist(me)
11:    plist = [:]
12:    setaprop(plist, #whichmodel, \
13:    [#comment:"Which Model to control", \
14:    #format:#integer, \
15:    #default:1, \
16:    #range:[min:1, max:scene.model.count]])
17:
18:    setaprop(plist, #whichmotion, \
19:    [#comment:"Which Motion to control", \
20:    #format:#integer, \
21:    #default:2, \
22:    #range:[min:1, max:scene.motion.count]])
23:
24:    return plist
25: end
26:
27: on beginsprite
28:    --store the duration of the motion that you want the
29:    --slider to control (makes typing easier)
30:    pduration = scene.motion[whichmotion].duration
31:
32:    --ptoggle determines if you are sliding the slider
33:    --or allowing it to move on its own
34:    ptoggle = true
35:
36:    -- when you grab the slider and drag it around, the
37:    -- pwasplaying property stores whether playback
38:    -- was playing or not.  When the slider is being
```

LISTING 21.2   Continued

```
39:    -- dragged, playback will be paused by this script.
40:    -- then, it will use this property to determine if
41:    -- it should start playback again when you let go.
42:    pwasplaying = false
43: end
44:
45: -- note that the mconstrainedvalue() handler is called from the
46: -- constrain to line behavior that is supplied with Director.
47: -- when called, this handler is sent three pieces of information:
48: -- the objectref, the number of the sprite and most importantly
49: -- the distance of the slider on the line in the range of 0 - 1
50: -- this allows you to multiply that value & duration to determine
51: -- the time that you should move the keyframeplayer playback to.
52: on mconstrainedvalue(me, num, val)
53:    newtime = val * pduration
54:    scene.model[whichmodel].keyframeplayer.currenttime = newtime
55: end
56:
57: -- the exitframe event moves the slider when you
58: -- are not dragging the slider around yourself
59: on exitframe
60:    if ptoggle and scene.model[whichmodel].keyframeplayer.playing then
61:      pcurrenttime = scene.model[whichmodel].keyframeplayer.currenttime
62:      percentage = pcurrenttime / float(pduration)
63:      --make sure that you offset the new location for the slider
64:      --by the amount of pixels from the left edge of the stage
65:      --in addition to currenttime expressed as distance in pixels
66:      newlocation = (percentage * 360) + sprite(spritenum - 1).left
67:      sprite(4).loch = newlocation
68:    end if
69: end
70:
71: --the mousedown handler will be used to pause the animation
72: --if playing and record the pwasplaying property.  In addition,
73: --it will set ptoggle to false so that the position of the
74: --slider will be dependent on the mouse position rather than
75: -- the exitframe event moving it automatically.
76: on mousedown(me)
77:    if scene.model[whichmodel].keyframeplayer.playing then
78:      sendallsprites(#pauseanim)
79:      pwasplaying = true
80:    end if
81:    ptoggle = false
82: end
83:
84: -- the mouseup handler will determine if the motion was
```

LISTING 21.2 Continued

```
85: -- playing prior to user interaction with the slider
86: -- if it was playing it will start it playing again,
87: -- but it will always set ptoggle to true so that the
88: -- slider will move on exitframes based on the currenttime
89: -- of playback of the given motion
90: on mouseup(me)
91:   if pwasplaying then
92:     sendallsprites(#playanim)
93:     pwasplaying = false
94:   end if
95:   ptoggle = true
96: end
97:
98: -- mouseupoutside is a safety handler that will make sure that
99: -- the mouseup event is received even if the mouse does not
100: -- go "up" on the slider (a likely possibility)
101: on mouseupoutside(me)
102:   mouseup(me)
103: end
```

Note that both these behaviors have been enhanced with the getpropertyde-scriptionlist() handler so that you can apply these scripts to control Models other than Model[1] and Motions other than Motion[2].

Motion Playlists and Multiple Motions

As soon as you begin to work with multiple Motions, the approach toward the Keyframeplayer Modifier in the previous demonstrations will not suffice. You will need to start examining some of the more intermediate levels of control that the Keyframeplayer Modifier offers you. Specifically, you must begin to learn about the keyframeplayer.playlist property, which is a linear list that contains information about Motions that are queued for playback by the Keyframeplayer.

The keyframeplayer.playlist property is interesting because although it is a linear list, you cannot set its value the way that you might expect to be able to. You must use Keyframeplayer commands designed to manipulate and manage this list. These Keyframeplayer commands are listed in Table 21.1.

TABLE 21.1   Keyframeplayer Playlist Commands

Command	Purpose
Play()	Plays the current (first) Motion in the Playlist.
Playnext()	Removes the current (first) Motion from the Playlist and begins playing the next Motion. Because you will have removed the first Motion, the second Motion is now the first Motion.
Queue()	Adds a Motion to the end of the Playlist.
Removelast()	Removes the last Motion from the Playlist.

When you're using the Playlist, it is important to understand that Playlist management is a bit different from how you might work with a normal linear list. The reason for this is that you can only add items to the end of the list and delete items from the front or end of the list. This can cause difficulties, but they are not insurmountable. We will be looking at several methods for managing the Playlist, such as using the commands provided with one Motion at a time, using the commands provided to manage multiple Motions within the Playlist, and using the commands provided in conjunction with other linear lists to control multiple Motions.

Part of your strategy for handling multiple Motions with the Playlist will be determined by the strategy you use to bring multiple Motions into a 3D Castmember. Remember that the Keyframeplayer allows you to apply any Motion in the 3D Castmember to the Model that the Keyframeplayer is attached to. There are several strategies for loading multiple Motions into a 3D Castmember.

The simplest form of loading multiple Motions involves creating several dummy objects in 3D Studio. Each of these dummy objects will be animated. In addition, you will create a single Model that will not be animated in 3D Studio (but will be animated in Director) to use the Motions that will export with the other Models. In this method, remember to keep the geometry of the dummy Models as simple as possible to reduce space.

Open the file named "Three Motions" on the CD and press Play. Figure 21.3 is a screenshot from this demonstration that shows the image of a 3D sphere whose Motion can be controlled by the buttons on the right side of the Stage.

FIGURE 21.3

Screenshot from the Three Motions demonstration.

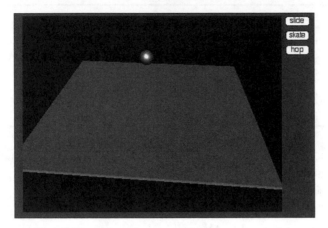

This demonstration contains three "cone" Models that are hidden during the initialization period of the movie by setting the model.visibility property for each to #none. You can check the number of Motions in the message window with the following syntax:

```
Put scene.motion.count
--4
```

Notice that there are four Motions within the 3D Castmember. Remember that motion[1] is the default Motion. We will not be working with that Motion, so the first Motion that is important to us is motion[2]. We can find out some basic information about motion[2] through motion[4] by checking their properties in the message window, like so:

```
put scene.motion[2].name
-- "dummy1-Key"
put scene.motion[3].name
-- "dummy2-Key"
put scene.motion[4].name
-- "dummy3-Key"
```

You can see from this naming convention that the suffix "-Key" has been appended to the names of the three dummy Models in order to create the

names of the Motions. The name of the Motion is important when we
begin to look at the use of the `keyframeplayer.play()` command. In
previous demonstrations, this command was called without any
arguments. However, in this example, it is important to understand that
`scene.model[x].keyframeplayer.play()` can accept the following syntax:

```
.play(motionname, looped, start, end, speed, offset)
```

When you call the `.play()` command in this fashion, the `motionname` you specify will be added to the front of the Playlist and immediately played. The
individual arguments for using the `play()` command in this way are optional,
except for `motionname`—this must be the name of a Motion currently within
the 3D Castmember. The `looped` argument is a Boolean that is used to determine whether playback of the Motion should be looped (True) or only played
once (False). The `start` and `end` arguments are given in milliseconds and allow
you to specify portions of a Motion to be played back. Note that you can set
the `playrate` property for the Motion playback with the `speed` argument.

Finally, the `offset` argument is a time in milliseconds that will ignore the start
time that you set only the first time through the Motion. For example, if you
were to specify a start time of 10 milliseconds and an offset of 5 milliseconds,
the first time the Keyframeplayer plays the Motion, it will start at 5 milliseconds. Then as the playback loops, it will subsequently go to 10 milliseconds.

In this demonstration, we will currently only be using the first two parameters—`motionname` and `looped`—because we are going to be managing the
Playlist in a rather simple manner. That is, when we want to play a Motion,
we will put a Motion in the Playlist and immediately play it. If we choose a
new Motion, the old Motion will be removed from the Playlist and then the
new Motion will be added. The scripts for each button in this example are
very similar to one another because of this. Take a look at Listing 21.3, which
shows the method of removing and playing Motions from the Playlist in this
manner.

LISTING 21.3   Playlist Management Script

```
1: on mousedown
2:    global scene
3:
```

LISTING 21.3   Continued

```
 4:   current = scene.model[5].keyframeplayer.playlist
 5:
 6:   if current <> [] then
 7:     scene.model[5].keyframeplayer.removelast()
 8:   end if
 9:
10:   scene.model[5].keyframeplayer.play("dummy1-key", 1)
11: end
```

In this fairly straightforward approach, we are able to quickly manage the Playlist without too much difficulty. Although it's a simple management solution, this strategy can be quite powerful, depending on the needs of your project. However, the Playlist is capable of more than this; therefore, we need to look at yet another method of managing the Playlist.

Sub-Motions and Motion Queuing

In this next example of working with multiple Motions, the strategy is quite different. Remember that in the last demonstration it was necessary to create a dummy object to export each Motion. This is often not a practical solution, especially if your file is going to contain many Motions. In addition, our management of the Playlist in the previous example was rather simple because we did not make use of queuing Motions (that is, storing several Motions in the Playlist).

By building a queue of Motions, we can cycle through a set sequence of Motions that will look seamless to the user. To the user, it just seems like one Motion rather than a composite of several Motions. At the same time, we will be looking at a strategy for reducing the number of dummy Models needed for multiple Motions.

Rather than build several Motions, in this demonstration, we will export a single Motion that contains several smaller Motions within it, which I will refer to as *sub-Motions*. Note that this strategy is going to make use of the fact that we can specify the start and end of Motions in milliseconds when we queue Motions onto the Playlist. Figure 21.4 illustrates how we'll set up the animation in the 3D animation software prior to export.

FIGURE 21.4

Multiple Motions existing within a single Motion track.

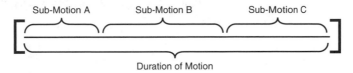

Note in Figure 21.4 that all these sub-Motions will be contained within one Motion for the 3D Castmember. It will be important to determine the number of milliseconds that comprise each of the sub-Motions. There are a variety of ways to do this. For a visual method, you could use the basic Keyframeplayer slider utility to scrub through the animation and then check the Currenttime property of the Keyframeplayer to determine the start and end times. Alternatively, you could note the start and end frames in your animation program, look up the Motion.Duration in Director, and then use the following formula to determine the start and end times of each motion:

startOrEndFrame * duration / Totalframes = startOrEndTime

In this strategy, determining the start and end times of each sub-Motion is of critical importance. Especially if you have created a large number of sub-Motions, this step can be time consuming. Once you have determined the start and end times of each sub-Motion in milliseconds, you are ready to begin.

Open the file named "Motion Queuing" on the CD and press Play. Figure 21.5 is a screenshot from this demonstration that illustrates the purpose of the controls for this demonstration.

Queuing motions onto the Playlist uses syntax that is extremely similar to the `play` command. Note that the format for
`scene.model[x].keyframeplayer.queue()()` is as follows:

```
.queue()(motionname, loop, start, end, speed, offset)
```

The difference between `.play()` and `.queue()()` is that queuing a motion will not cause the Motion to play. However, you should understand that the Keyframeplayer can technically be playing even if there is no Motion in the

Playlist. If this is the case, as soon as you queue a Motion, it will begin play-ing. Therefore, you may want to check before you queue a motion to see whether the Keyframeplayer is playing and pause it if it is not. Of course, you can use this to your advantage as well.

FIGURE 21.5

The Motion Queuing demonstration with explanations for the various controls.

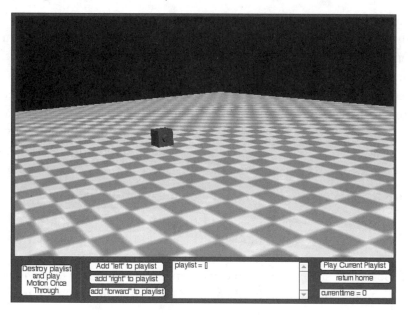

In this example, we will be building a short Playlist of sub-Motions that will each play once. Because we are not looping each sub-Motion, the Keyframeplayer will play the sub-Motion once, remove it from the front of the Playlist, and then play the next sub-Motion without stopping.

Cloning Motions from Other Castmembers

One of the drawbacks of the prior two methods has been the fact that the Motions have names that relate to Models rather than descriptions of what the Motions are themselves. In this next strategy, we will be looking at a method that is quite powerful for several reasons. First, we will be able to name Motions while in Director, allowing us to give them names that are immediately accessible and understandable. Second, we will be able to create multiple Motions that can either be sub-Motion based or simply use one Motion per keyframe movement. The latter option will allow us to name each movement. In addition, in this method we will be able to save the Motions in their own 3D Castmember.

All these options are made possible by the `clonemotionfromcastmember()` command. This powerful command allows you to clone a Motion from one Castmember and make a copy of it in another. When the copy is created, you will be able to change the name. In addition, we will be looking at a method of exportation that does not export the dummy Models but rather only exports the animation information itself. Note that the syntax of this command is as follows:

```
Scene.clonemotionfromcastmember(newName, oldName, Castmember)
```

In this syntax, `newName` is the name of the new Motion that we will create, `oldName` is the original name of the Motion, and Castmember is the name of the 3D Castmember we want to get the Motion named `oldName` from.

Here's the reason you'll want to use `clonemotionfromcastmember()`: If you are going to be working with a large number of Motions but are not satisfied with the sub-Motion option, you may want to use dummy models to export multiple Motions. However, if you did this and exported the dummy Models as well as the Motions, the size of the dummy Models could become prohibitive. More importantly, though, is the naming. If you are working with a large number of Motions, it can become very difficult to remember that dummy142-key is really the hop up and down Motion, for example.

In order to export Motion data only into a W3D file, you will need to alter some of the settings for the W3D exporter. Note that this example is for 3D Studio MAX; you will need to check with your exporter documentation if you are not using this program. Figure 21.6 illustrates the proper settings to use in order to export Motion only. Using these settings, you can create a file containing only Motions that can be cloned into other 3D Castmembers, as needed.

FIGURE 21.6

A screenshot from 3D Studio MAX showing how to set up the exporter for exporting Motions only.

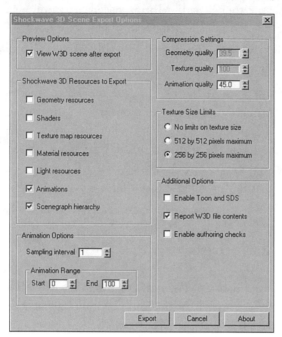

Note that in this strategy, we will be creating at least two W3D Castmembers. One will contain our Motions, and the other will contain our Models. This is also a good strategy if you are going to be applying Motions to Models that are created from scratch within Director. Realize that the Keyframeplayer Modifier can be added to any Model, regardless of where it was created.

Remember that cloning is a slow command, and for this reason, all the Motions are cloned at the beginning of the demonstration during the initialization phase of the movie. I would suggest cloning your Motions during points in the movie that you do not expect user interaction. In addition, note that before you clone anything from another Castmember, you must be sure that both Castmembers have a state of 4. This will ensure that the 3D Castmembers are prepared for the cloning operation.

NOTE

You may also want to consider that Motions can be loaded into your 3D Castmember with the loadfile() command, whose usage was discussed and demonstrated in the previous chapter.

> The advantage of using `loadfile()` is that you can compartmentalize the download of information so that users only need to download the specific assets required rather than all of them at once.
>
> The negative side of this command is that you will not have a chance to change the names of your Motions. Another negative aspect is that when you are loading a file, the state of that Castmember is no longer 4 until the loading process is finished.
>
> Because of these two issues, the most powerful strategy is to create a 3D Castmember that exists only in the cast. You'll load Motions into this 3D Castmember after the movie has downloaded and, perhaps, download your secondary Motions that users will not need until they are further into the project. Then, during a planned pause within the 3D environment, you clone the Motions that are needed into the project.

Motion Blending

Motion blending is one of the more intriguing capabilities of the Keyframeplayer. It gives you the ability to blend from one Motion to another. This functionality is useful if you are using the `playnext` command to switch between Motions while they are playing. Normally there is a slight blending of Motions, but you can cause this to be more pronounced. Without Motion blending, Motions will abruptly change from one to the next after the `playnext()` command is issued. With Motion blending, you can cause two Motions to slowly cross-fade their influence over the Motion of the Model for a much smoother transition. There are times when you might want one or the other, depending on the aesthetics of your overall Motion design.

There are two ways to implement Motion blending—you can either give Director automatic control of the blending or use custom manual control of the blend. Three properties are related to controlling Motion blending, as listed in Table 21.2.

TABLE 21.2 Keyframeplayer Motion Blending Properties

Property	Purpose
Autoblend	A Boolean that determines whether blending should be handled automatically by Director (True) or you will specify the amount of blending with Lingo for custom transitions between Motions.
Blendtime	Indicates the number of milliseconds it will take to linearly blend from the previous Motion to the current Motion. (This is only relevant if Autoblend is True.)

TABLE 21.2   Continued

Property	Purpose
Blendfactor	Used to manually control the percentage of blending from one Motion to another via Lingo. (This is only relevant if Autoblend is False.)

The main difference between autoblending and custom motion blending is that with autoblending, you must explicitly tell Director to play the next Motion. With custom blending, your options are actually quite different. Rather than telling Director to play the next Motion, you will control the amount of blending between the two Motions in real-time while they play. This gives you the option of creating transitions between Motions that are biased or not creating transitions at all. You can use custom Motion blending in such a way that the point of blending is to create the net Motion rather than the transition. Open the file named "Motion Blending" on the CD and press Play. Figure 21.7 illustrates the various controls available to you in this demonstration.

FIGURE 21.7

A screenshot from the Motion Blending demonstration.

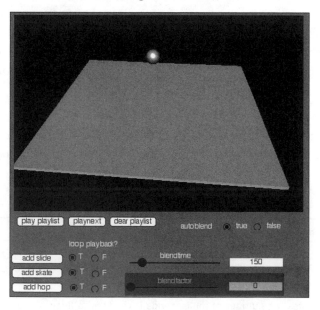

Remember that there are two methods of controlling Motion blending. When you are working with Autoblend set to True, the Blendtime property is important, but Blendfactor is not used. Conversely, when Autoblend is set to False, the Blendfactor property is used, but Blendtime is ignored.

Make sure that you queue at least two Motions when you work with Motion blending. If you do not, there will be nothing to blend between. In addition, try setting Blendtime to large as well as small values with the same Motions. This will allow you to see the dramatic differences that can take place. Motion blending is quite successful if you do not like abrupt changes between Motions or sub-Motions. However, the success of Motion blending depends on the quality of the Motions it is blending. For example, if you are blending between similar Motions, you may be able to use short blend times. With dissimilar Motions, you may require extended periods to switch from one to another.

NOTE

You can disable Motion blending by setting Autoblend to True and setting Blendtime to 0. This will force the Keyframeplayer to automatically switch from one Motion to the next. If you are working with fast animations, you may want to use this method and avoid Motion blending.

Cumulative Motions

In this last demonstration of the Keyframeplayer in this chapter, we will be looking at two properties of the Keyframeplayer that can change the way you work with Motions in general. The idea is that when a Motion reaches its end, the Model normally resets any rotation and positional changes that took place while the Motion was playing. However, it is possible to change this so that the effect of playing Motions is cumulative.

The two properties that we will be examining in this case are Rotationreset and Positionreset. The Positionreset property is a Boolean that is normally True. This tells the Keyframeplayer that after playing a given Motion to reset the Model to its initial position. With this property set to False, positional changes will accumulate. Rotationreset is more complex because it accepts a variety of symbols, as shown in Table 21.3.

TABLE 21.3   Possible Values for the Rotationreset Property

Value	Purpose
#all	Resets all axes of rotation
#X	Resets X axis rotation only
#Y	Resets Y axis rotation only
#Z	Resets Z axis rotation only
#XZ	Resets X and Z axes rotations
#XY	Resets X and Y axes rotations
#YZ	Resets Y and Z axes rotations
#none	Allows all rotations to accumulate

Note that the Positionreset and Rotationreset properties will cause accumulation even if you are looping playback of a single Motion. Open the file named "Cumulative Motions" on the CD and press Play. You should see the interface shown in Figure 21.8 for controlling the Cumulative Motions demonstration.

FIGURE 21.8

A screenshot from the Cumulative Motions demonstration.

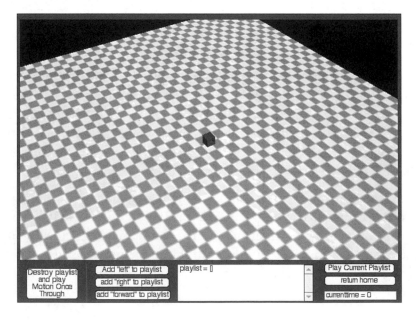

In this demonstration, first click the button to the far left, which will clear the Playlist and play the whole Motion once through. This will show you what each of the sub-Motions do to the cube. When you use this command, the cube will be reset to its identity() transformation, and the Motions will be set to reset their positions when done.

Next, build a small Playlist of forward, right, forward, right, forward, right, forward. Then press the Play Playlist button. By playing each of these sub-Motions and allowing each motion to accumulate, you cause the cube to move in a square. When playing the Playlist, I have set this demonstration to allow accumulation of both position and all rotation changes. Try building some Playlists of your own to move the cube in other ways, such as in zigzags or figure eights.

NOTE

Note that in this demonstration, I have turned Motion blending entirely off. Cumulative Motion and Motion blending can be difficult to control when used together.

Also, note that at this point, the level of control we have over the block with the Keyframeplayer is similar to the type of control we could easily build into the block using Lingo without the Keyframeplayer. However, in this example, the Motion of the block was kept simple. Instead of simply sliding forward, what if the block were to bounce forward or bounce and snake forward?

The Playlist allows you to build complex Motions in 3D animation software that would be difficult to replicate with code and then use the Keyframeplayer to play back these Motions. Of course, you have seen a variety of uses for the Keyframeplayer in this chapter, each of which is a viable use.

Try working with the Motions I have provided or learn about how to export your own Motions. If you are going to be working with Keyframe Motions, at some point you will need to learn how to integrate assets from 3D animation software with Director. It will be much better to do that now so that you learn the idiosyncrasies of converting from one program to Director before working on a project.

Summary

Two types of Motions can be exported with a W3D file: keyframe and bones. Keyframe Motions must be controlled with the Keyframeplayer Modifier and Lingo. Keyframe Motions cannot be created with code, and this is a limitation that can only be overcome with a 3D animation package that exports W3D. The Keyframeplayer offers you a range of features from Playlist management to Motion blending and cumulative Motion control.

Keyframe animation is the first area we have worked with that is extremely dependent on a 3D animation package. Much of how you use the Keyframeplayer Modifier will depend not only on the specific Motions that you export but also on the 3D animation package you are using. In this book, I am focusing only on 3D Studio MAX, but you should be aware that other 3D animation packages are available that may treat exportation differently.

It may be difficult to understand the role of the Keyframeplayer Modifier in the 3D environment because of the wide range of controls it offers. In addition, it is possible to replicate some of the functions we have been building from scratch. However, the strength of the Keyframeplayer is its ability to allow you to use complicated keyframe animations from many 3D animation packages.

Among the many possibilities for the Keyframeplayer Modifier are creating flythrough-style animations, creating product demonstrations that do not require user interaction, creating "trailers" for games or projects that are entirely animated, creating objects in a scene that are animated but not necessarily interacted with, and hardwiring complex Motions used for interaction without needing to code the path of the Motion.

FAQ

I am having trouble exporting rotations. My Model always rotates the wrong way. Why is this?

If you are trying to rotate a Model a large distance, you should add Keyframes at least every 90 degrees. The W3D exporter often has trouble determining which way to rotate when it feels there are multiple choices in terms of the direction of rotation.

I created an animated (space-warp, mesh deformation, and so on) MAX-modifier, but I can't get it to show up in Director after I exported to W3D. What can I do?

Shockwave 3D does not support Modifier-based animation. This means you will not be able to use any meshdeformation Modifier–based animation from within MAX, including morphing, twisting, and so on.

However, there is a possible workaround that you might look into if you absolutely must use Modifier-based animation. I caution you that this method can likely create very large W3D files, so you should use it strategically. Remember from Chapter 13, "A 2D Mouse in a 3D World," that it is possible to switch Modelresources for a Model. If you are working in 3D Studio MAX, create the animation using modifiers and then use the Snapshot tool to create a Model for each step of the animation. The meshes for these Models will be exported as Modelresources you can then use for the implementation of this technique. In Director, you would create a flip-book-style animation that cycles through the Modelresources you intend to animate.

This method can work particularly well if used in conjunction with multiple 3D Castmembers. Because you can decide to only export Modelresources into a W3D file, you could create a W3D that only contains Modelresources that are used as the source meshes for this flipbook style of animation. This technique will work with any animation based on MAX-modifier, and it's particularly useful if you're working with lip-synching and facial animation. However, there are also methods of lip-synching and facial animation that utilize bones animation.

CHAPTER 22

Bonesplayer Modifier

The focus of this chapter is the Bonesplayer Modifier included with Director 8.5 for the purpose of playing Bones-based Motions. We will be covering several aspects of Bones animation in this chapter, including tips on how to export Bones-based Motions from 3D Studio MAX 3.1. In addition, we will look at several strategies for controlling Bones. Some of the strategies that we will be examining are similar to those covered in the previous chapter dealing with the Keyframeplayer Modifier.

However, the Bonesplayer Modifier offers more capabilities, including the ability to synthesize composite Motions from existing Motion resources. In this chapter, we will be discussing the principles of what Bones animation is, how you can export Bones animation from 3D Studio MAX, and how to control the Bones Motions that you create with the Bonesplayer.

What Is Bones Animation?

Bones animation is a professional-level tool for 3D animation that allows animators to specify a skeletal structure for their Models. These skeletal structures have a definite hierarchy that is linked to the geometry of a Model. When the skeletal structure moves, the geometry that is linked to it moves as well. When the geometry moves, the shape of the Mesh can change position much the way our skin conforms to the underlying skeletal structure of our bodies as we move.

Within a given 3D animation package, you may be able to control these skeletal structures in a variety of ways; the two most common methods are known as *forward kinematics* and *inverse kinematics*. These two methods are important skills to master, but their specifics will vary depending on your 3D animation software. Specifically, the type of kinematics that is used determines how an animator will go about his business of specifying where the individual Bones in a skeletal hierarchy are at a given point in time.

Generally speaking, forward kinematics requires a small setup time for the Bones structure, but animating can be labor intensive because you will need to move every single Bone in the chain to make the Model look "just so." With inverse kinematics, there is a large setup time for the Bones structure, but the time spent animating that structure is reduced. The reason for this is that in inverse kinematics you place the last Bone in a chain where you would like it, and the computer determines the position of the rest of the Bones in the structure from that end point. The setup of the inverse kinematics chain is involved because you will set up constraints and rules for the links. For example, your elbow is constrained to rotate on essentially one axis and within a certain number of degrees.

However, neither of these types explains the most important aspect of Bones: What do Bones do? This will depend on whether the Bone hierarchy performs skeletal deformation. That is, with many Bones structures, the skeleton Bones will deform the geometry they are associated with (making it ideal for organic structures). With nondeformable Bones, the structure remains rigid as the skeleton moves (better for mechanical structures). Therefore, a Bone is a way for performing deformations on a Model's geometry that can be used for both character animation and machine animation.

Bones can be created in a variety of ways in 3D modeling software and will vary from package to package. 3D Studio MAX 3.1 has internal support for nondeformable Bones. In addition, its companion plug-in Character Studio is supported for deformable Bones animation export. When Bones animations are exported into Motions in a W3D file, all the individual Bones are treated as a single entity in terms of the Motion. That is, a single Bones Motion will contain information for each Bone in a skeletal hierarchy. Each Bone can move separately, but this must be defined within the 3D animation program.

NOTE

> In addition to controlling Bones hierarchies with Motions and the Bonesplayer Modifier, it is possible to control individual Bones with transformations as well. This means you can essentially use Lingo to build custom skeletal deformation from within Director. However, you will still need to have a skeletal structure created outside of Director for this option.

Exporting Bones Motions from 3D Studio MAX

When working with 3D Studio MAX and Character Studio, you can consider your toolset essentially complete in terms of 3D character animation. Character Studio is an impressive plug-in for 3D Studio MAX that allows you to control deformable Bones in a variety of ways. The possibilities for Bones animation are so numerous that I will only be listing some of the most popular uses in this section. Here are some of the possible uses for 3D Studio Max and Character Studio:

- Creating a Character Studio biped (a simulated human skeleton) to control a humanoid character. Character Studio ships with several methods for controlling bipeds. Among the most popular methods are the following:

    - Using Motion capture data. Character Studio supplies several hundred sample Motion capture files that can immediately control your biped, making it walk, kick, run, jump, and perform many other less-general activities, such as swatting bees and barbecuing.

    - Using "footsteps." Footsteps are Character Studio's method for allowing you to specify where a biped should step on a given frame. Character Studio figures out how to get the biped's feet to the correct locations.

- Creating a skeleton from native 3D Studio Bones and using Character Studio to tie the skeleton to a deformable body. This allows you to create a wide variety of nonbipedal organic structures, ranging from quadrupeds to snakes, fish, birds, and even plants and trees. These nonstandard skeletons can also be controlled with Character Studio. (Alternatively, you can bring them into Director and control them with Bones transformations.)

- Creating a skeleton from native 3D Studio Bones and tying these Bones to a skeleton without Character Studio to create a nondeformable body. If you are trying to create a "robotic" movement (ranging from bipedal robots to clocks, car engines, and other machinery) that does not need to deform, you would choose this option.

Guidelines for Bones Motion Export from 3DS MAX

You must follow several general rules if you are going to be working with the export of Bones Motions. These rules apply to the export of Bones Motions from 3D Studio MAX 3.1 with Character Studio. If you are working with a different 3D package, you will need to check with your specific exporter guidelines.

General Guidelines

First, do not group your Bones hierarchy because it will collapse upon export. Second, make sure you do not use any unconventional naming methods for your Bones hierarchies. Each Bone name should start with the name of the root Bone. If you are using bipeds from Character Studio, this will be set up for you. Third, if you are working with Character Studio, feel free to use the physique Modifier to attach your Bones to your meshes. However, be sure that the physique Modifier is the last Modifier attached to the mesh. This means that you should do your UVW mapping prior to adding the skeleton to your mesh.

Multi-Motion Guidelines

If you are working with Multi-Motion export, you are going to need a definite strategy from the very beginning. If you intend to animate a single skeleton with multiple Motions, you need to make sure each Motion you export is exported from the same skeleton. This is because the Motions that you create for a skeleton contain information for each Bone in the skeleton—the same names and the same number of Bones must be used.

In a vast majority of projects, you are going to be working with multiple Motions, and doing so successfully demands planning from the beginning. Develop your character and Bones structure, noting what types of Motions are going to be important to you. Once you have developed the character and you begin working on the Motions themselves, remember that each Motion must be created from the same skeleton. Also, consider a strategy that exports the character with the skeleton into a single W3D file; then for each Motion you want, export another W3D file with the Motion only. This way, you will use the `cloneMotionfromcastmember()` or `loadfile()` command to put it all together.

Using the Bonesplayer Modifier

The Bonesplayer and Keyframeplayer Modifiers have much in common in terms of usage. For this reason, much of what is covered in the previous chapter in terms of the Keyframeplayer can be applied to understanding the Bonesplayer. The Bonesplayer Modifier will be controlled with the Playlist and the Playlist commands—`Play()`, `Playnext()`, `Queue()`, and `Removelast()`. This means that if you understand the Keyframeplayer Modifier after reading the previous chapter, you already understand many of the basics about the Bonesplayer.

Keep in mind that the Bonesplayer can use Motion blending techniques as well as cloning motions and sub-Motions. Overall, Bones Motions tend to be more flexible because of an additional technique known as *Motion mapping*, which we will cover in this chapter. The first demonstration assumes you understand the basics of Playlist control as covered in the previous chapter.

NOTE

Unlike the Keyframeplayer, the Bonesplayer Modifier cannot be added to a Model at runtime. It must be attached during export of the W3D file that contains the Model to be animated with Bones.

Bones Animation Demonstration

In this demonstration, we will be examining the basic features of the Bonesplayer Modifier. First, this example uses the `cloneMotionfromcastmember()` function to load several Motions into a single 3D Castmember. Using `cloneMotionfromcastmember()` allows us to give each Motion a unique name upon cloning.

Second, we will be using the basic functions of the Bonesplayer.Playlist. Controlling the Playlist for the Bonesplayer is virtually identical to controlling the Playlist for the Keyframeplayer, except we will be using Bones Motions.

Contending with numerous small Motions is one of the difficulties of managing multiple Motions. Being able to refer to a specific Motion by name becomes extremely important. This is especially true with Bones Motions, because they tend to be small loops of animation, such as walk loops, or small "triggered" animations, such as punches or kicks.

On the CD accompanying this book is a file named "Basic Bonesplayer." Open this file now. Before we begin playing the movie, note that the 3D Castmember used on the Stage does not inherently contain any of the Motions we will be working with. Rather, if you look at the cast, you will see several 3D Castmembers that are not featured on the Stage. These other 3D Castmembers contain animation data only, and it is from these Castmembers that we will clone Motions, renaming them in the process.

First, we need to make sure the media of the 3D Castmembers we are cloning from is ready; otherwise, we will get a script error. Therefore, we will preload the 3D Castmembers with animation data only and check for their readiness before initializing the movie. The actual process of cloning is rather straightforward, as shown in Listing 22.1.

LISTING 22.1   Cloning Motions

```
 1: on exitFrame me
 2:   global scene
 3:   --clone the walk Motion
 4:   scene.cloneMotionfromcastmember("walk", "bip01", member("walk"))
 5:   --clone the run Motion
 6:   scene.cloneMotionfromcastmember("run", "bip01", member("run"))
 7:   --clone the yawn Motion
 8:   scene.cloneMotionfromcastmember("yawn", "bip01", member("yawn"))
 9:   go "run"
10: end
```

In this listing, the cloning of Motions involves a single command that requires three arguments: the name of the new Motion, the name of the old Motion, and the name of the 3D Castmember in which the old Motion can be found. Once we have cloned the Motions, we are able to refer to them by their new names.

NOTE

> The three 3D Castmembers that contain animation data only were created within 3D Studio MAX. This data was created specifically for use with the biped character in this demonstration. If you use these Motions on other bipeds, they will need to have the same number of Bones with the same hierarchy. For this reason (and also because a lot of fine-tuning is required between 3D Studio and Director), it is sometimes difficult to use the Motions of one character for another.

With the basic Bonesplayer movie open, press Play to begin the demonstration. Several controls can be found along the right side of the Stage, as you can see in Figure 22.1.

FIGURE 22.1

The Bonesplayer Modifier is controlled similarly to the Keyframeplayer, as you can see from the basic controls in this demonstration.

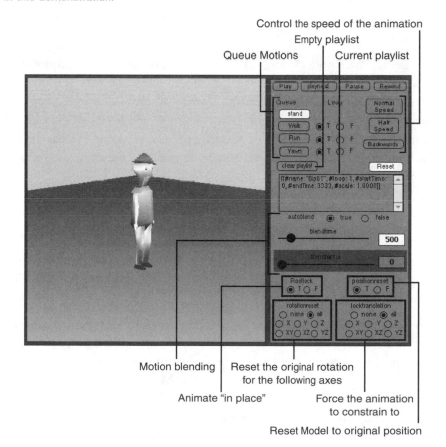

Among the various controls are several items you have control over that we have not worked with as of yet. In particular, we'll address the purpose of the Rootlock, Positionreset, Rotationreset, and Locktranslation properties.

NOTE

Note that the Rootlock, Positionreset, Rotationreset, and Locktranslation properties are available for the Keyframeplayer Modifier as well as the Bonesplayer Modifier.

The purposes of these properties are similar to one another in that they are designed to help you integrate Motions within the framework of your projects. How you set these properties depends on your specific approach toward Bones Motions. Rootlock is the most dramatic of these four properties. By setting Rootlock to True, the Bones Motion will affect the Model at the local level, but changes in World position will not take place. For example, if you were to play the walk Motion with Rootlock set to True, the character would walk in place.

However, the Rootlock property does not eliminate all translation of the Model in World space—you are still able to move the Model in World space using the translate function. In this way, you can create Motions that are intended to run "in place" and then change World positions via standard translations. Rootlock is also a great method of stopping the Model from walking off the screen. This way, you can examine the success of a looping Motion.

Positionreset is a useful property whose value is a Boolean; when it's set to True, any changes in World position a Model makes during the playback of a Motion will be removed. This causes the Model to seemingly "jump" back to its start position after looping through the Motion. Although setting this property to True is often helpful in testing the look of a particular Motion, you can also use this property to eliminate the drifting of Models over time.

You see, sometimes when you're working with Motions intended to return to the same spot, you may experience "drift." That is, if the end position and start position are intended to be the same but they are not (even in the slightest), this difference can accumulate. If the Motion is intended to play for long periods of time, this drift can cause the Model to slowly move unexpectedly, thus ruining the look of your project.

The next property, Rotationreset, is a bit different from Positionreset. This property limits rotation on some, all, or none of the axes. For this reason it is not a Boolean but rather accepts the following symbols: #none, #all, #x, #y, #z, #xy, #xz, and #yz. Rotationreset can be used to counter rotational drift, which is more common than positional drift. For this reason, you will most likely need to experiment with values for the Rotationreset in most cases.

Finally, the Locktranslation property is similar to Rotationreset in that it accepts values of #none, #all, #x, #y, #z, #xy, #xz, and #yz. However, these values do not refer to rotation axes but rather translational axes. By locking translation in a particular direction, you can bind a Model to a single plane. This is often helpful when you're working with walk loops if you want to limit a Model to a single ground plane. However, be aware that you will often need to set the Rotationreset property as well to counteract any rotational drift.

NOTE

The Locktranslation property can often be difficult to understand at first. The Locktranslation property allows changes to the translation of a Model during the playing of a Motion; however, when the Motion loops, the translation in a particular direction will be reset. For this reason, Locktranslation can often result in a slight "jumping" effect, in which the Model corrects its position at the end of a loop.

Another effect of the Locktranslation property is that it ignores any changes you make to the Model via Lingo. This means that even if the Locktranslation property is set for a particular axis and you specifically command the Model to translate along that axis, the command will be ignored.

Motion Mapping

Motion mapping is a powerful process that allows you to composite multiple Bones Motions. This process is often misunderstood because it is quite difficult to fine-tune its use. As with basic Keyframe and Bones animation techniques, the Motions you create in external 3D animation software is critical. Most likely you will need to work in both software packages simultaneously the first few times you create Bones Motions specifically for the purpose of mapping.

To understand what Motion mapping does, it is important that you clearly understand the scope of a Bones Motion. A Bones Motion contains information for the movements of an invisible skeletal hierarchy that is attached to the Modelresource of a given Model. A Bones Motion contains animation data on each Bone in a skeletal hierarchy—even if the Bone does not move.

Imagine that you have several Motions: punching, walking, and yawning. Each Motion would contain information for each Bone in the hierarchy, but some areas are more important than others for defining the essence of the Motion. For instance, the legs are the most important section of walking, whereas the arms are more important for punching and yawning.

Motion mapping allows you to decide which areas of the body will be controlled by which Motion. It is possible to use the walking Motion data for the legs only and apply this to the legs while also applying the punching Motion data only on the arms. You are not able to map two Motions to a single Bone: That is what Motion blending is for.

Motion mapping is powerful because it offers you many possibilities. It is possible to map two, three, or more different Motions together into a single composite Motion. Alternatively, you could choose to only use specific areas of a single Motion (imagine a walking Motion where the arms swing and the legs walk; you could use just the legs walking without the arms swinging).

Because of the variety of approaches toward Motion mapping, it is important that you carefully design the Motions with mapping in mind. A strong mapping strategy can be used to help reduce the number of Motions a user will need to download (and some Bones Motions can take up a good deal of space).

Overall, Motion mapping is an intriguing technique because the goal is to allow you to combine Motions similarly to how you might try to perform more than one action at once. Sometimes it will be successful, and other times the end result will look terrible—or even hilarious. Therefore, no matter how much planning you put into your Motions, how well they work together when synthesized with new Motions must be tested and retested heavily.

Motion Mapping Demonstration

To begin, we will be looking at a rather straightforward demonstration of Motion mapping. In this demonstration, you will have access to several Motions with the ability to apply parts of those Motions to a given Model.

On the CD is a file named "Motion Mapping." Open this file and press Play. Figure 22.2 is a screenshot from this demonstration with an explanation of how to use the interface.

FIGURE 22.2

The Motion Mapping demonstration allows you to synthesize new Bones Motions from existing Bones Motions.

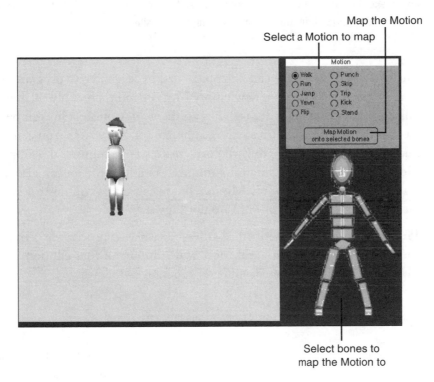

In this demonstration, you are able to select a visual representation of the Bones on the lower-right corner of the Stage. Note that when you select a given "Bone," all its child Bones will be selected as well. This is because when you map the Motion to a single Bone, all its children will automatically inherit the qualities of that Motion as well.

In this demonstration, if you select the pelvis, the Motion will be mapped to the whole skeleton. If you select any parent Bone, all its children will be selected. In addition, you will not be able to deselect a child whose parent is selected. This is because Motion mapping affects the skeleton hierarchy down the chain. The only Bones you can isolate are those at the end of the chain. You can, of course, isolate branches of the chain in order to build interesting effects.

NOTE

One method of working with this demonstration is to select the whole skeleton and apply a Motion and then select a section of the skeleton and apply a different Motion. In this way, you will be overwriting parts of the Motion while creating a composite.

The process of mapping can be approached in several ways programmatically. One method is to create a new empty Motion and then apply mapping to this empty Motion in order to build up the new Motion. This can be done on-the-fly so that mappings will accumulate (or overwrite). You can also do this in advance, meaning that you can create a large number of composite Motions for all the combinations you need in advance. You can also apply mapping directly to a source Motion, but because this will destroy some of the mapping for that Motion, I do not suggest it.

This method can be described as at least a two-step process involving the creation of an empty Motion and the actual mapping of that Motion. To create a Motion, you will use the newMotion() function as follows:

```
MyMotion = Scene.newMotion("newMotionname")
```

This will create a new Motion in the 3D Castmember referred to by scene. Before going on, if you check the type of myMotion, you will see that its type is #none:

```
Put myMotion.type
--#none
```

This is because no mapping has been applied to the Motion as of yet. In addition, this means that it is not currently a #Bones Motion. If you try to play this Motion with the Bonesplayer Modifier, it will generate a script error.

The second step necessary for Motion mapping is the actual process of mapping itself. The syntax for Motion mapping is as follows:

```
Scene.Motion("Motionname").map("MotionB", Bone)
```

In this syntax, `Scene.Motion("Motionname")` is the Motion the mapping will be applied to. `MotionB` must be the name of the Motion you want to get data from (and it must be a Motion of type #Bones). Finally, the `Bone` parameter is optional—if you omit this parameter, the Motion will be mapped to the entire skeleton. If you supply the name of a Bone, only that Bone and all its children will receive mapping from the source Motion.

The largest difficulty you may have with the `Bone` parameter is that you need to refer to the Bone by its name. Strangely enough, although you need to refer to the name of the Bone (there's a function for looking up Bone IDs if you know the name), you cannot look up the name of a Bone from its ID alone. This is extremely problematic. The solution is to carefully write down the names of the Bones so that you can refer to them later in Director.

NOTE

Note that if you are working with Motions of different lengths, the composite Motion will be as long as the longest Bone track. Therefore, if a particular Bone runs out of animation data while others are still animating, the Bone without data will stop moving. This can often be a problem if you are trying to loop a short Motion (such as walking) and then composite this with punching.

You should see that the man walks forward and then finishes his punch in a rather unnatural sort of pose. If you are working with combinations of Motions, you can avoid this problem by making sure your Motions are the same length.

Motion Mapping Strategies

Strategies and uses for Motion mapping range from simple to complex. Generally, some of the most simple methods of combining two Motions, such as running and jumping, can be extremely useful, especially if you are trying to build seamless interactive locomotion into your characters.

Other strategies include creating a large number of Motions that you can then join together on-the-fly through mapping. This can be very useful if you are working with the Motions of fingers. You might create several simple

Motions that merely contain positions for the hands. Then, depending on which hand position you want, you could map only the hand positions to the body.

Remember that in the Motion Mapping demonstration, we are simply playing any composite Motion you build. You could use the more advanced queuing features to only play selected areas of a composite Motion. Another possibility is to use Motion blending to your advantage. Imagine that you have three Motions: walking, punching, and a composite of both. You might blend from walking into the composite and then back into walking in order to build a seamless overall movement for a character.

Nonbipedal Bones

It is entirely possible to create skeletal hierarchies that are nonbipedal. That is, you can use Bones to control Models for organisms without arms or legs, such as fish and snakes. In addition, you can create quadrupeds such as cats, dogs, and horses. You might even use Bones systems for plant structures. What's more, you might use deformable Bones to create rope or chain. This is because Bones can deform the geometry of a mesh.

In addition to Bones hierarchies that deform the geometry of a mesh, it is possible to create hierarchies that are only used to translate geometry. That is, the geometry controlled by a Bones hierarchy is not a single Model but rather a group of Models. Those Models are then controlled by an underlying and invisible hierarchy that is more akin to machine or robotic Motion.

In this section, we will be examining two examples of nonbipedal Bones hierarchies. One is an example of nondeformable Bones, and the second is an example of deformable Bones. However, each will have a unique nonbipedal structure. Because we are still working with Motions, the techniques of using the Playlist, Motion blending, and Motion mapping still apply.

NOTE

Note that these examples are intended to show you some alternative methods of working with Bones animation. In addition, although the examples I am showing are rather basic, it is entirely possible to use the advanced features of the Playlist as well as Motion mapping with these methods for Bones Motions.

Nonbipedal, Nondeformable Bones Demonstration

In this example, we will be looking at Bones that are rigid rather than deformable. This means that when the Bones transform, the meshes associated with them will move more like a machine than an organism. To create a rigid Bone system like this, you may need to consult with the specific 3D modeling software you are working with. If you are using 3D Studio MAX, the process is quite approachable.

To create a rigid Bone system in 3D Studio MAX, create the Model that will animate from several meshes. Then, use the standard MAX Bones to create a skeletal structure. Finally, be sure to link each of the meshes to the appropriate Bone. This will force the meshes to collapse into a single Model. The Bones will animate rigidly in 3D Studio MAX as well as in Director. Figure 22.3 is a screenshot from 3D Studio MAX that shows the skeletal hierarchy as well as the meshes for a robotic arm drawn in wireframe.

FIGURE 22.3

A screenshot from 3D Studio MAX that shows the robotic arm and the underlying Bones structure.

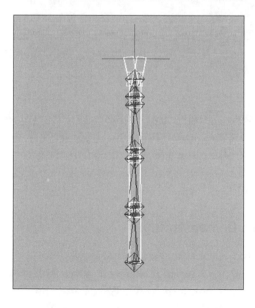

From Figure 22.3, you can see that the hierarchy for this robotic arm is made up of only a few links. In addition, this particular skeleton contains only one branch, so the overall structure is rather simple. If you open the file "Rigid

Hierarchy" on the CD and press Play, you will see this robotic arm. Figure 22.4 is a screenshot from the animation itself. Notice how the robotic arm swivels at its pivot points rather than bends at them.

FIGURE 22.4

A screenshot from Director showing the Rigid Hierarchy example.

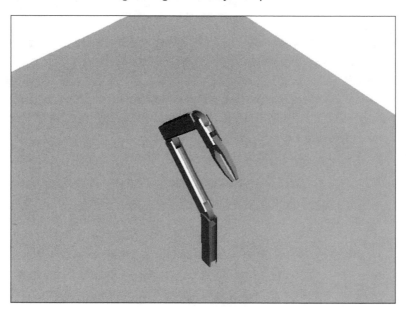

In this example, a simple Bones Motion has been saved with the 3D Castmember. This animation should play continuously, although you may want to try your hand at controlling the speed of the arm's movement with Playlist commands. As you can see from the demonstration, nondeformable bones are actually quite useful for storing complex mechanical animations.

Nonbipedal, Deformable Bones Demonstration

In this example, I have created a skeletal system that does deform the geometry of a Model, but it does not use a bipedal skeleton. This skeletal system was created in 3D Studio MAX with standard MAX Bones and the physique Modifier. If you are working with the physique Modifier in 3D Studio MAX, make sure it is the last Modifier on the stack; otherwise, it will not export to

Director. Figure 22.5 is a screenshot of the mesh with Bones from 3D Studio MAX prior to export.

FIGURE 22.5

A screenshot from 3D Studio MAX that shows the body of a snake and its underlying Bone structure.

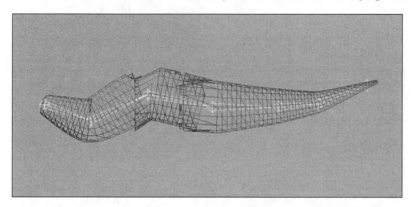

In this figure, it is impossible to see that the Bones and the mesh are linked through the physique Modifier. However, it is possible to see that the mesh is a single mesh and that several Bones control the geometry of that mesh. These Bones were then animated and exported to a W3D file. If you open the file "Deformable Hierarchy" on the CD and press Play, you will be able to see this animation. Figure 22.6 is a screenshot from the Deformable Hierarchy example that you can compare with Figure 22.5. Note the deformation of the geometry in this figure.

Remember that the Bones Motion attached to this Model can be controlled via the Playlist. In addition, you are still able to work with Motion mapping as well as all the other techniques we have discussed in this chapter and the previous chapter, such as Motion blending, cloning, and sub-Motions.

Overall, the past several demonstrations are intended to help you understand the range of possibilities for Bones Motions. If you are interested in learning more about Bones Motions, I suggest you begin looking for a 3D animation package that supports Bones animation export to Director. I mention this because the control of Bones Motions is relatively simple, as you can see from the demonstrations. The creation of the Bones Motions themselves is really the more difficult part.

FIGURE 22.6

A screenshot from the Deformable Hierarchy example in Director.

Summary

The Bonesplayer is a Modifier that is used to control skeletal hierarchies embedded within Models exported from 3D animation software. This Modifier has a wide range of uses because it can work with several types of skeletal hierarchies in addition to deformable and nondeformable structures. The Bonesplayer also has the ability to synthesize Motions as well as play Motions stored in 3D Castmembers.

The fact that Director can work with Bones animation is important. Bones animation can be extremely fluid and aesthetically appealing. In addition, it is a hallmark of 3D character animation as well as facial animation and lip-synching. It is also possible to add lifelike movements to plant structures and add rigid animation to machinery.

In terms of Bones Motions, the wide scope of possibilities available to the Bonesplayer is heavily dependent on your skill with 3D animation software packages. You should also know that we will be examining other methods of controlling Bones with Lingo but without Motions in Chapter 24, "Interactive Animation."

The fact that Director can capitalize on Bones Motions is one of its key strengths. This feature is particularly outstanding because it allows you to integrate elements of 3D animation created in long-standing professional 3D software with Director.

FAQ

I am having trouble making Bones and Keyframe animation look and perform well. What can I do?

Learning to control Bones and Keyframe animation is next to impossible if you do not have a 3D animation package capable of exporting these types of Motions. In addition, even if you do have a 3D animation package capable of exporting Motions, you may have trouble. There are a few areas that can be difficult: First, if you have not animated in 3D before, take a good long look at the 3D software you are working with. Learn how to animate with it before you try to incorporate it with Director. Second, if you already know how to animate, take a good look at the guidelines for exportation in this chapter and the previous chapter. Hierarchies you create in your 3D software may not always export the way you anticipate. Third, the Keyframeplayer and the Bonesplayer are approachable, but their success depends entirely on the Motions you create for them to use.

If you are having trouble with the look of the animation itself, first work on this in your 3D animation software. Finally, once you have working assets, take a look at them in Director. They may not play as smoothly, and you may notice moments when the animation stalls or skips. Most likely you are having trouble with the exportation of Motion from your 3D animation program. Experiment with the animation quality settings for your exporter as well as the sampling interval.

Lower sampling intervals will create large sets of animation data but can help if you are working with fast intricate Motions. High quality settings can often help with instability or jittering of the Bones but can lead to very large W3D files.

Is there a way to make Bones visible in Director?

Unfortunately, no. This is not possible. Bones cannot be rendered.

I hate the fact that I cannot find out the names of Bones, and I have so many Bones in my current project that I cannot feasibly write them all down. Is there anything that can be done?

Yes. Most 3D animation packages are going to have a way to assign a customizable Userdata property for a Model prior to export. This Userdata property is a property list that will be accessible to Director after export. This means you could carefully create a property list containing the names of all the Bones in a Model, saving it with the Model.Userdata property. Then you could access this list in Director. There are still drawbacks to this, but it is a better solution if you are working with a large number of Bones—or if you are working in a team.

Some 3D modeling solutions, such as Shapeshifter3D, will export a list of the Bone information stored within Userdata automatically for you.

Can I rename Bones in Director?

The creation, naming, and renaming of Bones must be done outside of Director. There are no methods to change or modify the hierarchy once inside of Director.

Are there any standards for naming Bones outside of Director?

When you name individual Bones in a hierarchy, make sure each Bone name begins with the name of the root Bone. For example, if the root Bone is named "fred," all its children would be named "fred FOO," where FOO is the name that distinguishes the Bone from the others. Note that no two Bones should be named the same. Most 3D modeling programs will not allow this.

Is there a way to have multiple Bone hierarchies on a single Modelresource?

This is not currently supported in Director. If you are going to have a skeletal hierarchy for a Modelresource, you must only use one.

Is there a way to control Bones without using Motions?

Yes. There is an interesting technique for controlling Bones with transformations that we will discuss in Chapter 24. In that technique, it is possible to control Bones without Motions, but you will still need to access the Bones through the Bonesplayer Modifier.

CHAPTER 23

Controlling Time

In this chapter we will be examining alternative methods for triggering events, controlling time, and manipulating the 3D environment. The techniques we will be discussing in this chapter are intended to broaden your understanding of the possibilities for time control via Lingo. However, I want to stress that the techniques in this chapter are alternatives—you should not go out of your way to use them unless you feel the benefits they offer are correct for your particular project. I want to be extremely clear about this: These techniques are not better or worse than the standard methods of dealing with events and the control of time. I present these techniques in order to widen your coding toolset and offer you choices in areas where it may seem that there are none.

Specifically, we will be examining two techniques: registering for events and building a custom scheduler. We will then apply these techniques to several situations so that you can gain an understanding of their use. Because both these techniques deal with the control of time, they are well suited for the control of animation.

Registering for events is a technique that allows you to associate scripts with specific Models and specific 3D Castmembers. Once associated with a Model, these scripts will wait for special events that are triggered automatically by the Bonesplayer or Keyframeplayer or even by collisions between Models (note, however, that we will be dealing with collisions in Chapter 29, "Collision Detection.")

Building a custom scheduler is a technique that can be as involved as your needs require. The essence of this technique is that we will not rely on the frame rate of the movie but rather update the environment based on changes in time. The advantages to doing this are related to the fact that your projects will run faster on some machines and much slower on others.

Registration Basics

Director is an event-driven environment. Handlers are triggered by events: system events, timeline events, user events, and custom events, to name a few. Handlers can be associated with Sprites and Castmembers. They can also exist within movie scripts or in child objects. Generally though, we think of a handler as a script that must receive a message from an event in order to execute.

Registering an event is a process that relies on the concept of a *callback*, which is a handler that is specified to run when a given event is triggered. This may seem as though it is exactly the same as the normal order of event messaging. That is, an event message is sent to scripts, and those scripts with the particular handler will execute, barring message interference from other scripts. The difference is that generally event messages are sent to event handlers. With callbacks, event messages are sent to custom handlers. In addition, callbacks send information about the system in the form of arguments attached to the event message to the custom handler.

Several commands are associated with the registration of events, and we will be working with these commands in the next several demonstrations. These commands are designed to work specifically with 3D Castmembers, and they will not function with others. Table 23.1 details the four commands used for registering events.

TABLE 23.1   Event Registration Commands

Command	Purpose
Registerscript()	Registers an event with a Node
Registerforevent()	Registers an event with a 3D Castmember
Sendevent()	Sends a custom message to a 3D Castmember (used to trigger custom events)
Unregisterallevents()	Removes all registered events from a 3D Castmember and its Nodes

Table 23.1 lists the commands we will be using to work with event registration, but it does not list the events we will be working with. We will be dealing with the registration of three types of events: timeMS, animationstarted, and animationended. In addition to these three predefined events, we will also examine how to create and trigger a custom event.

Basic Event Registration Demonstration

In this example, we will be examining the use of a simple persistent event to rotate a box. We will be working with the registerscript() command and the timeMS event to trigger a simple callback handler to rotate the box. First, open the file named "Simple Box Rotation" on the CD and press Play. You should see a green box in the center of the Stage that slowly rotates about its center.

This rotation is made possible via the timeMS event, which is essentially an event that waits a certain amount of time before triggering its callback. This event can be designed to persist, triggering its callback at a fixed frequency. It can also be set to delay before beginning its triggering or to only trigger a certain number of times. The syntax for registering the timeMS event with the registerscript command is as follows:

```
N.registerscript(#timeMS, #handlername, scriptNum, delay, \
period, repetitions)
```

In this example, N is a reference to a Node in a 3D Castmember, and #handlername is the name of the handler you want associated with this event. Also, scriptNum is the number of a script or a reference to a script object that the handler exists in. You can specify a value of 0, which will associate the first handler named handlername within a movie script.

The delay value is the number of milliseconds that should elapse before the first timeMS event is triggered. The period is the number of milliseconds that should elapse between all succeeding timeMS events. Finally, the repetitions parameter is the number of times the timeMS event should be generated. If you specify a value of 0 for the repetitions parameter, the timeMS event will trigger persistently.

In this example, the timeMS event is registered as a persistent event to occur every 41 milliseconds. The timeMS event is set to call a handler whose purpose is rotating the green box on the Stage. Therefore, the timeMS event is registered to persistently rotate the box. Note the syntax for this registration, which occurs in the initialization script for the movie:

```
mybox.registerscript(#timeMS, #rotatescript, 0, 0, 41, 0)
```

In this example, mybox is a reference to the first Node in the 3D Castmember: the Model of the box. You can see that the timeMS event is registered to trigger a handler named rotatescript from a movie script. In addition, the timeMS event should trigger immediately and then persist triggering every 41 milliseconds. The rotatescript handler itself is rather simple:

```
on rotatescript
  scene.model[1].rotate(1,1,0)
end
```

As you can see, this handler is quite basic; however, it's the method we use to call the handler that's important. There are some unfortunate difficulties you must know about when registering events this way. First, it is not possible to change the period of the timeMS event. Second, you may notice that although the event is registered with the scene.model[1] Node, the Node is still referenced directly in the handler. This is because the timeMS event does not return information concerning which Node it is attached to. Despite these discrepancies, you can still use methods of controlling timeMS to create a variety of effects.

NOTE

Although 42 milliseconds may seem like a random choice, it is, in fact, chosen quite specifically. Changing the rotation of the box every 42 milliseconds will, in effect, change the rotation 24 times per second. Therefore, an update of 42 milliseconds is equivalent to a rotation occurring at 24 frames per second (fps).

Two custom handlers can be found in a script named "Time Utilities" in the Simple Box Rotation movie. These two custom handlers—MSPF() and FPS()—convert frames per second into milliseconds per frame, and vice versa.

Each of these handlers requires a single argument. In the case of MSPF(), you supply a frame rate in frames per second. MSPF() will return the number of milliseconds that pass between each frame. In the case of FPS(), you supply a number of milliseconds, and FPS() will return the frame rate that should occur if you were to call an event with that period.

Nonpersistent Event Registration

In this example, we will be using the timeMS event to register a handler with a fixed period, but with a set number of repetitions. The reason for this is to create a rotating box that slowly grinds to a halt during rotation. Open the file named "Non-Persistent Rotation" on the CD and press Play. In the lower-right corner of the Stage is a button labeled "go." Each time you click this button, the box will begin its cycle of rotation and will eventually slow to a stop.

This script relies on two aspects of timeMS events. First, when registering for the rotation handler, rather than registering for a persistent event, we will specify a set number of repetitions. In this way, it is possible to trigger the rotation script a set number of times. The second aspect of timeMS events we will be using involves the callback arguments. Depending on the type of event you have registered, the event will send arguments along with the event message to the registered handler. In the case of timeMS, six arguments are passed to the registered handler. These six arguments and their purposes are listed in Table 23.2.

TABLE 23.2 TimeMS Event Callback Arguments

Argument	Purpose
Script Reference	Returns a reference to the registered handler.
Type	This is the type of registered event and will always be 0.
Delta	The number of milliseconds since the last timeMS event.
Time	The number of milliseconds since the first timeMS event.
Duration	The total number of milliseconds between registerforevent() and the last timeMS event (in case the timeMS event is persistent, this value is always 0).
SystemTime	The number of milliseconds since the Director movie started.

In order to make the rotation of the box slow down, we will use the time argument to change the amount of rotation over time. By decreasing the amount of rotation as the time increases, we cause the box to appear to slow down. Listing 23.1 shows two custom handlers: rotatescript() and loadscript(). When called, loadscript() sets up a timeMS event that will drive the execution of rotatescript().

LISTING 23.1   `Rotatescript()` and `Loadscript()` **Custom Handlers**

```
1: on rotatescript ref, type, delta, time, duration, systemtime
2:   global amount
3:   amount = amount - time / float(100)
4:   amount = amount * .001
5:   scene.model[1].rotate(aamount,aamount,0)
6: End
7:
8: on loadscript
9:   scene.unregisterallevents()
10:   global amount
11:   amount = 1000
12:   scene.model[1].registerscript(#timeMS, #rotatescript,\
      1, 110, 10, 110)
13: end
```

As you can see in Listing 23.1, the period of rotation remains the same over time, but the amount of rotation changes based on the amount of time that has passed. This has the overall effect of slowing the rotation of the box.

NOTE

> Another possibility for working with nonpersistent events is to create a nonrepeating event—that is, an event that is only triggered once but with some amount of delay. You can then trap the `delay` argument that is passed to the registered handler from the event. Then, from within the registered handler, you can register yet another `timeMS` event but change the delay time. This type of setup allows you to create what appears to be a persistent event with a changing period.

This demonstration capitalizes on the fact that the `timeMS` event will trigger a certain amount of times and then it will be released from memory. As we continue, we will be looking at events that prolong their influence on the environment by registering even more events to control time.

Fireworks

In this example, we will be examining how to integrate nonrepeating `timeMS` events and parent/child scripts to create an interactive fireworks demonstration. Open the file named "Fireworks" on the CD and press Play. Near the lower-right corner of the Stage is a button labeled "go." Each time you click this button, a firework will be launched with random speed and color. Note that it is possible to launch as many fireworks as you can click—the faster you click, the more fireworks that explode concurrently.

Each time you click the go button, a new instance of the Fireworks parent/child script is created. This script handles everything about the fireworks, including creation, motion, explosion, and removal from the environment. Listing 23.2 explains the code used to create this effect.

LISTING 23.2 Fireworks Parent/Child Script

```
 1: -- reference to the firework model
 2: property pObj
 3: -- reference to the explosion modelresource
 4: property pExpRes
 5: -- name of the firework
 6: property pName
 7: -- determines when firework will explode
 8: property pcount
 9: -- determines the speed of the firework
10: property pspeed
11:
12: global scene
13:
14: on new(me)
15:    -- use the milliseconds to generate a
16:    -- unique name for the firework
17:    num = the milliseconds
18:    pName = "firework" & num
19:
20:    -- I created a list of four colors that I choose
21:    -- from to determine the colors of the fireworks
22:    cList = [rgb(255,255,0), rgb(255,0,0), rgb(200,255,0),\
           rgb(250,250,250)]
23:
24:    -- choose the end color
25:    ecolor = cList[random(4)]
26:    -- choose the begin color
27:    bcolor = cList[random(4)]
28:
29:    -- set up the basic firework modelresource
30:    res = scene.newmodelresource(pname & "res", #particle)
31:    res.lifetime = 40
32:    res.emitter.maxspeed = 210
33:    res.emitter.direction = vector(0,-1,0)
34:    res.emitter.angle = 10
35:    res.sizerange.start = .5
```

LISTING 23.2 Continued

```
36:   res.sizerange.end = 0
37:   res.colorrange.start = bcolor
38:   res.colorrange.end = ecolor
39:
40:   -- create a new Model based on the firework modelresource
41:   pObj = scene.newmodel(pname, res)
42:
43:   -- create a second Modelresource and
44:   -- set it up to be an explosion
45:   pExpRes = scene.newmodelresource(pname & "explosion", #particle)
46:   pExpRes.lifetime = 1500
47:   pExpRes.emitter.maxspeed = 60
48:   pExpRes.emitter.minspeed = 50
49:   pExpRes.sizerange.start = 5
50:   pExpRes.sizerange.end = 0
51:   pExpRes.blendrange.start = 30
52:   pExpRes.blendrange.end = 100
53:   pExpRes.emitter.mode = #burst
54:   pExpRes.emitter.loop = false
55:   pexpres.gravity = vector(0,-.5,0)
56:   pexpres.colorrange.start = bcolor
57:   pexpres.colorrange.end = ecolor
58:   pexpres.drag = 1
59:
60:   -- determine the speed of the firework
61:   pspeed = .6 + random(10) / float(10)
62:   --set the initial value for pcount
63:   pcount = 0
64:
65:   -- determine the initial position of the firework
66:   pObj.translate(random(-40,40),-70,0)
67:   -- register the firescript event to repeat 100 times
68:   pObj.registerscript(#timeMS, #firescript, me, 0, 10, 100)
69:   return me
70: end
71:
72: on firescript(me)
73:   -- the purpose of the firescript event is
74:   -- to move the firework along the positive Y axis
75:   -- in addition, we will be checking to see how many
76:   -- times the firescript event has been called for an
77:   -- individual firework.
78:   -- if this is the last time (the hundredth) that the firescript
79:   -- will be called, then we will change the modelresource to the
80:   -- explosion and then register the cleanup event to occur
81:   -- after the explosion is done
82:
```

LISTING 23.2   Continued

```
83:    pcount = pcount + 1
84:
85:    if pcount = 100 then
86:      pObj.resource = pExpRes
87:      pObj.registerscript(#timeMS, #cleanup, me, 1500,0, 1)
88:    end if
89:
90:    pObj.translate(0,pspeed,0)
91: end
92:
93: on cleanup(me)
94:    -- delete all modelresources associated with this firework
95:    -- and delete the model for this firework as well
96:    scene.deletemodelresource(pName & "res")
97:    scene.deletemodelresource(pName & "explosion")
98:    scene.deletemodel(pName)
99: end
```

Note that the core of this parent/child script is driven by a timeMS event regis-tered to repeat 100 times. This initial timeMS event drives the motion of the firework as well as determines when to explode the firework. Once it has been determined that the firework should explode, a second timeMS event is regis-tered. This timeMS event waits until the firework is done exploding and then deletes all the Modelresources and the Model used by the parent/child script. In essence, this script is a compact set of instructions that handles all aspects of the lifetime of a given firework.

Motion-Based Events

In addition to the timeMS event, two events detect the beginning and ending of Motions played via the Keyframeplayer and Bonesplayer Modifiers. The animationstarted and animationended events occur whenever any Motion begins or ends. The animationstarted and animationended events do not require as elaborate an initialization as the timeMS event. In fact, the syntax for registering these events is as follows:

```
N.registerscript(#event, #handlername, scriptnum)
```

You can see that the syntax is extremely similar to registering the timeMS event, but you will not specify any arguments for time or period. This is important: `animationstarted` and `animationended` events persistently wait for any Motion to begin or end. Once one of these events is triggered, it calls the specified handler and sends it three custom arguments, as noted in Table 23.3.

TABLE 23.3   `Animationstarted` and `Animationended` Arguments

Argument	Purpose
Eventname	Specifies whether the event that triggered the script is `animationstarted` or `animationended`
Motion	Specifies which Motion started or stopped
Time	Specifies the current time of the Motion

These arguments allow you to identify which Motion either started or ended and what its current time is. This information can be very useful because the `animationstarted` and `animationended` events will send reports on every Motion that starts and stops.

NOTE

When you're working with looped animation, the `animationstarted` event will only be triggered for the first Motion in the loop. In addition, if you are working with Motion blending, the `animationstarted` and `animationended` events may trigger at the time when blending begins and ends rather than at the absolute beginning of the Motion.

Simple Animation Detection

In this demonstration, we will be using the `animationstarted` and `animationended` events to control the playback of sounds so that they correspond to the animation occurring on the Stage. On the CD is a file named "Basic Animation Events." Open this file and press Play. In the lower-right corner of the Stage is a button labeled "go." If you click this button, the character in the middle of the Stage will begin to animate.

More importantly, two events are registered during the initialization of this movie, as you can see in this excerpt from the initialization script:

```
obj = scene.model[1]
obj.registerscript(#animationstarted, #startsound, 0)
obj.registerscript(#animationended, #endsound, 0)
```

Note that I have registered Model[1] for two events: animationstarted and
animationended. Whenever any Bonesplayer or Keyframeplayer animation
starts or stops on Model[1], the startsound or endsound handler will be called,
respectively. These two rather simple handlers are shown in the following
code:

```
on startsound  puppetsound(1, "drumroll")
end

on endsound
  puppetsound(1, "success")
end
```

As you watch this particular demonstration, note that it is functioning as
intended: The drum roll begins as the character starts his back flip and then
the cymbal crashes after he is done. However, if you notice the timing on the
final cymbal crash in correlation with the end of the animation, you realize
that the cymbal crash is delivered a bit late. This is because the animationended
event occurs after the Motion has actually stopped, not when the major part of
the Motion has stopped.

The demonstration illustrates the fact that you can trigger events based on the
beginning and ending of Motion playback. In this case, we have triggered
sounds, but we could have just as easily triggered visual changes to the environment.

Enhanced Animation Detection

In this example, we will be using the animationstarted event in conjunction
with the timeMS event. Remember from the previous demonstration that when
the animated character lands, the congratulatory sound associated with his
landing is delivered a bit late. This is because the congratulatory sound is triggered from the animationended event, which is essentially too late.

Rather than wait for the animationended event, we will use our knowledge of
the length of the Motion. Because we can determine that the duration of the
back-flip Motion is roughly 3,000 milliseconds, it is possible to use the animationstarted event to register a delayed single-use timeMS event. This delayed
event will trigger before 3,000 milliseconds so that the congratulatory sound
will play right as the character is landing rather than afterward.

Open the file named "Enhanced Animation Events" on the CD and press Play. Again, a button labeled "go" appears in the lower-right corner of the Stage. Click this button to make the character do a back flip. In this example, the cymbal crash is delivered as the character lands on the ground and before the Motion actually stops.

Only two elements in this demonstration have changed. First, we do not register for an animationended event but rather only the animationstarted event, as in the last demo. However, the startsound handler that is registered with the animationstarted event has been modified as shown here:

```
1: on startsound
2:   puppetsound(1, "drumroll")
3:   obj = scene.model[1]
4:   obj.registerscript(#timeMS, #endsound, 0, 2300, 0, 1)
5: end
```

Notice that in this handler we are registering a timeMS event. The important part is that the last three parameters in the registerscript call in line 4: 2300, 0, 1. In this case, 2300 is the delay time in milliseconds that the timeMS event will wait to trigger the first time. Looking at the other two parameters, you see that I have not set a period and that the timeMS event is only scheduled to trigger once. Essentially, you can think of this as an event with a "fuse." You set the event to trigger once some time after you have set the event.

NOTE

You might also use this technique to trigger several repeating timeMS events. For example, imagine that you have a character and a Motion that enables it to walk. If you know that the character's feet will touch the ground every 30 milliseconds, you could use the animationstarted event to trigger several timeMS events, which would in turn play the sound of footfalls.

Custom Events

In addition to registering handlers with the events that are built in to Director, it is possible to specify your own custom events. When working with custom events, you will need to use the sendevent() command to trigger them. One reason you might decide to use a custom event is in order to consolidate other handlers under a single event.

One issue you need to be aware of is that when you create custom events you want to register, you need to register these events with the `registerforevent()` command. It is not possible to trigger custom events that are attached to Nodes; therefore, you should not create custom events with the `registerscript()` command because you will not be able to trigger them.

The only major difference between using `registerforevent()` and `registerscript()` is that when you use `registerforevent()`, the target of the event is a 3D Castmember rather than a Node in a 3D Castmember. This is the second difficulty of working with custom registered events. Because you cannot associate a custom event directly with a Node, the events you register this way will most likely affect the environment in more of a global way. It is possible to pass as many custom parameters along with the custom event as you like, but this is awkward, and we will be looking into alternatives to this method rather shortly. For now, we will examine a small custom event used to trigger a global change in a 3D Castmember.

NOTE

Note that in addition to the #timeMS, #animationstarted, #animationended, and custom events, the #collidewith and #collideany events will be used with collision detection, which is a process of determining when two Models intersect. For animating Models, this process is useful for a variety of reasons and, as such, has a wide variety of techniques associated with it. You can find more information about collision detection in Chapter 29, which is dedicated to this topic.

Basic Custom Events

In this demonstration, the focus is to show that you can create a simple handler that is called using the `sendevent()` command. On the CD is a file named "Custom Event." Open this file and press Play. In the middle of the Stage you should see several spheres slowly moving around the center of the environment. In the lower-right corner of the Stage is a button labeled "toggle debug mode." Clicking this button will set the `debug` property for all the Models to `true`. When you toggle debug mode on for all the Models, you are able to see that many of the Models are rotating about their axes as well as around the center of the environment.

NOTE

> The debug property must be set for each Model in the scene, but in this example, that action has been consolidated into a single event. This may seem strange though—why wouldn't we just put the code to toggle debug mode for all the spheres in the behavior attached to the button? Here's one reason: What if you are building a project where there is no button? What I mean by this is that you may be working on projects where there are several 3D Castmembers instanced on the Stage at one time. You can use registered events to send messages between two Castmembers. Therefore, perhaps actions you take on one 3D Castmember will affect the environment of a second or third 3D Castmember.

The functionality of the toggle debug mode button is broken into three areas of the scripts for this movie. First, in the initialization script, we need to register the debugtoggle handler to listen for the custom event named showaxis-toggle, as follows:

```
scene.registerforevent(#showaxisToggle, #debugtoggle, 0)
```

Of course, in this demonstration, the debugtoggle handler itself is rather important because it does the majority of the work, as you can see here:

```
 1: on debugtoggle
 2:   toggle = scene.model[1].debug
 3:   if toggle = 1 then
 4:     toggle = 0
 5:   else
 6:     toggle = 1
 7:   end if
 8:
 9:   repeat with x = 1 to scene.model.count
10:     scene.model[x].debug = toggle
11:   end repeat
12: end
```

The last part of this system is dependent on the behavior attached to the toggle debug mode button. This behavior actually triggers the showaxistoggle event. Remember that showaxistoggle is our custom event that cannot be triggered without a sendevent() message to the 3D Castmember. Here's the code to send a `showaxistoggle` event to the 3D Castmember when the toggle debug mode button is clicked:

```
on mousedown
  global scene
  scene.sendevent(#showaxistoggle)
end
```

It is very important that you understand that custom events registered with a 3D Castmember using `registerforevent()` cannot be triggered with any of the other methods available for sending messages in Lingo. Because of this, it is often difficult to build systems that include custom events registered with the 3D Castmember. Note that the concept of registering an event is extremely strong, but the implementation of that concept through the `registerforevent()` command has some difficulties. Before beginning the next section, we'll address the inherent difficulties associated with working with registered events.

Other than the facts that you can only register 3D Castmembers for events and that you must use the `sendevent()` command to trigger custom events, the weakest area of this particular part of the system is the process for "unregistering" events. When unregistering events, you can only use the `unregisterallevents()` function. Because this function will indiscriminately unregister every event currently registered, the management of your events is turned into a difficult chore.

In addition, no inherent list of registered events exists that you can refer to in order to track which Nodes or Castmembers have events tied to them. Because you can easily register several copies to a single Node or Castmember, you may run into situations where a single Node receives several copies of the same events—and it will trigger its handler every single time. This difficulty is then compounded by the fact that if you are in this situation, you will need to use `unregisterallevents()` in order to begin solving the problem. However, as I have stated, `unregisterallevents()` is indiscriminate in its method of removing events.

One workaround for these two problems is to maintain a linear list of your own that contains all the Nodes and the events registered to them. You would need to make sure that you remove registered events from the list that are not persistent and that have expired. In addition, when you need to unregister several events, but not all of them, you could quickly unregister all the events and then add the events that you would like to remain registered to the appropriate Nodes and Castmembers.

Overall, though, as you begin requiring detailed management of your events, the `registerforevents()` system begins looking like a weak method of implementation. I would suggest to continue reading through the second half of the chapter, where I will describe an alternative method of building a custom event structure with management capabilities. After you have reviewed both sections, it will be easier to understand the scope of the issues in custom event management, and you will be able to make choices about which system is correct for your project.

Building a Custom Scheduler

Building a custom scheduler is a dramatic approach to your projects that you should know about. However, you should also consider that if you are going to use a custom scheduler, you are going to need to create much of your code with parent/child scripts. In this section, we will slowly incorporate parent/child scripts as we work through several demonstrations.

But, first, what is a custom scheduler, and why would you want to use one? A custom scheduler is one of the final steps away from using the Score and Playback Head for controlling the speed of playback for your movies. A custom scheduler attempts to take as much control of timing away from the Playback Head and allows you to control time directly with Lingo.

There are many reasons why you might decide to develop your project using a custom scheduler. One of the most relevant reasons is to regulate the speed of playback on both very fast and very slow machines without needing to rewrite your projects. Another reason arises when you're working with elaborate custom animation, ranging from behavioral animation to complex AI routines. The idea is that you would want to separate the frame rate for your AI from the frame rate for redrawing the Stage. This type of approach allows you to stratify the importance of certain routines with increased or decreased regularity.

Unfortunately, the process of registering events that's covered in the first half of this chapter is not well suited to creating a custom scheduler. Although there are many positive benefits to the strategies for registering events, there are severe limitations as well. In this section, we will be examining a different approach toward registering custom events that is much more robust. The functionality that we will be working with will still rely on the notion of callbacks, but rather than using registered events, we will be using timeout objects.

Timeout Objects

This strategy relies on timeout objects, and it is therefore important that you understand what these are. A *timeout object* is a code object that is created with Lingo. Similar to the timeMS event, you register a script with a timeout object and specify a period of execution and whether the timeout object is persistent. However, timeout objects have many advantages. First, they are not associated with any Castmembers or Sprites at all—they exist independently from the Score. This makes them powerful because you can use them with 3D or 2D Sprites or without any Sprites at all.

Second, it is possible to change various aspects of a timeout object after it has been created, such as what handler should be called, what the period of execution is, and whether the timeout object is persistent. Perhaps most important is the fact that when you create a timeout object, it is automatically "registered" with a system-level list known as the *timeoutlist*. This list contains an object reference to every single timeout object currently registered with the movie. In addition to this information, you can remove individual timeout objects without destroying the other timeout objects currently running.

These features make timeout objects the obvious choice when building a custom scheduler, because you need as much control over time as possible in order to be successful. In this section, we will be looking at several demonstrations that build on one another so that you can become accustomed to the methodology of working with a custom scheduler.

How to Create and Manage Timeout Objects

Before we look at our first scheduler, it is important that you understand how to create a timeout object in addition to how you can control the various aspects of a timeout object. The primary task of creating a new timeout object is accomplished via the `new()` command using the following syntax:

```
Timeout("TimeoutName").new(period, #handlername, scriptref)
```

In this syntax, `TimeoutName` is the actual name of the timeout you will use later to refer to the timeout object and modify its properties. The `period` is the number of milliseconds that should elapse between timeouts. The `handlername` is the name of the handler that will be called when the timeout is triggered, and the `scriptref` is used if you need to specify which script the handler exists in. If the handler is in the same script, you will use the keyword `me`.

Once a timeout object has been created, it is automatically added to the time-outlist, which is a system property. This linear list can be accessed from any handler and contains all timeout object references in the movie. You can use references to timeout objects to access the variety of properties of timeout objects, as listed in Table 23.4.

TABLE 23.4   Timeout Object Properties

Property	Purpose
Name	Name of the timeout object.
Period	Speed in milliseconds between timeouts generated by the timeout object. When a timeout is generated, the `timeouthandler` will be triggered.
Persistent	A Boolean that determines whether the timeout object will repeat. The default for this property is `true`.
Timeouthandler	The name of the handler that is triggered by the timeout object.
Target	The script or Script object that contains the handler stored in the `timeouthandler` property.
Time	The system time in milliseconds of the next timeout for this timeout object.

One of the marked strengths of the timeout object is the fact that you can get and set the value of the `period`, `persistent`, `timeouthandler`, and `target` properties. This means that you can change the speed of a timeout object and turn the timeout object on and off repeatedly. In addition, you can change the handler that is triggered by a given timeout. Beyond that is the `target` property—with this property, you can actually change the location of the handler. For example, imagine that you have two parent/child scripts with similar handlers. You could change the timeout so that it not only uses a different handler but also uses a different handler in a different parent/child script.

When you begin working with these timeout object properties, you will need to access them with dot syntax. An example of this syntax in terms of a timeout object is as follows:

```
TimeoutObjectReference.property
```

Note that in this syntax, the `timeoutobject` reference can be any of the following:

- `Timeout("timeoutname")`
- `Timeoutlist[x]`
- A variable storing a reference to the timeout object

This wide variety of methods for controlling and accessing the properties of timeout objects is powerful. Timeout objects themselves are a well-designed aspect of Director's capabilities. They can be easily controlled as well as incorporated into a variety of strategies without you needing to build code to circumvent limitations (because they essentially do not need any workarounds).

NOTE

Also, note that the `time` property is the absolute system time for the next timeout for the timeout object. This means that it reports the time in terms of the movie's execution. For instance, imagine that a movie has been playing for 4,000 milliseconds and the timeout is scheduled to trigger in 300 milliseconds. The value of the `time` property would be 4,300 milliseconds, alerting you to the absolute time (relative to the execution of the movie) when the timeout will trigger next.

In addition to the `timeout()` function, there's a single timeout object function called `forget()` that allows you to actually destroy a timeout object. It also automatically removes the timeout from the timeoutlist. Although it is possible to modify the timeoutlist with standard list commands, I suggest using `forget()` instead if you are only destroying selective timeout objects. If you are going to destroy all the timeout objects in a movie, you can use the following line of code:

```
The timeoutlist = []
```

Finally, when you're working with timeout objects, realize that they persist beyond the life of a movie. This means that if you are working in the authoring environment, you will need to specifically destroy the timeouts that you have created in a movie when the movie stops. The easiest way to do this is to include the following handler with your movie:

```
on stopmovie
  the timeoutlist = []
end
```

Now that we have examined the basics of timeout objects, we will look at four examples of how to use them to build a custom scheduler. These four examples build on each other, so I highly recommend that you look at them in the order presented, especially if you are unclear about the implications of timeout objects.

Simple Scheduler

In this first example, we will be implementing a simple timeout object in order to combat a frequent problem with developing a project for a variety of delivery machines. One of the key problems that affects developers is that user machines may be much slower or faster than the development machine. Either of these can ruin the look of a project; projects that run too fast are just as bad as those that run too slow. What's required is some method of maintaining an even frame rate, regardless of the speed of the machine.

The difficulty with finding a solution to this problem is that the Score is typically driven by `exitframe()` handlers, which are in turn driven by the Playback Head. The speed of the Playback Head is driven by the frame rate that you have specified for the movie (or through `puppettempo`) or the timer channel on the Score. However, the frame rate that you specify is not necessarily the frame rate that will play. Even with the movie option to lock frame rate duration, you may find that working with a frame-based time system is just not efficient.

With timeout objects, we can build a system that largely avoids the use of the Playback Head to drive time in the movie. The basic setup for this system can be explained as follows: If we lower the frame rate of the movie to 1, the movie will only update once per second. Then we can create a timeout object that is scheduled to repeat at a certain interval based on `time`. This timeout object will trigger an event that manually updates the environment with the `updatestage` command.

NOTE

One strength of this system is that the `updatestage` command also generates a `stepframe` event. This means that if you are working with parent/child scripts and you would like them to receive an `exitframe`-like event, you can register them with the actorlist so that they will receive the comparable `stepframe` event.

In this method, the apparent "frame rate" of the movie is controlled via the change in time, specifically in milliseconds, rather than based on the frame rate property of the movie. This is important because on a very fast machine, the movie will only update when it is supposed to, based on `time`. On a slightly slower machine, some of the events may be skipped, but on much slower machines you will need to make sure you use additional optimization techniques, such as LOD. Beyond that, you must understand that there will be a minimum limitation to your projects: Real-time 3D will not be viable on every machine. If you can determine how slow of a machine will adequately run your project, you can alert users before they start.

Open the file named "Basic Scheduler" on the CD and press Play. You should see a semitransparent box that spins in the center of the Stage. You have seen examples in this book of spinning cubes before, but in this case we are using a timeout object to drive the Score. First, look at the Score itself, as illustrated in Figure 23.1.

FIGURE 23.1

Note how the timer channel is used to set the framerate to 999 at the beginning of the Score and then to 1 when the Playback Head reaches the main section of the movie.

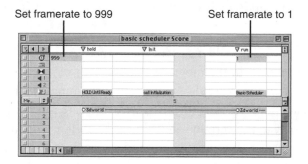

Note how in the timer channel of the score, the movie begins at 999 frames per second, but when the Playback Head arrives at the actual "run" segment of the movie, the frame rate is reduced to 1. The loop event that is attached to the frame labeled "run" contains three handlers. The first, an `exitframe()` handler, ensures that the Playback Head will remain on this frame. Even though the `exitframe` event will only be repeating once per second, this is good enough to keep the Playback Head in place.

The second part of the script is the `beginsprite()` handler. This handler will only be run once, when the Playback Head enters the frame. This `beginsprite()` handler creates a timeout object that will trigger every 41 milliseconds. This timeout object calls the third handler in this script: the `autorotate()` custom handler. This handler actually rotates the box and updates the Stage. Listing 23.3 is the actual code used to accomplish this effect.

LISTING 23.3   Basic Scheduler Script

```
 1: on exitFrame me
 2:   go the frame
 3: end
 4:
 5: on beginsprite me
 6:   --create the timeout object
 7:   timeout("basic_scheduler").new(41, #autorotate, me)
 8: end
 9:
10: on autorotate
```

LISTING 23.3   Continued

```
11:   global scene
12:   scene.model[1].rotate(3,3,0)
13:   updatestage
14: end
```

In a simple scheduler like this, all the scheduling events are placed in the same handler—in this case, autorotate(). This handler takes care of both the Model rotation as well as updating the Stage.

Enhanced Scheduler

The last example is good enough to explain the process of using a timeout object to drive a project, but it lacks finesse. Combining the rotation of the Model and the drawing of the environment within the same script does not take advantage of what can be done with a scheduler. Remember that this technique is good for regulating the timing of projects on many machines.

Part of the reason for this is that one of the slowest events in the system is the update of the Stage. Most importantly, with timeout objects, we can separate the update of the Stage from the update of modification of elements in the environment. This is not a statement to be taken lightly. With multiple timeout objects, we can create an environment that effectively has multiple timelines.

Open the file named "Enhanced Scheduler" on the CD and press Play. In this example, it is possible to control the update of the Stage and the speed at which the Model rotates separately. Note that you are not controlling the amount of rotation per update but rather the amount of times that rotation occurs. Figure 23.2 shows the two sliders that allow you to control the speed of these two separate timeout objects separately. Note that the update speed for the two timeout objects is in milliseconds and in TPS (the number of timeouts that will be triggered within one second).

This demonstration highlights several strengths of using timeout objects. First, note that we can change the period of an existing timeout object while it is running. Not to mention that it is possible to single out a timeout object. Both of these effects are possible with registered events, but the amount of work you would need to do to accomplish the same technique is not worth it.

FIGURE 23.2

A screenshot from the Enhanced Scheduler demonstration.

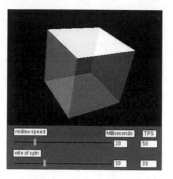

NOTE

In this demonstration, I have labeled the number of timeouts that will be triggered within one second as the *TPS*. You might just as easily think of this number as the apparent frames per second (fps) for a given timeline.

In Listing 23.4, you can see that I have consolidated all of the scripts required for building the enhanced scheduler within the initialization script for the movie.

LISTING 23.4   Enhanced Scheduler Initialization Script

```
 1: global scene
 2:
 3: on initialize
 4:    -- basic scene initialization
 5:    clearworld(scene)
 6:    obj = createbox("mybox", 80,80,80, rgb(10,20,190))
 7:    obj.shader.blend = 80
 8:    obj.visibility = #both
 9:    obj.shader.specular = rgb(0,0,0)
10:
11:    -- create the main Timeout that handles the
12:    -- update of the stage.
13:    timeout("drawspeed").new(41, #masterupdate)
14:
15:    -- create a second Timeout that handles the
16:    -- rotation of the box.
```

LISTING 23.4   Continued

```
17:    timeout("autorotate").new(12, #autorotate)
18: end
19:
20: on stopmovie
21:    the timeoutlist = []
22: end
23:
24: on masterupdate
25:    updatestage()
26: end
27:
28: on autorotate
29:    global scene
30:    scene.model[1].rotate(1,1,0)
31: end
```

As you work with this demonstration, I will suggest trying a few different settings for the speed of the timeout objects. Try setting drawspeed faster, slower,
and the same as the speed of rotation. Note that the speed of rotation does
not seem to change, although the smoothness of animation will become
"chunkier" as your frame rate decreases. However, the box still rotates the
same amount. Now, choose some median frame rate for the drawspeed timeout
object, such as 30 fps. Set the speed of rotation faster, slower, and the same.
You can see that certain settings are just impossible.

Depending on your machine, you will begin to see a point where it is difficult
to tell whether the rotation is actually speeding up. Around 100 fps and above,
I cannot really tell a difference. However, this is all right because persistence
of vision occurs at 8 fps. Animation is a process of showing a viewer an
ordered set of images at a given speed. Game developers often speak of
extremely high frame rates, such as 60 to 90 fps, as the target for their games.
This sort of range is not a realistic goal for Director, although many machines
can and do achieve these rates.

I suggest taking a look at other standard frame rates that are used for smooth
motion. As I have said, 8 frames per second is the recognized standard for
persistence of vision, but that is admittedly too slow. When drawing traditional animation, I will often animate at 12 fps. Silent films were projected at
a variety of speeds, ranging from 14 to 18 fps (although this had much to
do with the speed that the projectionist cranked the film). Modern film is

generally projected at 24 fps, and video runs at 29.97 fps (sometimes more easily referred to as 30 fps). IMAX films run at around 70 fps. The point is that the faster you play the frames, the smoother the motion, accepting that you have enough frames to show. With a computer simulation, we can show as many frames as we want hemmed by the speed of the target machine.

The point is this: If 18 to 30 fps is good enough for film and video, this standard should be sufficient for your Director projects. Shaving time off of the update of the project can help you use that time for other reasons, such as rotating the box, or hopefully, more complex operations. The concept is that your job during the design and development stages of your project is to decide which aspects of the project are more important than others. You cannot have all your code running at all times, so with timeout objects you can schedule important processes to update faster and less important processes to update slower.

Scheduler Management

In this next demonstration, we will be creating a management system for multiple timeout objects that builds on your understanding of a custom scheduler. When I speak of a management system, that system does not need to be extremely complicated, nor does it need to be universal. Most likely, as you begin building systems to manage your schedulers, you will build management services based on the requirements of a given project, although it is perfectly feasible that you might build an API to handle these tasks.

Let's begin by opening the file named "Scheduler Management" on the CD and press Play. This movie may take a moment or so to initialize because it needs to clone a variety of Modelresources before the main section of the movie can begin. In addition to the main focus of this example, which is scheduler management, in this particular demonstration I am also showing you a technique for quickly animating a Model's geometry using multiple Modelresources.

NOTE

As you know, it is not possible to export animation from 3D animation packages on the geometry of the Models. However, with most 3D animation packages, it is possible to take snapshots of a Model, thus creating multiple versions of the geometry. These multiple Modelresources can then be swapped out, similar to how you might create a flipbook-style animation. The difficulty with this technique is that it can create some rather large file sizes, so I suggest that you use it with caution. Note that the speed of changing from one Modelresource to another is rather quick, so the challenge of this technique truly is dependent on the size of the file.

While the movie is playing, you can click any of the Models in the scene to trigger a rippling effect. This ripple affects the Model at the geometry level, but the geometry is merely swapped out rather than actually changing the positions of Vertices and Faces. It is possible to modify geometry in real time as well using the Meshdeform Modifier, a technique that we will examine in Chapter 28, "Mesh Deformation and Detailed Picking."

Note that in this demonstration, once a Model has begun rippling, you won't be able to change the speed of its rippling. However, if you use the sliders to change the ripple and ripple decay speed and then click another Model, this new Model will ripple with the new settings. The idea is to demonstrate the fact that similar timeouts can be instanced at the same time so that each Model can animate at its own speed. At any given time in this movie, there may be as many as six timeout objects running (one for the update of the Stage and five for the Models). Figure 23.3 notes the various controls available to you while the movie plays.

FIGURE 23.3

The Scheduler Management demonstration treats Modelresources as though they are frames in a flip-book animation.

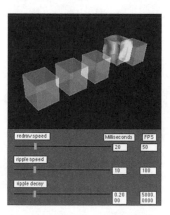

I suggest working with a variety of settings to test the different permutations of ripple speed and decay speed. Note that you can always alter the update speed of the Stage as well, but as in the other demonstrations, this does not affect the speed of the rippling, just the smoothness of its Motion.

A small behavior is attached to the 3D Castmember that handles mouse clicks; this script uses a bit of Picking Lingo to check if you have hit any Models. If you have hit a Model, a new child script will be spawned, and it is from this child script that the rippling and timeout object are managed. Listing 23.5 explains the Rippler parent/child script, which is called when you click a Model in this demonstration.

LISTING 23.5   Rippler Parent/Child Script

```
 1: -- reference to the model clicked
 2: property pModel
 3: -- counter used to determine which
 4: -- modelresource to use
 5: property pCount
 6: -- property used to determine the
 7: -- period of the Timeout Object
 8: -- that updates the current Modelresource
 9: property pSpeed
10: -- speed that the pSpeed variable
11: -- grows (thus Modelresource updating slows)
12: property pDecay
13: -- stores the name of the Timeout Object
14: property rname
15:
16: global scene
17: -- Rlist is a global variable that contains
18: -- the names of all of the ripple modelresources
19: -- in the order that they should be played back
20: global Rlist
21:
22: -- when the new handler is called, it is passed three
23: -- arguments: whichmodel to ripple, what the speed is
24: -- and what the speed of decay is
25: on new me, whichmodel, speed, decay
26:
27:    --set up the pModel and rName properties
28:    pModel = whichmodel
29:    rName = whichmodel & "rippler"
30:
31:    -- cycle through the timeoutlist to check
32:    -- and see if the Model is already rippling
33:    repeat with x = 1 to count(the timeoutlist)
```

LISTING 23.5   Continued

```
34:     if the timeoutlist[x].name = rName then
35:        -- if the model is already rippling
36:        -- jump out of the script
37:        return false
38:     end if
39:   end repeat
40:
41:   -- set up the pSpeed and pDecay properties
42:   pSpeed = speed
43:   pDecay = decay
44:
45:   -- Create a new timeout Object that references
46:   -- the ripplescript - this script actually handles
47:   -- the swapping of Modelresources
48:   timeout(rName).new(pSpeed, #ripplescript, me)
49:   -- set pCount = 1 (used to determine which
50:   -- modelresource should be currently displayed)
51:   pcount = 1
52:   -- return a reference to the child object
53:   return me
54: end
55:
56:
57: on ripplescript(me)
58:   -- set the modelresource of the current Model
59:   -- to the next modelresource in rList
60:   scene.model(pModel).resource = \ scene.modelresource(rlist[pcount])
61:
62:   -- add one to the value of pcount
63:   -- and make sure that it does not exceed the
64:   -- number of modelresources listed in rList
65:   pcount = pcount + 1
66:   if pcount > rlist.count then
67:     pcount = 1
68:   end if
69:
70:   -- slow the period of swapping modelresource
71:   pSpeed = pSpeed + pDecay
72:   timeout(rname).period = pspeed
73:
74:   -- if the speed is too slow forget the
75:   -- timeout object and reset the modelresource
76:   if pSpeed >= 50 then
77:     timeout(rname).forget()
78:     scene.model(pModel).resource = scene.modelresource[2]
79:   end if
80: end
```

As you can see from this code, the parent/child script handles the creation, destruction, and changing of the period for the timeout object that drives the changing of the ripple Meshes. Overall, this system is compact, but complete. Although it is obvious that the creation and destruction of the timeout objects is handled by the parent/child script, it is not clear how the child script reference is managed.

In this example, when the new handler returns a reference to the child object in line 53, this reference is not saved in a variable. Normally, you would want to store the reference because a child object will only live as long as there is a reference to it somewhere in memory. However, because the timeout object itself makes reference to the child object, it is the existence of the timeout object that maintains the existence of the child object. When the `ripple-script()` handler destroys the timeout object, it is also destroying the only reference to itself. Of course, allowing the timeout object to maintain the only reference to a child object will not always be sufficient, especially if you need to call handlers of the child object from other scripts. If that is the case, you will need to maintain the child objects in a variable reference as well—the way you normally would with parent/child scripts.

Enhanced Schedule Manager

In this demonstration, I will be combining many of the techniques we have been working on to develop a robust scheduler with management abilities. In this example, not only will we have parent/child scripts that manage their timeout objects, but we will also be able to send messages to the child objects. By maintaining a global linear list that contains references to all the child objects, we will be able to take advantage of one of the most powerful commands in all of Lingo: the `call()` function.

The `call()` function is similar to the `sendsprite()` and `sendallsprites()` functions and even somewhat similar to the `sendevent()` function. The idea is that the `call()` function can send an event message to a child object. This means that it is possible to use the `call()` function to trigger events inside of child objects, thus allowing you to build extremely robust behavior-like parent/child scripts. The usage of the call function follows this syntax:

```
Call(#handlername, childObject, argumentA, argumentB, …)
```

From this syntax, you can see that it is possible to quickly send a message to a child object with as many arguments attached to that message as you like. However, here's why the call() function is perhaps the most powerful function in Lingo: Although you can use call() to send a message to a single child object, another possibility exists. Rather than specifying a single child object with the childObject parameter, you can specify a linear list that contains references to all the child objects you want to send the event message to (with the same arguments).

In short, this command is powerful because with one line of code you can send a custom event message to a custom list of child objects, all at once.

It is this functionality that seals the timeout object with parent/child script-based schedule management system as the superior choice for the maximum amount of control. On the CD is a file named "Enhanced Management" that utilizes the power of the call() function in addition to the other tricks of schedule creation and management using timeout objects and parent/child scripts; open this file and press Play. Figure 23.4 shows the various controls at the bottom of the Stage.

FIGURE 23.4

The Enhanced Management demonstration allows you to control the Models in the environment with individual child objects, similar to how you use behaviors with individual sprites when working with non-3D assets.

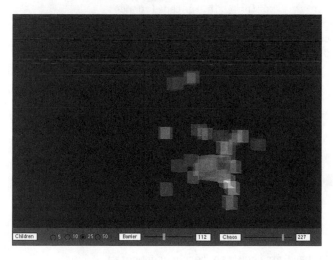

The controls at the bottom of this movie manage the small boxes that follow the main box. The main box is controlled by the position of the mouse using a parent/child script version of the Polar Mouse Cursor script from Chapter 13, "A 2D Mouse in a 3D World." The way that this schedule-management system is set up, each of the small boxes have their own child object and timeout object that controls their following of the leader box, how close they can come to the leader box, and their chaotic bouncing. Overall, this strategy allows us to build behavior-like scripts for each of the Models in the scene, and it is this type of control that allows us the most flexibility with the environment.

Three main scripts are used to create this system, beginning with the initialization of the environment. The other two scripts we will be looking at are parent/child script versions of the Polar Mouse Cursor script and the Tracker parent/child script behavior that causes the smaller Models to follow the main Model. I mention this because, as you look through the initialization script code in Listing 23.6, I will be referencing these two scripts, which are discussed later in this section.

LISTING 23.6   Enhanced Management Demo Initialization Script

```
 1: global scene
 2:
 3: on initialize
 4:     -- note that the actual initialization of the
 5:     -- environment has been separated into yet another
 6:     -- handler (later in this script)  The setenvironment
 7:     -- was created because I wanted to create a handler
 8:     -- that could be called from the controls on the
 9:     -- stage.  I could have done this with the initialize()
10:     -- handler, but I would prefer if the initialize()
11:     -- handler was standardized: therefore, no arguments.
12:     setEnvironment(5, 45, 75)
13: end
14:
15: on stopmovie
16:   the timeoutlist = []
17: end
18:
19: on masterupdate
20:   updatestage
21: end
22:
23: -- the setenvironment() handler required three arguments
24: -- the number of "follow" Models, the initial barrier distance
25: -- and the amount of chaotic bounciness for the follow Models
```

LISTING 23.6 Continued

```
26: on setEnvironment(numberoffollows, barrier, bouncy)
27:    -- the sList will be used to hold on to a linear list
28:    -- of references to all of the child Objects in the
29:    -- movie so that we can refer to them with the call()
30:    -- function all at once, later on.
31:    global sList
32:    sList = []
33:
34:    -- make sure that the timeoutlist is cleared as well as
35:    -- resetting the 3D Castmember
36:    the timeoutlist = []
37:    clearworld(scene)
38:
39:    -- create the main box that others will follow
40:    obj = createbox("master", 15,15,15, rgb(255,0,0))
41:    obj.shader.blend = 40
42:    obj.visibility = #both
43:
44:    -- create the number of follow boxes that was specified
45:    -- when this handler was called.
46:    repeat with x = 1 to numberoffollows
47:       --create a box with random color
48:       obj = createbox("follow" & x, 10, 10,10 ,\
49: rgb(random(200),random(50,200),random(200)))
50:       -- choose a randomvector (for initial placement)
51:       rand = randomvector() * 100
52:       -- move the box to its initial position
53:       obj.translate(rand)
54:
55:       -- in one line of code we are creating a new child object
56:       -- of the tracker parent/child script that is "attached" to
57:       -- the current model, and also we are adding the child object
58:       -- reference to the linear global list, slist.
59:       addat(slist, new(script "tracker", "master", obj.name, \
random(3,15), barrier, bouncy))
60:
61:       -- set up additional parameters for the box
62:       obj.shader.blend = 30
63:       obj.visibility = #both
64:    end repeat
65:
66:    -- create the main drawspeed timeout that controls the
67:    -- apparent framerate for the movie
68:    timeout("drawspeed").new(41, #masterupdate)
69:
70:    -- create a new instance of the 3D cursor script
71:    new(script "3d cursor", 1, 1)
72: end
```

The setup of the environment is rather straightforward: We are creating the main Model and all the "follow" Models, assigning the Tracker parent/child script to these follow Models, setting up the drawspeed timeout object, and instancing the Polar Mouse Cursor script. Because of the way that this is set up, it is possible to call the setenvironment() handler later on with different values in order to destroy the Nodes of the 3D Castmember and essentially reinitialize the scene.

The slist linear list is used by the two slider controllers on the Stage to call all the follow Models in order to change their barrier and bounciness properties with the call() function. Before we look at the Tracker parent/child script, take a look at the parent/child script version of the Polar Mouse Cursor in Listing 23.7. This listing does not go into detail about the Polar Mouse Cursor positioning, which is covered in Chapter 13, but it does show how a timeout object is used to update the cursor position rather than an exit-frame() event.

LISTING 23.7   Parent/Child Polar Mouse Cursor Script

```
1: Property centerofsprite, pmodel, pSprite
2:
3: global scene
4:
5: On new(me, whichsprite, whichmodel)
6:    pmodel = whichmodel
7:    pSprite = whichsprite
8:    centerofsprite = point((sprite(whichsprite).width / 2),\
      (sprite(whichsprite).height / 2))
9:
10:    -- right here we are creating a timeout object that
11:    -- will update the position of the mouse every
12:    -- 41 milliseconds, or 24 times per second
13:    timeout("cursor").new(41, #auto3dcursor, me)
14:    return me
15:
16: end
17:
18: on auto3dcursor(me)
19:    if inside(the mouseloc, sprite(pSprite).rect) then
20:      curloc = the mouseloc
21:      sideA = curloc[1] - centerofsprite[1]
22:      sideB = (curloc[2] - centerofsprite[2]) + .1
23:
24:      myangle = atan(sidea/sideb) * 57.29577951
```

LISTING 23.7   Continued

```
25:    if sideb < 0 then
26:      myangle = myangle + 90
27:    else
28:      myangle = myangle + 270
29:    end if
30:
31:    mymagnitude = sqrt(power(sidea,2) + power(sideb,2))
32:    scene.model[pModel].transform.identity()
33:    scene.model[pModel].translate(mymagnitude,-30,0,#world)
34:    scene.model[pModel].rotate(0,myangle,0,#world)
35:  end if
36: end
```

Notice how the update of the Polar Mouse Cursor script is driven by a time-out object as well as the reset of the environment. This means that the smoothness of the mouse positioning has a separate frame rate from the other elements in the demonstration. The final major component of this demonstration is the Tracker parent/child script. Listing 23.8 explains how this script controls each of the follow Models in the scene.

LISTING 23.8   Tracker Parent/Child Script

```
 1: -- which Model to follow
 2: Property pMaster
 3: -- which Model does the following
 4: Property pFollow
 5: -- how fast to follow the Master Model
 6: Property pfollowspeed,
 7: -- how chaotic the follow Model motion is
 8: Property pBounciness
 9: -- how close to the master Model the follow model can come
10: Property pBarrier
11:
12: global scene
13:
14: On new(me, whichMaster, whichFollow, whatspeed, barrier, bouncy)
15:    -- set up the basic properties
16:    pfollowspeed = whatspeed
17:    pMaster = whichmaster
18:    pFollow = whichfollow
19:    pBounciness = bouncy
20:    pBarrier = barrier
21:    -- create a timeout object to update this child script
22:    timeout(pfollow & "updater").new(41, #autoFollow, me)
```

LISTING 23.8   Continued

```
23:    -- return a reference to this child script
24:    return me
25: end
26:
27: on autoFollow(me)
28:    -- make sure that there is a follow object
29:    if pfollow <> void then
30:       -- find out where the master Model is in
31:       -- world relative space
32:       targetpos = scene.model(pMaster).getworldtransform()
33:       -- find out where the follow model is in
34:       -- world relative space
35:       mypos = scene.model(pFollow).getworldtransform()
36:
37:       -- only move the follow if it is further than the
38:       -- barrier distance to the master Model
39:    if mypos.position.distanceto(targetpos.position) > pBarrier then
40:          -- chaos is introduced by adding
41:          -- some amount of random vector to the
42:          -- position of the master Model - if
43:          -- bounciness = 0, then the randomvector will be 0
44:          rand = randomvector() * pbounciness
45:          targetpos.position = targetpos.position + rand
46:          -- interpolate the position of the follow model
47:          -- some amount toward the Master Model (if the amount
48:          -- of chaos was high, the follow model will move
49:          -- generally in the direction of the master model)
50:          newpos = mypos.interpolate(targetpos, pFollowspeed)
51:          scene.model(pfollow).transform = newpos
52:       end if
53:    end if
54: end
55:
56: -- two public handlers for changing the
57: -- pbounciness and pBarrier properties
58: on changeBounce(me, newbouncy)
59:    pBounciness = newbouncy
60: end
61:
62: on changeBarrier(me, newbarrier)
63:    pBarrier = newbarrier
64: end
```

You may note that within all three of these scripts, I did not use the `call()` function. I am, however, using it in the scripts attached to the slider controls at the bottom of the screen to change the pBounciness and pBarrier properties for all the follow Models in a single line of code.

In this demonstration, each of the follow Models have their own timeout object and therefore are capable of updating at different speeds. Another possibility would be to create a single timeout object for all of them and use the call() function to call the update of their positions. Because you can specify custom groups of follow Models with different lists, this can be a viable solution as well. Overall, this demonstration is the most advanced form of schedule management we will be working with in this chapter.

Throughout the chapter, the methods we have been looking at are alternatives you do not need to use. Although they require a bit more work to set up, the amount of flexibility that these alternative methods of time control provide make them extremely attractive. One might argue that the point of Director is to control media over time and that custom scheduling is the ultimate expression of that control. If you agree, why would you *not* want this amount of control?

Future Considerations

The examples of custom schedulers we have looked at have been rather straightforward. You should be aware that the notion of schedule management can be greatly expanded. This is especially necessary if you are going to be working on a project that requires intricate "registering" and "unregistering" of custom timeout objects as well as powerful techniques such as changing the target handler for a timeout object.

One of the primary reasons to create a custom scheduler is to build behavioral animation, which is sometimes also referred to as *rule-based animation*. The goal of behavioral animation is to create autonomous characters or agents in an environment that appear to have some intelligence of their own. The central tenet of behavioral animation is that you will use combinations of simple rules to create complex interrelationships between autonomous agents in an environment. Therefore, custom schedulers are important not only to regulate and control time but also to play a crucial role when you're building environments that contain characters that are not controlled directly by your users.

Custom schedulers are equally important when you're working with interactive animation—animation that is directly controlled by the user (which is discussed in the next chapter). The goal of interactive animation is to provide the user with the appearance of control over the environment to some extent. Whether that control is through a vehicle, character, or some other device, it is meant to extend the hand of the user into the environment. At the core of both of these techniques is the complete control of time, which can be provided with a great deal of flexibility via a custom scheduler.

Summary

Registering for events is a strategy that can be used to control a variety of aspects of your 3D environments. Some of the strongest reasons for learning how to control registered events include access to a customizable timer and detecting the beginning and end of Motion playback. Another critical reason that that we have not yet examined in detail is working with collision detection.

On the whole, the process of registering for events currently has several flaws that make it a difficult process to reconcile; however, the events that can be trapped with registering for events are difficult to duplicate. It is not the events themselves that are problematic, but the amount of control you have over those events once they are created.

In contrast, timeout objects make up an extremely robust subset of Lingo that tends to be overlooked. This is not without good reason, because many projects do not need the level of control they can provide. For those projects that do need custom scheduling and schedule management, timeout objects offer a range of unique capabilities that make them the obvious choice. Because there are certain events that can only be used with the registering process, it is not impossible that you might want to combine aspects of the two techniques. That is, you might decide to combine aspects of registering for events within the framework of a custom scheduler in order to take advantage of the benefits of both strategies.

Whatever your method, the goal of both techniques is to offer you new possible strategies for the control of time. Because animation is a time-based media, the control of time translates neatly into the control of animation. This is the fundamental and conceptual difference between several different modes of animation. When you're dealing with multimedia, animation can be approached as a simple action that does not rely on the user at all, nor is it aware of the user. A more intense approach is to control animation with code, allowing the user varying degrees of control over the environment.

The more the environment controls the animation, the more the animation seems autonomous to the user. The more the user "controls" the animation, the more he will feel he is interacting. The success of interaction and development of user experience in a given project is dependent on the perceived gradations between transparency of control. One might define opaque control as beyond the user's reach; transparent control is the intuitive level of self that a user should experience within an environment, and translucent control involves those elements that are affected by the user but also have the capability to act alone.

In short, custom scheduling, schedule management, and registering for events allow you to plan for such contingencies while providing you with enough room to expand the underlying control systems of your projects as your programming acumen sharpens.

FAQ

Which is better, a custom scheduler or the Score?

This is a question that has as many answers as there are Director developers. Many feel that a custom scheduler is overboard and unnecessary; others will not code without one. However, absolute rules are too rigid to be useful in the case of a custom scheduler. A custom scheduler is useful because it is one method of maintaining your target frame rate, regardless of the speed of the client machine. If you are working on a project that should not tax most machines—or one where timing is not a critical issue—perhaps you do not need a custom scheduler.

On the other hand, remember that you can use a custom scheduler to "skip" frames when the machine is running too slow, and you can also help force the frame rate within a target speed.

The decision could be made on these aspects alone, but really it depends on how much you expect to use callbacks. Remember that callbacks will play an important role in collision detection and interactive animation as well as AI routines.

Supplemental Resources

- www.red3d.com/cwr/

  This link is a Web-based resource created by Craig Reynolds—one of the pioneers of behavioral animation. This resource contains several useful articles, papers, code examples, and links that are essential to understanding how to build autonomous characters. If you are interested in behavioral animation, this link is an absolute necessity.

- www.atomicmedia.com/autonomous

  This is a link to Clint Hannaford's behavior library for autonomous character locomotion in Director. Note that these behaviors were designed for 2D characters, but they are extremely good examples of how you might approach developing a 3D autonomous character locomotion library of your own. Make sure you read through the usage license before you begin developing projects with this library.

CHAPTER 24

Interactive Animation

This chapter takes a critical look at the animation skills you have been learning in Part V, "Animation and Interactive Control Structures," and applies them outside of a laboratory-style demonstration. This chapter shows you how to use the skills and concepts we have covered in the previous chapters to create interactive animation. We will be combining a wide variety of skills and concepts from previous chapters into a single demonstration in this chapter. This demonstration is quite large, and it will be used not only to apply your current skills but also to introduce several new concepts.

Specifically, we will be looking at methods of using keyboard input to control a bipedal character within a 3D environment. In addition, this demonstration includes a method for creating false shadows that can add a sense of visual gravity for your Models. Finally, we will be examining a technique for creating custom proximity sensors used to gather information about the character's relationship to other Models in the scene, and we will use that information in a variety of ways.

All these tasks are combined to demonstrate a technique commonly referred to as *interactive animation*. The overall goal of this chapter is the application of skills and concepts toward creating interactive animation. However, the process of creation also includes understanding the design of interactive animation. Therefore, we will also be looking at design considerations for assets created outside of Director for helping you build your own interactive animations.

What Is Interactive Animation?

Interactive animation can be defined as animation that is controlled by or reacts to user input. In this chapter, I have applied this definition to the control of a bipedal character. We have looked at many different types of animation throughout the book so far, including Keyframe animation, Bones animation, interpolation-based animation, automatic animation, and behavioral or rule-based animation. The key difference between these and interactive animation is that the user makes the primary decisions that control the animation of a character or vehicle that the user will identify as *himself* in the environment.

In this chapter, I have defined two different aspects of control as constituting interaction. The first aspect is the ability for the computer to make decisions about user input as well as the lack of user input. The second aspect is the ability for the computer to determine the location of the character in the environment so that the environment can react to the character. These two aspects are interwoven to make the user feel as though he is controlling a character.

This feeling of control is best executed by a system that is moderately transparent to the user. The more transparent a system is, the easier it is for the user to suspend his disbelief. That is, he becomes willing to believe that he is interacting with the environment that you have created. In order to do this, there must be aspects of the environment that the user does have control over—and other aspects that he does not have control over or that act upon him. When a user is interacting with a project, he will be more open to actually experiencing the environment rather than simply looking at it. For this reason, understanding what interactive animation is as well as how to effectively create it is the exclusive focus for the remainder of this chapter.

Character Control Demonstration

In this demonstration, we will be examining a method for controlling a bipedal character via the keyboard. In addition, several new concepts and techniques will be used, including faked shadows and proximity sensors. Note that this demonstration makes extensive use of concepts and techniques you have learned in previous chapters, including the following:

- Cloning Motions from 3D Castmembers (Chapter 22)
- Bonesplayer Modifier (Chapter 22)
- Custom scheduling with management (Chapter 23)
- Registering for events (Chapter 23)
- Spatializing sound (Chapter 18)
- Controlling surface properties (Chapter 12)
- Camera Fog (Chapter 16)
- Toon Modifier (Chapter 15)

When explaining this demonstration, I assume that you are familiar with these concepts already.

To begin, open the file named "Character Control" on the CD and press Play. You should see a human character whose motion can be controlled with the arrow keys. The following keys are used for control:

- *Up arrow.* Speeds up the character's movement
- *Down arrow.* Immediately stops the character's movement
- *Left arrow.* Turns the character left (character relative)
- *Right arrow.* Turns the character right (character relative)

Move the character around the environment and also allow the character to wait for a few moments without input. As you can see in Figure 24.1, several areas on the floor stand out in the environment.

As you move the character toward these areas, you will be able to hear different sounds, depending on the character's distance from these areas. In addition, if the character enters any of these areas, the floor in that area will light up. These three areas represent proximity sensors in the scene. The sounds that you hear and the visible changes to the floor are two possibilities for the usage of our proximity sensors.

Finally, note the small circular shadow underneath the character that appears to follow the character as it moves around the environment. Director does not support cast Shadows, so as an easy alternative, I am using a small Model that approximates the shadow of the character on the floor. The shadow reinforces the sense of the floor as well as the presence of the character in the environment.

FIGURE 24.1

The Character Control demonstration uses the Toon Modifier to define the environment as an entirely non-realistic space.

NOTE

The 3D scene we will be working with in this demonstration was exported from 3D Studio. Because of that, remember that the axes for the environment will be shifted so that the Y axis and the Z axis are swapped. This can often cause confusion, so I want to draw your attention to it before it becomes a problem. This has been true in other demonstrations where Models and Motions were exported from 3D Studio, but in this example, we will be working with the axes heavily, so this issue is extremely important.

Keyboard Control

The main focus of this demonstration is the control of the bipedal character with keyboard input. The keyboard input is handled through a single parent/child script in conjunction with a timeout object. Note that this demonstration is run via a custom scheduling system that allows us to handle the different aspects and controls of the environment with multiple frame rates.

The Keyboard Control parent/child script is rather large because it has several functions. It is important that you realize the scope of what this script controls. However, when scripts are long, it is often difficult to discern their overriding logic. The Keyboard Control parent/child script consists of several handlers working in conjunction with one another to provide a range of services that fall into two categories: those services that evaluate user input, and those that make decisions for a character based on a lack of user input. Before we look at the code, I will first list the specific services provided by the Keyboard Control parent/child script:

- Constantly check for user input to move the character within the environment based on the arrow keys. This movement is not simply on or off; it speeds up and slows down based on the length of time the up-arrow key is depressed. The right- and left-arrow keys are used to rotate (turn) the character relative to itself.

- If the user has been moving the character but suddenly stops using the arrow keys for input, the speed of movement should slow down until the character eases to a stop.

- If character movement stops because of a lack of user input, the character will enter waiting mode. In waiting mode, the character plays the Motion named "wait," in which the character looks around while tapping its foot. This Motion is played at its full speed. The keyboard is still monitored for input that will release the character from waiting mode.

- If the character has been in waiting mode a very long time, the character will enter a special random motion mode. While the character is in waiting mode, a counter accumulates the time that is passing. After a certain amount of time without any user input, the character will perform a random motion. In this demonstration, the character will either yawn or sneeze.

- If the character is in waiting mode or random motion mode, the user should always be able to rotate the character around its Z axis.

- If the character is in waiting mode or random motion mode, the user should always be able to exit from those modes by pressing the up-arrow key.

- If moving the character about, the user should be able to instantly enter random motion mode by pressing the down-arrow key.

- Because the character is playing Bones-based Motions, small anomalies of rotation and position are often introduced that cause the character to look awkward, misplaced, or poorly aligned. To counteract this, a handler has been added to the parent/child script that removes unwanted rotation and position changes.

It is important that you keep these services in mind as you begin to look at the Keyboard Control parent/child script. Providing these services is the goal of the Keyboard Control parent/child script. Because it is a long script, I suggest reading through it once to get an idea of its scope. Then you can backtrack to look at specific sections that seem unclear.

NOTE

You may have noticed from the goals listed for the Keyboard Control parent/child script that I have not included any methods for limiting character movement. This goal has not been included with the other scripts in this chapter; therefore, no boundaries exist for character movement in X/Y space. The limitation of user movement can be broken down into two main areas: collision detection and boundary management. We will be looking at both of these in Chapter 29, "Collision Detection." They are large concepts that require the full scope of a chapter.

Before you look at the actual script, you should keep in mind that the script is comprised of several handlers, each with different responsibilities. Table 24.1 provides a list of these handlers and their general purposes.

TABLE 24.1   Keyboard Control Parent/Child Script Handlers

Handler	Purpose
New()	Creates a new instance of the parent script and timeout object to drive the input of data from the keyboard.
Checkkeys()	A main handler that checks for user input from the keyboard.
Constraintransform()	A minor handler run from checkkeys() that forces the character to constrain its movements to a single plane while remaining perpendicular.
Setpwait()	Used to switch the character into wait mode. This handler is used when there is no user input.

TABLE 24.1   Continued

Handler	Purpose
Unsetpwait()	Used to switch the character out of wait mode.
Randommotion()	Used to switch the character into random motion mode. This handler is used when there has been no input for a while.
Unrandom()	Used to switch the character out of random motion mode. Note that this handler is called via a timeMS event.

As you can see from this table, the checkkeys() handler is the largest handler, but it's also the most general. Most of the other handlers will be directly called from checkkeys() when they are needed. Out of all the handlers, you should focus on this one as you look through the Keyboard Control parent/child script in Listing 24.1.

LISTING 24.1   Keyboard Control Parent/Child Script

```
 1: --used to determine the speed of playback
 2: --for the bones Motions (controlled by keys)
 3: property pspeed
 4: --used to determine if the character is
 5: --waiting for user input
 6: property pwait
 7: --used to determine how long the character
 8: --has been waiting for user input
 9: property pcount
10: --used to determine if the character is
11: -- currently executing a random movement
12: property pRandom
13: -- stores a reference to the model that
14: -- will be animated and controlled
15: property pModel
16:
17: global scene
18:
19: on new(me, aModel)
20:    -- initialize properties
21:    pspeed = 0
22:    pcount = 0
23:    pModel = scene.model(amodel)
24:    --by default the model is not waiting
25:    pwait = false
26:    pRandom = false
27:    -- set up a timeout object that will
```

LISTING 24.1   Continued

```
28:    -- run the checkkeys script 24FPS
29:    timeout("keyboard").new(42, #checkkeys, me)
30:    return me
31: end
32:
33: on checkkeys(me)
34:    -- first, determine if the character is
35:    -- waiting for input or not.
36:    if pwait then
37:    -- if the character is waiting for input
38:    -- make sure that the movement (up) key
39:    -- has not been pressed
40:     if keypressed(126) then
41:    -- if the character is waiting, but the up
42:    -- key has been pressed, we will call a handler
43:    -- that changes the motion to a walking motion
44:    -- and sets the pwait variable to false
45:       unsetpwait(me)
46:     end if
47:
48:     -- when pwait is true, the speed is always 1
49:     pspeed = 1
50:
51:     -- if the character is not playing a random
52:     -- waiting behavior, the add one to the counter
53:     -- the counter is used to determine if enough
54:     -- time has passed waiting for user input
55:     -- for the character to do a random movement
56:     if pRandom = false then
57:       pcount = pcount + 1
58:     end if
59:
60:     -- check to see if the counter is high enough
61:     -- to perform a random movement
62:     if pcount > random(150,200) and pRandom = false then
63:       randommotion(me)
64:     end if
65:    else
66:    -- If the character is not waiting for user input
67:    -- then there is a different set of tasks
68:
69:    -- make sure that the counter is 0
70:     pcount = 0
71:
72:    -- the speed of animation constantly slows
73:     pspeed = pspeed - .03
```

LISTING 24.1   Continued

```
 74:    -- if the speed of animation is very slow,
 75:    -- then we will actually go in to wait mode
 76:      if pspeed < .2 then
 77:        setpwait(me)
 78:        pspeed = 1
 79:      end if
 80:
 81:      -- make sure that the speed of animation
 82:      -- does not exceed a playrate of 1.5
 83:      if pspeed > 1.5 then pspeed = 1.5
 84:
 85:      -- set the playrate of the bonesplayer
 86:      pModel.bonesplayer.playrate = pspeed
 87:
 88:      -- check to see if the up key is currently
 89:      -- pressed.   If it is, then add .4 to the
 90:      -- speed of animation
 91:      if keypressed(126) then
 92:        pspeed = pspeed + .4
 93:      end if
 94:
 95:       if the down key is pressed, automatically
 96:      -- switch to waiting mode
 97:      if keypressed(125) then
 98:        setpwait(me)
 99:      end if
100:    end if
101:
102:    -- Note that the following code is performed outside of
103:    -- the first if/then statement, thus, the following code
104:    -- executes regardless of whether the character is
105:    -- waiting or moving.
106:
107:    -- if the left or right arrows are pressed, rotate
108:    -- in that direction (character relative)
109:    if keypressed(123) then
110:      pModel.rotate(0,0,5,#self)
111:    end if
112:
113:    if keypressed(124) then
114:      pModel.rotate(0,0,-5,#self)
115:    end if
116:
117:    -- constraintransform() is a custom handler designed
118:    -- to make sure that the character remains perpendicular
119:    -- to the ground, and at the same height above the ground
```

LISTING 24.1   Continued

```
120:    constraintransform(me)
121: end
122:
123: on constraintransform(me)
124:    -- find out what the current position of the character is
125:    curpos = pModel.getworldtransform().position
126:    -- create a vector that constrains the z position to 180
127:    -- but uses the x and y position (so the character remains
128:    -- in the same x/y location, but is on one plane
129:    fixedpos = vector(curpos.x, curpos.y, 180)
130:    -- move the model in to place
131:    pModel.transform.position = fixedpos
132:
133:    -- find out what the current rotation of the character is
134:    currot = pModel.getworldtransform().rotation
135:    -- remove all rotations except for those around the Z axis
136:    -- which are used to turn the character
137:    fixedrot = vector(0,0, currot.z)
138:    -- set the rotation of the character to the fixed rotation
139:    pModel.transform.rotation = fixedrot
140: end
141:
142: on unsetpwait(me)
143:    -- make sure that there is a bit of motion
144:    -- blending before playing the next motion
145:    pModel.bonesplayer.blendtime = 50
146:    -- set the playrate down to 0
147:    pModel.bonesplayer.playrate = 0
148:    -- queue up the walking animation
149:    pModel.bonesplayer.queue("bip01", 1)
150:    -- transition to the walking motion
151:    pModel.bonesplayer.playnext()
152:    -- make sure that if we were leaving
153:    -- the wait state while a random motion
154:    -- is playing, that we eliminate the
155:    -- random motion as well, in addition to
156:    -- resetting the value for pRandom
157:    if pRandom then
158:      pModel.bonesplayer.playnext()
159:      pRandom = false
160:    end if
161:    -- make sure that pspeed is also 0
162:    pspeed = 0
163:    -- make sure that pwait is false
164:    -- so that checkkeys() can monitor
165:    -- input from the keyboard
```

LISTING 24.1   Continued

```
166:    pwait = false
167: end
168:
169: on setpwait(me)
170:    -- make sure that pwait is true
171:    pwait = true
172:    -- prandom should be false
173:    prandom = false
174:    -- the blendtime between motions
175:    -- should be relatively high
176:    pModel.bonesplayer.blendtime = 500
177:    pModel.bonesplayer.playrate = 1
178:    -- queue the basic wait motion
179:    pModel.bonesplayer.queue("wait", 1)
180:    -- play the basic wait motion
181:    pModel.bonesplayer.playnext()
182: end
183:
184: on randommotion(me)
185:    -- first, choose which random motion is going to play
186:    if random(0,1) = 0 then
187:      whichmotion = "yawn"
188:    else
189:      whichmotion = "sneeze"
190:    end if
191:
192:    -- queue the random motion to play (not looped)
193:    pModel.bonesplayer.queue(whichmotion, 0)
194:    -- play the random motion
195:    pModel.bonesplayer.playnext()
196:    -- queue the wait motion (to play looped)
197:    pModel.bonesplayer.queue("wait", 1)
198:    -- determine the amount of time to wait to set the
199:    -- prandom flag to false.  This amount of time is
200:    -- determined based on the duration of the random motion
201:    unwaittime = scene.motion(whichmotion).duration - 100
202:    -- registering a timeMS event.  Note that this timeMS event
203:    -- is scheduled to trigger only once.  Therefore it will
204:    -- automatically destroy itself
205:    pModel.registerscript(#timeMS, #unRandom, me, unwaittime, 0, 1)
206:    -- make sure that pcount is 0
207:    pcount = 0
208:    -- prandom is currently true, this way, in case the user
209:    -- breaks out of the random motion, the process will know to
210:    -- remove both the random motion and the queued wait motion
211:    -- from the playlist
```

LISTING 24.1   Continued

```
212:    prandom = true
213: end
214:
215: on unrandom(me)
216:    -- set the prandom flag to false
217:    prandom = false
218: end
```

Once the Keyboard Control parent/child script is instantiated, it essentially manages itself. Generally, you are going to want to set the frequency for the timeout object that checks for user input equal to or faster than the frame rate of the movie. Because user input is one of the most important aspects of interaction, you should put as much effort as possible into making sure the interaction feels natural and fluid. In the case of a character-control script, it is very important that you allow others to test your methods of interaction. Just because it performs as designed will not always mean it is intuitive to use. Often, when you're developing, it is easy to lose sight of the fact that users will be relying on your code to interact with the project.

Finally, note that the Keyboard Control parent/child script relies on the existence of several Motions that have been cloned into the main 3D Castmember. Therefore, it is important to ensure that this script is instantiated after these Motions are cloned. Figure 24.2 shows the Score for the movie.

FIGURE 24.2

The Character Control demonstration score consists of several scripts that are called in sequence rather than all at once, to initialize the environment.

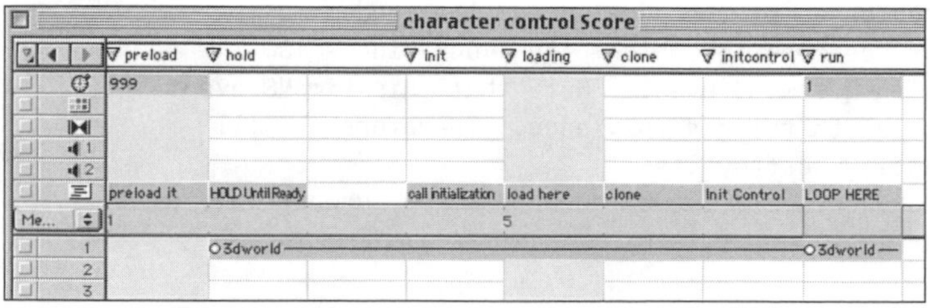

In this figure, note that the Score channel contains a frame behavior named *initcontrol* directly after cloning has occurred. This frame behavior initializes the Keyboard Control script. This Score has been set up to be rather explicit in terms of describing what tasks are being taken care of at a given time; this makes it easier to reconfigure when you need to insert additional minor initializations at a specific time during execution.

Future Considerations

You might consider making several enhancements to this Keyboard Control script in the future. Currently, the speed of walking accelerates and decelerates based on user input. You might want to apply acceleration and deceleration to the input for turning left and right. You could also introduce secondary actions for the user to control, such as reaching for a door handle or picking items up off of the floor. You can always expand the number of random Motions that the character has, but remember that too many of these can unnecessarily bloat your file size.

You may want to consider adding the ability to toggle user control on and off. This can be useful in conjunction with proximity sensors, which you will be learning about later in this chapter. For example, when the character gets very close to a door, the computer might take control of the character temporarily, moving it automatically through the door. In order to do this, you will need a method of suspending user input.

In addition to adding controls for additional character movements, you might want to consider adding methods to go to an application menu or an options screen. Once the user is in an options screen, the purpose of the keys will change, but users will still be able to exit out of the options screen. Essentially, I am speaking about building a level of control that can be toggled between different modes. This does not need to be as opaque as a traditional menu. Imagine that the menu is a pad of paper that the character removes from his back pocket. When a user enters menu mode, the character might take out the pad of paper while the camera zooms in to look at it, and interaction continues from within the environment.

Keeping the user experience as transparent as possible expands from simple menu and options systems into having multiple modes of character control. Imagine that the user can switch between several modes—walking mode, examining mode, and configuration mode. An obvious addition to this list for making a game would likely be fighting mode or running/jumping mode. Once the user is within a different mode, the purpose of the keys will change slightly to accommodate for the new actions, motions, or method of interaction.

Not only should you be concerned with how the code works in this demonstration, you should pay careful attention to the Motions that were selected to be used in this demonstration. The movement of the Motions should be smooth, and the timing of the Motions is critical as well. For those Motions that are looped, you should make sure the beginning and end of the Motions are as transparent to the user as possible. For Motions that are triggered to run once, such as the sneeze or the yawn, you should make sure they are short and concise.

Similar to issues you might consider in the design of sounds, think about the attack and decay of a Motion while you are designing your interactive animation. In short, consider that outstanding Motions can be ruined with poor code, but no amount of coding can fix a poorly created Motion. Therefore, you will want to spend a serious amount of time working with the planning and creation of assets in conjunction with the code. It is not enough to simply say that you will be using a walk loop; you need to really think about how long the loop is and how it will fit into the other Motions you are planning to incorporate.

This often means you will need to tweak canned Motions or create Motions of your own. Just as you would not expect a stock Model, Texture, sound, or other asset to be immediately ready for your project, you may need to do a fair amount of tweaking to the Motions you use to make them fit your project. Finally, although this point is extremely obvious, as with any asset-tweaking, be sure to save everything you do. I do not recommend overwriting files. Instead, you should create new ones as you make changes. You may be surprised how many times you may need to change a Motion or the position of a Bone—or you many need to revert to previous versions. For this reason, it is easier to save your work than have to re-create it.

False Shadow

Although cast shadows are not supported in Director 8.5, it is possible to create effects that can convey a general sense of shadows. In this demonstration, when you move the character close to the Camera, note that a small dark circle underneath the character moves along with it. By walking the character over different areas of the floor, you will find that this circle is semitransparent.

In this technique, the *circle* you see is actually a sphere that has been scaled almost completely flat in one direction. This has the effect of removing the sense of dimensionality to the sphere, but it retains its model-like qualities.

Once the sphere has been created, there is still the task of forcing it to follow the Model. Normally, this would be a rather trivial task of adding the sphere as a child of the Model that you want it to follow. However, in this case (and in other cases with bipeds), the local origin of the biped will often rotate and translate in World space as the biped moves. In terms of the Motion for the biped, these changes are important and represent changes to the position of the root Node in the skeletal hierarchy.

NOTE

To see these changes to the local coordinate system, try setting the debug mode "on" while working with this demonstration with the following code in the message window:

```
scene.model[1].debug = true
```

Remember that debug mode will not work if you are using software rendering. As the character walks, you can see that the local axes are moving in local coordinate space and that the character is moving in World space.

The fact that the local coordinates of the biped will rotate in World space is important because if you were to add the sphere as the child of the biped, it might move around unexpectedly. In addition, if the biped were to jump or otherwise change its distance to the floor, the shadow would unrealistically retain its distance to the biped. Rather than altering the scenegraph hierarchy, we will use a parent/child script to automatically position the sphere a set distance below the character. This parent/child script is shown along with comments in Listing 24.2.

LISTING 24.2   False Shadow Parent/Child Script

```
1: -- stores a reference to the shadow model
2: property pModel
3: -- stores a reference to the Model to follow
```

LISTING 24.2   Continued

```
 4: property pFollow
 5:
 6: global scene
 7:
 8: on new(me, follow)
 9:   -- initialize the properties
10:   pFollow = scene.model(follow)
11:   -- create the shadow model
12:   pmodel = createsphere("myshadow", 80, rgb(30,30,30))
13:   -- set the blend of the shadow model such that
14:   -- it is semi-transparent
15:   pmodel.shader.blend = 30
16:   -- create a timeout object that will handle
17:   -- the task of causing the shadow to
18:   -- automatically follow the biped character
19:   timeout("floorshadow").new(42, #floorfollow, me)
20:   return me
21: end
22:
23: on floorfollow(me)
24:   -- find out the position of the target Model
25:   targetpos = pFollow.getworldtransform().position
26:   -- create a new transform object
27:   mypos = transform()
28:   -- translate this transform to the same position
29:   -- as the target model
30:   mypos.translate(targetpos)
31:   -- move this transform (in this case) -133 units on
32:   -- the Z axis so that the shadow lies on the ground plane
33:   mypos.translate(0,0,-133)
34:   -- scale the shadow model so that it is essentially flat
35:   mypos.scale(1,1,.01)
36:   -- move the shadow model so that it is in position
37:   -- on the floor underneath the biped Model
38:   pmodel.transform = mypos
39: end
```

In addition to using a sphere to accomplish this technique, you might simply use a plane with a carefully mapped Texture with an alpha channel. If you are working with jumping bipeds, you should consider scaling the size of the shadow larger and the blend fainter the farther the biped is from the ground. Finally, you should consider looking at examples that others have created to fake shadows in Shockwave 3D, several of which are listed at the end of this chapter in the "Supplemental Resources" section.

Overall, faking shadows is an interesting concept that can be approached in several ways. In this demonstration, I have shown a very direct, simple method of implementing a fake shadow that grounds the character in the environment. The examples in the "Supplemental Resources" section demonstrate more aggressive mathematical approaches that produce believable cast shadows. However, the goal is still the same: to ground the character or object in the environment with signifiers of reality.

Proximity Sensors

In this section, you will learn about proximity sensors. A proximity sensor is not a built-in method or type of object in Director but rather a concept that you must implement on your own. I mention this because other 3D systems, such as VRML, have built-in proximity sensors. A proximity sensor is usually defined by having at least a location in space. Then, it is possible to use Lingo to determine how close to that point the character is in the environment. This information about distance is used to control various aspects of the environment or provide feedback for the user.

A proximity sensor can simply determine where a character is in the environment and use the distance information, or it might also include information for a trigger zone (that is, a location that you specify might also have a radius or sphere of influence). Within that sphere, certain actions might take place. Outside of that sphere, other actions take place. In this section, we will be looking at a type of proximity sensor that uses the proximity information for both of these purposes.

Make sure you have first walked the character around the environment, making note of how the sound in the environment reacts to the position of the character. Also note that three hotspots on the floor of the environment light up as the character steps on them. Both of these effects are handled by the Proximity Sensor parent/child script, which is explained in Listing 24.3.

LISTING 24.3   Proximity Sensor Parent/Child Script

```
1: -- stores the position of the center of the
2: -- proximity sensor in world units
3: property pWorldposition
4: -- stores the radius of the proximity sensor
```

LISTING 24.3　Continued

```
 5: property pRadius
 6: -- stores a reference to the timeout object
 7: property pTimeout
 8: -- stores a reference to the Model that is associated
 9: -- with the proximity sensor's active zone
10: property pModel
11: -- the targetmodel stores a reference to the Model that
12: -- should be tracked by this proximity sensor
13: property pTargetmodel
14: -- the distance from the targetmodel to the center
15: -- of the proximity sensor
16: property pProximity
17: -- the sound channel used by this proximity sensor
18: property pSound
19: -- boolean which stores true if the pproximity
20: -- is smaller than the pradius, and stores false
21: -- if it is not.  Essentially, this property stores
22: -- whether the targetmodel is within the proximity
23: -- sensor's zone or not.
24: property ptrigger
25:
26: global scene
27:
28: on new(me, targetmodel, aModel, worldpos, influence, aSound)
29:    -- initialize the properties
30:    pSound = asound
31:    pWorldposition = worldpos
32:    pRadius = influence
33:    pModel = scene.model(aModel)
34:    ptargetmodel = scene.model(targetmodel)
35:    ptrigger = false
36:    --create a unique name for the timeout object
37:    -- based on the name of the sensor, target and
38:    -- also the milliseconds.  This will ensure that
39:    -- the name is unique.
40:    ctime = the milliseconds
41:    timername = aModel & "_sensor_" & targetmodel & ctime
42:    -- note that we are registering the sensor() handler.
43:    -- it is this handler that does the majority of the work
44:    pTimeout = timeout(timername).new(42, #sensor, me)
45:    return me
46: end
47:
48: on sensor(me)
49:    -- first, determine where the targetmodel is in the world
50:    targetlocation = ptargetmodel.getworldtransform().position
```

LISTING 24.3   Continued

```
51:    -- figure out the distance between the target
52:    -- and the sensor in world units
53:    pProximity = pworldposition.distanceto(targetlocation)
54:
55:    --this if/then/else if statement contains four possibilities
56:    -- either the targetmodel is inside or outside of the
57:    -- sensor range, or it has just triggered leaving or entering
58:    -- the range.  In each case, a unique handler is called.
59:
60: if pProximity < pRadius and ptrigger = false then
61:    -- if the user just triggered the sensor
62:    -- by entering its "zone" then run the following handler
63:      triggerzone(me)
64:    else if pProximity < pRadius and ptrigger = true then
65:     -- if the user has already triggered the sensor
66:     -- but remains within the zone
67:      withinzone(me)
68:    else if pProximity > pRadius and ptrigger = true then
69:       -- if the user has triggered the sensor
70:       -- but is no longer within the zone
71:      exitzone(me)
72:    else
73:       -- if none of the others are true, the user is simply
74:       -- outside of the zone
75:      outsidezone(me)
76:    end if
77: end
78:
79: -- when the user triggers the zone, it will illuminate the
80: -- model associated with this proximity sensor
81: on triggerzone(me)
82:    ptrigger = true
83:    pModel.shader.emissive = rgb(200,200,0)
84: end
85:
86: -- when the user leaves the zone, it will cancel the
87: -- illumination for the model associated with this sensor
88: on exitzone(me)
89:    -- note that after we leave the zone, the ptrigger
90:    -- property is reset to false again
91:    ptrigger = false
92:    pModel.shader.emissive = rgb(0,0,0)
93: end
94:
95: -- when within the zone, ensure that the corresponding
96: -- sound is at maximum volume
```

LISTING 24.3   Continued

```
 97: on withinzone(me)
 98:    sound(pSound).volume = 255
 99: end
100:
101: -- when outside of the zone, modulate the volume of the
102: -- sound so that as the character retreats from the zone
103: -- the volume will diminish
104: on outsidezone(me)
105:    newvol = 255 - integer((pProximity * 255) / 4000)
106:    sound(pSound).volume = newvol
107: end
```

As you can see from this script, determining where the character is relative to the proximity sensor is handled in only a few lines of code (lines 50 and 53). The majority of the script is used not to detect proximity but rather to decide what to do with the proximity information.

You already know that the purpose of a proximity sensor is to provide a concise method of handling information about the location of the character in the environment. In this demonstration, the main concern of proximity sensors is to use this information to control the environment, but the sensors can also be used to control the character as well. In terms of the functionality for these basic proximity sensors, you may want to consider the following basic enhancements:

- The ability to turn sensors on and off
- Moving the location of the sensor
- Changing the size of the region
- Using multiple radiuses for a single sensor
- Speeding up or slowing down the period of sensing based on the distance to the sensor
- Using reporting utilities to send proximity messages to other scripts, or even a proximity sensor manager

Although you may not require all these enhancements, you should at least consider them. The proximity sensor is one of the basic tools of interactive 3D programming that allows you to build complex environments. Because of this, it is important to understand that although we can add functionality to proximity sensors, it's more important how we decide to use them. For this reason, I suggest the following list of possible uses for proximity sensors:

- *Alarm/trigger.* The most basic use of the proximity sensor is to create an alarm, either visual or aural. Effectively this means that the proximity sensor is used as a simple switch.

- *Silent alarm/trigger.* Rather than triggering some response in the environment, the alarm or trigger can be invisible to the user. You might be collecting data about the character's movements or current location, how long it stays in a particular area, and so on.

- *Hot/cold sounds.* Similar to the use of sound in the Character Control demonstration, you might use proximity sensors as a way to control the volume of sound rather than just triggering it.

- *Temporary loss of keyboard control.* A common use for proximity sensors that you may be familiar with from 3D games is the temporary loss of control. For example, your character might approach a door that is a proximity sensor. When the character reaches the threshold distance, the user loses control of the character, and the character is automatically animated to open the door and walk through it. Then, control is returned to the user.

- *Changing the scope of control.* Similar to the temporary loss of control, changing the scope of control is often used to switch from one mode of movement to another. For example, a character might approach a ladder or staircase until he is within the threshold distance. Then, the user will temporarily lose control as the character moves to the "start" of the ladder or staircase. When the user regains control of the character, the scope of the controls he was using to make the character walk has now changed into the controls for moving the character up and down the ladder or staircase.

- *Changing the Camera angle.* If you are working with multiple camera angles, using proximity sensors is a concise method of switching between Cameras as the character moves through the environment.

- *Combining input from multiple proximity sensors.* You could use multiple proximity sensors to build complex reactions from the environment to the user. For example, imagine that you have two proximity sensors, A and B, that have zones that overlap at certain locations. When the character is within A, one action triggers. When the character is within B, a different action triggers, and when the character is within A and B, a third action triggers. This example can be expanded to include dozens of sensors and interrelationships.

Of course, these lists of enhancements and purposes are general and cannot include all possibilities for proximity sensors. However, I believe that from these lists you can begin to glean the scope of the purposes they can be used for. Overall, proximity sensors are an integral component, not only for building rich environments that can interact with your users but also for providing information about the character to autonomous agents. In addition to controlling autonomous agents, if you are interested in developing multiuser environments, proximity sensors can play an important role as well, providing information about a character to other clients within the same environment.

Summary

Interactive animation is a technique for developing projects that combine techniques of Motion control, user input, and environmental response. The overall goal for interactive animation is to encourage the users to lose themselves in the environment you have created so that they will be able to engage with your project to the point where they might actually "experience" the environment.

Building a solid interactive animation depends as much on your code as the assets you use, including the Motions themselves. You will often need to work with Director and your 3D animation software simultaneously while tweaking the Motions in order to get the look you want.

Beyond proper planning and execution of the Motions and the control of those Motions is the reaction of the environment itself. An environment that does not react to the character will only reinforce the fact that it is not real, rather than draw users in. One technique that is often used to build a rapport between the character and the environment is the use of proximity sensors.

In the past several chapters, we have been examining a wide variety of animation techniques, including Keyframe animation, Bones animation, interpolation animation, and behavioral animation. Of all these techniques, interactive animation is the most difficult to create, because it calls upon your understanding of all the others. However, it is equally important that you do not forget how powerful these other techniques are.

To put these techniques in context, Keyframe, Bones, and interpolation animation should be looked at as the specific methods for making Models move within an environment. Behavioral and interactive animation describe the methods you will use to control how and when the Keyframe, Bones, and Interpolation animation techniques should be applied. Whereas interactive animation effectively describes a method for building user input, behavioral animation hints at the beginnings of artificial life (AL) and artificial intelligence (AI).

Although these two topics are well beyond the scope of this book, you might think about using AI and AL as methods for controlling the nonplayer characters in an environment, including aspects of the environment itself. Interactive animation includes user control of a character in the environment, but it also deals with how that character will interact with the environment itself—and therefore those elements controlled via your AI and AL techniques.

For this reason, we have been focusing on the use of custom schedulers and multiple frame rates for different pieces of code. As you begin to build large, complete environments, you will find that certain tasks are much more important than others. It is your job to prioritize the tasks according to their usage of processor time. You should immediately consider that drawing the environment and allowing for user input are high priorities. Control of the environment and nonplayer characters may play a secondary role, and other system-level tasks, such as downloading new Textures for other areas of the environment, might take a tertiary role.

The job is difficult, so the goal must be clear: Define your characters and your environment on paper before you sit down to work on them. This is especially true with the design and implementation of your Motions. No matter what, before you begin working on your first implementation of an interactive animation system, remember this rule: Good Motions can be ruined by poor coding, but poor Motions cannot be fixed with great code. The point is, you need to create outstanding assets as well as code in order to create convincing, engaging, interactive animations that users will remember.

FAQ

The demonstration in this chapter uses a custom scheduler. Is it possible to build interactive animation without custom scheduling?

Of course you can use frame-based controls for building interactive animation, but in the case of interactive animation, you will have a much stronger system if you drive it with a custom scheduler. This becomes exponentially more important the larger your environments become.

The demonstration in this chapter has a Camera with a fixed viewpoint. I need the Camera to move. What can I do?

The next chapter, "Advanced Camera Control," covers several methods for building Camera movements within an environment. In addition, you may want to consider looking at Chapter 27, "Creating Meshes from Code," for examples of terrain following, and Chapter 29, "Collision Detection," for examples of collision detection and boundary management.

In this chapter, you mentioned the development of multiuser environments. Is this topic covered in this book?

Unfortunately, no. Multiuser environments are well beyond the scope of this book. In general, if you are planning on learning how to create multiuser 3D environments and you have not created any multiuser applications in the past, my advice to you is this: First learn how to create single-user environments while concentrating on the use of time-based (rather than frame-based) control. Once you have mastered the creation of a single-user environment, it will be easier for you to learn how to create a multiuser environment. So many issues are involved in the creation of an environment that to introduce multiuser techniques at the same time would be simply overwhelming.

Supplemental Resources

This section provides several online resources from which you can benefit. Here's a list individuals in the Director 3D development community who have put together some amazing demonstrations for faking cast shadows with Director:

- Foster Langbein

Foster Langbein has two demonstrations for faking cast shadows that are worth taking a look at. The first link demonstrates a technique for faking cast shadows that is fast and reasonably accurate, and the second link demonstrates a slightly slower but noticeably more accurate method for creating cast shadows:

```
http://www.forestint.com.au/testing/sw3d/shadowDemo.html
```

```
http://www.forestint.com.au/testing/sw3d/shadowDemo2.html
```

- Jerry Charumilind

  Jerry Charumilind has several outstanding demonstrations at the following link that are worth looking at. Among the demonstrations is a shadow demo that uses multiple Camera renders to create cast shadows:

  ```
  http://poppy.macromedia.com/~jcharumi/
  ```

- Barry Swan

  Barry Swan has put together an interesting demonstration, complete with a tutorial and available code, that fakes cast shadows in Shockwave 3D. If you follow this link, make sure to look for the tutorial named "Faking Shadows" (consider looking at his other demonstrations and tutorials for advanced techniques as well):

  ```
  http://www.theburrow.co.uk/d85/
  ```

PART VI

Advanced Techniques

This section on advanced techniques is intended to help you learn how to control several of the most intriguing and impressive tools in Director's 3D environment. We will begin by examining several Camera techniques that will expand your ability to create immersion and interaction. Next, we will take an advanced look at transformations and vector math, which you will need to understand before proceeding to the last three chapters. The last three chapters explore the topics of creating Meshes from code, where we will center on methods of terrain generation. Then we will examine the topic of Mesh Deformation—a tool that allows you to control the geometry of your Models down to the level of Vertices. Finally, we'll examine the built-in collision-detection routines in the 3D environment. You'll learn where you might use them and where you might need to build custom solutions.

CHAPTER 25

Advanced Camera Control

In this chapter we will be examining several techniques that call upon the skills and topics you have learned previously in this book. Specifically, we will examine several advanced techniques involving Cameras: Camera animation, Camera zoom, Camera navigation, Camera following, Camera examination, and Multiple viewports. Each of these techniques is presented with considerations for how to apply them in specific situations. In addition, suggestions for future enhancements are made when necessary.

Camera Animation

When you're changing the orientation or position of a Camera, it is often desirable to animate the Camera between two "looks" rather than "cutting" from one view to another. Many of the examples in this chapter build on the basic concepts you'll learn here in this section. This technique of animation capitalizes on the `interpolate()` and `interpolateto()` transform commands.

You are familiar with the concept of interpolation from Keyframe animation, where keyframes are defined and Director *interpolates* between positions, rotations, scale, and so on. This technique is known as *in-betweening*. However, it is more of a mathematical process made simple for us through the visual control of the Score. The `interpolate()` commands allow us to build similar functionality—with code.

So that you better understand what the `interpolate()` command is going to do before we use it, let's look at the syntax rather generally applied to a Node:

```
Node.transformA.interpolate(transformB, percentage)
```

This command is interesting because it allows you to determine the transformC that exists some percentage between two other transforms. For example, if you were to move your coffee mug from one side of your desk to the other, you could use interpolate() to find out where the mug was 30 percent of the way through its trip.

The difference between the interpolate() and the interpolateto() command, as demonstrated by the sample syntax, is that interpolate() creates a new transformC and returns it to you, leaving transformA unmodified. Interpolateto() acts directly on transformA and therefore is more of a destructive process—but many times this is exactly what you want.

Open the file named "Animated Camera Pointing" on the CD and press play. You may recognize the general layout of this demonstration from the Camera Pointing demo in Chapter 6, "Understanding Cameras." This demonstration is essentially identical except for one thing: Click the buttons and watch how smoothly the Camera *interpolates* to its new orientation. Alone, interpolateto() cannot animate, but when it is used in an exitframe handler, it can become quite powerful.

Two scripts in the movie work in conjunction with another to make this effect possible. More accurately, the initialization script creates a clone of the Camera that the Sprite uses. The following section of code is taken from the end of that script:

```
1:   --clone the first camera
2:   scene.camera[1].clone("dummycam")
3:
4:   --create a global variable
5:   global newtrans
6:   --store the transform of the dummy camera in the global
7:   newtrans = scene.camera[2].getworldtransform()
8:
9: end
```

We are creating a dummy Camera so that we can run the pointat() commands on the dummy Camera. Then, we will use the modified transform of the dummy Camera and the interpolateto() command, as shown in the following script, which is used to create this animation:

```
1: property pWM  -- model number to point at, set in GPDL
2:
3: global scene
4:
5: global newTrans  --newtrans is given an initial \
   value in the init script
6:
7: -- set up the pWM property
8: on getpropertydescriptionlist me
9:   set plist = [:]
10:   setaprop(plist, #pWM, [#comment:"Which Model #", \
   #format:#integer, #default:0])
11:   return plist
12: end
13:
14: on mousedown
15:   --find out the position of the Model you want to point at
16:   obj = scene.model[pWM].getWorldTransform().position
17:   -- set the up vector
18:   up = vector(0,1,0)
19:   -- point the second (dummy) camera at the object
20:   scene.camera[2].pointAt(obj, up)
21:   --note that up until now, even though we have moved
22:   --the dummy camera, the camera used by the sprite
23:   --has not changed.
24:
25:   --set the global variable newtrans equal to the
26:   --new transform of the dummy camera
27:   newtrans = scene.camera[2].getworldtransform()
28: end
29:
30: on exitframe
31:   --every exitframe, move the camera that is used
32:   --by the sprite 3% of the way toward the position
33:   --of the dummy camera
34:   scene.camera[1].transform.interpolateto(newtrans, 3)
35: end
```

Notice in the exitframe handler that we are constantly moving camera[1] toward the orientation of camera[2]. Because we are constantly only moving 3 percent of the way to the new transform, we slowly "ease" into place. Try experimenting with the percentage argument to see the visual effect of having a value of 20, 50, or 90. By changing that percentage, the overall motion of the Camera changes dramatically. Finally, note that the interpolate() commands are available to all Nodes: Cameras, Lights, Models, and Groups.

Camera Zoom

Controlling the `fieldofview` or `orthoheight` property of the Camera can be used to create a Camera zoom effect. This effect can be controlled directly by the movie or incorporated into the amount of control the user has over the environment. I will explain how to create a general zooming behavior that relies on the mouse, and therefore user interaction. In addition, we will examine a technique that combines picking, repositioning, and zooming in on specific objects also controlled via the mouse.

General Camera Zoom

The type of Camera projection you use will determine the specific property of Camera zoom you will need to control: either `fieldofview` or `orthoheight`. In this example, we will create a Camera zoom behavior that can be used for perspective Cameras, although you could modify the script rather easily to use it with orthographic Cameras.

NOTE

In this example, I am setting up an "absolute" zoom—in other words, specific locations on the 3D Sprite will always produce the same zoom amount for the Camera. Another possibility is to create a "constant" zoom—that is, whenever the mouse is down, the Camera zooms in; otherwise, it zooms out.

The logic that I will employ in this example is essentially flag driven, meaning that the heart of this script relies on the `exitframe` handler's ability to actually perform the zooming action. The rest of the script determines how the user will interface with that action—the `mousedown` and `mouseup` handlers determine whether the zooming should occur.

Open the file named "Basic Zoom" on the CD and press Play. Click the Sprite, and while the mouse remains down, move the mouse vertically. Notice how in this example, moving the mouse lower on the Sprite correlates to zooming in. Also notice how moving the mouse outside of the Sprite does not change the zoom. This is because the range of the Camera zoom is constrained within the height of the Sprite. This behavior is accomplished through the following script:

```
 1: property spritenum
 2: property pZooming --boolean flag variable
 3: property pMAXZoom, pMINzoom  -- maximum and minimum values for FOV
 4: property pZoomrange -- range between pMaxZoom & pMinZoom
 5:
 6: on getpropertydescriptionlist me
 7:   plist = [:]
 8:   setaprop(plist, #pMAXzoom, [#comment:"Maximum FieldofView?",\
      #format:#integer, /
 9: #default:120, range:[min:1, max:179]])
10:   setaprop(plist, #pMINzoom, [#comment:"Minimum FieldofView?",\
      #format:#integer, /
11: #default:30, range:[min:1, max:179]])
12:   return plist
13: end
14:
15: on beginsprite me
16:   --set up initial value for pZooming
17:   pzooming = false
18:   --initialize pZoomRange based on GPDL values
19:   pZoomRange = pMaxzoom - pMinZoom
20: end
21:
22: on mousedown me
23:   pzooming = true
24: end
25:
26: on mouseup me
27:   pzooming = false
28: end
29:
30: on mouseupoutside me
31:   --make sure that you turn zooming off
32:   -- in case the user mouseup's outside the sprite
33:   mouseup(me)
34: end
35:
36: on exitframe
37:   --only zoom the camera if pzooming is true
38:   if pzooming then
39:
40:     -- convert the mouseloc into a field of view
41:     FOV = (((the mouseloc[2] - sprite(spritenum).top) *\
      (pZoomRange)) / sprite(spritenum).height)
42:
43:     -- invert sequence of numbers
```

```
44:      -- this way, the lower the mouse is on the sprite
45:      -- the smaller the FOV, the larger the scene will appear
46:      -- therefore: Down on the sprite = Zoom In
47:      FOV = pMaxZoom - FOV
48:
49:      -- ensure that the FOV value is constrained \
            within the Max & Min Ranges
50:      FOV_CONSTRAINED = min(pMAXzoom, max(FOV, pMinZoom))
51:
52:      -- set the field of view
53:      sprite(1).camera.fieldofview = FOV_CONSTRAINED
54:   end if
55: end
```

There are several points to note on the structure of the exitframe handler. First, lines 47, 50, and 53 could be combined into one single line of code, but this would have made it too difficult to read—if you like, combine them to conserve room, but there is little benefit. Second, line 41 performs the calculation of a proportion through an algebraic construct known as *cross-multiplication*. This construct can be used to convert a specific value between two ranges of numbers; hence, we are performing a change in units. It is important that you know the two ranges (in this case, the height of the Sprite and the range of zoom) and a specific value within one of those ranges. Therefore, to convert from the height of the Sprite into the corresponding zoom amount, the following equation was used:

(Specific Height * Zoom Range) / Sprite Height

Remember that this formula can be used in many situations when programming. It can be especially important in multimedia programming, because you are almost always building visual interfaces to your information. Therefore, many times you will need to correlate Stage or 3D environment positions into some other range of numbers. I am making a point of this equation for a reason: If the values are going to be constant (a specific location on the Stage always refers to a specific amount of zoom), you might want to consider creating a look-up table rather than using multiplication and division. Part of the reason for this is more obvious when you're using a small range of zoom, where you would need to use floating-point division to get accurate zoom data.

Constant Zoom

In this example, rather than creating an absolute zoom, where the `fieldofview` property of the Camera correlates to specific locations on the Sprite, we will create a "constant" zoom that zooms in as long as the mouse is down and zooms back to an initial position when the mouse is up. In addition, we will reposition the Camera to point at a specific object or location based on where the user has clicked. The idea is to reinforce how you can use code to create a method of interaction.

Open the "Constant Zoom" file located on the CD and press Play. It may take you a moment to learn how to interact with this movie. As the mouse is down, the Camera zooms in constantly. When the mouse is release, the Camera zooms out constantly. In addition, the camera repositions itself; you may notice after working with this movie for a moment that the farther from the center of the screen you move the mouse, the faster the Camera moves in that direction. Also, the Camera movement is limited to the grid in the background. This is so the camera doesn't go flying off into empty space.

In this example, some small cubes are hidden among the grid and are difficult to find unless you zoom in. If the mouse is on top of one of these cubes, the Camera will "lock in." Although the amount and speed of zooming is dramatic in this example, the concept should be clear: The Camera zooms in while the mouse is down and zooms out while the mouse is up. The code to create this effect is as follows:

```
1: property spritenum
2: property pZoom, pHomeZoom
3:
4: global scene
5:
6: on beginsprite me
7:    -- by default we are not zooming
8:    pZoom = false
9:    -- gather information about the
10:   -- default field of view for the camera
11:   pHomeZoom = sprite(spritenum).camera.fieldofview
12: end
13:
14: on mousedown me
15:    --on mousedown set the zoom to true
16:    pZoom = true
```

```
17: end
18:
19: on mouseup me
20:    --on mouseup release the zoom
21:    pZoom = false
22: end
23:
24: on mouseupoutside me
25:    --also release the zoom on mouseupoutside
26:    mouseup(me)
27: end
28:
29: on exitframe
30:    if pZoom then
31:      --if pZoom is true, we Zoom the camera in
32:
33:      --collect fieldofview
34:      curFOV = sprite(spritenum).camera.fieldofview
35:      -- subtract from that amount
36:      curFOV = curFOV - 4
37:      -- constrain fieldofview, larger than 6
38:      if curFOV < 6 then curFOV = 6
39:      --zoom the camera
40:      sprite(spritenum).camera.fieldofview = curFOV
41:
42:      --check to see if the cursor is pointing at a model
43:      hitMODEL = scene.camera[1].modelunderloc(the mouseloc)
44:
45:      --if we are pointing at a model
46:      if hitMODEL <> void then
47:        --and if the model is not the "backgroundgrid model"
48:        if hitMODEL.name <> "backgroundGrid" then
49:          -- automatically "lock on" to the model
50:          hitPOS = hitMODEL.getworldtransform().position
51:          scene.camera[1].pointat(hitPOS,vector(0,1,0))
52:        else
53:          -- otherwise allow the camera to "wander"
54:          -- but only within the "backgroundgrid" model
55:          hitPOS = scene.camera[1].spritespacetoworldspace(the mouseloc)
56:          scene.camera[1].pointat(hitPOS)
57:        end if
58:      end if
59:    elzse
60:      -- if pZoom is false, rather than zooming in
61:      -- we will slowly zoom out until the camera
62:      -- fieldofview matches its original fieldofview
63:      -- which was stored in pHomeZoom
```

```
64:
65:       --collect fieldofview
66:       curFOV = sprite(spritenum).camera.fieldofview
67:       --add .5 to current fieldofview
68:       curFOV = curFOV + .5
69:       --constrain results to original zoom
70:       if curFOV > pHomeZoom then curFOV = pHomeZoom
71:       --zoom camera
72:       sprite(spritenum).camera.fieldofview = curFOV
73:    end if
74: end
```

Note that in this example, without the background grid, the Camera would be next to impossible to control. Other enhancements you might consider include creating a zoom in/out that zooms in slowly and increases speed and combining the zoom effect with Overlays to create a "binocular" effect. Finally, you might capture the initial transform of the Camera, and when the mouse is up, not only zoom out but also slowly interpolate the Camera back to its initial orientation.

Basic Camera Navigation

In this section, we will examine two methods of implementing Camera navigation. In the first example, we will implement a rather straightforward system of correlation between keys on the keyboard and changing the World position of an orthographic Camera. In the second example, we will explore the topic of creating first-person perspective Camera navigation within an environment.

Isometric Navigation

This example utilizes a specific variation on an orthographic Camera projection known as an *isometric view*. An isometric view is special because distances in the X, Y, and Z directions that are objectively the same length will be visually described as the same length. Just because an orthographic Camera does not have a vanishing point does not mean that the visual description of distances can't be changed—think about a top view or a side view in a 3D modeling program. These views are defined to point along the World axis toward the World origin and have the effect of creating views of your geometry without any depth. Now imagine that the Camera is still pointed at the

World origin but is oriented in the "corner" of the scene, as illustrated in Figure 25.1.

FIGURE 25.1

Placement of an orthographic Camera for an isometric view11

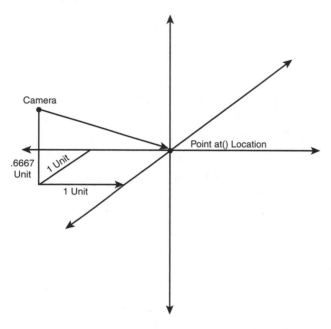

The most important thing about the placement of this Camera is that the distances from the origin (or more specifically, the pointat() position) to the Camera along these axes have the ratio 1, 1, .6667, as noted in the figure. The idea is that because the Camera has no vanishing point, you can put the isometric Camera as far away as you need to from the scene in order to "fit more" into the view plane. That way, regardless of whether you decide to put your orthographic Camera at vector(45,45,30) or vector(5000,5000,3333.5), as long as you point at vector(0,0,0), you should end up with an isometric Camera.

The addendum to this is that if you move the Camera and do not change the 1, 1, .6667 ratio created by pointing at vector(0,0,0), you will continue to have an isometric view of the environment: You can move the Camera, but this does not change its orientation. Isometric views are quite common in a genre of video games known as *iso-games*, such as Zaxxon and Ultima Online. Classically, iso-games have been created through "tile/sprite" methods (2D image compositing), but there are many "modern" 3D engine–based games that use isometrics as well. The isometric view is also heavily used in architectural and technical illustration because it allows you to objectively describe your subject.

In this example of isometric navigation, the initial setup of the isometric Camera was done visually in 3D Studio MAX. Then the Models and Camera were exported into a W3D file for Director to use. Open the file named "Iso Camera Navigation" on the CD and press Play.

While the movie plays, use the arrow keys to control the navigation of the Camera through the city scene. Now use the arrow keys in conjunction with the Shift key. Notice how the Shift key changes the way you navigate through the city. The reason for this is that in an isometric view, there are two dominant sets of coordinates we can use to move the Camera. First, we can move the Camera along a single World axis, as with the unmodified arrow keys. Second, we can move along two world axes at the same time, as with the arrow keys modified by the Shift key. The degrees of motion possible through these two methods are illustrated in Figure 25.2.

FIGURE 25.2

Two methods of organizing movement coordinates with arrow keys for isometric views.

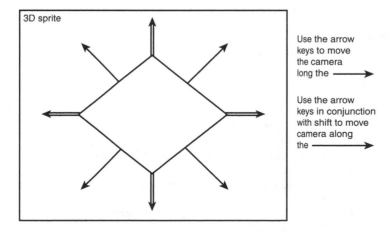

In addition to using the Shift and arrow keys, experiment with the Option key (Macintosh) or Alt key (PC) while this demo plays. I have built a variation of the Constant Zoom demo for an orthographic Camera and have tied it to the Option key.

One issue that must be addressed is that the ratio created in 3D Studio might not be perfect, due to perhaps a lack of precision (even though you could use the transform input tool in 3DS MAX). Also, depending on how much you compress your geometry in the exporter, small changes in geometry or positions may take place. In order to eliminate any discrepancies in the placement on the Camera, we will reposition and orient the Camera, as shown in the following excerpt from the initialization script:

```
1:   --make sure that the camera is iso
2:
3:   scene.camera[1].transform.position = vector(512,-512,341)
4:   scene.camera[1].pointat(vector(0,0,0), vector(0,0,1))
5:
6: end
```

Once the Camera has been set up initially, the key to moving the Camera is to make sure you transform it relative to World coordinates. Building this tiered system of navigation is handled through the following script:

```
 1: property spritenum
 2: property pHomeZoom
 3:
 4: global scene
 5:
 6: on beginsprite me
 7:   pHomeZoom = sprite(spritenum).camera.orthoheight
 8: end
 9:
10: on exitframe
11:   if the shiftdown then
12:     case(chartonum(the keypressed)) of
13:       30: --up (stage relative)
14:         scene.camera[1].translate( -1.5, 1.5, 0.0000,#world)
15:       31: --down (stage relative)
16:         scene.camera[1].translate(1.5,-1.5, 0.0000,#world)
17:       28: --left (stage relative)
18:         scene.camera[1].translate( -.8, -.8, 0.0000,#world)
19:       29:  --right (stage relative)
```

```
20:        scene.camera[1].translate( .8, .8, 0.0000,#world)
21:      end case
22:    else
23:      case(chartonum(the keypressed)) of
24:        30: --up
25:          scene.camera[1].translate(0,1,0,#world)
26:        31: --down
27:          scene.camera[1].translate(0,-1,0,#world)
28:        28: --left
29:          scene.camera[1].translate(-1,0,0,#world)
30:        29: --right
31:          scene.camera[1].translate(1,0,0,#world)
32:      end case
33:    end if
34:
35:    --ZOOM Controls: based on the constant zoom demo
36:    --but updated to use the orthoheight property of
37:    --the camera rather than the fieldofview.
38:    --also, this zooming behavior is tied to the
39:    --option/alt key rather than the mouse down.
40:    if the optiondown then
41:      curFOV = sprite(spritenum).camera.orthoheight
42:      curFOV = curFOV - 7
43:      if curFOV < 30 then curFOV = 30
44:      sprite(spritenum).camera.orthoheight = curFOV
45:    else
46:      curFOV = sprite(spritenum).camera.orthoheight
47:      curFOV = curFOV + .3
48:      if curFOV > pHomeZoom then curFOV = pHomeZoom
49:      sprite(spritenum).camera.orthoheight = curFOV
50:    end if
51: end
```

You can see that driving the Camera via the keys is quite simple in this example, as compared to the precision that was required to set the scene up initially. Notice also that whenever we move the Camera, we always move it in World space. What's more, and perhaps more importantly, when we move the Camera in two directions at once, we need to make sure the absolute value of the displacements are the same. If they are different, we would alter the orientation of the Camera, and although it make look isometric, we would not have an isometric view. This may seem like a small point, but if we were working with a much larger city map, the effect of moving "north" with the Camera as if we were moving in an isometric view would eventually lead us northwest or northeast.

NOTE

> Not all iso-games and architectural/technical illustrations use strict isometry. You see, a truly iso-metric view is very descriptive, but sometimes it needs to be "sweetened," so to speak. This sweetening results in changing the 1, 1, .6667 ratio mentioned earlier.
>
> When this happens, you will end up with either a dimetric or trimetric viewpoint. Therefore, the clinical definition of an isometric view is a rendering of a 3D environment where distances on the X, Y, and Z axes are displayed the same. In dimetric views, distances on two of the axes are displayed as the same, and in trimetric views, the distances on all three axes are displayed differently.
>
> Therefore, especially in game development, the term *isometric* is loosely used to refer to view-ports that are reminiscent of isometry: dimetric or trimetric. In this case, it is just easier to use one term than many.

The beauty of working with isometric-based projects this way is that, unlike working with isometric with tile-based methods, zooming in is much easier to do. A future consideration for you to think about is changing the Camera view from isometric to dimetric, or even to perspective for dramatic changes in point of view. Imagine a city demo where you click a window and then suddenly the Camera "flies" into the scene directly in that room. The idea is that you can use the 3D engine to blend methods of describing your visual environment to excite and engage your viewers.

Simple Camera Navigation

This example demonstrates a rather straightforward method of "driving" a perspective Camera through a relatively flat world using the arrow keys. The Camera moves with linear acceleration and deceleration as you drive through the environment. Open the file named "Camera Driving" on the CD, press Play, and use the arrow keys to "drive" the Camera within the environment. The script used to create this type of navigation is as follows:

```
1: property spritenum
2: property pSpeed
3: property pMaxSpeed, pMinSpeed
4: property pAccel, pDecel
5: property pFriction
6: property pTurnAmount
7:
```

```
 8: global scene
 9:
10:
11: on beginsprite
12:   pspeed = 0  --current speed (velocity) of the camera
13:   pMaxSpeed = 20 --maximum speed of the camera
14:   pMinSpeed = 0 --minimum speed of the camera
15:   pFriction = .99 --per-frame rate of slowing down for camera
16:   pAccel = 4 --how fast the camera accelerates toward max speed
17:   pDecel = 2 --how fast the camera decelerates toward min speed
18:   pTurnAmount = 5 --how fast the camera turns
19: end
20:
21:
22: on exitframe
23:   --Slow the camera down by the friction amount
24:   pspeed = pspeed - pFriction
25:   --make sure that the camera stops if it is
26:   --moving too slow
27:   if pspeed < pMinSpeed then pspeed = pMinSpeed
28:   --make sure the camera is limited to the max speed
29:   if pspeed > pMaxSpeed then pspeed = pMaxSpeed
30:
31:   --move the camera on its own negative Z axis
32:   --therefore, propelling us, into the scene
33:   --the distance prescribed by the pspeed property
34:   scene.camera[1].translate(0,0,-pspeed, #self)
35:
36:
37:   --Accelerate
38:   if keypressed(126) then
39:     --notice that accelerating only
40:     --changes the value of the "pspeed"
41:     --the actual movement is handled
42:     --separately
43:     pSpeed = pSpeed + pAccel
44:   end if
45:
46:   --Brake
47:   if keypressed(125) then
48:     --same thing here:  deceleration
49:     --changes the value of pspeed,
50:     --but the realization of this is
51:     --handled separately
52:     pSpeed = pSpeed - pDecel
53:   end if
54:
```

```
55:
56:    --Turn Right
57:    if keypressed(123) then
58:      --rotate the camera on its Y axis, therefore
59:      --the Z axis will point in a different "world"
60:      --direction, and the camera will move to the right
61:      scene.camera[1].rotate(0,pTurnAmount,0,#self)
62:    end if
63:
64:    --Turn Left
65:    if keypressed(124) then
66:      --rotate the camera on the Y axis, but to the left
67:      scene.camera[1].rotate(0,-pTurnAmount,0,#self)
68:    end if
69: end
```

This script defines the values of several properties during the beginsprite() handler. You should consider tinkering with the initial values of pFriction, pMaxspeed, and pAccel to change the overall quality of Camera motion. The prime concept to understand in this demo is that pressing the up- and down-arrow keys does not translate the Camera—it changes the pSpeed property (velocity) used to translate the Camera. This is important, because it allows us to introduce the idea of accelerating, friction, and deceleration by allowing velocity to accumulate over time.

The second item of importance in this code is that the keypressed() function is used rather than chartonum(the keypressed). The reason for this is that keypressed() is a function which returns true or false, which allows us to check whether a key has been pressed, rather than blindly checking which the last key pressed was. In short, this change allows the user to keep his finger on the up-arrow key while momentarily tapping right or left to steer.

There are many areas in which we might enhance this code. One area would be to create the same type of accumulative velocity for the turning of the Camera. That way, the longer you press to the left- or right-arrow key, the farther your "steering wheel" is turned.

Here's another area where we could add to the visual style of this demo: Notice how the blue pyramids "appear" out of the horizon? This effect is created by setting the far-clipping plane of the Camera through the yon property relatively close to the Camera. In this example, that value is 2000. Try experimenting with different values for yon to see how this changes the relationship of velocity and the horizon.

Camera Following

Camera following is a term used to refer to a type of Camera navigation that essentially follows a Model, rather than the Camera itself being directly navigated. However, because a Model will be in front of the Camera, it is often necessary to enhance the method of following, depending on your situation. There are two situations in which you will most likely need advanced Camera following: building a driving game and building a first-person adventure. We will examine the reason why strict Camera following is generally not good enough for either of these situations, and then we will examine how to create a stronger candidate for our Camera following code.

Simple Camera Following

The Simple Camera Following demo is intended to show you how to create a Camera that follows a Model. Open the file named "Simple Following" on the CD, press Play, and then "drive" through the environment using the arrow keys.

This demo is intended to show how following the Model very strictly can feel very awkward and lacks a sense of presence in the scene. Therefore, essentially, this is a demo that is intended to show you what *not* to do. However, it is still an important demo, because you have to set up the Camera so that it follows the Model, which is actually easier than it sounds.

We will create a Model and then add the Camera as a child of that Model so that when the parent Model moves, the Camera moves with it. This is accomplished in the following excerpt from the initialization script of the Simple Camera Following demo:

```
1: --create the Model to follow
2: obj = createbox("mybox", 10,10,10,rgb(255,0,0))
3:
4: --translate it up (so that it is on top of the ground plane)
5: obj.translate(0,5,0)
6:
7: --reset the camera transform
```

```
 8: scene.camera[1].transform.identity()
 9: --add the camera as a child of the Model
10: scene.model("mybox").addchild(scene.camera[1], #preserveparent)
11:
12: --set the camera field of view
13: scene.camera[1].fieldofview = 45
14:
15: --Move the camera behind the Model
16: scene.camera[1].translate(0,20,85,#parent)
```

The second part of making this demo work involves modifying the navigation script so that we move the Model rather than the Camera. This forces the Camera to follow its parent (the Model), but technically we are navigating the Model.

Advanced Camera Following

The problem with the previous demo is that the movement of the Camera is just too rigid. If you are in a car and you accelerate very rapidly, you may experience a certain amount of force jerking you backward. The car will probably accelerate faster than you, which is what pushes the back of your head into the seat. Again, this is more evident with extreme acceleration. When your head moves back, your eyes move with it, and therefore the "view" accelerates away from you. Then, you eventually catch up to the acceleration of the car, you can sit forward, and you "catch up" to the view. Similar effects happen when you turn while moving very quickly.

Camera following is a technique that tries to compensate for the fact that a first-person viewpoint may not immediately track the Model that the Camera is trying to follow; instead, the Camera is constantly "catching up" with the Model that it is following.

At the heart of this demonstration is the interpolateto() transform command. We used interpolateto() in the first demonstration in this chapter to reorient the Camera. Because Interpolateto() can animate both position and orientation, we can use it to build a Camera following script. But in order to utilize this command, we need to enhance the initialization script for the movie.

First, open the "Advanced Following" file on the CD and press Play. Drive the Model using the arrow keys and make sure you take some "hard" turns. Notice how the driving in this demo is much more engaging than the previous demo.

In this demonstration, after creating the Model and parenting and positioning the Camera, I made a clone of the Camera, named "dummy." The dummy Camera is a clone, so its parent is also the Model. Then, I change the parent of the original Camera back to the World so that technically, at this point, the Camera that the Sprite is using does not move or follow anything. The cloning and reparenting of the original Camera are handled in the following code excerpt from the initialization script:

```
1:   --create the Model to follow
2:   obj = createbox("mybox", 10,10,10,rgb(255,0,0))
3:
4:   --translate it up (so that it is on top of the ground plane)
5:   obj.translate(0,5,0)
6:
7:   --reset the camera transform
8:   scene.camera[1].transform.identity()
9:   --add the camera as a child of the Model
10:  scene.model("mybox").addchild(scene.camera[1], #preserveparent)
11:
12:  --set the camera field of view
13:  scene.camera[1].fieldofview = 45
14:
15:  --Move the camera behind the Model
16:  scene.camera[1].translate(0,10,35,#parent)
17:
18:  --clone the original camera
19:  scene.camera[1].clone("dummy")
20:  -- "un-parent" the original camera from the Model
21:  scene.camera[1].parent = scene.group("world")
```

The last step is then to modify the exitframe handler from the navigation script so that the Camera interpolates to the position and orientation of the dummy Camera. Remember, the dummy Camera will automatically follow the Model. If we were to look through its "eyes," we would see the same view of the World that was presented in the previous demo. Instead, the navigation behavior has the following enhancement, located at the end of the exitframe handler:

```
1: --capture the current position and orientation of the dummy camera
2: trans = scene.camera[2].getworldtransform()
3:
4: --interpolate camera[1] 15% of the way to the current
5: --position and orientation of the dummy camera
6: scene.camera[1].transform.interpolateto(trans, 15)
```

These changes may seem minute, but the overall effect is quite convincing. The one parameter you might consider changing is the percentage argument for the interpolateto() command. If you use a higher value, the Camera will follow the Model more closely; with a lower value, the Camera will act a bit looser.

Here are some other enhancements you might think about incorporating into your system:

- Allowing user to "turn his head"
- Attaching a Camera to an animated character's head
- Adding a bit of vertical Camera shake
- Switching between first-person and third-person Cameras

Regardless of the method of Camera following you use, remember that this topic is quite large, and you can learn much about this subject through observing camera treatment in video games. Some good examples include Diablo, Mario Kart, Descent, and Dynasty Warriors II.

Camera Examination

A frequently used method of building user interaction with the environment through the Camera is a technique I will refer to as *Camera examination*. Basically, Camera examination is a method of "grabbing" the Camera view and rotating it in any direction around a subject in order to examine it. In this section, we will explore three variations on a method of implementing this technique.

Simple Camera Examination

The first example creates a rather straightforward, linear correlation between the location of the mouse on the Sprite and the position of the Camera. Open the file named "Simple Examine" on the CD, press Play, and try to grab the book and move it around. Now grab anywhere on the Stage and move the book around.

The point is that, in this example, we are not actually rotating the book around the center of the Stage; rather, we are rotating the Camera around the book. You might wonder why I would go through so much trouble to do this; however, think about a situation where instead of needing to rotate around just one book, there are hundreds of Models to rotate around. This technique allows you to alter the way you see the environment rather than the Models in the environment.

This technique is achieved in a similar way to the examples of Camera following you just learned. The Camera is assigned as the child of a Model that the user manipulates via the mouse. Because the Camera is the child of a Model that is moving, the Camera will move. In order to make this effect quite efficient, I have created a small Model in the center of the World and added the Camera as its child in the initialization script of this movie, as follows:

```
1: --create a dummy box at the center of the environment
2:   obj = createbox("dummy", 1,1,1, rgb(0,0,0))
3:  --set the resource of the box model to void
4:  --because we dont want to see a little bitty
5:  --box floating in the middle of our scene.
6:   obj.resource = void
7:  -- note that without a modelresource, there
8:  --can still be a Model, but it wont have any
9:  --geometry... (but it still has a transform)
10:
11:  --make the camera a child of the "dummy" model
12:   obj.addchild(scene.camera[1], #preserveworld)
```

Creating the dummy Model and then assigning the Camera as its child is not very difficult, but it is critical. Calculating the rotation of the Camera around a point in space can be difficult, and this method is intended to alleviate much of the guesswork.

NOTE

There is an item of conceptual importance in this demonstration that you should take time to grasp. Notice that I have set the resource of the #box Model to void. As it says in the comments of the code, a Model without a resource has no geometry, but this does not stop it from having a transform (that is, a position and orientation).

I have used this setting so that the Model is not visible. This is important, because the Model is technically our rotational pivot for the Camera, and in some situations, that rotational pivot may need to be positioned where it would be visible, rather than inside of another Model.

Once the scene has been established, the behavior of the Camera is controlled via the position of the dummy Model. In this case, the majority of the task is handled by an exitframe event controlled by flag-based logic, as shown in the following script:

```
1: property spritenum
2: property poldtrans
3: property pdrag
4:
5: global scene
6:
7: on beginsprite me
8:   --pdrag will be used to determine whether we are
9:   --dragging the Dummy Model or not.
10:   pdrag = false
11:   --poldtrans is used to make sure that when you drag
12:   --the dummy object, it drags relative to its
13:   --last known transform (the position that you dragged
14:   --it to last time, rather than its identity transform)
15:   poldtrans = scene.model("dummy").getworldtransform()
16: end
17:
18: on mousedown me
19:   pdrag = true
20: end
21:
22: on mouseup me
23:   pdrag = false
24:   --record the transform of the dummy
25:   poldtrans = scene.model("dummy").getworldtransform()
26: end
27:
28: on mouseupoutside me
29:   mouseup(me)
30: end
31:
```

```
32: on exitframe me
33:    -- if you are dragging...
34:    if pdrag then
35:       --figure out the difference in pixels
36:       --between where the mouse clicked down
37:       -- and where the mouse is now.
38:       deltaPOS = the clickloc - the mouseloc
39:       --reset the dummy object to its last known transform
40:       --that way when we rotate the dummy, it will rotate
41:       --respective to this position rather than the
42:       --identity transform for the dummy.
43:       scene.model("dummy").transform = poldtrans
44:       --transform the dummy based on the current
45:       --delta in position between clickloc and mouseloc
46:
47:       --first rotate around the x axis (by the vertical delta)
48:       scene.model("dummy").rotate(vector(deltapos[2],0,0), #world)
49:       --now rotate around the z axis (by the horizontal delta)
50:       scene.model("dummy").rotate(vector(0,0,deltapos[1]), #world)
51:    end if
52: end
```

Before going any further, I would like to say that there are many variations on this technique, ranging from the axis rotated around, to the amount of rotation applied to the Camera. Also, because we are rotating the Camera in these demos, the lighting in the scene will not change. This could be a good thing, unless you are trying to rotate a Model that has reflections. Because you are moving the Camera, the relationship of the Model to the Lights in the scene will not change, and therefore the reflections will look "baked" onto the surface of the Model. If this is the case, you might want to consider rotating the Lights along with the Camera—or if you only need to rotate the one Model, then rotate the Model rather than the Camera.

Friction Camera Examination

The second example of Camera examination introduces an element of simulated friction so that the Camera can be "grabbed and thrown." This way, when you let go of the Camera, it eases into place rather than just stops. Open the file named "Friction Examine" on the CD, press Play, and then try to "grab and throw" the Model of the toaster.

The initial setup of the movie is identical to the previous movie; the difference is in the complexity of the behavior script. The majority of work is still done by the `exitframe` handler and is driven by flag-based logic. However, the value of the `pDrag` property will determine how the `exitframe` handler moves the dummy Model. Take careful note of this expansion of tasks for the `exitframe` handler in the following script:

```
 1: property spritenum
 2: property pdeltapos
 3: property pFriction
 4: property plastloc
 5: property pdrag
 6:
 7: global scene
 8:
 9: on beginsprite me
10:   pdrag = false
11:   -- amount of simulated friction to slow
12:   -- the camera rotation by each frame
13:   pFriction = .5
14: end
15:
16: on mousedown me
17:   pdrag = true
18: end
19:
20: on mouseup me
21:   pdrag = false
22:   -- notice that on mouseup, rather than recording
23:   -- the last position of the dummy Model, I am
24:   -- recording the delta between the location of the
25:   -- mouse at the last exitframe and the current
26:   -- mouse position.  This means that the amount of
27:   -- "throw velocity" is determined in a very small
28:   -- amount of time.
29:   pdeltaPOS = plastloc - the mouseloc
30: end
31:
32: on mouseupoutside me
33:   mouseup(me)
34: end
35:
36:
37: on exitframe me
38:
39:   if pdrag then
40:     --check the distance of dragging
```

```
41:     pdeltaPOS = the clickloc - the mouseloc
42:     --rather than using the last position of the
43:     -- dummy model, I will issue an identity() command
44:     -- this is what makes the Camera return to its initial
45:     -- position when you "tap" the mouse… If you do not like
46:     -- this, you can always retro-fit this part of the demo
47:     -- to use the poldtrans property from the previous demo…
48:     scene.model("dummy").transform.identity()
49:     scene.model("dummy").rotate(vector(pdeltapos[2],0,0), #world)
50:     scene.model("dummy").rotate(vector(0,0,pdeltapos[1]), #world)
51:     --record the last position of the mouse, so that if the
52:     --user lets go of the mouse, the computer can determine the
53:     -- "velocity" of the drag & throw.
54:     plastloc = the mouseloc
55:
56:  else
57:     -- This is the Friction section.
58:     -- in case the user is not dragging
59:
60:     --and that pdeltapos is not void
61:     -- because if it were void, it would
62:     -- mean that the Model was never dragged,
63:     -- and therefore does not need to "slow down"
64:      if pdeltapos <> void then
65:
66:        --this repeat loop will quickly check the values
67:        -- of the vertical and horizontal elements of the
68:        -- pdeltapos property. What it will do is cause
69:        -- each of these elements to approach zero – whether
70:        -- they are a positive value or a negative value
71:        repeat with x = 1 to 2
72:
73:          --determine whether the vertical or horizontal
74:          -- element of pdeltapos is greater than zero,
75:          -- and if it is, diminish it by the pFriction amount
76:          -- until it reaches zero
77:          if pdeltapos[x] > 0 then
78:            pdeltapos[x] = pdeltapos[x] - pFriction
79:            if pdeltapos[x] < 0 then pdeltapos[x] = 0
80:
81:          else if pdeltapos[x] < 0 then
82:            --determine whether the vertical or horizontal
83:            -- element of pdeltapos is less than zero,
84:            -- and if it is, increase it by the pFriction amount
85:            -- until it reaches zero
86:
87:            pdeltapos[x] = pdeltapos[x] + pFriction
```

```
88:            if pdeltapos[x] > 0 then pdeltapos[x] = 0
89:          end if
90:        end repeat
91:
92:        -- once the velocity of the dummy model has been modified
93:        -- via pFriction, rotate the dummy Model.
94:        scene.model("dummy").rotate(vector(pdeltapos[2],0,0), #world)
95:        scene.model("dummy").rotate(vector(0,0,pdeltapos[1]), #world)
96:      end if
97:   end if
98: end
```

There are many areas in which you might consider enhancing this particular
variation on the technique. One change would be to never allow the dummy
Model to reach a zero velocity so that the view always "floats." Another possibility is to set the pFriction property very low so that it takes a very long time
for the dummy Model to slow down.

Zeroing Camera Examination

In the final variation of this technique, the Camera will "zero" back to its initial position after the user has examined the object, as if the Camera were
attached to a rubber band. In other words, when you let go of the Camera, it
unwinds to its initial position. This can be helpful if you want to ensure that
the user can examine the Model without worrying about "messing up" the
view. The variation in this case is, again, quite small and takes place in the
exitframe() event, as indicated here:

```
1: property spritenum
2: property pdeltapos
3: property pZeroFactor
4: property pdrag
5:
6: global scene
7:
8: on beginsprite me
9:   pdrag = false
10:   pZeroFactor = .5
11: end
12:
13: on mousedown me
14:   pdrag = true
```

```
15: end
16:
17: on mouseup me
18:    pdrag = false
19: end
20:
21: on mouseupoutside me
22:    mouseup(me)
23: end
24:
25: on exitframe me
26:
27:    -- if the user is dragging the mouse this time, we
28:    -- reset the view to the identity() transform, but
29:    -- we also skip the step of recording "friction"
30:    -- because the dummy Model always springs back
31:    -- to the same position.
32:
33:    if pdrag then
34:      pdeltaPOS = the clickloc - the mouseloc
35:      scene.model("dummy").transform.identity()
36:      scene.model("dummy").rotate(vector(pdeltapos[2],0,0), #world)
37:      scene.model("dummy").rotate(vector(0,0,pdeltapos[1]), #world)
38:    else
39:
40:
41:      if pdeltapos <> void then
42:        repeat with x = 1 to 2
43:
44:          if pdeltapos[x] > 0 then
45:
46:            -- this is one of the critical differences
47:            -- rather than subtracting some amount of friction
48:            -- we will multiply by the "pzerfactor" which must
49:            -- be a float between 0-1.  I know this may seem
50:            -- impossible but, if you continue to multiply
51:            -- a value by a float 0-1 you will continue
52:            -- to divide that number. that number can become
53:            -- so small that the leading number of zeroes
54:            -- will turn the value into zero eventually…
55:            pdeltapos[x] = pdeltapos[x] * pzerofactor
56:            if pdeltapos[x] < 0 then pdeltapos[x] = 0
57:          else if pdeltapos[x] < 0then
58:            pdeltapos[x] = pdeltapos[x] * pzerofactor
59:            if pdeltapos[x] > 0 then pdeltapos[x] = 0
60:          end if
61:        end repeat
```

```
62:
63:        -- no matter what, if the user is not dragging, use the
64:        -- identity() function on the dummy model.  This will ensure
65:        -- that when you rotate the dummy model by the amounts in the
66:        -- pdeltapos (that are decreasing by half until they reach zero)
67:        -- you will eventually appear to settle back to the original
68:        -- orientation.
69:        scene.model("dummy").transform.identity()
70:        scene.model("dummy").rotate(vector(pdeltapos[2],0,0), #world)
71:        scene.model("dummy").rotate(vector(0,0,pdeltapos[1]), #world)
72:    end if
73:  end if
74: end
```

In this section, we have covered many variations on this one basic idea: What appear to be small changes can have a great impact on the scene. More importantly, notice how the identity() transform is used in these demonstrations. Just because you set a Model to its identity() transform momentarily does not mean the user will need to see that. For this reason, identity() can help you create effects involving transformation that would be difficult to create otherwise.

Multiple Viewports

In this section, we will look at two methods of implementing multiple viewports for a single 3D World. These two examples are quite different from one another in that the first example utilizes multiple Sprites of the same Castmember, whereas the second method utilizes a single Sprite with multiple Cameras drawn within it.

Viewports with Multiple Sprites

The rootnode property is an interesting Camera property that can be used to exclude Nodes from being drawn by a Camera. This property is similar to setting the parent property for a Node. Instead of changing the scenegraph hierarchy, this property will change which Models are drawn by a Camera. By default, a Camera's rootnode is the World; therefore, it draws the World Group and all its children. If you change this property to a different Node, the Camera will only draw that Node and its children.

However, if you set the rootnode property to be a Node that is not a Light or does not have a Light as one of its children, there will be no Light to light that Model. For this reason, it can be awkward to initialize your scenes to utilize rootnode.

If you open the "Dual Sprites" file on the CD and press Play, you will see two Sprites on the Stage. These two Sprites are both views of the same 3D Castmember, but they utilize different Cameras. In addition, each of the Cameras utilizes different root nodes. Examine the following excerpt from the initialization script to see how the scene has been set up:

```
1:   --make sure that sprite 1 uses camera 2
2:   sprite(1).camera = scene.camera[2]
3:   --make sure that sprite 2 uses camera 3
4:   sprite(2).camera = scene.camera[3]
5:
6:   --assign light 1 as the child of model 3 (glass)
7:   scene.model[3].addchild(scene.light[1], #preserveworld)
8:   -- assign light 2 as the child of model 4 (plant)
9:   scene.model[4].addchild(scene.light[2], #preserveworld)
10:
11:    --assign the tableleg as child of the table
12:   scene.model[1].addchild(scene.model[2], #preserveworld)
13:   --create a clone of the table and tablelef
14:   scene.model[1].clone("tableclone")
15:
16:   --assign the original table as a child of the wineglass
17:   scene.model[3].addchild(scene.model[1], #preserveworld)
18:
19:   --assign the table clone as a child of the vase
20:   scene.model[4].addchild(scene.model("tableclone"), #preserveworld)
21:
22:
23:   --set the rootnode of camera 2 to the glass
24:   scene.camera[2].rootnode = scene.model[3]
25:   --set the rootnode of camera 3 to the plant
26:   scene.camera[3].rootnode = scene.model[4]
```

This code creates two separate scenegraph hierarchies—to the point of cloning any Models that need to appear in both Cameras. Then, after the scenegraphs have been created, the rootnode property of each Camera is assigned to the topmost Node of each hierarchy. Admittedly, this process is both powerful and cumbersome, especially because of the way we need to clone Nodes that will appear in both Cameras. If you needed to create two views of the same exact scene, using multiple Sprites of the same Castmember is certainly viable, but it lacks certain possibilities that are possible in the next demo.

Viewports with Multiple `camera.rect` Values

A more interesting and more robust approach toward using multiple Cameras is to create multiple Camera viewports inset within a Sprite. Rather than using one Sprite per Camera, this technique creates Cameras that overlap, grow, shrink, disappear, and react to the user in more interesting ways than the multiple-Sprite approach.

Open the file named "Nav With Top View" on the CD and press Play. This demo is taken from the earlier Advanced Following demo. However, the enhancement in this case is a view from above the Model to follow that inset near the top of the Sprite. Notice how as you drive around, this top-view Camera is quite accurate. Another possibility would be to create a rearview mirror–type effect with this technique.

In order to create inset cameras like this, you need a second Camera to inset. Then you need to do two things: Add the Camera to the Sprite Active Camera list and then set the `camera.rect` property for the "inset." Observe the code used to create the camera, and then create the inset:

```
1:   --camera 2 creation and initialization
2:   cam = scene.newcamera("topview")
3:   cam.fieldofview = 90
4:   cam.transform.identity()
5:   scene.model("mybox").addchild(cam, #preserveparent)
6:   cam.translate(0,40,0)
7:   cam.pointat(scene.model("mybox"))
8:
9:   -- first, add the new camera to the sprite
10:  -- active camera list
11:   sprite(1).addcamera(cam)
12:   --second set the rect of the topview camera
13:   --so that it is inset near the upper left
14:   -- of the sprite.
15: scene.camera("topview").rect = rect(400,10,630,210)
```

Note that the `camera.rect` values should be given relative to the top-left corner of the Sprite. Overall, this technique can be very rewarding for several reasons. First, it is possible to change the position of the `camera.rect` property on-the-fly, so you can create Camera views that "travel" through the scene. Second, you can scale up and down `camera.rect` properties, thus creating pop-up windows. Third, you can manage multiple overlapping Cameras that change into single Cameras, and back again, much easier than you can with a multiple-Sprite setup. The point that should be clear with this method is that you have a much wider scope of control over the final result, making this the obvious choice over using multiple Sprites.

Summary

The Camera is a vital component of every 3D environment and has the potential to be controlled in extremely specific ways. We have looked at techniques, such as Camera zoom and Camera examining, that can be used as interface elements. In addition, we have looked at techniques that utilize the Camera as if it were the eyes of a first-person or third-person viewer. Finally, we examined two methods of creating multiple views of a single 3D World on the Stage at the same time.

Each of these techniques has the following in common: Although the Camera can be controlled through a small number of properties, it is the functions and commands you use in conjunction with those properties that help you to build behaviors. Also, the behaviors we have examined, especially in the "Camera Examination" section, demonstrate how seemingly small changes in the code can change the overall method of user interaction.

Finally, the techniques presented in this chapter are powerful because they can be combined, enhanced, and iterated upon to create a wide array of interfaces that involve the Camera as a primary motivating force. Remember, the Camera is a vital component of the 3D environment, not just because without the Camera there is nothing to see, but because the Camera helps users build a visual relationship with the environment. Therefore, understanding how to control the Camera is the cornerstone of controlling your 3D environments, and in turn your projects.

FAQ

What about Camera collision detection?

There are several ways to build Camera collision detection. We will be examining this subject in Chapter 29, "Collision Detection."

What about Camera headlights?

Camera headlights are easier to create than you might think. Create a spotlight that points in the same direction as the Camera, and then add that Light as a child of the Camera. Now when you move the Camera, the Light will move with it. You can use this effect to create "headlights" for Models as well.

CHAPTER 26

Advanced Transforms and Vector Math

The focus of this chapter is to take a close look at the mathematics involved in 3D programming. Specifically this means that you will be learning vector math. Vector math is a powerful tool that you may have avoided until now for a variety of reasons. If you have not been exposed to mathematics in quite a while or have not worked with vectors at all in the past, do not worry. We will be walking, not running, through the concepts of vector math. Although I will be presenting some techniques, my goal for this chapter is that you walk away understanding the basics of vector math.

Because of this, you will find that the format for this chapter is a bit different from the others in this book. Namely, you may find that we will be spending much time building concepts before actually applying them. Because of the nature of mathematics, and because I'm assuming you have had no experience with vector math in the past, there is no way around this. This leads to my next point: If you have had experience with vector math in the past, you may find this chapter rather slow. I am presenting this chapter now because the remainder of the book requires some knowledge of the concepts we will be covering. Therefore, other than the examples in this chapter, consider that the concepts you are learning here will be applied in the remaining chapters of the book. The techniques shown in this chapter are good on their own, but to truly harness the power of vector math, you will need to see how it is applied in the remaining chapters.

Finally, you must understand that this chapter is not a replacement for a solid course in vector mathematics, nor should it be considered your only source for learning this material. Although I feel this chapter explains vector mathematics in a clear, concise method that follows the speed of the rest of the book, you may not agree. If you are having trouble with mathematics in general, be sure to consult the resources listed at the end of the chapter.

In addition to vector math, you should notice that the chapter title also mentions *advanced transforms*. The last third of the chapter is dedicated to several transformation issues we have not yet had time to address. Specifically, we will be looking at how and why you might invert a transform and how to change a transform from local coordinates to World coordinates. Also, explanations of gimbal lock, Euler angles, and using axisangle rotations are provided. I suggest you read through the chapter entirely, making notes where you have trouble, so that you can return to the troublesome areas later.

Who Should Read This Chapter?

If your initial response to this chapter is "I hate/fear math; how much should I read?" you are not alone. This is a fair question, and I want to answer it for you before you read the chapter. Whether you hate or fear math, I consider this chapter a prerequisite for the remaining chapters in the book. In short, if you are interested in learning about creating Meshes from code (Chapter 27), Mesh deformation (Chapter 28), or collision detection (Chapter 29), you need to read this chapter. So, the answer to this question is not so much how to alleviate your hatred or fear of mathematics but rather how to point toward your goals. Without a clear understanding of vector math and advanced transformations, it will not be possible to fully explain the aforementioned topics.

To continue, Director is an authoring tool with a high-level scripting language, Lingo. Because Lingo is a high-level tool, you should not expect the same amount of low-level control that you would in C or C++. When we begin working with vector mathematics, this becomes a bit of a sticking point. You see, Director 8.5 is one of the first high-level authoring tools for 3D programming that bridges a conceptual gap. 3D programming has traditionally been left out of authoring packages or implemented in amazingly crippled ways. In Director 8.5, we have an extremely deep amount of control over the environment, considering the fact that Lingo is basically a high-level scripting language.

In terms of vector math, Lingo takes the same conceptual stance that you would expect it to: It hides much of the low-level control from you as a developer. This is great, because in terms of vector math, it means we will avoid having to perform much of the actual algebra, trigonometry, and matrix methods. Most of these tasks are performed by the vector math functions we will be looking at.

Although this amount of high-level control makes *using* vector math very easy, the fact that many concepts are kept hidden from developers can often make the task of *learning* vector math very difficult. This, in turn, leads to the point I wish to make: Just because you can avoid having to do the arithmetic does not get you out of learning the concepts behind vector math. This is all further complicated by the fact that 99 percent of the texts that you are going to find on 3D programming and 3D math in general are written at a very abstract level.

Generally, texts for 3D programming are written with C or C++ programming in mind. This does not mean that you cannot translate the information in those books into knowledge for Director, but you will have to cut through a majority of information geared toward explaining exactly how to manipulate the algebra, trigonometry, and matrix methods of vector math.

In short, this chapter is unique because in it you will find that the topic of vector math has been tailored for those learning Director 8.5. If you have worked with vectors in the past, this chapter may seem painfully slow, but if you have not worked with vectors or do not understand them, this chapter is essential.

Vectors

You know from Chapter 4, "Transformations," that vectors represent dynamic information—a displacement in space; a change from one location to another. You also know that vectors quantify two vital pieces of information: a direction and a magnitude. Finally, you know that in Director, these two pieces of information—direction and magnitude—are not represented directly but rather through three components of a vector: X, Y, and Z.

You may recall that there is a difference between a vector and the uses for the vector data type in Director. In addition to representing displacements, component vectors can be used to represent locations or orientations. Director also uses the vector data type for scaling transforms, attenuation, and UVW mapping coordinates. When covering vector math in this chapter, we will be primarily concerned with discussing the use of the vector data type to represent locations in 3D space.

Scalars

You know that a vector is an important way of describing two vital pieces of information: a direction and a magnitude. Because of this, vectors are extremely useful in a wide variety of fields, including architecture and physics. Although I have defined a vector as a displacement, physicists often use vectors to represent physical forces. For example, if we were trying to describe acceleration or velocity, we would need to talk about both direction and strength. Using a vector allows us to describe both of these qualities within a single data type.

Also, many physical properties do not need information about direction but rather only magnitude. Examples of these are temperature, time, and volume. Because these properties only need to be represented by one number, we do not use vectors for them. Instead, these numbers will be referred to as *scalars*. Scalars are actually quite easy to understand—just think of them as normal numbers that represent one quantity. Another term for a scalar that you might encounter is a *real number*. In short, a scalar can be an integer or a floating-point number, and it can be positive or negative.

Vector Math

As you begin to learn about vector math, the first lesson is to understand what types of operations are actually possible. In scalar arithmetic, you expect to have the ability to add, subtract, multiply, and divide, but there are differences when it comes to vectors.

It is possible to add and subtract vectors. When we add or subtract vectors, the result is a vector. These two operations should be considered the easiest to understand. Next, it is also possible to multiply a scalar and a vector, which also results in a vector. Multiplying scalars and vectors is very useful because it provides a method of scaling vectors. In addition, it is possible to divide a vector by a scalar to produce a scaled vector as well.

Vector math becomes rather confusing when we begin multiplying vectors by other vectors. What you might find strange is that there are actually two different ways in which vectors can be multiplied by other vectors. With one method, the result will be a scalar; with the other method, the result will be a vector. Often, the multiplication of vectors is the part of vector math viewed as the most difficult or challenging.

NOTE

If you are concerned that I have left the division of two vectors off of this list, don't be. Dividing one vector by another vector is an operation that is not defined in Director—or by most (if any) 3D engines. This is because there is no one unique solution to the equations used to perform vector division. Note that this is not only true inside of Director—it's an issue that applies to vector math in general.

In the following subsections on vector math, we will begin by working with 2D vectors. In addition, we will be looking at the equations from a geometric point of view before imposing the algebraic methods of doing the same. This will provide a visualization of the concepts we will be dealing with, which I believe can help in the long run.

Vector Addition

Vector addition is the simplest of all the vector operations and also remains the most approachable. We will draw vectors in the form of an arrow the length of the magnitude of the vector, pointing in the direction of the vector. We will call the end of the arrow with the arrowhead the "head of the vector," and we will call the opposite end the "tail." Vector addition can be visualized geometrically by arranging vectors head to tail. In Figure 26.1, you can see that I have arranged two vectors so that the head of vector A ends where the tail of vector B begins.

FIGURE 26.1

Head-to-tail demonstration of geometrically adding two vectors together.

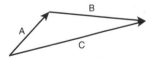

In this figure, vector C represents what is often referred to as the *net displacement*. Essentially, vector C visually represents the sum of adding vector A and vector B together. Vector addition has two interesting properties: First, it is said to be *commutative*, which means that if you add A + B or B + A, the result is C in both cases. This important point leads to what is known as the *parallelogram law of vector addition*, as illustrated in Figure 26.2.

FIGURE 26.2

Illustration of the parallelogram law of vector addition.

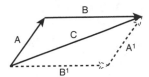

This law is a visual way for you to remember that regardless of the order in which you add vectors, you will always end up with the same resultant. In addition to being commutative, adding vectors is also *associative*. This is important when you begin adding more than two vectors together. Essentially, if we were to add vectors A + B + C, we would end up with the same result as adding B + C + A or A + C + B. The order of addition does not affect the resultant. The fact that vector addition is associative is clearly demonstrated in Figure 26.3.

In this example, vectors A, B, and C result in vector D. Regardless of the order in which we add vectors A, B, and C, we will always arrive at vector D.

One situation that often arises with vector addition that you should be aware of is that the resultant can often cancel out the effect of all vectors. For example, imagine that you have three vectors you are adding together, as shown in Figure 26.4.

As you can see from this figure, it is possible that the resultant of the vectors might not have a magnitude larger than the sum of the component vectors. Remember, you are not just adding the magnitudes of vectors but also the magnitudes and the directions of those vectors.

FIGURE 26.3

Illustration of the addition of multiple vectors.

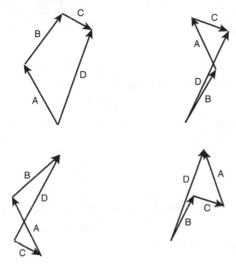

FIGURE 26.4

Adding vectors whose net resultant is `vector(0,0,0)`.

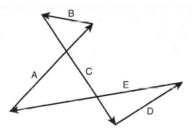

Next, we will take a look at the syntax used for vector addition. Note that the following example is intended to be executed in the message window. First, we need to create two vectors:

```
VectorA = vector(10,20,0)
VectorB = vector(2,12,0)
```

Next, we will add them together:

```
Put vectorA + vector B
-- vector(12,32,0)
```

As you can see, to arrive at the resultant vector—`vector(12,32,0)`—you add the individual components of each vector together. If we were to describe any vector A as `vector(Ax, Ay, Az)` and another vector B as `vector(Bx, By, Bz)`, to solve for the resultant vector of A + B, we would use the following formula:

Vector C = ((Ax + Bx), (Ay + By), (Az + Bz))

However, this algebraic information is provided merely as a background to help you see the conceptual leap from the geometric solution for vector addition to the algebraic solution. This process of adding the individual components is automated for you when simply using the + operator with two (or more) vectors as the operands.

Vector Subtraction

The next operation we will be looking at is vector subtraction. We can solve vector subtraction geometrically, but our method is a bit different from addition. Rather than placing all the vectors head to tail, we will align all the vector tails at a common starting point, as shown in Figure 26.5.

FIGURE 26.5

A demonstration of vector subtraction.

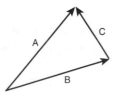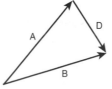

Note from this figure that the process of vector subtraction is not commutative. This means that the order of vector subtraction is extremely important. You can see from this example that A–B = C, and B–A = D. Note that C and D are not equivalent because their directions are not the same. These two vectors, C and D, do have the same magnitudes, but as you know, this is not enough for vector equivalency.

Next, we will do some investigation of vector subtraction in the message window, similar to our experiment with vector addition. First, we will define two vectors:

```
VectorA = vector(10,10,0)
VectorB = vector(4,7,0)
```

Now we will subtract vectorB from vectorA:

```
Put vectorA - vectorB
-- vector(6,3,0)
```

If you look at this resultant, vector(6,3,0), you might start thinking that something is wrong. How can it only be vector(6,3,0)? Is this correct? Let's use what you have learned to check both ourselves and Director using geome try. To illustrate this vector subtraction, let's think back to the parallelogram law of vector addition. You know that vector addition is commutative, and because of this, you know that the following mathematical statement is true:

vectorA + vectorB = vectorB + vectorA

Essentially, this statement tells us that regardless of the order in which we add vectors together, we will get the same resultant. You know that we cannot make the same statement for vector subtraction, because vector subtraction is not commutative. However, subtraction and addition are related in strange ways. Note that the following mathematical statement is true:

vectorA - vectorB = vectorA + -(vectorB)

In this mathematical statement, I have proposed that vector subtraction is equivalent to adding a negated version of the second vector. With this in mind, we are able to make the next, most important mathematical statement:

-(vectorB) + vectorA = vectorA + -(vectorB)

If you look at this proof, you see that vector addition retains its commutative properties even though we are essentially subtracting two vectors. But as I said, this is easier to understand (and also check ourselves) if we look at this example using geometry. Figure 26.6 illustrates three vectors: vector A, vector B, and the resultant from their subtraction.

FIGURE 26.6

Using addition to subtract two vectors by negating one of the vectors before addition.

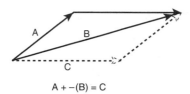

$$A + -(B) = C$$

Again, we are presented with the parallelogram law of vector addition, but we are using the parallelogram in a different way. Although this may seem redundant, think about what you have learned about vector addition and vector subtraction. First, you know that there is a relationship between adding and subtracting. Second, this diagram shows that if you have two vectors, you can derive a variety of other vectors from them. Third, and most important, both vector addition and vector subtraction have the capability to change the magnitude and direction of a vector.

Scalar Multiplication

The next operation we will be looking at with a great deal of scrutiny is the process of multiplying vectors and scalars. In case you read other texts about vector mathematics at some point, you should know that this process is often referred to as *scalar multiplication*. In this section, I will be addressing the multiplication of both scalars and vectors as well as the division of vectors by scalars.

When you multiply a scalar and a vector, the result will be a vector that has the same direction but a different magnitude. Essentially, this process has the effect of scaling the magnitude of a vector. If the scalar is positive, the direction of the vector will remain the same; if the scalar is negative, the direction of the vector will reverse. Note that Figure 26.7 shows two vectors, A and B, where B represents A * 3.

FIGURE 26.7

Basic vector scaling with multiplication.

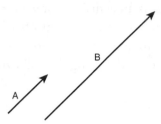

You should keep in mind that it is also possible to scale a vector by dividing it by a scalar. Dividing a vector by a scalar will change the magnitude of a vector as well, but it will scale the vector smaller than its magnitude was originally. You can see this process represented geometrically in Figure 26.8, which shows two vectors, C and D, where D represents C / 2.

FIGURE 26.8

Basic vector scaling with division.

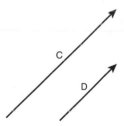

Even though it is possible to scale vectors with division, I will advise you to use caution when working with it. The reason for this caution is that as with any other division process, you cannot divide by zero. If you mistakenly divide by zero, this will result in a script error. Also, note that division is not commutative, so you cannot reverse the order of scalar and vector. If you do, you will get a script error. The beauty of using scalar multiplication to scale vectors is that you can eliminate both of these issues. Because a scalar can be a floating-point number, you can use multiplication to scale vectors smaller as well as larger. It is this flexibility that makes scalar multiplication the obvious choice.

Even if you are working with scalar multiplication, there are a few issues we need to address. If you multiply any vector by the scalar value 0, Director will return 0 rather than an error. Note that this is an actual 0, not `vector(0,0,0)`. Therefore, if your code is expecting a vector, you could run into trouble. If you need to scale a vector and you are planning to use vector division, as in the case of vectors C and D from Figure 26.8, consider using the following mathematical equivalency:

(C / scalar = D) = (C * (1.0000 / scalar) = D)

If you want to scale a vector (let's say by half), the method of scaling demonstrated on the left side of this formula would be to divide the vector by 2. On the right side of this equation, you are shown that you could just as easily multiply the vector by 0.5.

Of course, this still leaves us with a problem concerning zero. If we process 1 / `scalar`, where `scalar` is 0, we will get a script error. One possibility would be to check ourselves with an `if`/`then` statement before dividing. The logic for this process is represented with the following pseudocode:

```
If scalar = 0 then
 D = C * 0
 Return D
Else
 D = C * (1 / scalar)
 Return D
End if
```

However, one issue still remains concerning zero: When you're multiplying by zero, the result will *not* be an empty vector: `vector(0,0,0)`. Rather, the result will be a scalar: 0. This is important, because if you mistakenly treat the scalar as though it were a vector (for instance, by assigning it as a position or rotation of a transform), this will produce an error. Therefore, the following pseudocode provides a better way to work with this problem:

```
If scalar = 0 then
 Return vector(0,0,0)
Else
 D = C * (1 / scalar)
 Return D
End if
```

As you can see, the major issues of scaling vectors simply involve being careful about scaling by zero. Fortunately, the process itself is rather straightforward. Because of this, scalar multiplication is often considered the easiest or most basic of the vector mathematics. However, this is not entirely true. Scalar multiplication in itself is conceptually and algebraically approachable, but some of the techniques it is used for need further explanation.

In the examples we have looked at so far, the scalar has always been a positive number. If the scalar were a negative number, an interesting thing happens to our vector. Namely, in addition to any changes in magnitude that it receives, it will reverse its direction. Depending on the value of the scalar used in "vector * scalar" operations, you can make certain assumptions about the resulting vector, as shown in Table 26.1.

TABLE 26.1   Expected Scaling from Vector * Scalar Operations

Value of Scalar	Expected Scaling of Vector
scalar > 1	The vector magnitude increases.
scalar = 1	The vector magnitude remains the same.
scalar > 0 < 1	The vector magnitude decreases.
scalar = 0	The scalar 0 is returned.
scalar < 0 > -1	The vector magnitude decreases and the vector direction reverses.
scalar = -1	The vector magnitude remains the same and the vector direction reverses.
scalar < -1	The vector magnitude increases and the vector direction reverses.

You may find that these rules prove highly effective—especially if you want to reverse the direction of a vector, because you can simply multiply it by −1. This will prove useful later in this chapter in the section on transforms, as we begin to look at how to use vectors to manipulate translations in space.

Normalization

As I have mentioned, some of the techniques that scalar multiplication is used for are not entirely clear. To take scaling one step further, you need to learn about a process known as *normalization*. In order for you to clearly understand what normalization is, I want to clarify several points about vectors. First, no matter the direction of a vector, its magnitude will always be positive. It may be pointing in a negative direction, but the magnitude taken on its own will always be a positive number. Second, you know that if you scale a vector with a positive value, the only possible effect will be that the magnitude will change, but you also know that the direction will remain the same. Third, the magnitude of a vector must be greater than or equal to the largest component of the vector.

Because of these three facts, if you take each component of a vector and divide it by the magnitude of that vector, you will end up with what is known as a *normalized vector*. Luckily, this process has been simplified for us in Director with the `normalize()` and `getnormalized()` functions. The `normalize()` function is a destructive process that does not return any data. Therefore, when you call it, you will use the following syntax:

```
Myvector.normalize()
```

Note that because this is a destructive process, in this example, the value of `myvector` will be changed after you execute this line. Another possibility you should consider if you need to preserve the original vector is the `getnormalized()` function. You would use `getnormalized()` with syntax similar to the following:

```
Put myvector.getnormalized()
```

Alternatively, to store the normalized vector in a separate variable, use this:

```
MyvectorNormalized = myvector.getnormalized()
```

Remember, the `normalize()` and `getnormalized()` commands generate a result that is exactly equal to the following:

```
Put Myvector / myvector.magnitude
```

Note that the only reason I have shown the division of the magnitude in this example is to help you better understand where the results for the `normalize()` and `getnormalized()` commands are derived from.

Aside from these details of how to normalize a vector, you might still be curious as to what exactly a normalized vector is. In short, a *normalized vector* is a vector whose magnitude equals 1. Another common name for a vector whose magnitude equals 1 is a *unit vector*. Overall, the fact that we can normalize a vector at all may seem like a small point, but its complexity is deceptive and requires further explanation.

In order to explain this complexity, I must introduce yet another concept, known as the *unit circle*. The unit circle applies to 2D vectors, but we will quickly expand our understanding to include 3D vectors. Remember that a normalized vector has a magnitude of 1, but its direction remains exactly the same as it was before normalization. If we were to plot a point for every 2D vector whose magnitude is 1 by placing the tail of each vector at a unique origin, we would end up with what's shown in Figure 26.9.

FIGURE 26.9

The unit circle.

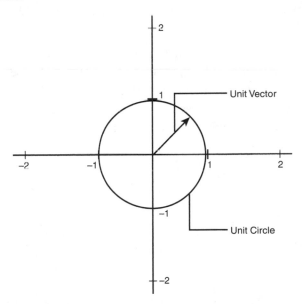

As you can see, the unit circle is a circle whose radius is 1, formed by the locus of points one unit distant from a common origin. The *locus of points* merely means all the points. If we apply the concept of a locus of points to three-dimensional vectors, the unit circle becomes what is known as the *unit sphere*.

Each of the vectors represented by the displacement between the origin and any point surface of this sphere has a magnitude of exactly 1. The only difference represented by these vectors is that they each have a unique direction.

NOTE

> Essentially, the unit sphere represents every possible *direction vector*. Often, a vector that is normalized is referred to as a *direction vector* because its magnitude is 1. The importance of the magnitude equaling 1 is related to the fact that when we begin working with the unit sphere, we are able to begin thinking about how elements of trigonometry can be used in three dimensions.

With the fact that every point on the unit sphere represents a different direction in mind, I can introduce you to the `randomvector()` function. You know that the `random()` function is used to generate random numbers. The `randomvector()` function is used to generate a random unit vector—literally, one of the vectors represented by the surface of the unit sphere. This is very important, especially if you are going to be randomly placing Models in your scene.

You see, because the `randomvector()` function always produces unit vectors, you can assume that the maximum value for any component of `randomvector()` will be between 0 and 1. Remembering that you can scale any vector by multiplying it by a scalar, you can combine `randomvector` with scalar multiplication to generate random vectors whose scope is anywhere within the 3D environment.

For example, consider the following code:

```
Put randomvector() * 100
-- vector( -51.6703, 1.3569, 85.6057 )
put vector( -51.6703, 1.3569, 85.6057 ).magnitude
-- 100.0000
```

In this code example, you see that it is possible to choose a random vector—a single vector on the unit sphere—and then scale the magnitude of this vector with certainty that no matter where the vector points to, it is (in this case) exactly 100 units in XYZ space from the origin.

Vector Multiplication

Next, we will be looking at two methods for multiplying vectors together: the *dot product* and the *cross product*. These two methods of multiplication have their own functions with specific names in Director: dot() and cross(). You should also be aware that these two methods of vector multiplication have other names:

- The dot product, or *scalar product*, is a method of multiplying two vectors that will result in a *scalar*.

- The cross product, or *vector product*, is a method of multiplying two vectors that will result in a *vector*.

I prefer the names *scalar product* and *vector product* because they immediately describe the results you should expect from the mathematical operation. However, these two terms have many names—you may even see them referred to as the *inner product* and *outer product*. I only offer this information in case you are reading other texts on the subject and are confused with the myriad of terms. Both of these methods of vector multiplication have a series of implications and uses, but you first need to learn what they are and what they do.

Dot Product

As I have mentioned, the dot product will return a scalar value. If the two source vectors you use to generate the dot product happen to be normalized, the scalar value returned to you is a special number. Specifically, this number will be the cosine of the angle between the two vectors on which you performed the dot product.

You could take this cosine value and determine the actual angle between the two vectors in degrees. However, there are other built-in functions in Director that allow you to do this without a hand-coded arccosine function. Therefore, you might still be curious regarding why we would want to evaluate the dot product at all.

Let's walk through three scenarios. In all these scenarios, we have two vectors, A and B, that are normalized. If the scalar that is returned to us after the dot product of A and B equals 0, we know that the cosine of the angle between A and B is 0. There is only one angle that generates a cosine of 0, and that angle is 90 degrees. Therefore, if the dot product of two normalized vectors returns 0, you know that the two vectors are perpendicular.

In the second scenario, suppose that the scalar returned to us is 1. If the scalar that represents the cosine of the two angles is 1, we know that the directions of the two vectors are parallel. Finally, in the third scenario, if the scalar returned to us is –1, we know that the two angles are both parallel and point exactly opposite one another in 3D space. In order to help you understand this concept, Figure 26.10 illustrates several vectors.

FIGURE 26.10

Illustration of the dot product.

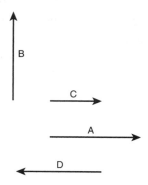

In this illustration, all the dot products have been calculated between vector A and the other vectors. However, Figure 26.10 only shows two-dimensional vectors. Because we are working in three dimensions, the angle between vector A and the other vectors is not unique. To explain what I mean by this, let's consider the following demonstration. Take your right arm and point it directly to the right of you. You might say that your arm is pointing down your positive X axis. If we were to write out the direction of your arm as a normalized vector, we would write vector(1,0,0).

Now, with your arm still extended, rotate it 30 degrees. Immediately you should be thinking, in what direction? Up, down, left, right, or some combination? This is the problem: There are so many possible 30-degree angles from the current position of your arm, it is impossible to tell which one is which.

To continue with this demonstration, rotate your arm 30 degrees up from your positive X axis. Your arm should be pointing in the same direction as vector A in Figure 26.11.

FIGURE 26.11

Illustration of vector A pointing 30 degrees above the positive X axis.

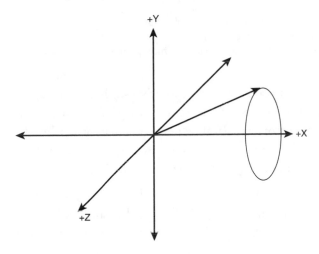

Note in Figure 26.11 that a circle is drawn around the positive X axis; this circle describes all the possible positions for a vector 30 degrees from the positive X axis. The point is this: If you are working in two dimensions, there will only be two angles 30 degrees from the positive X axis. If you are working in three dimensions, there will be an infinite number of angles 30 degrees from the positive X axis.

To continue your understanding of how to utilize the dot product, let's create several vectors in the message window:

```
A = vector(1,0,0)
B = vector(0,0,-1)
C = vector(-1,0,0)
D = vector(.7071, .7071, 0)
```

Now, let's evaluate the dot product between vector A and each of the other vectors (note that the .dot() function is a typing shortcut for the .dotproduct() function):

```
put A.dot(B)
-- 0.0000
-- since the cosine of the angle is 0, the vectors are perpendicular
put A.dot(C)
-- -1.0000
-- since the cosine of the angle is -1, the vectors
-- are parallel and collinear
put A.dot(D)
-- 0.7071
-- since the cosine is neither 0 or 1, without
-- arccosine the best we can say is
-- that the angle between A and D is neither perpendicular nor parallel.
```

Remember that the dot product is commutative so that A.dot(B) is equivalent to B.dot(A). In essence, this most basic use of the dot product is a quick way to test whether two vectors are parallel, perpendicular, or neither. Just remember that even if you determine that an angle is perpendicular, it might be perpendicular to the left or right, up or down, or some combination.

In addition to this quick perpendicular/parallel test, there is another possible use for the dot product. The second use for the dot product is to determine the projection of a vector. A projection of a vector determines how far in some direction another vector extends. This concept is very difficult to understand without several diagrams. Begin by examining Figure 26.12, which illustrates a vector (A), a direction vector (B), and the projection of A along B.

In Figure 26.12, I am showing how the projection of a vector can be thought in terms of the length of the shadow cast by a stick struck by the rays of the sun at noon. Note that in this example, the stick is vector A, the direction of the ground is defined by a unit vector, B, and the projection of vector A onto B is the length of the shadow. Remember this: The projection is a scalar. The dot product produces a scalar—if vector A is of any length and vector B is of unit length, the scalar product will be the length of the projection.

The geometric subtleties that are involved in this are often difficult to understand. That is why Figure 26.13 illustrates two different projections to give you an idea of the relationships between vector A and vector B.

From the two projections shown in Figure 26.13, note that the common factor between them is the fact that vector C and the ground plane are always perpendicular. Finding the length of a vector in the direction of another is a useful tool in 3D programming.

FIGURE 26.12

Illustration of the projection of vector A along vector B.

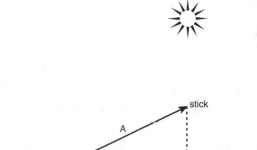

B is a direction
vector; a magnitude
of 1, which points in
the direction of the
ground.

Shadow of stick
on ground
—
also, the projection
of A onto B

FIGURE 26.13

Illustration of the projection of vector A along vector B.

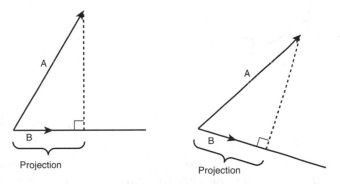

NOTE

Note that the projection of vectors is a process that is used by all 3D environments, all 3D rendering. If we were building a 3D engine of our own, we would use projection to figure out how to
draw the lines that exist in 3D space on the single plane of the screen.

Cross Product

The second method of vector multiplication we will be dealing with is the cross product (or *vector product*). As I have mentioned previously, the cross product will return a vector. The most important aspect of this returned vector is that it will be perpendicular to both of the source vectors. The nature of what this vector means is quite interesting, as you will soon see.

There are many ways to describe a plane in 3D space. For example, a plane is described any three points in space, as long as the three points are non-collinear. That is, as long as the three points are not all on the same line. Another way to describe a plane is with two noncollinear vectors. If we were to take two noncollinear vectors, A and B, and evaluate the cross product for those two vectors, this would return to us a third vector, C, that will be perpendicular to both of the source vectors. In addition, vector C would be perpendicular to the plane described by AB. This concept can be difficult to understand without a visual. Figure 26.14 illustrates the cross product of vectors A and B, which is noted as vector C.

FIGURE 26.14

Illustration of the cross product of vectors A and B.

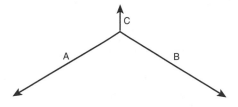

The vector labeled C is the cross product of vectors A and B and is also known as the *normal* of the plane formed by the two source vectors. For short, you can refer to this vector as a *normal*. Note that vector C is perpendicular to plane AB in all directions; to emphasize this point, when a line is perpendicular to a plane, we say that it is *orthogonal to the plane*.

NOTE

Normal is one of those overloaded words that you should be very cautious of when you hear it. Already, you have learned about a process known as *normalization*. Normals and normalization are not the same thing. They do not refer to the same processes or concepts, and they remain unique entities of 3D programming. For now, you must take caution to keep these two items conceptually separate. Also, keep in mind that in future chapters I will introduce several variations on the concept of *normals*, but without the basic understanding of what a normal is, these specific variations will be impossible to understand.

Whereas the dot product is commutative, the cross product is not. Therefore, the order of operands is of extreme importance when you're evaluating the cross product. Keep in mind that the order of operands raises an interesting issue. Imagine that you have two noncollinear vectors, A and B, that describe a plane. If you determine that the cross product of A.cross(B) equals some vector, C, the cross product of B.cross(A) refers to the vector that could also be described as c * -1. In Figure 26.15, I refer to this vector as *D*. This concept is explained geometrically in Figure 26.15. Note that in this figure you are looking at four vectors in three-dimensional space: vectors C and D are collinear.

NOTE

The .cross() function is a shortcut for the .crossproduct() function. You may use either interchangeably, but I prefer .cross() for the minor typing relief.

FIGURE 26.15

Illustration of the effect that the order of operands has on the cross product.

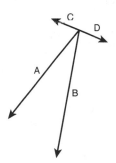

From this figure, you can see that if you reverse the order of operands for the cross product, the result will be a vector that is the same magnitude as C but whose direction is exactly 180 degrees opposite. We will call this second result

D. Remember that A and B describe a plane, AB. Vector C points in the direction of everything above plane AB, whereas vector D points in the direction of everything below plane AB. In short, plane AB bisects the 3D environment, and vectors C and D describe the two halves.

Flexing Our Vector Math Muscles

Now that we have looked at a myriad of concepts, terms, and processes for vector math, I want to show you a practical example that makes use of these concepts. I have chosen a topic that makes use of each of the topics we have covered, with special attention on the dot product and cross product.

We will be implementing a custom handler for the purpose of determining whether a given 3D point is on the surface of a plane, in front of a plane, or behind a plane. First, however, you need to understand several givens. When speaking about a plane, I am not talking about a plane Modelresource, although the lesson could be extended to include them. Instead, I am speaking about a plane in 3D space that extends infinitely in two directions. The orientation of this plane, as well as "in front of" and "behind," are determined by a normal for the plane. The normal will point in the direction of "in front of" the plane, but we will define which way the normal points.

This concept may be difficult to understand with only a written description. That is why I have provided Figure 26.16, which shows a plane (AB), the normal to plane AB (labeled *N*), and a 3D point labeled *P* for which we will determine whether it is in front or behind the plane.

FIGURE 26.16

Inside/outside testing.

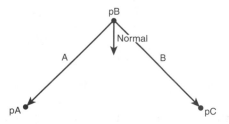

Note that this figure contains three points on the surface of the plane: pA, pB, and pC. In this demonstration, we only need four points in 3D space. We will use three of these points to define a plane. The fourth point is the point for which we will determine whether it's in front of, behind, or on the plane.

Several steps are involved in this process. I will list these first so that you understand the scope and flow of the overall process:

- Two points can be used to define a location vector. Because we have three points on a plane, we can use these three points to define two vectors.

- With these two vectors, we will use the dot product to find the normal of the plane, and we will also normalize this result. This will make sure that the normal is a unit vector and essentially a direction vector, which we will call *N*.

- Once we have the normal to the plane, our next job is to create a vector that points from the plane to the point we are trying to determine the status of. This vector should also be normalized, because we are only interested in it as a direction vector, which we will call *D*.

- Finally, we will calculate the dot product of N and D—essentially, `N.dot(D)`. Because both of these vectors are normalized, the dot product will be the cosine of the angles between the two.

- Therefore, if the dot product equals zero, the point is on the plane. If the dot product is greater than zero, the point is on the side of the plane opposite the direction of the normal. If the dot product is less than zero, the point is on the side of the plane in the same direction as the normal.

Note that this process is merely taking the skills and concepts you have learned and applying them to a real problem you may have when working with 3D. Literally, we are writing a custom function that will determine what side of a plane a given 3D point is on.

The first item in this process involves finding the World coordinates of three points on a plane, which we will label *pA*, *pB*, and *pC*. Once we have determined what these coordinates are, we will be using vector subtraction to determine two of the vectors between the points. In order to evaluate the exact value of these two vectors, we will use the following code:

```
VectorA = pA - pB
VectorB = pC - pB
```

Remember as you look at these two lines of code that pA, pB and pC are location vectors. Each of the points contains three coordinate values that we are subtracting in order to find out the value of two of the vectors between the points. Remember that vector subtraction is not a commutative process; therefore, the order of operands that I have suggested in this case is highly important, as you will continue to see.

These vectors will, in turn, be used to calculate the normal of the plane. This process is a rather simple cross product of vector A and vector B, as follows:

```
MyNormal = vectorA.cross(vectorB)
```

Remember that the cross product is not commutative; therefore, the order of operands is highly important because it determines the direction of the normal used in this demonstration. Be aware that the last two examples of code I have shown are in a specific order; you can change this order, but do not do so until you have read through the rest of this demonstration.

I mentioned earlier that two possible vectors can represent the normal to a plane. These two possible normals are collinear and point in opposite directions. In the case of this demonstration, this point is tantamount. You see, which of the two normals we choose will determine which side of 3D space is "inside" and which is considered "outside." If you examine Figure 26.17, you will see that I have offered two possible ways to label the three points on the plane.

Figure 26.17 shows two possible methods for labeling the three points on the plane. In the example on the left, the points are labeled counterclockwise; on the right, the points are labeled clockwise. Take your right hand and make a fist, placing the heel of your hand against the center of the diagram on the left. Now raise your thumb so that it is pointing directly away from the book. Note how your fingers are curling in the same direction as the labeling of the points and how your thumb points away from the book. This is known as the *right hand rule*—your thumb points in the direction of the normal that will be used if you order the points counterclockwise.

FIGURE 26.17

The direction of the normal is defined by the order of points.

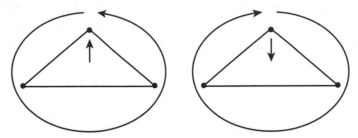

Now, turn your fist over 180 degrees so that your thumb is pointing at the book (this hurts my wrist); your fingers will curl in the direction of the labeled points in the illustration on the right. This is still the right hand rule (you're still using your right hand, correct?), and your thumb points in the direction of the normal. The bottom line is this: The order in which you define your points is critical because the direction of the normal will depend on this information. If you go through the whole demo and realize that the inside space and the outside space are calculated exactly opposite, do not fret—simply change the order in which you label the points.

NOTE

I cannot stress enough how important this seemingly small issue is. Note that this issue of point ordering (which determines the direction of the normal of a plane) will be examined again in further depth in the next chapter, "Creating Meshes from Code." In that chapter, you will learn how the normal will be used to determine which side is the "front" and which is the "back" for our custom meshes.

Once we have determined the normal, the next step is to use vector subtraction once again. This time we will determine the vector between the point that we are checking for being inside/outside and *any* point on the plane. The easiest way to do this is to simply use one of the points we used when defining the plane itself (for instance, pA). Note that the code to determine the vector between pA and the point that we are checking is as follows:

```
dVector = the_point - pA
```

The order of this operation is extremely important because we are primarily interested in the direction of this vector. By subtracting a point on the plane from the point itself, we are finding a vector that points from the plane to the point. In Figure 26.18, you can see that I have drawn in dVector, noting the direction of the vector that extends from the plane toward the point we are checking.

FIGURE 26.18

We need to find the direction of the vector from the plane to the point that we are checking.

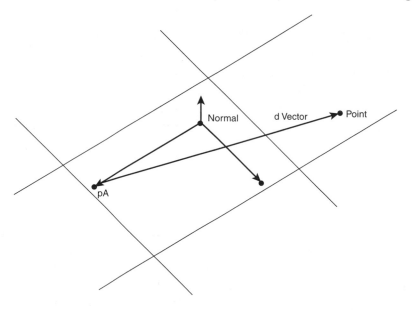

The next step is quite simple; because we are interested in the directions of dVector and myNormal, we will normalize these two vectors. Normalizing these vectors will ensure that each of their magnitudes equals 1 and that they are now unit vectors. This is because we are interested in the directions of these two vectors. Because they are both unit vectors, the next step is quite simple. We will calculate the dot product of dVector and myNormal as follows:

```
Testresult = dvector.dot(myNormal)
```

Because both dVector and myNormal are unit vectors, their dot product will be the cosine of the angle between the two. This information is enough for us to determine whether the point is on the inside or outside of a plane. Here's a summary of the possibilities for the value of testresult:

- If testresult equals zero, the point is on the plane.
- If testresult is greater than zero, the point is in back of the plane.
- If testresult is less than zero, the point is in front of the plane.

Remember that which side is "front" and which side is "back" is determined by you; they are relative to the order in which you set up your code. Because I am sure you will find this process very useful (and because I want to ensure that you understand the process), I have set up a small demonstration file that utilizes this example in a Director movie. If you look on the CD accompanying this book, you will find a file named "Inside Outside Test." Open this file and press Play. The Stage should look relatively similar to what's shown in Figure 26.19.

FIGURE 26.19

Screenshot from the Inside Outside Test demonstration.

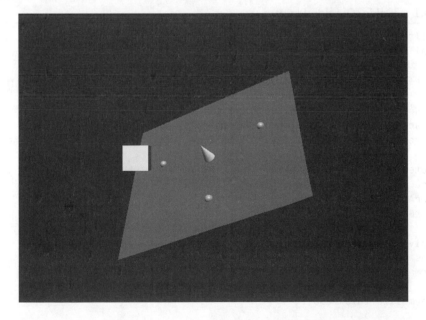

As you can see in Figure 26.19, I have created several models to represent the plane, the three points on the plane, and the normal to the plane. In addition, there is a box that represents the point we are checking to determine which side of the plane it is on.

In order to work with this demonstration, you can click and drag either the plane or the box. If you click the plane, you will be able to rotate it around two axes. As you rotate the plane, you may notice that it is actually semitransparent; this was done to help you in case you drag the box instead of the plane. When you drag the box, you will be able to move it on the X/Z plane in space. If the box is on the same side of the plane that the normal points in, the box will be a light cyan color. If the box is on the side opposite the plane, the box will be a light yellow color. If the box happens to be exactly on the plane, it will turn white.

Play with the demonstration for a while if you are having trouble with the concepts I have presented. Once you feel like you understand what is going on in the environment, take a look at the code that checks for inside/outside in Listing 26.1. If you are still having trouble, refer to the explanation for this demonstration or even return to the sections on normalization, the dot product, and the cross product.

LISTING 26.1   Inside/Outside Script

```
 1: on exitframe(me)
 2:   global scene
 3:
 4:   -- save a reference to the location vectors of
 5:   -- the three red spheres in world-space coordinates
 6:   pA = scene.model("pntA").getworldtransform().position
 7:   pB = scene.model("pntB").getworldtransform().position
 8:   pC = scene.model("pntC").getworldtransform().position
 9:
10:   -- determine the vectors between pA - pB
11:   -- and pC - pB.
12:   vectorA = pA - pB
13:   vectorB = pC - pB
14:
15:   -- solve the cross product, which will return
16:   -- the normal of the plane
17:   myNormal = vectorA.cross(vectorB)
18:
19:   -- normalize this result
```

LISTING 26.1   Continued

```
20:    myNormal.normalize()
21:
22:    -- determine the location of the point that you want to
23:    -- check, making sure this is in world space coordinates
24:    the_point = scene.model("mover").getworldtransform().position
25:
26:    -- determine the vector between the_point and any
27:    -- point on the plane.  In this case, I will choose
28:    -- pA, since we know that it is on the plane.
29:    dVector = the_point - pA
30:    -- normalize dVector
31:    dvector.normalize()
32:
33:    -- solve the dot product of the normal and dvector.
34:    -- because these two vectors have been normalized
35:    -- the result will be the cosine of the angle
36:    -- between these two vectors
37:    testresult = mynormal.dot(dvector)
38:
39:    -- check to see if the point in on the plane,
40:    -- in back of the plane, or in front of the plane.
41:    if testresult = 0 then
42:      scene.model("mover").shader.diffuse = rgb(255,255,255)
43:    else if testresult > 0 then
44:      scene.model("mover").shader.diffuse = rgb(200,200,0)
45:    else if testresult < 0 then
46:      scene.model("mover").shader.diffuse = rgb(0,255,200)
47:    end if
48: end
```

As you can see from this demonstration, the script to test whether a point is on one side of a plane or the other is not very long, but it is extremely effective. In addition, this demonstration is meant to underscore the fact that vector mathematics is an indispensable tool for advanced control of the 3D environment. I assume at this point that you have many questions and concerns about vector mathematics. Specifically, I assume that your questions fall into two groups: Either you still feel shaky on the mathematics or you want to know where to go from here. If you are having trouble, I recommend looking through the concepts again. If you are curious as to what else you might apply vector mathematics to, there are several resources listed at the end of the chapter to aid you.

NOTE

I doubt that anyone will actually get the box on the plane, ever. The reason I say this is that the point we are checking is the *centroid* of the box. Literally, it is the three-dimensional center of the box. If you think about it, this is only one very tiny point, and unless that point is exactly on the plane, the box will not turn white. You may notice that because of this: It is possible to have the plane bisect the box, and you can actually see the moment when the center of the box moves from one side of the plane to the other.

If you think about it, if the centroid of the box were exactly on the surface of the plane, the cosine of the angle between the two vectors would be 0, and this would tell you that the angle between the two vectors was exactly 90 degrees.

If you wanted, you could change line 27 in the preceding code so that it reads as follows:

```
testresult = myNormal.anglebetween(dVector)
```

Note that the `anglebetween` function will return the actual angle between the two vectors in degrees. Because getting the angle to be exactly 90 degrees might be too strict, you could consider searching for angles that are greater than 85 degrees or so. This would allow you to create a "zone" around the plane that can be detected. Note that `anglebetween` does not return the direction of the two `anglebetween` vectors but rather only the angle.

I hope this example reminds you of some of the lessons you have learned in previous chapters—specifically, the examples of proximity sensors covered in Chapter 24, "Interactive Animation." Using this demonstration as a guide, you should be able to combine the proximity sensor techniques with the inside/outside test to define more complex zones for your proximity sensors.

Another possibility you might want to consider is using invisible planes to divide the space of your environment into discreet areas. What are some reasons why you might do this? Aggressive download optimization, performance optimization, and AI. Remember that the planes we are defining do not need an actual plane Model or Modelresource—the planes we are talking about are mathematical constructs that bisect all of three-dimensional space.

If we were to partition the space of our environment, we might use this information to determine which parts of the environment need to exist at a certain point in time. Imagine if you were working on a massively large 3D environment, where it is impossible to keep the entire environment in RAM at once. It's so large that you need to download other parts of the environment while the user is looking at previously downloaded parts. If the environment is extremely large, you would need a way to determine which parts to download and when. Partitioning the space in this way is exactly the answer.

Another possibility is to use this information for aggressive performance optimization. If you created a Doom-style game, and the levels are very large, you would not want to draw all the Models in a level all the time, would you? You would not even want them in the World. Using a method similar to the example for "when to download," you could couple your partitioning of 3D space with code that adds and removes Models from the World on-the-fly.

Finally, sticking with the subject of a Doom-style game, once again you might apply partitioning to your AI. Imagine that you developed some behavioral animation code that controls the "bad guys" in your Doom-style game. AI costs a lot in terms of performance, so you would not want all your bad guys walking around, making semiautonomous decisions, all the time. You could use partitioning of the space to control which bad guys' timeout objects are set to update frequently and which are simply turned off. Think of it as a method for turning on and off the puppets in a funhouse. When you aren't in the funhouse, do you think they waste the electricity for the zombie man? Of course not, and neither should you.

If you have read through this section and you are concerned that you may not be ready for the remaining chapters of the book, go ahead and advance to those chapters, even if you feel shaky with this material. Often, it is difficult to get a handle on abstract concepts without several applications of those concepts. If you look at the techniques in the remaining chapters and have problems, you can always come back and review the points that seem unclear.

Advanced Transforms

In this section of the chapter, we will be looking at some of the advanced features and issues related to transform objects. Remember that vectors and transforms are used in conjunction with one another to determine the position, orientation, and scale of Models in the 3D environment. Also recall that although every Model Node has its own transform object, it is possible to create independent transform objects in code.

As you begin fine-tuning your vector math skills, you will need to understand an important concept about the origin for vectors. Recall that a vector does not have a location in space—only a displacement. You have also learned that if a vector is a component vector, it is possible to use the vector to represent a location. In order for there to be components of a vector, we need to have some sort of origin point from which to measure the coordinates.

This leads to one of the final concepts about vectors that you need to know about: The difference between free vectors and fixed vectors. A *free vector* does not have a location, it does not have a starting point, and it therefore cannot be represented by components. You know that all the vectors we have worked with are represented by components, because all the vectors we have worked with are fixed vectors.

But to where are they fixed? Vectors have a local origin that is not the same as the World origin, and this can be the problem. Often you need data about vectors that are in World coordinates, and this is where transforms can come in. You see, it is possible to multiply a transform by a vector in order to generate a vector that is in World coordinates. Let's take the following syntax example of converting a local vector into a World-coordinate vector. First, we need to create a local vector:

```
MyLocalVector = vector(a,b,c)
```

If you were going to translate between world and local coordinates, you would most likely have a meaningful transform() object in World coordinates derived from the position of a Node. In this example, we do not have this luxury, so our next step will be to create a transform and then translate this transform so that it is not at the origin point. In this example, I have translated myworldtransform to vector(200,40,10):

```
Myworldtransform = transform()
Myworldtransform.translate(200,40,10)
```

Now, the last step is to find out the value of the local vector in World coordinates by multiplying mylocalvector by the transform object located at the new origin for the vector:

```
myWorldCoordVector = myworldtransform * mylocalvector
```

This method will work equally well if you are generating transforms from Models or Nodes from within a scene. In this way, it is possible to find out where a vector would be in World space relative to any given Node.

Another frequent requirement you might have is being able to convert a vector from World coordinates back into local coordinates. This process is only slightly different, but it involves the use of the `transform.inverse()` function. The `transform.inverse()` function is a nondestructive process that returns an inverted version of the transform(), where the `transform.invert()` function will invert a transform but is destructive. The inversion of transforms is important for many reasons.

You may recall that the order of operations for transformations is extremely important. You know that if you rotate and then translate a Node, you get vastly different results than if you do the opposite. Translation also has another strange property: If you translate a Node multiple times, it is not possible to simply translate the Node in the reverse order to return to the point at which you started. Rather, you need to get the inverse of the transform in order to transform back to your start point.

With this in mind, what we need to do to convert from World coordinates into local coordinates is to first take the inverse of the World transform, as follows:

```
MyInvertedTransform = myWorldTransform.inverse()
```

Then, to convert a vector into local coordinates, we would use the following:

```
MyLocalVector = MyInvertedTransform * MyWorldCoordVector
```

Although this may seem like a small issue, converting vectors between local and World coordinates is often the cause of many problems when you begin working with advanced vector math. Luckily, transforms widen the amount of flexibility we have with our vectors. This issue will become especially important in the next two chapters, so be aware that this, too, is a topic that will be revisited shortly.

Gimbal Lock

As you continue to work with rotations, you may eventually run into certain situations where your rotations act unexpectedly. You may notice your Models rotating smoothly and then wildly flipping orientation when approaching 90 degrees on one of the axes of rotation—or worse, rotation on one of the axes may become "locked up."

First, this is a known issue that affects everyone working in 3D animation and 3D programming. This issue is related to the way we normally rotate Models in 3D space using angles of rotation around the X, Y, and Z axes. When we rotate Models on these axes, we are using what are properly referred to as Euler angles (pronounced *oiler*). Euler was a mathematician who lived in the 18th century; among the many things he did, he defined a method for rotating objects in 3D space about the X, Y, and Z axes.

The primary drawback to using Euler angles to rotate your Models is that the computer does not actually rotate the Model along all three axes at once. Rather, the Model is first rotated along the X axis, then the Y, and then the Z. This leads to a problem known as *gimbal lock*, whose effects are often cited as "wildly flipping orientations" (when gimbal lock is being approached). In a complete gimbal lock, you will lose a degree of freedom of rotation.

Why? Because when the computer rotates along the axes one at a time, after an axis has been rotated, it does not move again. If one of the axes becomes collinear with another axis, the Model will experience gimbal lock. There is a secondary issue that underscores this difficulty. When you're using Euler angles, there is always more than one way to describe a given rotation, especially when the rotations approach 0, 90, and 180 degrees. Specifically, the orientation of (0,90,0) can equally be written as (180,0,180).

As I have said, the primary problem of Euler angles is based on the fact that the angles are rotated one at a time. Although this is a limitation, you have some options for rotation that you ought to consider. First, gimbal lock will not affect you if the rotation is on one axis. If the rotation is on two axes, the percentage is high only if the rotations are large, such as 45-degree or 90-degree rotations. If the rotation is on all three axes at the same time, this is where you will run into gimbal lock the quickest.

If you must perform rotations on all three axes at once, you can try two different solutions—one is weak, the other is strong. The weak solution is to split the rotations up so that you can handle the order of rotations manually. Literally, if you need to rotate scene.model[x].rotate(40,90,-180), you would instead break this up into the following:

```
Scene.model[x].rotate(40,0,0)
Scene.model[x].rotate(0,90,0)
Scene.model[x].rotate(0,0,-180)
```

This can still sometimes cause problems. For this reason, I want to provide you with a much stronger option. However, I caution you that you most likely will not need this solution for quite a while.

Among many other clever thoughts on mathematics, Euler observed the fact that no matter how many times you rotate something, the final rotation can always be described with a single rotation. However, this single rotation is not necessarily along any of the local axes. Rather, this single rotation takes place around a single arbitrary axis that can be defined as a unit vector.

To see exactly what it is I am talking about, let's look at a small demonstration. First, create an empty transform object with the following code in the message window:

```
T = transform()
```

Now we have an identity transform, named T, that we will proceed to rotate using the standard Euler angle method, as follows:

```
T.rotate(45,0,0)
```

Now, let's look at the value of the axisangle property:

```
Put T.axisangle
-- [vector( -1.0000, 0.0000, 0.0000 ), -45.0000]
```

Note that vector(-1,0,0) is a unit vector whose direction points down the negative X axis. In addition, notice that there is a scalar value −45, which tells us how many degrees around the axis defined by `vector(-1,0,0)` we have rotated the transform. Admittedly, this first example is very simple. For the next example, let's again create a transform object, but this time we will subject it to several rotations:

```
--create a new transform
t = transform()
-- rotate that transform
t.rotate(34,12,10)
-- show the axisangle property
put t.axisangle
-- [vector( -0.9007, -0.4005, -0.1681 ), -36.3492]
-- we can access the axisangle property with bracket access
put t.axisangle[1]
-- vector( -0.9007, -0.4005, -0.1681 )
-- note that the axisangle vector is a unit vector
put t.axisangle[1].magnitude
-- 1.0000
```

In this example, we are still using Euler angles to rotate the transform object. In this next example, we will create a transform and use a variation on the `rotate()` function that rotates about an axisangle directly:

```
-- create a new transform
t = transform()
-- rotate that transform using the following syntax:
-- t.rotate(point, axis, angle)
-- where point is the start point of the axis
-- and axis is a normalized vector which will
-- be used for its direction.  The angle specified
-- is the number of degrees around this arbitrary
-- vector that you will rotate.
t.rotate(vector(0,0,0), vector(0,1,0), 34)
-- just to show you what we have actually done,
-- look at the current rotation of the transform
-- when displayed using standard Euler Angles:
put t.rotation
-- vector( 0.0000, 34.0000, 0.0000 )
```

In this example, you can see that we have rotated around the Y axis in a unique way. However, our rotation is still no more complex than what I would expect you to do with standard Euler angle rotations. The next step is to look at how we might actually rotate around a truly arbitrary axis. For example, note that Figure 26.20 illustrates a unit vector, A, on the unit sphere.

FIGURE 26.20

Illustration of an arbitrary unit vector that we will use as an axis for rotation.

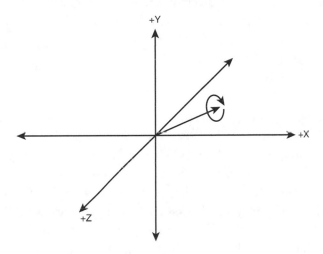

This vector can be described as vector(10,5,0); when normalized, this vector is vector(0.8944,0.4472,0.0000). The angle between vector(1,0,0) and vector A is 26.5 degrees. Only because there is no Z component to this vector do I know that vector A describes a displacement that is 26.5 degrees directly above the positive X axis. Using this information, we can freely rotate the transform about this axis with the following:

```
-- create transform
T = transform()
-- define axis
A = vector( 0.8944, 0.4472, 0.0000 )
-- rotate about that axis
T.rotate(vector(0,0,0), A, 45)
-- report on the Euler Angle Rotation
put t.rotation
-- vector( 41.8103, 18.4349, 7.0938 )
```

Therefore, in the final report on the rotation of the transform, you can see that we successfully rotated about all three canonical axes with a single function. Note that the axisangle-style rotations do not suffer from gimbal lock because there is only one rotation performed at a time on the arbitrary axis we provided. Also, note that I have been specifying the point for axisangle rotation as vector(0,0,0). If you want to rotate around an axis that passes through the origin of a Model, then use this vector. Otherwise, you can just as easily specify axes of rotation that are outside of the Model or offset from the centroid of the Model.

Summary

Vector math encompasses many concepts that build on one another. Included in this vast array of concepts are the processes of vector addition, vector subtraction, scalar multiplication, scalar product, and vector product. Vector math is a powerful tool that is often difficult to understand or harness because it may be hard to visualize what you are doing. In addition, small mistakes in math or logic can result in major setbacks. You might have an idea for using vector math to create a script that is very good, but even one small mistake can make you think that your basic idea is wrong. In short, if you run into trouble the first time you use vector math on your own, do not fret. This is entirely expected—remember that several of the processes are not commutative, and simply reversing the order of your operands can sometimes destroy or save a script.

Of course, there is no substitute for understanding. If you are having trouble with the concepts in this chapter, I suggest you reread it before moving on. In addition to vector math, we have addressed two important issues about transforms. First, we looked at a method for converting vectors between local coordinates and World coordinates. This process is extremely important and will be revisited in the remaining chapters of the book.

Second, we examined the problem of gimbal lock—the loss of a degree of rotational freedom that can occur when Nodes or transforms are rotated using Euler angles. Gimbal lock is a problem that eventually affects every developer, but you may be able to avoid it for years. The first time it happens, you will come back to this chapter and read about how to fix the problem; until then, just be aware that this is something that can happen and that your day to deal with this problem is coming.

Finally, as has been said many times throughout this chapter, vector math is a powerful tool. If you feel you understand the concepts I have presented in this chapter, then by all means go on to the next chapter. If you are having trouble, you might want to consider some of the resources suggested in the "Supplemental Resources" section of this chapter, shortly following this summary.

FAQ

I have never run into gimbal lock. Do you think that I should worry?

Anyone using Euler angles for rotation will generally run into problems with gimbal lock at some point during his or her career. Many simply do not understand that this is a predictable, known limitation of Euler angles. Others simply build strategies that eliminate the possibility for gimbal lock.

If you are truly having major issues with gimbal lock, have tried to use the axisangle techniques, and are still having trouble, there is still one last resort. Unfortunately, this method requires a large amount of mathematics bravado and is well beyond the scope of this book. However, I will at least point you to a topic known as *quarternion rotation*. Quarternions provide a special way of defining rotations that are extremely robust but mathematically challenging to implement. If you are interested in this possibility, I would suggest looking into the online articles I have cited in the "Supplemental Resources" section.

Supplemental Resources

In this section, I provide online links to tutorials about vectors as well as articles on quarternion rotation and gimbal lock. In addition, you'll find a subsection dedicated to books on math that you might want to consider reading.

Online Resources

- chortle.ccsu.ctstateu.edu/vectorLessons/vectorIndex.html

  This is a link to an outstanding online tutorial that covers the basics of vector math. In general, this tutorial progresses much slower than our current chapter, but it's also much more concerned about teaching the algebra of vector math, and it is not tailored to those working with Director.

- `www.gamasutra.com/search`

  If you go to the Gamasutra Web site and search for the word "vectors," you will get a list of about 70 links to articles about vectors, many of which are about vector mathematics and how to apply it in 3D programming. Note that these articles will be written with C and C++ programmers in mind, but the concepts can be applied to Director as well.

- `www.darwin3d.com/gamedev/articles/col0398.pdf`

  This is a link to a PDF document written by Jeff Lander. In this article, he provides an extremely good explanation of Euler angles, gimbal lock, and quarternion rotations.

Books

I have suggested two books on mathematics that you will find diametrically opposed in terms of approach. The first book is considered the primer for writing 3D engines in C++ and is often used in college courses. It represents an amount of information that I do not expect you will need to know, including topics such as matrices, topologies, Bézier curves, and constructive solid geometry.

- *Mathematics for Computer Graphics Applications*, by Michael E. Mortenson (Industrial Press, ISBN 083113111X)

  This book is an advanced account of mathematics for computer applications that approaches the subject of vectors, matrices, and transformations. In short, this book is amazing, but it will not be for the mathematically fearful. If you have worked through this chapter without any problems and you want an extremely inclusive view of the mathematics behind 3D environments, you might want to look into this book.

- *Maths: A Student's Survival Guide: A Self-Help Workbook for Science and Engineering Students*, by Jenny Olive (Cambridge University Press, ISBN 0521575869)

  Jenny Olive's book on explaining math is geared toward those who have either not been introduced to the concepts of math or who have been away from a math class for quite some time. Her approach is impeccable, and this book is well worth the investment if you are having trouble with mathematics, algebra, trigonometry, and up through calculus.

CHAPTER 27

Creating Meshes from Code

In this chapter, we will be examining the process of creating Meshes from code. This process requires that you have a basic understanding of vector math. Until now, we have been relying on geometry that has been created either visually in an external 3D modeling program or with predefined primitive shapes. In this chapter, we will be focusing on the creation of Meshes from code. Whereas we have had the luxury of predefined Mesh primitives in the past, in this chapter you will be learning how to use Lingo to generate Modelresource geometry from scratch that will then be used to create Models.

I will preface this chapter by stressing that this is an introduction to Mesh creation. Mesh creation is an enormous subject that could fill several books the size of this one—but we need to begin somewhere. Once you have covered this chapter, you may wish to continue learning about this subject from some of the supplemental resources listed near the end of the chapter.

In this chapter, we will be examining several aspects of Mesh creation. To begin, you will learn what a Mesh is comprised of. We'll continue by exercising your understanding of a Mesh using Lingo to create several simple Models. After we have examined several simple shapes, we will look at methods for devising Mesh-based grids with code—a task that is a bit more complicated than it first sounds.

We will then combine your understanding of grid creation with Imaging Lingo to build a system for terrain generation. Finally, we will examine a method for creating a terrain-following script—a script that allows you to navigate the terrain while staying some distance above it. Building this terrain-following script will involve an explanation of an advanced Picking Lingo command: `modelsunderray()`.

Looking at this list of objectives for the chapter, you should be able to quickly see that Mesh creation from code has at least one immediate practical application: terrain generation. However, the subject of Mesh creation has many more applications than just this—we just do not have time to look at them. I cannot stress enough that this chapter is only the first of many documents you will need to reference on the subject. For that reason, you will find at the end of this chapter a list of supplemental resources, including books and online material, you should consider looking into if you are interested in this powerful branch of 3D Lingo.

Before we begin, I want to mention that the fact we can create Meshes from code with Lingo is proof of the depth and power of 3D programming in Director. Although learning this technique may not be as easy as using a 3D modeling program, it offers you possibilities that are generally only available to those who program 3D worlds with OpenGL and DirectX using low-level languages such as C and C++. With this in mind, we can begin examining the fundamentals of Mesh creation, realizing that this is an advanced topic within the advanced topic of 3D programming.

What Is a Mesh?

The more I mention Mesh creation, the more you should be asking yourself, What is a Mesh? I have previously defined a Mesh as the geometry that describes the shape of a Model. This definition tells you what a Mesh does, but it leaves out the details of how it does it.

Because we are talking about the creation of geometry, let's first think about how you might draw a shape in two dimensions. For example, if you want to draw a square, you might draw four points on paper and then connect the four points with lines. If you have done a good job making sure the four sides of the square are of equal distance and that they are all perpendicular at the corners where they meet, you should end up with a square. Looking at the square, you would probably say that the square is a *two-dimensional shape* and is comprised of the geometric elements *points* and *lines*.

As you begin to think about how to create three-dimensional shapes, your understanding of points and lines needs to be reexamined and expanded. In two dimensions, you create points and connect them with line segments. But points only exist in two dimensions—you need to begin with the most basic building block of 3D geometry—the 3D point, or more correctly, the *Vertex*.

However, Vertices are not connected by mere lines; rather, they are connected by *Faces*. Therefore, the two building blocks for three-dimensional shapes, which we know are called *Meshes*, are created from Vertices and Faces.

Vertices and Faces

No sooner than we answer the question of what a Mesh is, we are presented with another question: What are Vertices and Faces? Vertices are actually quite easy to understand—they are 3D points. Literally, you might think of them as locations in 3D space. You know that we have used component vectors to describe locations in 3D space, even though vectors are not locations themselves—they are displacements. Vertices *are* locations, but they use vectors to describe their position. The other item Vertices use to describe their position is a common origin. This origin is the origin of a local coordinate system.

Explaining what a Face is involves a slightly more involved answer. A Face connects Vertices together. You might recall that any two-dimensional shape with three sides is a triangle. Specifically, a Face connects three Vertices to create a triangle. But this triangle is not a simple two-dimensional triangle. Rather, we must draw upon the fact that in 3D space, we can describe a plane with any three points. Putting all these facts together, we would say that a Face describes a triangular segment of a plane in 3D space described by the positions of three Vertices.

Face Normals and Vertex Ordering

You now know that a Face is a 3D triangle that essentially connects three Vertices. If you think about a 3D triangle, you know that in 3D space it must have two sides (we'll call them the "front" and "back"). When you're working with 3D, by default the Renderer will only draw the front Face. But how does the Renderer know which Face is the front one? The answer to this is tied up in Face normals and Vertex ordering.

To understand the implications of Vertex ordering, you need to understand a normal. Imagine that you have a sheet of paper with a triangle drawn in the middle that's lying flat on a table. If you place a pencil eraser down in the middle of the triangle, the point of the pencil should be sticking straight up in the air. As long as the pencil is making a right angle with the paper, we might say that the pencil describes the *normal* of the triangle. Alternatively, we might simply call this normal a *Face normal*. But this only reinforces the original question: What made us decide to make the pencil point upward, away from the triangle, rather than downward into the table?

To understand the answer to this question, we need to back up to the point when the triangle was drawn on the paper. To continue with this example, go ahead and actually draw a triangle on a piece of paper. First, draw any three points on the paper. Next, put your pencil down on one of the points and draw a line to one of the other points. Without raising the tip of your pencil, draw a line to the remaining point. Finally, connect the last point and the first point, and you should have a triangle.

If someone else were to look at your triangle, it would be impossible for him to determine whether you connected the lines going clockwise or counterclockwise, but you did draw the triangle going in one of these directions. The point is that without lifting your pencil, there are only two directions you could have gone in. This information is what is used to determine whether the pencil will point away from the table or toward it. The direction in which the pencil points depends on whether the triangle was drawn clockwise or counterclockwise.

In terms of creating meshes from code, the "drawing of a triangle" is analogous to defining the Vertices of a Face. The direction of the normal of a Face is defined by whether those Vertices are connected in clockwise or counterclockwise order. Figure 27.1 illustrates how a Face can be defined by connecting three Vertices in clockwise or counterclockwise order.

FIGURE 27.1

Vertex ordering defines the direction of a Face normal.

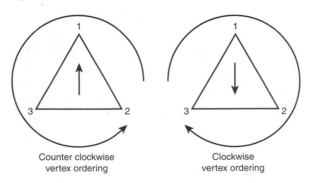

Counter clockwise
vertex ordering

Clockwise
vertex ordering

You might remember this discussion from the previous chapter. In this chapter, however, we will be applying your knowledge of normals to Faces instead. Because it is good practice, continue by taking your right hand and make a fist. Now stick your thumb straight up in the air. While your thumb is pointing straight up in the air, place the bottom of your fist in the center of the triangle on the left. Your fingers curl around into a fist counterclockwise, mimicking the order of the Vertices. This is known as the *right hand rule*, which describes the direction of the Face normal when your Vertices are connected counterclockwise. If you turn your fist so that your thumb is pointing at the floor, your fingers will be curling around clockwise; therefore, the Face normal is pointing in exactly the opposite direction.

Backface Culling

Exactly why is the normal to a Face so important, you might ask. The answer to this question involves a bit of discussion about the Camera. You know that the Camera has a property called `pointatorientation`—two vectors that describe "forward" and "up" relative to the Camera. I am glad that I have a "pointatorientation"—my eyes point in *front* of me, and the sky is *up* (most of the time). All the Faces whose normals form an angle with the Camera's front direction Vector that is between 0 and 90 degrees will be drawn. All other Faces will not be drawn. This includes the back Faces of a given Face, which brings up the technique known as *backface culling*.

Backface culling has its roots in performance optimization. If we could suddenly cut the number of Faces the Renderer has to draw in half, we should be able to speed up performance. Luckily, this process is already set up for us by Director. In addition, we have some degree of control over this technique with the `model.visibility` settings. With settings of #front, #back, #none, and #both, we can control which Faces of a Model are drawn at a given time.

Therefore, in terms of Mesh creation, we are presented with a single, overriding understanding. Because we can create Faces by connecting Vertices in either a clockwise or counterclockwise direction, neither direction is more correct than the other. For some Meshes, you will actually need to define some of the Faces counterclockwise and others clockwise so that they all point toward the outside of the geometric form you are trying to create. The only time you will have made a mistake is if your Mesh looks like it has a strange triangular-shaped hole or holes in it.

One immediate way to fix this is to use `model.visibility` = `#both`, but that's an ugly workaround to what should be viewed as a problem with your Mesh that can be better fixed by standardizing the way you define your Faces. In this chapter, we will primarily be defining faces by connecting Vertices counterclockwise, but there is at least one Mesh (the pyramid) in which we will need to use both. Because we will have control over Vertex ordering when building Meshes with Faces, we will spend much time making sure our Face normals are pointing in the correct directions.

NOTE

As a side note about `model.visibility` = `#both`, you know that when you're creating Meshes in Director, you have complete control over how the Faces are defined. If you are creating Models in external 3D modeling programs, issues with the normals can sometimes be introduced. This is often true in cases where you have converted Models between 3D programs several times before exporting to W3D.

If the normal information about Faces in a Mesh becomes corrupted, lost, or damaged, you will have a problem, because the Renderer will simply guess as to which Faces are facing toward the Camera and which are facing away from it in every frame! This results in Meshes with strange triangular holes in them that "blink" on and off.

In this situation, you should either re-create the Model altogether or look for a utility in your 3D modeling program that has the ability to unify or optimize normals. Essentially, such a command will make sure all the Faces are defined in the same order. If that is not an option for you, use `model.visibility` = `#both`, but realize that you will be losing some performance in your project. If your Mesh has 10 Faces, then 20 Faces will need to be drawn. If your Mesh has 5,000 Faces, then 10,000 Faces will need to be drawn. You can see that this problem is not trivial.

Mesh Modelresource

Although we will be creating Vertices and Faces to build a Mesh, it is important to understand that a Mesh is a special type of Modelresource. It is the most advanced Modelresource, because it provides functions and properties for the purpose of defining Vertices and Faces as well as building the Mesh itself.

Although a Mesh is a type of Modelresource, we will not be creating new Meshes with the `newModelresource()` command. Rather, new Meshes are created with the `newMesh()` command. The syntax for the `newMesh()` command can take up to five parameters, as shown in the following example:

```
Scene.newmesh(Name, Faces, Vertices, Normals, Colors, Texturecoordinates)
```

As you look at these parameters, there are several points to note. The Name parameter is the most obvious; this will be the name of the Mesh Modelresource you are creating. The Faces parameter controls how many Faces you will be creating in the current Mesh, and Vertices controls how many Vertices you will be using to define the Faces. Note that in many cases, multiple Faces will be sharing Vertices, so the number of Faces to Vertices is not always as clear cut as you might think.

The value that you set for Vertices indicates the number of entries that will be expected in a linear list of Vectors, each of which will describe the location of one Vertex in the Mesh. This Vertexlist will then be cross-referenced with individual Face numbers in order to create the connections between Vertices that define the Faces themselves. When we work on the first demonstration, this process will be described in fuller detail.

The next parameter, Normals, is used if you are going to be generating your own normals with math rather than allowing Director to do it for you. We are not going to be doing this, so in all the examples we will be looking at, the Normals parameter will be set to 0. We will allow Director to generate the normals based on how we define our Faces.

The Colors parameter is interesting because it offers us a method for controlling the colors of the Mesh on a per-Vertex level, essentially coloring Faces prior to the application of a Shader. We will be examining the specifics of what this means as we continue. For now, understand that the Colors parameter controls the number of RGB colors that you can define in a specialized Colorlist for the Mesh to be used with the Vertices.

The final parameter, Texturecoordinates, offers you a method for defining custom UV Texture coordinates for each Face in your Mesh. In Chapter 14, "Multitexturing," we spoke about how, by default, primitive Modelresources are automatically assigned UV coordinates. You also know from Chapter 14 that we can use different shader.texturemode settings to determine whether UV coordinates are used or Textures are mapped onto the Model using a variety of mapping methods.

Although it is possible to specify UV coordinates, we will be using mapping methods to apply Textures to our Meshes and will therefore not be working with setting custom Texturecoordinates. For this reason, in the demonstrations in this chapter, the Texturecoordinates parameter will be left at 0.

Once you have created your mesh Modelresource with the newMesh command, it is still not ready to be used. The next steps that you will need to perform include setting the values of all the Vertices in the Mesh and defining Faces by connecting these Vertices. This process is accomplished by setting the values of several Modelresource properties that are exclusively available to the Mesh Modelresource type. These properties are listed in Table 27.1.

TABLE 27.1   Mesh Modelresource Properties

Property	Purpose
Vertexlist	A linear list containing one item per Vertex. Each item consists of a single vector.
Colorlist	A linear list containing one item per color. Each item consists of a single RGB color.
Face[x]	A property that allows you to reference individual Faces by number. The Face property is not used alone but rather in conjunction with a variety of subproperties.

In addition to these properties are the Normallist and Texturecoordinatelist properties, but we will not be working with these lists in this chapter. We will be working with the Vertexlist, Colorlist, and Face properties. The order of entries in the Vertexlist is important: item 1 corresponds to vertex 1; item 2 to Vertex 2, and so on. The order of entries in the Colorlist is not as important as the order of the Vertexlist, although if you are going to be working with per-vertex coloring, you will need to know which entries correspond to which colors.

The Face property is not as simple as the Vertexlist and Colorlist properties of a Mesh Modelresource. This is because the Face property contains a variety of subproperties that will be used to define which Vertices are used for a given Face and which colors will be used for a given Face. These two subproperties are noted in Table 27.2.

TABLE 27.2   Mesh Modelresource Face Subproperties

Property	Purpose
Face[x].vertices	A linear list of three integers. Each integer corresponds to an item in the Vertexlist.

TABLE 27.2 Continued

Property	Purpose
Face[x].colors	A linear list of three integers. Each integer corresponds to an item in the Colorlist.

Because each item in the Vertexlist property refers to a specific Vertex, you are essentially assigning the Vertices that will be used by a Face as well as their order. As you know, the order of Vertices is of tantamount importance to the director of a Face normal. Therefore, the order of the list you set the Face[x].vertices property to is extremely important as well.

An individual Face can use as many as three colors from the Colorlist property. The Face[x].colors property accepts a linear list of three integers, which correspond to colors in the Colorlist property. This means that an individual Face can actually be comprised of more than one color at a time. This may seem confusing, but it shouldn't be. Recall our example of a triangle defined by three points. Imagine that at each of the points of the triangle is a specified color, and as you travel over the surface of the triangle toward a different point, the color will slowly fade to the color at the new point. In essence, this means that there will be a slight (or dramatic) gradation in color between the Vertices on an individual Face. We will be examining this technique in further detail when we begin looking at the actual Mesh-creation demonstrations.

NOTE

In addition to these two subproperties of the Face property are the .normals, .shader, and .texturecoordinates subproperties. As mentioned before, we will not be working with these properties in this chapter.

Once you have set up all the values for the Vertices and Faces for a Mesh, you need to issue two commands before you can use the Mesh with a Model. The first command, generatenormals(), will use the vertex ordering information to generate the Normallist property automatically. The syntax for the generatenormals() command is quite simple, as you can see here:

```
Scene.modelresource[x].Generatenormals(method)
```

Note that `modelresource[x]` must correspond to the Mesh Modelresource you are building. Of equal importance is the `method` parameter. You must specify a value of either #flat or #smooth for this command. Generally, #flat will attempt to make the edges of the Mesh look sharp and faceted, whereas #smooth attempts to blend the edges of the Mesh so that it looks like one continuous surface. The differences and subtleties between these two techniques are actually much more complex than this explanation, but this explanation should suffice for the moment. In our first few demonstrations, we will be exclusively using #flat, and for this method, you can simply go on with the understanding of Face normals as you have learned so far. When we begin using #smooth in the later demonstrations, I will explain exactly what the differences are between these two methods of normal generation.

NOTE

The number-one way to get a script error when creating Meshes from code occurs when you're generating normals. Specifically, if you do not specify the `Face[x].vertices` for every Face that you created via the `Faces` parameter in the `newMesh` command, you will get a "`generatenormals()` object has been deleted" message. This frustrating message hardly informs you of the fact that the Mesh Modelresource object has been deleted because of this reason. In short, if you get this message, it means you have not accounted for every Face in your Mesh.

After you have successfully generated the normals for your Mesh (which you must do if you want to see your Mesh), you still need to actually build the Mesh. This is one of the easiest steps of all, as noted by the following syntax:

```
Scene.modelresource[x].Build()
```

The process of building the Mesh is the most time consuming of all the processes for the computer in this scenario. The speed of building an individual Mesh will correspond with the number of Faces that are being used to build the Mesh. Once you have actually built the Modelresource, you can issue a `newModel` command—something along the lines of this:

```
Scene.newmodel(Modelname, scene.modelresource[x])
```

In summary, the process of creating a Mesh Modelresource is broken into several general tasks. Although there will be additions to this list, the general order of tasks for creating a custom Mesh Modelresource from code is as follows:

1. Create Mesh Modelresource with the `newMesh()` command.

2. Set the value of the `Vertexlist` property.

3. Correlate the `Vertexlist` entries to create Faces.

4. Generate normals for the Mesh.

5. Build the Mesh.

6. Create a Model from the Mesh Modelresource.

With this order of tasks in mind, we will turn our attention from the abstract outline of Mesh creation and begin with our first demonstration of creating a custom Mesh with code.

Building a Triangle

In this demonstration, we will be examining the code to create a Mesh comprised of a single Face. You know that a Face is always the shape of a triangle, so this demonstration could equally be thought of as building a single-faced Mesh. On the CD is a file named "Building a Triangle." Open this file and press Play. You should see a single triangle rotating around the Y axis in the center of the Stage, as shown in Figure 27.2.

Note that you have the ability to switch between several `model.visibility` settings: #front, #back, and #both. Also note in this example (which is impossible to truly see from Figure 27.2) that we are using per-Vertex shading for the Face. That is, each Vertex on the Face has a different color, and there is a ramp of color between these three across the surface of the Face. Before we look at the code for this example, take a look at Figure 27.3, which illustrates several key elements used to create this Mesh.

Note from Figure 27.3 that this Face is comprised of three Vertices, numbered 1, 2 and 3. Also note that I have centered the Vertices for this single Face so that the origin of the local coordinate system and the logical center of the triangle are essentially in the same place. This will allow you to rotate the triangle around its center without any complicated axisangle transforms.

FIGURE 27.2

Screenshot from the "Building a Triangle" demonstration.

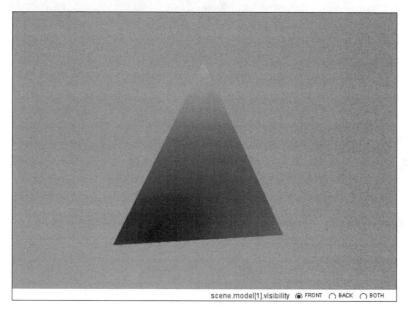

scene.model[1].visibility ⦿ FRONT ⚬ BACK ⚬ BOTH

FIGURE 27.3

An illustration of how to build a single triangle.

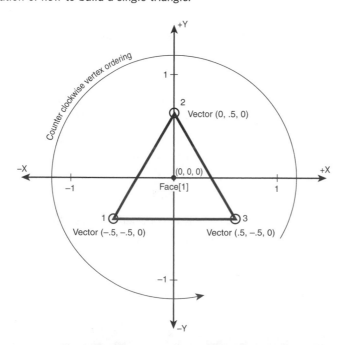

Also note that the locations for the Vertices of this Face are decimal values. I have done this so that we can easily scale the Mesh at the Model level using transformation to the size we want. There is nothing wrong with defining your Meshes at "actual scale," but for small Models such as this, it is often easier to use this method for Mesh creation.

Finally, note that the Vertex order for this Face has been defined as counterclockwise. How this face definition has been made is best understood by looking at the actual code used to create this triangle (see Listing 27.1).

Listing 27.1   Initialization for the "Building a Triangle" Demo

```
 1: global scene
 2:
 3: on initialize
 4:   clearworld(scene)
 5:
 6:   -- first, create a mesh resource.  Note that in this
 7:   -- example, I have specified that "triangleres" will
 8:   -- consist of 1 face, 3 vertices, ignore normals
 9:   -- 3 colors and 0 texturecoordinates
10:   meshRes = scene.newMesh("triangleres", 1 , 3, 0, 3, 0)
11:
12:   -- next, we will populate the Vertexlist with our
13:   -- vector values.  There must be one vector entry
14:   -- for each of the Vertices that you specified for the mesh
15:   -- note that these three vertices will be referred to by their
16:   -- position in the list, 1, 2 and 3
17:   meshRes.vertexList = [vector(-.5, -.5, 0), vector(0,.5,0), \
       vector(.5,-.5,0)]
18:
19:   -- next, we will specify the values for the colorlist, note
20:   -- that these three colors :red, green, blue will be referred
21:   -- to by their item number in the list: 1, 2 and 3 respectively
22:   meshRes.colorlist = [rgb(255,0,0), rgb(0,255,0), rgb(0,0,255)]
23:
24:   -- now, we must assign the Vertices to the Face.
25:   -- Note that the order of assignment is important
26:   -- where 3,2,1 is counterclockwise because of the
27:   -- locations of the 3 vertices in 3D space not
28:   -- because of the numbers of the vertices themselves.
29:   meshRes.face[1].vertices = [ 3,2,1 ]
30:
31:   -- next, we will assign the colors that each Vertex
32:   -- in the face should use.  Remember that these numbers
33:   -- refer to values in the colorlist property for the mesh
```

Listing 27.1   Continued

```
34:    meshRes.face[1].colors = [1,2,3]
35:
36:    -- now that we have defined the Face, generate its normal
37:    meshRes.generateNormals(#flat)
38:
39:    -- build the mesh
40:    meshRes.build()
41:
42:    -- create a Model based on the mesh
43:    obj = scene.newModel("triangle", meshRes)
44:
45:    -- scale it up (so that we can see it, remember that we
46:    -- are creating Meshes with coordinates in the range of
47:    -- 0-1, which allows us to easily scale to any size.
48:    obj.scale(100,100,1)
49:
50:    -- just setting the background color of the sprite here.
51:    scene.camera[1].colorbuffer.clearvalue= rgb(100,100,100)
52: end
```

There are two additional notes I would like to make concerning this script. First, notice that line 17 defines the Vertexlist and line 29 defines the order of Vertices for Face[1]. This is important because the Vertex ordering defined via the Face[1].vertices statement in line 29 is affected by the order in which the Vertices are defined in the Vertexlist in line 17.

Second, note that at line 48 we are actually scaling up the Model using the triangle Mesh 100 times in both the X and Y directions. Because the triangle Mesh is one unit wide from Vertex 1 to 3 prior to scaling, this means that the width at the base of the triangle should be 100 units.

As you can see from this rather simple example, organization is the key to success for creating Meshes from code. Because we have only just created a single Face, I cannot stress enough how important organization will be as we continue. Although you may look at Figure 27.3 as simply a figure for this book, I highly recommend that you draw just such a figure each time you go to create a new Mesh until you get the hang of the process. Even if you have been doing this for years, there are going to be many times when using paper and pencil is going to help you out more than staring at your code for hours and hours.

Building a Square

In this demonstration, we will be examining how to build two Faces, such that we will end up with a single square Mesh. Before I tell you the answer, what is the smallest number of Vertices you will need to define in order to create two Faces comprising a single square Mesh? If you said four, you are correct.

Now, for those of you who said six, let me clear this up right away. If we needed three unique Vertices to define a given Face, your answer would have been correct. But we don't need unique Vertices to define a Mesh, which leads to an important point in Mesh creation: Faces can share Vertices.

Shared Vertices means your role as the creator of Meshes becomes a little more complicated, but your role as the optimizer of performance has been given another area for efficiency. In order to understand how we will use two triangular Faces to define a single square Mesh, consider the illustration shown in Figure 27.4.

FIGURE 27.4

How to build two Faces from four Vertices by sharing Vertices.

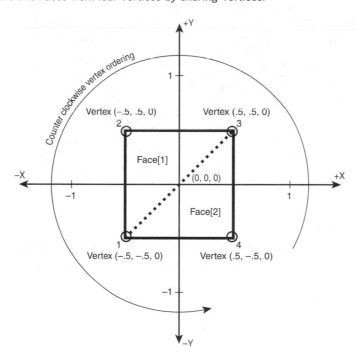

As you can see from Figure 27.4, Face[1] is comprised of the Vertices numbered 3, 2, and 1, whereas Face[2] is comprised of Vertices numbered 4, 3, and 1. Note that for an individual Face, it is unimportant which Vertex of the Face you begin with, as long as you continue to define the Face in the correct order—in this case, counterclockwise.

If you open the file named "Building a Square" on the CD and press Play, you will be able to see this Mesh. Figure 27.5 is a screenshot from this demonstration. Notice that I have colored each Face dramatically different so that you can see the hidden edge between the two Faces.

FIGURE 27.5

Screenshot from the "Building a Square" demonstration.

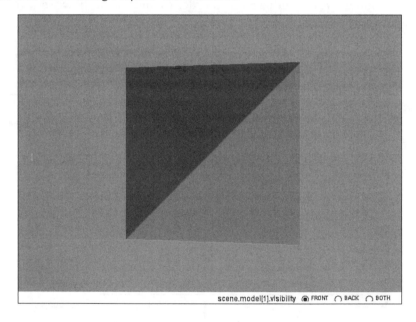

scene.model[1].visibility ● FRONT ○ BACK ○ BOTH

If I had not colored each Face differently, you would not be able to see the fact that this Mesh is created from two Faces. It would look like one smooth surface. Next, take a look at the code used to create this Mesh, as shown in Listing 27.2.

Listing 27.2   Initialization for the "Building a Square" Demo

```
1: global scene
2:
```

Listing 27.2   Continued

```
 3: on initialize
 4:   clearworld(scene)
 5:
 6:   --create the mesh resource: 2 faces, 4 vertices, 2 colors
 7:   meshRes = scene.newMesh("squareres", 2 , 4, 0, 2, 0)
 8:
 9:   --create the vertexlist
10:   meshRes.vertexList = [vector(-.5, -.5, 0), \
      vector(-.5,.5,0),vector(.5, .5, 0), vector(.5,-.5,0)]
11:   --create the colorlist
12:   meshRes.colorlist = [rgb(200,200,0), rgb(0,200,200)]
13:
14:   -- assign the vertices for face 1
15:   meshRes.face[1].vertices = [3,2,1]
16:   --assign the colors for the face[1] vertices
17:   meshRes.face[1].colors = [1,1,1]
18:
19:   --assign the vertices for face 2
20:   meshRes.face[2].vertices = [4,3,1]
21:   -- assign the colors for the face[2] vertices
22:   meshRes.face[1].colors = [2,2,2]
23:
24:   -- now that we have defined the Faces, generatenormals
25:   meshRes.generateNormals(#flat)
26:
27:   -- build the mesh
28:   meshRes.build()
29:
30:   -- create a Model based on the mesh
31:   obj = scene.newModel("square", meshRes)
32:   -- scale it up
33:   obj.scale(100,100,1)
34:
35:   scene.camera[1].colorbuffer.clearvalue= rgb(100,100,100)
36: end
```

You already know that we have shared Vertices to create this square Mesh, so I want to point out lines 17 and 22 in this script, where we assign the colors to the Vertices for each Face. If you think about it, Vertex 1 and Vertex 3 are given two different colors. If you look again at the square in Figure 27.5, you can see that the two Faces are clearly defined. Note that the color assignments are Face-level properties; this is why a Vertex not only can be shared by two or more Faces but it can have a different color for each Face that references it.

Building a Pyramid

We have looked at two demonstrations so far, but we have not yet actually created a three-dimensional geometric form. In this demonstration, we will be doing just that. Specifically, we will be applying your understanding of Mesh creation to build a simple pyramid. Begin by examining Figure 27.6, which illustrates how a fifth Vertex will allow us to define the six Faces required to build a square-bottomed pyramid.

FIGURE 27.6

How to build a square-bottomed pyramid from five Vertices and six Faces.

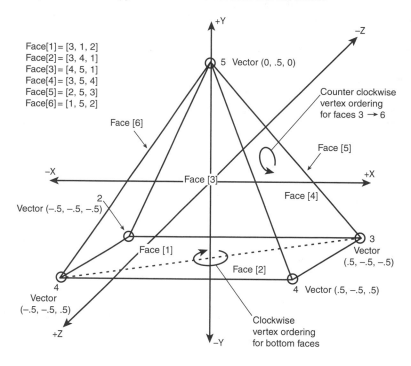

Note that even in three dimensions, Vertex ordering still relies on whether the Vertices are defined clockwise or counterclockwise. In this demonstration, I have defined the majority of the Faces counterclockwise. But notice how the two Faces on the bottom have been defined clockwise; this is so that the pyramid looks like a solid object. If I had defined all Faces counterclockwise, you would be able to "see into" the pyramid when looking at it from the bottom.

If you open the file named "Building a Pyramid" on the CD and press Play, you will be able to see this example in action. Rather than show the screenshot for this demonstration and the code listing, I will refer you to the demonstration directly. Comments are included with the code in the demonstration file. When you look at the code in that example, you will notice that it is only slightly more complex based on the fact that the Vertexlist is larger and the number of Faces we need to define is larger. But structurally, other than the fact that the bottom Faces of the pyramid are defined clockwise, the script is essentially identical to the previous examples we have looked at.

Creating Grids

At this point, the focus of the chapter will shift slightly. We will change from the general goal of learning how to create a Mesh to the specific goal of how to use Mesh creation to create terrain.

I have broken the demonstration of creating terrain into two demonstrations. This is because there are two major issues we will be dealing with that can easily be confused. Our first task for creating terrain is to build code that will be able to generate a simple grid. Although the grid might be simple—or at least simple to imagine—creating it is one of those coding challenges that will test your repeat loop savvy.

Before we begin looking at code though, we need to examine different styles of grids that are commonly used for generating terrain. This will allow us to decide which method of grid creation works best. Figure 27.7 illustrates two of the most common styles of grids used in 3D programming.

Note that in Figure 27.7, I have drawn in the individual Faces that comprise the grids. Although each of these grid styles has its own strengths and weaknesses, we will be using the square grid method because it is the easiest to code. If you examine Figure 27.8, you can see that I have expanded the illustration for the square grid method. You can see how the Faces and the Vertices are numbered in a square grid with two columns and two rows. Note that the grid is shown on the X/Z plane; therefore, you are technically looking straight down at the grid from overhead.

FIGURE 27.7

Different grid styles.

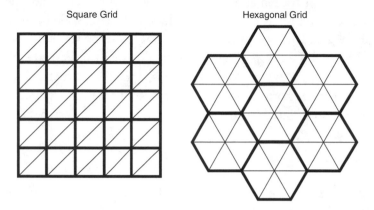

Square Grid   Hexagonal Grid

FIGURE 27.8

A square two-by-two grid with numbered Vertices and Faces shown.

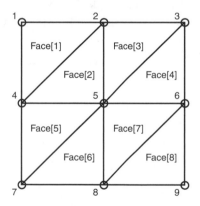

Without a diagram such as Figure 27.8, you would be hard-pressed to create the code for a grid Mesh of this complexity off-the-cuff. In this demonstration, it would be silly to hard-code the size of an individual grid into a custom handler. Rather, because we are going to go out of our way to build the code to create a grid anyway, it would be better to create a handler that can define a grid of any size, meaning that we should be able to control the width, length, and number of divisions that comprise the grid via a single handler.

First, we need to figure out the algorithms capable of evaluating how many Faces and how many Vertices are required for a given Mesh. We know how many columns and how many rows of Faces span the width and length of the grid. We also know that each square is made up of two Faces. Therefore, the number of Faces can be calculated with the following formula:

Number of Faces = columns * rows * 2

In addition, we know that each column and each row contains one more Vertex than the number of Faces in that row or column. Therefore, the number of Vertices we need for a Mesh can be determined as follows:

Number of Vertices = (columns + 1) * (rows + 1)

Once we have figured out how many Faces and Vertices are required, we will be able to generate the rough Mesh Modelresource. Setting the locations for the Vertices themselves is actually straightforward, because the Vertices are numbered from left to right. When we reach the end of a row, the numbering continues at the left side of the next row. Overall, the numbering is simple enough that a repeat loop should be able to handle the creation of the Vertices. We will eventually nest two repeat loops for this purpose in order to set the correct increments between the Vertices.

Once the Vertexlist has been set, the major part of our task is before us. Specifically, we will need to assign the Vertices to the Faces in the Mesh. In order to do this efficiently, we will need to come up with some general rules about how the order of Vertices affects the numbering for Faces. This is because we are going to encapsulate the code for defining the Faces within a repeat loop; therefore, we need some form of an algorithm that can routinely determine which Faces are based on which Vertices, regardless of the size of the grid.

Table 27.3 lists all the Faces for the grid in Figure 27.8 as well as the corresponding Vertices for each Face (in counterclockwise order), which I have labeled V1, V2, and V3. We are trying to see whether there is some common link between the numbers. In short, we are trying to determine whether there's a series to the numbers that we can use to create an algorithm for assigning Vertices to Faces.

TABLE 27.3   Breakdown of the Vertices Used for Each Face

Face Number	V1	V2	V3
1	1	4	2
2	2	4	5
3	2	5	3
4	3	5	6
5	4	7	5
6	5	7	8
7	5	8	6
8	6	8	9

We will begin by examining how V1, V2, and V3 relate within a given row. You may be able to see the correlation better if you look at the odd Faces first and then look at the even Faces. If you haven't seen it yet, the odd numbered Faces and the even numbered Faces follow their own algorithms for determining which Vertices comprise them! These rules for Vertex numbering apply only to the square grid:

- Odd faces = [V1, V1 + columns + 1, V1 + 1]
- Even faces = [V1 + 1, V1 + columns + 1, V1 + columns + 2]

If you begin by looking at the values in the V2 column, you can see that they are in groups of twos. However, there's a strange discrepancy: The values in this column skip Vertex 6. What is so special about Vertex 6 that we should have to skip it? Looking back at Figure 27.8, note that Vertex 6 is on the right edge of the grid. But, we can't just say that we will always skip Vertex 6, because it might not always be on the right edge. This rule can be expressed as follows:

```
If V1 mod (columns + 1) = 0 then

  V1 = V1 + 1
End if
```

Admittedly, all these rules can become confusing—who would have ever thought that creating a simple grid would be so difficult? Once you have assigned the Vertices to the Faces, the only things left to do are quite simple: Generate the normals using the generatenormals() command and then build the Mesh using the build() command.

Open the file named "Building a Grid" on the CD and press Play. You will be presented with the end result of this demonstration: a square grid. Note that I have colored alternating Faces different colors so that you can see the hidden edges between Faces. I have also colored Face[1] blue so that you can easily see the position of the first Face in the Mesh. In this demonstration, I have created a single custom handler named grid() that can create square grids of any number of columns and any number of rows. To call the grid() custom handler, you will use the following syntax:

```
Obj = Grid(name, columns, rows, spacing)
```

Note that the grid() custom handler will return a reference to the grid Model. The columns and rows parameters refer to the number of Faces you want to create across the surface of the grid, whereas spacing is used to determine the width and height of each Face. Therefore, in this script, the width of the grid in units is "columns * spacing," and the length of the grid is "rows * spacing." With these last two pieces of information in mind, let's look at the grid() custom handler, which is shown with comments in Listing 27.3.

Listing 27.3   Grid-Creation Custom Handler

```
 1: global scene
 2:
 3: on grid(gname, columns, rows, spacing)
 4:
 5:    --based on the params figure out
 6:    --how wide and how long the final
 7:    --grid dimensions will be
 8:    gridwidth = columns * spacing
 9:    gridlength = rows * spacing
10:
11:    -- determine the number of faces
12:    nFaces = columns * rows * 2
13:    -- determine the number of vertices
14:    nVerts = (columns + 1) * (rows + 1)
15:
16:    --create a new mesh modelresource
17:    --that defines the number of faces
```

Listing 27.3   Continued

```
18:   --and vertices from the lines above
19:   meshRes = scene.newmesh(gname & "res", nFaces, nVerts, 0, 3, 0)
20:   meshRes.colorlist = [rgb(255,255,0), rgb(255,0,255),\
      rgb(0,100,255)]
21:
22:   --since we are going to be using a nested
23:   --repeat loop to generate our vertexlist,
24:   --we will temporarily add the vertices to
25:   --this list, before assigning the value of
26:   --this list to the vertexlist all at once
27:   tempvertexlist = []
28:
29:   -- determine, based on the width and length
30:   -- of the final grid, where in local coordinates
31:   -- the X/Z starting position should be for the
32:   -- first vertex in the grid.  -- this will make sure
33:   -- that the center of the grid is located at the
34:   -- center of model relative coordinate space
35:   startwidth = -(gridwidth / 2)
36:   startlength = -(gridlength / 2)
37:
38:   -- next, we will be generating the vertices for
39:   -- the vertexlist by cycling through all of the
40:   -- vertices that we need to create from
41:   -- -X to +X and -Z to +Z
42:   repeat with length = 1 to (rows + 1)
43:     repeat with width = 1 to (columns + 1)
44:
45:       -- this next line of code adds
46:       -- the a vertex to the temporary vertex list
47:       -- Note, that the Y component of this
48:       -- list is currently 0, because the grid
49:       -- we are creating is flat.  When we revisit
50:       -- this script, this line in particular will
51:       -- be different because we will be setting
52:       -- a Y value (to create terrain)
53:       addat(tempvertexlist, vector(startwidth, 0,  startlength))
54:
55:       -- add the correct amount of units to the
56:       -- current value of startwidth
57:       startwidth = startwidth + spacing
58:
59:     end repeat
60:     --once we have created all of the vertices in
61:     -- a given horizontal row, we need to advance
62:     -- the value of startlength, so that the vertices
```

Listing 27.3   Continued

```
63:     -- are "closer towards the viewer" on the +Z axis
64:     startlength = startlength + spacing
65:     --also, when we move to the next row, make sure
66:     -- that we reset the position of the X component
67:     -- to the starting position of the grid entirely
68:     startwidth = -(gridwidth / 2)
69:   end repeat
70:
71:   -- once all of the vertexlist have been assigned
72:   -- in the temporary list, set them to the actual list
73:   meshRes.vertexlist = tempvertexlist
74:
75:   --next, you will need to assign all of the vertices
76:   --to the faces in the grid.  This is the most complicated
77:   --part of the script.
78:
79:   -- first, I will create several counters that will be used
80:   -- to determine "which face" we are on and "which vertex"
81:   -- is the first vertex for the current face
82:   startvert = 1
83:   facenumber = 1
84:   -- multiple is used to make sure that when we are counting
85:   -- the value of startvert, that its increment goes something
86:   -- like 1, 2, 4, 5, (for a 2 face X 2 face grid)
87:   multiple = columns + 1
88:
89:   -- notice that the repeat loop only goes through
90:   -- 1/2 the number of faces: why? because the vertices
91:   -- for odd faces and even faces will be determined
92:   -- using two different schemes!  This way, within
93:   -- one cycle of the repeat loop, we will define
94:   -- an odd face, and then an even face and essentially
95:   -- "jump" the counters by two
96:   repeat with length = 1 to (nFaces / 2)
97:     --odd face
98:     faceVerts =[startvert, startvert+columns+1, startvert+1]
99:     meshRes.face[facenumber].vertices = faceverts
100:    meshRes.face[facenumber].colors = [1,1,1]
101:
102:    --even face
103:    faceVerts =[startvert+1, startvert+columns+1,\
                startvert+columns+2]
104:    --(note how I am adding one to facevalue temporarily
105:    -- in order to reference the even numbered face)
106:    meshRes.face[facenumber + 1].vertices = faceverts
107:    meshRes.face[facenumber + 1].colors = [2,2,2]
108:
```

Listing 27.3   Continued

```
109:      -- jump the current facenumber by two
110:      facenumber = facenumber + 2
111:      --add one to the value of startvert
112:      startvert = startvert + 1
113:      --but make sure that if we are at the end of a row
114:      --that we skip two vertices and not just one!
115:      if startvert mod multiple = 0 then startvert = startvert + 1
116:   end repeat
117:
118:   -- I am setting the color of face[1] different
119:   -- so that you can locate it in the grid.
120:   meshres.face[1].colors = [3,3,3]
121:
122:   --generate normals
123:   meshRes.generatenormals(#flat)
124:   --build the mesh
125:   meshRes.build()
126:   --create the model
127:   obj = scene.newmodel(gname, meshRes)
128:   -- in true OOP style, we will return
129:   -- a reference to the object we just created
130:   return obj
131: end
```

Pay special attention to the note beginning at line 45 that refers to line 53 in this script. The Model we are creating with this script is a flat grid. In order to make terrain, we need to modify the Y values for the Vertices in this grid, but nothing else. For example, try changing line 53 so that it reads as follows:

```
addat(tempvertexlist, vector(startwidth, random(10),  startlength))
```

Changing line 53 to this will create a random-looking terrain. However random terrain using random numbers generated by the random() function creates an extremely noisy unrealistic surface. We need a method for actually creating a surface that looks like terrain. This method is the topic of the next section.

Building Terrain

We have now solved one half of the problem of generating terrain; we have created a script that can generate a square grid of any size. We need a way of specifying the Y values for the Vertices in that grid, and we will be able to build terrain. After quickly realizing that random numbers in themselves will not be able to help us without building extremely complex random number–generation tools (which would run pretty slow in Lingo), you might wonder how exactly we are going to create realistic terrain without overdoing it.

For a moment, let's put aside the creation of terrain randomly, as that was never the goal. The goal was to create terrain. A frequently used technique in both 3D animation and 3D programming to create terrain is to use what is often referred to as a *height field*, which is an 8-bit grayscale bitmap. Because an 8-bit bitmap can represent 256 individual levels of gray value, you can use the gray value of each pixel in a height field bitmap to control a terrain with 256 individual levels of height; this will be more than sufficient for our purposes. Figure 27.9 is an example of a height field bitmap that was created in Adobe Photoshop by using the clouds filter. The levels for the image were then adjusted to ensure strong areas of contrast.

FIGURE 27.9

A height field bitmap used to generate terrain.

Note that in the script we will be building, the light areas are low, and the dark areas are high. If all the values for the terrain are stored in a bitmap, you might wonder, why not just save them in a linear list? If you were going to be using a terrain that was the same each time, this is exactly what I would tell you to do. However, there is still the issue of extracting the height field data.

Evaluating the grayscale levels for the pixels in the height field bitmap is a job for Imaging Lingo if there ever was one. Specifically, we will be using the `getpixel()` function to cycle through the pixels in the bitmap to determine the corresponding height values. The syntax for `getpixel()` is as follows:

```
ImageObject.Getpixel(point(x,y))
```

If the bitmap is 32 bits, this will return an RGB value; if the bitmap is 8 bits (as it is in our case), `getpixel()` will return a `paletteindex()`, which is simply a number from 0 to 255. Now, if I told you that the height field we are working with is 256-by-256 pixels, you might quickly calculate that there are 65,536 pixels in a bitmap of that size.

Two obvious issues are involved here: First, there is no way you want users to have to wait while you cycle through 65,536 `getpixel()` calls, because these calls are kind of slow in general. Second, you probably don't want to create a list with 65,536 items in it. So, what can we do? Look at the height field in Figure 27.9. What if rather than checking every single pixel we were to sample the pixels at a regular interval?

What if we were to sample every other pixel? This would mean a total of 16,384 required samplings. Sample every four pixels, and that number drops to 4,096. This is much better in terms of the number of `getpixel()` calls as well as the size of the linear list. If you think this will not be specific enough, open the file on the CD named "Building Terrain" and press Play. I will refrain from showing you a screenshot of this demonstration because the terrain slowly spins while the movie plays, and the overall effect is not captured in the same way with a static image.

As you can see from the demonstration, not only have I created terrain, but I have applied a full-color terrain texture to it, thus enhancing the overall effectiveness of the height field technique. You can also switch between looking at the terrain using the landscape Texture, alternating colored Faces or wireframe mode via radio buttons at the bottom of the Stage.

This demonstration capitalizes on the use of three scripts. The first script we will be looking at is the `buildarray()` custom handler, which cycles through the values of the height field in order to extract the Y values for the terrain. The syntax for calling the `buildarray()` script is as follows:

```
MyArray = buildarray(Castmember, Sample, Maxheight)
```

Here, `Castmember` must refer to an 8-bit bitmap Castmember, `Sample` is the number of pixels we want to skip, and `Maxheight` is the maximum height in Model-relative coordinates we want to create our terrain. In short, the `buildarray()` script takes the 256 levels in an 8-bit bitmap and converts them into 256 levels of height that are scaled as steep or shallow as you like. With this single script then, it is possible to create gigantic mountains (with large `Maxheight` values), gentle foothills (with float values for `Maxheight` between 0 and 1), and everything in between. Examine the code for the `buildarray()` custom handler, as shown in Listing 27.4.

Listing 27.4   `Buildarray()` **Custom Handler**

```
1: on buildarray(whichmember, sampling, maxHeight)
2:    -- create empty linear list
3:    heightarray = []
4:
5:    -- determine if scaling has been set
6:    -- for the maximum height value.  If not,
7:    -- set the maximum height to 1.
8:    if maxheight = void then maxheight = 1
9:
10:   -- create a duplicate image object
11:   -- of the height field bitmap
12:   img = member(whichmember).image.duplicate()
13:
14:   -- cycle through all of the pixels
15:   -- as determined by the sampling.
16:   -- as you can see, higher sampling
17:   -- values produce coarser results
18:   repeat with y = 1 to (img.height / sampling)
19:     repeat with x = 1 to (img.width / sampling)
20:       --figure out the position of the current pixel
21:       whichpoint = point((x * sampling - 1), (y*sampling - 1))
22:       -- get the value of that pixel
23:       pixel = img.getpixel(whichpoint)
24:       -- make sure that you change from a
```

Listing 27.4   Continued

```
25:        -- paletteindex into a number
26:        num = pixel.paletteindex
27:        -- trap the 0 value
28:        if num.paletteindex = 0 then num = 0
29:        -- divide the number by 255
30:        -- this will force the value
31:        -- of num to a float number between
32:        -- 0 and 1
33:        num = num / float(255)
34:
35:        -- then, multiply the float value by
36:        -- the maximum height that you want
37:        -- for your terrain.
38:        num = num * maxheight
39:
40:        -- finally add num to the heightarray
41:        addat(heightarray, num)
42:     end repeat
43:   end repeat
44:
45:   return heightarray
46: end
```

As you can see from this code, the higher the sample rate, the smaller the linear list we will be creating. Also, note that it is entirely possible to use height fields that are much larger or much smaller than 256×256, but as you can see from the demonstration, we are able to create quite large landscapes with just 256×256 bitmaps.

The next script we will be looking at is an excerpt from the terrain() custom handler. The majority of this script is based on the grid() custom handler, so there is no sense in looking at the parts of the script that are unchanged. In Listing 27.5, I have only placed comments on those lines in the excerpt from the beginning of the terrain() custom handler that are new or have changed. After line 37, the script remains exactly the same as the grid() custom handler.

Listing 27.5   Terrain() Custom Handler

```
1: on terrain(gname, columns, rows, spacing, hArray)
2:
3:   gridwidth = columns * spacing
```

Listing 27.5 Continued

```
 4:    gridlength = rows * spacing
 5:    nFaces = columns * rows * 2
 6:    nVerts = (columns + 1) * (rows + 1)
 7:
 8:    --make sure that there are enough items in the
 9:    --hArray for the number of vertices you are creating
10:    if hArray.count <> nVerts then
11:      return false
12:    end if
13:
14:    meshRes = scene.newmesh(gname & "res", nFaces, nVerts, 0, 3, 0)
15:    meshRes.colorlist = [rgb(255,255,0), rgb(255,0,255), rgb(0,100,255)]
16:
17:    tempvertexlist = []
18:    startwidth = -(gridwidth / 2)
19:    startlength = -(gridlength / 2)
20:
21:    --create a counter to get
22:    --height positions from hArray
23:    arraypos = 1
24:    repeat with height = 1 to (rows + 1)
25:      repeat with width = 1 to (columns + 1)
26:
27:        --notice how this next line of code now
28:        -- uses values from the hArray for the Y Vertex values
29:        addat(tempvertexlist, vector(startwidth,(hArray[arraypos]),\
startlength))
30:
31:        startwidth = startwidth + spacing
32:        --add one to the arraypos counter
33:        arraypos = arraypos + 1
34:      end repeat
35:      startlength = startlength + spacing
36:      startwidth = -(gridwidth / 2)
37:    end repeat
```

As you can see from line 1 of Listing 27.5, the terrain() custom handler requires a fifth parameter: hArray. The hArray parameter is a linear list created by the buildarray() custom handler. Note that there must be as many entries in hArray as there are Vertices in the grid; these values are checked in lines 10–12.

The final part of this demonstration worth looking at is the initialization script that calls both the buildarray() and terrain() custom handlers as well as applies the landscape Texture to the terrain Model. This script is shown in its entirety in Listing 27.6.

Listing 27.6   Terrain Initialization Script

```
 1: global scene      -- we will reference the SW3D in this script
 2:
 3: on initialize
 4:   clearworld(scene)
 5:
 6:   --build the array
 7:   myarray = buildarray("heightfield", 4, 3024)
 8:   --create the terrain
 9:   obj = terrain("terrain", 63,63,800, myarray)
10:   --create a shader for the terrain
11:   shd = scene.newshader("grd", #standard)
12:   --set the terrain shader to the new shader
13:   obj.shader = shd
14:   --create a new texture from the landscape bitmap
15:   txt = scene.newtexture("lndscape", #fromcastmember, \
member("landscape"))
16:   --assign the shader texture
17:   obj.shader.texture = txt
18:   --set the mapping mode to #wrapplanar
19:   obj.shader.texturemode = #wrapplanar
20:   --use replace (rich colors)
21:   obj.shader.blendfunction = #replace
22:   --note that I am rotating the mapping coordinates
23:   --for the texture 90 degrees in this next line:
24:   shd.wraptransform.rotate(90,0,0)
25:   -- make sure the visibility is set to #front
26:   obj.visibility = #front
27:   -- and that the faces are filled in
28:   obj.shader.renderstyle = #fill
29:   --set the camera background color to a sky blue
30:   member(1).camera[1].colorbuffer.clearvalue =  rgb(210,210,255)
31:   -- move the terrain downward somewhat
32:   obj.translate(0,-1000,0)
33: end
```

Pay special attention to lines 19 and 24 in this code listing. Using the #wrapplanar Texturemode, we are using Texture mapping rather than Texture coordinates. Because of the orientation of the default mapping coordinates, we need to rotate the wraptransform in line 24 so that the landscape Texture aligns correctly with the landscape itself. Overall, this demonstration shows how it is possible to use the Mesh-creation tools to generate realistic, believable terrain.

Terrain Following

The final demonstration we will be looking at in this chapter does not so much deal with the creation of the terrain as to what to do once you have created the terrain. In the last demonstration, the Camera was simply situated in the center of the terrain as it spun slowly so that you could look around. That method might be good for a demonstration, but if we are going to go through all the trouble of generating a complex terrain, we ought to have a way to explore it. For this reason, we will be taking the next logical step in this series of demonstrations—you will learn how to build a terrain-following script.

What is a terrain-following script? If you remember the Camera navigation demonstrations from Chapter 25, "Advanced Camera Control," you may recall that we built a method to control the driving of a Camera within an environment. That environment happened to be very flat. Because our terrain is not flat, we need to create a script that can raise and lower the vertical position of the Camera based on the height of the terrain. In this demonstration, we will be combining this general idea with dummy objects and interpolation animation to create a believable and dramatic experience.

Before I continue to explain how we will be creating our terrain-following script, open the file on the CD named "Terrain Following" and press Play. You will drive the Camera using the arrow keys. Note that for added dramatic effect, I have increased the maximum height of the terrain to create steep hills, and I increased the Camera's field of view to 90 degrees. Try driving the Camera around the terrain for a little while. Notice what happens as you approach an uphill or downhill grade. The Camera not only maintains its distance above the terrain, but it also maintains a sense of actually moving up and down with the grade of the terrain.

NOTE

If you do happen to drive "off" the terrain, simply turn around 180 degrees to the left or right and drive into the terrain. When you reach the terrain, the terrain-following script will automatically "right" itself. Note that is just a terrain-following script; we will examine boundary management in Chapter 29, "Collision Detection."

Modelsunderray()

To understand exactly how the terrain-following script works, you must first learn about an advanced command from Picking Lingo that you have not yet encountered: `Modelsunderray()`. Before now, we have strictly been using `Modelsunderloc()`. `Modelsunderray()` is similar, except for the fact that it is not tied to any specific Camera in the scene.

Allow me to explain it this way: `Modelsunderloc()` draws a line from the current Camera position in the World through a point specified as the `loc()` in Sprite coordinates. This imaginary line continues on "forever" into 3D space, reporting back about those Models that are in its way. `Modelsunderray()` takes a point in 3D space and a direction Vector. It then draws an imaginary line (or *ray*, if you will) from the 3D point in the direction of the direction Vector, "forever" through 3D space. Any Models that are in its way are reported.

This means you can take any arbitrary position in the 3D environment and point a ray in any arbitrary direction from that point and find out what Models lie in the path of this ray. It gets better! So far when looking at any of the Picking Lingo commands, we have only been requesting simple data—the default. This simply returns a list with the names of the Models that have been intersected.

In this demonstration, we will be requesting detailed data from the Picking Lingo command `Modelsunderray()`, which will provide us with several powerful pieces of information. The scope of detailed Picking Lingo data is explained in Table 27.4.

TABLE 27.4   Detailed Picking Lingo Data

Property	Purpose
Model	The name of the model intersected
Distance	The distance from the 3D point to the point of intersection with the Model
Isectposition	The point of intersection in World coordinate space
Isectnormal	The normal of the intersected Face
MeshID	The number of the intersected Mesh (if you're working with a multiple-Mesh Model)
FaceID	The number of the intersected Face in the Mesh

TABLE 27.4   Continued

Property	Purpose
Vertices	The Vertices of the intersected Face in the Mesh in World space
UvCoord	The UV Texture coordinates of intersected Face

Note that this detailed information is available in the form of a property list nested inside of a linear list. The linear list contains a property list entry containing the detailed picking data noted in Table 27.4 for *each* Model that is intersected by the ray. As you may have been able to guess, Picking Lingo just became exponentially more impressive as well as useful.

For our purposes in this demonstration, the only properties we are interested in are Model and Isectposition. Keep in mind that we will be working with detailed Picking Lingo in the next chapter as well. In terms of the Isectposition property, note that this is the point of intersection between the ray and a Face in World coordinate space. This is not the position of one of the Vertices (although that data is available as well); instead, this is the exact Vector location of the intersection with the Face. The process of using modelsunderray() is often referred to as *shooting a ray*.

If we were to shoot a ray from some position directly above ourselves in the environment in the direction of our position, we could determine the elevation of the terrain at the point of intersection between the ray and the terrain. The point of intersection would be given as a World-coordinate vector that we could then strip out all but the precious Y-axis location data in order to position the Camera some distance above the terrain. This process is illustrated in Figure 27.10.

As you'll notice from actually driving the Camera, the process described in Figure 27.10 could not possibly account for the way the Camera accelerates and decelerates, nor how it obeys the grade of the terrain. Although Figure 27.10 is enough to explain the basics of the modelsunderray() command, it is not exactly the way that the terrain-following script is set up.

Rather, in order to understand the terrain-following script, you should have already covered the Advanced Camera Navigation demonstration from Chapter 25. If you have not, you need to look at that demonstration first—or perhaps look at it again to refresh your memory. The key to the Advanced Camera Navigation demonstration is that the position and orientation of the

Camera interpolates to the position and orientation of a dummy Camera. In turn, the dummy Camera is attached to a Model that is the actual Model driven through the scene via the keyboard input.

FIGURE 27.10

Modelsunderray *example.*

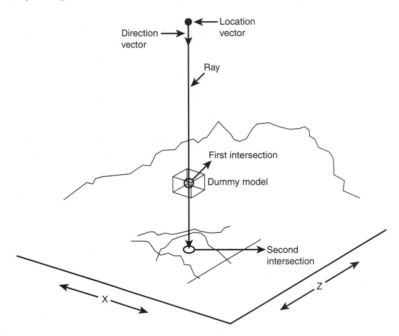

In this demonstration, I have taken this process several steps forward. Rather than creating just one dummy object, I have created two. The first dummy object is an invisible box that is driven through the scene with the arrow keys. In this demonstration, a dummy Camera is also parented to the first dummy object. The second dummy object is an invisible box that travels 550 units in front of the first dummy box. I use two modelsunderray() calls to make sure both the first and second dummy boxes maintain a height 15 units above the terrain at their respective X/Z positions. Then, I use the pointat() command to point the dummy Camera at the position of the second dummy object. The final step is to interpolate the current position and orientation of the active Camera some percentage toward the position and orientation of the dummy Camera. This elaborate technique produces the results you have experienced in the terrain-following demonstration. I have drawn a cross-section view of the environment in Figure 27.11 to help you visualize what is actually going on in the scene.

FIGURE 27.11

Illustrated explanation of how two dummy Models, a dummy Camera, two `modelsunderray()` *commands, and interpolation can be used to build a robust terrain-following script.*

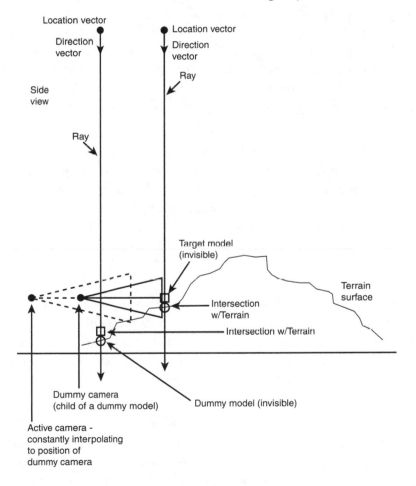

As you can see from this illustration, this technique relies on a combination of both a dummy object for Camera position and a second dummy object as a Camera targeting device. Because the terrain-following script is over 200 lines long, including comments, and because many of the lines exceed 100

characters wide, I have decided to refrain from listing the code for the terrain-following script at this point. I suggest that you finish this demonstration by reading through the code and the extensive comments in the file itself, because it will be easier to read from within Director. In addition to examining the terrain-following script, be sure to examine the heavily documented initialization script as well.

Where to Go from Here?

In addition to the topics of generating your own normals and Texturecoordinates, you should look into several other areas of investigation if you are interested in pursuing Mesh generation further. Note that these areas of inquiry can be pursued through the supplemental resources I have listed at the end of this section.

For continued study of terrain generation, you should consider looking into alternative grid methods, random terrain generation, Perlin noise, noise synthesis, fractal noise, and digital elevation maps (DEM), to name a few. In terms of Mesh creation in general, you should consult a strong text on topologies, curves, surfaces, and convex hulls, such as Michael Mortenson's book mentioned in the "Supplemental Resources" section of the previous chapter.

Summary

Mesh creation from code is a gigantic subject. We have touched only the fundamentals of this topic and applied them in several examples. The process of Mesh creation draws heavily upon your understanding of vector math, specifically location vectors and normals. If you find the topics of vertex ordering and normals to be unclear, I suggest reviewing the previous chapter before reviewing this one again.

Because the subject of Mesh creation is so large, once we covered the fundamentals of Mesh creation, it was better to explore a common technique in detail—in this case, terrain generation—so you could learn more about Mesh creation. Although terrain generation is a common technique, it is hardly a simple one. The two most complex areas of this technique include the part of the terrain-generation script that handles the assignment of Vertices to Faces in order to create a grid, and the method for determining the height of the terrain at a given point.

Finally, after we created the terrain-generation script, the last demonstration we examined introduced the concept of *terrain following*, which is made possible through advanced options for Picking Lingo that can provide detailed data about intersections between Faces and arbitrary rays in the 3D world.

FAQ

What is the difference between normals that are generated with the #smooth setting versus the #flat setting for the generatenormals() *command?*

The difference is that with the #flat setting, each Vertex will receive one normal for each Face it belongs to. The three Vertices in a given Face will use only one normal, but note that an individual Vertex can have several different normals, depending on the number of Faces it belongs to. This is what creates the #flat appearance.

If you use the #smooth setting, each Vertex is assigned a single normal, and the normals of the Vertices in a given Face will generally be different from one another. A way to understand this difference is to think about the surface of a sphere. If you choose any one point on the surface of the sphere, the normal at that point is probably vastly different from the normals at a point immediately adjacent it.

Now, it just isn't possible to have normal data for every single point on the sphere, so the #smooth setting is an attempt to take the "average" of the normals for a given area of a Mesh. You will find that the success of the technique relies on the crease angle between Faces. At points where this angle is extremely sharp, no amount of smooth normals will help. When the crease angle is relatively shallow, smooth normals can be extremely convincing.

Supplemental Resources

- www.andrew.cmu.edu/user/sowen/survey/index.html

This truly amazing resource, created by Steve Owen, contains a wide variety of information about the scope of Mesh generation as well as an extensive bibliography. In addition, you'll find links to online articles, symposiums, conferences, and an active Listserv, all dedicated to mesh generation.

- *Curves and Surfaces in Geometric Design*, by Jean H. Gallier (Morgan Kaufmann Publishers, ISBN 1558605991)

  If you feel confident in your math skills and you would like an excellent text dedicated to the subject of created surfaces, this is it. Although this book will most likely exceed the needs of most users, it does an outstanding job of correlating algebra, geometry, and algorithms in an accessible format (considering the subject matter).

- *Geometric Modeling*, by Michael Mortenson (John Wiley & Sons, ISBN 0471129577)

  Although the mathematical requirements for most geometric modeling can be difficult to grasp, this book is an extremely thorough examination of geometric modeling that is presented extremely well. The strength of this particular book is its ability to explain the math of geometric modeling of complex shapes without alienating its audience.

CHAPTER 28

Mesh Deformation and Detailed Picking

In the previous chapter, you learned about how to create 3D geometry purely with Lingo. In this chapter, we will be focusing our attention on two areas of 3D Lingo that provide both feedback and control of geometry at a low level. These two areas, Mesh deformation and Detailed Picking, build upon the lessons of previous chapters—specifically Chapter 26, "Advanced Transforms and Vector Math," and Chapter 27, "Creating Meshes from Code." I expect you have already completed, and hopefully understand, the concepts presented in those chapters.

Mesh deformation and Detailed Picking Lingo complement each other quite well. Whereas Detailed Picking Lingo can provide accurate information about user interaction with geometry, Mesh deformation is a tool that can be used to allow you to create geometry that reacts to user input. This means that in addition to the fact that geometry can be transformed in 3D space according to the input of users, the shape of that geometry can be changed as well.

Although this is an extremely powerful level of control, such power comes with responsibilities. Your responsibility will be to continue learning how to control vectors and vector math in conjunction with the new tools you will be learning about. This chapter presents the concepts of Mesh deformation as well as its application. In addition, you will be learning how to combine Mesh deformation and Picking Lingo. The overall goal is to show you how to approach using Mesh deformation, but the presentations in this chapter by no means exhaust the subject of Mesh deformation.

Mesh Deformation

As you have seen throughout the book, Lingo provides you with control of Modelresource geometry in many ways—from creating Models, transforming geometry in 3D space, using Bones skeletal deformations, and even creating geometry with code. Lingo also provides a much lower level of control over geometry with the Meshdeform Modifier.

This Modifier allows you to change the positions of Vertices and Faces of Modelresources in real time. Mesh deformation can be applied to Mesh primitives, Meshes created from code, or Meshes imported from external modeling programs. This is an important point: You do not need to build your geometry from scratch in order to use the Meshdeform Modifier to control that geometry.

However, because the Meshdeform Modifier is an abstract tool for controlling geometry, the success of your ideas in this area will depend on the organization of your code. In addition, many times building the geometry with code will give you the critical advantage of understanding the structure of the geometry—that way, you will understand how to change the structure.

Meshdeform Modifier

The Meshdeform Modifier is applied to Models in the 3D environment using the syntax we have encountered when applying other Modifiers to Models. Specifically, you will add the Meshdeform Modifier to Models with the following code:

```
Scene.model[x].addmodifier(#Meshdeform)
```

Once you have added the Meshdeform Modifier to a Model, you will have access to detailed information about the Model's geometry that you can examine and also change. However, you must understand that while the Meshdeform Modifier is applied to a Model, it changes the Modelresource.

NOTE

The implications of the Meshdeform Modifier being able to change the Modelresource geometry are important. If you have Models that share a Modelresource, adding the Meshdeform Modifier to one of those Models will add the Meshdeform Modifier to all of them. Put another way: When you apply the Meshdeform Modifier through a Model, the Modifier attaches itself to that Modelresource.

If you clone a Model using the `clone()` command, the clone will use the same Modelresource; therefore, the changes you make to one Model will be made to the other. If you clone a Model with the `clonedeep()` command, the clone that is created will also create a clone of the Modelresource. The cloned Modelresource will not have the Meshdeform Modifier attached.

The Meshdeform Modifier has one property, `mesh[x]`, that in turn has several subproperties that allow for direct control of the Mesh information. This is actually an important point. You may remember that some Modelresources, such as boxes and cylinders, have more than one Mesh. In addition, it is possible to import Modelresources from 3D modeling programs that contain multiple Meshes. The Meshdeform Modifier allows you to access the properties of each Mesh of a Modelresource, in case there is more than one. To find out how many Meshes a Modelresource has, you can use the following syntax:

```
Scene.model[x].Meshdeform.mesh.count
```

For a vast majority of Modelresources, the Mesh count will be 1. If you are going to be working with multiple Mesh Modelresources, be sure you are accessing the correct one. Also, make sure you understand that the Faces and Vertices of each of the Meshes are exclusive to one another, meaning that changes you make to one Mesh will not change another in a multiple-Mesh Modelresource.

Once you have determined which Mesh you are going to be working with, all the examinations and changes to geometry you make will be performed via subproperties of the `mesh[x]` property, as shown in the following syntax:

```
Scene.model[x].Meshdeform.mesh[x].sub-property
```

Pay close attention to this syntax, because making a typographic error here is easy to do. Many times people forget about typing the `mesh[x]` property or the `Meshdeform` property, but these cannot be left out. This problem is coupled with a discrepancy in the standard of 3D Lingo that does not allow you to save a variable reference to a Mesh. Specifically, you cannot do the following because it will generate a script error:

```
MeshReference = scene.model[x].Meshdeform.mesh[x]
```

This issue may seem small, but it really becomes bothersome to have to type out `Meshdeform.mesh[x].property` all the time—and there is no way around it.

Because all the Mesh deformation properties we will be accessing and modifying are subproperties of `mesh[x]`, we only need to look at those subproperties before we begin the demonstrations. Table 28.1 lists these subproperties and provides an explanation of their purposes.

TABLE 28.1   Meshdeform Modifier Properties

Property	Purpose
Colorlist	Allows you to get/set the list of colors used by the Faces in a Mesh.
Vertexlist	Allows you to get/set the list of vectors, which is then referenced to build the Faces of a Mesh.
Face[x]	Allows you to get (but not set) a linear list of index numbers that refers to vectors in the Vertexlist that comprise a given Face.

As you look at Table 28.1 for the first time, you may notice that the properties for the Meshdeform Modifier have striking similarities with the Mesh Modelresource–type properties—and you must be very careful on this point. Pay special attention to the fact that not all these properties can be set—for example, `face[x]` and `face[x].neighbor`. We will be using the information these properties provide, but the fact that you cannot change them is very important, because it means the Meshdeform Modifier does not allow you to change the *continuity* of a Mesh.

The continuity of a Mesh is one of the areas of research for geometric topology—a branch of geometry concerned with morphing operations that stretch, bend, twist, or shrink a Mesh *without* adding, removing, or modifying Faces by changing the *order* of Vertices. Think of a piece of fabric that you can stretch, bend, twist, and shrink—as long as you do not cut the fabric or sew it together anywhere. In terms of Mesh deformation, Meshes are like this fabric.

Of the items in this list, we will be working heavily with the `Vertexlist` property in order to change the vectors used to define the locations of the Vertices.

In addition, we will be using the vertex indexing information provided by face[x], which returns a linear list containing three integers that refer specifically to the index numbers of the items in the Vertexlist.

NOTE

In addition to the subproperties of the mesh[x] property listed in Table 28.1, we have four additional subproperties: normallist, texturecoordinatelist, texturelayer, and face[x].neighbor. We will not be working with these properties, but I want to address the following points about each.

The normallist property is a linear list that contains the normals used by a Mesh. If you are using a Mesh Modelresource that was generated with code, the number of entries in this list will depend on whether you used the #flat setting or the #smooth setting with generatenormals(). If you used #flat, you are using Vertex normals, and there will be three normals per Face. Therefore, the number of entries in the Normallist will be equal to the number of entries in the Vertexlist. If you used #smooth, you are using Face normals, and there will only be one normal per Face. In this case, the number of entries in the Normallist will be equal to the value of scene.model[x]. Meshdeform. mesh[x]. face.count.

The texturecoordinatelist property is a linear list that contains UV coordinate data about the Mesh, and it's used by the Shader to place Textures on the Mesh. In addition, the texturelayer property allows you to access the UV coordinates used by up to eight layers of Textures with scene.model[x].Meshdeform.mesh[x].texturelayer[x].texturecoordinatelist.

The face[x].neighbor property returns a nested linear list that can be retrieved but not changed. This property provides you with information about Faces that share more than one Vertex with a given Face.

Detailed Picking

Mesh deformation and Detailed Picking work rather well together. Detailed Picking can provide you with information about the Mesh a user is interacting with, and Mesh deformation changes aspects of the Mesh based on that information. As you know from the previous chapter, #detailed is an optional setting for the modelsunderray() command. In this chapter, we will be using the optional #detailed setting with the modelsunderloc() command. Table 28.2 is provided as a refresher on the scope of information available via Detailed Picking.

TABLE 28.2   Detailed Picking Lingo Data

Property	Purpose
Model	The name of the Model intersected
Distance	The distance from the 3D point to the point of intersection with the Model
Isectposition	The point of intersection in World coordinate space
Isectnormal	The normal of the intersected Face
MeshID	The number of the intersected Mesh (if you're working with a multiple-Mesh Model)
FaceID	The number of the intersected Face in the Mesh
Vertices	The Vertices of the intersected Face in the Mesh in World space
UvCoord	The UV Texture coordinates of the intersected Face

The beauty of this information is that it is cross-referenced with the Meshdeform Modifier properties. Therefore, if you click a Model and determine that you clicked FaceID number 12, you can use that information to find out from the Meshdeform Modifier which Vertices that Face is using. Then, you can use the Meshdeform Modifier to change values about those Vertices. Although it may initially sound difficult, the overall process for Mesh deformation is quite accessible, as you will see in the following demonstrations.

Detailed Picking Demonstration

In this demonstration, we will be using `modelsunderloc()` and the Meshdeform Modifier to modify the geometry of a plane with the mouse in real time. If you open the file named "Detailed Picking" on the CD accompanying this book and press Play, you should see a Stage set up as shown in Figure 28.1.

You can click the plane in this demonstration to alter the surface of the Model. Note that the surface will not return to its original state, unless you click the Reset button. When you click the plane, a behavior script is called that finds Detailed Picking information at the location you clicked. It then takes this information and moves the Vertices of the Face that was clicked. You can see this process in action by playing with the demonstration. After you have experimented for a while, refer to Listing 28.1 to see how the code is structured.

FIGURE 28.1

A plane whose geometry can be altered by combining Mesh Deformation with Detailed Picking.

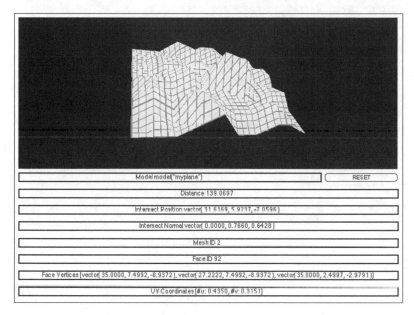

LISTING 28.1   Detailed Picking Script

```
1: property spritenum, origin
2:
3: global scene
4:
5: on beginsprite
6:   origin = point(sprite(spritenum).left, sprite(spritenum).top)
7:
8: on mousedown
9:   pt = the clickloc - origin
10:
11:   -- get detailed info
12:   modellist = sprite(spritenum).\
     camera.modelsUnderLoc(pt, 1, #detailed)
13:
14:   --send the detailed info to a custom handler
15:   --that puts the information into fields on stage
16:   reportpick(modellist)
17:
18:   --make sure that a model has been hit
19:   if modellist <> [] then
20:     -- find out which face was hit
```

LISTING 28.1   Continued

```
21:     whichface = modellist[1][#faceID]
22:     -- find out the 3 vertices that face uses
23:     vertlist = scene.model[1].Meshdeform.mesh[2].face[whichface]
24:
25:     --cycle through the 3 vertices
26:     repeat with x = 1 to 3
27:       --find the exact vertex location
28:       vert = scene.model[1].Meshdeform.mesh[2].vertexlist[vertlist[x]]
29:       -- add a small amount to that location
30:       newvert = vert + vector(0,0,5)
31:       -- set the vertex to the modified position
32:       scene.model[1].Meshdeform.mesh[2].\
        vertexlist[vertlist[x]] = newvert
33:     end repeat
34:   end if
35: end
```

Note that at the end of line 12 in this script, the #detailed parameter forces Director to return Detailed Picking information, which is returned to you in the form of a linear list of property lists. Each property list in the linear list represents one intersection of the ray and a Mesh in 3D space. If we were working with more Models, we might need to actually parse the list to see which Model was hit, or even which Mesh of the Model was hit. In this demonstration, the only checking I am doing is with the if/then statement beginning at line 19. This checks to make sure you have clicked the plane.

NOTE

If you are working with a Model with multiple Meshes or if you are working with Multiple Models, you will need to parse the list more thoroughly to determine which Model and which Mesh was intersected with the ray used by Picking Lingo.

Healing Surface Demonstration

In this demonstration, we will be deforming the surface of a Mesh based on the location of the mouse. In addition, the Mesh will be continually "healed" back to its original position. This gives the overall effect of pressing on a sponge. After you press on a sponge, the sponge expands to its original shape. Open the file named "Healing Surface" on the CD and press play. If you click the plane, drag around, and then let go, you will see this sponge-like behavior. Figure 28.2 shows this effect.

FIGURE 28.2

Healing Surface screenshot.

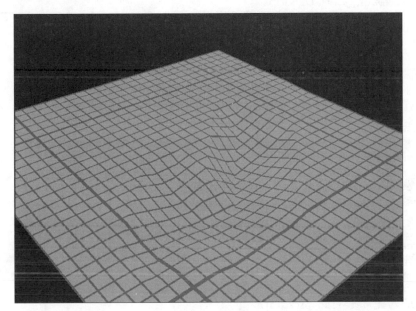

This demonstration is not too different from the previous demonstration, except for two points. First, the Mesh is deformed by the mouse in the opposite direction from the last demonstration; therefore, the Mesh looks like it is being depressed. Second, a `repeat` loop checks the position of each Vertex versus its original position. If it is in a different position, the Vertex is moved slightly upward.

The process of moving the displaced Vertices can be approached in many ways. In this demonstration, I have decided to interpolate the position of the Vertices so that they slowly return to their original positions, but not linearly (that is, so that the "healing" happens fast at first and then slows down). However, if you remember, the `interpolate()` command only works on transform objects, not on Vertices. Therefore, I have created two temporary transform objects and translated them by the amounts given in the original and current Vertex positions. Then, I interpolate the two transform objects.

Finally, I extract the new position information, which is a vector, and use this position information to move the Vertex. This process is slightly convoluted, but the end result is worth it. You can see the script of this process in Listing 28.2.

LISTING 28.2   Healing Surface Script

```
 1: property spritenum
 2: property origin
 3: --stores the original vertex values
 4: property originalVertexList
 5: --vector to push mesh
 6: property  pushvector
 7:
 8: global scene
 9:
10: on beginsprite
11:   origin = point(sprite(spritenum).left, sprite(spritenum).top)
12:   pushvector = vector(0,0,-3)
13:   originalVertexList = scene.model[1].meshdeform.mesh[2].vertexlist
14: end
15:
16: on exitframe
17:   --determine if the mouse is stilldown
18:   if the stilldown then
19:     pt = the mouseLoc - origin
20:     --find out detailed pick info
21:     modellist = sprite(spritenum).\
        camera.modelsUnderLoc(pt, 1, #detailed)
22:     --check to make sure that the model was selected
23:     if modellist <> [] then
24:       -- figure out which face was selected
25:       whichface = modellist[1][#faceID]
26:       -- find out the vertices for that face
27:       vertlist = scene.model[1].meshdeform.mesh[2].face[whichface]
28:
29:       --cycle through the vertices
30:       repeat with x = 1 to 3
31:         -- move them all down
32:         cur = scene.model[1].meshdeform.mesh[2].\
          vertexlist[vertlist[x]]
33:         cnew = cur + pushvector
34:         scene.model[1].meshdeform.mesh[2].\
          vertexlist[vertlist[x]] = cnew
35:       end repeat
36:     end if
```

LISTING 28.2   Continued

```
37:    end if
38:
39:    --cycle through all vertices in the mesh
40:    repeat with x = 1 to 100
41:      --get original vertex vector
42:      originalVertex = originalVertexList[x]
43:      -- get current vertex vector
44:      currentVertex = scene.model[1].meshdeform.mesh[2].\
         vertexlist[x]
45:      -- if the original and the current are not the same
46:      if originalVertex <> currentVertex then
47:        -- check to see how close they are
48:        -- if the difference is greater that .05 units...
49:        if originalvertex.distanceto(currentvertex) > .05 then
50:          --create two temporary transforms
51:          tA = transform()
52:          tb = transform()
53:          --translate them to the currentvertex
54:          --and original vertex positions
55:          tA.translate(currentvertex)
56:          tb.translate(originalvertex)
57:          -- create a third temporary transform
58:          -- interpolated 10% between the other two
59:          tc = ta.interpolate(tb, 10)
60:          -- extract the position information from the
61:          -- third, interpolated transform
62:          vertfinal = tc.position
63:          -- move the vertex to the interpolated position
64:          scene.model[1].meshdeform.mesh[2].\
             vertexlist[x] = vertfinal
65:        end if
66:      end if
67:    end repeat
68: end
```

As you can see from this demonstration, it is possible to use transform objects simply for the purpose of interpolating two Vertices. I could have written code to do the interpolation, but this method is a little easier. Note that the vectors used in lines 55 and 56 have been expressed in World coordinates, or relative-to-World coordinates, and it is this fact that allows the code to function correctly.

Sine Wave Surface Demonstration

In this demonstration, we will be deforming the surface of a plane with values generated from the mathematical function for a sine wave. This technique can be used to produce a gentle, rolling motion or more dramatic expressions of the sine wave. On the CD is a file named "Sine Surface." Open this movie and press play to see an animated version of the screenshot shown in Figure 28.3.

FIGURE 28.3

Sine Surface demonstration screenshot.

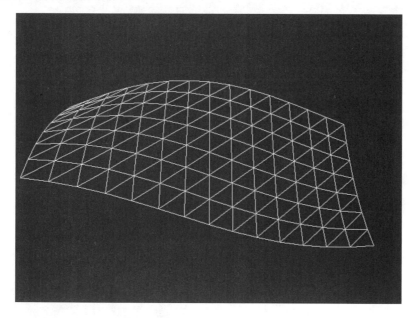

The focus of this demonstration is for you to understand how to use the Meshdeform Modifier to achieve this animation, but it is equally important that you understand the basics of how the sine wave is being generated. For that reason, I will begin by explaining how to generate a sine wave in general before explaining how to use that information to animate the surface of a plane.

To begin with, it is important that you understand what a sine wave looks like in 2D. Figure 28.4 illustrates important features about a sine wave that are used in the mathematical function to derive the value of the specific amplitude of the wave at any given point in time.

FIGURE 28.4

An illustration of a sine wave and its principle components.

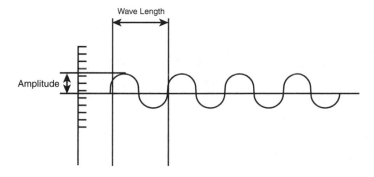

The mathematical function we will be using can determine the amplitude of the sine wave using information about the frequency of the wave and time. In terms of this demonstration, the value for time is easily understood: You will provide values for time to the sine wave generator. If you provide time values that incrementally become larger, the resulting amplitude values will oscillate between the maximum amplitude and the minimum amplitude for a given wave.

The *frequency* of the wave is a single value that describes the rate at which it passes a fixed point. The frequency is a constant value that is derived from two variables about a wave: the hertz and the wavelength. The wave should be thought of as a cycle. The number of times a given wave can oscillate from 0 to its maximum amplitude, then down to its minimum amplitude, and finally up to 0 again in one second is stored in a value known as *hertz*. Therefore, hertz is a measure of the cycles per second of a wave. The *wavelength* is the distance of one cycle of the wave.

Using the following formula, we are able to calculate the exact frequency of a given wave:

```
Frequency = (2 * pi * hertz) / wavelength
```

Once the frequency has been determined, there is little left to do in order to actually generate the sine wave values. We can determine the amplitude of the wave at a given point in time with the following formula:

```
CurrentAmplitude = (amplitude * (sin(frequency * time)))
```

Notice in this formula that we are using the `sin()` function. This is no accident, because we are generating the values for a sine wave. With this formula, you could change `sin()` to `cos()` to generate a cosine wave if you like. Note that in this equation, `(sin(frequency * time))` generates values between −1 and 1. Multiplying this number by the maximum amplitude thereby scales the wave the its current value at a given point in time. Therefore, if we simply feed this function increasing values for time (1, 2, 3, 4, and so on), we can generate an animation of this wave.

Now that you have a basic understanding of the components of a sine wave, we can begin looking at the implementation of the Sine Surface demonstration. To begin with, you need to understand that in this demonstration I have taken the amplitude values as they change over time and perturbed the Y axis location of Vertices on the surface of a plane. If you look at Figure 28.5, you can see that the sine wave travels across the surface of the plane from the lower-right corner through the upper-left corner.

FIGURE 28.5

Expressing the sine wave moving across a surface.

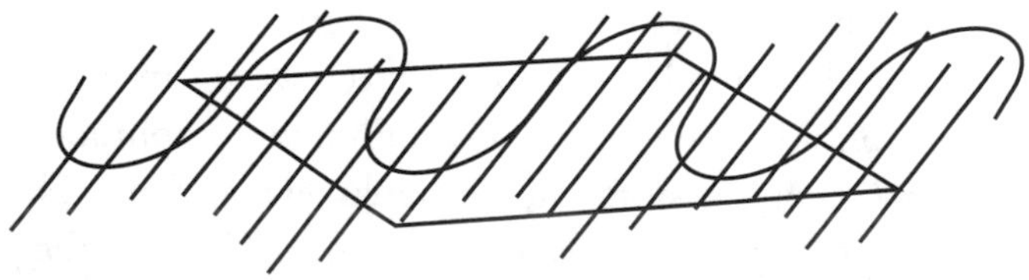

I could have simply expressed the sine wave as moving from left to right across the surface of the plane, but we are able to touch upon more sophisticated control of the Meshdeform Modifier by shifting the direction of the wave in 3D space. In this demonstration, the only purpose for using the Meshdeform Modifier is to change the Y axis component of the Vertices of the plane. If you think about it, there are a lot of Vertices in the plane. To express the sine wave across the surface of the plane, we need to continuously change the Y axis component of all the Vertices.

However, not all the Vertices are going to have the same exact Y axis value at the same time. If you remember, the Y axis value expresses the amplitude of the sine wave at a specific point in time. If we were to set the value of one Vertex to an amplitude derived from `sin(frequency * 1)`, we would need to set the next Vertex an amplitude derived from `sin(frequency * 2)`, and so on.

You should note that I said *not all the Vertices*, meaning that some of the Vertices *are* going to be at the same exact Y axis value at the same time. This is extremely important. Deciding which Vertices are at the same Y axis value at the same time will determine the direction the wave will travel through the surface of the plane. In order to make the process of choosing the correct Vertices easier, I have decided to utilize the `grid()` custom handler that was used in the previous chapter. If you have not read the previous chapter, this demonstration will be difficult for you at best.

I have chosen to use a Mesh created by the `grid()` custom handler because if you understand how that handler works, you understand how the Vertices and Faces are numbered within the Meshes created by that handler. If we were to divide the Vertices of the Mesh into small groups of Vertices that will all be at the same Y axis value at the same time, we could write a handler that controls the Y axis value of these groups of Vertices. Figure 28.6 illustrates the method of numbering Vertices that is used by the `grid()` custom handler as well as the division of groups of Vertices that we will be using.

Figure 28.6 is intended to illustrate the primary task of the script that we will be using in this demonstration. Specifically, the first task is to be able to dynamically generate the groups of Vertices. After this task is completed during the initialization phase for the script, the overall flow of the script can be described as follows:

- Initialization handler

  1. Set up groups of Vertices in nested linear lists.

  2. Set up the hertz, wavelength, amplitude, and base value for the time of the wave.

  3. Instantiate a timeout object to repeatedly call the handler, which updates the Y axis positions of the Vertex groups.

- Vertex update handler

    1. Calculate the amplitude of the wave at a given point in time. Move all Vertices in the first group to this Y axis location.

    2. Take the base time value and offset it by a set amount. This offset time value will be used to calculate the amplitude of the wave for the next group of Vertices.

    3. Increase the offset time value again and repeat this step until all groups of Vertices have been updated.

    4. Change the base time value by a set amount. This way, the next time the Vertex update handler is called, the first group will move the Y axis position of the second group, and so on.

FIGURE 28.6

This figure is intended to help you visualize how groups of vertices have been organized.

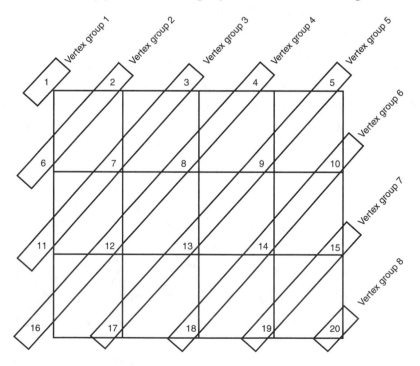

The most difficult part of this script is the section of the initialization handler that sets up the groups of Vertices in nested linear lists. In an effort to make this demonstration slightly easier to understand, I have limited the capability of the Sine Wave Generator script such that it will only work correctly with grid Meshes that are wider than they are long or that are square. You see, it is easiest to set up the groups in two steps consisting of two sets of nested repeat loops.

The first set of nested repeat loops sets up the groups of Vertices in an order that needs to be slightly corrected by the second set of nested repeat loops. This issue is difficult to understand without an illustration. Figure 28.7 illustrates the groups created by the first set of nested repeat loops as well as the correction of those groups that is performed by the second set of repeat loops.

FIGURE 28.7

The organization of Vertices into groups is a two-step process as illustrated in this figure.

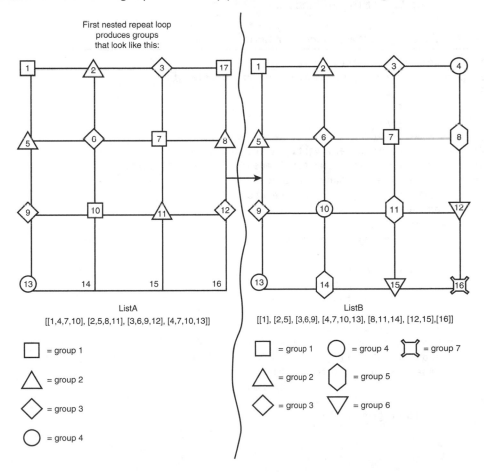

If we were to use the groups noted in Section A of Figure 28.7, the resulting surface would look like the lower-right corner is broken. This is because the surface would be in the same positions as the opposite corner of the surface, which are generally not the correct positions to be in. In Section B of Figure 28.7, you can see that I have corrected for this problem. Also, notice that in this figure, you can see the nested linear lists that represent the result of each set of nested `repeat` loops. In ListA, each nested list has the same number of items; in ListB, the structure is a bit different.

Remember, creating the sine wave itself is not too difficult. The success of this demonstration is based on how the Vertices are treated as groups. The next step is to actually look at the parent/child script used to drive the animated Mesh deformation. Listing 28.3 explains the two primary handlers of this script. These two handlers are used to instantiate the script and to drive the update of the animation.

LISTING 28.3   Sine Wave Generator Script

```
1: property timecounter, vertGroups
2: property frequency, amplitude, hertz, wavelength
3:
4: global scene
5:
6: on new(me, columns, rows, hz, amp, WL)
7:    -- find out how many vertices are in the model
8:    numVertices = scene.model[1].meshdeform.mesh[1].vertexlist.count
9:    -- determine how many vertices
10:   -- are in a single row of the mesh
11:   singleRow = columns + 1
12:   -- vertgroups is the list that
13:   -- we are going to generate
14:   vertGroups = []
15:   -- tgroup is a temporary list
16:   -- that we use as a utility
17:   -- for building the vertgroups
18:   tgroup = []
19:   --FIRST nested repeat loop set
20:   repeat with i = 1 to singleRow
21:     addat(tgroup, i)
22:     repeat with x = 1 to (rows )
23:       whichvert = (i + (x * (columns)))
24:
25:       addat(tgroup, whichvert)
26:
```

LISTING 28.3   Continued

```
27:      end repeat
28:      addat(vertGroups, tgroup)
29:      tgroup = []
30:    end repeat
31:
32:    --second nested repeat loop set
33:    tgroup = []
34:    wrongcount = 1
35:    repeat with x = 1 to rows
36:      repeat while vertGroups[x].count > x
37:        r = vertGroups[x].count
38:        cc = vertGroups[x][r]   + (columns + 1)
39:        addat(tgroup, cc)
40:        deleteat(vertGroups[x],r)
41:      end repeat
42:
43:      addat(vertGroups, tgroup)
44:      wrongcount = wrongcount + 1
45:      tgroup = []
46:    end repeat
47:
48:    --set up the wave properties
49:    hertz = hz
50:    amplitude = amp
51:    wavelength = WL
52:    timecounter = 0
53:    --instantiate the timeout object
54:    timeout("wavewatch").new(42, #updatewave, me)
55:    --return a reference to the script
56:    return me
57: end
58:
59: on updateWave(me)
60:    --update the base time
61:    timecounter = timecounter + 100
62:    -- determine the frequency of the wave
63:    frequency = (2 * pi * hertz) / float(wavelength)
64:    --cycle through all of the items in vertgroups
65:    repeat with x = 1 to vertGroups.count
66:        -- build a temporary time counter that
67:        -- if offset from the base time
68:        -- by an increasing interval
69:        currentcounter = timecounter + (50 * x)
70:        -- determine the amplitude based on the temporary time counter
71:        currentAmplitude = float(amplitude * \
         (sin(frequency * currentcounter)))
```

LISTING 28.3   Continued

```
72:      -- cycle through all vertices in the
73:      -- current group
74:      repeat with m = 1 to vertGroups[x].count
75:        --find the current Vertex index
76:        whichvertex = vertGroups[x][m]
77:        --find the current vertex vector
78:        v = scene.model[1].meshdeform.mesh[1].\
           vertexlist[whichvertex]
79:        --set the Y component equal to the currentamplitude
80:        v = vector(v.x currentamplitude, v.z)
81:        -- set the vertex position
82:      scene.model[1].meshdeform.mesh[1].vertexlist[whichvertex] = v
83:      end repeat
84:    end repeat
85: end
```

Note that several small custom handlers are included with this script that are not shown in Listing 28.3. These small handlers allow you to change the wavelength, hertz, and amplitude of the wave while the animation is playing. Refer to the script in the Director movie for further information about how to use these additional custom handlers.

Summary

Detailed Picking and Mesh deformation do not need to be used together, but they do complement each other quite well. Mesh deformation allows you to modify the geometry contained within the Modelresources of your movies. However, there are limitations to how it can affect the geometry. Specifically, you must understand that it is not possible to use the Meshdeform Modifier to change the Vertices used for a Face, or even the order of Vertices used for a Face.

The result of this is that you are not able to use the Meshdeform Modifier to cut or tear the Mesh. However, you can perform any operations that stretch, bend, or twist the Mesh. In addition, although we have not examined these areas, you can use the Meshdeform Modifier to change Texturecoordinates or the normals of a Mesh.

Overall, Mesh deformation and Mesh creation are very large, interrelated topics. We have examined the basics of these two topics, but there is certainly more. If you are interested in pursuing these two areas further, I suggest you look into the resources I have listed at the end of this chapter as well as the resources listed in the previous chapter. Specifically, you will need to learn more about the subjects of geometric and algebraic topology. These two areas of study can help you understand the mathematics required to change a Mesh without breaking the structure.

Of course, you don't need a degree in mathematics or an extremely robust understanding of topology to use the Meshdeform Modifier. The examples in this chapter are perfect evidence of that. Finally, although the examples in this chapter focus on using the Meshdeform Modifier to change a Mesh, you could easily use the Meshdeform Modifier to find out additional information about a Mesh. The possibilities presented to you by this powerful tool are impressive. Learning to control this tool can be a daunting task because of the mathematics involved, but the rewards are really worth it.

FAQ

I want to make a Model explode into tiny fragments. How can I do that?

The problem with doing this is that you would need to be able to break the structures of the Faces in a Mesh from one another. Specifically, you need to duplicate Vertices in order to create Faces that are not attached to one another (in different Meshes). Although I will not say that this is impossible with Director, it is prohibitive. If you are really interested in doing this, I suggest two different options.

First, you might consider using the flipbook Modelresource technique from Chapter 23, "Controling Time." That technique explains how you can take snapshots of a Mesh animated with deformation modifiers external to Director in 3D modeling programs. If you did it that way, the explosion would have to be the same each time.

Second, you might consider swapping out the Modelresource with a Modelresource that has one Face per Mesh. Then, you could deform each of these as separate Meshes. It is not a pretty solution, but it could work.

I want to create rippling water. Is that effect possible?

It is possible to build a surface that reacts like water or Jell-O to the input of your users. Unfortunately, explaining how to do this is a bit too long for the FAQ. If you look in the "Supplemental Resources" section, you'll see that I have provided a link to an article on Gamasutra.com that can help you get started.

Supplemental Resources

In this section, I have suggested an online resource that addresses Mesh deformation and surface perturbation. Also, in addition to the book on topology listed here, I suggest you begin reading the books mentioned at the end of Chapters 26 and 27 for an introduction to the subject (particularly the Mortenson books).

- www.gamasutra.com/features/20001110/oliveira_01.htm

  This excellent article, titled "Refractive Texture Mapping," by Gustavo Oliveira, can help you understand how you might go about building a rippling water surface. This article contains pseudocode written for C++, but you should be able to translate the logic.

- *Three-Dimensional Geometry and Topology*, by William P. Thurston (Princeton University Press, ISBN 0691083045)

  This is an advanced book on geometry and topology that you might consider reading if you are comfortable with abstract mathematics. Overall, this is perhaps the best book on the subject, although you will find that it is written for mathematics students, not for programmers.

CHAPTER 29

Collision Detection

This chapter covers the fundamentals of one of the largest subjects in advanced 3D programming—collision detection. In addition to covering the built-in tools of collision detection provided with Director, we will also be examining methods for building custom collision-detection routines using vector math. As is the case with the other chapters in this section of the book, I assume you have read through at least Chapter 26, "Advanced Transforms and Vector Math."

Collision detection is the process of determining whether two polygons in a 3D environment will intersect and taking the appropriate action depending on the answer. It is a process you will most likely be using if you are going to develop games with Director 3D, generally for the purpose of limiting character movement and resolving whether bullets have hit their mark. In this chapter, we will discuss two of the three methods of collision detection you will want to consider when designing your projects. Specifically, we will examine the use of the Collision Modifier and implementing boundary management (hand-coding your own solution). The third method for collision detection, using the Havok Xtra, is beyond the scope of this book. However, you will find a brief discussion of the Havok Xtra in Appendix G.

This chapter includes a demonstration that shows a method for using the Collision Modifier to handle bullet-like objects in a 3D environment. It also includes a demonstration that provides a custom boundary-management solution—specifically, to show you how to build walls that deflect characters so that they slide along the walls as they move within a 3D environment.

Collision Modifier

The Collision Modifier provides a basic level of collision detection for the Models in your environments. You add the Collision Modifier to individual Models; therefore, only the Models with the Collision Modifier attached will be checked for collisions. Checking for collisions on only select Models is meant to serve as a method for speeding up the collision-detection process. However, even with this corner-cutting, the Collision Modifier is slow, and it can slow your projects down dramatically.

The Collision Modifier must be built in to an elaborate system of callback handlers that use the `registerscript()` command. Also, when working with the Collision Modifier, you must not use the `updatestage` command—at all. This means that the custom scheduling techniques that we have been using for updating the Stage cannot be used with the built-in collision detection that Director provides. Adding the Modifier to a Model is not very difficult; it uses a syntax that you are no doubt familiar with by now:

```
Scene.model[x].addmodifier(#collision)
```

It is important that you understand that for collision detection to work, you need to assign the Collision Modifier to at least two objects you want to check for collisions between with each other. Once you have assigned the Collision Modifier to an object, you will have access to properties via the following syntax:

```
Scene.model[x].collision.property
```

Here, *property* is the name of one of the Collision Modifier properties. This Modifier only has four properties used to control it, as listed in Table 29.1.

TABLE 29.1   Collision Modifier Properties

Property	Purpose
`Enabled`	A Boolean that determines whether collision events are checked for this Model. The default is `True`.
`Resolve`	A Boolean that determines whether detailed collision information will be generated and sent to the callback handler. The default is `True`.

TABLE 29.1   Continued

Property	Purpose
Immovable	A Boolean that is set to True if you will not be animating the Model with the Collision Modifier attached (for example, for walls). The default is False.
Mode	This property accepts three symbols as its value: #sphere, #box, and #mesh.

Of these four properties, Enabled and Immovable need no more explanation, but Mode and Resolve do. I will continue this discussion by explaining the Collision.Mode property in detail. In an effort to minimize the amount of time the Collision Modifier uses per frame, you can force the Collision Modifier to check for collisions with geometry that is not as detailed as the actual Models.

If you have an extremely complex Model (let's say, a bipedal character), you might want to check to see whether it has collided with another Model. If the Mode property is set to #mesh, the Collision Modifier will check whether the actual Model geometry has collided with any other geometry per frame. Now, as you can imagine, with a complex Model, this can be very costly in terms of performance. The default Collision.Mode setting is #sphere, which uses a Model's bounding sphere to check for collisions with other Models. It works much faster, but it's more imprecise. The last method, #box, uses the Model's bounding box rather than its bounding sphere. This is useful for walls and other objects that would not be represented well by the #sphere setting.

In itself, the Resolve property seems simple, but its implications are quite complex. When the Resolve property is set to True, you can find out information about the collision, such as which models collided, where the collision was located, and what the normal at the point of collision was. The problem is that when you resolve a collision, the Models will move to their last position before the collision, and then they will not move at all. Therefore, you are able to find out quite a bit of information, but it comes at a cost.

In order to understand how you gain access to the collision information, you first need to recall our discussion of registering events in Chapter 23, "Controlling Time." In addition to the #timeMS, #animationstarted, and #animationended events, there are two more collision events that are registered similarly:

- #collideany. Used with `registerforevent()`, this event sends a message to its associated handler any time a collision occurs within a given 3D Castmember.
- #collidewith. Used with `registerscript()`, this event is associated with a specific Model. It sends a message to its associated handler any time a collision occurs involving the Model the #collidewith event is registered with.

The syntax for assigning these two scripts does not differ from the syntax you have seen in the past. The following examples offer a refresher on these methods:

```
Scene.registerforevent(#collideany, #myhandler, me)
```

Alternatively, to register to receive collision events for only one Model in a scene, you might use the following:

```
Scene.model[x].registerscript(#collidewith, #myhandler, me)
```

In addition, here's a shortcut method for registering the #collidewith script:

```
Scene.model[x].collision.setcollisioncallback(#myhandler, me)
```

In case you were wondering, yes, it is more of a conceptual shortcut rather than a typographical one. Once a Model or 3D Castmember has been registered to receive collision events, as in the preceding examples, you can begin understanding how to access the collision information. Imagine that the handler we are registering to receive collision events looks like this:

```
On myhandler(me, collisiondata)
  Put collisiondata.modelA
  Put collisiondata.modelB
  Put collisiondata.pointofcontact
  Put collisiondata.collisionnormal
End
```

The purpose of this simple handler is merely to explain that the collision information is sent as an argument. That argument is actually a code object named collisiondata. The collisiondata object has properties you can access via dot syntax, as explained in Table 29.2.

TABLE 29.2   Collisiondata Properties

Property	Purpose
ModelA	A Model reference to the Model that caused the collision
ModelB	A Model reference to the Model that was collided with
Pointofcontact	The World space coordinate vector where the two Models collided
CollisionNormal	The normal at the point of collision

As you can see, the Collisiondata that is available to resolve collisions is quite useful. Not only can you determine which Models were hit, but you can determine where they were and how they hit each other. The collisiondata object will always contain information about ModelA and ModelB. In order for the Pointofcontact and CollisionNormal information to be available, the Resolve property for both Models must be set to True. If Resolve is set to True, the Models will not be able to move after the collision has been resolved.

NOTE

Here's one possibility that we will not be exploring: You can quickly disable and then reenable the Collision Modifier after a collision has occurred and you have retrieved the Collisiondata information. This allows you to move the Model again while gaining access to the Collisiondata. However, it involves precise timing that can easily get thrown off.

The Collision Modifier has both positive and negative qualities. In its favor, it does a pretty good job of performing collision detection on complex Models. In addition, the level of detailed information about a resolved collision can be extremely useful. However, the functionality of the Collision Modifier comes with an extreme performance penalty that becomes more and more apparent depending on the number of Models you are checking for collisions. The following demonstration is intended to highlight the versatility of the Collision Modifier as well as the performance issues that can become prohibitive.

Collision Modifier Demonstration

On the CD accompanying this book, open the file named "Bullet" and press Play. You will see crosshairs that follow the position of the mouse. If you click, a sphere "bullet" will fire in the direction of the crosshairs. In this demonstration, the Camera is slowly spinning around its Y axis. There are several spheres within the scene; if you shoot at a sphere and hit it, the sphere will change colors. Sounds are associated with hitting and missing, and a counter for hits appears at the bottom of the screen.

The initialization script for this demonstration is worth looking at, because you can see how I have applied the Collision Modifier to the spheres and set their Immovable property to True. Remember, in this demonstration, the Camera is moving, not the spheres. Two main parent/child scripts provide the functionality for this movie. The first script handles the positioning of the crosshairs and a handler to call the second script when the mouse is pressed. The second script creates the bullet and handles all aspects about each bullet fired separately. The Crosshairs script is shown in Listing 29.1.

LISTING 29.1   Crosshairs Script

```
 1: property poffset
 2:
 3: global scene
 4:
 5: on new(me)
 6:   --offset position, for the overlay
 7:   poffset = point(32,32)
 8:   --timeout that updates the position of the crosshairs
 9:   timeout("mousefollow").new(82, #mousefol, me)
10:   return me
11: end
12:
13: on mousefol(me)
14:   -- move the overlay to the position of the mouse
15:   -- (minus the offset amount)
16:   scene.camera[1].overlay[1].loc = the mouseloc - poffset
17:   cursor 200
18:   cursor 200
19: end
20:
21: on fire(me)
22:   -- we want bullets to fire at the middle of the
```

LISTING 29.1   Continued

```
23:    -- overlay, so we will calculate that position as follows:
24:    thepoint = the mouseloc - (poffset/2)
25:    --find out the world space position of this point
26:    directionvect = sprite(1).camera.\
       spritespacetoworldspace(thepoint)
27:    --normalize that vector (just want the direction)
28:    directionvect.normalize()
29:    --scale the vector back up to a standard magnitude
30:    directionvect = directionvect * 56
31:    -- instantiate a new bullet, passing it the
32:    --value of directionvect as its argument
33:    new(script "bullet", directionvect)
34: end
```

As you can see from this example, moving the crosshairs is handled in essentially one line of code (at line 16). In addition to moving the crosshairs, this script handles the firing of bullets with the fire() handler. Upon closer examination of the fire() handler, you may notice that I am using the spritespacetoworldspace() command in line 26 in order to find the World space vector of the mouse click. In this handler, I use this vector to determine the direction in which the bullet should travel; however, the magnitude of this vector is simply too large.

In the fire() handler at lines 28 and 30, I first normalize the vector and then scale it up. This scaled version of the vector is used as the speed of the bullet—literally it is used as the distance in World units that the bullet will travel per update of the bullet's location.

Also, note that this handler must be called by referencing the child object of this script. In this demonstration, a movie script such as the following is used:

```
On mousedown
  Global mouseref
  Mouseref.fire()
End
```

The purpose of the fire() handler is to determine the direction and speed of the bullet and then to call the Bullet script. The Bullet script handles the majority of the work in this demonstration. In addition to creating the new bullet Model, it handles the update of the bullet's position and contains the code that is referenced by the bullet's callback handlers for collision information. Finally, the Bullet script handles destroying the object in case of hits—or misses. The Bullet script is shown in Listing 29.2.

LISTING 29.2   Bullet Script

```
 1: --direction and magnitude of bullet travel
 2: property pdirection
 3: --reference to the bullet model
 4: property obj
 5: --pcounter determines if bullet has
 6: --traveled too far without a hit
 7: property pcounter
 8: -- name of Model and Timeout Object
 9: -- used by the model
10: property pname
11:
12: global scene
13:
14: on new(me, mdir)
15:    --save the pdirection
16:    pdirection = mdir
17:    -- generate a unique name for the bullet
18:    pname = "bullet" & the milliseconds
19:    -- create a new bullet (note that I have already
20:    --created a bullet modelresource in the initialization
21:    -- of the movie, to save time)
22:    obj = scene.newmodel(pname, scene.modelresource("bulletres"))
23:    -- add the collision modifier to this model
24:    obj.addmodifier(#collision)
25:    --set up the callback handler in case of collisions with the bullet
26:    obj.collision.setcollisioncallback(#hit, me)
27:    --set up a timeout object that will "move" the bullet.
28:    timeout(pname).new(42, #firing, me)
29:    pcounter= 0
30:    return me
31: end
32:
33: on firing(me)
34:    --move the bullet
35:    obj.translate(pdirection)
36:    --add one to pcounter
37:    pcounter = pcounter + 1
38:    --check the value of pcounter,
39:    -- if it is too high, this is a miss
40:    if pcounter >=20 then
41:       --play the miss sound
```

LISTING 29.2   Continued

```
42:      puppetsound(1, "miss")
43:      --destroy the timeout object for this bullet
44:      timeout(pname).forget()
45:      --destroy the model of this bullet
46:      scene.deletemodel(pname)
47:    end if
48: end
49:
50: -- this handler will only be called if there
51: -- is a collision with this bullet
52: on hit(me, data)
53:    --determine which model was hit
54:    whichmodel = data.modelB
55:    -- if the model that was hit was one
56:    --of the spheres then…
57:    if whichmodel.name contains "hitter" then
58:      -- choose a random color
59:      randomcolor = rgb(random(255),random(255),random(255))
60:      -- change the diffuse color of the hit model
61:      whichmodel.shader.diffuse = randomcolor
62:      -- add one to the count, shown on stage
63:      thecount = value(member("outbox").text)
64:      thecount = thecount + 1
65:      member("outbox").text = string(thecount)
66:      --play the collision sound
67:      puppetsound(1, "collide")
68:    else
69:      --play the miss sound
70:      puppetsound(1, "miss")
71:    end if
72:
73:    -- forget the timeout object
74:    timeout(pname).forget()
75:    -- destroy the model
76:    scene.deletemodel(pname)
77: end
```

Note that the speed of this demonstration is actually quite slow considering the number of Models we are working with. Overall, the Collision Modifier is sufficient for simple uses such as this. However, I suggest *not* using it—mainly because of the performance penalties, but also because it cannot be integrated well into the custom scheduler strategy I presented in Chapter 23. To be honest, this demonstration could have easily been re-created by checking the distance between the bullets and all the Models in the scene. When the distance between a bullet and another Model is too low, a collision occurs. If we were working in an environment where accurate bullet placement is necessary (such as when shooting enemies), the Collision Modifier would be a bit better choice.

Boundary Management

Director 8.5 provides so many tools and unique resources that we are able to build our own collision-detection routines with Lingo itself. The Collision Modifier tends to be too slow and designed with *any* situation in mind, rather than a specific situation. Instead of relying on the Collision Modifier, with a little bit of Picking Lingo and vector math, we can build a much faster, much more useful version of collision detection of our own.

The Collision Modifier sends out messages when a collision has just happened in the environment. This is useful for bullets, grenades, and so on, but it does not give us the ability to predict when two Models are *going* to collide. In this section, we will be looking at how to build a system for detecting where the boundaries in your environment are and how to take appropriate action when a boundary has been reached.

Boundary Management Demonstration

Open the file named "Boundary Management" on the CD and press Play. You will be presented with an environment in which you can drive around a cylinder by using the arrow keys. The Camera will automatically follow the cylinder. Note that if you drive too close to the walls in the environment, you are deflected. If you were approaching the wall at a steep angle, you simply decelerate until you stop—prior to hitting the wall.

You should notice that the cylinder has three Models associated with it that are used as part of our boundary-management system in this demonstration. Because this is a demonstration, I am making these three objects visible so that you can see how they work. If I were going to be creating a real project, though, I would make these three objects invisible.

I will refer to the plane as the *safeplane*. Notice how the safeplane moves as you speed up and slow down your movement of the cylinder. The reason for this is that the safeplane is part of an early-warning system: The faster the cylinder is moving, the farther from the cylinder the safeplane will be. You see, the two boxes mark the starting position of two rays that are shot into space with the modelsunderray() command toward the safeplane. These rays are perpendicular to the safeplane, so essentially the setup looks like what's shown in Figure 29.1.

FIGURE 29.1

An illustration showing how the safeplane, two boxes, and modelsunderray() commands are used to determine whether any Models are "too close" to the cylinder.

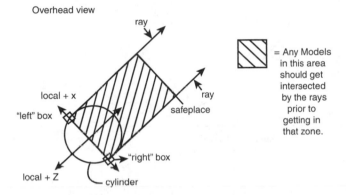

The modelsunderray() commands are called such that they only return the first Model they hit. If that Model is the safeplane, the cylinder will not hit anything on that side. It is possible that you might hit something with both rays, in which case our code will determine which hit is actually closer to the cylinder. Every single time an intersection occurs, the speed of the cylinder will be slowed down a bit. When the cylinder slows, the safeplane moves slightly closer to the cylinder.

It is important to understand that the cylinder will slow down upon an intersection, but it is equally important to understand how much the cylinder will slow down. You see, intersections that occur very close to the Model need to be treated with higher priority than those that happen farther away. Technically, the safeplane is simply used to filter out all the intersections with the ray that are unimportant to the immediate future position of the cylinder. Figure 29.2 illustrates how the amount of deceleration increases dramatically as the distance from the cylinder to the intersection point decreases.

FIGURE 29.2

A graph that correlates the distance of the intersection from the cylinder with the amount of deceleration for the cylinder.

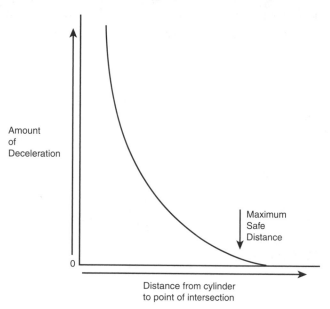

When intersections with the rays happen extremely close to the cylinder, the deceleration is great enough to ensure that the cylinder simply stops moving in that direction. Essentially, this is enough to build a simple collision-avoidance system that can manage boundaries for a Model. Note that as a user of the demonstration, you are limited to the area I have walled you into.

However, simply slowing the cylinder down is only one half of this demonstration. You might also notice that when you are about to collide with a Model, you are also slightly deflected from hitting it. After the code determines whether the rays intersect a Model that is too close to the cylinder and which one of the rays is intersecting a Model closest to itself, there is a simple matter of steering the cylinder. The steering of the cylinder is done automatically so that it tends to slide along walls rather than simply stop. You can see from Figure 29.3 that several pieces of information are required to perform this deflection.

Notice that in Figure 29.3, we need to determine the normal of the obstacle and the direction of the cylinder. The normal will be provided by the Detailed

Picking Lingo information from the modelsunderray() command. The direction of the cylinder is not very complicated, but it is derived from a property we have not talked about yet.

FIGURE 29.3

An overhead view illustrating what happens when our cast rays hit a Model that is not the safeplane.

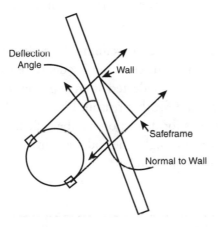

If we were to simply use the rotation of the cylinder in World space, we would not be using the correct information. Rather than the rotation around an axis, what we are really more interested in is the direction that the cylinder is pointing. In this demonstration, the forward direction of the cylinder is its local negative Z axis. Therefore, if we can determine the position of the local Z axis of the cylinder in World space, we will have our direction vector. Luckily, there is a property that can provide this information with the syntax shown here:

```
Dirvect = -(Scene.model[x].getworldtransform().zaxis)
```

Notice that I am negating this value; this is not a mistake. I said that the .zaxis property returns the local Z axis, but it's the *positive* Z axis. We need to negate this in order to find the correct direction vector. Note that this information is also used as the direction to shoot the rays with the modelsunderray() commands.

Once these two pieces of information—the normal and the direction vector of the cylinder—have been secured, determining how much to deflect the cylinder is as simple as determining the dot product of the two vectors. Because both the normal and the direction vector will be normalized, the result of the dot product will tell us the angle between the normal and the direction vector. Once this amount has been determined, we divide this angle in half and then automatically steer the cylinder that amount away from the impending collision.

The last issue I would like to address before we examine the code for this demonstration concerns the deflection. You see, if the Model were to hit an obstacle at a very steep angle, it would be deflected at an angle up to 45 degrees. That is actually quite a lot, and for that reason, I have decided to limit the angles on which our routines for deflection will be called. In Figure 29.4, you can see that depending on the angle, the code will either decelerate the cylinder or decelerate and deflect the cylinder.

FIGURE 29.4

Determining deceleration only or deceleration and deflection.

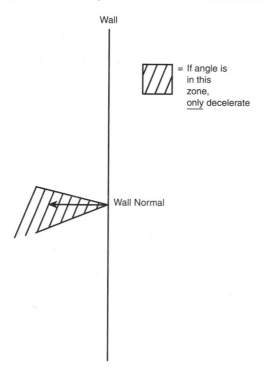

Try driving the cylinder at an obstacle while maintaining near perpendicularity upon collision. The cylinder should simply slow down. This allows users to approach a wall without being thrown away from it.

This demo is made possible through two parent/child scripts, although you should check the initialization script as well if you are interested in seeing how the environment is set up. The two parent/child scripts are versions of the Camera Following/Driving script from Chapter 25, "Advanced Camera Control," and the boundary-management script that takes care of deceleration and deflection as well as maintaining the safeplane. The Camera Following/Driving script is explained in Listing 29.3, although I have only included comments on those areas that are different from our previous encounter with the script.

LISTING 29.3   Camera Following/Driving Script

```
 1: property spritenum
 2: property pSpeed
 3: property pMaxSpeed, pMinSpeed
 4: property pAccel, pDecel
 5: property pFriction
 6: property pTurnAmount
 7:
 8: global scene, avoider
 9:
10: on new(me)
11:    pspeed = 0
12:    pMaxSpeed = 20
13:    pMinSpeed = 0
14:    pFriction = .99
15:    pAccel =
16:    pDecel = 2
17:    pTurnAmount = 5
18:    timeout("camfollow").new(42, #drive, me)
19:    return me
20: end
21:
22: on drive(me)
23:    pspeed = pspeed - pFriction
24:    if pspeed < pMinSpeed then
25:       pspeed = pMinSpeed
          -- if the cylinder is not moving, then
          -- tell the boundary management script
          -- not to look for boundaries
26:       avoider.toggleDeflection(#off)
```

LISTING 29.3   Continued

```
27:    end if
28:
29:    if pspeed > pMaxSpeed then pspeed = pMaxSpeed
30:    scene.model("mycyl").translate(0,0,-pspeed, #self)
31:
32:    if keypressed(126) then
33:      pSpeed = pSpeed + pAccel
         -- if the cylinder is moving, make sure that
         -- the boundary management script is checking
         -- for the boundaries
34:      avoider.toggleDeflection(#on)
35:    end if
36:
37:    if keypressed(125) then
38:      pSpeed = pSpeed - pDecel
39:    end if
40:
41:    if keypressed(123) then
42:      scene.model("mycyl").rotate(0,pTurnAmount,0,#self)
43:    end if
44:
45:    if keypressed(124) then
46:      scene.model("mycyl").rotate(0,-pTurnAmount,0,#self)
49:    end if
50:
51:    trans = scene.camera[2].getworldtransform()
52:    scene.camera[1].transform.interpolateto(trans, 12)
53: end
54:
55: --the following custom handler allows
56: --us to brake from outside this script
57: on braking(me, decel)
58:    pspeed = pspeed - decel
59:    if pspeed < pMinSpeed then
60:      pspeed = pMinSpeed
61:      avoider.toggleDeflection(#off)
62:    end if
63: end
64:
65: --following handler allows us to
66: --turn from outside this script
67: on deflect(me, theta)
68:    scene.model("mycyl").rotate(0,theta,0, #self)
69: end
70:
       -- custom handler to find out the
```

LISTING 29.3   Continued

```
    -- current speed of the cylinder
71: on getspeed(me)
72:   return pspeed
73: end
74:
    -- public handler to find out the
    -- maximum speed of the cylinder
75: on getmaxspeed(me)
76:   return pMaxspeed
77: end
```

A global variable named avoider references the Boundary Management script. It is used at lines 34 and 26 to turn deflection on and off. The reason for this is in case the cylinder has stopped moving, we want to free up a little bit of processor time and not do all the modelsunderray() calculations.

Notice how this script has been enhanced with four custom handlers: braking(), deflect(), getspeed(), and getmaxspeed(). These handlers allow the Boundary Management script to control this script externally. Specifically, the braking() handler allows us to slow the cylinder externally, and the deflect() handler allows us to steer the cylinder externally. The other two handlers, getspeed() and getmaxspeed(), are simply concise public methods for finding out information about the speed of the cylinder.

As you can see from the Camera Following/Driving script, the actual mechanics of deflecting and decelerating are in place, but they need to be called from outside the script. This will be done from the Boundary Management script, as shown in Listing 29.4.

LISTING 29.4   Boundary Management Script

```
 1: --boolean, determines if modelsunderray()
 2: --advanced warning system should be active
 3: property deflectActive
 4: --the maximum safe distance, used to place
 5: --the safe plane.  At maximum speed, the
 6: --plane will be the maximum safe distance away
 7: property pMaxSafe
 8: --the maximum speed of the cylinder
 9: property pmaxspeed
10:
11: global scene
```

LISTING 29.4   Continued

```
12: --object reference to the camera following script
13: global driver
14:
15: on new(me)
16:    -- in the beginning, we are not moving,
17:    --so do not check for boundaries
18:    deflectActive = false
19:    --find out the maximum speed of the cylinder
20:    pmaxspeed = driver.getmaxspeed()
21:    --calculate the maximum safe distance
22:    pMaxSafe = pmaxspeed * 5
23:    --instantiate a timeoutobject that
24:    --takes care of boundary management
25:    timeout("avoid_obstacles").new(42, #foresight, me)
26:    return me
27: end
28:
29: on foresight(me)
30:    --make sure that we should be checking boundaries
31:    if deflectActive then
32:       --call the custom handler that
33:       --takes care of the safeplane
34:       handlesafeplane(me)
35:       --call the custom handler that
36:       --takes care of boundary checking
37:       checkForHits(me)
38:    end if
39: end
40:
41: on handleSafePlane(me)
42:    --find out the current speed of the cylinder
43:    cspeed = driver.getspeed()
44:    -- determine the distance from the cylinder
45:    -- that the safeplane should be placed.  note
46:    -- that this is a simple ratio.  Also note that
47:    -- this number is negated because we want to
48:    -- move the plane down the -Z axis
49:    newsafe = -((cspeed * pMaxSafe) / float(pmaxspeed))
50:    -- identify the safe plane
51:    scene.model("safeplane").transform.identity()
52:    -- move safe plane to new position
53:    scene.model("safeplane").translate(0,0,newsafe, #parent)
54: end
55:
56: on toggledeflection(me, newvalue)
57:    case(newvalue) of
```

LISTING 29.4   Continued

```
58:    #on:
59:      deflectactive = true
60:    #off:
61:      deflectactive = false
62:    #otherwise:
63:      return false
64:  end case
65: end
66:
67: on checkForHits(me)
68:   --will be used to determine if the
69:   --math heavy section of this code
70:   -- can be skipped due to the fact that
71:   -- no boundary will be hit.
72:   activehit = false
73:   --find the direction of the cylinder in world space
74:   dirvect = -(scene.model("mycyl").getworldtransform().zaxis)
75:   dirvect.normalize()
76:   --find the position of the two boxes
77:   leftEdgepos = scene.model("leftedge").getworldtransform().position
78:   rightEdgepos = scene.model("rightedge").\
       getworldtransform().position
79:
80:   --shoot a ray from each box toward the direction vector
81:   --return only the first model that is encountered.
82:   lefthit = scene.modelsunderray(leftedgepos, dirvect,  1, #detailed)
83:   righthit = scene.\
       modelsunderray(rightedgepos, dirvect, 1,  #detailed)
84:
85:   --check to see if the "left" ray did not hit the safeplane
86:   if lefthit[1][#model].name <> "safeplane" then
87:     --find out how close the obstacle is
88:     leftDistance = lefthit[1][#distance]
89:   else
90:     --hit the safeplane, so set this distance
91:     --ridiculously high
92:     leftDistance = pmaxsafe * 5
93:   end if
94:
95:   --check to see if the "left" ray did not hit the safeplane
96:   if righthit[1][#model].name <> "safeplane" then
97:     --find out how close the obstacle is
98:     rightDistance = lefthit[1][#distance]
99:   else
100:    --hit the safeplane, so set this distance
101:    --ridiculously high
```

LISTING 29.4   Continued

```
102:      rightDistance = pmaxsafe * 5
103:    end if
104:
105:    --determine if either the left or right ray hit something
106:    if leftdistance <= pmaxsafe or rightdistance <= pmaxsafe then
107:      --determine which side hit closer
108:      if leftDistance > rightdistance then
109:        --change the value of activehit to a copy of
110:        -- the list returned by modelsunderray()
111:        activeHit = righthit.duplicate()
112:        -- save a symbol telling us which way to turn (later on)
113:        turn = #right
114:      else
115:        --note that if they are equal, the script
116:        --defaults to the left
117:        activeHit = lefthit.duplicate()
118:        turn = #left
119:      end if
120:    end if
121:
122:    -- figure out if we have hit anything
123:    if activehit <> false then
124:      --if we have...
125:      --first slow speed down
126:      adecel = activehit[1][#distance]
127:      --this line slows the speed of the
128:      --deceleration logarithmically.  it also
129:      -- makes sure that the closer to the
130:      --cylinder the collision occurs, the
131:      --higher the rate of deceleration
132:      decel = power((log(pmaxsafe * 2) - log(adecel)), 4)
133:      --call the braking script
134:      driver.braking(decel)
135:
136:      -- get the normal at the point that we hit
137:      --(the normal is already normalized)
138:      i = activehit[1][#isectnormal]
139:      --figure out the angle between the direction
140:      --and the normal, and convert from radians to degrees.
141:      theta = ((i.dot(dirvect)) * 57.295779576)
142:
143:      --divide that angle in half (angle of deflection)
144:      theta = theta / float(2)
145:
146:      -- if we are turning right, negate the angle
147:      case(turn) of
148:        #right:
```

LISTING 29.4 Continued

```
149:         theta = -theta
150:       #left:
151:         nothing
152:     end case
153:
154:     -- make sure that the angle is within
155:     -- our range for deflection before
156:     -- auto-steering the cylinder.
157:     --(try commenting this out and driving around)
158:     if theta > -26 and theta < 26 then
159:       driver.deflect(theta)
160:     end if
161:   end if
162: end
```

The foresight() handler, which is shown in lines 29 to 39 in Listing 29.4, is the primary handler, and it's called every 42 milliseconds. The foresight() handler, in turn, calls the handleSafePlane() and checkForHits() handlers. These two handlers perform the majority of the work for this script.

The last few points I would like to make on this demonstration have to do with the walls. Notice that some of the walls are light blue and some are dark purple. The dark purple walls are thinner than the light blue walls. This is important. You see, the dark purple walls are actually thinner than the distance between the two rays we are shooting to check for future collisions. With proper alignment, it is possible to drive the cylinder directly through these walls. Note in Figure 29.5 that I have shown an overhead view of how this is possible.

To fix this, we can either make wider walls or place the rays closer together. If we place the rays too close together, the cylinder will be able to brush up against the wall (and sometimes enter it). This can also be a problem if we have very sharp corners, as shown in Figure 29.6.

You should avoid creating wall structures that look like this—possibly by simply removing the corners of this shape. Another method for avoiding these corners would be to actually shoot a third ray from the middle of the cylinder, although if the angle were sharp enough, this would not help.

You may also have trouble maneuvering if the interior corners of your walls form angles less than 90 degrees. In those cases, driving into these corners may cause the cylinder to bounce around a little, because it is being deflected from one corner wall to the next. The easiest way to avoid this is to avoid designing areas that have sharp interior corners for your players to get lost in.

FIGURE 29.5

Overhead illustration showing how the cylinder can be driven through walls that are not as wide as itself.

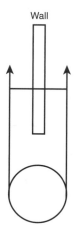

FIGURE 29.6

Extremely sharp corners can cause unrealistic breaches of the wall surface.

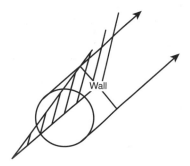

Summary

Collision detection must be included in your plans from the very beginning of a project; too much about the structure of the scenegraph and code hierarchies depends on whether you will need collision detection. In general, there are three areas of collision detection: the Collision Modifier, your own collision solution, and the Havok Xtra. We have only touched on the first two possibilities. Of these, building your own collision solution is superior in terms of speed.

Creating your own collision-detection routines involves the use of Picking Lingo and your knowledge of vector math. You might even consider coupling your knowledge of Mesh deformation with collision detection to create dents or markings on Models where collisions have occurred.

In the demonstrations in this chapter, I have shown that there are essentially two approaches toward collision detection. You can use built-in routines to detect when a collision has already happened. This is very good when you are creating bullets or other types of interactions that depend on a cause-and-effect situation. When the bullet collides with an object, it is then that you take action. The second approach is to build a custom system to avoid having Models collide at all. This type of system is useful if you are trying to contain the movements of a user within a specific area of your 3D world.

FAQ

I am designing a game and I need accurate collision detection for rigid body physics. Where should I start?

The Havok Xtra is included with Director. It is extremely robust. I suggest reading through Appendix G, "Havok Xtra," which will point you toward resources for getting started.

You seem to discourage the use of the Collision Modifier. Is this correct?

Yes. I don't think it works all that well, and I think it is too slow. Considering that 99 percent of projects that need collision detection are going to involve games in which speed is not optional, creating your own solution is much more effective (although time consuming).

Supplemental Resources

- *Convex Hull Simplification with Containment*, by Stan Melax
  (`http://www.cs.ualberta.ca/~melax/hull/consimp.html`)

  This is an outstanding article on convex hulls—how to create them and how to utilize them. A convex hull is a low-polygon-count Model that is "shrink wrapped" around a complex Model. This article has several illustrations that explain the concept.

- *BSP Collision Detection as Used in MDK2*, by Stan Melax
  (`http://www.gamasutra.com/features/20010324/melax_01.htm`)

  Another outstanding article by Stan Melax that explains collision detection and the use of binary space partition (BSP) trees. In addition, Melax addresses sliding, corner reduction, and managing multiple-height floors.

- *Advanced Collision Detection Techniques*, by Nick Bobic (`http://www.gamasutra.com/features/20000330/bobic_01.htm`)

  An excellent article that explains different techniques for working with custom bounding boxes and the benefits of each. Bobic also mentions BSP trees and convex hulls, although not in detail. However, he does reference several more articles at the beginning of this article that do go into detail about these issues.

- BSP Tree FAQ (`http://Reality.sgi.com/bspfaq`)

  This is an outstanding resource for BSP trees. It contains an answer to the all important question, "What is a BSP tree?" It also provides examples and links to other resources you might be interested in.

PART VII

Appendixes

The appendixes in this section cover several pertinent topics that I expect will help you gain greater control over the 3D environment. In this section, I will explain how to work with the 3DS MAX W3D Exporter. This exporter has been publicly available the longest. If you have worked with 3DS MAX before, there are many items that you will need to know about before you export from 3DS MAX that change the way you will build hierarchies. Next, I will explain the relevant issues that affect the OBJ Importer. I will give a brief demonstration of Imaging Lingo and show how to work with 2D trigonometry in Director. I have also put together an optimization cheat sheet—essentially an optimization top 10. Next, I provide you with a custom parent/child script dedicated to helping you work with color in Director. This script provides you with methods of converting between RGB and HSB color spaces, choosing color via names, and creating custom palettes of unlimited size. In addition, a dedicated application is included for helping you create palettes and name colors. After the appendix on color, I provide an introduction to the Havok Physics engine. Finally, this section includes a compilation of online resources for 3D programming, game programming, 3D modeling, 3D animation, and Director in general.

APPENDIX A

3D Studio MAX W3D Exporter

The purpose of this appendix is to provide you with a set of tips and tricks as you begin to work in 3D Studio MAX for the purpose of exporting W3D Models. This appendix assumes that you have some knowledge of 3D Studio MAX, 3D modeling, and 3D animation in general.

NOTE

You should realize that 3D Studio MAX is not the only 3D modeling/animation package that offers W3D export. However, it has had a W3D exporter available since the beta cycle of Director 8.5.

During the writing of this book, other exporters became available. Unfortunately, these exporters were not made available readily enough to be included. I can say that of the other major 3D modeling/animating software packages, the creators of Maya, Lightwave, Softimage, Truespace, and Cinema4D have all announced plans for W3D exporters for their software. You can find information about these and other modelers in Appendix H, "Online Resources."

Most likely, by the time this book is published, these 3D software manufacturers will have all released W3D exporters for their respective software packages.

This appendix is not a guide for learning how to model or animate in 3D Studio MAX, nor is it the final document that you will need to read on W3D export. Instead, it is a reference that can help you avoid mistakes the first time you are creating Models or animation for export from 3D Studio MAX. At the end of this appendix are links to two documents on the Macromedia site that can help you continue to learn about specific issues that not all users may encounter.

How to Export Models from 3D Studio MAX

Once you have created your scene in 3D Studio and are ready to export, you should select the viewport that you would like to have as the default viewport for the W3D file. Then simply select Export from the File menu. Once you select W3D as the file type to export, the dialog box in Figure A.1 will pop up on your screen.

FIGURE A.1

The 3D Studio MAX 3.1 W3D Exporter.

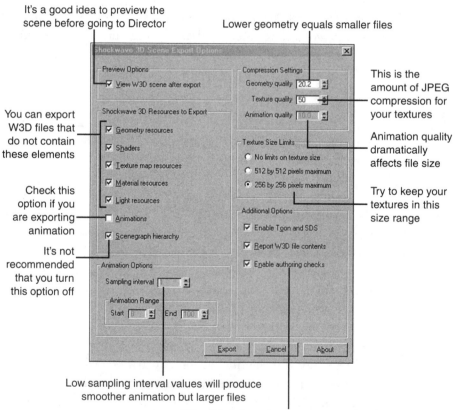

It's a good idea to preview the scene before going to Director

Lower geometry equals smaller files

This is the amount of JPEG compression for your textures

You can export W3D files that do not contain these elements

Animation quality dramatically affects file size

Check this option if you are exporting animation

Try to keep your textures in this size range

It's not recommended that you turn this option off

Low sampling interval values will produce smoother animation but larger files

This will alert you to any unsupported options you may have used in your scenes

Figure A.1 contains explanations of each of the settings that you can change from this dialog box. One topic you should be aware of is *precision*. Due to the method of geometry compression that offers such small file sizes, many times high geometry compression will not preserve your locations with extreme precision. Be aware that you may need to sacrifice compression for precision if your projects demand it. Compression and precision issues can affect extremely precise Camera and lighting placements as well. However, with Cameras and Lights, you can reset these positions very quickly via Lingo— the same might not be true for geometry.

Critical Issues with W3D Export

This section addresses the main issues that will affect your workflow as a 3D artist outside of Director in 3D Studio MAX. In addition to this appendix, I highly suggest that you refer to the tech notes on the Macromedia site on W3D exportation. These cover a range of issues you will encounter when working with this exporter. However, you should begin with this section because it lists the most critical issues with W3D export that affect the choices you will be making when creating scenes in 3D Studio MAX.

Canonical Axis Discrepancies

The first difficulty you'll face when working on a project that incorporates 3DS MAX and Director 8.5 is understanding the differences in the canonical world axis. You have learned that in the Director 8.5 3D environment, the X axis is left and right, the Y axis is up and down, and the Z axis is into or out of the screen. In 3D Studio, the X axis is still left and right, but the Y axis is into the screen, and the Z axis is up and down. This can cause problems of disorientation. In general, you should come up with a strategy for dealing with this, especially if you are going to be working with multiple 3D Castmembers.

Naming Conventions

It is important that you name your models uniquely. In addition, 3D Studio will name Models for you as you are creating them. Try to set the names for these Models before you export, because the names set for the Models at export time are the names the programmers will need to use. It is much easier to refer to "doorknob01" than it is to refer to "sphere14."

Cameras

When you export, the current view will become the default Camera view for the W3D file. Make sure you have selected the correct viewport or Camera for the initial view that you would like to see in your 3D World. Also, you can define multiple Cameras in 3D Studio and give them unique names—this is a wonderful way to set up multiple Cameras visually. Finally, the Cameras in Director are always free Cameras; if you use a target Camera, it will be converted to a free Camera.

Shaders and Textures

Materials tend to be the hardest hit during a conversion between 3D Studio and Director. You will most likely be able to get the effect you need, but you will probably need to re-create the effect through code in Lingo rather than be able to export directly from 3D Studio without any problems in terms of Textures. One addendum to this is that UV coordinates work very well—and the 3D Studio UV coordinate editor is a powerful tool. If you are not familiar with this tool in 3D Studio, I suggest you learn it.

Lights

Some aspects of Lights are not supported in Director and will not export; instead, they will be converted to acceptable values or ignored. Atmospheric effects, projections, and rectilinear spotlights are all not supported, and they will be ignored on export. In addition, Target spotlights will be converted to free spotlights.

Models

Director can handle many tens of thousands of vertices in its 3D environment, but if you are designing an online project, you most likely will want to keep this number much lower. Also, if you are designing games, you are going to want to use standard "low polygon count" modeling techniques. Finally, Director does not support Nurbs, but you can model with Nurbs and then export a Mesh snapshot.

Animation

You cannot export animated Mesh deformation modifiers or space warps. Only keyframe- or Bones-based animation will export for geometry. If you need to animate a Camera or a Light's position, you will need to group it with a Model. If you need to animate Camera or Light properties, you will need to do so in Lingo.

Hierarchies

If you want to preserve a hierarchy, group it in 3D Studio before export.
If you want to create a single Model with multiple Meshes, link Models
together in 3D Studio. Link Models that will become sub-Meshes to the
Model that will become the main Mesh. After you export, the W3D version
of this Model will only look like one Model with multiple Meshes, each capable of having its own Shader.

Bones

If you are working with Bones hierarchies, make sure you name all the Bones
with the same root name. In addition, make sure you group the Bones before
export so that their hierarchy does not collapse.

Character Studio

If you do not have Character Studio for 3D Studio, consider purchasing it. It
expands the power of 3D Studio dramatically. In addition, it integrates very
well with Director. If you are planning on working with Bones animation to
perform skeletal deformation, you will need to use Character Studio. The
Bones created in 3DS itself can not be used to deform the skeleton, but only
for simple hierarchies.

Supplemental Resources

The following two documents are excellent resources on many specific issues,
and they expand greatly on the list I have presented in this appendix. Many
subtle issues exist, depending on the exact tools you prefer to use. In addition,
several optimizations for streaming are worth examining.

- Tech Note 15295: Exporting W3D Files from 3D Studio MAX

    www.macromedia.com/support/director/ts/documents/3d_exporters.htm

- Preparing Content for Shockwave 3D

    www.macromedia.com/support/director/work_3d/models_use_in_sw/models_
    use_in_sw.html

APPENDIX B

OBJ Converter

In this appendix, I will explain the strengths and weaknesses of the OBJ Converter. Also, I will show you some locations to get stock OBJ files as well as address some concerns you many have when using OBJ files. I will also provide a general explanation of what this tool makes possible.

In terms of 3D file formats, Director 8.5 can only import native W3D files. Director 8.5 ships with a converter that converts Wavefront OBJ files to the W3D standard. Included with the OBJ Converter is an excellent document that highlights the usage of the OBJ Converter and known issues. This appendix addresses several items of key importance for successfully importing OBJ files.

The OBJ File Format

The OBJ file format has existed for quite some time and has a history of its own developments, long prior to the W3D format. Although it is sometimes still referred to as a *Wavefront OBJ*, this format has been used as a transfer format for quite some time. That is, many non-Wavefront applications have supported OBJ import and export for a long time. Unfortunately, this has led to variations and irregularity in both the quality of the data and the specific structure of the data. In short, until you actually do the conversion process and import the W3D file, you cannot be sure that your OBJ data will accurately import. This has obvious implications for your testing cycle: Test early and test often.

Issues

Although the OBJ Converter document lists several known issues with popular 3D modeling tools, the list is not inclusive. If you can use your 3D software to export to the W3D format natively, by all means do so. There are many free 3D model repositories on the Web, and even some inexpensive royalty-free model CDs. However, these sources tend to have unreliable OBJ data. The OBJ file format stores its material and texture information separately from the OBJ file. Many times, this data is lost or not included with free 3D models. Also, many OBJ exporters do not save the MTL files required. If this is the case, you can still convert the OBJ file, but you will need to manually texture the object with Lingo. Finally, although the OBJ standard has limited support for NURBS surfaces, they are not supported in W3D.

Strategy

With these issues in place, you may be concerned over the viability of the OBJ Converter as a production tool. Keep in mind that there are several consignment-based model repositories on the Web that have extremely reliable OBJ files, among them Turbosquid.com. Also, if you are working with a 3D tool that does not support OBJ, you may want to consider Polytrans from Okino Software. Polytrans is a very reliable converter that creates OBJ files that work well with the OBJ-to-W3D converter.

Advanced

Perhaps one of the strongest arguments I can make for the OBJ Converter is as follows: The OBJ file format is well documented, and it is an ASCII (plain-text) document. For this reason, it is feasible to write applications to generate OBJ files. Here are two resources that can guide you in this endeavor:

- *3D Graphics File Formats*, by Keith Rule

  Rule's book is dedicated to explaining the concepts behind many 3D file formats and strategies for writing code for converting between them.

- http://www.neutralzone.org/home/faqsys/docs/obj~1.spe

  This is an OBJ file format "white paper" that explains the inner structure of the format, with detailed examples.

APPENDIX C

Imaging Lingo

This appendix is intended to offer you a basic introduction to Imaging Lingo. This subset of Lingo is often regarded as being difficult to learn because it is an abstract, low-level tool that can be used to develop custom imaging APIs. Imaging Lingo was introduced in Director 8, but you may not have had a chance to learn what it can do or why you might want to use it. There are certainly many opinions of the usefulness of Imaging Lingo, but one thing is certain: Imaging Lingo offers you deep control over the 2D environment of Director. Therefore, the integration of Imaging Lingo and 3D Lingo offer you the widest possible control over the visual environment that is worth understanding.

What Is Imaging Lingo?

Imaging Lingo is a subset of Lingo commands, functions, and properties that centers on the creation and manipulation of the image code object. Unlike bitmaps or other visual Castmembers, the image code object exists entirely in RAM—the way that you would expect a child object or color object to exist. Specifically, the information it contains is bitmap information, and this information can be applied to bitmap Castmembers—but in itself, it is merely a code object.

You can create image code objects from several different Castmember types or create empty image objects from scratch. You can use Imaging Lingo to find out information about specific pixels in an image as well as change the color of specific pixels. One of its most powerful tools allows you to composite images into new images, or with themselves. In addition, imaging commands and functions allow you to work with alpha channels in much the same manner.

In addition to the commands and functions dealing with the image code object are Lingo commands that are not specifically Imaging Lingo but that you might not be familiar with. These commands can aid you when using Imaging Lingo. Among these helper commands are tools that enable you to create bitmap Castmembers at runtime and manipulate `point()`, `rect()`, and quad code objects.

What Can You Do with Imaging Lingo?

In terms of the robust method in which Imaging Lingo has been implemented, it is safe to say that Imaging Lingo is to 2D what the Shockwave 3D Castmember is to 3D in Director. Other than stating what Imaging Lingo can do from a purely technical standpoint, it is important for you to understand what is actually possible with this tool.

The ability to composite bitmaps at runtime is a powerful method of accomplishing a variety of techniques, including creating painting programs and tile-based games. Even some users have used it to implement 3D environments without the Shockwave 3D Castmember. Although you may not need this tool for those specific tasks, it would be a mistake to overlook its power at creating bitmaps and textures in real time, providing methods to build a purely code-based interface.

In terms of the 3D environment, this tool offers building real-time Textures. One of the many goals you should be thinking about is trying to keep file sizes as small as possible. If you can reduce a file size by creating a bitmap that will be used for a Texture after the movie has downloaded, you will have saved the user some amount of download time.

Because Texture objects in the 3D environment are used as Textures for Models and as the basis for Backdrops and Overlays, you can use Imaging Lingo in conjunction with the 3D environment in several useful ways:

- For real-time menu systems
- For 3D compass/radar/navigation systems

- For animated Textures
- For compositions of large textures from multiple small bitmaps
- For the creation of small textures from sections of large bitmaps
- For the simulation of Sprite ink effects

The possible uses for Imaging Lingo are very broad, and this can often make learning a powerful tool seem daunting. In addition, this tool is robust from a programming sense, meaning that the commands appear very simple but are powerful when used in conjunction with one another to achieve a specific goal. More so than when you program other aspects of Lingo, you are probably going to work through some amount of pseudo-code before you begin.

Imaging Basics

The core of Imaging Lingo is based on a code object known as an *image object*. Image objects can be created on-the-fly, but they are not Castmembers. Instead, they are code objects that exist in RAM only at runtime. This is why they must be created from code, and they are not saved with a movie.

NOTE

Even though you cannot save image objects, you can create bitmap Castmembers from image objects and then save those bitmaps in a cast or movie.

You can create empty image objects and then paste information into them, or you can duplicate the visual information from a Castmember or the Stage into a new image object. Once you actually have an image object or objects to work with, you are able to crop, cut, paste, and otherwise manipulate the image data. Then, you can put the image data back into a new bitmap Castmember or into an existing Castmember, or you can use it directly as a Texture in the 3D environment.

There are quite a few commands dealing with imaging Lingo that can be found in the Lingo Dictionary under Lingo By Feature in the Bitmaps section. However, the list that you will find in the help file does not list all of the commands that you might find immediately useful in conjunction with the imaging Lingo properties, commands, and functions. I have created a list of properties, commands, and functions for specific, as well as those related to, imaging Lingo and a brief description of each as shown in Table C.1.

TABLE C.1   Imaging Lingo and Related Commands and Properties

Property/Command	Purpose
Image	Allows access to the image object of various Castmembers and movie elements
Image()	Used to create new, empty image objects
Copypixels()	A fast and recommended method of copying pixels from one bitmap to another
Crop()	Crops an image object
Draw()	Draws lines or unfilled shapes on the image
Fill()	Draws lines or filled shapes on the image
Duplicate()	A recommended method of creating a duplicate image object
Rect()	Rectangle code objects defined by left, top, right, and bottom coordinates
Quads	A quad code object defined by four points: upper-left, upper-right, lower-left, and lower-right corners
usefastquads	A Boolean that determines whether fast or slow algorithms are used when manipulating quads (default is false)
Setpixel()	A slow but powerful command that allows you to set the color of a specific pixel in an image object or bitmap
Getpixel()	A slow but powerful command that returns information about a specific pixel in an image object or bitmap
Extractalpha()	A function that returns a new 8-bit image object created from the alpha channel of a 32-bit image object or bitmap
Setalpha()	A function that allows you to specify an 8-bit image to function as the alpha channel for another 32-bit image
Usealpha	A Boolean that determines whether the alpha channel information in a bitmap or image object should be used (default is true)
Depth	A testable property that only returns the bit depth of a bitmap or image object
Createmask()	Returns a special mask object that is used in conjunction with copypixels() for simulating the mask Sprite ink

TABLE C.1   Continued

Property/Command	Purpose
Creatematte()	Returns a special mask object created from alpha channel information that is used in conjunction with copypixels() for simulating the mask Sprite ink
Not Specifically Imaging Lingo	
Member.duplicate()	A command that will create a duplicate of any Castmember, including bitmaps
Member.erase()	A command that will erase any Castmember
New(#bitmap)	A command that can be used to create a new, empty bitmap Castmember

As you can see from Table C.1, an extensive number of commands, functions, and properties comprise the tool known as Imaging Lingo. But understanding how to use Imaging Lingo requires more than these explanations—we will be covering several concepts in the next section that are as important as the entries in Table C.1. Understanding these critical concepts and strategies is often the key difference between deciding to use or avoid Imaging Lingo altogether.

Image, `Image()`, and `Duplicate()`

The basis for most of Imaging Lingo centers on the image code object. Therefore, it is important that you understand the variety of methods available to you for creating image objects. The simplest method utilizes the `image()` function, which returns an empty image object. The basic syntax for the `image()` function is as follows:

```
ImageObjectRef = image(width, height, bitdepth)
```

There are several optional parameters for setting the alphadepth or palette, but these three parameters are required to create an empty image object. In addition to creating empty image objects from scratch, you can also create image objects from the Castmembers in the following list:

- Bitmap Castmembers
- Stage or MIAW

- RealMedia Castmembers
- 3D Castmembers
- Texture objects in a 3D environment
- Text Castmembers
- Vector shape Castmembers
- Flash Castmembers

When you want to create an image object from any of these elements, you should use the duplicate() function. This will allow you to work on a copy of the image data in one of these elements without changing that data itself. In addition, the duplicate() function is the recommended method because it avoids recursive pointers and, in short, memory leaks. The syntax for creating a new image object based on a Castmember is as follows:

```
ImageObjectRef = member("membername").image.duplicate()
```

If you need to duplicate the Stage, use the following:

```
ImageObjectRef = The stage.image.duplicate()
```

If you need to duplicate a Texture, use this:

```
Scene.texture("texturename").image.duplicate()
```

Note that although you can get the image from any of these elements, you can only set the image of a bitmap Castmember or a Texture object in a 3D environment.

The Rect() Code Object

Rect() is a function and a code object that is used to define a rectilinear area. That area can be the bounding rectangle of an image object or a Castmember, or it can simply be an arbitrary rectangular shape that you may need to hold onto. For example, imagine that you have an image object that is 100 pixels high by 1,000 pixels long, and it contains a photograph of a sunset. You could define an arbitrary rectangle that is 100 by 100 pixels that can be used to find a specific part of the image object.

There are several ways to define a rect. We will look at two. To create a rect from scratch, use this:

```
RectRef = rect(left, top, right, bottom)
```

Here, `left`, `top`, `right`, and `bottom` are pixel values describing the boundaries of the rectangle. Another method you might use is to grab the rect of an image object with this:

```
Rectref = imageObjectRef.rect()
```

Once you have created a rect code object, you can use several commands to manipulate the rectangles themselves. Table C.2 lists some of the functions you might find useful when learning about rects in conjunction with Imaging Lingo.

TABLE C.2   Basic Rect Manipulation Functions

Function	Purpose
Inflate()	Expands or compresses a given rectangle
Offset()	Moves a given rectangle some distance
Union()	Takes two rectangles and returns the smallest rectangle that includes both of the source rectangles
Intersect()	Takes two rectangles and returns the rectangle where they intersect
Map()	Takes two rectangles and a point and returns the point inside the second rectangle relative to the relationship between the first rectangle and point

NOTE

Keep in mind that rects have uses outside of Imaging Lingo as well. Other rect functions, such as `inside()`, `mapmembertostage()`, and `mapstagetomember()`, are helpful when you're working with Sprites and rects. However, the functions listed in Table C.2 tend to be the most useful in terms of Imaging Lingo.

To further explain these functions, let's suppose that we have a rectangle defined by the following:

```
TestRect = rect(0,0,300,100)
```

Now offset `TestRect` with the following code:

```
Testrect = Testrect.offset(40,50)
```

Here's the current value of `TestRect`:

```
Put testrect
--rect(40,50,340,150)
```

Now, inflate `TestRect` with the following code:

```
Testrect = testrect.inflate(10,20,0,20)
Put testrect
--rect(30,30,350,170)
```

As you can see from these examples, it is possible to manipulate a rectangle that exists in an essentially arbitrary space.

Quads

A quad is a unique entity that is similar to a rect in that it describes a four-sided space, but as its name suggests, a quad describe quadrilaterals. Now, a rectangle is a special quadrilateral, because each of its angles is 90 degrees—that is why it can take the form of four coordinates.

To describe a quad, we need more information; quads are described by a linear list of four points. The form of a quad looks like this:

```
Myquad = [point(x,y), point(xx,yy), point(xxx,yyy), point(xxxx,yyyy)]
```

These four points are used to describe the upper-left, upper-right, lower-right, and lower-left corners of a quadrilateral, respectively. It is possible to create quads that cross over themselves, so be aware of this when setting the points.

Quads can be used for Sprites to add perspective types of effects, but they also come into play with Imaging Lingo in terms of the `copypixels` command, which we will be looking at next.

Copypixels()

You might be wondering why we have spent so much time looking at rects and quads, with little mention to Imaging Lingo. We have examined these items because you must understand rects and quads if you want to learn about what is arguably the most powerful function available to you in Imaging Lingo. `Copypixels()` is a very fast executing command that will most likely serve as the basis for many of your intricate imaging strategies.

`Copypixels()` can copy pixels from one image object to another. It can also scale those pixels up or down or skew them into non-rectilinear shapes via quads. In addition, it can simulate effects of Sprite inks or changes in opacity, and it can even use masks and mattes created from other image objects.

Because of the wide variety of uses for this command, there are a wide variety of syntaxes you will want to consider. The most basic syntax is as follows:

```
ImageObjectRef.copypixels(sourceImage, targetRect, sourceRect, parame-
terlist)
```

The `parameterlist` argument is optional. It can contain the parameters as shown in Table C.3.

TABLE C.3   Copypixels() Optional Parameters

Parameters	Purpose
#color	Determines the foreground color of the image.
#bgcolor	Determines the background color of the image.
#ink	Applies one of the Sprite inks to the image.
#blendlevel	Sets the opacity for the copied pixels.
#dither	Dithers the area of copied pixels.

TABLE C.3   Continued

Parameters	Purpose
#usefastquads	A Boolean that determines which algorithm should be used if the `targetrect` parameter was actually a quad rather than a rect.
#maskimage	A mask image object created from `createmask()` or `creatematte()`. Some of the Sprite inks (such as mask) require that you use a maskimage.
#maskOffset	The `point()` value offset for the mask.

In order to best explain this function, I have put together a small file named "Imaging Demo" that you can find on the CD. Open this file, the Stage, and the message window. The imaging demo contains several bitmap Castmembers that we will use to explore the syntax and usage of the `copypixels()` function.

In the center of the Stage you should see a small black square. If you look at the cast, you will see that there are two versions of this square: test and backup. The Castmember named test was used to create the Sprite on Stage. When we are done altering the image properties, we will use the Castmember named backup to revert to the original version of test.

First, let's perform a simple `copypixels()` function (note that I have taken some preliminary steps in order to make the typing less of a burden). First, create a rectangle object that is 128 by 128 pixels; we will use this in our `copy-pixels()` function (note that the following commands are intended to be executed from the message window):

```
r1 = rect(0,0,128,128)
```

Then, copy the image from the grid Castmember into the image used by the test Castmember:

```
member("test").image.copypixels(member("grid").image, r1, r1)
```

The results of this operation are instantaneous—the Sprite updates as soon as you execute this command. Now, revert to the original image with the following code:

```
member("test").image = member("backup").image.duplicate()
```

Realize that this works only because I had previously made a copy of the original test Castmember. Now let's try a more difficult operation. This time, we are going to create a mask from one image and then copy the pixels of a second image, masking out parts of it from the first. This will require several steps that do not have an apparent visual effect, but I will explain what is happening as we execute the commands.

First, create a rectangle for the source image and another rectangle for the destination rectangle:

```
sourceR = rect(0,0,160,100)
targetR = rect(15,50,170,150)
```

Now, create an image object from the text Castmember named "textmask," which will then be used to create a matte object:

```
img = member("textmask").image.duplicate()
mask - img.creatematte()
```

Finally, copy pixels from the image of the sky using the matte object created from the text Castmember. In addition, by using the source and target rects that we set up previously, we are able to position the result into the center of the test image. Use the following command to perform all these functions:

```
member("test").image.copypixels(member("sky").image,\
 targetR, sourceR, [#maskimage:mask])
```

The result of this operation should leave you with the same image I saved in the file in a bitmap Castmember named demoA.

Finally, the last demo involves using the copypixels() command in conjunction with quads to add perspective to an image. There are several steps to this operation, so as you are working through the individual steps in the message window, be aware that until the last step you will not see any results on the Stage.

First, create a duplicate of the image object from the bitmap Castmember named "backup":

```
member("test").image = member("backup").image.duplicate()"
```

Next, define a quadrilateral with the following code:

```
Myquad = [point(0,0), point(100,40), point(100,120), point(0,160)]
R1 = rect(0,0,128,128)
```

Now, copy pixels from the house Castmember into the destination quad we just set up as well as the source rect:

```
member("test").image.copypixels(member("house").image, myquad,r1)
```

This operation shows you how you can use quads to alter and distort images. I put a copy of the finished demonstration into a bitmap Castmember named demoB.

I suggest that you continue experimenting with the images in this demonstration to see whether you understand the copypixels() command. As mentioned earlier, copypixels() is the most powerful of all the imaging commands, and it will likely play a central role in most any imaging technique you build.

Where to Go from Here

Chapter 17, "Special Effects," offers several examples of how you might use Imaging Lingo in the 3D environment. In addition, at the end of that chapter are several online resources you may want to consult when learning about Imaging Lingo. Finally, read through the Macromedia help to get specific syntax information about all the commands and functions introduced in this appendix.

APPENDIX D

2D Mathematics and Utilities

This appendix is intended to aid you primarily with 2D mathematics rather than 3D vector-based mathematics. Although this appendix is not a replacement for a solid foundation in algebra, geometry, and trigonometry, it will help guide you in the creation of several custom functions for solving trigonometry problems. The custom functions in this appendix are included in the Math Utilities file that appears on the CD included with this book.

These custom functions fall into two categories. First are basic mathematical tools, such as arccosine, arcsine, and radian-to-degree converters, that extend the capabilities of Lingo. These basic mathematical tools are then used to develop the second set of functions, whose purpose is solving basic problems of trigonometry.

Modulus Operator

The modulus operator (mod) is built into Lingo, but many times it is overlooked. I mention it because it is an extremely useful mathematical operator that can be used in a variety of situations. Technically, mod divides two numbers and returns the remainder rather than the quotient. The mod operator can be used to cycle through a range of numbers. For example: 0 mod 3 = 0, 1 mod 3 = 1, 2 mod 3 = 2, 3 mod 3 = 0, 4 mod 3 = 1, and so on. For this reason, mod can be used to generate events with a periodic nature. The following code example creates a jittering effect, and it's implemented in the file "jitter":

```
Property pcounter, pperiod, spritenum

On beginsprite me
```

```
  Pcounter = 0 -- set the counter to 0
  pperiod = random(8) - decide what the period of this sprite will be
End

On exitframe me
 Pcounter = pcounter + 1 -- add 1 to the counter
-- if we reach the period of this sprite, trigger the event
 If pcounter mod pperiod = 0 then

   jit(me)   --the event to trigger
 End if
End

on jit me
-- find out the current location of the sprite
cloc = sprite(spritenum).loc  -- decide how far to move the sprite on X axis
 nx = random(-3,3)
 -- decide how far to move the sprite on Y axis
 ny = random(-3,3)
 -- find out the new location
 nloc = cloc + point(nx,ny)
 -- move the sprite to the new location
 sprite(spritenum).loc = nloc
end
```

In addition to creating periodic events, mod can be used in other ways. Imagine that we've rotated a sphere 8,320 degrees. Using mod, we can solve the following:

```
8320 mod 360 = 40
```

Therefore, although we know that the sphere has made several revolutions, what is important is that the sphere appears to be rotated 40 degrees from its original position. This usage of mod will become important when we create look-up tables for sine and cosine values.

Radians and Degrees

Many times you will need to convert between radians and degrees, and vice versa. This is especially true because the native cos() and sin() functions require that you pass values to them in radians. In addition, we will be creating some custom trigonometry functions which will expect angles in radians as well. The file Math Utilities contains the following handlers:

```
On deg2rad degrees
 Return degrees / 57.295779576
End

On rad2deg radians
 Return radians * 57.295779576
End
```

You may be curious where 57.295779576 comes from. The formulas for converting from radians to degrees and degrees to radians always involves (pi / 180). Because (pi / 180) is a constant, we can reduce it to 57.295779576 and gain a minute performance boost. Small optimizations like this may seem irrelevant, but time wasted on unnecessary operations accumulate and eventually slow your projects down. When you can optimize in a situation this clear, it is worth taking advantage of.

Sin() and Cos() Look-up Tables

Both sin() and cos() need to be used for developing our basic trigonometry custom functions. These two functions require that you pass angles to them in radians rather than degrees. Utilizing the deg2rad() custom handler, you can quickly pass values as follows:

```
Put deg2rad(30).cos

Put deg2rad(30).sin
```

If you can sacrifice a bit of precision for added speed, it is possible to use sine and cosine look-up tables rather than the sin() and cos() functions. The following custom functions were constructed such that they expect degrees rather than radians.

```
On fastSIN pangle
 SinLUT = [0.0175, 0,0349 LOOK-UP VALUES ARE IN THE FILE]
```

```
      --make sure that the angle is an integer, positive and between 0 - 360
pangleFIX = integer((pangle mod 360))

  if pangleFIX > 0 then
   sign = 1
  else
   sign = -1
  end if

  panglefix = abs(panglefix)

  if pangleFIX = 0 then
   return 0.0000
  else
   return (sinLUT[pangleFIX] * sign)

  end if

end

On fastCOS pangle
 cosLUT = [0.9998, 0,9994 LOOK-UP VALUES ARE IN THE FILE]
 --make sure that the angle is an integer, positive and between 0 - 360
 pangleFIX = integer(abs(pangle mod 360))
 if pangleFIX = 0 then
  return 1.0000
 else
  return cosLUT[pangleFIX]
 end if
end
```

Notice that these two custom functions, fastCOS() and fastSIN(), are very similar to one another. Also notice the use of the modulus operator for limiting the angle between 0 and 360 degrees. This way, if you ask for the fastCOS() value of 8,034 degrees, the function will reduce it to 114 degrees. The cos() value of 8,034 is exactly equal to the cos() value of 114 degrees. Fastcos() and fastsin() are included in the Math Utilities file.

ATAN(), COTAN(), ACOS(), and ASIN()

The arccosine and arcsine custom functions, acos() and asin(), can be derived from the arctangent function, atan(), that is built into Lingo. In addition, the cotangent custom function, cotan(), can be derived from the tangent function, tan(). Here's an example:

```
On acos ratio
  return -atan(ratio/sqrt(-(ratio*ratio)+1))+1.5708
End

On asin ratio
  Return atan(ratio/sqrt(1 - (ratio * ratio)))
end

on cotan pangle
 if pangle <> 0 then
  return float(1) / tan(pangle)
 else
  return void
 end if
end
```

Square Root and Coding

The square root function is traditionally a slow mathematical operation. This is not aided by the fact that Lingo is not fully compiled into machine code and must be interpreted at runtime. The square root function can slow a program down, and you need to be aware of this when you decide to use it. One method of working around the square root function is to use look-up tables (LUT) for arcsin and arccos.

Right Triangle Theorems

Given limited information about a right triangle defined by sides a, b, and c and opposite angles A, B, and C, we can use trigonometry to determine the missing distance and angle information. If you know the location of two points, you can determine the distance between them as well as the angle between them using these custom functions. Table D.1 lists the theorems that we will use to create our custom functions.

TABLE D.1   Right Angle Theorems

Theorem	Requires
ASA Theorem	Two angles and the distance of the side between them
AAS Theorem	Two angles and the distance of the adjacent side
SAS Theorem	Distance of two sides and the angle between them
SSS Theorem	Distance of three sides

There are several things to note about the following code examples. First, because Lingo is not case sensitive, we must not use a and A to represent two separate variables. Rather, we use AA, BB, and CC for the angles and a, b, and c for the sides. Second, be aware that these functions rely on sqrt() and have not been optimized to use fastCOS() or fastSIN(), in favor of accuracy. Here are the code examples:

```
On AAS_c(AA, BB, a)
 return (a * sin(BB)) * (cotan(AA) + cotan(BB)))
end

on ASA_a(AA, c, BB)
 return ((sin(AA) / sin(pi - AA - BB)) * float(c))
end

on ASA_b(AA, c, BB)
 return ((sin(BB) / sin(pi - AA - BB)) * float(c))
end

on SAS_b(a, BB, c)
 return sqrt(power(a,2) + power(c,2) - 2 * a * c * cos(BB))
end

on SAS_AA(a, BB, c)
 return asin((a * sin(BB)) / (sqrt(power(a,2) + power(c,2)\
 - 2 * a * c * cos(BB))))
end

on SAS_CC(a, BB, c)
 return asin((c * sin(BB)) / (sqrt(power(a,2) + power(c,2) \
- 2 * a * c * cos(BB))))
end

on SSS_AA(a, b, c)
```

```
   return acos((power(b,2) + power(c,2) - power(a,2)) / (2 * b * c))
end

on SSS_BB(a, b, c)
  return acos((power(a,2) + power(c,2) - power(b,2)) / (2 * a * c))
end

on SSS_CC(a, b, c)
  return acos((power(a,2) + power(b,2) - power(c,2)) / (2 * a * b))
end
```

Summary

The range of applications for these basic trigonometry functions extends well beyond the limits and suggestions of this appendix. On a mathematical level, these functions can be used to determine the distance between two points and the angle between those points. Here are some practical applications of trigonometry in Director:

- Firing bullets in a 360 degree arc in a game environment
- Determining the distance between players and enemies in a game environment
- Creating measurements of area and volume for charting and e-commerce applications
- Spatializing sound within an interface

In conclusion, trigonometry is a powerful tool that has a range of applications in Director. At times, the actual processing power for particular math functions, such as square root, can become prohibitive. If you can use look-up tables, I would suggest doing so. However, if you need precision, you ought to consider looking for other ways to speed up the code, such as consolidating constants and avoiding those functions that drain the most resources.

APPENDIX E

Optimization Cheat Sheet

Optimization is not a spice added after you have cooked a meal. It is the main ingredient. I encourage you to read through Chapter 19, "Performance Optimization," and Chapter 20, "Download Optimization," to learn how to apply the tips listed in this appendix. This appendix serves as a cheat sheet, listing the 10 most common areas needing performance and download optimization. Most of the following file-size optimizations would most likely not be used on a CD-ROM project, but the performance issues will affect all projects.

- File Size and Textures

  The "heaviest" part of any Shockwave 3D project is probably going to be the Textures. Try to limit the number of Textures that you need. When you need them, try to reuse them often in order to get as much mileage as possible.

- Performance and Textures

  The dimensions of textures should be powers of 2. Reduce the size below 256×256 (or even 128×128) if possible. Also, it is alright to use rectangular aspect ratios, as long as each side of the Texture is a power of 2, such as 128×256. Remember that large Textures increase file size as well as decrease performance. When a texture is on a Model that is moving, it is difficult to tell the difference between a 256×256 and a 128×128 Texture. Users will appreciate acceptable frame rates at the cost of low-quality Textures faster than they will accept the reverse situation.

- Performance/File Size and Textures

  32-bit textures use a lot of video RAM, and many users' video cards might not be able to support them (although this is quickly changing).

If you do not need an alpha channel in a texture, absolutely remove it from the texture. If you do need an alpha channel, make sure that it is an absolute necessity.

- File Size and Geometry

Primitives are created from code and take up no space to download. They are created relatively quickly, although some complex extrusions can bog down a processor for a moment. If you are trying to reduce file size, try to use primitives as much as possible.

- Performance and Geometry

The 3D Renderer renders each Model, one at a time. Try to use as few Models as possible or combine Models that are static into single Models. If you have one extremely complex Model, it will render faster than if you use the same geometry across 30 simpler objects.

- File Size and Sound

Sound can dramatically increase the file size of a movie. Try reducing the sound by changing stereo sounds to mono and 44.1KHz sounds to 22.5KHz or 11.025KHz. Also try using the Shockwave audio compression from the Publish Settings dialog. As an absolute last resort, change your sounds from 16 bit to 8 bit (note that I almost never recommend doing this because it reduces the quality of most sounds unbearably).

- Performance and Stage Size

Reduce the size of the Stage and the 3D Sprite—the smaller the viewing area, the faster the rendering rates you can achieve. Use Direct to Stage as often as possible. Try to avoid designing projects that need Ink effects. If you must have Ink-like effects, attempt to use Imaging Lingo and Backdrops to accomplish the same goals. Reduce the number of overlapping Sprites, and eliminate Sprites overlapping the 3D Sprite. If you need multiple views of the 3D environment, consider multiple Cameras via the Camera.Rect rather than multiple 3D Sprites.

- Performance and Lighting

Complex lighting can be beautiful but very costly. Try to accomplish your needs with as few Lights as possible. One technique is to bake lighting into textures (remember to be careful about too many textures). A general rule is to try to use fewer than five Lights in a scene.

- General Performance

  Software Rendering relies on the speed of the CPU rather than the video card. Because of this, Software Rendering will use cycles that could have been used for other code in your project. On very fast machines with very slow video cards capable of 3D acceleration, you may get faster speeds in software rendering. My advice is to always use 3D acceleration if it is present, and if it is, make sure that you do not cause the environment to switch to Software Rendering. Changing the screen resolution or color depth will cause a drop into Software Rendering, and using too many textures (running out of VRAM) will drop you into software rendering as well.

- General File Size

  No matter what, don't forget to recompile all scripts and then save and compact them. This will optimize your code; then it will reorder the data inside your casts so that they are ready for optimal downloading. It can reduce file size dramatically because it removes all references to deleted Castmembers that might still be present in a file. I have seen 3MB files reduce to 140KB—it is the easiest way to reduce the size of your files.

APPENDIX F

Colorlut Custom Color Management System

Throughout Shockwave 3D, we must specify colors with the rgb(R,G,B) standard, where R, G, and B are values between 0 and 255. If you have ever tried to determine the settings for a specific color, you have probably had a hard time doing this without a visual aid. In addition, it's cumbersome to remember that rgb(121,198,17) was just the shade of orange you were looking for. Worse yet, if you have ever tried to develop or design a palette of colors in Director, choosing evenly weighted, complementary colors can be a nightmare via rgb(R,G,B).

This appendix presents a parent/child script called *colorlut*, which is a robust and dynamic Color Look-Up Table information system. In addition to the runtime colorlut script, we will be looking at ColorTool, an application created in Director for the creation of color palettes that conform to the colorlut standard.

Benefits of Colorlut

There are several benefits to using the colorlut system that are not present in Director. The advantages of colorlut palettes are as follows:

- Large palettes that can handle well over 256 colors.
- You can access colors by user-defined names (orange, pale blue, and so on).
- RGB-to-HSV and HSV-to-RGB conversion utilities are built in.
- H, S, and V real-time sorting methods are available.
- You can add and remove colors to and from the palette at runtime.
- You can use multiple simultaneous palettes.

- ColorTool can save and load palettes for development over time.
- ColorTool has RGB and HSV color picking built in.

The colorlut system was designed with concern for creating a lightweight solution with few public methods. It is concise so that you have the option of enhancing the format of the data as well as strategizing the usage of the palettes. In order to control these custom palettes, we must examine three main areas: how to create and maintain the palettes through custom handlers, the structure of the palette format, and an overview of the ColorTool application.

Creating a New Custom Palette

The Color Utilities cast file contains a parent script called colorlut. Several key public handlers are used to create and control the custom color palettes. You can create and maintain as many palettes as your strategy calls for. In the examples in this appendix, the palettes will reside in global variables; however, you could just as easily place the palettes inside a list of palettes or use them as properties of sprites. The following code is used to instantiate a new palette object and assumes that Mypal is a global variable:

```
Mypal = New(script "colorlut", paletteData)
```

Mypal now contains a reference to a child object for rgb(r,g,b) and hsv(h,s,v) color information and for specifically naming that information. The paletteData argument is optional. If you create a new colorlut object without this argument, it will create an empty palette. If you want to define several colors when you create the new colorlut object, paletteData has a very specific structure that it expects.

Palette Data Structure

Palette data is a linear list that contains a linear list of information for each specific color in the palette. The structure of this list is as follows:

```
[["colornameA", rgb(R,G,B)], ["colornameB", rgb(R,G,B)], …]
```

Notice that this list only contains rgb(R,G,B) color information. The hsv(h,s,v) data will be generated for you by the colorlut parent script. Because the custom palettes that we are building are essentially a nested linear list, you can have a very large amount of entries before there would be problems. However, I encourage you to work with concise color palettes. One strategy for using this system is to create many small palettes that have very specific functions. Finally, I suggest that you keep the length of the color names reasonable—anything over eight characters may become difficult to remember.

Custom Handlers for Palette Control

Table F.1 lists the names of the public methods and their purposes. Once you have created a colorlut custom palette, the parent script generates an internal list format that contains the color names, RGB information, and HSV information. The first utility that you should be aware of is the CLUTnames() function. CLUTnames() will return a linear list of the names of the colors only; it is called with the syntax mypal.CLUTnames().

TABLE F.1   Colorlut Public Methods

Public Methods	Purpose
CLUTnames()	Returns a linear list of color names only
CLUTadd(name, rgb)	Associates name and RGB data and adds this date to the list
CLUTget(name)	Retrieves RGB data associated with the name
CLUTdel(name)	Removes color data from the list
CLUTsort(type)	Sorts colors by hue, saturation, or value

Be aware that CLUTadd() will allow you to add multiple colors with the same name or with the same color information. I suggest avoiding this because it may lead to difficulties with your sorting the lists. What's more, it will always lead to difficulties when you're accessing from the list because CLUTget() only searches for the first name that matches. CLUTget() and CLUTdel() can access color data from the list by name or by number. This allows you to access color information in sequential order as well as by name.

The type argument for CLUTsort() must be passed as hue, sat, or val. This will sort the colors in the list according to the type of sorting you choose. HSV colors are more intuitive than RGB colors. *Hue* refers to the chromatic part of the color and is expressed in degrees. Red is at 0 degrees, Green is at 120 degrees, and Blue is at 240 degrees. If you sort via hue, the colors will be ordered from 0 to 360 degrees. *Saturation* refers to the density of the color information. Saturation is expressed in the range of 0 through 100, where 0 is gray (no color information) and 100 is fully saturated. *Value* is sometimes referred to as *brightness*; it designates whether the color is pure or mixed with black. At 0, the color is black; at 100, it is as bright as possible (at the current hue and saturation).

ColorTool

The ColorTool interface was designed as an immediate visual method of defining colors (see Figure F.1). Bear in mind that because you can save and load color palette information, it is possible to develop reusable sets of color palettes over time. I want to forego the usage of the export button. This button will dump the current palette information into the message window. This information is preformatted for use with the new (script colorlut, paletteData) handler as the paletteData argument. This makes it easy to visually define your colors, name them, and then create the code based on the color palette. Finally, notice that you can choose your colors with an RGB picker or an HSV picker. You may find that the HSV picker is easier to use when developing color correlations.

FIGURE F.1

The Color Tool interface.

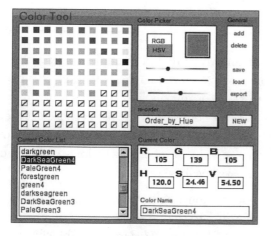

Palette Strategies

It is possible to approach the custom color palettes with many different strategies. You may want to consider the following suggestions:

- Use single, large, interchangeable palettes for movies or when shared between MIAW.

- Use multiple, small palettes relating to individual Sprites or Models.

- Use palettes optimized for specific geometry, such as terrain or foliage.

- Maintain small, interchangeable palettes with color names that correspond to clients or projects.

Whatever your strategy for working with color may be, the colorlut parent script can simplify the chore of remembering specific RGB values. Also, keep in mind that the colorlut parent script is open to your enhancement. Feel free to expand on the custom handlers in the utility to suit your needs.

APPENDIX G

Havok Xtra

The purpose of this appendix is to provide you with a basic explanation of what the Havok Xtra is and what you will need to begin working with it. However, this appendix does not explain how to use the Havok Xtra itself—this is a large subject that is beyond the scope of this book. I suggest learning 3D programming in Director prior to tackling the task of learning the Havok Xtra. Once you are ready, I strongly encourage you to learn how to use the Havok Xtra because it is an impressive feature.

What Is the Havok Xtra?

The Havok Xtra is a real-time physics engine that is included with Director 8.5. If you own Director, this plug-in is available to you. In addition, there are several behaviors supplied with Director 8.5 that were created to be used with the Havok Xtra. These Havok behaviors can be found in the library palette. If you do not find them there, they will be on the Director 8.5 installation CD in the "goodies" folder. If you purchased Director 8.5 via Web download, there is a link to the Havok Web site where you can find these behaviors at the end of this appendix.

There are several reasons why this Xtra is an exciting tool for Director 8.5. The first reason is simple: This tool allows you to add real-time physics simulations to your environment. Havok's real-time physics engine can be used to simulate gravity, friction, and car suspension and steering, in addition to many other simulations. Note that these are not effects that are added to an environment but rather a simulation that can be used to control Nodes in the 3D environment.

It is often difficult to understand what is meant by a 3D environment with a real-time physics engine. Imagine that you have just created a box Model. If the movie is playing, nothing happens to the box—it just stays there. However, if you use the physics engine to assign a mass to the box, the box will begin to fall. If you created a floor for the box to fall to, it will strike the floor with momentum and bounce some distance, depending on how elastic it is. Mass, gravity, and collision are among some of the basic features of a real-time physics engine.

The second reason why access to the Havok engine is exciting is also simple: The full Havok physics engine is a professional software development kit that can be licensed for $75,000. You get many of its tools with your purchase of Director. These tools include rigid-body dynamics in addition to springs, linear dashpots, and angular dashpots.

What Do I Need to Work with Havok?

Havok uses the Shockwave 3D Castmember in addition to a special Castmember known as an *HKE scene*. HKE scenes can be created and exported from an external modeler, such as 3D Studio, or you can set up HKE files directly through Lingo. Therefore, although you can create HKE files visually in 3D Studio, you do not need to use any product other than Director to access the powerful Havok engine.

Behaviors

Director 8.5 ships with several behaviors designed to help you begin working with the Havok Xtra. These behaviors are quite functional, and you may find that they are suitable for a wide variety of projects. Of course, if you decide that you would rather customize the control of the Havok Xtra, it is entirely possible to develop your own behaviors. Depending on the requirements of your project, you might want to consider developing a custom scheduling system to interface with the Havok Xtra rather than working with the behaviors at all. Whichever route you decide to pursue, the Havok behaviors are important. They are well documented, and you can learn how to build a custom control for the Havok Xtra from these tools.

HKE Export

Any 3D modeling product that can export HKE physics scenes can be used with Director. However, you do not need to use a 3D modeling product in conjunction with Havok. How you decide to work with Havok will depend on your needs. If you are familiar and comfortable with creating scenes entirely through Lingo, using the Havok Xtra similarly should not be too difficult of a leap. If you are more comfortable with a visual tool, 3D Studio or some other modeling product that supports HKE export may prove beneficial.

Havok Online

The link www.havok.com/xtra will guide you to the pertinent section of the Havok Web site regarding the Havok Xtra. Several subsections of this site are worth looking at. In addition to the most recent version of the Xtra and exporters, there is a PDF of Lingo terminology and usage, a quickstart guide, and many Open Source examples that are well worth looking at. Finally, you'll find several examples of projects created with the Havok Xtra by Director developers working with Shockwave 3D.

APPENDIX H

Online Resources

As you begin to search for useful information about 3D programming, 3D animation, AI, and so on, you may find that this task is more work than you thought. There are so many Web sites that use the term *3D* for one reason or another that the term begins to lack meaning. Therefore, in this appendix, I provide you with a guide toward some of the locations of information you should start with if you are going to be working with 3D in Director. The resources in this appendix range from online work by Director developers to software you might be interested in learning more about.

Director 3D Work Online

In this section are several links to individuals working with 3D programming in Director who are worth knowing about. In addition, these are highly visible members of the 3D community who can be found in most public forums.

Noisecrime

http://www.noisecrime.com

Noisecrime has been developing 3D with Director since before Shockwave 3D, using some fairly powerful methods that rely on quads. His recent work with Shockwave 3D is quite impressive, including a clone of Quake.

Allen Partridge

http://insight.director-3d.com/studio/

Allen Partridge has been developing games for quite some time. One look at his "17 Keys" game, completed in Shockwave 3D, and you will see that he is able to create visually appealing work that falls outside of mainstream game conventions, and he's highly successful in the process. In addition, Allen has included some examples of his work for you to examine on the CD.

Barry Swan

http://www.theburrow.co.uk/

Barry Swan is well known for the T3D engine—a 3D engine that works entirely in Lingo without the Shockwave 3D Xtra. There is no doubt that Barry will be sharing many of his experiments with Shockwave 3D as well.

Clevermedia

www.clevermedia.com/3D/

Clevermedia is a well-recognized force in the Shockwave games market and has many games on its site, now including several games made with Shockwave 3D.

Nonoche

www.metapages.com/games/

Nonoche developed the game Frenzirynth, which is impressive for its playability, number of levels, addictiveness, and very small download size.

Robert Walch

www.entermation.com/games/

Robert Walch has developed a great example of a 3D multiuser chat room that demonstrates his skill with both 3D and multiuser applications.

skeletonmoon

www.skeletonmoon.com

Here's where you'll find some of the 3D projects I have been working on. Recently, I have been working on a collection of experiments with a 3D interface and narrative that can be found at skeletonmoon.

General Director Resources

The following resources are important to know about for all Director developers, whether working in 3D or not. Each of these sites contain development information and links that you will find valuable while learning and working.

Macromedia

www.macromedia.com

Macromedia is a great reference for examples of 3D and non-3D tech notes, sample movies, developer resources, and Director in general.

Director Online

www.director-online.com

Director Online is at the forefront of the thriving Director development community. Visit this site for tons of interesting articles on programming methods, specific applications, and examples of source code.

Director University

www.directoru.com/community

Director University has a great community-building section that includes links to many 3D developers using Director, an online glossary, 3D resources, and the classes that are offered through the university.

Director 3D

www.director-3d.com

Director 3D was developed as an information exchange for all things 3D with Director.

Director Web

www.mcli.dist.maricopa.edu/director

Director Web is an impressive collection of demos as well as online and offline work. It has been servicing the Director development community since version 3.

Mediamacros

`www.mediamacros.com`

Mediamacros is a great source of information about general Director news, including sites, awards, and new Xtras.

James Newton

`perso.planetb.fr/newton`

James Newton has an impressive array of both 3D and non-3D online demonstrations that you may find useful.

Listserv

The following listservs are valuable sources of information you should seriously consider subscribing to. You will find many representatives of Macromedia engineering as well as Director development veterans and new users.

3Ddirector-L

`www.trevimedia.com/mailinglists/`

3Ddirector-L is a fast-growing community of Director developers using Shockwave 3D with a variety of experience levels. Keep in mind that this is probably the best area to ask your 3D questions, although it is likely that this listserv will begin to stratify in the coming months.

dirGames-L

`nuttybar.drama.uga.edu/mailman/listinfo/dirgames-l/`

dirGames-L is a community of Director game developers that is quite impressive for its collective amount of skills. However, unless your questions are 3D-game related, dirGames-L requests that you ask elsewhere. However, I have found that even if you are not developing games, dirGames-L is a good resource to learn many tricks from that can be applied to non-game projects.

Lingo-L

www.penworks.com/LUJ/lingo-l.cgi

Lingo-L is a great community that has existed for quite some time, where the questions are related to any Lingo concerns you might have. It is a good place to ask questions that are basic to intermediate and can certainly include questions of 3D.

3D Modeling and Animation Software

In this section, I have listed those 3D modeling and animation software packages that currently have W3D output or that have announced W3D output within the next several months (at the time of this writing).

Maya

www.aliaswavefront.com/en/Home/homepage.html

Maya is an extremely powerful 3D modeling and animation package that is available for the Mac, PC, and Unix platforms. Maya is developed by Alias/Wavefront and is widely regarded as the pinnacle of professional 3D modeling, animation, and cost.

Softimage

www.softimage.com

Softimage is a widely used 3D modeling and animation package that is available on PC and Unix. Users of Softimage often cite the interface as the strongest characteristic of this environment.

3D Studio MAX

www.discreet.com

3D Studio MAX is an affordable 3D modeling and animation package for the PC that has had many years to perfect its professional features and accumulate a wide base of users. This package has many tools for low-poly-count modeling, animation, and scripting the environment that easily competes with the features of much more expensive solutions.

Lightwave

www.lightwave6.com

Lightwave offers an impressive suite of modeling and animation tools that is available at an extremely affordable price. In addition, Lightwave is available for both the Mac and PC platforms. For the price, Lightwave is an impressive tool with a unique interface that many 3D artists prefer.

Cinema 4D

www.maxon.net/usa/index.html

A powerful cross-platform modeling and animation environment, Cinema 4D is well known and well respected for its gentle learning curve and its integration with sister product Bodypaint 3D, a 3D painting package. Cinema 4D is supported on both the Mac and PC platforms.

Truespace

www.caligari.com

Truespace is a relatively inexpensive modeling and animation solution, but by no means is it crippled. Many of the tools that are standard with Truespace are only available as plug-ins for the larger systems. Other than its affordability and intuitive interface, perhaps one of its most impressive offerings is its use of Python as its built-in scripting language. Currently, Truespace is only available for the PC.

Shapeshifter

www.shapeshifter3d.com

Shapeshifter is a modeling tool, but it's not an animation tool. However, it has two particular strengths. First, it is a cross-platform tool Xtra. This means that Shapeshifter runs within the Director environment. Shapeshifter can create models from scratch or import them from other tools. In addition, Shapeshifter has a built-in UV coordinate editor. Finally, Shapeshifter exports directly to the W3D format. Its extremely competitive price makes Shapeshifter a very good choice even for those developers who want a system of modeling integrated within the Director environment.

Support Software

This section is dedicated to support software that you may find helpful when working with 3D. Also, several of the tools in this section are mentioned because they are freely available.

DeepPaint

www.us.righthemisphere.com

DeepPaint is a powerful painting tool that many 3D artists use to develop textures. It is particularly good at painting with textures. In addition, it is capable of importing models from 3D software and allows you to paint textures directly onto the surface of your models.

MeshPaint

www.texturetools.com/meshpaint.shtml

MeshPaint is another 3D painting tool that allows you to paint directly onto objects imported from 3D modeling software.

Painter and Painter 3D

www.corel.com

Painter is a powerful natural-media paint tool that takes full advantage of pressure-sensitive tablets. The brushes are realistic, convincing, and customizable. In addition, a similar version of Painter (Painter 3D) allows you to import 3D models and paint directly on them.

Lightscape

www.lightscape.com

Lightscape creates both photorealistic and photo-accurate data. It utilizes actual physical information about the objects in your scene to create a real-time rendering of the lighting in your scene. Lightscape contains a tool called Mesh-to-Texture, which allows you to take the high-quality real-time rendering from Lightscape and create texture maps for your environments from it.

Polytrans

www.okino.com

Polytrans is a powerful 3D file format conversion utility that supports a wide array of formats. In addition, it creates OBJ files that the Director 8.5 OBJ Importer translates into W3D flawlessly.

Rhinoceros

www.rhino3d.com

Rhino is a powerful Nurbs-based modeler that many prefer for the creation of objects that will then be imported into other animation packages. Although Nurbs are not supported by W3D, you can still model with Nurbs and then export a Mesh.

AnimaTek World Builder

www.digi-element.com

AnimaTek World Builder is to Bryce what Photoshop is to Superpaint. If you want to create terrain and you need a professional feature set and detailed level of control, then World Builder is it. World Builder can be used alone or as a plug-in for a variety of modeling environments—for example, 3DS MAX, Lightwave, and Maya. As a tool to develop models, backgrounds, and textures, World Builder is impressive.

Blender

www.blender.nl

Blender is an outstanding tool that has two main reasons for its inclusion here. It is a powerful modeling/animating and rendering tool that has been compiled for a wide array of platforms. More importantly, it is free. Although it does not currently have W3D export capabilities, it does have several export options, and it has Python built in as its native scripting language.

3D, AI, and Game Programming

Although not specifically Director related, these resources have information that you may find extremely helpful when working with 3D programming or AI or when building games in general. Because these topics have existed for quite some time before Director had a 3D environment, you may find it necessary to learn from those using other methods of development.

Amit's

www-cs-students.stanford.edu/~amitp/gameprog.html

Amit's is one of those "best kept but not so secret" Web sites dedicated to game programming. There is much to be gleaned from this gigantic site.

Gameai

www.gameai.com/ai.html

The Game AI page is a good place to start learning about how AI is applied to games and to discover the differences between AI and game AI. Many resources and links can be found at this site.

Gamedev

www.gamedev.net

Gamedev is a solid community of game developers that has tons of resources and many articles about game development in general. In addition, there are several links and articles about game AI that can be accessed via the Gamedev.net search engine.

Gamasutra

www.gamasutra.com

Gamasutra is a great site filled with news and articles about the game-development industry. You can find a wide range of information from inside development news to resources and links.

General 3D Information

The following resources are not specifically Director related, but they do offer information about 3D. These links are especially geared toward 3D animation as well as the creation and distribution of 3D assets.

3D Café

www.3dcafe.com

3D Café is a highly visible 3D resource, and among other things, it has several good tutorial sections about how to create certain types of Models in your preferred modeling package. It also has a wide variety of product information, including information about 3D texture and model CD-ROMs.

3D Ark

www.3dark.com

3D Ark is an interesting site devoted to 3D animation, modeling, and rendering that is very user driven. There are many discussion forums, tutorials, and product reviews that you may find helpful as you begin to work.

3D Models

The next few links are both providers of 3D Models and service bureaus for the creation of 3D Models for your projects. Often, there is not enough time to develop all the Models you will need for a project; these service providers can help you find stock 3D Models that can reduce your costs.

Turbosquid

www.turbosquid.com

Turbosquid has attracted a robust community of 3D artists who use the Turbosquid site to promote their Models. The Models that you will find on this site are professional, top quality, and (for a small fee) royalty free. In addition, and perhaps most importantly, Turbosquid specifically has models saved in the W3D format.

Viewpoint Data Labs

`modelbank.viewpoint.com`

The Viewpoint Modelbank sells quality models at a variety of detail levels, depending on the requirements of your project. The plant and animal models are particularly impressive, although all models are of superior quality.

Kaon Interactive

`www.kaon.com`

Kaon Interactive is an interesting company that will create models for you from photographs or drawings of your products. Many times you may own extremely high-resolution Models for rapid prototyping that cannot be used for the low-poly-count requirements of the Web. Kaon will essentially use an existing product or product photograph to create a detailed, low-poly-count model for you.

Arius 3D

`www.arius3d.com`

Arius 3D is a service provider that uses a 3D scanning process that yields extremely high-resolution scans of any object you would like. In addition, its particular scanning method scans the surface of objects to create highly detailed textures.

GLOSSARY

2.5D   Two and a half dimensions. In terms of 3D programming, this is an environment comprised of 2D elements that has been treated to look like a 3D environment. Although many 2.5D solutions are successful, they are not truly 3D.

3D Lingo   3D Lingo is a branch of Lingo dedicated to controlling 3D environments in Director. Therefore, 3D Lingo extends the capabilities of Lingo.

3D Speedport Xtra   The 3D Speedport Xtra is included with all versions of Director. This Xtra allows you to convert OBJ files into W3D format.

alpha channel   An alpha channel refers to information stored within a bitmap whose purpose is to control the amount of transparency per pixel. Alpha channels are generally referred to by their bit depth, which describes how many levels of transparency they are capable of. 1-, 4- and 8-bit alpha channels are common, which provide 2, 16, and 256 levels of transparency, respectively.

Ambient (Shader)   The Ambient property of the standard Shader is used to determine the color of the shaded regions on the surface of a Model.

Ambient Light   The Ambient Light in a scene is used to approximate a general light level for an environment. Specifically, the use of Ambient Light is an attempt to approximate the amount of reflected, incidental, and bounce light within a scene.

animated Textures   In 3D programming, the use of animated Textures refers to any process that changes the material qualities of a Model over time. This may range from flipbook-style animations to transformation-based animations.

API (Application Programming Interface)   An API is used to refer to a subset of instructions used by programmers to simplify common tasks for a programming language.

attenuation   Attenuation is a term that applies to both lighting and sound design in 3D programming. In Director, attenuation has only been defined for lighting; this property controls how fast and with what bias, if any, the light intensity will fall off to darkness.

Backdrop   A Backdrop is a 2D image that has been pasted behind all the other elements in a scene. Backdrops are applied to Cameras.

backface culling   Backface culling is a process used in 3D rendering to speed the drawing of an environment. This is accomplished by determining which Faces are pointing at the active Camera and drawing them, ignoring those that are facing backward.

behavioral animation   A process for creating autonomous and semiautonomous animations. Specifically, in this process, the programmer defines rules for animation that will sometimes conflict with each other. These conflicting rules can force complex and beautiful patterns of animation to arise. Behavioral animation arises from a simple premise: Many simple rules can describe highly complex Motions.

billboard   A billboard is a special type of element in a 3D environment that is actually just a flat plane. In order for this plane to truly be called a *billboard*, it must always rotate so that it is constantly aligned with the Camera.

bit depth   Bit depth is a term used to refer to the number of colors available to a monitor, to a bitmap, or to a program.

bitmaps   A bitmap contains information about location and color that can be used to store photographic or illustrated images.

Bones   Bones provide a method for controlling and animating Models in a 3D environment that can be used to create highly complex systems of movement.

Bonesplayer Modifier   The Bonesplayer Modifier is automatically attached to every Model with a Bones hierarchy. With the Bonesplayer, you can play back Bones-based Motions using a given Model.

boundingsphere   The boundingsphere of a Model is an invisible sphere that encompasses a Model and all its children. Boundingspheres are generally used in collision detection in order to ease the burden of checking for extremely complex collisions.

bump mapping   Bump mapping is a technique that is not supported in Director. Bump mapping refers to a process for using a Texture to affect the surface normals for a Model in such a way that the surfaces appears to contain ridges or dents.

Camera   A Camera is one of the most basic Nodes in a 3D environment. The Camera is considered the eyepiece of the viewer in a 3D scene. Without a Camera, the user cannot see the 3D world.

clipping planes   The clipping planes are integral parts of a Camera. There are two clipping planes: a far-clipping plane and a near-clipping plane. All models closer than the near-clipping plane and all Models farther than the far-clipping plane will not be drawn.

collinear   When two or more points or vectors exist on the same line, they are collinear.

collision detection   A memory-intensive process that checks to see whether Models are intersecting.

coplanar   When two or more lines, planes, vectors, or points exist on the same plane, they are coplanar.

cross product   The cross product is one of two methods of multiplying two vectors together. The process produces a vector that is perpendicular to the two original vectors. This resulting vector is known as a *normal*.

D3D (Director 3D)   Developers often refer to the process of programming or developing 3D content in Director as *D3D*.

dot product   The dot product is one of two methods of multiplying two vectors together. This process produces a scalar value. If the two original vectors were unit vectors, this scalar value is the cosine of the angle between the two vectors.

Fog   Fog is a property of Cameras that attempts to add a bit of atmospheric distortion to an environment.

Group   A Group is one of the primary Nodes in the 3D environment. Essentially, a Group is comprised of other Nodes.

Havok Xtra   The Havok Xtra is a powerful physics-simulation engine provided with Director. This physics-simulation engine can be used to determine high-quality collision detection and to create springs and levers.

Imaging Lingo   Imaging Lingo is a branch of Lingo that is used to create, composite, and otherwise modify 2D image objects on-the-fly. These 2D image objects are essentially bitmaps that exist in RAM and can be displayed on the Stage or used as Textures in the 3D environment.

inner product   See *dot product*.

interactive animation   A methodology for creating animations controlled by the user. This methodology includes building a set of rules that defines the reactions of the environment to user input as well as to a lack of user input.

local coordinates   When measuring locations in a 3D World, you need to measure from a starting point. If that starting point is not the origin of the 3D World, such as a Node, the measurements you make are in local coordinates.

Mesh   A Mesh is a special type of Modelresource that allows you to build the geometry of a Model from scratch with Lingo.

Mesh deformation   Mesh deformation is a process of manipulating the geometry of a Modelresource using the Meshdeform Modifier.

mip-mapping   Mip-mapping is a process that creates several successively smaller versions of a Texture. This allows the 3D Renderer to choose a version of the Texture that is correctly sized, given that the size of Texture will vary depending on its location in the 3D environment.

Model   A Model is one of the primary Nodes in a 3D environment. Models are used to represent the objects in a scene.

Modelresource   A Modelresource contains information about the geometry of a Mesh. This geometric Mesh is used to provide information to Models. Essentially, a Modelresource is the geometric information that defines what a given Model will look like.

Modifier   There are several different types of Modifiers that can be applied to Models. The uses for Modifiers range from controlling the playback of animation to modifying the complexity of Modelresources on-the-fly.

Motion   A Motion is a special element in a 3D scene that must be exported from a 3D animation program. Motions can contain either Keyframe or Bones animation data, which can then be played back by Models in the scene.

Motion blending   Motion blending is a process that is used with both Keyframe and Bones Motions. When switching from the playback of one Motion to another, you can decide to have the Motions switch immediately or to slowly fade one Motion into the other.

Motion mapping   Motion mapping is a process that can only be used with Bones Motions. It allows you to synthesize new Motions from existing Motions.

nearfiltering   Nearfiltering is a process that slightly blurs Textures that are close to a Camera.

Node   Node is a generic term used to refer to Cameras, Lights, Models, and Groups. Each of these items plays a primary function in any 3D environment; classifying them as Nodes stresses their importance. Also, Nodes share certain common qualities, such as how they are transformed.

normal   A normal is a vector that is perpendicular to another vector, line, or surface. Normals are used in the 3D environment to determine which side of a Model should be drawn and which side should be ignored.

normalization   Normalization is a process that divides all components of a vector by the original magnitude of that vector. This process forces all vectors to a magnitude of 1.

NPR (non-photo-realistic rendering)   NPR is a process that focuses on the rendering of Models in a nonrealistic manner, such as trying to paint the Models or etch them.

OBJ file format   The OBJ file format is an old standard that has existed for quite some time; it is possible to convert OBJ files into W3D format using the 3D Speedport Xtra.

OOP (object-oriented programming)   OOP is a method of programming that involves the encapsulation and reuse of handlers, functions, and properties. This method of programming is more difficult to set up but easier to maintain.

outer product   See *cross product*.

Overlay   An Overlay is a property of a Camera that allows you to assign a Texture to exist in front of all the Models in a scene.

parent/child hierarchy   A parent/child hierarchy refers to a process in 3D environments that creates linkages between Nodes. These hierarchies are used to create systems of inherited transformations.

parent/child script   A parent/child script is the basic component of OOP in Director. Parent scripts are instantiated, thereby creating child objects that exist independently of their parents, maintaining their own handlers and properties.

particle system   A particle system is a primitive in Director's 3D environment that should be thought of as a primitive of movement and not of geometry. Particle systems are typically used to create explosions, fireworks, exhaust, and other effects that would be difficult, if not impossible, to model.

Picking Lingo   Picking Lingo is a branch of 3D Lingo that is used to determine whether any 3D Models are under the position of the mouse, an arbitrary location on the screen, or an arbitrary location in the 3D World.

plane   A plane is the simplest primitive type. It exists as a flat surface, similar to a piece of paper.

primitives   Primitives are the five built-in Modelresource types and are easily defined by Lingo; specifically, these five primitives are boxes, cylinders, spheres, planes, and particle systems.

rule-based animation   See *behavioral animation*.

scalar   A scalar is a number that represents a single property, such as a magnitude.

scalar multiplication   Scalar multiplication is the process of multiplying a vector by a scalar. This will not change the direction of the original vector, but the magnitude of the vector will be scaled based on the value of the scalar.

scalar product   See *dot product*.

scaling   Scaling is one of the three primary methods of transformations used to increase or decrease the size of Models.

scenegraph hierarchy   The scenegraph hierarchy refers to all the parent/child linkages in a 3D environment. All Nodes have some placement in the scenegraph hierarchy. All linkages in the hierarchy can eventually be traced to a single common origin: the root node.

SDS (Subdivision Surfaces)   A process of increasing the complexity of a Modelresource in real time, which is implemented with the subdivision Modifier.

Shader   A Shader is an element of 3D environments used to define the surface qualities of a Model, such as its color and how shiny it is.

skeletal deformation   Skeletal deformation refers to the process of Bones animation that deforms the geometry of a Model according to the movements of invisible "Bone" resources, which must be exported from 3D modeling and animation software. These "Bone" resources cannot be created with Director.

software rendering   Software rendering is a process of drawing 3D environments that does not take advantage of any 3D video hardware a user might have. Typically, software rendering is reliable, but slow.

SW3D (Shockwave 3D)   SW3D is a term often used to refer to the overall process and product involved with creating real-time 3D projects in Director. It's also sometimes referred to as *D3D* or *Director 3D*.

Texture   A Texture is an element of 3D environments used in conjunction with a Shader to define the material qualities of a Model, such as whether the Model looks like it's made out of wood.

timeout object   A timeout object is a special code object that effectively acts as a timer. Timeout objects are used to trigger a given handler after a certain amount of time has elapsed.

transform object   A transform object is a special code object that can store information about position, orientation, and scale, independently of any given Node.

transformation   Transformation is a term that is used to refer to processes that orient, position, or scale the Nodes in a 3D environment.

translation   Translation is one of the three types of transformation. Translation is the process of positioning Nodes within the 3D environment.

unit circle   A unit circle is a circle comprised of all the endpoints of 2D unit vectors.

unit sphere   A unit sphere is a sphere comprised of all the endpoints of 3D unit vectors.

unit vector   A unit vector is a vector with a magnitude of 1.

UV coordinates   UV coordinates are used when applying Textures to a Shader. The letters U and V are used to ease confusion between texture coordinates and world coordinates. UV coordinates do not exist in the same space as XY coordinates—rather they exist in a separate Texture coordinate space.

UVW mapping   UVW mapping is the process of applying a Shader to a Model. Shaders are applied to Models in Model-relative 3D space. In order to ease confusion between these mapping coordinates and normal coordinates, the letters UVW are used, although they technically refer to XYZ coordinates.

vector   A vector is a data type used to represent two pieces of data: a direction and a magnitude. In Director, these two pieces of data are not represented directly but rather with three components representing a displacement in space.

vector product   See *cross product*.

Vertex   A Vertex is the simplest component of a Modelresource. You can think of it as a single point in 3D space.

Vertices   The plural form of Vertex.

W3D file format   The W3D file format is a Director-native file format used to import Models and Motions created in external modeling programs.

World coordinates   When measuring locations in a 3D World, you need to measure from a starting point. If that starting point is the origin of the 3D World, the measurements you make are in World coordinates.

Index

Symbols

A

H

J-K

N

U–V

Other Related Titles

Special Edition Using Director 8.5
Gary Rozensweig
ISBN: 0-7897-2667-X
$49.99 US/$74.95 CAN

Real-Time Interactive 3D Games
Allen Partridge
ISBN: 0-672-32285-4
$59.99 US/$89.95 CAN

Special Edition Using Photoshop
Richard Lynch
ISBN: 0-7897-2425-1
$39.99 US/$59.95 CAN

Special Edition Using Mac OS X
Brad Miser
ISBN: 0-7897-2470-7
$39.99 US/$59.95 CAN

www.photoshop.imageready
Greg Simsic
ISBN: 0-7897-2551-7
$45.00 US/$67.95 CAN

Coming Early 2002

Lingo Line by Line
Darrel Plant
ISBN: 0-7897-2721-8
$59.99 US/$89.95 CAN

Special Edition Using Adobe After Effects X
Rick Gerard
ISBN: 0-7897-2646-7
$49.99 US/$74.95 CAN

Sepcial Edition Using Adobe Premiere X
Michael Velte
ISBN: 0-7897-2669-6
$39.99 US/$59.95 CAN

Special Edition Using Adobe Illustrator X
Peter Bauer
ISBN: 0-7897-2704-8
$39.99 US/$59.95 CAN

3ds Max 4 Workshop
Duane Loose
ISBN: 0-7897-2546-0
$45.00 US/$67.95 CAN

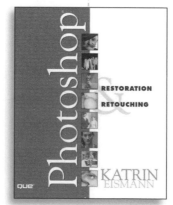

Photoshop Restoration and Retouching
Katrin Eismann
ISBN: 0-7897-2318-2
$49.99 US/$74.95 CAN

www.quepublishing.com

All prices are subject to change.

License Agreement

By opening this package, you are agreeing to be bound by the following agreement:

You may not copy or redistribute the entire CD-ROM as a whole. Copying and redistribution of individual software programs on the CD-ROM is governed by terms set by individual copyright holders.

The installer and code from the author(s) are copyrighted by the publisher and the author(s). Individual programs and other items on the CD-ROM are copyrighted or are under an Open Source license by their various authors or other copyright holders.

This software is sold as-is without warranty of any kind, either expressed or implied, including but not limited to the implied warranties of merchantability and fitness for a particular purpose. Neither the publisher nor its dealers or distributors assumes any liability for any alleged or actual damages arising from the use of this program. (Some states do not allow for the exclusion of implied warranties, so the exclusion may not apply to you.)

What's On the CD-ROM?

The companion CD-ROM contains all of the project files used in the book, sample models, and converters.

Installation Instructions

Windows

1. Insert the disc into your CD-ROM drive.
2. From the Windows desktop, double-click the My Computer icon.
3. Double-click the icon representing your CD-ROM drive.
4. Double-click on readme.htm.

Macintosh

1. Insert the disc into your CD-ROM drive.
2. Double-click the Director's Third Dimension icon when it appears on your desktop.
3. Double-click on readme.htm.